ECONOMIC, SOCIAL AND CULTURAL RIGHTS IN ACTION

Economic, Social and Cultural Rights in Action

Edited by
MASHOOD A. BADERIN
ROBERT MCCORQUODALE

OXFORD
UNIVERSITY PRESS

OXFORD
UNIVERSITY PRESS

Great Clarendon Street, Oxford OX2 6DP

Oxford University Press is a department of the University of Oxford.
It furthers the University's objective of excellence in research, scholarship,
and education by publishing worldwide in

Oxford New York

Auckland Cape Town Dar es Salaam Hong Kong Karachi
Kuala Lumpur Madrid Melbourne Mexico City Nairobi
New Delhi Shanghai Taipei Toronto

With offices in

Argentina Austria Brazil Chile Czech Republic France Greece
Guatemala Hungary Italy Japan Poland Portugal Singapore
South Korea Switzerland Thailand Turkey Ukraine Vietnam

Oxford is a registered trade mark of Oxford University Press
in the UK and in certain other countries

Published in the United States
by Oxford University Press Inc., New York

© The several contributors, 2007

British Library Cataloguing in Publication Data
Data available

Library of Congress Cataloging in Publication Data
Economic, social and cultural rights in action / edited by Mashood Baderin,
Robert McCorquodale.
    p. cm.
Includes bibliographical references and index.
ISBN 978–0–19–921790–8 (alk. paper)
    1. Human rights. 2. Social rights. 3. Economic policy. 4. Cultural policy.
5. International Covenant on Economic, Social, and Cultural Rights (1966)
I. Baderin, Mashood A. II. McCorquodale, Robert.
    K3240.E26 2007
    341.4′8—dc22

                                                            2007003106

Typeset by Newgen Imaging Systems (P) Ltd, Chennai, India
Printed in Great Britain
on acid-free paper by
Biddles Ltd, King's Lynn

ISBN 978–0–19–921790–8

1 3 5 7 9 10 8 6 4 2

Foreword

What word best describes how Professor David Harris is regarded in the world of international law and in the human rights community? Perhaps 'inspiring', or 'appreciated'. Clearly, as everything that follows attests, he has inspired all the contributors to this volume, and many, many more besides. He has been valued as a teacher and appreciated for his long years of unstinting service to the University of Nottingham, both as an academic and as an administrator. But the word that springs to my mind above all, when thinking of David Harris, is 'respect'. This volume is prepared to honour a man for whom his colleagues have profound 'respect'. That respect stems from a combination of several things: David Harris' work on human rights is solidly grounded in an impressive familiarity with international law generally; and his knowledge of economic, social, and cultural rights is second to none: his contribution to this field has been both pioneering and enormous.

David Harris' interest in rights other than political and civil rights was certainly not a mere product of the entry into force of the ICESCR in 1976. He was already in the 1960s a leading expert on the European Social Charter, and from 1990 to 1996 was a member of the Strasbourg Committee of Independent Experts on the European Social Charter. He wrote much, and spoke at conferences on this topic in many countries, including the UK, the Netherlands, Slovakia, Russia, Estonia, and the former Yugoslavia. He readily lent his experience to the building of human rights infrastructure in such places as China, Cuba, India, Indonesia, Italy, Latvia, Mongolia, Ukraine, and Iraq. He has advised the Council of Europe on human rights matters relating to Slovenia, Albania, Georgia, and elsewhere. Unsurprisingly, he was the UK's national legal expert in the Programme for Legal Support for Newly Independent OSCE States.

Along with these practical contributions, there has been a continuous stream of high quality books and articles. His book *Cases and Materials on International Law* has been very widely relied on. He has written and/or co-edited the standard works (sometimes with co-authors) on the inter-American system of human rights, the law of the European Convention on Human Rights, and the International Covenant on Civil and Political Rights. For years he provided the annual survey of decisions on the European Convention of Human Rights for the *British Yearbook of International Law*. He edited journals and encyclopaedias, and has written much, much more than can here be mentioned.

He has given so much to our understanding of economic and social rights, with a minimum of fanfare and much self-effacement. This is a man for whom the subject of human rights has been everything and self-promotion nothing. This is the stuff of respect.

It is thus entirely fitting that colleagues, many of whom are former students, all specialists in the field of economic, social, and cultural rights, should wish to pay tribute to David Harris. And it is fully in keeping with Professor Harris' substantive writings and meticulous way of going about things that this volume should itself be a serious contribution to scholarship. There are some excellent studies on economic, social, and cultural rights; but none yet does what is attempted here— a combination of survey of the conceptual debates on such rights, a recounting of the complicated history of the drafting and coming into effect of the Covenant, and an analysis of where things now stand. This book provides all that a reader can want in understanding the history (and politics) of economic, social, and cultural rights. It is also fully up to date in addressing the work of the Committee under the ICESCR Covenant, as well as drawing on the now considerable literature on the matter. The decision to bring all of this together under three main themes— structure and scope of obligations under the ICESCR, regional and comparative understandings of ESC rights, and application of these rights, is in my view perceptive. Further, it is successfully brought to fruition by writers who are true scholars in this field and whose expertise is incontestable.

This volume provides the reader with a carefully thought out deployment of the law-in-context on economic, social, and cultural rights. Contributors and editors have produced a balanced and scholarly contribution to understanding. And in so doing they have honoured one who has dedicated his life to the law of human rights.

Judge Dame Rosalyn Higgins
President, International Court of Justice

The Hague
December 2006

Contents

Table of Cases

Table of Statutes

List of Contributors

Jane Ansah is currently the Attorney General of Malawi. She was previously a Judge of the High Court of Malawi and obtained her PhD on the Right to Development from the School of Law, University of Nottingham under the supervision of Professor David J Harris.

Mashood A Baderin is Professor of Law at Brunel Law School, Brunel University, London. He is an expert in international human rights and Islamic law. He obtained his PhD from the School of Law, University of Nottingham under the supervision of Professor David J Harris. He teaches and researches in international and comparative human rights law.

Ed Bates Lecturer, University of Southampton, has written chapters for D Harris, M O'Boyle, and C Warbrick *The Law of the European Convention on Human Rights* (2nd edn, OUP, forthcoming). His book, *The Evolution of the European Convention on Human Rights 1948–1998*, began life as a PhD research under Professor David J Harris' supervision at the School of Law, University of Nottingham and is to be published by OUP in 2008.

Richard Burchill is Director of the McCoubrey Centre for International Law and Senior Lecturer, Law School, University of Hull, UK. His publications include *International Conflict and Security Law: Essays in Honour of Hilaire McCoubrey*, with Justin Morris and Nigel White (Cambridge University Press, 2005) and *Defining Civil and Political Rights: The Jurisprudence of the United Nations Human Rights Committee*, with Scott Davidson and Alex Conte (Ashgate, 2004).

Robin R Churchill is Professor of International Law at the University of Dundee. Before that he had been a member of staff at Cardiff University for many years. His primary teaching and research interests lie in the fields of Public International Law (especially relating to the sea, the environment, and human rights) and EU Law.

Matthew Craven is Professor of International Law, School of Oriental and African Studies, University of London. His book, *The International Covenant on Economic, Social and Cultural Rights* (OUP, 1997) originated in a PhD at the University of Nottingham under the supervision of Professor David J Harris.

Verónica Gómez has been a Human Rights Specialist at the Executive Secretariat of the Inter-American Commission on Human Rights (IACHR) since 1998. She studied law and international law at the University of Buenos Aires (1990) and was both a fellow at the CONICET (National Institute of Scientific and Technical Research) (1991–92) and the British Council (1993–94). She obtained an LLM degree in International Law at Nottingham University (1994) and thereafter was privileged to conduct research in the area of international law of human rights under Professor David J Harris.

Paul Hunt is Professor of Law at the University of Essex (UK) and Adjunct Professor at the University of Waikato (New Zealand). In 1998, Paul Hunt was elected by the UN to serve as an independent expert on the UN Committee on Economic, Social and Cultural Rights. In 2002, he was appointed UN Special Rapporteur on the right to the highest attainable standard of health. His books include (co-editor), *World Bank, IMF and Human Rights* (Wolf Legal Publishers, 2003).

Sarah Joseph is Professor of Law and the Director of the Castan Centre for Human Rights Law at Monash University, Melbourne. She has published widely on human rights, and is currently a lead Chief Investigator on an Australian Research Council project on the WTO and Human Rights.

Urfan Khaliq is a Lecturer at Cardiff Law School, Cardiff University. His teaching and research interests encompass Public International Law, EU Law, and Human Rights Law. He is currently completing a book for Cambridge University Press on the legal issues that an ethical dimension to foreign policy raises.

Robert McCorquodale is Professor of International Law and Human Rights at the University of Nottingham. He is co-author of one of the leading texts in international law; *Cases and Materials on International Law* (4th edn, OUP, 2003), as well as having published widely on issues of international law and on international human rights law in particular. He has also provided advice to governments, international organizations, non-governmental organizations, and individuals on a range of international legal issues.

Dominic McGoldrick is Professor of Public International Law and Director of the International and European Law Unit, Liverpool Law School, University of Liverpool. He is a specialist in Human Rights Law. In 1999–2000 he was a Fulbright Distinguished Scholar and a Human Rights Fellow at the Harvard Law School. He has authored four books: *Human Rights Committee* (Clarendon Press, 1991), *International Relations Law of the European Union* (Longman, 1997), *From 9–11 to the Iraq War 2003: International Law In An Age Of Complexity* (Hart, 2004) and *Human Rights and Religion—The Islamic Headscarf Debate in Europe* (Hart, 2006). He was the co-editor of *The Permanent International Criminal Court—Legal and Policy Issues* (Hart, 2004).

Gillian MacNaughton is a human rights lawyer. She is currently reading for the DPhil in Law at the University of Oxford where her research focuses on equality and social rights. Previously, she worked as a senior research officer to the UN Special Rapporteur on the right to the highest attainable standard of health.

Michael O'Flaherty is Professor of Applied Human Rights and Co-director of the Human Rights Law Centre at the University of Nottingham. He is a member of the (UN) Human Rights Committee. He has published extensively, including on the role of human rights treaty bodies and on the law and practice of human rights field operations. He has served, among other positions, as Co-ordinator of the UN's Asia and the Pacific human rights programme and as head of its human rights programmes in Sierra Leone and Bosnia-Herzegovina. He is a member of the boards of and otherwise advises numerous international human rights organizations.

Manisuli Ssenyonjo is a Lecturer in Law at Brunel University. He has previously held full-time lectureships at the Universities of the West of England, Bristol, and Makerere University, Uganda. He is an experienced Barrister and Solicitor of the High Court of Uganda. He has published several articles in leading academic journals, and acted as a consultant to governments, intergovernmental organizations, and non-governmental organizations.

Jennifer Tooze is a Home Office lawyer. She completed her PhD in the field of economic and social rights at the School of Law, University of Nottingham, under the supervision of Professor David J Harris and has since undertaken human rights and development work for several organizations. She was called to the Bar in 2003.

Patrick Twomey is a Barrister, and since 2003, has been Director of the International Human Rights Network (IHRN). IHRN is an NGO based in Ireland which specialises in supporting others in applying human rights-based approaches to their work. Previously he was Co-Director of the Human Rights Law Centre, University of Nottingham.

Colin Warbick is Professor of Law in the School of Law, University of Birmingham. He is a co-author of D Harris, M O'Boyle, and C Warbrick, *The Law of the European Convention on Human Rights* (2nd edn, OUP, forthcoming). He has written on several aspects of international law and human rights. He has been a consultant to the Council of Europe and the Organization of Co-operation and Security in Europe.

Nigel D White is Professor of International Law at the University of Sheffield and Director of the Centre for Law in its International Context. He was formerly Professor of International Organizations in the School of Law, University of Nottingham 2000–05. He is author of numerous articles and books including *Keeping the Peace: The United Nations and the Maintenance of International Peace and Security* (Manchester University Press, 1997), *The Law of International Organisations* (Manchester University Press, 2005), *The UN System: Toward International Justice* (Lynne Rienner, 2002), editor of *Collective Security Law* (Ashgate, 2004), co-editor of *European Security Law* (OUP, forthcoming 2007), and co-editor of the *Journal of Conflict and Security Law* published by Oxford University Press.

PART I

INTRODUCTION

1

The International Covenant on Economic, Social and Cultural Rights: Forty Years of Development

*Mashood A. Baderin and Robert McCorquodale** *

I. Introduction

We, the unarmed, the economically under-developed, the technologically under-privileged, have no strength except the strength of law . . . . [and so] we are pleased to vote for the draft Covenants on Human Rights.[1]

On 16 December 1966, the United Nations General Assembly voted unanimously for the adoption of the International Covenant on Economic, Social and Cultural Rights (ICESCR).[2] Those present noted that this adoption was 'historic'[3] and provided 'a new frame of reference'[4] for the protection of human rights in the future for those who, as indicated in the quotation above, have no economic, social, and cultural power. Forty years later—and thirty years since it entered into force[5]—it is important to reflect on the extent to which the ICESCR has created a new frame of reference for considering economic, social, and cultural issues, and has provided a strong law for the protection of these rights.

With over 150 states having now ratified the ICESCR, representing more than three-quarters of the members of the United Nations (UN), and from across all regions and all political and economic systems of the world, there can be no doubt

* Both authors are grateful for the support, care, and intellectual stimulation that David J Harris has provided to them throughout their academic careers.

[1] Mr Ornes-Coiscou (Dominican Republic) speaking at the General Assembly Plenary Meeting, 21 General Assembly Official Records (GAOR), 1495th meeting (16 Dec 1966) paras 137–138.

[2] General Assembly Resolution (GA res 2200 (XL)), incorporating the International Covenant on Economic, Social and Cultural Rights (ICESCR), the International Covenant on Civil and Political Rights (ICCPR) and the Optional Protocol to the ICCPR. The ICESCR was adopted by 105 votes to zero with no abstentions.

[3] Mr Tinoco (Costa Rica) 21 GAOR, 16 Dec 1966, para 177.

[4] Mr Rossides (Cyprus) 21 GAOR, 16 Dec 1966, para 174.

[5] The ICESCR entered into force on 3 Jan 1976, three months after the deposit of the thirty-fifth ratification of the treaty (in accordance with art 27(1) of the ICESCR).

that it is accepted as an important frame of reference in human rights. Yet, despite this history, there remains considerable debate, both academically and within the international community more generally, about the concepts, substance, and application of economic, social, and cultural rights (ESC rights) as reflected in the ICESCR. The consideration and analysis of some of the key issues in relation to these matters forms the substance of this book.

This chapter aims to provide an outline of the context within which each of these issues will be examined in other chapters. After clarifying the history of the drafting of the ICESCR, it will set out some of the core conceptual debates about ESC rights, including their justiciability and the nature of the relevant legal obligations. Within the discussion of the three main themes of the book—the structure and scope of obligations under the ICESCR; regional and comparative understandings of ESC rights; and applications of these rights—a summary of the main arguments of the authors of the chapters will be provided. These three themes were chosen as being an effective means to consider the ICESCR forty years on, as being distinctive from the (all too few) books dealing with ESC rights,[6] and as reflective of the work of Professor David J Harris of the University of Nottingham, who has inspired all those who have contributed to this book.

II. Drafting the ICESCR

Barely had the excitement died down about the adoption on 10 December 1948 of the Universal Declaration of Human Rights (UDHR),[7] before the drafting of a legally binding treaty on human rights was commenced. Indeed, it had been decided in 1947, at only the second session of the UN Commission on Human Rights (the HR Commission), that the HR Commission should draft a Declaration, a human rights treaty (to be called a 'Covenant') and a document setting out measures of

---

[6] Examples of books that deal with the whole legal area of ESC rights include M Craven, *The International Covenant on Economic, Social and Cultural Rights: A Perspective on its Development* (Clarendon Press, 1995), A Eide, C Krause, and A Rosas (eds), *Economic, Social and Cultural Rights* (Nijhoff, 2001), and Y Ghai and J Cottrell, *Economic, Social and Cultural Rights in Practice: The Role of Judges in Implementing Economic, Social and Cultural Rights* (Interights, 2004), as well as there being a collection of documents in B Ramcharan, *Judicial Protection of Economic, Social and Cultural Rights: A Textbook* (2nd edn, Nijhoff, 2005). There are also some excellent books dealing with a specific ESC right. It is interesting that no book dealing comprehensively with the *travaux préparatoires* of the ICESCR has been published, in contrast to the position with many of the other major human rights treaties.

[7] The then President of the General Assembly, Dr HV Evatt of Australia, stated: '[T]he adoption of the Declaration is a step forward in a great evolutionary process... the first occasion on which the organised community of nations has made a declaration of human rights and fundamental freedoms. That document is backed by the authority of the body of opinion of the United Nations as a whole and millions of people, men, women and children all over the world who would turn to it for help, guidance and inspiration': UN (GAOR), 183rd Plenary Meeting (10 Dec 1948), p 934. See also A Devereux, *Australia and the Birth of the International Bill of Human Rights 1946–1966* (Federation, 2005).

implementation.[8] The drafting process for the Covenant ended up taking nearly twenty years and was so difficult to do that, barely half-way through the process, it was declared to be 'a probable failure'.[9] The drafting process involved a range of UN bodies, principally the HR Commission (comprised of members voted on by governments and chaired for the first five years by Eleanor Roosevelt), the Economic and Social Council (ECOSOC), which had responsibility for the HR Commission), the Third Committee (being the Committee on Social, Humanitarian and Cultural Questions), and the General Assembly (GA). There was also a great deal of influential input from those UN specialized agencies which had responsibilities that covered aspects of ESC rights, especially the International Labour Organization (ILO), the World Health Organization (WHO), the UN Educational, Scientific, and Cultural Organization (UNESCO), and the Food and Agriculture Organization (FAO),[10] as well as from non-governmental organizations (NGOs).[11]

In the very early stages of their drafting work, the HR Commission took the decision not to include any ESC rights at all in this Covenant.[12] This was despite the fact that the UDHR included specific ESC rights (in articles 22–27) and that the UN Charter provided that the UN shall promote 'higher standards of living, full employment, and conditions of economic and social progress and development; [and] solutions of international economic, social, health, and related problems; and international cultural and educational cooperation'.[13] This decision 'was not reached without spirited and lengthy controversy' between the members of the HR Commission.[14] The HR Commission's decision was overruled by the GA (to which the matter had been referred by the ECOSOC), which resolved that:

[W]hen deprived of economic, social and cultural rights, man does not represent the human person whom the Universal Declaration regards as the ideal of the free man ... [and so requests that the Covenant includes] a clear expression of economic, social and cultural rights in a manner which relates them to the civil and political freedoms proclaimed by the draft Covenant.[15]

The HR Commission thus prepared a single draft Covenant containing seventy-three articles grouped into six parts covering both ESC rights and CP rights.[16]

---

[8] HR Commission, 2nd session, UN doc E/600, ECOSOC OR, 6th session, supp 1 (1948), para 18.

[9] JF Green, *The United Nations and Human Rights* (Brookings Institute, 1956) p 67.

[10] For a comprehensive analysis of the role of these UN specialized agencies in the drafting of the ICESCR, see P Alston, 'The United Nations' Specialized Agencies and Implementation of the International Covenant on Economic, Social and Cultural Rights' (1979) 18 Colombia J of Transnational L 79.

[11] See D McGoldrick, *The Human Rights Committee* (Clarendon Press, 1991) p 10.

[12] HR Commission, 5th session, UN doc E/1371, ECOSOC OR 9th session, supp 10 (1949).

[13] UN Charter, art 55 (a) and (b).

[14] A Holcombe, 'The Covenant on Human Rights' (1949) 14 L and Contemporary Problems 413 at 421.

[15] GA res 421 (V), 4 Dec 1950. See also J Simsarian, 'Economic, Social and Cultural Provisions in the Human Rights Covenant' 24 (626) *Department of State Bulletin* 1003 (1951).

[16] HR Commission, 7th session, UN ESCOR, supp 9 (E/1992) (24 May 1951), pp 20–26.

However, this was not the end of the issue as some states indicated their unwillingness to be parties to a Covenant that would commit them to provisions on ESC rights.[17] Both the ECOSOC and the GA debated the matter again, with the final decision being to request that the HR Commission:

[D]raft two Covenants on human rights... one to contain civil and political rights and the other to contain economic, social and cultural rights, in order that the General Assembly may approve the two Covenants simultaneously and open them at the same time for signature, the two Covenants to contain, in order to emphasize the unity of the aim in view and to ensure respect for and observance of human rights, as many similar provisions as possible.[18]

This decision to draft two separate Covenants was deeply divisive. Most commentators consider that this was a reflection of the dominance of western liberal states in the UN, with their emphasis on international supervision of civil and political rights (CP rights).[19] A participant at the time considered that there were four main reasons underpinning this decision to have separate Covenants: it would enable states to ratify one or other Covenant; CP rights were 'rights' to be given effect to promptly, while ESC rights were 'goals' to be achieved progressively; CP rights would be implemented primarily by legislation, whilst ESC rights would be implemented by a variety of methods, both public and private, would be costly and would not be immediate; and ESC rights could not be defined precisely and were not justiciable by a legal body, in contrast to CP rights.[20] As will be seen, both below and in other chapters in this book, these reasons have proved to be mistaken or overstated,[21] though they were decisive at this point in the drafting process. From this time onwards, two separate Covenants were drafted: one to deal with CP rights and one to deal with ESC rights. Yet, it should not be overlooked that the GA resolution that decided that there were to be two Covenants also affirmed the position that 'the enjoyment of civil and political freedoms and of economic, social and cultural rights are interconnected and interdependent.'[22] Indeed, the Preambles of each of the final Covenants confirm, in essentially the same terms, that:

[I]n accordance with the Universal Declaration of Human Rights, the ideal of free human beings enjoying civil and political freedom and freedom from fear and want can only be

---

[17] See LB Sohn, 'A Short History of United Nations Documents in Human Rights' in *United Nations and Human Rights* (18th Report of the Commission to Study the Organization of Peace, 1968) p 38 at 105–106.   [18] GA res 543 (VI), 5 Feb 1952.
[19] See eg, A Cassese, *International Law in a Divided World* (OUP, 1986), especially pp 297–300, A Eide, 'Economic, Social and Cultural Rights as Human Rights' in A Eide, C Krause, and A Rosas (eds), *Economic, Social and Cultural Rights: A Textbook* (2nd edn, Nijhoff, 2001), 9, 9–11 and M Nowak, *Introduction to the International Human Rights Regime* (Nijhoff, 2003), pp 78–79.
[20] J Simsarian, 'Progress in Drafting Two Covenants on Human Rights in the United Nations', (1952) 46 AJIL 710 at 710–712. See also J Simsarian, 'Economic, Social and Cultural Provisions in the Human Rights Covenant' 24 (626) *Department of State Bulletin* 1003 (1951).
[21] See comments in A Eide, 'Economic, Social and Cultural Rights as Human Rights' in A Eide, C Krause, and A Rosas (eds), *Economic, Social and Cultural Rights: A Textbook* (2nd edn, Nijhoff, 2001), 9, 10.   [22] GA res 543 (VI), 5 Feb 1952, preamble.

achieved if conditions are created whereby everyone may enjoy his economic, social and cultural rights, as well as his civil and political rights.[23]

The contention about drafting one or two Covenants was inextricably linked to the perceived differences between the two groups of rights and the issue of implementation. The debates on drafting appropriate implementation procedures for the ICESCR were, as one member of the Commission noted, 'the most difficult and controversial aspect of the covenant'.[24] As early as 1951, a detailed proposal for a 'Committee on Economic, Social and Cultural Rights', comprising fifteen members elected by ECOSOC, was put forward but rejected.[25] Interestingly in light of subsequent events, two of the reasons for rejection were that a separate body would lend support to the contention that ESC rights and CP rights were different, and that 'the time had come to call a halt to the process of setting up new committees'.[26]

A proposal that the Human Rights Committee (HRC), established under the ICCPR, should also have responsibility for considering reports under the ICESCR was not pursued.[27] Instead, it was accepted by the HR Commission, once it had been decided that there were to be two Covenants, that the implementation procedure for the ICESCR was to be by periodic reports, where states would submit regular reports to ECOSOC on the measures that they had adopted and the progress they had made in achieving the observance of the rights recognized in the ICESCR.[28] This position was supported even by the ILO, which had been operating a complaints procedure for decades.[29] In fact it was not until 1966 (the year that the ICESCR was adopted) that an alternative proposal was made. This proposal suggested that a committee of independent experts should be created to review state reports.[30] The proposal was not supported, probably because the then recent decision of the International Court of Justice (ICJ) in the

---

[23] Preamble to the ICESCR. The preamble to the ICCPR merely reverses the order of the rights at the end ie 'everyone may enjoy his civil and political rights, as well as his economic, social and cultural rights'.

[24] E/CN.4/SR.424 (1954), 12 (statement by Polish member).

[25] This was a proposal by Lebanon (E/CN.4/570 (1951)) and revised (E/CN.4/570/rev 1 (1951)).

[26] Statements by the Chinese and Pakistani members of the Commission in 1951, quoted in P Alston, 'The Committee on Economic, Social and Cultural Rights' in P Alston (ed), *The United Nations and Human Rights: A Critical Appraisal* (Clarendon Press, 1992), pp 476–477.

[27] This was a proposal by France: E/CN.4/L.388 (1954). The French member argued at the time that ESC rights will, after all, 'tend to become semi-enforceable or even fully enforceable by judicial action': E/CN.4/SR.432 (1954), 10.   [28] See art 16 ICESCR.

[29] 13 ESCOR 1, E/2057/add 2. It is likely that the reason for the lack of support by UN specialized agencies for a complaints procedure in the ICESCR was to maintain their own authority and to prevent duplication: P Alston, 'The United Nations' Specialized Agencies and Implementation of the International Covenant on Economic, Social and Cultural Rights' (1979)18 Columbia J of Transnational L 79 at 90–92.

[30] There was a proposal by Italy (A/C.3/L.1358 (1966)) and by the United States of America (A/C.3/L.1360 (1966)), the latter being influenced by the establishment of such a committee under the Convention on the Elimination of All Forms of Racial Discrimination, which had been adopted the year before (GA res 2106, 21 Dec 1965).

South-West Africa cases[31] appeared to create doubt in the minds of many state representatives about the roles of expert bodies.[32]

After the ICESCR entered into force in 1976, ECOSOC established Working Groups of governmental experts to assist it with reviewing state reports, though the first Working Group only came into existence in 1979.[33] These Working Groups were generally acknowledged to be an unsatisfactory means of supervision,[34] though little was done until a Working Group itself suggested in 1985 that it should become a committee of independent experts. This was endorsed by ECOSOC (as a simple 'renaming') with surprisingly little discussion.[35] This resolution of ECOSOC created a Committee on Economic Social and Cultural Rights, comprising eighteen independent experts (who serve in their 'personal capacity'), voted for by states parties for four-year terms, 'with due consideration being given to equitable geographical distribution and to the representation of different forms of social and legal systems'.[36] This change in the composition and independence of the body supervising the ICESCR has had a significant effect on its status. Most commentators agree that the Committee on Economic Social and Cultural Rights (ESCR Committee) now operates in practice (and is treated by states) in much the same way as the other bodies that supervise compliance with the global human rights treaties.[37] This is despite the fact that the ESCR Committee is still subject to the power of ECOSOC to alter its composition and operation, and it does not have the security of being a treaty-based body.

The ESCR Committee's role in supervising the obligations that states have undertaken under the ICESCR is, of course, affected by the content of those obligations. The substantive issue of obligations will be discussed below, yet the extent of these obligations was a matter of debate during the drafting process. During the early debate, it was stated that '[i]ndividuals must be allowed to enjoy human rights beyond those specifically conceded by the State. Freedom to enjoy such rights must be established, otherwise economic, social and cultural rights would be illusory and devoid of real meaning'.[38] Once it was clear that there were two Covenants to be drafted, in 1952 the HR Commission largely adopted a (revised) draft proposal of the United States of America (US) concerning state

---

[31] *South-West Africa Cases (Ethiopia and Liberia v South Africa)* ICJ Rep 6 (1966).
[32] One representative in the Third Committee said: 'The peoples of Africa had recently seen an eg of what experts were capable of, and they would never forget what the judges of the International Court of Justice had done to the people of South West Africa': A/C.3/SR.1410 (1966), para 11.
[33] ESC res 1988 (LX) (1976).
[34] See M Craven, *The International Covenant on Economic, Social and Cultural Rights*, p 40–42.
[35] ECOSOC res 1985/17: forty-three votes in favour to one against (USA—due to the 'need for budgetary austerity': E/1985/SR.22, para 11) with four abstentions (Bangladesh, Brazil, Japan, and Malaysia).   [36] Ibid, para (b).
[37] See, eg, P Alston, 'The Committee on Economic, Social and Cultural Rights' in P Alston (ed), *The United Nations and Human Rights: A Critical Appraisal* (Clarendon Press, 1992), pp 487–489 and M Craven, *The International Covenant on Economic, Social and Cultural Rights*, pp 49–51.
[38] E/CN.4/SR.269, p 6 (Eleanor Roosevelt).

parties' obligations under the Covenant.[39] This remained essentially the same through to the final version of the ICESCR.[40]

When the final version of the ICESCR was adopted it had been through nearly twenty years of drafts, debate, disagreements, and disavowal. It entered into force ten years later as 'the first comprehensive international human rights instrument to be legally binding on state parties.'[41] Its adoption, entry into force, and widespread ratification has been important, and has been a significant part of the considerable debate on a range of key issues in regard to ESC rights and about human rights more generally.

III. The nature and scope of obligations of economic, social, and cultural rights

Within the provisions of the ICESCR, ESC rights consists of the right to work,[42] the right to enjoy just and favourable conditions of work,[43] the right to form and join trade unions,[44] the right to social security and social insurance,[45] the right of family to protection and assistance,[46] the right to an adequate standard of living,[47] the right to the highest attainable standard of physical and mental health,[48] the right to education,[49] and the right to cultural life and benefits of scientific progress.[50] This group of rights is considered to be essentially humanitarian and aimed at providing human beings with a right to those basic subsistence needs that make life liveable in dignity, because no dignity can be said to be inherent in a jobless, hungry, sick, homeless, illiterate, and impoverished human being.[51] Thus, by their intrinsic nature, ESC rights 'imply a commitment to social integration, solidarity and equality and include tackling the issue of income distribution... [which]...are indispensable for an individual's dignity and the free development of their personality.'[52] Shue has observed that ESC rights are very important basic rights and that '[n]o one can fully, if at all, enjoy any right that is supposedly protected by society if he or she lacks the essentials for a reasonably healthy life'.[53]

Traditionally ESC rights are referred to as the 'second generation' of human rights in contrast to CP rights, which are traditionally referred to as the 'first generation' of human rights, owing to these rights being drafted later in time, at

---

[39] See the discussion in P Alston and G Quinn, 'The Nature and Scope of State Parties' Obligations under the International Covenant on Economic, Social and Cultural Rights' (1987), 9 Human Rights Q 156, pp 223–229.　　[40] Art 2(1) ICESCR.

[41] E/CN.4/SR. (1987), 7 (statement by Mr Smirnov, USSR).　　[42] Art 6.

[43] Art 7.　　[44] Art 8.　　[45] Art 9.　　[46] Art 10.　　[47] Art 11.　　[48] Art 12.

[49] Arts 13 and 14.　　[50] Art 15.

[51] J K Mapulanga-Hulston, 'Examinining the Justiciability of Economic, Social and Cultural Rights' (2002) 6 The Intl J of Human Rights No 4, 29–48.　　[52] Ibid at 34.

[53] H Shue, *Basic Rights: Subsistence, Affluence and US Foreign Policy* (1979) pp 24–25.

least in terms of national constitutions.[54] This very unhelpful terminology has often led to the misconception of ESC rights as second-class rights to CP rights. But, as noted above, the decision to have separate Covenants for CP rights and ESC rights respectively was based mainly on disagreements regarding the technical nature of ESC rights and the obligations of states in relation to these rights. Yet, to some extent, these disagreements continue to haunt the development of ESC rights today. Indeed, the arguments about the technical nature and obligations of ESC rights have been debated and challenged in various ways over the years in publications and at conferences, by academics, government officials, and human rights activists.[55]

The first key argument was that, unlike CP rights, ESC rights were perceived, especially by some industrial states, as not being 'real' human rights but seen merely as aspirational 'societal goals' to be determined by social policy.[56] For example, the US government deleted the sections dealing with ESC rights from the US State Department's annual *Country Reports on Human Rights Practices* submitted to the US Congress in 1982,[57] with the then US Assistant Secretary of State arguing that 'the rights that no government *can violate* [i.e. civil and political rights] should not be watered down to the status of rights that government should *do their best to secure* [i.e. economic, social and cultural rights]'.[58] Of course, the adoption and entry into force of the ICESCR as a human rights treaty should have put to rest, at least for the states parties to it, any pre-adoption legal arguments that ESC rights were not human rights per se.[59]

Second, ESC rights were perceived as vague and non-justiciable, and could thus not be claimed against a state in the same manner as CP rights.[60] Whilst there is

---

[54] K Vasak, 'Human Rights, A Thirty Years Struggle' (Nov 1977) *UNESCO Courier*, pp 29–32.

[55] See generally, G van Hoof, 'The Legal Nature of Economic, Social and Cultural Rights: A Rebuttal of Some Traditional Views' in P Alston and K Tomasevski, (eds) *The Right to Food* (Nijhoff, 1984); A Eide and A Rosas, 'Economic, Social and Cultural Rights: A Universal Challenge' in A Eide, C Krause, and A Rosas (eds), *Economic, Social and Cultural Rights: A Textbook* (Nijhoff, 1995) p 15; JK Mapulanga-Hulston, 'Examining the Justiciability of Economic, Social and Cultural Rights' (2002) 6 The Intl J of Human Rights No 4, pp 29–48; AA An-Na'im, 'To Affirm the Full Human Rights Standing of Economic, Social and Cultural Rights' in Y Ghai and J Cottrell (eds), *Economic, Social and Cultural Rights in Practice: The Role of Judges in Implementing Economic, Social and Cultural Rights* (Interights 2004) 7–22. See also the Limburg Principles on the Implementation of Economic, Social, and Cultural Rights, UN doc E/CN.4/1987/17 and NGO Coalition for an Optional Protocol to the ICESCR, Fact Sheet no 7 'The Question of Justiciability'.

[56] See the discussion in DJ Harris, *Cases and Materials on International Law* (6th edn, Sweet & Maxwell, 2004) p 655.

[57] *See* P Alston, 'US Ratification of the Covenant on Economic, Social and Cultural Rights: The Need for an Entirely New Strategy' 84 AJIL 367 (1990) at 372–375. See also DJ Harris, *Cases and Materials on International Law*, above at p 655, fn 18: 'During the Reagan Presidency, the US took the view that such rights were "societal goals" rather than human rights: see the US statement in UN doc A/40/C.3/36, p 5 (1985)'.

[58] P Alston, ibid, p 373 (emphasis and brackets in the original).

[59] See P Alston and G Quinn, above at p 158 for same view.

[60] EW Vierdag, 'The Legal Nature of the Rights Granted by the International Covenant on Economic, Social and Cultural Rights' (1978) 9 Netherlands Ybk of Intl L 99.

some vagueness and lack of conceptual clarity of ESC rights, Alston has noted that this is not peculiar to ESC rights but that the difference is the extent of elaboration enjoyed by CP rights.[61] Since 1989, the ESCR Committee has provided considerable conceptual clarity and elaboration to the nature and scope of many ESC rights contained in the ICESCR, especially through the publication of General Comments.[62] Of more significance is the question of non-justiciability, which seems to have been the most impeding factor against the development and judicial enforceability of ESC rights. The argument of non-justiciability is to the effect that courts and quasi-judicial institutions cannot adjudicate on ESC rights because they involve policy decisions that fall within the functions of the legislature and executive of a state rather than that of the judiciary and that the courts (or any international human rights supervisory body) cannot take over policy making from governments in relation to ESC rights.[63]

This view has been challenged in the following terms:

Adjudicating economic, social and cultural rights claims does not require courts to take over policy making from governments. Courts have neither the inclination nor the institutional capacity to do so. Rather, just as in civil and political rights cases, courts and other bodies adjudicating economic, social and cultural rights review governmental decision-making, to ensure consistency with fundamental human rights. Holding governments accountable to human rights [whether CP rights or ESC rights] enhances democracy. It does not undermine it.[64]

The ESCR Committee similarly observed that the classification of ESC rights as non-justiciable rights is arbitrary and 'would drastically curtail the capacity of the courts to protect the rights of the most vulnerable and disadvantaged groups in society'.[65] In its Concluding Observations on the report submitted by Zambia in 2003, the ESC Committee expressed regret at the view expressed by the Zambian delegation that ESC rights were not necessarily justiciable.[66] The jurisprudence of the African Commission on Human and Peoples' Rights on ESC rights under the African Charter on Human and Peoples' Rights (ACHPR),[67] equally negates the notion of non-justiciability of ESC rights, as have national courts, with the South African Constitutional Court specifically rejecting the argument that ESC rights

---

[61] P Alston, 'The Committee on Economic, Social and Cultural Rights' in P Alston (ed), *The United Nations and Human Rights: A Critical Appraisal* (1992) p 490.

[62] Other human rights supervisory bodies have also contributed significantly to the clarification of ESC rights, such as seen in the chapter on the European Social Charter in this book.

[63] See the discussion of this issue in R Beddard and D Hill (eds) *Economic, Social and Cultural Rights: Progress and Achievement* (Macmillan, 1992).

[64] Coalition for an Optional Protocol to the ICESCR's Fact Sheet No 7, 'The Question of Jusiticiability', para 3.   [65] ESCR Committee, *General Comment 9*, para 10.

[66] UN doc E/C.12/1/add 88 at para 11, See also *Concluding Observations of the Committee on Economic, Social, and Cultural Rights: United Kingdom of Great Britain and Northern Ireland*, E/C. 12/1/add 79, 5 June 2002, para 11, discussed in the chapter by Ed Bates in this book.

[67] See particularly the case of *The Social and Economic Rights Action Center for Economic and Social Rights v Nigeria*, Communication no 155/96 (2001).

were not justiciable.[68] Thus the argument of non-justiciability of ESC rights can no longer be legitimately sustained in international law.

A related argument to that of non-justiciability was the view that, unlike CP rights that mostly required 'negative obligations' on the part of states, ESC rights required 'positive obligations' on the part of states to fulfil them and, consequently, ESC rights were more resource demanding than CP rights, and so could only be progressively implemented depending on the availability of resources.[69] The obligations of states parties are recognized under the ICESCR as being subject to the availability of resources and require only the 'progressive realization' of the recognized rights.[70] Although it has been argued accurately that some CP rights also require resources to be protected,[71] it is clear that ESC rights generally require greater resources to achieve. This has greatly affected the full development and realization of the ESC rights over the years, especially in developing states. The ESCR Committee has, however, indicated that these differences must not be seen as watering down the obligations of states under the ICESCR. It has stated that 'while the Covenant provides for progressive realization and acknowledges the constraints due to the limits of available resources, it also imposes various obligations which are of immediate effect'.[72] For example, the obligation to ensure the right of everyone to form and join a trade union (article 8) is of immediate effect.

The obligations of states under the ICESCR are perceived as a combination of 'obligations of conduct' and 'obligations of result'.[73] While the undertaking of states parties 'to take steps' under article 2 (1) to realize the rights protected in the Covenant is an 'obligation of conduct' and has immediate application, the realization of the relevant rights, in most cases, is an 'obligation of result' that may be achieved progressively.[74] In its *General Comment 3*, the ESCR Committee stressed the 'obligations of conduct' as follows:

[W]hile the full realization of the relevant rights may be achieved progressively, steps towards the goal must be taken within a reasonably short time after the Covenant's entry into force for the States concerned. Such steps should be deliberate, concrete and targeted as clearly as possible towards meeting the obligations recognized in the Covenant. The

---

[68] See, particularly, *Soobramoney v Minister of Health, KwaZulu Natal* 1997 (12) BCLR 1696 and *The Government of the Republic of South Africa and Others v Grootboom*, 2000 (3) BCLR 277(C). See also COHRE, Leading Cases on Economic Social and Cultural Rights: Summaries, Working Paper 3 (ESC Rights Litigation Programme, COHRE (2006)) <http://www.cohre.org/view_page.php?page_id=62#1368> accessed 21 Nov 2006.

[69] For a comprehensive analysis see P Alston and G Quinn, 'The Nature and Scope of State Parties' Obligations under the International Covenant on Economic, Social and Cultural Rights' (1987), 9 Human Rights Q 156–229.

[70] Art 2 ICESCR. See also HJ Steiner and P Alston, *International Human Rights in Context: Law Politics Morals* (2nd edn, OUP, 2000) p 246.   [71] See eg, M Craven, above at p 15.

[72] ESCR Committee, *General Comment 3*, para 1.

[73] See eg, Report of the International Law Commission (1977) 2 Ybk of the Intl L Com 20, para 8.

[74] See P Alston and G Quinn, above pp 107–109.

means which should be used in order to satisfy the obligation to take steps are stated in article 2(1) to be 'all appropriate means, including particularly the adoption of legislative measures.'[75]

The ESCR Committee explained the 'obligations of result' and the progressive realization of the rights as follows:

[T]he fact that realization over time, or in other words progressively, is foreseen under the Covenant should not be misinterpreted as depriving the obligation of all meaningful content. It is on the one hand a necessary flexibility device, reflecting the realities of the real world and the difficulties involved for any country in ensuring full realization of economic, social and cultural rights. On the other hand, the phrase must be read in the light of the overall objective, indeed the *raison d'etre*, of the Covenant which is to establish clear obligations for States parties in respect of the full realization of the rights in question. It thus imposes an obligation to move as expeditiously and effectively as possible towards that goal. Moreover, any deliberately retrogressive measures in that regard would require the most careful consideration and would need to be fully justified by reference to the totality of the rights provided for in the Covenant and in the context of the full use of the maximum available resources.[76]

Although the Committee confers upon itself 'the ultimate determination as to whether all appropriate measures have been taken' in respect of the above obligations,[77] there is no doubt that in respect of both 'obligations of conduct' and 'obligations of result' much will still depend on the humane volition and good faith of the states parties to take the appropriate steps towards the realization of the ESC rights.

In appreciation of the resource-demanding nature of ESC rights, article 2(1) of the ICESCR indicates the obligation of states parties to 'take steps *individually and through international assistance and co-operation, especially economic and technical'*[78] to realize the rights guaranteed. Developing states would certainly favour the argument that this places some level of obligation on the international community, especially on the economically powerful states to assist and co-operate with the developing states in the realization of the ESC rights.[79] The ESCR Committee also seemed to have suggested this when it emphasized that:

[I]n accordance with Articles 55 and 56 of the Charter of the United Nations, with well-established principles of international law, and with the provisions of the Covenant itself, international cooperation for development and thus for the realization of economic, social and cultural rights is an obligation of all States. *It is particularly incumbent upon those States which are in a position to assist others in this regard.* The Committee notes in particular the importance of the Declaration on the Right to Development adopted by the General

---

[75] ESCR Committee, *General Comment 3*, paras 2 and 3.   [76] ibid, para 9.

[77] ibid, para 4.   [78] Emphasis added.

[79] See, eg, Chile's argument during the drafting of the Covenant that 'international assistance to under-developed countries had in a sense become mandatory as a result of commitments assumed by States in the United Nations'. E/CN.4/SR.1203, at 342, para 10 (1962).

Assembly in its resolution 41/128 of 4 December 1986 and the need for States parties to take full account of all of the principles recognized therein. *It emphasizes that, in the absence of an active programme of international assistance and cooperation on the part of all those States that are in a position to undertake one, the full realization of economic, social and cultural rights will remain an unfulfilled aspiration in many countries.*[80]

Most industrial states do not seem to accept that they have a legal obligation under the ICESCR to provide international assistance and co-operation to developing states for the realization of economic, social, and cultural rights. In their view, while developing states may seek the assistance and co-operation of developed states, they can not claim it as a legal right in the strict sense of the word.[81] They make reference, for example, to the wording of article 11 of the ICESCR which, in recognizing the right of everyone to an adequate standard of living, also recognizes that international co-operation in that regard is 'based on free consent' of states.[82] Assistance and co-operation for the full realization of ESC rights in developing states tends therefore to depend on the moral will and humane-volition of industrial states, rather than any international legal obligation on their part. It must be emphasized however, that the developing states must themselves make a conscientious effort in meeting their ESC rights obligations to the maximum of their available resources through a careful balancing of the available resources, in a way that will encourage international assistance and co-operation from industrial states.

Therefore, it is clear that there have been considerable debates about the nature and scope of the obligations of ESC rights, both during the forty years of the existence of the ICESCR and beforehand. The essence of the arguments that doubted the nature, the justiciability, and the scope of obligations of ESC rights have, in our view, now all been comprehensively rebutted in the literature and jurisprudence, both through strong conceptual analysis and clear applications of ESC rights.

IV. Economic, social, and cultural rights in action

In order to determine the impact of the ICESCR after forty years, assess how far the obligations have been fulfilled, and to see the effect of the legal protection of ESC rights now, this book explores the conceptual, comparative, and practical applications of these rights. In doing this, the authors seek also to honour the extraordinary legal scholarship of Professor David J Harris. David Harris, CMG, is Emeritus Professor of International Law and Co-Director of the Human Rights

---

[80] ESCR Committee, *General Comment 3*, para 14 (emphasis added). See also ESCR Committee, *General Comment 2 (International Technical Assistance Measures)*; UN doc HRI\GEN\1\Rev 1 at 45 in E/1990/23.   [81] See M Craven (1995), above at 148–150.
[82] Ibid.

Law Centre at the University of Nottingham, and is one of the leading international experts on ESC rights. In his over forty years of extremely high quality legal scholarship,[83] he has done, and continues to do, a great deal to change the perception of international human rights law, especially ESC rights, so that it is seen as a matter of necessary academic discussion and policy application world-wide. His books and other publications have shown deep insight into ESC rights at the conceptual and structural level,[84] with a regional and comparative analysis,[85] and including examinations of substantive applications of ESC rights.[86] Indeed, when he was appointed to the University of Nottingham in 1963, the ICESCR was still not finalized and yet one of his very first publications was on ESC rights.[87] His impact on ESCR rights has not been solely in his writings and talks, but also in

[83] One of the most well-known and respected books on general public international law is DJ Harris, *Cases and Materials on International Law*, first published in 1973 and now in its sixth edition (Sweet & Maxwell, 2004).

[84] See, eg, DJ Harris, 'Commentary of the Rapporteur on Consideration of State Parties Reports and International Co-operation: Limburg Principles of the Implementation of the International Covenant on Economic, Social and Cultural Rights' (1987), 8 Human Rights Q 147–155; DJ Harris, 'The System of Supervision in the European Social Charter: Problems and Options for the Future' in L Betten (ed), *The Future of European Social Policy* (Kluwer, 1991) pp 1–34; DJ Harris, 'International Rights of Petitions for Economic Social and Cultural Rights' in R Burchill, DJ Harris, and A Owers (eds), *Economic Social and Cultural Rights: Their Implementation in United Kingdom Law* (University of Nottingham, 1999), pp 14–31; and D J Harris, 'Lessons from the European Social Charter' in J Crawford and P Alston (eds), *The Future of Human Rights Treaty Monitoring* (Cambridge University Press, 2000), pp 347–360. See also, amongst many conference presentations and guest lectures: DJ Harris, 'The Justiciability of Economic and Social Rights' at the British Council Seminar on Establishing and Protecting Human Rights (1995) and DJ Harris, 'The International Covenant on Economic, Social and Cultural Rights: An Effective Guarantee of Human Rights', in M Pentikainen (ed), *Proceedings of the EU-China Human Rights Legal Seminar* (University of Lapland, 1999).

[85] See, eg, DJ Harris, 'The Protection of Economic and Social Rights in Common Law Countries' in F Matscher (ed), *Die Durchsetzung Wirtschaftlicher und Sozialer Grundrechte: Eine Rechtsvergleichende Bestandsaufnahme* [The Implementation of Economic and Social Rights: National, International and Comparative Aspects] (Engel, 1991), pp 201–222; DJ Harris, 'A Fresh Impetus for the European Social Charter' (1993), 41 Intl and Comparative L Q pp 659–676; DJ Harris, 'Human Rights Standards in the European Social Charter', J Rovšek (ed), *Uveljavljanje Politiènih, Državljanskih, Ekonomskih in Socialnih Pravic v Pravnem Sistemu Republike Slovenije* (1994), pp 108–138; DJ Harris, 'The European Social Charter and Social Rights in the European Union', in L Betten and D MacDevitt (eds), *The Protection of Fundamental Rights in the European Union* (Kluwer, 1997), pp 107–111; DJ Harris and S Livingstone (eds), *The Inter-American System of Human Rights* (Clarendon Press, 1998); DJ Harris, 'The European Social Charter', in R Hanski and M Suski (eds), *An Introduction to the International Protection of Human Rights: A Textbook* (Åbo Akademi University, 1999), pp 243–263; and DJ Harris and J Darcy (eds), *The European Social Charter: The Protection of Economic and Social Rights in Europe* (Transnational, 2001). See also, amongst many conference presentations and guest lectures: DJ Harris, 'Lessons for the UN Reporting System in the Experience of the European Social Charter', University of Cambridge Research Centre for International Law Conference on the United Nations Reporting System, 1997.

[86] DJ Harris, 'Comments on the Rights to Health: The Rights to Complain' in F Coomans and F Van Hoof (eds), *The Right to Complain about Economic, Social and Cultural Rights* (1995), pp 103–106. R Burchill, DJ Harris, and A Owers (eds), *Economic Social and Cultural Rights: Their Implementation in United Kingdom Law* (University of Nottingham, 1999).

[87] DJ Harris, 'The European Social Charter' (1964), 13 Intl and Comp L Q 1076.

his national and international activities, most notably, his membership of the Committee of Independent Experts of the European Social Charter, on which he sat from 1990 to 1996. He also regularly trains and advises government and non-government officials on human rights matters.

This long and distinguished career has been marked by vision, courage, and flair, albeit in a very modest way, in the creation of innovative ways to advance the knowledge and application of human rights.[88] This has included the pioneering of the Masters in Human Rights Law at the University of Nottingham, the founding of the Human Rights Law Centre[89], and the creation of the Human Rights Law Review. Above all, he has demonstrated a commitment to assisting new and less experienced people working in human rights. This is seen in his collaborative publications, sharing of teaching and consultancies, and, above all, in his unstinting support, careful supervision, and fostering of the careers, of research students, many of whom have gone on to write and work on ESC rights.

Thus David Harris' influence on ESC rights has been across a wide array of issues, though primarily in three main areas: the structure and the scope of obligations under the ICESCR; regional and comparative understandings of ESC rights; and the applications of these rights. These are also three areas that allow thorough consideration of the impact of the ICESCR forty years after its adoption.

A. The structure and scope of obligations under the ICESCR

The ICESCR created some specific legal obligations on states parties. Over time, as was shown above, these obligations came to be supervised by the ESCR Committee. Whilst the role of the Committee is crucial, there is also a need to see how the ICESCR has influenced other parts of the UN system, including whether ESC rights are being included and protected across the system, in order to determine the extent to which these rights are accepted and applied more generally.[90] In this section of the book, the integration of ESC rights within the broader UN human rights treaty body approaches, including whether human rights have an extra-territorial obligation dimension, is considered, as is their effect on the Security Council and on development, as well as on the roles and responsibilities of non-state actors.

Michael O'Flaherty begins this section with an examination of the general need for the integration of the recommendations of the seven principal UN

---

[88] He has also had the wonderful support of his wife, Sandra, and his two sons.
[89] The Human Rights Law Centre was founded in 1992. Its activities can be found at <http://www.nottingham.ac.uk/law/hrlc> accessed 27 Oct 2006.
[90] See, eg, P Alston, 'Beyond "Them" and "Us": Putting Treaty Body Reform into Perspective' in J Crawford and P Alston (eds), *The Future of Human Rights Treaty Monitoring* (Cambridge University Press, 2000) 501, especially p 524, M Sepúlveda, *The Nature of Obligations under the International Covenant on Economic, Social and Cultural Rights* (Intersentia, 2003), 45–72 and M Robinson, *A Voice for Human Rights* (University of Pennsylvania Press, 2006), especially p 115.

human rights treaty bodies. He analyses the weaknesses of the current system of unco-ordinated recommendations between the treaty bodies, which, he argues, could give rise to 'clashes of approach' and cases of 'inconsistent or contradictory recommendations' by the treaty bodies. He considers examples, such as the question of deportation of trafficked children from Greece addressed by the HRC and the ESCR Committee differently in their respective Concluding Observations on the issue. He argues that an integration of the approaches of the treaty bodies based on a human rights-based approach can enhance the structure and fulfilment of the obligations under the main human rights treaties, including the ICESCR, as well as the work of the respective Committees, including the ESCR Committee.

There is a strong link between respect for human rights, especially ESC rights, and development within states,[91] which links the structure and obligations of ESC rights to development. This is considered by Patrick Twomey in his analysis on human rights approaches to development, through which he considers how ESC rights can be integrated into all stages of development and have a central role in human rights-based development. The development of a state depends largely on the level of human development within the state,[92] and human development is a principal objective of human rights, especially through the guarantee of ESC rights. Where states uphold their obligations to respect, protect, and fulfil human rights generally, and ESC rights in particular, they would consequently fulfil their developmental obligations. In that regard, he refers to the fact that development as defined in the 1986 UN Declaration on the Right to Development covers 'all areas of national life such as health, environment, housing, education, distribution of resources, enhancement of people's capabilities and widening of people's choices'. He identifies the importance and need for effective evaluation indicators for the obligation of states and proposes that adopting a human rights approach to development can provide clear indicators of accountability, by which the developmental efforts of relevant states can be evaluated. This approach, he argues, 'introduces the notion of obligations and entitlements deriving from international human rights law and makes the enjoyment of human rights an explicit objective of development'.

But can the obligations to promote and protect ESC rights be delimited by territoriality? Mathew Craven discusses the issue of extraterritoriality and ESC

---

[91] See eg, former UN High Commissioner for Human Rights, Mary Robinson's lecture on: 'Bridging the Gap between Human Rights and Development: From Normative Principles to Operational Relevance' Presidential Fellows' Lecture, World Bank Washington DC, 3 Dec 2001. See also P Alston and M Robinson (eds), *Human Rights and Development: Towards Mutual Reinforcement*, (OUP, 2005) and the second preambular paragraph of the UN Declaration on the Right to Development (1986), GA res 41/128 of 4 Dec 1986, which recognizes development as 'a comprehensive economic, social, cultural and political process with the objective of constant improvement of the well-being of the entire population and all individuals'.

[92] See, eg, art 2(1) of the UN Declaration on the Right to Development, ibid, which provides that: 'The human person is the central subject of development and should be the active participant and beneficiary of the right to development'.

rights, where he considers the limitations of territoriality as a 'violence of dispossession' against disempowered, marginalized, or deprived people (i.e. the 'community of the dispossessed') who ESC rights are principally intended to protect. In relation to the enforcement of economic sanctions, he revisits the important question of whether state obligations under the ICESCR 'extended extra-territorially to the point at which states imposing sanctions in another state might be held responsible for any consequential deprivation (of the right to food or health care for example) even if the sanctioning state exercised no formal jurisdiction or control over the population concerned.' He observes that, despite the obligation for international co-operation under the ICESCR and the various comments by the ESCR Committee to the effect that states parties to the ICESCR assume some substantive obligations of an extra-territorial nature,[93] the question still remains a contentious one. Against this contentious background, he argues that a territorial conception of ESC rights puts into question the very rationale of ESC rights and that 'the conditions for legitimising the discourse of ESC rights necessarily involve placing the issues of poverty, disease or malnutrition within a global, rather than a local framework, so as to make possible the idea that the dispossessed are legitimate agents, capable of articulating meaningful claims on their own behalf'.

Nigel White analyses the applicability of ESC rights to the UN Security Council, to see if it is bound to respect human rights law generally, and ESC rights in particular, when acting under Chapter VII of the UN Charter. This includes when it imposes economic sanctions against states and against individuals (such as those suspected of terrorism), and when it establishes a post-conflict administration in a state. He explores the source of such obligations and what mechanisms exist, if any, to ensure compliance. He concludes that the Security Council is legally bound to respect core ESC rights in all those circumstances. However, he finds that 'the UN system is woefully inadequate in ensuring the accountability of the Security Council in this, or in any other, regard' and goes on to propose some ways by which that shortcoming may be corrected.

This section is concluded by Manisuli Ssenyonjo, as he examines the role of non-state actors (NSAs) in the realization of ESC rights. He addresses a range of relevant questions, including whether states can be held accountable for human rights violations caused by NSAs, whether NSAs can ignore ESC rights as long as states do not hold them accountable, and whether NSAs can be directly accountable under human rights law for any violations of ESC rights by them. He considers all the different views and concludes that 'the era of NSAs to respect ESC rights has arrived, but the question is "how can this be legally realized"'. He then goes on to identify and suggest some possible means of meeting that challenge.

---

[93] Eg ESCR Committee, *General Comment 8*, UN doc E/C.12/1997/8; ESCR Committee, *General Comment 12*, UN doc E/C.12/1999/5.

This section of the book addresses some of the major and most important theoretical and practical questions regarding the structure and scope of obligations under the ICESCR. It deals with a wide variety of substantive and institutional issues, and demonstrates the wide ramifications for the international legal system due to the adoption of the ICESCR.

B. Regional and comparative understandings of ESC rights

If ESC rights are to form a strong frame of reference globally then it is vital that they are seen by all those affected, including states and individuals, as being of relevance to them. Because cultures, socio-economic systems, and community interests are particularly significant in the understanding of ESC rights, the regional and comparative context must be explored.[94] Therefore in this section, the African, American, and European (both under the European Social Charter (ES Charter) and the European Convention on Human Rights (ECHR)) human rights systems are considered, as well as a specific national legal system.

The section starts with the examination by Mashood Baderin of the role of the African Commission on Human and Peoples' Rights (African Commission) in the implementation of ESC rights in Africa. He assesses the implementation of ESC rights under the African human rights system through a critical evaluation of the activities of the African Commission and highlights possible ways of enhancing the realization of the ESC rights guaranteed under the ACHPR. He provides an analysis of all the communications on ESC rights that have been decided by the African Commission. He observes that the jurisprudence of the African Commission on ESC rights 'boldly establishes the justiciability of ESC rights and thereby challenges the outdated notion of the non-justiciability of ESC rights' but concludes that there can be further improvement to ensure the full and practical realization of the ESC rights under the African regional human rights system and suggests some ways for such improvement.

Verónica Gómez considers the development of the protection of ESC rights within the inter-American human rights system. The protection has been enhanced with the Additional Protocol on ESC Rights,[95] as well as some very strong decisions by the Inter-American Commission and Court about the positive legal obligations on states and that extend the range of reparations and protective measures. This has had significant impacts on the implementation of ESC rights

---

[94] See eg, C Anselm Odinkalu, 'Implementing Economic, Social and Cultural Rights under the African Charter on Human and Peoples' Rights', in M Evans and R Murray (eds), *The African Charter on Human and Peoples' Rights* (Cambridge University Press, 2002) 178, especially pp 183–187.

[95] Additional Protocol to the American Convention on Human Rights in the Area of Economic, Social and Cultural Rights, adopted at San Salvador, El Salvador, on 17 Nov 1988: see *Basic Documents Pertaining to Human Rights in the Inter-American System* OEA/Ser.L/V/I.4 rev 10 (2004), p 85.

in the region, including in relation to the protection and recognition of matters affecting indigenous peoples. This analysis also shows the ability for ESC rights to be judicially considered and applied by a regional human rights body, and then accepted by the relevant states.

The chapter by Robin Churchill and Urfan Khaliq follows with an examination of the collective complaints system under the ES Charter. They critically examine the practical operation of the collective complaints system of the ES Charter since the Collective Complaints Protocol (CCP) entered into force in 1998. They analyse the CCP within the general overview of mechanisms for ensuring compliance with ESC rights under other treaties and consider the likely utility and effectiveness of the collective complaints system under the CCP. They offer recommendations as to how the system can be improved to achieve its objectives.

The concept of the indivisibility and interrelatedness of all human rights has strongly been promoted, particularly after the adoption of the Vienna Declaration on Human Rights, which stated emphatically that 'all human rights are universal, indivisible and interdependent and interrelated'.[96] Colin Warbrick, in his examination of economic and social interests under the ECHR, argues that this does not necessarily merge ESC rights with CP rights. He argues that, with the exception of the right to education, the ECHR does not explicitly or impliedly protect ESC rights and that, even though there may be overlaps between certain CP rights and ESC rights, that does not result in the transformation of ESC rights into CP rights or vice versa. Through a theoretical and case law analysis, Colin shows that the ECHR may only sometimes protect economic and social aspects of explicit ECHR (CP) rights and not the protection of ESC rights per se. He concludes that, while reference to 'economic and social interests might expand the substance of civil and political rights under the ECHR, there is less evidence that this process will work in reverse'.

Some states are very reluctant to accept that ESC rights can be judicially considered, as Ed Bates shows in his chapter on the United Kingdom (UK) government and the ICESCR. He shows how the UK government's views on the nature and legal status of ESC rights have affected the (lack of) incorporation of these rights into UK law. Indeed, in the latest exchanges, the ESCR Committee (in its Concluding Observations on the UK's report):

[R]eiterate[s] its concern about the state party's position that the provisions of the Covenant, with minor exceptions, constitute principles and programmatic objectives rather than legal obligations that are justiciable, and that consequently they cannot be given direct legislative effect.... [In contrast, the Committee's clear view is that] all economic, social and cultural rights are justiciable.[97]

---

[96] Vienna Declaration on Human Rights, 1993, para 5, 32 Intl Legal Materials 1661 (1993).
[97] *Concluding Observations of the Committee on Economic, Social, and Cultural Rights: United Kingdom of Great Britain and Northern Ireland*, E/C. 12/1/add 79, 5 June 2002, para 11.

He follows the processes and procedures within the UK, where strong pressure is being placed on the UK government to implement ESC rights, but he is not optimistic that implementation will occur in the near future.

This section of the book thus provides very useful analyses of regional and comparative understandings of ESC rights across the three main regional human rights systems. It shows the influence of the ICESCR within these systems and cross-currents of influence between systems, though its influence within states remains less secure.

C. Applications of ESC rights

There are a wide range of ESC rights and this book does not attempt to deal with each one in detail. Rather, this section deals with some cross-cutting issues that can affect the application of many ESC rights. Hence, matters concerning the use of effective indicators and appropriate analytical frameworks, applying ESC rights in relation to poverty, democracy, and development, and dealing with cultural issues, form the basis for this section.

In 1993, the World Conference on Human Rights urged the examination of 'a system of indicators to measure progress in the realization [of ESC rights]'[98] because the use of specific human rights indicators gives clarity to the level of compliance by states and so could prevent 'recalcitrant States' using the ICESCR obligation of progressive realization as an 'escape hatch'.[99] Thus Paul Hunt and Gillian MacNaughton consider this important issue with reference to the right to health. They demonstrate that indicators have an important role to play in measuring and monitoring the progressive realization of the right to health. However, they demonstrate that, no matter how sophisticated the indicators might be, they will never give a complete picture of the enjoyment of the right in a specific jurisdiction. They also show how indicators must have certain qualities, such as appropriate disaggregation, and allow for external factors to be taken into account.

In the following chapter, Jennifer Tooze discusses the right to social security and social assistance, and argues that both rights 'can be translated into state obligations that can be effectively monitored and enforced' in international law. She gives an overview of the rights and provides an analytical framework within which the provisions of social security and social assistance can be monitored under article 9 of the ICESCR. She compares the approaches of the ESCR Committee with that of the ILO on different aspects of interpreting and measuring the realization of the rights to social security and social assistance and concludes that,

[98] Vienna Declaration and Programme of Action, World Conference on Human Rights, A/CONF.157/23 (12 July 1993) para 98.

[99] S Leckie, 'Another Step Towards Indivisibility: Identifying the Key Features of Violations of Economic, Social and Cultural Rights' (1998), 20 Human Rights Q 81 at p 94.

where the ESCR Committee works in close consultation with the ILO, meaning can also be given to the rights to social security and social assistance under the ICESCR.

Richard Burchill considers the relationship between democracy and ESC rights, though he notes that the ESCR Committee has not articulated any clear ideas on this relationship. He makes clear that a minimalist, market-based definition of democracy is inappropriate and instead needs to be one that is inclusionary and emancipatory, so that it addresses the social and economic aspects of the human experience and society. This is a challenging conclusion that could enable a range of aspects of the application of ESC rights, such as how participation in society can be effected, to be clarified.

Similarly, Sarah Joseph seeks to bring together another cross-cutting issue, that of trade and human rights, to see how they impact on ESC rights, especially poverty. As Skogly has noted:

[P]oor people experience violations of a large range of rights, all of which would—if they were respected, protected and fulfilled—contribute to moving people out of poverty. Part of the problem is a lack of respect for the right to an adequate standard of living.... The ability to exercise one's right to food, to housing, clothing, medical care and education, through the exercise of a right to participation, expression and other civil and political rights, is vital for individuals if they are to move away from being poor, and for society to eradicate poverty.[100]

It is in this context, and the real concerns expressed about the role of the World Trade Organization (WTO), that she explores the WTO rules, decisions, and practices. By use of specific examples, in considering the arguments made by industrialized and developing states, and in exploring some of the core economic theories, she offers a way forward so that the WTO can be a means to assist those in poverty and aid development for all.

Development is also a key aspect examined by Jane Ansah. She considers the legal status of the right to development in international law and its inclusion as an ESC right. She then applies it to the particular national example of Malawi, which has the right to development protected by its Constitution. Whilst the case law and practice is still relatively small, she analyses this, combined with comparative examples, to show the vital importance of this right in a poor, developing state. She also argues that lawyers and the judiciary need to take it seriously.

Dominic McGoldrick concludes this section by dealing with cultural rights, which are often neglected or given a cursory discussion when ESC rights are considered, even by the ESCR Committee. One of the reasons for this, as he discusses, is the difficult task of definition, with Lyndel Prott noting that 'any attempt to talk about cultural issues in terms of rights may be slippery and

---

[100] S Skogly, 'Is There a Right not to be Poor?' (2002) 2 Human Rights L Rev 59, 65.

difficult. Culture is not a static concept: cultures change all the time'.[101] However, in 2005, with the ESCR Committee's *General Comment* 17[102] and the UNESCO Convention on the Protection and Promotion of the Diversity of Cultural Expressions,[103] he argues that there is now a possibility of significant normative improvements in the understanding and application of cultural rights. He considers that an ESC rights framework offers a positive structure for addressing difficult tensions that arise from states' multicultural and pluralist policies.

Therefore, this section demonstrates the impact that the ICESCR has had on a range of global issues that affect the daily lives of many people. The authors show that there is a need to apply ESC rights to these issues in an effective way.

V. Conclusion

For most of the world's population, issues of food, water, education, health, and work are part of the pressing reality of their daily lives. For many governments, ESC rights appear to be a long way from implementation. Indeed, '[some argue that] the incorporation of economic and social rights in the human rights canon is simply spitting in the wind, when hundreds of millions suffer from malnutrition and vulnerability to disease and starvation. Worse, it is an insult to them to insist on their "human rights" when there is no realistic prospect of these being upheld'.[104] However, as the ESCR Committee has made clear,

[w]hile the common theme underlying poor people's experiences is one of powerlessness, human rights can empower individuals and communities. The challenge is to connect the powerless with the empowering potential of human rights. Although human rights are not a panacea, they can help to equalise the distribution and exercise of power within and between societies.[105]

This is one of the challenges and one of the transformation possibilities of ESC rights.

Just as with the drafting of the ICESCR, the protection of ESC rights remains a contentious, difficult, and challenging matter. Indeed, it has been stated that 'there hardly exists another human rights treaty which has been more frequently misinterpreted, downplayed or intentionally abused' than the ICESCR.[106] Yet, as

---

[101] L Prott, 'Cultural Rights as People's Rights' in, Crawford (ed), *The Rights of Peoples* (OUP, 1988) 93 at 95. See also L Prott, 'Understanding One Another on Cultural Rights' in *Cultural Rights and Wrongs* (Paris, UNESCO, 1998) 165.

[102] ESCR Committee, *General Comment 17* (2005) 13 Intl Human Rights Rep (2006) 613.

[103] See <http://unesdoc.unesco.org/images/0014/001429/142919e.pdf> accessed 27 Oct 2006.

[104] D Beetham, 'What Future for Economic and Social Rights?', 43 *Political Studies* (1995) 41, 43–44.

[105] ESCR Committee, *Statement on Poverty and the International Covenant on Economic, Social and Cultural Rights* (2001) E/C.12/2001/10, para 6.

[106] B Simma, 'The Implementation of the International Covenant on Economic, Social and Cultural Rights' in F Matscher (ed), *The Implementation of Economic and Social Rights: National, International and Comparative Aspects* (Engel, 1991), p 79.

is clear from this book, after forty years of debate, development, and application since the adoption of the ICESCR, ESC rights are now accepted as being part of the international human rights legal obligations of states and there are institutional supervisory bodies—global, regional, and some national—that are able to check compliance with these obligations. In addition, the protection of ESC rights has affected a very wide range of issues of concern to the international community, from peace and security to world trade and poverty. At the same time, the 'unarmed, the economically under-developed, and the technologically under-privileged' referred to at the very beginning of this chapter, remain reliant on a law that is stronger than it was forty years ago but is still far from being strong enough. For this law to be strengthened, it also relies on action, so that the law has an effect—a meaning—on daily lives, as was acknowledged by the first chair of the HR Commission:

Where after all, do universal human rights begin? In small places, close to home—so close and so small that they cannot be seen on any map of the world. Yet they are the world of the individual person: the neighborhood he [or she] lives in; the school or college he [or she] attends; the factory, farms or office where he [or she] works. Such are the places where every man, woman, or child seeks equal justice, equal opportunity, equal dignity without discrimination. Unless these rights have meaning there, they have little meaning anywhere.[107]

[107] Eleanor Roosevelt, remarks at presentation of booklet on human rights, *In Your Hands*, to the Commission on Human Rights, New York, 27 March 1958.

PART II

THE STRUCTURE AND SCOPE OF OBLIGATIONS UNDER THE ICESCR

2

Towards Integration of United Nations Human Rights Treaty Body Recommendations: The Rights-Based Approach Model

Michael O'Flaherty

I. The nature of treaty body recommendations

The seven principal United Nations (UN)-sponsored human rights treaties stipulate that states parties submit periodic reports to the respective treaty monitoring bodies on their implementation of the treaty obligations. Following the review of a report, the treaty body in question issues a set of 'Concluding Observations', containing its collective assessment of the state's record and recommendations for enhanced implementation of the rights in question. Arguably, the issuance of Concluding Observations is the single most important activity of human rights treaty bodies—it provides an opportunity for the delivery of an authoritative overview of the state of human rights in a state and for the delivery of forms of recommendation which can stimulate systemic improvements.[1]

There is a more or less common structure for the Concluding Observations of all of the treaty bodies.[2] They comprise an introduction which identifies the documents considered—normally the state party report, core document, list of issues, and replies to the list of issues—and the dates on which they were examined; positive aspects (in which the treaty bodies acknowledge the measures taken to implement the treaty and note the areas in which significant progress was made); and principal areas of concern and recommendations directed to the state party by the treaty body (these sub-sections constituting the main body of the Concluding Observations). The Human Rights Committee (HRC), the Committee on the Elimination of Racial Discrimination (CERD), and the Committee on the Rights

---

[1] See M O'Flaherty, *Human Rights and the UN: Practice before the Treaty Bodies* (Nijhoff, 2002) ch 1.
[2] See *Methods of Work Relating to the State Reporting Process: Background Note by the Secretariat*, UN doc HRI/ICM/2002/02.

of the Child (CRC) merge the sub-sections on concerns and recommendations into one, with a recommendation usually suggested for each concern identified. Concluding Observations also commonly include a 'factors and difficulties' sub-section.[3] The Concluding Observations of CRC remain the most extensive, frequently exceeding fifteen–twenty pages, while those of other committees rarely exceed five pages in length.[4]

Treaty bodies do not have judicial powers and in no case have they been empowered to determine violations of the treaties by states parties. It is thus clear that Concluding Observations, as such, impose no legal obligation on states parties. In any case, the plain text of all Concluding Observations adopted thus far makes clear that the treaty bodies see their role as advisory and recommendatory.[5]

The non-binding nature of Concluding Observations is all the more evident when account is taken of the extent to which treaty bodies make recommendations on matters extraneous to the actual treaty obligations of the states parties, such as for the ratification of other treaties[6] and additional protocols,[7] withdrawal of reservations[8], and implementation of the declarations and plans of action adopted at world conferences.[9] Likewise, recommendations which associate the treaty body with one of a range of legitimate forms of treaty compliance can not be considered to have normative effect: the issue is commonly exemplified by treaty bodies recommending to states parties that they incorporate the provisions of the treaties in domestic law in a 'monist' manner, notwithstanding that it is for the state to determine how best to implement the treaty at the domestic level.[10]

The present author has undertaken an analysis of the legal status of Concluding Observations elsewhere.[11] Having essayed the various arguments regarding their legal status and having concluded that they do not have binding effect, he observed:

Any (further effort) at the articulation of any form of obligation which may arise from concluding observations would be unhelpful and inappropriate. Concluding observations emerge from a process of dialogue, notable for its non-adversarial nature.[12] The according of a compulsive quality to the subsequent findings by the treaty body would be inconsistent

---

[3] The UN secretariat reported in 2002 that HRC had abandoned the practice: *Methods of Work Relating to the State Reporting Process: Background Note by the Secretariat*, UN doc HRI/ICM/2002/02 at para 92. However, such a sub-section was included in Concluding Observations on a report of Colombia which were adopted in 2004: UN doc CCPR/CO/80/COL.

[4] The practice of CRC has been described by committee members as necessitated by the wide range of issues addressed by the Convention on the Rights of the Child (author's discussions with committee members).

[5] See C Tomuschat, *Human Rights: Between Idealism and Realism* (OUP, 2003), pp 154.

[6] See eg, the practice of ESCR Committee.　　　　[7] See eg, the practice of CRC.

[8] All of the treaty bodies.　　　　[9] See eg, the practice of CEDAW.

[10] See *Concluding Observations of ESCR Committee on Ireland*, UN doc E/2003/22 at para 126. On the issue of the nature of the implementation obligation see ESCR Committee *General Comment 3* of and HRC *General Comment 31*, both at UN doc HRI/GEN/1/rev 7, as well as M O'Flaherty and L Heffernan, *International Covenant on Civil and Political Rights—International Human Rights Law in Ireland* (Brehon/Sweet & Maxwell, 1996) ch 1.

[11] M O'Flaherty, 'The Concluding Observations of United Nations Human Rights Treaty Bodies', (2006) 6 (1) Human Rights L Rev.　　　　[12] M O'Flaherty (n 1 above) at 1.

with this model and is likely to meet with the resistance of states and their further unwill-ingness to participate in the reporting process.[13] In any case, much of the content of con-cluding observations simply does not lend itself to normative expression. Apart from the elements which have nothing to do with the treaties themselves, a considerable proportion of the analysis and recommendations may have a hortatory quality.[14] It is also common-place for recommendations to propose approaches which are either very case-specific or are of an experimental or untried nature—approaches of a type which may change radically over time or according to regional specificities and that are hardly the stuff of law.[15]

Given the non-binding and operational nature of the guidance, it is evident that the crafting of the recommendations is not constrained by the formal nature of state obligation and may propose strategies and address issues to the extent useful in the interest of comprehensive enjoyment of human rights. Examples of such an approach are replete across the treaty bodies. For example, the Committee on Economic, Social and Cultural Rights (ESCR Committee), in its 2005 Concluding Observations on a periodic report submitted by Zambia,[16] recommended that resources be provided to a national human rights institution in a manner compliant with the clearly non-binding and extraneous (for purposes of the International Covenant on Economic, Social and Cultural Rights) 'Paris Principles'.[17] It also recommended that Zambia codify its customary law[18]—a matter on which the Covenant is silent.

II. Weaknesses of the current system of unco-ordinated recommendations

Taking account of the purpose of Concluding Observations and their essentially practical and unregulated nature, it is striking that their only commonalities

[13] This point has been made by state representatives to the author on numerous occasions.

[14] See n 13 above.

[15] Ibid. In a recent paper Martin Scheinen seems to approach the issue somewhat differently. He characterizes the review of state party reports and the issuance of Concluding Observations as, '(application of) a normative grid over a set of facts: assessing laws, practices or situations *in abstracto* for the purpose of addressing their compatibility with human rights'. He does concede that Concluding Observations may include recommendations on policy, 'as long as any such recommen-dations flow directly from a normative finding made through interpreting the applicable standards'. It is suggested this characterization by Scheinen does not correspond with the actual practice of treaty bodies which, as noted above, frequently make policy proposals that do not appear to be based on normative considerations. See M Scheinen, *Background Paper N 3, Use of Indicators by Human Rights Treaty Bodies—Experiences and Potentials* (Expert Meeting on Human Rights Indicators, Turku/Abo, 11–13 March 2005) at pp 3 and 7, available at: <http://www.abo.fi/instut/imr/degree_programmes/norfa/Expert.doc> accessed on 23 May 2006.

[16] *Conclusions and recommendations of the Committee on Economic, Social, and Cultural Rights, Zambia*, UN doc E/C.12/1/add 106 (2005).

[17] Ibid at para 33. The proper title of the Paris Principles is, *Principles relating to the status and functioning of national institutions for protection and promotion of human rights*, available at: <http://www.unhchr.ch/html/menu6/2/fs19.htm#annex> accessed on 23 May 2006.

[18] *Conclusions and recommendations of the Committee on Economic, Social, and Cultural Rights, Zambia* (n 16 above) p 4, UN Doc E/C.12/1/add 106 para 37.

concern the issue of their structure. On matters of substance they stand alone, with each treaty body considering and adopting its own recommendations without reference to the activities of the other committees. No cross referencing or other such mutuality can be detected in those Concluding Observations that have been adopted so far, even in situations where two or more treaty bodies have addressed implementation of the same or similar human rights or have examined the same situation within a state.[19] As a result, states must address multiple sets of recommendations, often concerning the same or closely related issues. In so doing they require to take account of differing indications of prioritization.[20] They may also have to contend with clashes of approach by distinct treaty bodies including cases of inconsistent or contradictory recommendations. This was illustrated by the distinct manner in which two treaty bodies, the ESCR Committee and the HRC, addressed the issue of the deportation of trafficked children from Greece. In Concluding Observations adopted in 2004, the ESCR Committee recommended that, 'the State party ensure respect for the necessary procedural safeguards when deporting victims of trafficking in persons, particularly when such victims are children'.[21] Notably, there is no reference to such issues as the propriety of or the acceptability of such safeguards, and the reference could be understood as to be no more than to the existing Greek standards. The HRC, in 2005, went considerably further and recommended that Greece, 'develop a procedure to address the specific needs of unaccompanied non-citizen children and to ensure their best interests in the course of any immigration, expulsion, and related proceedings'.[22]

The weakness of such fragmented and mutually unsupportive approaches appear to be obvious in terms of diminished impact and missed opportunities. They may also be perceived as inconsistent with the very nature of human rights as indivisible and inter-related.[23] Fragmented forms of recommendation are also at odds with the actual experience of human rights denial and violation which is commonly one of vulnerable groups suffering from multiple and closely inter-related forms of suffering, deprivation, and discrimination, all of which require to be addressed in a coherent and integrated manner.[24]

The situation would appear to be one that is ripe for attention and correction. Surprisingly though, the consolidation and integration of treaty body

---

[19] Eg, observe the absence of cross referencing between the Committee on the Elimination of Racial Discrimination's recommendations in 2005 regarding the Zambian Human Rights Commission (UN doc CERD/C/ZMB/CO/16 at para 20) and those issued by the ESCR Committee, referred to above.   [20] Ibid.

[21] ESCR Committee, *Concluding Observations, Greece* UN doc E/C.12/1/add97 (2004) at para 39.

[22] HRC, *Concluding Observations, Greece* UN doc CCPR/CO/83/GRC (2005) at para 17.

[23] *World Conference on Human Rights, Vienna Declaration and Programme of Action*, 12 July 1993, UN doc A/157/23. (1993).

[24] See eg, the analysis of sexual abuse and its relationship to other forms of human rights abuse, in Amnesty Internatonal USA, 'A fact Sheet on Sexual Violence: A Human Rights Violation' at: <http://www.amnestyusa.org/women/pdf/sexualviolence.pdf> accessed 27 Oct 2006.

recommendations has not featured as an element thus far in the various treaty body reform discussions. The 2002 proposals of the UN Secretary-General[25] did not address the issue and nor do the more recent proposals by the UN High Commissioner for Human Rights for an integrated treaty body.[26] These latter proposals do, however, provide an appropriate context for the discussion since consolidated recommendations would seem to be an obvious form of output from the review of state reports by a single integrated treaty body.[27]

III. Towards a model for the integration of recommendations

Superficially, it is easy to imagine how a common set of recommendations might be developed—for instance, it might be no more than a consolidated form of what now exists in several distinct treaty body outputs, with the imposition of some overall coherence and the avoidance of inconsistent elements. While this might already constitute an improvement on the current situation, it would also represent change on the most modest of scales. It would miss an opportunity for development of a form of recommendations which has as its objective the optimal comprehensive implementation of human rights within the given context of a particular state.

It is necessary to devise a model framework for such a recommendatory system, containing all of those elements that must be considered in any given case, albeit their relevance will vary according to the particular circumstances of each state. None of these elements is particularly original since each of them is addressed, to a greater or lesser extent, by at least some of the treaty bodies, though in each case with regard to just the specific treaty that is monitored by the treaty body, and in a fragmented, inconsistent, and unsystematic way. The first such element concerns the need for the model to integrate attention to all of the human rights contained within the human rights treaties that are monitored by the treaty bodies. The attention requires to be non-hierarchical and, to the extent possible, respectful of the principle of indivisibility.

Second, the model must engage comprehensively with the full extent of the state's implementation obligation. The scope of this obligation is well explicated in various General Comments[28] of the treaty bodies as well as in academic

---

[25] *An Agenda for Further Change*, UN doc A/57/387.

[26] *Plan of Action of the United Nations High Commissioner for Human Rights*, 2005, UN doc 59/2005/add 3 at para 99.

[27] For the single most comprehensive contemporary (Dec 2005) survey of the issue and commentary by interested parties see OHCHR Treaty Body Reform Discussion Forum: <http://ohchr.org/English/bodies/treaty/reform.htm> accessed on 13 Oct 2006.

[28] See in particular, ESCR Committee, *General Comment 3*; HRC, *General Comment 31*; CERD, *General Recommendations I and II*; CRC, *General Comment 5*; all contained in UN doc HRI/GEN/1/rev 7.

discourse.[29] Notably, the categorization of the obligation as tripartite—to respect, protect, and fulfil—has proved helpful in charting its extent.[30] The state obligation, at least with regard to its fulfilment component, is sometimes addressed from a distinct but more or less complementary perspective, that of what the CRC describes as 'general measures of implementation'.[31] That committee has elaborated on such measures which it identifies as law reform, independent national child rights institutions, comprehensive national agendas for the rights of the child, children-focussed permanent institutions in government, allocation of resources for children, systematic monitoring of child rights, education/ training/awareness raising, and involvement of civil society. The general measures of implementation approach diverges from a strict obligation-related one in that it also deals with issues of implementation that go beyond formal treaty-based requirements.[32]

The focus on implementation brings us to the third requirement for the model, that is to incorporate attention to the actual enjoyment of human rights rather than just to the state's legal obligation. This consideration has particular resonance in the context of the review of enjoyment of economic, social, and cultural rights and it is certainly reflected in the longstanding practice of the ESCR Committee in its drafting of Concluding Observations, as was noted earlier.[33] The concern with the actual enjoyment of rights also highlights the need for recommendations to be based on an analysis of patterns of vulnerability to human rights abuse or violation within a state and to the precise identification of whatever actor is impeding full enjoyment of the rights, be it the state, a non-state domestic actor (in which case, obviously, circumstances may engage state responsibility), or such other actor as an intergovernmental organization or a transnational commercial enterprise. It is no less necessary to base recommendations on a power analysis of a state, identifying its elites and the extent and manner of 'elite capture' of power and resources that may affect the given society.[34]

Finally, recommendations must be constructed in a manner whereby they can be acted upon in an effective manner. This consideration has preoccupied a number of commentators on the quality of the current form of treaty body Concluding Observations. The UN Independent Expert on Enhancing the Long-term Effectiveness of the UN Human Rights Treaty System, Philip Alston, in 1997, expressed concern regarding Concluding Observations and recommended that their quality be improved in terms of, 'clarity, degree of detail, level of accuracy

---

[29] For a recent review see C Tomuschat, *Human Rights: Between Idealism and Realism* (OUP, 2003) ch 5.

[30] For a survey of the literature and a critical review see E Koch, '*Dichotomies, trichotomies or waves of duties*' (2005) 5 Human Rights L Rev, no 1.   [31] CRC, *General Comment 5* (n 28 above) at 8.

[32] See Summary Report, *Study on the Impact of the Implementation of the Convention on the Rights of the Child* (UNICEF 2005).   [33] See nn 18 and 19 above.

[34] C Johnson and D Start, *Rights, Claims and Capture: Understanding the Politics of Pro-Poor Policy* (Overseas Development Institute, Working Paper 145, 2001).

and specificity'.[35] The present author elsewhere has examined the extent to which treaty bodies have addressed such concerns.[36]

For our present purposes it is sufficient to suggest, borrowing from the language of business, that recommendations be 'SMART', that is, specific, measurable, attainable, realistic, and time-bound.[37]

IV. The relevance of the 'rights-based approaches' model

Having identified the elements necessary to the model it becomes possible to identify the extent to which some form of it is already in existence and may be adapted to the work of the treaty bodies. The present author suggests that such a model does indeed exist and is at least partially suited to the purpose. The model may be found within the discourse and practice of Rights-Based Approaches to Development (RBA).

RBA refers to efforts to undertake development activities in a manner that serves to promote the human rights of the affected populations.[38] It has multiple origins.[39] One of these is the writings of development scientists who, concerned for human wellbeing, grew disaffected with prevailing economic models and development strategies such as that of structural adjustment.[40] Another is the manner in which some development agencies perceived a duty on their part to implement law—this particularly having been the case for the UN Children's Fund (UNICEF) which presented its ultimate goal to be that of promotion of implementation of the Convention on the Rights of the Child.[41] Prominent theories of the nature of poverty also contributed greatly to the first stirrings of RBA. In particular, Amartya Sen's capability approach[42] to poverty laid the foundations for an analysis which would highlight the extent to which poverty is caused by and may be understood as a failure to enjoy certain human rights.[43]

Out of roots such as these, a wide range of academic, policy, and practical initiatives emerged.[44] Through the 1990s and into the present decade, rights-based

[35] UN doc E/CN.4/1997/74 at para 109.

[36] M O'Flaherty (n 1 above) at 3. See also, M Schmidt, *The Follow-Up Activities of the UN Human Rights Treaty Bodies and the OHCHR* (paper delivered to the Meeting on the Impact of the Work of UN Human Rights Treaty Bodies on National Courts and Tribunals, ILA Committee on Human Rights Law and Practice, Turku, Finland, Sept 2003) (on file with the author).

[37] The writing on this topic is vast. See eg, materials at: <http://www.standards.dfes.gov.uk> accessed on 23 May 2006.

[38] See H Slim, *Making Moral Low Ground, Rights as the Struggle for Justice and the Abolition of Development*, XVII Praxis: Fletcher J Development Studies (2002).

[39] See M Darrow and A Tomas, 'Power, capture and conflict: a call for human rights accountability in development cooperation', (2005) 27 Human Rights Q 2 pp 471–538.

[40] See n 34 (above).

[41] *UNICEF Guidelines for Human-Rights Based Programming Approach* (UNICEF, 1998) (on file with the author).

[42] A Sen, *Inequality Reexamined* (Harvard University Press, 1992); A Sen, *Development as Freedom* (Knopf, 1999). [43] OHCHR, *Human Rights and Poverty Reduction* (Geneva, 2004).

[44] See Darrow and Amparo (n 39 above) at 11.

approaches to development took shape in a disparate and sometimes inconsistent manner and with a notable variety of emphases. Some approaches considered human rights to be no more than one of a range of tools to be applied or disregarded according to particular circumstances,[45] whereas others treated human rights as a non-negotiable normative framework for development work.[46] Some core perceptions did, however, inform most all approaches, notably the principle of non-discrimination and the recognition that a principal purpose of development is the empowerment of the most marginalized members of society.

Recent years have seen a considerable degree of further clarification of the core principles of RBA, or at least the development of one more or less articulated school thereof. This school is that of RBA as understood by the UN. Individual UN agencies, especially UNICEF and the UN Development Programme (UNDP), had been at the forefront of early RBA developments[47] and the UN High Commissioner for Human Rights had made the matter a priority issue for her office.[48] The UN actors had also sought, from the late 1990s and within the framework of the UN Development Group,[49] to identify core aspects of RBA which might inform their co-ordinated action—a process which was spurred on by the various UN reform initiatives of the UN Secretary-General[50] as well as the linkages between human rights and development which were contained in the Millennium Development Goals.[51] The process of reflection led, in May 2003, to a common UN position on RBA, contained in what is known as the Statement of Common Understanding, adopted at Stamford, Connecticut, USA (the Stamford Statement).[52] The Stamford Statement asserts that all programmes of development co-operation, policies, and technical assistance should further the realization of human rights as laid down in the

[45] For an example of an instrumental use of the human rights-approach see World Bank, *Engendering Development: Through Gender Equality in Rights, Resources and Voice*, Washington, 2001, available at: <http://www.wds.worldbank.org/external/default/WDSContentServer/WDSP/IB/2001/03/01/000094946_01020805393496/Rendered/PDF/multi_page.pdf> accessed on 12 Mar 2007.

[46] For instance, U Jonsson, *Human Rights Approach to Development Programming* (UNICEF, 2003).

[47] See UNDP, *Integrating Human Rights with Sustainable Human Development* (New York, 1998).

[48] See eg, the OHCHR presentation, *Human Rights in Development*, 2000 at <http://www.undg.org/search.cfm?by=keywords&q=human%20rights&page=2&num=10&sort=Score&view=basic&archives=0> accessed on 23 May 2006.

[49] See the multiple materials at: <http://www.undg.org/search.cfm?by=keywords&q=human+rights&opt=any&section=1&page=1&archives=1&detailed=&basic=&num=10&sort=postdate> accessed on 23 May 2006.

[50] Secretary-General's Reports, *Renewing the United Nations: A Programme for Reform*, UN doc A/51/950, *An Agenda for Further Change*, UN doc A/57/387, *In larger freedom: towards development, security and human rights for all!*, UN doc A/59/2005.

[51] *United Nations Millennium Declaration*, UN doc A/55/2; see also, *World Summit Outcome*, 2005 UN doc A/60/L.1 at paras 119–134.

[52] Report of the Second Interagency Workshop on Implementing a Human Rights-Based Approach in the Context of UN Reform (Stamford, Connecticut, 5–7 May 2003) at: <http://www.undg.org/documents/4128-Human_Rights_Workshop_Stamford_Final_Report.doc> accessed on 23 May 2006.

Universal Declaration of Human Rights (UDHR) and other international human rights instruments and that:

(h)uman rights standards contained in, and principles derived from, the UDHR and other international human rights instruments guide all development cooperation and programming in all sectors and in all phases of the programming process [...] Development cooperation contributes to the development of the capacity of 'duty-bearers'[53] to meet their obligations and/or of 'rights-holders' to claim their rights.[54]

The Statement identifies a number of elements which it considers as 'necessary, specific and unique to a human rights-based approach':

(i) assessment and analysis in order to identify the human rights claims of rights-holders and the corresponding human rights obligations of 'duty-bearers'[55] as well as the immediate, underlying, and structural causes of the non-realization of rights;

(ii) programmes assess the capacity of rights-holders to claim their rights and of duty-bearers to fulfil their obligations. They then develop strategies to build these capacities;

(iii) programmes monitor and evaluate both outcomes and processes guided by human rights standards and principles; and

(iv) programming is informed by the recommendations of international human rights bodies and mechanisms.[56]

Of most direct interest for the present discussion are the principles derived from human rights law which are identified as integral to RBA. These are described in the Stamford Statement to be: universality and inalienability; inter-dependedness and inter-relatedness; non-discrimination and equality; participation and inclusion; and accountability and the rule of law.

V. Applying the RBA approach for treaty body recommendations

A. Relevance

At first sight it may seem odd to propose that a methodology intended for the integration of human rights concerns into a discrete discipline, development, has

---

[53] In RBA discourse the terms 'duty-bearer' and 'obligation', when applied outside the context of the state, tend to refer to roles and responsibilities relevant to the effective implementation of rights rather than to any form of formal legal responsibility. See eg, U Jonsson at 12. See also, M O'Flaherty, Address to: *Our Rights, Our Future Human Rights Based Approaches in Ireland, Amnesty International Conference* Dublin, 27 Sept 2005 (n 46 above) available at: <http://www.amnesty.ie/user/content/view/full/4648> accessed on 23 May 2006.   [54] Note 52 (above) at 13.
[55] Ibid.   [56] Ibid at 12.

anything at all to say to the work of such core institutions of the human rights system as the treaty bodies. It might even be suggested that to propose as a model for treaty body work that which is itself encouraged to pay better attention to treaty body findings (see above) is at best ironic and at worst entirely inappropriate. The present writer would, however, suggest that there are multiple reasons for its consideration.

In the first instance it is possible to demonstrate the global relevance of RBA, albeit it has its origins in and is principally considered with regard to the developing world. As extrapolated at Stamford, and notwithstanding the immediate context of the development work of the UN, one can identify the extent to which that articulation of RBA is essentially about the comprehensive implementation of all human rights in an indivisible manner.[57] Its focus accordingly may be understood to be of global reach. Its preoccupation is with comprehensive implementation of what the Office of the UN High Commissioner for Human Rights has termed, 'all human rights for all'.[58] Accordingly, the commonality of purpose between RBA and treaty body recommendations may also be identified.

The universal relevance of RBA can be indicated further by means of an acknowledgement of the significance of its reinterpretation of poverty/underdevelopment as a state of lack of opportunity among members of marginalized communities rather than as some form of mere income disparity/economic disadvantage. So understood, myriad forms of poverty can be identified in any state of the world.

Application of RBA outside developing states has been demonstrated by initiatives on the part of civil society and governments. There is an increasing number of instances in the relatively wealthy states of the world to apply RBA approaches for specific social sectors. For instance, poverty eradication schemes are incorporating such methods[59] as are campaigns concerned with the place of children in society.[60] Attempts can also be identified for the application of RBA systemically across developed world societies. In Ireland, for instance, the NGO Amnesty International, in 2005, launched a campaign to place RBA at the heart of the national public policy, budgeting and programming framework.[61]

A second requirement for our analysis is that of determining whether RBA and treaty body recommendations are sufficiently related in form and function for them to have mutual relevance. When account is taken of the extent to which each

---

[57] See M O'Flaherty (n 53 above) at 13.

[58] <http://www.ohchr.org/english/about/mission.htm> accessed on 23 May 2006.

[59] See eg, Combat Poverty Agency, *Working for a Poverty-Free Ireland: Strategic Plan 2005–2007*, available at: <http:www.cpa.ie/publications/strategicplans/2005–2007_strategicplan.pdf> accessed on 23 Oct 2006.

[60] See eg: The Child-Rights Project, Child Friendly Cities: <http://www.childfriendlycities.org> accessed on 23 May 2006.

[61] Amnesty International, *Our Rights, Our Future, Human Rights Based Approaches in Ireland: Principles, Policies and Practice* (Dublin, 2005).

of them is perceived to be concerned with issues of both process and output, such a relationship becomes easy to locate. The concern of RBA with process and output is easy to identify since its pre-occupation is with the implementation of development (process) and the attainment of development goals (output). Treaty body recommendations can also be described in such terms. In the first instance, and most obviously, they constitute an output. But they are also intimately related to issues of process in at least two regards: their content is dependent on the nature of the preceding investigatory actions of the treaty body and the recommendations themselves propose elements of process to be undertaken within states. The adoption by treaty bodies of RBA may also suggest still further process-related implications which will be discussed at a later point in the present chapter.

B. The impact of RBA categorizations

A further consideration regarding the relevance of RBA for treaty body work is that of the extent to which its application would actually make a difference in practice. The first difference is, of course, the self-evident one that it would provide a framework for a form of integrated set of recommendations as distinct from the current discrete outputs of the several treaty bodies. But would this compendium amount to anything more than just the sort of minimalist consolidated text referred to earlier? The present author would suggest a positive response to such a query. It may be demonstrated by means of a reflection on what issues might be addressed were RBA categories to be applied. As has already been observed, there is no fixed list of such categories and, for our purposes, those which are used are the ones identified within the principles in the Stamford Statement. It may also be recalled that the issues to be addressed within the context of each principle include both elements which are matters of legal obligation for the state and others which, while not of a binding nature, go to the heart of actual implementation/enjoyment of rights. These are:

Universality and inalienability: The first of the Stamford principles recalls a central tenet of international human rights law.[62] In so doing it provides a compelling context for the commonplace but contested treaty body practice of the review of the legitimacy of reservations[63] and insistence on the extra-territorial application of the treaties.[64] It also provides a context for investigation of such issues of actual

---

[62] Universal Declaration of Human Rights (UDHR), *Preamble and art 1*; World Conference on Human Rights, *Vienna Declaration and Programme of Action*, 12 July 1993, UN doc A/157/23 (1993).

[63] See HRC, *General Comment 24*, UN doc HRI/GEN/1/rev 7 (2004) at 161. For practice in the context of Concluding Observations see eg, CERD, *Concluding Observations on a report of the United States*, UN doc A/56/18 at para 391.

[64] HRC, *General Comment 31*, UN doc HRI/GEN/1/rev 7 at 192 (2004). For practice in the context of Concluding Observations see eg, HRC, *Concluding Observations, United States of America*, 3 Oct 1995, CCPR/C/79/add50 (1995) at para 284.

implementation (as opposed to state obligation) as the extent to which a state has limited enjoyment of rights by means of legitimate reservations.[65] Attention to issues of enjoyment of the rights also provides an appropriate context for treaty bodies to locate their commonplace arguments regarding the relative merits of direct incorporation of treaties by states.[66]

Interdependence and interrelatedness: These categories provide context for an insistence by treaty bodies on the non-hierarchical nature of the human rights system, with no category of rights having a greater status than another. Instead, it can be proposed that the protection and promotion of human rights be undertaken in a manner reflective of integrative human experience, as noted earlier in this chapter. Furthermore, issues of interdependence and interrelatedness draw concentrated attention to the interplay of rights and to the need for the recommendations to consistently address all relevant categories of rights. They point, for instance, to the systemic significance of discrimination against women, racial discrimination, and promotion of the rights of the child, as well as to the impact for the enjoyment of all human rights of such prohibited practices as torture.[67] Beyond matters of legal obligation the context is compellingly provided for suggestions by treaty bodies that states ratify additional human rights treaties and implement recommendation of World Conferences and the various other 'soft-law' outputs of international human rights mechanisms.

Non-discrimination and equality: These principles offer a cornerstone for the undertaking by treaty bodies of vulnerability analysis—identifying the most marginalized, overlooked, or actively discriminated against of communities and assessing action required to address their plight. In essence, the principles put the most powerless of a state's population at the heart of the process, making clear the appropriateness of the sometimes apparently disproportionate attention paid by treaty bodies to sometimes tiny and often invisible groups.[68] The quest to assess a response to the plight of such groups (and individuals) requires a treaty body to undertake a form of analysis of the power-distribution within a state, taking account of whatever

---

[65] See eg, HRC, *Concluding Observations, United Kingdom of Great Britain and Northern Ireland*, UN doc CCPR/C/79/add119 (2000) at para 13.

[66] See the discussion of this practice in C Tomuschat (n 28 above), at 9. For practice in the context of Concluding Observations see eg, ESCR Committee, *Concluding Observations, Ireland*, UN doc E/C.12/1/add77 at para 12.

[67] For recent discourses on the relationship between torture and the enjoyment and violation of other human rights see Louise Arbour, *Message of United Nations High Commissioner for Human Rights, on the occasion of Human Rights Day 2005* at: <http://www.unhchr.ch/huricane/huricane.nsf/view01/3B9B202D5A6DCDBCC12570D00034CF83?opendocument> accessed on 23 May 2006; and Irene Khan, Secretary-General of Amnesty International, *The Inaugural Paragon Human Rights Lecture* (Nottingham, 9 Dec 2005), available at: <http://www.nottingham.ac.uk/law/hrlc/paragon.htm> accessed on 23 May 2006.

[68] Following review by HRC of a state report in 2005, a senior representative of the state expressed surprise and concern to the author regarding what the diplomat perceived to the inordinate attention paid by the Committee to the plight of a numerically tiny community within that state.

manifestation there may be of the phenomenon of 'elite-capture'.[69] Such an examination will typically throw light on locations of power, authority, and capacity for responsive action within and beyond government, including at the transnational level. Context is thus provided for recommendation which, of necessity, must address actors and issues beyond the framework of formal state treaty obligation.

Participation and inclusion: This principle captures the essence of the RBA: the empowerment of the rights-holder and the manifestation of that power in all of the processes and outputs which impact for their wellbeing.[70] Each of the human rights treaties does contain provisions supporting some form of a right of participation on the part of the holders of human rights, with the nature of the right most directly addressed and articulated in the practice of the Committee on the Rights of the Child.[71] The participation/inclusion principles invite treaty bodies to explore the extent to which such involvement takes place and is effective. The exploration will of necessity require an assessment of the extent to which consultation and dialogue frameworks exist and are used within a state, from the local to the national levels.[72] Since participation/inclusion seems to demand some level of awareness and human rights competency on the part of rights-holders, the principle also provides an appropriate context for the examination by a treaty body of the extent to which a state undertakes and otherwise promotes human rights education and public information.

Accountability and rule of law: Neither accountability nor the rule of law are particularly novel in terms of the goals of treaty body recommendations.[73] The RBA principle does, however, provide a context in which to locate a number of issues which may otherwise be addressed somewhat disparately. For instance, it recalls the importance of consistently insisting with states on the justiciabilty of all rights, including those of an economic, social, or cultural nature.[74] It also encourages a sociological analysis of issues of access to justice, focusing on the extent to which the most marginalized of right holders actually have effective and appropriate redress for human rights violations and how access might be systemically improved. Within this context it is also possible to locate any recommendations which may address forms of community justice and redress, for instance in the context of transitional justice frameworks.[75]

---

[69] Johnsson and Start (n 34 above) at 10.   [70] See Amnesty International (n 61 above) at 16.

[71] See *General Comment 5*, UN Doc HRI/GEN/1/rev 7 at para 12.

[72] See M O'Flaherty (n 53 above) at 13.   [73] See Tomuschat (n 29 above) at 8.

[74] The treaty body which most consistently raises the issue of the justiciability of economic, social, and cultural rights is the ESCR Committee, see eg, *Concluding Observations on a report of New Zealand*, UN doc E/C.12/1/add88 at para 11. The practice is not consistent—the ESCR Committee omitted reference to the issues with regard to another state in which such rights are not currently justiciable, Solomon Islands, see *Conclusions and recommendations of the ESCR Committee, Solomon Islands*, UN doc E/C.12/1/add84 (2002).

[75] For a recent example of a treaty body addressing issues of transitional justice see *Concluding Observations on Brazil*, adopted in 2005 by HRC, UN doc CCPR/BRA/CO/2 at para 18.

An examination of issues of accountability leads to a highlighting of the need for transparency on the part of duty bearers. Transparency is closely related to the issue of participation since the rights-holder can only become involved on the basis of insight into the nature and operation of whatever process is at issue. Questions may thus be raised, for instance, regarding any opacity in the work of governmental services and agencies. Concerns might also be raised with regard to the extent to which such operations occur outside the framework of formal accountability and review procedures.[76] Likewise, context is provided for a review of the extent to which a state has put in place effective procedures to ensure the accountability of any non-governmental actor, the actions of which impact the enjoyment of human rights.

It is important for transparency to be in place at all levels of governance, from the local to the national, hence RBA focuses attention on the need for all levels of local government to be engaged with its human rights responsibilities—a context for the increasing treaty body attention to the protection of human rights in pro-grammes of governmental decentralization and concerning the human rights responsibilities of municipal government.[77]

VI. Some further consideration of the merits of an application of the RBA by treaty bodies

The brief review of how an application of RBA to treaty body recommendations might affect content illustrates the extent to which current recommendation con-tents would survive, albeit often relocated or re-contextualized. It also demon-strates how a more profound and systemic investigation might be encouraged which integrates attention to the actual enjoyment of all human rights. In this regard there would be specific merit in considering the extent to which RBA data gathering and monitoring tools, including quantitative indicators and bench-marking,[78] might be better and more systematically integrated in the work of the treaty bodies.[79]

---

[76] Such as when governments bypass the civil service bureaucratic structures and employ the ser-vices of the private sector or political appointees.

[77] See International Council on Human Rights Policy, *Local Rule: Decentralisation and Human Rights*, Versoix, 2002; and L Joy, *Decentralisation and Local Government Enhancement: A Human Rights Checklist*, undated, available at: <http://www.undp.org/governance/guidelines-toolkits.htm> accessed on 23 May 2006.

[78] See I Byrne, 'Mainstreaming of human rights: a tentative operational approach to monitoring and enforcing human rights in MEDA development projects' (2004) (9:3) *Mediterranean Politics*.

[79] See generally, M Scheinen, *Background Paper No 3, Use of Indicators by Human Rights Treaty Bodies—Experiences and Potentials* (Expert Meeting on Human Rights Indicators, Turku/Abo, 11–13 March 2005) at pp 3 and 7, available at: <http://www.abo.fi/instut/imr/norfa/Expert.doc> accessed on 23 May 2006.

Also, RBA invariably emphasizes the importance for a state to undertake human rights planning. Indeed, outside of a systematic planning and programming process, RBA loses its coherence.[80] The RBA approach to treaty body recommendations would accordingly lead to a heightened emphasis on the development, review, and implementation of such plans and programmes, with what, outside the practice of the ESCR Committee,[81] is currently no more than an occasional component of Concluding Observations[82] becoming an invariable and central tenet.

RBA experience in the development context can be of some assistance for the manner in which treaty bodies may address the issues of national human rights planning. In particular, there are lessons to be learned from how considerations of human rights have been integrated into the UN development planning and programming frameworks, especially the Common Country Assessment (CCA) and the UN Development Assistance Framework (UNDAF).[83] Recent revisions of the guidelines for these frameworks have highlighted the manner in which human rights programming must be 'mainstreamed', cutting across all social sectors, rather than itself categorized as a niche issue that is severable from other aspects of national life.[84] They also take account of and propose means for the participation of rights-holders and other 'stake-holders' in all stages of the planning process.[85] The UN humanitarian assistance framework, the Consolidated Appeals Process (CAP), is also of some utility, particularly for the design of national vulnerability assessment programmes.[86]

Another source of assistance for treaty bodies in formulating recommendations relating to issues of planning is the guidance developed on matters of national human rights plans of action and national human rights education plans of action. Both of these forms of process were considered at the Vienna World Conference on Human Rights[87] and continue to be promoted in the programme of the Office of the UN High Commissioner for Human Rights.[88] These models will have particular resonance for developed states that do not already have

---

[80] U Jonsson (n 46 above), ch 6 at 12.

[81] See eg, *Concluding Observations on Azerbaijan*, 2004, UN doc E/C.12/1/add104.

[82] See eg, *Concluding Observations on Ecuador*, 2003, UN doc CERD/C/62/CO/2.

[83] According to the United Nations Development Group, '(t)hese tools are designed to enhance the UN's collective analysis and programming in support of national goals and priorities, including the MDGs. Quality CCAs and UNDAFs should clearly demonstrate the linkages with national poverty reduction strategies and plans', see: <http://www.undg.org/content.cfm?id=830> accessed on 23 May 2006.

[84] See United Nations Development Group, *CCA and UNDAF Guidelines (2004)* at: <http://www.undg.org/content.cfm?id=840> accessed on 23 May 2006.   [85] Ibid.

[86] See *Technical Guidelines for the CAP 2006*, at: <http://www.reliefweb.int/cap/CAPSWG/CAP_Policy_Document/Guidelines/2006CAP%20Technical%20Guidelines.pdf> accessed on 23 May 2006.

[87] World Conference on Human Rights, *Vienna Declaration and Programme of Action*, 12 July 1993, UN doc A/157/23 at para 68.

[88] See OHCHR Professional Training Series No 10, *Handbook on National Human Rights Plans of Action* (Geneva, 2002).

national development planning process into which human rights considerations might be inserted.

More generally, experience in the application of RBA in the humanitarian and development context is capable of yielding a wide range of experiences from which lessons might be derived for purposes of the crafting of recommendations by the treaty bodies.[89] A growing number of RBA-inspired state-level programmes are now coming under review and generating specific lessons. The experience concerning the situation of children is particularly revealing, with such actors as UNICEF deriving clear guidance from the review of its programmes and county-level strategies.[90] One significant feature of such lessons is that they are all derived from experience in developing states, especially states of the South. This is of particular significance for treaty body practice as it might contribute to a changing of the baseless perception that the states of the North have some form of supremacy in terms of the protection of human rights.

It would be misleading to suggest, however, that there is a vast array of guidance from which the treaty bodies might draw. The derivation of lessons and best/good practices from development experience remains a somewhat ad-hoc process.[91] Also, such practices as do exist focus mainly on issues related to economic, social, and cultural rights, for instance on participation of rights-holders in development of physical infrastructure and in strategies for job creation and enhanced social welfare systems. Given the developmental context in which the activities take place this bias is not surprising. It is not, however, reflective of the inclusive and non-divisible approach to human rights which should lie at the heart of RBA. It is possible that the adoption of RBA by treaty bodies may actually serve to generate the experiences and practices across all areas of human rights and thus redress this imbalance. In this regard it must, however, be acknowledged that treaty bodies themselves lack any extensive experience of identification of good practice (of any kind) in one state that is then proposed for emulation in another. This latter consideration raises the distinct issue of the extent to which treaty bodies may be already missing opportunities to render their work more effective—with them, in this case, failing to utilize their pivotal role to identify, 'harvest', and propose generically good practice among states and, in so doing, to stimulate and support a practice of state peer to peer assistance and skills transfer.[92]

---

[89] See eg, the many case studies cited in Inter Agency Standing Committee, *Growing the Sheltering Tree* (Geneva, 2002).

[90] See, *inter alia*, UNICEF, *Programme Cooperation for Children and Women from a Human Rights Perspective*, UN doc E/ICEF/1999/11, and more recently, C Moser and A Moser, *Moving Ahead with Human Rights: Assessment of the Operationalisation of the Human Rights Based Approach in UNICEF Programming*, 2002 (on file with the author) and J Theis, *Consolidation and Review of the Main Findings and Lessons Learned of the Case Studies on Operationalising HRBAP in UNICEF* (2004) (on file with the author).

[91] See Mac Darrow and Tomas Amparo 'Power, Capture, and Conflict: A Call for Human Rights Accountability in Development Cooperation' 27 Human Rights Q 7(2) at 479.

[92] Concluding Observations do commonly include a subsection addressing 'positive aspects', ie acknowledging areas where a state has made progress or otherwise been successful in the promotion

VII. Conclusion

RBA does not dictate any set format for integrated treaty body recommendations and it can be implemented both in the context of the current system of multiple treaty bodies and in any future unified system which may emerge. However, it must be acknowledged that the adoption of RBA, in whatever context, would not be a simple or straightforward matter. RBA will require to, on the one hand, high-light particular concerns and problems and, on the other hand, accord adequate weight to all of the applicable human rights. In every case the approach requires to be systemic and profound, taking account of underlying causes of problems as well as of solutions. It requires an appreciation of and a willingness to address the manner in which a society operates and evolves, as well as of the role that human rights does and should play in that evolution.

Considerations such as these draw attention to issues of the competence and the range of technical and geographical skill of treaty body members and their secretariats. They also raise issues of the quality and breadth of the available information on the situation within a state under review. For instance, they invite an examination of the appropriateness of the structure and recommended contents of state reports and of the most useful means for states to provide additional information.[93] The matter of the extent to which additional sources of information are required is also highlighted as is the importance of the role in the report review process of non-governmental organizations.[94]

More generally, RBA, predicated as it is on a process of engagement with and empowering of rights-holders, suggests an important role for civil society at all stages of report preparation and review and for the implementation of recommendations. Methodologies would have to be developed which take account of the full engagement of this crucial stakeholder but which are compatible with the practical constraints of the system. It is notable in this regard that a number of models already exist for effective participation in report review by local civil society;[95] for instance, NGOs have effectively developed and managed coalitions of national groups that have lobbied and interacted with the CRC[96] and CEDAW.[97]

---

and protection of the human rights under review (for a recent and fulsome example, see HRC, *Concluding Observations on Brazil*, UN doc CCPR/C/BRA/CO/2 at paras 3–4). However there are no systems in place for the bringing of such instances to the specific attention of other states parties.

[93] See M O'Flaherty (n 1 above) at 1 and W Vandenhole, *The Procedures before the UN Human Rights Treaty Bodies* (Intersentia, 2004).   [94] M O'Flaherty (n 1 above) ch 1 at 1.

[95] See M O'Flaherty, 'The Reporting Obligation Under art 40 of the International Covenant on Civil and Political Rights: Lessons Learned from the Consideration by the Human Rights Committee of Ireland's First Report' (1994) 16 Human Rights Q 3 pp 513–538.

[96] NGO Group for the Convention on the Rights of the Child, <http://www.crin.org/NGO GroupforCRC> accessed on 23 May 2006.

[97] International Women's Rights Action Watch, 'Producing NGO Shadow Reports: A Procedural Guide CEDAW' available at <http://iwraw.igc.org/shadow.htm> accessed on 23 May 2006.

Michael O'Flaherty

Some of the practical issues of enhanced implementation are already being considered in the discussions on treaty body reform,[98] albeit without reference to RBA. The place of such issues within the reform agenda does, however, point to its ultimate goal—the optimal impact of the human rights treaties. It is suggested that the adoption by the treaty bodies of RBA may contribute significantly to the attainment of that goal by providing it with an overarching framework directed towards the promotion and protection of 'all human rights for all'.

[98] See OHCHR Treaty Body Reform Forum, <http://ohchr.org/English/bodies/treaty/reform. htm> accessed on 13 Oct 2006.

3

Human Rights-Based Approaches to Development: Towards Accountability

Patrick Twomey[*]

I. Introduction

The concept of human rights-based, or human rights-based approaches (HRBAs) to, development has featured as an emerging commitment by a range of development actors in recent years.[1] There is widespread recognition of the need to identify lessons from past development interventions both to further the transition towards HRBAs and ensure greater accountability towards those rights-bearers most in need of or affected by development.[2] However, despite greater clarity as to its core principles, significant steps remain if HRBAs are to be transplanted from policy statements and made operational in a coherent fashion. The growing formal commitment to HRBAs raises many questions. Most fundamentally, what does the commitment mean in terms of revisiting the planning, implementation, and evaluation of development interventions? What is the relationship between best practice in development as understood heretofore and human rights-based development? How are socio-economic rights, in particular, to be integrated into all stages of development? How can existing indicators and measurement tools be developed so that data and information yielded is human rights relevant?

---

[*] The author wishes to acknowledge with appreciation the opportunity as Co-Director of the Nottingham Human Rights Law Centre to work with and learn from David Harris.

[1] The acronym HRBAs is used in this chapter to refer to the various approaches to development that qualify as being categorized as human rights-based.

[2] A growing body of literature on HRBAs includes; Unicef, *Guidelines for Human Rights-Based Programming Approach* (UNICEF, 1998); ODI, *What Can We Do With A Rights-Based Approach To Development?* (1999); J Häusermann, *A Human Rights Approach to Development* (Rights and Humanity/DFID, 1998); *2003 Report of the Second Inter-agency Workshop on Implementing a Human Rights-based Approach in the Context of UN Reform* <http://www.un.or.th/ohchr/file_download/llp/HisStamford.pdf> accessed 10 Jan 2006; Theis, *Promoting Rights-Based Approaches: Experiences and Ideas from Asia and the Pacific* (Save the Children, 2004), Amnesty International/International Human Rights Network, *Our Rights, Our future. Human Rights Based Approaches in Ireland: Principles, Policies and Practice* (2005).

HRBAs require new thinking not only of development actors, but also those classically categorized as human rights actors; the revisiting of programme methodologies, indicators, and impact assessment.[3] The lack of conceptual clarity regarding HRBAs, the historic monopolization of human rights by lawyers, the fear that human rights are 'political', the lack of substantive knowledge and empowerment necessary for effective participation, all represent challenges that require ongoing research and dialogue.

This chapter[4] outlines HRBAs' core concepts and explores the evolution of human rights-based approaches to development including the United Nations (UN) commitment to integrate human rights into all its work, national development plans, the role of socio-economic rights in development problem analysis, impact assessment, and key challenges to undertaking human rights-based development. The chapter also highlights the issue of measurement of human rights change as a critical factor in development planning, implementation, and evaluation towards ensuring accountability for both process and impact.

II. Human rights defined

The term human rights is used throughout as encompassing the full spectrum of internationally recognized human rights: civil, cultural, economic, political, and social. Given their nature, socio-economic rights have a central role in human rights-based development. The emergence of human rights-based development has been impeded by old ideological battles regarding recognition of some categories of human rights. The equal status of all human rights was reaffirmed in 1993, when 170 states reached consensus at the World Conference on Human Rights at Vienna. The Vienna Declaration and Programme of Action re-stated the legal principles that all internationally recognized human rights are *universal, inalienable, interrelated, and interdependent.*[5] The universality of human rights means that they are to be enjoyed by everyone, without discrimination. Their inalienability means that they are inherent in each individual, not a gift or privilege given by authorities. The principle that human rights are inter-dependent and inter-related recognizes that the full enjoyment of any particular human right depends upon the enjoyment of others. For example, the enjoyment of the right to health is dependent on the right to housing and the right to education

---

[3] The UNDP Evaluation Office core document *Managing for Results: Monitoring and Evaluation in UNDP: A Results-Oriented Framework* (Nov 2001), for example, makes no reference to human rights.

[4] The chapter is based on Part I of *Our Rights, Our future. Human Rights Based Approaches in Ireland: Principles, Policies and Practice* (2005). The report, written by International Human Rights Network (IHRN) and commissioned by Amnesty International's Irish section, reviews the experience of applying HRBA principles by key state and non-state actors in Ireland. The report is available at <http://www.ihrnetwork.org/development-ireland.htm> accessed 10 Jan 2006.

[5] A/CONF.157/23 12 July 1993, para 5 (emphasis added).

(eg regarding diet/lifestyle, transmission of HIV/Aids, etc). As UN-Habitat has noted, housing rights need not only to be disaggregated according to the different impact on different groups but seen in their wider framework.

Housing cannot be thought of as merely having four walls and a roof, but involves an intricate consideration of adequacy, health, security, and the law.[6]

Similarly, in many states the exercise of the right to vote is dependent on the vindication of the right to housing while the right to equality underscores all of these rights.

Under human rights law, the state has primary responsibility to *respect, protect, and fulfil* the human rights of all those in its territory. To respect human rights means the state has a duty not to interfere directly or indirectly with their enjoyment. Protecting human rights means the state must proactively provide a system which prevents, protects from, and provides redress for, interference by non-state actors (such as neighbours, spouses, companies). The state obligation to fulfil human rights requires it to ensure that they are fully enjoyed, whether through adopting appropriate legislative, administrative, budgetary, judicial, or other measures.

Modern international human rights law is the product of a consensus reached by states as to the *minimum standards they agree to be bound by*, e.g. in the right to education, health, etc. The *methods* by which those standards are met are a matter of discretion for each state. While the standard required to ensure the right to a fair trial are clear and detailed (right to a defence, presumption of innocence, etc)—a wide variety of types of legal system (Civil Law, Common Law, etc) meet those standards throughout the world. Moreover, international human rights is an evolving body of law, as reflected in moves to make non-state actors accountable and to develop rights based approaches to new issues such as the environment.[7]

By their participation in the international human rights framework, states undertake to ensure that their constitutions, laws, policies, budgets, etc, reflect these legal obligations and achieve, rather than undermine, the minimum standards which they have agreed to be bound by. This applies to all branches of the state and to all levels, including local authorities. States are legally obliged to ensure that their own development plans (whether social or economic), as well as development assistance to other states, are assessed in terms of their human rights impact before and during implementation. This obligation extends to regulating the behaviour of third parties involved in, or otherwise impacting on,

---

[6] UN-HABITAT, *Monitoring Housing Rights: Developing a Set of Indicators to Monitor the Full and Progressive Realisation of the Human Right to Adequate Housing* (United Nations Housing Rights Programme, (2003)) p iv.

[7] Eg, see the chapter on 'Non-State Actors and Economic, Social, and Cultural Rights' by Manisuli Ssenyonjo in this book.

development processes—e.g. corporations—to ensure that all human rights are
effectively enjoyed.

III. Development defined

The 1986 *Declaration on the Right to Development*, adopted by the UN General
Assembly,[8] defines development as:

a comprehensive economic, social, cultural and political process with the object of the
constant improvement of the well-being of the entire population and all individuals, on
the basis of their active, free, and meaningful participation.[9]

This understanding applies to all states, whether they might be classified as
developing or otherwise. The definition involves therefore, not just economic
growth or macroeconomic performance, but covers all areas of national life such
as health, environment, housing, education, distribution of resources, enhancement of people's capabilities, and widening of people's choices. It includes, but is
broader than, those areas that are commonly prioritized by donor development
assistance.[10]

The definition's emphasis on *process* as well as *outcomes* means that development
is a composite of civil, political, economic, social, and cultural human rights. It is
rooted in the provisions of the UN Charter, the Universal Declaration of Human
Rights (UDHR), and the key international human rights treaties, including the
International Covenant on Civil and Political Rights (ICCPR),[11] the International
Covenant on Economic, Social and Cultural Rights (ICESCR),[12] and the Con-
vention on the Rights of the Child (CRC),[13] etc. In 1993, the Vienna World
Conference on Human Rights affirmed the right to development by consensus.

IV. Human rights-based approaches

Human rights-based approaches[14] to development are processes which apply a
number of core principles. Adherence to these core principles requires that the

---

   [8] Res 41/128 of 4 Dec 1986.   [9] ibid, preamble, para 2.
   [10] The ESCR Committee *General Comment 2 on International Technical Assistance* E/1990/23
highlights the fact that economic development itself does not necessarily mean the achievement of
economic, social, and cultural rights, noting that many activities undertaken in the name of 'development' do not contribute to improving the situation in the field of human rights or are even counter
productive.   [11] 999 UNTS 171.
   [12] 993 UNTS 3.   [13] 1577 UNTS 3.
   [14] Sometimes referred to as human rights 'mainstreaming' or 'integrating' human rights. As indicated in n 1 above, the expression 'human rights-based approaches' is used in the plural in this chapter
to reflect the fact that different approaches can be applied.

means and the results of all development seek to ensure the full enjoyment of human rights by all. It is important to emphasize that a range of human rights-based approaches have been developed. Which approach is likely to be most effective varies according to the particular sector being addressed, the social and political context and the different actors seeking to employ HRBAs. HRBAs are, however, united by a common purpose and core principles even if different actors adopt different formulations.

HRBAs seek to ensure that human rights are a central frame of reference in policy-making and political choices by ensuring people have the political, institutional, and material means to demand, exercise, and monitor their human rights, and to participate actively in decision-making processes.

It entails going beyond human development, based on best practice insofar as it introduces the notion of obligations and entitlements, deriving from international human rights law and making the enjoyment of human rights an explicit objective of development. It entails a shift from past approaches which sometimes conceived human rights endeavours as self-standing interventions related to development efforts. Rather than conceiving human rights as an 'add-on' compliment to development, HRBAs has been described as the 'scaffolding of development policy'.[15] It entails more than formal commitment to respect the human rights norms and standards. It requires the integration of those minimum standards into all plans, policies, budgets, processes, and institutions. By definition, HRBAs is as concerned with the *process* as well as the *outcome* of development.

In the context of poverty reduction, for example, HRBAs require not only that alleviation strategies and goals be explicitly based on the norms and values of international human rights law, but also that those strategies be identified, applied, and reviewed with active and informed participation of the poor. The use of human rights language and participatory processes empowers the poor both to assert their human rights and hold accountable those legally responsible for their delivery. The inter-connected principles, which have been internationally recognized as forming the core of HRBAs, are:

  (i) express application of the international human rights framework;
 (ii) empowerment;
(iii) participation;
 (iv) non-discrimination and prioritization of vulnerable groups; and
  (v) accountability.

Outlined below, these principles are themselves part of the legally binding framework. The principles are employed as the lens through which each state's on-going economic, social, cultural, and political progress—ie its development—must be evaluated.

[15] ODI, *What Can We Do With A Rights-Based Approach To Development?* (1999), p 1.

V. The core principles of human rights-based approaches

A. Express application of the international human rights framework

This requires that the goals of all development are defined in terms of the relevant international human rights commitments of the state—as legally enforceable entitlements on the national level. This necessarily includes:

(i) explicitly taking human rights obligations into account at every stage of national and local development processes (from the identification of needs through to policy and programme identification as well as implementation, monitoring, and evaluation);

(ii) addressing the full spectrum of indivisible, interdependent, and interrelated rights: civil, cultural, economic, political, and social;

(iii) ensuring that all sectors of national planning reflect the human rights framework (for example, health, education, housing, justice administration, political participation); and

(iv) building the capacity of public representatives, civil servants, local officials so that they apply the human rights framework in their work (eg through recruitment, training, specialized advice).

HRBAs place development assistance within a universal framework (comprising both law and principles) of rights and duties, which must prevail over individual policy choices, logframe terminology, etc. As a normative framework common to all states, HRBAs provide legitimacy to policy discourse between donor and recipient states which otherwise might be perceived as 'interference', and linked to the elements below, ensure that development is understood by beneficiaries as being undertaken within a human rights framework.

The need for precision as regards the nature and content of the applicable legal framework is all the more acute in light of divergent and shifting terminology of donors, intergovernmental organizations, and other development actors. New terms are invented for existing well-defined international legal commitments resulting in conceptual confusion and risk of diluting many existing obligations from rights and obligations to mere objectives for progressive achievement etc. In this context, there is evidence that core human rights norms (developed through case law and other interpretation) which are the constituent parts of *'democratic principles'* and *'rule of law'* and *'good governance'* are undermined through vagueness of language prompted by political sensitivity of identifying human rights violations.[16]

---

[16] Contrasting definitions of good governance highlight the deviation in emphasis on human rights. See World Bank and OHCHR definitions of 'good governance' respectively:

Governance can be broadly defined as the set of traditions and institutions by which authority in a state is exercised. This includes (1) the process by which governments are selected, monitored and replaced, (2) the capacity of the government to effectively formulate and implement sound policies,

A related challenge is inconsistent selection of international instruments by different development actors as the basis for their interventions. The European Commission, for example, commonly cites its May 2001 Communication on *Human Rights and Democratisation in Third Countries*[17] as the basis of its donor assistance. While its reference to the norms in the European Convention on Human Rights (ECHR) is common, it only rarely refers to the Revised European Social Charter (ESC) in its Regional and Country Strategy Papers[18] or other development instruments, even in jurisdictions where the ESC is applicable law.[19] Similarly we find reference to 'EU standards' on issues where no such norms exist or where they are themselves questionable in terms of the applicable human rights framework e.g. with regard to asylum or justice sector.[20] Even within the UN system, one finds misinterpretation of the Millennium Development Goals[21] as representing *the* framework for human rights-based development when they constitute only part of that framework. Benchmarks or indicators that represent a lower standard than applicable human rights norms must be clearly identified as such. This does not mean that all other indicators are irrelevant, but that clarity is needed regarding the fundamentally different nature of those that derive from the applicable legal framework. Similarly, where indicators purport to be human rights-based, legal accuracy is of fundamental importance. Thus, for example, matters that represent immediate obligations ought not to, by virtue of inappropriate indicators, be reduced to progressive realization, etc.

The divergent ideological positions of different bilateral donors also impede the shift towards human rights-based development. Thus, for example, the United States Agency for International Development (USAID) *Handbook of*

---

and (3) the respect of citizens and the state for the institutions that govern economic and social interactions among them. <http://info.worldbank.org/governance/kkz2002/q&a.htm#1> accessed 10 Jan 2006.

Governance is the process whereby public institutions conduct public affairs, manage public resources, and guarantee the realization of human rights. Good governance accomplishes this in a manner essentially free of abuse and corruption, and with due regard for the rule of law. The true test of 'good' governance is the degree to which it delivers on the promise of human rights: civil, cultural, economic, political, and social rights. The key question is: are the institutions of governance effectively guaranteeing the right to health, adequate housing, sufficient food, quality education, fair justice, and personal security? <http://www.unhchr.ch/development/governance-01.html> accessed 10 Jan 2006.

[17] COM(2001) 252 final.

[18] <http://europa.eu.int/comm/development/body/csp_rsp/csp_en.cfm> and <http://europa.eu.int/comm/external_relations/ceeca/pca/index.htm> accessed 10 Jan 2006.

[19] Eg, in 2000 the European Commission piloted a 'Democratic Dialogue and Analysis Grid' (DDAG) in Uganda, guidelines to which stated that the 'aims included in the grid are the component elements of the definition of democratic principles, human rights and the rule of law *as given in the Commission Communication*'. [ie May 2001, EC Communication on *Human Rights and Democratization in Third Countries*]—equating international treaties with an internal EC administrative document.

[20] See, eg, EC, *Federal Republic of Yugoslavia Country Strategy Paper* 2002–2006 p 27.

[21] <http://www.un.org/millenniumgoals/> accessed 10 Jan 2006.

Democracy and Governance: Program Indicators places on a par the benchmarks of 'strengthened rule of law and respect for human rights' and 'laws, regulations and policies [that] promote a market-based economy'.[22]

Mechanisms for co-ordination and information sharing are often weak in-state. This is one factor behind the narrow conception of human rights of many donors, associating them with the justice system or otherwise as a distinct 'sector' rather than as a cross-cutting issue. The European Commission, for example, commonly uses human rights language and principle in its political situation analysis but not in its analysis of a state or region's 'social situation'. Similar challenges derive from the fractured nature and volume of project-base development which has seen emphasis on activity indicators and the limited attention devoted to framing indicators of human rights outputs, though the trend away from projects to programmes and sectoral approaches in itself facilitates progress towards HRBAs.

B. Empowerment

In practice this principle requires that policies and programmes be based on empowerment as opposed to charity. Requiring that people have the power, capacity (including education and information) as well as access needed to improve their own communities and influence their own lives, it presupposes that a wide range of rights are acknowledged and vindicated.

It requires that rights-holders and duty-bearers share a common understanding of human rights goals and the duties to respect, protect and fulfil them. This means systematically educating and raising awareness of government, public representatives, civil servants, service providers, and other duty-bearers. The test for empowerment of any development intervention or agency purporting to apply HRBAs requires that it be:

interrogated for the extent to which it enables those whose lives are affected the most to articulate their priorities and claim genuine accountability from development agencies, and also the extent to which the agencies become critically self-aware and address inherent power inequalities in their interaction with those people.[23]

C. Participation

Recognition of the need for participation is now commonplace in the field of development and is seen as an essential element of good development practice.

[22] USAID *Handbook of Democracy and Governance: Program Indicators* (Centre for Democracy and Governance, Aug 1998) p 31.

[23] C Nyamu-Musembi and A Cornwall, 'What is the "Rights-based Approach" All About?' Perspectives from International Development Agencies, IDS Working Paper 234 (Institute of Development Studies, Brighton, 2004) p 47.

It is accepted as a means to improve relevance and effectiveness of programming. Since the 1980s, concepts such as participatory monitoring and evaluation have been adopted by larger donor agencies and development organizations. However, this evolution has stemmed from donor's perspectives than by a demand for empowerment (the basis for all human rights change). Factors include the shift towards 'management by results', growing scarcity of funds leading to a demand for demonstrated success, and moves towards decentralization and devolution.

A series of major international innovations have on paper committed UN Agencies to participatory processes. These include United Nations Development Assistance Framework (UNDAF) and the Poverty Reduction Strategy Papers (PRSPs) of their sister organizations the World Bank/International Monetary Fund (IMF). Yet, this undertaking is commonly met without applying participation as a human right in itself. Both processes have been criticized for failing to adequately apply in practice their policy commitment to civil society participation. When the UNDAF was piloted in Guatemala it was criticized as 'an exercise between the Government and an inter-agency entity [the UN Country Team]'.[24]

Participation in all stages of development needs to be active, free, and meaningful—including communities, civil society, and all stakeholders; mere formal consultation is not sufficient. In turn, this requires that national and local development processes and institutions are accessible and that information is transparent and timely. Ensuring meaningful participation raises questions such as: who should participate? Who decides who participates? In what form/process is participation ensured? Where should ultimate decision-making power rest? Participation, for example, needs to be managed so that voices that are not commonly heard in decision-making processes (women, rural populations, etc) are included, which in turn raises challenges of literacy and empowerment. True participation also necessitates that donors do not set priorities in isolation from beneficiaries, but are prepared to make changes on the basis of unexpected results which participation yields.

HRBAs require a fundamental rethink of long accepted notions of partnership. A true process of participation inevitably raises issues of ownership of programmes and development processes; it involves stakeholders in all stages of the decision making process. Participation as a process means, for example, that local actors are not only involved in project implementation or project evaluation, but most fundamentally in the identification of priorities, in project design, etc. These processes in turn need to be based on human rights principles, transparency, non-discrimination, etc. Participatory evaluations are an important opportunity to advance dialogue on common objectives.

It is too common for donor aid management systems to focus on activity and outputs (e.g. reports were produced, training events took place) to measure the

---

[24] Ricardo Stein, Secretariat of Peace, speaking of the Country Strategy Note, see IHRN, *The Right to Participate in International Human Rights Fieldwork* <http://www.ihrnetwork.org/human-rights-fieldwork.htm> accessed 10 Jan 2006.

'success' of a programme, while too little time and funding is allocated to designing processes of participation which empower. Ultimately participation needs to be reflected in the allocation of programme time, resources, and expertise.

D. Non-discrimination and prioritization of vulnerable groups

Human rights-based approaches require that discrimination and protection of vulnerable groups be treated as a priority. Who is vulnerable here and how is this question to be answered at national and local level? Answering the question with certainty is subject to available official data disaggregated, by race, religion, ethnicity, language, sex, migrants, age, and any other category of human rights concern.

Many development actors have begun to pay particular attention to the 'feminization' of poverty, its causes and remedies. Gender-proofing is central to ensuring this principle is met; it assesses the implications for women and men of any planned action, including policies, legislation and programmes, in any area and at any level. HRBAs require a fundamental shift in mindset addressing some past practices whereby gender impact of development interventions was confined to identifying numbers of women participating in development 'activities' or 'gender impact assessment' checklists annexed to programme designs. HRBAs also require that gender-proofing be part of the wider human rights-proofing of all programming.

E. Accountability

Accountability requires that human rights impact assessment be applied to all development plans, policies, budgets, and programmes to determine progress in human rights terms. This requires identification of both claim-holders (and their entitlements) and corresponding duty-holders (and their obligations) and in turn the positive obligations of duty-holders (to protect, promote, and provide) and negative obligations (to abstain from violations) of the full range of relevant actors, including local authorities and private companies.

Establishing accountability has to become a central consideration for ensuring development effectiveness. It is not enough to find fault or pass the buck when some policy or programme fails. It is critical to understand why the intervention failed, who is responsible and what actions need to be taken collectively to meet the commitments. Only by identifying and establishing accountability for failures (or development ineffectiveness) can meaningful solutions be found. A rights-based approach to development effectiveness brings out the importance not just of outcomes but also of the processes bringing these outcomes about.[25]

---

[25] UNDP, *Development Effectiveness—Spotlight On Performance: Why Some Countries Do Better Than Others* (United Nations Development Programme, 2003) p 7.

As outlined in Section III of the 2002 Office of the United Nations High Commissioner for Human Right (OHCHR) *Draft Guidelines: A Human Rights Approach to Poverty Reduction Strategies*,[26] accountability is a multifaceted concept. It encompasses the state as the principal duty-bearer with respect to the human rights of those within its jurisdiction but also the international community insofar as it too has responsibilities to help realize universal human rights. Weak as the mechanisms for ensuring state accountability are, the challenge is even greater in the case of global actors whether intergovernmental organizations (IGOs), international non-governmental organizations (NGOs), and transnational corporations.

Ultimately, accountability in the human rights sense is about translating universal standards into local benchmarks for measuring progress and developing effective laws, policies, institutions, procedures, and mechanisms of redress that ensure delivery of entitlements and redress for denial and violations.

VI. The evolution of global commitment to HRBAs

Today there is consensus among states regarding the universal framework and core standards which international human rights entail. It is perhaps best illustrated by the near universal adoption by the world's states of the CRC as binding minimum standards regulating states in that regard. From agreement on the core standards in the various treaties, attention has increasingly turned to the effective implementation of such standards and the tools and mechanisms necessary to achieve this.

While a range of actors have made important contributions to the evolution of HRBAs, the UN has been central. Development agencies of the UN system, especially the UN Development Programme (UNDP), have long pioneered people-centred approaches. This is not surprising, as the UN and its member states are charged with collective and individual responsibility to promote universal respect for human rights—a founding principle and purpose of the UN. The full integration of human rights throughout the UN system is, and always has been, a legal imperative flowing from the UN Charter.

The acknowledgment that the enjoyment of human rights is *both the means and the goal* of development is therefore of long-standing, and the concept of human rights-based approaches is not new. The policy commitment was reaffirmed by the UN system as a whole in its 1997 *Programme of Reform* for all parts of the system, from the UNDP to the World Bank. This reform programme drew on the UN General Assembly's *Declaration on the Right to Development* of 1986[27] which indicated the necessity of a human rights framework for effective development. Designed to streamline the UN's work while improving its

---

[26] <http://www.unhchr.ch/development/povertyfinal.html> accessed 15 April 2006.
[27] Note 8 above.

co-ordination and management structures, the Programme acknowledged human rights as both a principal goal of the organization and a means by which its other goals could be advanced.[28] A similar commitment to HRBAs is reflected in the 1990s world conferences on social development, gender, human rights, and racism, as well as in the Millennium Development Goals agreed by UN members in 2000.[29]

The 2000 UN Human Development Report represented a landmark statement on the human rights-based approach to development, noting;

Poverty eradication is a major human rights challenge of the 21st Century. A decent standard of living, adequate nutrition, health care, education decent work and protection against calamities, are not just development goals- they are also human rights[30]

Leading development NGOs, such as Oxfam, Action Aid International, and Care International also work to apply HRBAs/acknowledging the imperative of being human rights implementing agencies as opposed to providers of charity. Not only NGOs active in development but also many engaged in humanitarian response and peace processes see the added value of human rights-based approaches in securing sustainable solutions. The largest combined aid donor in the world, the European Union (EU), has committed to apply human rights in its aid relationships with third states, through implementation by the European Commission and its state-level offices world-wide.[31] A range of bilateral donor states (such as the United Kingdom (UK), Sweden, the Netherlands, and Denmark) as well as regional organizations take a similar approach. A wide range of international actors have now made explicit their legal and policy commitment to base their development work on human rights standards. Changing practices to reflect these commitments is, however, a slow process of learning from experience.

VII. Progress in international practice

An established body of HRBAs experience is available from a range of states and other actors. Some illustrations of this experience are outlined here. A range of actors are revisiting policies, practices, and institutional structures in moving beyond recognition in principle that their work should be based in human rights. This has seen the development of a growing body of methodologies and practical

---

[28] *Renewing the United Nations: A Programme for Reform*, UN doc A/51/950 (July 1997), paras 78–79, hereafter the Programme for Reform.

[29] <http://www.un.org/millenniumgoals/> accessed 10 Jan 2006.

[30] UNDP, *Human Development Report 2000*, p 8.

[31] See *Communication from the Commission to the Council and the Parliament: the European Union's role in Promoting Human Rights and Democratisation in Third Countries*, COM (2001) 252 final (8 May 2001).

tools. Some of these initiatives are led by multilateral agencies, others are the result of national efforts. In some cases, the way is being led by NGOs, academics or community groups. In others, states take the lead through ministries responsible for national planning or various sectors (health, education, environment, etc).

A number of bilateral donors have also been at the forefront of making human rights-based approaches central to their overseas development programming, including the Canadian International Development Agency (CIDA), the Norwegian Agency for Development Co-operation (NORAD), the Danish International Development Agency (DANIDA), the Swedish International Development Cooperation Agency (SIDA), and the UK Department for International Development (DFID).

Within the UN system,[32] the United Nations Children's Fund (UNICEF) has led the way in developing programming tools and placing human rights at the centre of assessing its own impact; it explicitly adopted the CRC as its framework for programming as soon as the treaty came into force in the early 1990s. The World Health Organization (WHO) supports governments towards applying HRBAs in national health policies and strategies through a designated health and human rights team.[33] A joint UNDP-OHCHR programme, Human Rights Strengthening (HURIST), works to support national governments in their development planning by developing methodologies and identifying best practices in HRBAs.[34]

In May 2003, the second UN inter-agency workshop on 'Implementing a Human Rights-Based Approach to Development in the Context of UN Reform' was held in Stamford, Connecticut. Participating agencies, in what is sometimes referred to as the 'Stamford consensus', distinguished between human rights-based approaches and 'good programming practices' and agreed on a Common Understanding on HRBA within the UN system. This consensus covered a number of aspects including agreement that all programmes, policies, and technical assistance should further the realization of human rights; that the human rights standards in the UDHR and other international human rights instruments form the basis for all development co-operation. In addition it was stressed that UN programming in all sectors and in all phases of the programming process

---

[32] The International Labour Organization (ILO), which predates the UN itself, has operated within a human rights framework since it was founded in 1919.

[33] A Strategy Unit within WHO serves as focal point for developing its health and human rights approach. WHO works to advance health as a human right in close collaboration with OHCHR and the UN's independent Special Rapporteur on the Right to Health. Of particular importance is the human rights-based approach to combating AIDs pioneered at the Harvard School of Public Health and Human Rights influencing the UNAIDS agency (empowering women, addressing discrimination, etc).

[34] The programme's specific aim is to support the implementation of UNDP's undertakings in its policy document *Integrating Human Rights with Sustainable Human Development*. See also, the April 2005 UNDP note of its experience integrating human rights in its own work in *Human Rights in UNDP: A Practice Note*.

should contribute to the development of the capacities of duty-bearers to meet their obligations and of 'rights-holders' to claim their rights.

While the range of work on HRBA has increased very rapidly in recent years, much of it remains fragmented. Pooling of experience and identification of positive lessons for replication remains the exception rather than the rule. In particular, little has been done to transplant lessons from the more extensive application of HRBAs in developing world contexts to industrialized states.

A seminal process aiming to provide a systematic approach to state-level efforts to apply HRBA is the UN Development Assistance Framework, which is applied in most states which have UN offices present and engaged in development work. A second process that has been promoted by the UN in all states, regardless of their stage of development is the National Human Rights Action Plans. These two processes are potential key tools for applying HRBAs at state level. The two processes are introduced here, not to suggest their success in any particular state, but to indicate models for practical approaches to give real meaning to HRBAs, assuming lessons are learned from their applications elsewhere.

VIII. UN Development Assistance Framework (UNDAF)

The UN Secretary-General's reform programme has involved encouragement of the myriad of UN agencies to work together *as a team* at state level. The UN Country Team[35] is expected to agree, in conjunction with the government concerned, on a common analysis of the state's challenges and solutions. This analysis leads to a multi-year development plan to frame the government's future planning. Most significantly, this process, intended to shape the vision and allocation of development resources by UN agencies for a period of years, is expressly founded on the human rights obligations of the state concerned, and is designed so as to help it fulfil its obligations. The UN guidelines require that the process be participatory, with civil society input and access to information—not simply a UN-government dialogue.[36] The 2004 revised version states explicitly that

---

[35] The composition of the Country Team will vary according to the UN agencies present in a particular state, but generally include: the UNDP Resident Co-ordinator and Resident Representative, as well as representatives of UNICEF, the Department of Economic and Social Affairs, the World Bank, ILO, WHO, the UN Population Fund, World Food Programme, UN Volunteers, High Commissioner for Refugees, the head of any UN Peacekeeping/Peacebuilding mission, UNESCO, and International Organization for Migration, etc.

[36] For CCA/UNDAF Integrated Guidelines 2004 see <http://www.un.org.lb/un/awms/uploadedfiles/CCA-UNDAF%20Guidelines-English.doc> accessed 10 Jan 2006. Among the Stated Guiding principles for UNDAFs is 'Integrate systematically human rights principles and gender equality as well as sustainable development concerns' though even then the list of principles suggest lack of clarity regarding the legal imperative involved with, for example, MDGs listed ahead of human rights commitment and 'reduce vulnerabilities of the poorest, including indigenous peoples and migrants' listed separately from the human rights commitment.

the Common Country Assessment (CCA) and UNDAF should 'support government and civil society in pursuit of the universal, indivisible, and interdependent human rights, as set out in the Universal Declaration of Human Rights and other international human rights instruments'.[37] In addition, account is to be taken of UN supervision or monitoring bodies that may have identified development-related problems.

The effectiveness of UNDAF processes has been undercut by the fact that parallel processes were promoted by other UN bodies. Thus, for example, while the World Bank takes part in UNDAF as part of the UN Country Team, it also promotes PRSPs with the IMF.[38] First introduced in 1999 by the IMF and the World Bank as a replacement for Structural Adjustment Programs, PRSPs are meant to be developed on a state basis after thorough participatory processes. PRSPs are a precondition for loans and debt relief and enshrine what the International Financing Institutions (IFIs) term 'good governance' commitments by the aid recipient state. Significantly, PRSPs are not designed to be human rights-based and there is no systematic attempt to ensure that the decisions made based on each process are compatible with human rights. This contributes to incoherent and inconsistent policy processes among donors and facilitates those governments who wish to play them off against each other.

National Human Rights Action Plans (NHRAP) are another state-level planning process intended to bring together all relevant national actors to produce a time-bound set of priorities for achieving human rights change. The concept originates with the Vienna Declaration and Programme of Action, which called upon states to consider implementing such a process. While the title varies from state to state, such plans have been developed in states as diverse as Brazil, South Africa, Moldova, Latvia, Sweden, and Australia. An NHRAP is meant to constitute an action-orientated process, which includes strong participation, benchmarks, and targets along with mechanisms for on-going monitoring and evaluation. The process itself facilitates national debate on the nature of human rights and the choices to be made. The process is recognized as being as important as the outcome, with participation generally facilitated through committees, public meetings, and hearings. Central to an NHRAP's success or failure has been the extent to which it is linked to any over-arching development process such as a state's National Development Plan. Equally it needs to be linked to policy planning and budget decisions in sectors such as health, education, and law enforcement to ensure that human rights are not 'quarantined' as a distinct sector.

In the case of the UN-promoted NHRAPs, they too have been criticized for not being linked into other state-level development plans and budgets and for being marginalized from the UNDAFs happening in the same country.

---

[37] Common Country Assessment and United Nations Development Assistance Framework Guidelines for UN Country Teams preparing a CCA and UNDAF (2004), p 7.
[38] <http://www.imf.org/external/np/prsp/prsp.asp> accessed 10 Jan 2006.

Development practitioners have identified some of the reasons behind this incoherence as including agency-specific mandates, agendas, jargon, and turf battles. Sometimes individuals within an agency can impede or promote HRBAs at state level while a contradictory message comes from their headquarters. Isolated sectoral approaches continue to be applied where more holistic approaches are needed, challenging national level harmonization by development actors, especially in joint or multi-sectoral programming.

IX. Challenges faced in seeking to apply HRBAs

A selection of the challenges that typically arise in seeking to implement human rights-based development or are raised in opposition to such approaches are mentioned briefly here. The challenges include:

(i) competing rather than co-ordinated development processes;[39]

(ii) participation not seen as a human right and inadequately applied;

(iii) weak capacity to undertake HRBA programming or support from specialized focal point (e.g. human rights expertise lacking in delegations of one of the most significant global development actors, the European Commission, development timelines driven by donor financial year timelines, etc);

(iv) distorted public perception of human rights, human rights associated with criminals/terrorists, or ideologically suspect;

(v) low public awareness of human rights and low expectations of change;

(vi) prevalent view that 'we cannot afford human rights' or that poverty is by definition addressed by economic growth;

(vii) lack of clarity regarding the core meaning of HRBA. In particular, confusion between the freedom to choose from various human rights-based approaches and the fact that the core elements of HRBA as legal imperatives are not optional; and

(viii) failure to match the commitment to human rights-based development with systematic human rights-based measurement and indicators.

The following section focuses on this latter challenge as perhaps the most commonly highlighted practical lacuna of HRBAs and critical to establishing the added value of HRBAs.

---

[39] A factor not aided by an array of terminology. The UK DFID, for example, uses as its overarching principles, *Participation, Inclusion,* and *Fulfilling Obligations* to encapsulate its commitment to HRBA. On the other hand, the UN HURIST Programme uses the acronym PANEL representing *Participation; Accountability, Non-discrimination, Empowerment, Linkage to normative standards.* For a range of definitions employed by various actors, see <http://www.crin.org/docs/resources/publications/hrbap/Interaction_analysis_RBA_definitions.pdf> accessed 10 Jan 2006.

X. Measuring human rights-based development

If growing acceptance of the merits of development based upon human rights can be assumed, a key issue is what this means for how we measure and assess development as a process and in terms of its impact. At the heart of HRBAs is the issue of measurement.

The range of actors engaged in measurement of development includes evaluation units of states, multilateral organizations including IFIs, individuals, UN agencies and larger NGOs, etc. Evaluation networks include the OECD's Development Assistance Committee (DAC) Network on Development Evaluation and a network of development practitioners and evaluators, International Development Evaluation Association (IDEAS), and the UN Evaluation Group (UNEG) established in January 1984.

Measurement in HRBA terms means measurement of the immediate, underlying, and structural causes of the non-realization of rights; measurement of the capacity of rights-holders to claim their rights, and of duty-bearers to fulfil their obligations; measurement of development processes and outcomes to ensure that they are informed by the recommendations of international human rights bodies and mechanisms, etc.

Fundamentally, human rights-based measurement of development (both in terms of process and impact) needs to encompass the full spectrum of human rights—civil, political, economic, social, and cultural, mirroring the nature of the obligations of 'conduct' and 'result'. In turn, appropriate indicators also help address some of the shibboleths that still cloud the debate regarding socio-economic rights versus civil and political rights in terms of their concreteness and justiciability.

Many development actors have been far ahead of what might be conceived as the human rights community in focusing on measurement of their interventions and a range of methodological tools are also available from humanitarian actors, such as Vulnerability Assessment Mapping (VAM), or base-line surveys. Extensive work has been done on the merits and pitfalls of using various types of indicators—qualitative, quantitative, objective, subjective, etc.[40] Actors such as the World Bank, the IMF, ILO, UNESCO, and UNDP collate and analyse volumes of data on their work. However, much of these focus on economic development, or on the human side, or confined to measurement of poverty. The annual UNDP Human Development Reports are perhaps among the most well known, with its Human Development Index (HDI), Human Poverty Index (HPI), Gender-related Development Index (GDI), and Gender Empowerment Measure (GEM). From the first Human Development Report in 1990, these annual reports have

---

[40] See, eg, various manuals and guides at <http://www.eldis.org/participation/pme/Eldis_selection.htm> accessed 10 Jan 2006.

sought to measure development through a combination of indicators, including life expectancy, educational attainment, and income to produce a composite human development index (HDI). They represent a departure from earlier emphasis on economic indicators. The HDI sets a minimum and a maximum for each dimension and then places each state on these scales—expressed as a value between 0 and 1.[41] The human poverty index (HPI) uses indicators of the most basic deprivation: life expectancy, lack of basic education, and lack of access to public and private resources. The first indicator highlights the percentage of people expected to die before age forty. The second measures the percentage of a state's adult population that is illiterate, while the third constitutes a composite of three variables: the percentage of people with access to health services and to safe water and the percentage of malnourished children under five.

The gender-related development index (GDI) also represents a refinement of the HDI by factoring in inequality in achievement between women and men. The greater the gender disparity in basic capabilities, the lower a state's GDI compared with its HDI. The gender empowerment measure (GEM) examines whether women and men are able to participate actively in economic and political life and take part in decision-making.[42]

The 2000 Human Development Report represented a departure insofar as it linked indicators to the issue of human rights accountability, noting that 'Indicators can be used as a tool for:

(a) Making better policies and monitoring progress.
(b) Identifying unintended impacts of laws, policies and practices.
(c) Identifying which actors are having an impact on the realization of rights.
(d) Revealing whether the obligations of these actors are being met.
(e) Giving early warning of potential violations, prompting preventive action.
(f) Enhancing social consensus on difficult trade-offs to be made in the face of resource constraints.
(g) Exposing issues that had been neglected or silenced.'[43]

More recently, the Millennium Development Goals (MDGs) have provided additional benchmarks for development. However, the gain in terms of political momentum needs to be viewed in light of a certain regression in human rights

---

[41] Eg with the minimum adult literacy rate set as 0% and the maximum at 100%, the literacy component for a state with a literacy rate of 50% would be 0.50. Similarly, the minimum for life expectancy is twenty-five years and the maximum eighty-five years, so the longevity component for a state where life expectancy is fifty years would be 0.5. For income the minimum is $100 (Purchasing Power Parity (PPP)) and the maximum is $40,000 (PPP). Income above the average world income is adjusted using a progressively higher discount rate. The scores for the three dimensions are then averaged to produce an overall index.

[42] UNDP, Human Development Report Office (HDRO), *Analytical tools for human development [the conceptual basis for UNDP Human Development Index / development indicators]* (HDRO, 2005).

[43] UNDP, *Human Development Report 2000*, Ch 5, Using Indicators for Human Rights Accountability, (OUP, 2000) p 89.

terms, insofar as they have become the litmus test for many development actors, almost as a replacement framework for human rights.[44] The gap between development based on the MDGs and the wider human rights framework has prompted the OHCHR's Advisor on the MDGs to describe the MDGs and human rights as ships passing in the night.[45] The pre-eminence of the MDGs may be seen as an understandable reaction to what has been described as 'current considerable confusion over the purpose, methodology, terminology and typology of indicators',[46] but taken as an alternative to the wider human right framework they represent the triumph of measurability over applicable law.

In addition to the array of initiatives and measurement models in the traditional development sector, a range of human rights actors have been engaged in development of indicators, checklists, and quantitative measurement systems in the past decade or so.[47] Many human rights indicators however are rudimentary at best, the standard being the state of ratification of international human rights standards. Examples include civil and political rights initiatives of institutions such as Freedom House, American Association for the Advancement of Science, etc. A 2003 EU study identified some 170 'measurement' initiatives across areas variously categorized as 'democracy', 'human rights', or 'good governance'.[48]

To identify whether development is good or bad in human rights terms requires that the indicators themselves be human rights-based. The core problem is not shortage of measurement initiatives or even data but rather shortage of *human rights relevant* data. Despite the volume of activity, the 2003 study referred to above, for example, still noted a lack of indicators and data in key areas, including economic, social, and cultural rights. A more recent survey comments on

a near absence of a conceptual framework in these initiatives that could be readily considered as a starting point for undertaking a meaningful work on human rights indicators.[49]

[44] Eg, the UNDP Human Development Index 'data sources' links the MDGs and a range of UN agencies but NOT OHCHR or the human rights treaty bodies. Similarly, the DevInfo database system contains indicators, time periods and geographic areas organized to monitor global and national commitments to sustained human development is based on forty-eight quantitative indicators for monitoring progress towards the MDGs but omits the wider human rights framework.

[45] P Alston, 'Ships Passing in the Night: The Current State of the Human Rights and Development Debate seen through the Lens of the Millennium Development Goals' (2005) 27 Human Rights Q 3.

[46] Organization for Economic Co-operation and Development, *Guidelines for the use of indicators in country performance assessment* (2002) <http://www.oecd.org/dataoecd/51/36/33670318.pdf> accessed 10 Jan 2006.

[47] For brief overview of some of these initiatives see H Sano and L Lindholt, *Human Rights Indicators 2000. Country Data and Methodology* (2000) at <http://www.humanrights.dk/departments/international/PA/Concept/Indicato/> accessed 10 Jan 2006.

[48] T Landman, and J Häusermann, 'Map making and analysis of the main international initiatives on developing indicators on democracy and good governance' (Report for the Statistical Office of the Commission of the European Communities (EUROSTAT) University of Euex, Human Rights Centre, 2003).

[49] R Malhotra and N Fasel, 'Quantitative Human Rights Indicators: A survey of major initiatives' (Background paper for the UN Expert Meeting on Human Rights Indicators, Turku, 2005).

The evolution of such coherent rights-based indicators has also been bedevilled by conflicting processes and benchmarks for collecting data and most fundamentally the failure to marry the methodological head-start that the development actors with the substantive precision of the applicable human rights legal framework. As noted in the context of housing rights:

In creating a set of housing rights indicators, it is important to identify the particular elements, which comprise the construct being measured, in this case 'housing rights'. Working from those elements, it then becomes possible to identify different 'indicators,' or the quantifiable measures, which may be used to collect data with respect to the particular element in question.[50]

It is here that the body of jurisprudence on socio-economic rights, General Comments, Reporting Guidelines and Concluding Observations, etc, need to be utilized more coherently and comprehensively as a foundation for developing context-specific indictors and as the ultimate litmus test for 'good development'.[51]

That the exercise requires more than adding-on to existing measurement models and indicators is illustrated by the 2003 Report of the Second Inter-Agency Workshop on Implementing a Human Rights-based Approach in the Context of UN Reform. The report acknowledged that there is sometimes 'a disconnect between UN Country Teams and the treaty-bodies'. Moreover, the various Treaty Bodies have not systematically sought to ascertain whether states parties base their development on human rights.[52] Work on developing indicators of human rights-based development requires a process of inter-disciplinary and inter-agency learning and which also links global and regional human rights mechanisms. Currently, a range of agencies, some within the UN family, have developed indicators for their specific subject matter or beneficiary group, sometimes developing indicators based on the three-pronged state obligation to respect, to protect and to fulfil human rights. UNICEF, for example, has long taken a rights-based approach to its programming and developed indicators on that basis. In the narrower field of human rights, the development of indicators is only recently being given attention.

Socio-economic rights present some specific challenges that are posed by the inherent nature of the obligations involved, in particular, concepts such as 'progressive realization' and 'maximum of available resources', etc. Difficulties

---

[50] UN-HABITAT, 'Monitoring Housing Rights: Developing a Set of Indicators to Monitor the Full and Progressive Realisation of the Human Right to Adequate Housing', United Nations Housing Rights Programme, (UN-HABITAT, OHCHR, Nairobi, 2003) p 9.

[51] Among a number of initiatives to review human rights-based impact assessment is an ongoing project co-ordinated by the Dutch NGO *Humanist Committee on Human Rights* which includes the development of monitoring tools (eg Health Rights of Women Assessment Instrument (HeRWAI)) and more generally facilitating information exchange between organizations concerned with human rights impact assessment to identify and measure impact (positive and negative) of policies and programmes.

[52] See the chapter on 'Towards Integration of United Nations Human Rights Treaty Body Recommendations: The Rights-Based Approach Model' by M O'Flaherty in this book.

defining even the minimum core content have been seen as creating the risk of focus shifting from the essence of the rights to more readily observed procedural aspects of the rights concerned.[53] This challenge of formulating indicators to capture distinctions between immediate and progressive obligations (sometimes presented as a distinction between state's positive and negative obligations) can, however, be overstated. Important foundations have been laid, including the Committee for ICESCR's 'minimum threshold approach' of minimum standards to be achieved by all states, irrespective of their economic situation. Further elaboration is found in the Committee's *General Comment 3* on the Nature of States Parties Obligations,[54] various guidelines such as the 2002 OHCHR Draft Guidelines on a Human Rights Approach to Poverty Reduction Strategies, the Maastricht Guidelines on Violations of Economic, Social, and Cultural Rights, as well as the work of various rapporteurs and working groups.[55] These sources provide a starting point to address challenges involved in measuring progress against resource availability, speculating as to alternative courses of action, or of acquiring evidence of state responsibility. In effect this entails shifting the 'burden of proof' where significant numbers of people live in poverty, by obliging the state to show that the situation is beyond its control.

Indicators are of fundamental importance in the case of accountability, on several perspectives. Firstly, as the Maastricht Guidelines on Violations of Economic, Social, and Cultural Rights[56] list 'the failure to monitor the realization of economic, social and cultural rights, including the development and application of criteria and indicators for assessing compliance' as an example of violation of economic, social, and cultural rights by omission of states insofar as it is required by legal obligations.

Indicators are recognized as central to both states' and supervisory bodies' ability to evaluate effectively the extent to which progress has been made towards the realization of international human rights obligations. The Committee for the ICESCR, for example, has called on states parties 'to set specific goals or benchmarks with respect to the reduction of infant mortality, the extent of vaccination of children, the intake of calories per person, the number of persons per health care provider, etc.'[57] The various other supervisory committees and UN Treaty Reporting Guidelines place similar emphasis on the need for indicators.

Indicators are fundamental to assessing whether the applicable standard has been met as a matter of law but also to encompassing political, professional

---

[53] IHRIP and Asian Forum for Human Rights and Development, *Circle of Rights, Economic Social, and Cultural Rights Activism: A Training Resource* (Module 8 Defining the Content Of ESC Rights—Problems and Prospects) (Institute of International Education, IHRIP, 2000).
[54] E/1991/23.
[55] Eg, Disaggregation of rights such as that developed with regard to the right to education by former Special Rapporteur, Katerina Tomaševski—'Four A's'—acceptability, accessibility, affordability, and adaptability.   [56] Maastricht 22–26 Jan 1997.
[57] ESCR Committee *General Comment 1, Reporting by States Parties*, E/1989/22, 24 Feb 1989.

commitments to development based on human rights. Accountability in this context necessarily needs to go beyond accountability as encapsulated in what has been termed a 'violations approach' but it includes political, contractual, and professional accountability of the various actors involved in development. While indicators and measurement are key to establishing an evidentiary basis for judicial enforcement of ESCR in national contexts, they are also critical for this wider notion of accountability, to take account of the range of development actors, multilateral, bilateral donors, IFIs, aid agencies, NGOs, etc.

XI. What difference can HRBAs make?

Proposals for the integration of human rights into development activity can too easily remain at the level of generality—the sweeping commitments in the introduction of plans or policy documents. Development activity does not *automatically* promote respect for human rights simply by expenditure on health, education, etc. Many activities undertaken in the name of 'development' are subsequently recognized as ill-conceived where money is wasted, or even counter-productive in human rights terms, where certain groups are discriminated against.

As has been emphasized above, there is no single human rights-based approach. Rather, as outlined below, there are principles to be applied to achieve human rights standards. The selection of methods and tools is left to states to choose, according to what is *most effective*. Identifying examples of human rights-based approaches which are *effective in achieving positive human rights change* is a question of:

(i) assessing the *human rights impact* of current approaches (taking account of the full spectrum of human rights, the range of affected groups, their specific circumstances, etc); and

(ii) adjusting those approaches through effective learning across all areas of the state's sphere of responsibility.

Inherent in the universal human right framework from which HRBAs derive, as former High Commissioner for Human Rights, Mary Robinson has noted, is that 'a commitment to a human rights-based approach should apply equally to developed and developing countries'. Applying such human rights-based approaches to development necessitates that development reflects the five core principles outlined in section V above.

In her opening statement to the General Assembly Special Session on Social Development in Geneva in June 2000, Mary Robinson noted that human rights-based approaches bring the promise of more effective, more sustainable, and more rational development processes. This added value of HRBAs is outlined below.

XII. The value-added of human rights-based approaches to development

A central challenge for HRBAs has been to identify the value-added of this approach in the face of what many see as 'passing fashions' offered as rationale for development interventions. The key added value might be seen as the greater legitimacy that HRBAs entail, grounded in, and gaining legitimacy from, the inherent human rights recognized in international law. These human rights are minimum agreed standards. Human rights are sometimes opposed as Western constructs inappropriately 'imposed' on other cultures. The legitimacy of HRBAs is grounded in their universality, which takes as a fundamental starting point the fact that states adhere to these human rights treaties as a matter of choice and as an exercise of state sovereignty. HRBAs facilitate greater transparency and wider endorsement of national development processes, as development objectives, indicators, and plans are based on the agreed universal standards of the international human rights instruments.

HRBAs offer an authoritative basis for advocacy by civil society. The relevant international legal obligations empower development advocates to promote basic social services over the sometimes competing interests of those in power. HRBAs provide civil society advocates with international mechanisms (both judicial and non-judicial) to highlight policy choices by the state which impede or reverse the progressive realization of economic and social rights.

HRBAs shift the focus from the fact that the vulnerable in society have needs to the fact that they have human rights. By requiring meaningful participation of a community (itself a human right) HRBAs require that people be empowered as a result and that the development itself constitutes a process of empowerment.

HRBAs mean greater coherence across sectors through normative clarity. The international instruments and the authoritative interpretations of treaty bodies and human rights mechanisms define the content of development (including the requirements of, for example, health, education, housing, and governance). These are public, accessible tools detailing the institutional and developmental requirements arising from the minimum standards states have undertaken.

HRBAs provide a more complete and rational development framework for all areas of human development, whether health, education, housing, personal security, justice administration, or political participation. They provide a common template for coherence between all aspects of state responsibility and action (both domestic and external): from the processes and content of macro policy priorities, strategic plans, and fiscal allocation to training and performance assessment of state employees.

HRBAs offer a framework for more effective analysis and identify the wider range of solutions needed; traditional poverty analysis bases judgments on income and economic indicators alone. A human rights analysis reveals additional concerns of the poor themselves, highlighting poverty as more than material need but as powerlessness and social exclusion, as highlighted by the World Bank's *Voices of the Poor* study.[58]

As an example, economic growth alone is not sufficient to reduce poverty— growth needs to be combined with policies designed to reduce inequality. Donors such as DFID recognize this by a policy commitment to 'broad based economic growth'. Clearly higher rates of growth can contribute to more rapid poverty reduction. Where the income growth rate rises faster, the incomes of poor people tend to also rise faster. However, there is variation among states in the relationship between growth and poverty reduction. These variations reflect differences in *what has happened as regards income inequality*—which is central to HRBA concerns to address poverty effectively.

Local ownership of, and participation in, development process, inherent in HRBAs, are fundamental to designing development initiatives that are tailored to local realities and needs and maximize impact and sustainability and yield greater impact and sustainability. HRBAs offer integrated safeguards against unintentional harm by development by ensuring that human rights protection measures are organically incorporated into development plans, policies, and projects from the outset.

By identifying specific duties and duty-bearers, human rights-based development moves from the realm of charity to one of obligation. This includes identifying those responsible for respecting, protecting, and fulfilling human rights, and holding them accountable for these responsibilities. HRBAs empower communities and individuals to identify relevant duty-holders and assert their rights accordingly.

HRBAs require that root causes be addressed, which requires the equitable distribution of power and resources based on the recognition that human beings' inherent dignity entitles them to a core set of rights that cannot be taken away. HRBAs challenge vested interests and power structures, recalling that development is an inherently political process. They provide a basis for assessment of development progress made, beyond mere expenditure, or increased Gross Domestic Product (GDP), and provide a specific set of criteria to which the state and its agents must answer.

XIII. Conclusion

When we use the phrase human rights and development we sometimes seem to imply that the two are quite different. [...] fundamentally the ultimate goal is the same: to

---

[58] <http://www1.worldbank.org/prem/poverty/voices/> accessed 10 Jan 2006. See also Pro-Poor Growth Briefing Note 1: *What Is Pro-Poor Growth and Why Do We Need To Know?* (DFID PD Growth Team, Advanced Draft 12 Dec 2003); other sources: M Lipton and R Eastwood, *'Pro-Poor Growth and Pro-Growth Poverty Reduction'*, (presented at the Asia and Pacific Forum on Poverty Reduction, Asian Development Bank, Manila, 5–9 Feb 2001); S Klasen, 'In Search of the Holy Grail: How to Achieve Pro-Poor Growth' (IDEAS, 2001). Also see D Dollar and A Kraay, 'Growth is Good for the Poor', (2002) 7 *J of Economic Growth*, 195–225.

contribute to enhancing the dignity of people's lives. Development aims at improvement in the lives and the well-being of all people. It does this through the delivery of services and the expansion of government capacities. This is also the process of realizing many human rights.[59]

The debate regarding human rights based development has necessitated both a conceptual and language shift. This debate has benefited from advances made in asserting the legitimacy of socio-economic rights but has suffered also from some of the scepticism and resistance that has impeded the realization of socio-economic rights and been a feature, for example, of the debate on an Optional Protocol to the ICESCR. A certain degree of conceptual clarity as to what it means to understand development from a human rights perspective can be said to have been secured. This is in no small part due to those, such as David Harris, who have long promoted the legitimacy of socio-economic rights. However, many development actors have yet to make the commitment to change how they do things. For those actors who have embraced HRBAs in principle, the next challenge is to operationalize the commitment that has been made. To achieve this requires that human rights lawyers, armed with half a century of jurisprudence and other norms, work with traditional development actors. It requires that substantive human rights expertise be married to long-standing work on participation, impact assessment, etc in development and humanitarian fields.

Most fundamentally, HRBAs require a shift in mindset by a range of actors with common goals albeit working in different disciplines. This shift is required of actors that traditionally saw themselves as part of the human rights or development communities. Many of the human rights community have been said to:

remain reluctant to venture outside their areas of expertise narrowly defined. They have happily endorsed calls for development and humanitarian agencies to take on human rights functions but have not seen it to be necessary or even desirable for themselves to reach out with a more developmental contribution to the overall agenda.[60]

Highlighting the legal imperative inherent in HRBAs is critical to expanding the reach of HRBAs but it alone is not likely to deliver the potential of this approach. Moreover, without the necessary resources, and political energy, there remains the risk that it becomes another competing theory for addressing

---

[59] Mehr Khan Williams, United Nations Deputy High Commissioner for Human Rights, (addressing 7th Annual Irish Department of Foreign Affairs-hosted NGO Forum on Human Rights, 11 June 2005).   [60] P Alston, 'Ships Passing in the Night' (n 47 above), at 827.

4

The Violence of Dispossession: Extra-Territoriality and Economic, Social, and Cultural Rights

*Matthew Craven**

I. Introduction

In his article 'The Politics of Utopia' Frederic Jameson suggests that the present climate appears unpropitious for utopian theorizing. He points out that the explanation for this may lie in the 'extraordinary historical dissociation' of two distinct worlds that characterizes globalization today:

In one of these worlds, the disintegration of the social is so absolute—misery, poverty, unemployment, starvation, squalor, violence and death—that the intricately elaborated social schemes of utopian thinkers become as frivolous as they are irrelevant. In the other, unparalleled wealth, computerized production, scientific and medical discoveries unimaginable a century ago as well as an endless variety of commercial and cultural pleasures, seem to have rendered utopian fantasy and speculation as boring and antiquated as pre-technological narratives of space flight.[1]

Jameson's point, in part at least, was clearly not that different people may stand in different temporal relations to the 'other world' that a utopian theorist may attempt to conjure into existence (that some may be closer, others more distant from that ideal), but that the temporal horizon is in fact a spatial one—for some, in certain parts of the world, the idea of a life without poverty, disease, malnutrition, and the like, renders utopian speculation utterly lifeless, whereas for others, in other places, that speculation appears little more than a faintly modified description of daily life. What Jameson's description of the apparent sterility of

* I would like to express my enormous gratitude to David Harris, as supervisor for my doctoral thesis, who not only directed me towards researching in the field of economic, social, and cultural rights (ESC rights), but who has also provided continued advice and support in my academic career. My thanks also go to Susan Marks whose comments on an earlier version of this chapter were invaluable.

[1] Jameson F, 'The Politics of Utopia' (2004) 25 *New Left Rev*, p 35.

utopian discourse thus appears to communicate is two things. First is a dissipation
of the sense of time or history in what he takes to be the post-modern experience
of late capitalism (underpinned by its refutation of narratives of progress, and
stories of development and fruition). Second, is a coeval concretization of a spatial
differentiation between the experience and outlook of different people in different
places, in which each potential protagonist appears to be locked into an imaginative stasis.

Jameson's argument was by no means directed towards the contemporary discourse of human rights, let alone that accompanying the recognition of economic,
social, and cultural rights (ESC rights). But his comments have some resonance in
that context nevertheless. Here, from one perspective, ESC rights embody a kind
of reformist agenda (linked to a progressive narrative of 'development') that has
particular purchase or meaning for those living in poverty or destitution in certain
parts of the world, but which is ultimately confronted by an array of obstacles
ranging from those concerning the inadequacies of local systems of governance
and social order, to those that condition the international environment (such as
might relate to trade, investment, debt or technology). From another perspective,
by contrast, the ESC rights agenda appears far more mundane—concerned as it
appears to be with the staples of political debate in modern democratic societies
(health, education, equality, etc), and to which the language of 'rights' seems to
have very little positive to add.

Within this debate, the question of space—or more specifically territory—
seems to assume a significant place. Those for whom the ESC rights agenda
appears too remote, see the difficulties as lying largely beyond the confines of the
nation state: domestic political or social reform always appears possible, whilst
international reform seems inconceivable. Those, by contrast, who see the project
as mundane, do so largely by refusing to engage with the possibility that their lives
may be somehow connected to those living in poverty elsewhere in the world (that
the accrual of wealth and resources in the North is unconnected to their lack in
the South). And it is, thus, in respect of the existence or otherwise of international
(or extra-territorial) obligations in respect of ESC rights that much appears to
depend.

In the course of this chapter I want to explore the significance of the ideas of
space or territory for the contemporary understanding of ESC rights. In the
process, I will touch upon the debate surrounding the imposition of economic
sanctions and the position adopted in respect of the question of extra-territoriality
by the United Nations (UN) Committee on Economic, Social and Cultural
Rights (ESCR Committee). But the main focus will be to place the discussion of
extra-territoriality and its relation to justificatory arguments about ESC rights in
the context of the Arendt's critique of the 'Rights of Man' as developed in the work
of Agamben and Balibar. It will be argued that the Arendt's warning that the
advancement of human rights might justify processes of exclusion and dispossession at precisely the same moment at which it opposes them, retains considerable

force for the contemporary ESC rights project, particularly when the latter is framed in territorial terms.

Two points ought to be made at the outset about the title of this chapter. First of all, although I use the term 'dispossession' in relation to the non-enjoyment of ESC rights, I do not intend by that to restrict analysis to those instances in which individuals or communities may have been deprived of some existing (legal) entitlement, but I also include within it the simple condition of 'being in poverty or destitution' (however problematic those terms may be). Dispossession remains the preferred terminology, however, insofar as it appears peculiarly expressive of the idea that poverty and destitution are not merely natural 'Malthusian Phenomena', but rather are socially generated and may themselves be produced through the legal relations of entitlement and exchange to which the narrower definition might refer. Secondly, dispossession is referred to as an act of 'violence'. The purpose here, is to direct attention to two plausible equivalences: one between the kinds of act that are typically regarded as violent (the use of force or coercion), and those that result form other 'technologies of power' (social organization and legal entitlements perhaps); the other between the consequential physical manifestation of each (for which a differentiation between physical pain and starvation, for example, is clearly problematic). To see poverty as violence, in other words, is to forefront both the catastrophic nature of poverty and the extent to which it is managed or produced through social, political, economic, or legal arrangements.

II. The UN Committee and extra-territorial obligations

In December 1997, the ESCR Committee issued a General Comment on the 'relationship between economic sanctions and respect for economic, social and cultural rights'.[2] The main purpose of that General Comment was to encourage the UN Security Council, and member states participating in its decision-making, to spend more time considering the impact that such sanctions may have upon the ESC rights of the inhabitants of 'target' regimes. It was an issue that had been brought to the Committee's attention in several state reports,[3] and had assumed particular prominence in the case of Iraq. A number of studies that had been undertaken by the World Health Organization (WHO), amongst others, in assessing the impact of the sanctions regime on Iraq in the aftermath of the first

[2] ESCR Committee *General Comment 8*, UN doc E/C.12/1997/8.
[3] The Committee was to make note of the fact that, at that stage, UN authorized sanctions had been imposed upon South Africa, Iraq/Kuwait, parts of the former Yugoslavia, Somalia, the Libyan Arab Jamahiriya, Liberia, Haiti, Angola, Rwanda, and the Sudan. To this list might have been added Sierra Leone, Cambodia, Afghanistan, Eritrea, Ethiopia, the Democratic Republic of the Congo, and the Côte d'Ivoire.

Gulf War,[4] indicated that whilst the UN had moved to mitigate the adverse effects of its sanctions regime—particularly through its operation of the 'Oil for Food' programme[5]—the imposition of sanctions had had a catastrophic effect upon the health and well-being of the Iraqi population. There were undoubtedly causal questions here relating to the relationship between the sanctions imposed and the consequential effects (for example, the extent to which humanitarian assistance was being diverted for the profit of the local elite) but even with such qualifications, the evidence was clear enough to suggest that the compatibility of sanctions regimes with states' commitments under the International Covenant on Economic, Social and Cultural Rights (ICESCR) could not be taken for granted.[6]

If the Committee felt itself compelled to respond to the issue—to point out, at least, that economic sanctions, if not carefully targeted, structured, and monitored, might constitute something analogous to the deliberate starvation of the population, or the purposeful deprivation of medical assistance—there was the inevitable question as to how it might do so within the framework of the obligations under the Covenant itself. There were two obvious difficulties. First of all, there was a general question concerning the applicability of the Covenant in case of sanctions duly authorized by the Security Council acting under Chapter VII of the UN Charter insofar as article 103 of the Charter provides that, in case of conflict, obligations under the Charter should prevail over those under any other

---

[4] FAO/WFP/WHO, 'Assessment of Food and Nutrition Situation in Iraq' (May/June 2000) noted that 800,000 children under five years of age were chronically malnourished and high levels of anaemia in school children. Two million children were registered as suffering from protein, calorie, and vitamin-related malnutrition in 1998. The Infant Mortality Rate has risen from 47 in 1984–89 to 108 in 1994–99, *Child and Maternal Mortality Survey* (UNICEF, 1999).

[5] This was initially ill-fated. A scheme was proposed in SC res 706 (1991) and a basic structure for its implementation laid down in SC res 712 (1991). Neither of these resolutions was ever implemented. On 14 April 1995, the Security Council (SC) created a new arrangement to the same end in SC res 986 (1995). This 'temporary' arrangement allowed for the sale of $2 billion of Iraqi oil ($1 billion in each of two 90-day periods), the terms of which were agreed with Iraq in a Memorandum of Understanding (S/1996/356) followed by the adoption of the necessary procedures by the Sanctions Committee in Aug (1996) (S/1996/636). On 10 Dec 1996, states were finally authorized to import petroleum and petroleum products from Iraq during specified periods (SC res 1111 (1997); SC res 1129 (1997)). In 1998, the Council extended the scope of the programme (SC res 1153 (1998); 1210 (1998)) and at various points further extended the period of allowable trade. The sanctions were finally terminated pursuant to SC res 1483 (2003).

[6] In his Supplement to the Agenda for Peace in 1995, for example, the UN Secretary-General admitted that: 'Sanctions, as is generally recognized, are a blunt instrument. They raise the ethical question of whether suffering inflicted on vulnerable groups in the target country is a legitimate means of exerting pressure on political leaders whose behaviour is unlikely to be affected by the plight of their subjects. Sanctions also always have unintended or unwanted effects. They can complicate the work of humanitarian agencies by denying them certain categories of supplies and by obliging them to go through arduous procedures to obtain the necessary exemptions. They can conflict with the development objectives of the Organization and do long-term damage to the productive capacity of the target country. They can have a severe effect on other countries that are neighbours or major economic partners of the target country. They can also defeat their own purpose by provoking a patriotic response against the international community, symbolized by the United Nations, and by rallying the population behind the leaders whose behaviour the sanctions are intended to modify.' *Supplement to an Agenda for Peace* (1995), UN doc S/1995/1, para 70.

international agreement. Secondly, and in some respects more fundamentally, there was a question as to whether or not state obligations under the Covenant extended extra-territorially to the point at which states imposing sanctions in another state might be held responsible for any consequential deprivation (of the right to food or health care, for example) even if the sanctioning state exercised no formal jurisdiction or control over the population concerned. Whilst the question whether the effect of Security Council resolutions is to automatically nullify inconsistent conventional obligations is certainly of some general importance,[7] it is with respect to the second of these issues that this paper is concerned.

The ICESCR itself, unlike the majority of other human rights treaties, makes no explicit mention of its scope of application. Whereas article 2(1) of the International Covenant on Civil and Political Rights (ICCPR) speaks of the obligation of states to respect and ensure the rights of all individuals 'within its territory and subject to its jurisdiction', the parallel provision in article 2(1) of the ICESCR avoids any reference to 'jurisdiction' or 'territory'. It does, however, impose an obligation upon all states to 'take steps, individually and through international assistance and cooperation' with a view to achieving the full realization of the rights recognized on a progressive basis. The reference to international co-operation, here, is further reiterated in several other articles (such as articles 11(2) and 15(4)), and it is 'agreed' under the terms of article 23 that 'international action for the achievement of the rights recognized' should include 'such methods as the conclusion of conventions, the adoption of recommendations, the furnishing of technical assistance and the holding of regional meetings and technical meetings for the purpose of consultation and study'.[8] Whilst clearly implying that states parties assume certain obligations of an external or international nature, the exhortation to 'co-operate' does not appear to go very far beyond a commitment to participate in certain types of international activity of a humanitarian character (such as through the provision of a certain amount of aid or assistance to a number of undefined states). It certainly leaves open the larger question as to whether states parties may assume obligations directly in respect of individuals in third states.[9]

Despite the absence of an unambiguous textual provision determining the nature and extent of extra-territorial obligations, the Committee in its General Comment on Sanctions reaffirmed what had largely been hinted at in its earlier

[7] See the chapter on 'The Applicability of Economic and Social Rights to the UN Security Council' by Nigel White in this book on this point.

[8] Art 22, in addition, authorizes the Economic and Social Council to 'bring to the attention of other organs of the United Nations, their subsidiary organs and specialized agencies . . . any matters arising out of the reports [submitted by states parties] which may assist such bodies in deciding, each within its field of competence, on the advisability of international measures likely to contribute to the effective progressive implementation of the present Covenant.'

[9] Coomans suggests, however, that in consequence of these provisions 'a certain extraterritorial (in the sense of international) scope was intended by the drafters and is part of the treaty'. F Coomans, 'Some Remarks on the Extraterritorial Application of the International Covenant on Economic, Social and Cultural Rights', in F Coomans and M Kamminga, *Extraterritorial Application of Human Rights Treaties* (Intersentia, 2004) p 183 at 185.

practice[10] concerning the activities of international lending agencies and transnational corporations[11] by asserting that states parties did assume certain substantive obligations of an extra-territorial nature:

Just as the international community insists that any targeted State must respect the civil and political rights of its citizens, so too must... the international community itself do everything possible to protect at least the core content of the economic, social and cultural rights of the affected peoples of that State (see also *General Comment 3* (1990), paragraph 10).[12]

States imposing sanctions thus were under an obligation to take ESC rights fully into account when designing an 'appropriate sanctions regime',[13] to monitor and protect those rights[14] and take appropriate steps 'in order to respond to any disproportionate suffering experienced by vulnerable groups within the targeted country'.[15] The Committee's general position in this respect has subsequently been reaffirmed in later practice. In its General Comment on the Right to Food, for example, the Committee maintained that

States parties should take steps to respect the enjoyment of the right to food in other countries, to protect that right, to facilitate access to food and to provide the necessary aid when required.[16]

This implied, in the view of the Committee, not only an obligation to 'refrain at all times from food embargoes or similar measures which endanger conditions for food production and access to food in other countries', but also an obligation to 'provide disaster relief and humanitarian assistance in times of emergency'.[17] Similarly in its General Comment on the Right to Water, the Committee insisted that states parties ensure that water is never used 'as an instrument of political and economic pressure', that they should 'prevent their own citizens and companies from violating the right to water of individuals and communities in other countries' and that, when acting as members of international organizations, should take steps to ensure that those organizations take the right to water into account in their various activities.[18]

---

[10] See M Craven, *The International Covenant on Economic, Social and Cultural Rights: A Perspective on its Development* (OUP, 1995) pp 144–150.

[11] See eg, *General Comment 2* (1990), UN doc E/C.12/1990/para 9; *General Comment 3* (1990), UN doc E/C.12/1990/, para 13.   [12] *General Comment 8*, UN doc E/C.12/1997/8, para 7.

[13] Ibid, para 12.

[14] Ibid, para 13 ('When an external party takes upon itself even partial responsibility for the situation within a country (whether under Chapter VII of the Charter or otherwise), it also unavoidably assumes a responsibility to do all within its power to protect the economic, social and cultural rights of the affected population').   [15] Ibid, para 14.

[16] *General Comment 12*, UN doc E/C.12/1999/5, para 35.   [17] Ibid, para 37.

[18] *General Comment 15*, UN doc E/C.12/2002/11, paras 32, 33, and 36. The Committee has also repeatedly called upon 'other actors' such as UN Agencies, the World Bank and the International Monetary Fund (IMF) to incorporate a concern for ESC rights more directly in their work. See eg, *General Comment 2*; *General Comment 14*, UN doc E/C.12/2000/4, paras 63–65; *General Comment 15* (2002), UN doc E/C.12/2002/11, para 60.

For all the Committee's insistence that the Covenant does impose certain extra-territorial obligations upon states—at least as regards a duty to 'respect' or 'protect' the enjoyment of ESC rights on the part of those living in other states[19]—the issue has clearly remained a contentious one. In recent years, for example, the United States of America (US) has responded very sharply to the suggestion of the UN Commission's Special Rapporteur on the Right to Food that states were burdened with a range of extra-territorial obligations in the fulfilment of that right.[20] In the 2004 session of the UN Commission on Human Rights, for example, the US representative declared his support for the idea of the 'progressive realization' of the right to food, but emphasized categorically that such a right 'did not give rise to international obligations'.[21] He suggested, furthermore, that the Special Rapporteur should be chastised for his 'irresponsible and unfounded statements' in that regard.[22] Similarly, in the 2006 session, the US representative again objected to the 'novel legal assertions' concerning extra-territorial obligations of states found in the Special Rapporteur's reports on the right to food.[23] Whilst the US may have been most vocal in this regard, it has clearly not been alone. In critical votes on such issues in the Commission, the US was joined by several other Western European and Northern states, and a number of the same states raised similar concerns in debates surrounding the drafting of an Optional Protocol to the Covenant.[24]

The UN Committee's position relating to the extra-territorial effect was briefly discussed by the International Court of Justice in the *Legal Consequences case*[25] but its conclusion really took the matter no further. There the Court emphasized, in light of the position adopted by the UN Committee, that the obligations under the Covenant could be thought to extend to occupied territory, or territory otherwise falling within a state's 'jurisdiction' albeit not under its sovereignty.[26] But in this respect, it merely reprised the position that had otherwise been established

[19] For an analysis of extra-territorial obligations in terms of the tripartite category of obligations see Coomans (n 9) above p 7; S Skogly and M Gibney, 'Transnational Human Rights Obligations', (2002) 24 Human Rights Q 781.

[20] J Ziegler, 'The Right to Food', UN doc E/CN.4/2005/47.

[21] Williamson (USA), E/CN.4/2004/SR.51, p 16, para 84. Comments made in respect of draft resolution E/CN.4/2004/L.24.   [22] Ibid.

[23] Piedra (USA), E/CN.4/2005/SR.50, p 17, para 95.

[24] Report of Open-ended Working Group, UN doc E/CN.4/2005/52, para 76 ('The representatives of the United Kingdom, the Czech Republic, Canada, France, and Portugal believed that international co-operation and assistance was an important moral obligation but not a legal entitlement, and did not interpret the Covenant to impose a legal obligation to provide development assistance or give a legal title to receive such aid.')

[25] *Legal Conseqeunces of the Construction of a Wall in the Occupied Palestinian Territories* [2004] ICJ Rep para 112.

[26] In case of Israel's obligations with respect to the West Bank, therefore, it suggested that 'the territories occupied by Israel have for over 37 years been subject to its territorial jurisdiction as the Occupying Power. In the exercise of the powers available to it on this basis, Israel is bound by the provisions of the International Covenant on Economic, Social and Cultural Rights.' *Legal Consequences*, para 112.

in cases such as *Loizidou*,[27] and gave little indication as to whether the Committee's more general position regarding extra-territorial obligations was a sound one. Ultimately, its explanation for the absence of a jurisdictional clause in the Covenant—namely that the guarantees were 'essentially territorial'[28]—tends to affirm the inference that extra-territorial obligations only exist in largely exceptional cases.

The purpose of this chapter is not to revisit the general arguments as to what might represent the most legitimate construction of the terms of the Covenant as regards 'international' or 'extra-territorial' obligations, nor seek to articulate how sanctions may be made more 'human rights friendly'. Studies of that particular nature have been undertaken elsewhere.[29] Rather, the purpose is to explore the significance of the notion of 'territorialism' (which I take to be the idea that ESC rights should be understood exclusively in terms of a relationship between a single sovereign and its subjects within a bounded space) for the project of ESC rights as a whole. The particular argument developed in this chapter is that a territorial conception of economic, social, and cultural rights not only, and rather obviously, provides a convenient analytical space for the deployment of coercive economic measures internationally, but also, and more invidiously, puts into question the very rationale of ESC rights. It is suggested that whilst instruments for the protection of ESC rights (for which I take the ICESCR to be paradigmatic) are built upon the premise that they may advance or substantiate the claims of the disempowered, marginalized, or deprived, precisely that some 'community of the dispossessed' is excluded from being able to represent themselves as rights-claimants when their experience is located within a specific territorial framework. To put the argument in a different way, the cost of resistance to the idea of extra-territorial responsibility, is not simply an incidental one (one that may be articulated, for example, in terms of 'collateral damage', or 'necessary suffering') but rather a cost which may seriously prejudice any continued commitment to such rights.

III. Arendt's critique

In the development of my argument, I want to take as my starting point, Hannah Arendt's critique of the rights of man in the second part of her work *The Origins of*

---

[27] *Loizidou v Turkey* (Preliminary Objection) Series A no 310, ECtHR (1995) para 57. Here, the European Court of Human Rights took the view that Turkey could be held responsible for acts of interference in the applicant's enjoyment of her property rights in Northern Cyprus by reason of its 'effective control' over that territory.

[28] The one provision which appears to support this interpretation is art 14 of the Covenant which provides that any state party which, at the time of becoming a Party 'has not been able to secure in its metropolitan territory or other territories under its jurisdiction compulsory primary education, free of charge' should formulate a plan for doing so.

[29] See eg, A Reinisch, 'Developing Human Rights and Humanitarian Law Accountability of the Security Council for the Imposition of Economic Sanctions' (2001) 95 AJIL 851; C Joyner, 'United Nations Sanctions after Iraq: Looking Back to Look Ahead' (2003) 4 Chinese J of Int'l L 329.

Totalitarianism.[30] As Balibar has subsequently suggested,[31] Arendt famously inverted the terms of traditional political philosophy in two important ways. First of all, Arendt brought to the fore—in terms reminiscent of Schmitt[32] and, more recently, Agamben[33]—the place of the excluded (and specifically the stateless) in the constitution of European politics in the early 20th century. She was to make clear that the inherited tradition of political philosophy in Europe came to be based upon, or function through, the exclusion of those who were not citizens and therefore lacked rights (those who were 'thrown back, in the midst of civilization, on their natural givenness'[34]), and in exposing the tragedy, she also exposed the fragility of the political order—particularly in terms of its capacity to resist the totalitarian urge.[35]

In the second place, Arendt brought to the fore the relationship between human rights and political rights: whereas originally the former were thought to be the basis for the latter (the identification of universal rights preceding their articulation in particular constitutional documents), in Arendt's view this relationship was subsequently reversed through the conflation of human rights with popular sovereignty: the enjoyment of civil rights, of membership in a community, thereafter came to be the basis for human rights (the condition under which rights might be enjoyed).[36] The point, however, was not, as one might be inclined to suppose, that this was a case of 'faulty transposition' or a failure in the political project of emancipation, but rather a failure that cut to the heart of the humanitarian ideal. As Arendt put it,

> the conception of human rights... based upon the assumed existence of a human being as such, broke down at the very moment when those who professed to believe in it were for the first time confronted with people who had indeed lost all other qualities and specific relationships—except that they were still human.[37]

Arendt thus understood the value of being 'human' to which the idea of 'human rights' refers in a quite specific way. For her, being 'human' was not something

---

[30] H Arendt, *The Origins of Totalitarianism* (Harcourt, 1968) pp 267–302.

[31] E Balibar, *We, The People of Europe? Reflections on Transnational Citizenship* (Princeton University Press, 2004) pp 117–118.

[32] C Schmitt, *Political Theology* (trans G Schwab; MIT Press, 1985). Schmitt's insight was to bring the concept of the 'exception' to the centre of political philosophy. He thus defines the sovereign as 'he who decides on the exception' (pp 5–7).

[33] G Agamben, *Homo Sacer: Sovereign Power and Bare Life* (Stanford University Press, 1995); *id. State of Exception* (trans K Attell, University of Chicago Press, 2004).

[34] Arendt, (n 30 above) p 302.

[35] Arendt was fiercely critical, in that respect, of the 'liberal identification of totalitarianism with authoritarianism' (*Between Past and Future* (Faber and Faber, 1961) p 97) and was keen to demonstrate the conditions under which democracy may move in precisely the same direction.

[36] She remarks '[t]he people's sovereignty... was not proclaimed by the grace of God but in the name of Man, so that it seemed only natural that the 'inalienable' rights of man would find their guarantee and become an inalienable part of the right of the people to self-government.... The whole question of human rights, therefore, was quickly and inextricably blended with the question of national emancipation; only the emancipated sovereignty of the people, of one's own people, seemed to be able to insure them.' Arendt (n 29 above) p 291.   [37] Ibid, p 299.

that connoted, as Hegel might have put it, the notion of seeking and enjoying recognition within society. Rather, it was the opposite; a quality that lacked specificity or particularity, a quality of being that was neither spatially nor temporally determinate, a quality that ensued from being excluded (whether internally or externally) from community. What the quality of being 'human' lacked, above all else, was the 'right to have rights', and in that respect, the stateless were able to conceive of themselves as little more than savages awaiting civilization.

The central feature of Arendt's critique in this respect—particularly as it has been conceived in the work of Agamben, Balibar, and others—is the instrinsic relationship between the idea of human rights on the one hand, and the categories of the nation-state on the other (citizenship/sovereignty). Agamben insists, for example, that:

> it is time to stop regarding declarations of rights as proclamations of eternal, metajuridical values binding the legislator (in fact, without much success) to respect eternal ethical principles, and to begin to consider them according to their real historical function in the modern nation-state.[38]

For him, declarations of rights were the means by which 'natural life' was inscribed in the 'juridico-political order of the nation-state' and became the 'earthly foundation of the state's legitimacy and sovereignty'.[39] At the same time as sovereignty came to be based upon the assumed relationship between man and the citizen, birth and nationality, the figure of the refugee or the stateless immediately placed that 'originary' fiction in crisis.[40] For Agamben, the stateless were not merely as those who were *incidentally* excluded from the politics of the nation state, but were rather the *central referent* for Western 'biopolitics'.[41] They represented, in his terms, the symbolic figure of the sacred person (*homo sacer*) whose perilous existence on the one hand recalled the juridical foundation of political society (to render secure the life of the individual within society), but whose insecurity was also, and paradoxically, produced through that legal-political order. *Homo sacer*, understood as the person who may be 'killed yet not sacrificed' (whose body is regarded as sacred, yet whose exclusion from the political order is such as to allow them to be killed without punishment) thus represented the personification of a constitutive paradox within Western biopolitics.

For present purposes, I am less concerned with exploring the complexities of this account of the underpinnings of sovereignty in the nation-state or the terms of the contemporary Western biopolitical order, than with developing a more simple idea, but one which is yet implicit in the work of Agamben and Arendt: that the humanitarian ideals that underpin the contemporary commitment to ESC rights are put to the test precisely at those critical moments in which the

---

[38] Agamben, *Homo Sacer* (n 32 above) p 127.   [39] Ibid.   [40] Ibid, p 131.
[41] Agamben draws upon Foucault for his account of biopolitics. See M Foucault, *History of Sexuality Volume 1: An Introduction* (Random House, 1978).

individuals or communities who stand to be empowered, are themselves excluded from the discourse. I adopt from Arendt, therefore, the idea that it is the socially peripheral—the marginalized, dispossessed, or subaltern—who stand at the centre of any concern for ESC rights as part of a discourse of human rights. I adopt from Agamben the idea that the exclusion of the socially peripheral from the enjoyment of rights may not only remain the cause for any continued commitment to ESC rights (in the sense that is their rights which are to be fulfilled), but may also be a product of the processes through which those rights have come to be legally articulated in the first place.

IV. Including the excluded

In order to understand the central place of this process of inclusion/exclusion within the framework of the discourse of ESC rights, it is necessary to step back once again into the realm of extra-territoriality. In its most basic form, one might be inclined to take the view that the relationship between an individual and the state assuming authority over that individual is fully expressive of the content of the rights in question. Just as, it might be argued, a state's territorial sovereignty is exclusive, so also, it must have exclusive responsibility for the fulfilment of the rights of those that come within its jurisdiction or under its control. In some ways this makes obvious sense—who else is going to take responsibility for education, housing, or health care? Who else may assume obligations here? If there is a right to housing, then it surely only makes sense to say that it is opposable as against those who have the capacity to provide it. To argue otherwise, is to move beyond the sanctified boundaries of moral agency, and maintain a view which is simply utopian. Just as an 'ought' seems to imply a 'can', obligations must surely be built upon a contingent capacity.

Of course, pushed to its extreme, asserting an inextricable nexus between capacity and obligation may be such as to render the idea of ESC rights largely incoherent—we are all too aware of the resource limitations that affect the realization of ESC rights in many parts of the globe, and that prefiguring obligations by reference to any momentary capacity to fulfil them would not only undermine the conditions for their universality but would render that distribution immutable. One finds in article 2(1) of the Covenant, therefore, the idea not merely that the realization of ESC rights is dependent upon available resources, but also the idea that they should be realized in a progressive manner.[42] The idea of progress thus brings into view, on the horizon, the possibility of universality

---

[42] The text of art 2(1) reads as follows: 'Each State party to the present Covenant undertakes to take steps, individually and through international assistance and co-operation, especially economic and technical, to the maximum of its available resources, with a view to achieving progressively the full realization of the rights recognized in the present Covenant by all appropriate means, including particularly the adoption of legislative measures.'

(encapsulated in the idea of the 'full realization' of ESC rights), through the unspoken medium of a change in the global distribution of resources. It allows, thereby, a certain mediation between the idea that the contemporary global context precludes universal realization of ESC rights, and the idea that there exists an immanent potential for their realization. Progressivism, to put it in a different way, seems to be a means of negotiating in, a temporal sense, between an apologia for destitution and a utopian fable of 'rights enjoyment'.

This temporal separation between present and future, however, does not overcome the difficulties associated with the relationship between the imaginative ideal of rights-fulfilment on the one hand and the particular constraints that face states committed to their realization on the other. The problem, here, arises most clearly when one seeks to articulate the terms of the relationship between rights and obligations within the Covenant. In typical Hohfeldian terms,[43] one might be inclined to insist that the content of all rights (including ESC rights) must be capable of being described in terms of correlative obligations: where there is no right there is no obligation and *vice versa*. When describing that relationship by reference to the terms of article 2(1) of the Covenant, however, certain difficulties arise: if the obligation is to realize the rights in a progressive manner, does that render the rights themselves 'progressive'? Might a state be capable of violating a procedural obligation (for example, in failing to establish a plan of action to implement the right to free primary education as required by article 14) but yet not violate a substantive right?

The aporia, here, is particularly evident when one comes to speak about ESC rights in terms of their violation.[44] To illustrate the point, reference might be made to an introductory paragraph in the ESCR Committee's General Comment on the Right to Water in which it made the following remark:

The Committee has been confronted continually with the widespread denial of the right to water in developing as well as developed countries. Over one billion persons lack access to a basic water of supply, while several billion do not have access to adequate sanitation, which is the primary cause of water contamination and diseases linked to water.[45]

As a justification for concerning itself with the question of access to water when considering state reports, the Committee might be forgiven for believing that the facts spoke for themselves. But could the Committee rightly claim that lack of access to a basic water supply constituted a 'widespread denial of the right to water'? Surely, prior to any such claim, the Committee would have had to undertake an evaluation as to whether the states concerned had sufficient resources to make such water available, and whether their efforts at distribution were adequate

---

[43] W Hohfeld, *Fundamental Legal Conceptions as Applied in Judicial Reasoning* (Yale University Press, 1923) ch 1.

[44] For the advancement of a 'violations approach' to ESC rights see A Chapman, 'A "Violations Approach" for Monitoring the International Covenant on Economic, Social and Cultural Rights' (1996) 18 Human Rights Q 23.   [45] *General Comment 15* (n. 17 above) para 1.

in the circumstances. Even if, as the Committee has maintained, states have an obligation to fulfil the 'core content' of rights (for which one supposes the Committee means a minimum essential level of enjoyment[46]) it is clear that the presence or absence of resources would still be relevant to the evaluation, and hence no categorical statement in that respect can be made merely on the facts themselves.[47] There is, thus, an apparent disjunction between the proclamation of rights, on the one hand, and the contingent conditions for their fulfilment on the other—a disjunction that appears may only effectively be resolved in this context either by reformulating the rights (in the sense such as the 'right to the progressive realization of the right to housing, education', etc), or by conceptually separating what it means to have a right on the one hand, and what it means to have an obligation on the other.

The most obvious way of understanding this problem, however, is to think of the Committee as speaking about the rights in question in two different ways. On the one hand is the legal conception of right—one whose fulfilment or denial is determined by an exhaustive evaluation of the circumstances and conditions in which it occurs (in accordance with the terms of article 2(1) of the Covenant). On the other hand is the idea of 'right' in a metajuridical, ethical, or 'pre-legal' sense whose referent is the metaphorical figure or image of the starving child, the homeless family or the dispossessed community. In this latter sense, one might be encouraged to speak of a person's rights being denied or violated by virtue of the very fact of deprivation, and quite apart from any tangible legal chain of responsibility being identified.

The key question, here, however, is what function is served by this metajuridical notion of right? What is its relationship to the legal conception of rights? Why should the ESCR Committee invoke that idea when seeking to articulate obligations incumbent upon states in the context of the right to water? The answer appears plain enough. Just as the idea of progress that lies at the heart of the articulation of obligations under the Covenant reaches out towards a (forever postponed) moment of 'rights fulfilment', so also it moves away from a dystopian understanding of contemporary society—one beset by disease, illness, malnutrition, and homelessness. That dystopia, however, is not (or at least not merely) a representation of some fictional past, cast back in order to give sense to the idea of progress or as an apology for institution building, but far more importantly as an idea that forms a central feature of arguments that justify the enunciation of rights in the first place. Just as it is evident that a particular social context shaped the articulation of rights in the Universal Declaration of Human Rights (UDHR) and the two Covenants (excluding, for example, reference to minority rights or refugees, to the elderly or those with disabilities) so also an enduring and dynamic sense of injustice (the injustice of deprivation or loss of freedom), provides the continuing justification for resort to the language of human rights.

---

[46] Ibid, paras 37–8.
[47] For the initial elaboration of the 'core content' see *General Comment 3* (1990) para 10.

At this point it becomes apparent that, as with the stateless in Arendt's critique, the dispossessed become both central and marginal to the account of ESC rights. They are clearly central in the sense that they provide the continuing imperative for the articulation of rights claims. Without the images of suffering or dispossession with which we are constantly confronted no universal project of ESC rights would plausibly be maintained.[48] At the same time, however, the dispossessed are also evidently marginal in the sense that they are constantly one step away from being able to represent themselves as rights-holders. At every moment, they are faced with the impossibility of being 'claimants' by virtue of the fact of destitution—having to precede any such claim by reference to some original enactment of ownership or by some evaluation as to the adequacy of social resources and the inadequacy of their distribution. The destitute are thus the original category of the excluded—the category whose exclusion provides the constitutional impulse for the development of institutional initiatives for the protection and promotion of ESC rights, and the category whose continued exclusion is lamentably its point of immanent critique. The violence of their destitution may thus be thought to be a privileged one, but also one that denies the sense of any such privilege.

In some degree this bears upon a fundamental ambivalence within the category of 'victimhood'. As Mutua has suggested, the presentation of human rights victims as a 'horde of nameless, despairing, and dispirited masses'[49] is such as to view them as incapable of capacity for action or initiative and to present them as objects of possible intervention. It obscures, thereby, the extent to which their capacity for action 'may be a source of residual and ongoing pleasure: the pleasure of solidarity, the pleasure of expression, the pleasure of re-imagining the world'.[50] The point being made here, however, is that these two different senses, or experiences, of victimhood (the passive sense of the victim as an 'object of intervention', the active sense of the victim as 'agent') are separated in the discourse of ESC rights. In this context the dispossessed may be identified by others (states, non-governmental organizations, etc) as the reason for action, and their plight the inducement for adoption of protective or ameliorative measures, but they are prevented in the terms of the existing discourse from presenting *themselves* as victims in the sense of having any entitlement to specific claims or capacity for legal agency.

V. Expanding horizons

Thus far, I have sought to suggest that the exclusion of the dispossessed from the discourse of ESC rights follows from the immediate resource constraints that

---

[48] See U Baxi, 'Voices of Suffering and the Future of Human Rights' (1998) 9 Transnational L and Contemporary Problems 125 at 159–162.

[49] Cf M Mutua, *Human Rights: A Political and Cultural Critique* (University of Philadelphia Press, 2002) pp 28–29.

[50] S Marks and A Clapham, *International Human Rights Lexicon* (OUP, 2005) p 404.

impinge upon the capacity of many governments to deal effectively with that dispossession, and have suggested that the discourse itself is imperilled as a consequence. I have only hinted, however, at the relationship between this narrative of dispossession and the question of territoriality, and have largely left untouched the significance of territorial borders. In the work of both Agamben and Balibar, the 'excluded' are seen to inhabit particular space—for Agamben it is the 'camp',[51] for Balibar the urban ghetto, the detention zone, or more broadly, and figuratively, the 'South'. Balibar, in particular, is vexed by the apparent multi-locational nature of 'the border' which, when taken to describe the boundaries of the *demos* (the 'nondemocratic condition of democracy'),[52] may come to be located on some occasions in the 'middle of political space'[53] and, on others, outside the limits of a state's formal jurisdiction.

For present purposes, I am not so much concerned for the way in which borders are representative of the point at which the nature of coercive authority subtly changes character, (the point at which, as Balibar puts it 'the status of citizens returns to the condition of a "subject"'[54]) but their role in excluding the dispossessed from being able to represent themselves, as such, in the language of ESC rights. The conditions described above that underpin the inability of the dispossessed to speak of the violation of their rights are, in the main, a function of a territorial framework that ultimately encourages an association of poverty with the inadequacy, and/or mismanagement, of national resources. When located within an exclusively national context, poverty, and dispossession tend to be seen as local problems—problems associated with 'lack of development', economic mismanagement, corruption, or lack of knowledge or expertise—for which aid, development assistance, or other forms of international intervention may act as suitable palliatives. In some respects, and as is emphasized in the work of Sen amongst others, questions of governance and the mechanics of local distribution will frequently be critical to an individual's enjoyment of access to food, housing, water, and other rights and freedoms.[55] At the same time, however, the presentation of the problem in this way not only obscures the broader international context in which those problems are socially produced, but would also mean that the dispossessed are constantly faced by the economic incapacity of their national governments, and hence only ever able to represent themselves as potential claimants or aspirational rights-holders.

If the key condition that prevents the dispossessed from representing themselves as 'rights claimants' is the problem of resource scarcity, then one way of avoiding that exclusionary framework is by broadening the horizons of the engagement.

---

[51] Agamben describes the 'camp' as 'a piece of land placed outside the normal juridical order' but which is not simply 'an external space' but which is 'included' in the juridical order 'through its own exclusion' (n 32 above) pp 169–70.   [52] Balibar (n 30 above) p 109.
[53] Ibid.   [54] Ibid.
[55] Sen emphasizes, here, the significance of 'capabilities' in the conception of development. See eg, A Sen, *Development as Freedom* (OUP, 1999) pp 3–5.

It has long been fairly clear, that problems of dispossession (poverty, malnutrition, etc) are not exclusively local—that they also implicate questions of trade, debt, or investment that may be configured within or through the international environment. This much at least, was the insight of those proponents of the New International Economic Order and the Right to Development[56] even if those projects are no longer the focus of sustained attention. The importance of this emphasis upon the international environment, however, is found in the way it shifts the emphasis away from the problem of scarcity, and places greater importance instead upon the question of distribution. The issue becomes, in other words, less a matter as to whether a particular government may have at its command, sufficient resources to 'lift' the dispossessed out of poverty, and rather more a matter of understanding the various, and multiple, ways in which both the local and international environment may condition an individual's access to the necessary resources for their survival, well-being and active social agency.[57] If that is the starting point, one may then think about resources on a global scale being available but unevenly distributed, and thereby allow the dispossessed to speak of themselves literally in those terms—as having been *dis-possessed* of their rights rather than awaiting their conferral.

An insistence upon the importance of the global context for an understanding of social rights is not, ultimately, a polemical rejection of local responsibility for problems of distribution or lack of access to resources or the means to ensure basic subsistence, nor an attempt to insist that the only response may be to hold accountable international actors (international financial institutions, multinational corporations, foreign governments) for the crises that affect millions around the globe. Rather, and more simply, it is to observe that the conditions for legitimizing the discourse of ESC rights necessarily involve placing the issues of poverty, disease, or malnutrition within a global, rather than a local framework, so as to make possible the idea that the dispossessed are legitimate agents, capable of articulating meaningful claims on their own behalf. Without this, it is hard to avoid Arendt's conclusion that being 'human' for purposes of human rights, is to mean little other than being the object of an exclusionary politics.

VI. Conclusion

In the course of this chapter I have suggested that, insofar as the debates concerning the question of extra-territorial obligations seem to suppose that one can readily demarcate between different realms of rights and responsibilities in the field of ESC

---

[56] For an insightful discussion see A Orford, 'Globalization and the Right to Development', in P Alston (ed), *Peoples' Rights* (OUP, 2001) 127.

[57] For an investigation into the disconnect between local poverty and global wealth see T Pogge, *World Poverty and Human Rights* (Polity Press, 2002).

rights (the internal/external, the national/international), these configurations ultimately put in jeopardy any continued commitment to the discourse. One response, of course, may be to suggest that the discourse itself is inherently problematic—that it attempts to depoliticize inherently 'political' struggles over the form or structure of public projects, over distribution of resources within a given society, or over the legitimacy of different kinds of social arrangements. Framing such struggles in terms of individual rights, it might be argued, does little to advance the cause of those who are dispossessed (insofar as it fails to understand the issues as being social rather than strictly individual) and may ultimately be the cause of further dispossession (through the shifting of social resources away from other vulnerable groups or individuals). At the same time, it is important to recognize that arguments advancing the idea that ESC rights effectively 'depoliticize' issues of social contestation don't go very far if they merely entail a call for such issues to be dealt with through existing political procedures rather than through judicial intervention, or if they are seen to emphasize the obvious fact that the values in question are themselves opaque. Both of these might, in turn, be regarded as 'depoliticizing' moves if their sense is such as to merely reaffirm the ongoing marginalization of those who do not have access to social resources and whose voices are not heard within the current political order; and if one is looking towards the elaboration of a new brand of politics, then talking about ESC rights as a way of allowing the dispossessed to express their sense of injustice, or otherwise become active social and political agents, may not be quite so out of place.

Another objection, of course, is that even if one may recognize the significance of the international context for purposes of maintaining a commitment to ESC rights, this is still confronted by the idea of sovereignty. How might a state retain a simultaneous commitment to the idea that it has a domestic political constituency to which it is responsible, with the notion that it also has responsibility for the lives and livelihood for those living beyond its borders? As both Agamben and Balibar intimate, it is the inextricable relationship between the idea of sovereignty on the one hand and human rights on the other, that makes the elaboration of a non-exclusionary, 'humane', political project peculiarly difficult. Jameson echoes this observation in a somewhat different way in his discussion of the idea of a 'utopia of full employment':

As the economic apologists for the system today have tirelessly instructed us, capitalism cannot flourish under full employment; it requires a reserve army of the unemployed in order to function and to avoid inflation. That first monkey-wrench of full employment would then be compounded by the universality of the requirement, inasmuch as capitalism also requires a frontier, and perpetual expansion, in order to sustain its inner dynamic. But at this point the utopianism of the demand becomes circular, for it is also clear, not only that the establishment of full employment would transform the system, but also that the system would have to be already transformed, in advance, in order for full employment to be established.[58]

[58] (Note 1 above) p 38.

Just as, for Jameson, the social potential of the idea of full employment is dependent upon a prior transformation of the system that it seeks to transform, so also the idea of social rights might seem dependent upon the prior reconfiguration of the idea of sovereign competence in relation to resource distribution that it seeks to bring into effect. Jameson, however, is nonetheless clear as to the significance of the utopia he propounds, and his observations are equally pertinent for the project of ESC rights in general, as they are for the specific idea of full employment:

To foreground full employment [ESC rights] in this way, as the fundamental utopian requirement, allows us, indeed, to return to concrete circumstances and situations, to read their dark spots and pathological dimensions as so many symptoms and effects of this particular root of all evil identified as unemployment [dispossession] .... At this point, then, utopian circularity becomes both a political vision and programme, and a critical and diagnostic instrument.'[59]

Perhaps we ought to think, then, about the 'critical' and 'diagnostic' function of ESC rights advocacy and, in the process, broaden what might otherwise be a dangerously parochial engagement with the pathology of dispossession.

[59] Ibid. (Words in parentheses added.)

5

The Applicability of Economic and Social Rights to the UN Security Council

*Nigel D. White**

I. Introduction

The United Nations (UN) is obliged to promote human rights but is it bound by human rights law, including economic and social rights? This chapter will concentrate on the activities of the UN Security Council, which, because of its unique mandatory powers under Chapter VII of the Charter, can take decisions that would otherwise constitute intervention in the sovereignty of the state or states concerned.[1] This creates the potential for conflict with human rights norms, which regulate the relationship between sovereign and subject within states. When the Security Council imposes economic sanctions against a state, or sanctions actions against individuals suspected of terrorism, or sets up a post-conflict administration, is it bound to respect human rights law? If so what is the source of the obligation and what mechanisms exist, if any, of accountability to ensure that the Security Council does not violate human rights? Focusing on economic and social rights, this chapter will consider the inadequacies of the human rights regime applicable to the Security Council and will consider whether the current reform debate offers any prospect of improvement.

II. The UN and the promotion of human rights

The human rights provisions in the UN Charter are relatively few and far between. The preamble reaffirms 'faith in human rights, in the dignity and worth

* Thanks to Dr Robert Cryer for his comments on an earlier draft. Many thanks as well to David Harris for his advice and guidance over the years, first as my PhD supervisor and then as a colleague.
[1] Art 2(7) of the UN Charter provides that 'Nothing contained in the present Charter shall authorize the United Nations to intervene in matters which are essentially within the domestic jurisdiction of any state or shall require the Members to submit such matters to settlement under the present Charter; *but this principle shall not prejudice the application of enforcement measures under Chapter VII*'. (Emphasis added.)

of the human person, in the equal rights of men and women', and further aspires to 'social progress and better standards of life in larger freedom', and 'the economic and social advancement of all peoples'. In the purposes of the UN in article 1, the 'self-determination of peoples' is mentioned in the context of developing friendly relations among nations. Article 1(3) states another purpose to be the achievement of international co-operation in solving problems 'of an economic, social or humanitarian character, and in encouraging respect for the principle of human rights and for fundamental freedoms for all without distinction as to race, sex, language, or religion'. That these are by and large aspirational treaty provisions is confirmed by article 55 which states that the UN shall 'promote', *inter alia*, solutions to international economic, social, and health-related problems; international cultural and educational co-operation and 'universal respect for, and observance of, human rights and fundamental freedoms for all without distinction as to race, sex, language or religion'.[2]

Familiarity with these provisions sometimes leads to their import being overlooked. First of all, human rights are listed alongside the provisions of the preamble and purposes that cover what is often seen as the 'primary' purpose of the United Nations,[3] namely the maintenance of international peace and security.[4] Secondly, the provisions mentioned implicitly cover all three generations of human rights, though, self-determination and non-discrimination apart, no specific rights are mentioned. Thus, although it was not until the Universal Declaration of Human Rights (UDHR)[5] was adopted by the UN General Assembly in 1948 that the UN developed a more specific set of human rights, it could be argued that such rights were embedded in the UN Charter in 1945.

However, those provisions are, as stated, largely aspirational. The UN and member states were, at most, being obliged to *promote* human rights. In addition, by the terms of the UN Charter cited above, economic and social issues were seemingly not issues of rights but of social progress which added to their aspirational quality, a fact not fully rectified by their inclusion in the UDHR in 1948, at least at that time, since that Declaration was 'soft' law even before we knew what that term meant.[6]

Finally, although human rights and human rights issues did seem to receive (almost) equal billing with peace and security concerns in the preamble and article 1,[7] their equal status is eroded by the remainder of the Charter. While Chapter IX of the Charter on International and Economic Co-operation is the

---

[2] See further art 56, which states that 'all Members pledge themselves to take joint and separate action in co-operation with the Organization for the achievement of the purposes set forth in article 55'.   [3] *Certain Expenses* case [1962] ICJ Rep 167.
    [4] See eg, art 1(1).   [5] GA res 217(A), 1948.
    [6] See C Chinkin, 'The Challenge of Soft Law: Development and Change in International Law', (1989) 38 ICLQ 850; H Hillgenberg, 'A Fresh Look at Soft Law' (1999) 10 Eur J of Int'l L 499; KW Abbott and D Snidal, 'Hard and Soft Law in International Governance' (2000) 54 *International Organization* 421.   [7] Peace and security issues are listed first.

foundation of a relatively weak system for the supervision of the protection and promotion of human rights by member states, the Economic and Social Council (ECOSOC) and a number of the Specialized Agencies, Chapter VII of the UN Charter, in combination with the 'hard' treaty obligations in articles 2 and 25, underpin the value of peace and security with significant institutional powers.

Admittedly many parts of the UN system have competence over aspects of human rights. In addition to the greatly criticized Human Rights Commission established by ECOSOC in 1946,[8] there are a number of Specialized Agencies with some human rights competence: for instance the United Nations Educational, Scientific and Cultural Organization (UNESCO) in relation to cultural and education rights, the International Labour Organization (ILO) in relation to labour rights, the World Health Organization (WHO) in relation to the right to health, the Food and Agriculture Organization (FAO) in relation to the right to food, and subsidiary organs such as the United Nations Industrial Development Organization (UNIDO) and the United Nations Development Programme (UNDP) with concern over the right to development. The purpose of these organizations, however, is not directly to promote and protect human rights but to facilitate co-operation and development in education, health, labour, etc. Of more relevance to human rights protection are the bodies of experts established by the human rights treaties—for instance the Human Rights Committee (HRC) and the Committee on Economic, Social and Cultural Rights (ESCR Committee) established by the two International Covenants[9] respectively, which are treated as part of the UN human rights system.[10]

The Security Council's explicit powers to take non-military and military measures to maintain or restore peace and security, when combined with the obligation on member states to refrain from the threat or use of force except in self-defence,[11] were designed not only to give the Council power to act on the international stage against the external sovereignty of a member (and arguably non-member)[12] state, but also to take enforcement action that affected states' internal sovereignty.[13] This was in part fuelled by the realization that the Second World War was not simply a result of action to repel aggressor states, but also to defeat a state guilty of committing the most horrendous crimes against individuals and groups. Hence the Security Council was empowered not only to police the interstate obligation to refrain from uses of force which might be acts of aggression or breaches of the peace, but also to consider situations that might constitute threats

---

[8] The World Summit of the UN in 2005 decided to replace the Human Rights Commission with the Human Rights Council—see the World Summit Outcome Document in GA res 60/1, 24 Oct 2005, paras 157–160.

[9] The International Covenant on Civil and Political Rights (ICCPR) 1966, and the International Covenant on Economic, Social and Cultural Rights (ICESCR) 1966.

[10] See ND White, *The United Nations System: Toward International Justice* (Lynne Rienner, Boulder Col, 2002) pp 7–8.   [11] Art 2(4) and 51 of the UN Charter.

[12] Art 2(6) of the UN Charter.   [13] Art 2(7) of the Charter.

to the peace as well.[14] Threat to the peace is a term that can be deployed to cover situations of extreme violence against individuals within states.[15] Thus, although the Charter gives 'primary responsibility' to the Security Council for the mainten-ance of international peace and security,[16] and appears to give the General Assembly primary concern for the promotion of human rights,[17] the division is not complete with significant overlapping competence between the two organs in both human rights and security matters.[18]

III. The Security Council unbound?

While the Security Council, along with the other component parts of the UN, is bound to promote, and in extreme cases protect, human rights, there is little in the Charter that suggests it is itself bound by human rights.[19] The same is true as regards member states at least in relation to the Charter, though this was remedied to some extent by the UDHR and then more so in terms of hard law by the two International Covenants of 1966 and subsequent human rights treaties.

To tackle the issue of whether or not the UN is bound by human rights law, it is necessary to start at the general level of whether or not international organizations are subject to international law. There is a conceptual problem here given that traditionally it is states that are viewed as the creators as well as the subjects of international law. Treaties are made by states and are normally ratified solely by states, while custom is a product of state practice combined with the *opinio juris* of states. The applicability to organizations of these two main forms of international law is not immediately apparent. Organizations do not (except in relatively rare and specific cases) become parties to treaties, and they do not normally purport to consent to customary international law.[20] However, to deny that general prin-ciples of international law are applicable to organizations is in a sense to deny that

---

14 Art 39 of the UN Charter.

15 B Simma (ed), *The Charter of the United Nations* (2nd edn, OUP, 2002) pp 723–724.

16 Art 24(1) UN Charter.

17 Art 13(1)(b) UN Charter states that the 'General Assembly shall initiate studies and make rec-ommendations for the purpose of . . . promoting international co-operation in the economic, social, cultural, educational and health fields, and assisting in the realization of human rights and funda-mental freedoms for all without distinction as to race, language, or religion.'

18 On the General Assembly's competence in human rights and security matters see ND White, *Keeping the Peace: The United Nations and the Maintenance of International Peace and Security* (2nd edn, Manchester University Press, 1997) pp 169–182.

19 The provisions of the Charter strongly indicate that it is the General Assembly, ECOSOC, and the Agencies that are obliged in the main to promote human rights. In relation to the Security Council art 24(2) states that 'in discharging these duties the Security Council shall act in accordance with the Purposes and Principles of the United Nations'. However, as has been stated, the purposes and principles oblige the UN (and therefore the Security Council) to promote human rights not to abide by human rights itself.

20 The UN Secretary General's statement as to the applicability of International Humanitarian Law to UN Forces is a rare instance—UN doc ST/SBG 1999/13, 6 Aug 1999.

they can be international legal persons, with rights and *duties* on the international plane.[21] Many intergovernmental organizations have legal personality on the international plane separate from the international legal personalities of their member states. In international institutional law it is not necessary for the organization to claim international legal personality. Indeed, the vast majority of organizations do not make an express claim, personality is derived from the way the body is constituted and empowered.[22]

There appears to be no doubt that organizations possessing international legal personality and being active in international relations are subject, at the very least, to *jus cogens* or peremptory norms of international law, such as those prohibiting aggression and genocide, and other basic principles, for example, of human rights, such as non-discrimination, or those governing the environment, such as the no harm and precautionary principles.[23] Furthermore, to isolate organizations from treaties or custom disregards the fact that organizations do contribute to the making of both of these sources of international law.[24] In addition, it is not acceptable for states to belong to organizations that are not bound by the basic principles of international law that bind states.[25] This suggests that states cannot establish international bodies that can carry out acts prohibited for its members, though in the case of the UN it was created before or at least at the same time as the basic principles. Finally, in the case of the UN and organizations in the UN system, there is a strong case for arguing that the fundamental values enshrined and enhanced by the UN, including the UDHR, are binding not only on the member states but also on the organization itself. This is the application of a theory of constitutionalism to the UN system.[26]

Such a theory dictates that the Charter is not just an inter-state compact but a 'kind of public law transcending in kind and not merely in degree the ordinary agreements between states'.[27] 'A constitution typically sets out the fundamental rules of a political order and establishes the basic political institutions'.[28] Furthermore, a constitution both constitutes a political order and regulates that order in terms of the competences of different institutions and in terms of the relations between the subjects of that order.[29] This signifies that the laws produced

[21] CF Amerasinghe, *Principles of the Institutional Law of International Organizations* (Cambridge University Press, 1996) p 78.

[22] *Reparation for Injuries Suffered in the Service of the United Nations* [1949] ICJ Rep 174 at 178–9.

[23] See also P Sands and P Klein, *Bowett's Law of International Institutions* (5th edn, Sweet & Maxwell, 2001) pp 458–459.

[24] See generally JE Alvarez, *International Organizations as Law Makers* (OUP, 2005).

[25] *Matthews v United Kingdom*, 28 (1999) EHRR 361 at para 22 .

[26] See ND White, *The United Nations System*, pp 14–17.

[27] AD McNair, 'The Functions and Different Legal Character of Treaties' (1930) XI *British Yearbook of International Law* 100 at 112. But see G Arangio-Ruiz, 'The Federal Analogy and UN Charter Interpretation: A Crucial Issue' (1997) 8 Eur J of Intl L 1 at 9.

[28] H Abromeit and T Hitzel-Cassagnes, 'Constitutional Change and Contractual Revision: Principles and Procedures' (1999) 5 Eur L J 23 at 34.

[29] ND White, *The Law of International Organisations* (2nd edn, Manchester University Press, 2005) p 15.

by the UN's legal order potentially have applicability to both institutions and states, depending upon the nature of the activities undertaken.

Of course in practice, an organization may not be sufficiently active in international affairs to encounter any rules of international law. But as organizations increasingly move from debate and standard setting, towards application and operation, they will increasingly be subject to international law. Can it be argued that the World Bank, when funding a large dam project in a developing state, is not bound by fundamental axioms of environmental and human rights law? Can it be argued that the North Atlantic Treaty Organization (NATO), when using its military might, is not subject to the rules governing the use of force in international relations as well as the principles of international humanitarian law? Of course, there are issues of when responsibility lies with the organization and when liability is with the member states, an issue returned to later. In general terms, an organization that has international legal personality bears responsibility for acts carried out in its name and under its authority.

In 2003 the International Law Commission (ILC) commenced discussions on the responsibility of International Organizations. Draft article 3 recognizes that 'every internationally wrongful act of an international organization entails the international responsibility of the international organization'. Further, it declared that 'there is an internationally wrongful act of an international organization when conduct consisting of an action or omission: (a) is attributed to the international organization under international law; and (b) constitutes a breach of an international obligation of that international organization'.[30] By mirroring the provision in its 2001 Articles on State Responsibility,[31] the ILC indicates that by similarly viewing institutions as being responsible for breaches of international law, it must be the case that they are bound by international law.

The Final Report of the International Law Association (ILA) Committee on Accountability of Organizations in 2004 makes it clear that acts of organizations 'may be in accordance with the letter or spirit of the constituent instrument... but this does not prevent them from being wrongful under international law because of their non-conformity with other applicable rules of international law'.[32] The ILA Committee's examples include organizations incurring 'internationally legal responsibility if their use of force and their imposition of economic coercive measures are not in conformity with relevant rules of international law, and in particular the humanitarian law principles of proportionality and of necessity'. Further, organizations 'may incur international legal responsibility if the exercise of discretionary powers entails a sufficiently serious breach of a superior rule of law such as the right to life, food and medicine of the individual or guarantees for due process of law'.[33]

---

[30] ILC, *Report of the 55th Session 2003*, UN doc A/58/10, 31 (hereinafter ILC Report 2003).

[31] Arts 1 and 2 of the Articles on Responsibility of States for Internationally Wrongful Acts 2001.

[32] ILA Committee on the Accountability of International Organizations, *Final Report* (Berlin, 2004) 34.   [33] Ibid.

IV. Human rights and the Security Council

According to the International Court of Justice (ICJ):

International organizations are subjects of international law and, as such, are bound by any obligations incumbent upon them under general rules of international law, under their constitutions or under international agreements to which they are parties.[34]

The primary rules of international law applicable to an international organization depend, in the words of the ILA Committee on the Accountability of International Organizations, on its 'institutional acts, operational activities, as well as the omissions' of the organization.[35] Human rights obligations are normally applicable to institutional activities that have an effect on the lives of individuals within states. According to the ILA the:

Human rights obligations, which are increasingly becoming an expression of the common constitutional traditions of States, can become binding upon [organizations] in different ways: through the terms of their constituent instruments; as customary international law; or as general principles of law or if an [organization] is authorised to become a party to a human rights treaty.[36]

Thus, when the Security Council is involved in the temporary administration of territory (as in Kosovo), or when imposing non-military measures against states, it is bound by basic provisions of human rights law, and is responsible for any breach caused by its actions.[37] The ILA Committee recommends that wherever possible non-forcible measures should be 'directed against particular individuals and entities rather than against the population as a whole'. But when listing individuals and entities for the purpose of targeted sanctions the organization should establish the 'necessary mechanisms to ensure compliance with basic human rights guarantees'.[38]

In relation to peacekeeping and peace enforcement activities the Council is potentially responsible for violations of human rights law and, where appropriate, international humanitarian law when it is engaging in activities of the kind regulated by that legal regime.[39] The ILA Committee declares that 'troop-contributing

---

[34] *Interpretation of the Agreement of 25 March 1951 between the WHO and Egypt* [1980] ICJ Rep 73 at 89–90.   [35] Note 32 above.

[36] Ibid 27.

[37] This is in addition to the obligations (if any) placed on the Security Council under art 50 of the UN Charter which states that 'if preventive or enforcement measures against any state are taken by the Security Council, any other state ... which finds itself confronted with special economic problems arising from the carrying out of those measures shall have the right to consult the Security Council with regard to a solution of those problems'. Bryde and Reinisch view art 50 as granting discretionary powers to the Council in B Simma (ed), *The Charter*, 785, thus making it an unsuitable mechanism for addressing violations of economic, social, and cultural rights in states, other than the target state, affected by the sanctions.   [38] (Note 32 above) 28–29.

[39] For a wider discussion see MC Zwanenberg, *Accountability under International Humanitarian Law for United Nations and North Atlantic Treaty Organization Peace Support Operations* (EM Meijers

states remain responsible for violations of the applicable international humanitarian laws, but [organizations] bear a coordinate responsibility with troop-contributing states for ensuring compliance with the applicable principles of international humanitarian law in peacekeeping or other operations conducted under the control or authority' of the organization.[40] The same argument must apply to human rights law. Peacekeeping forces have responsibility to uphold basic human rights, including economic and social rights, although the protection of these rights will arguably only be an obligation in areas or situations under their 'effective control'.[41]

Although the ILA Committee's general principles provide the framework for apportioning responsibility between organization and member states in peacekeeping operations, the final answer as to where responsibility lies will depend on the circumstances of control in each specific case. As Hirsch states:

Each individual case must be examined as to whether the specific legal act was performed under the control of the organization or the sending state. If a member of such force performs an act under the direction of its national government, that government will be the proper addressee of any claim arising from that act; this conclusion will not be altered even in cases where the contingent to which that member belongs is generally under the operational control of the organization.[42]

There will often be issues in the activities of peacekeeping operations of whether it is the organization or the state that is responsible for activities carried out on the ground, though in the case of a refugee camp under the control of the UN for instance, that body can have no excuse for discriminating against women and girls in the provision of basic education.[43]

At the level of organizational decision-making though, human rights obligations are directly applicable to the Security Council. The fact that it is made up of states and that the permanent members may have too great an influence on particular decisions does not shift responsibility for Security Council decisions

Institute of Legal Studies, 2004); I Scobbie, 'International Responsibility', in R-J Dupuy (ed), *A Handbook on International Organizations* (2nd edn, Nijhoff, 1998) p 886.

[40] On responsibility of organizations for harm to individuals caused by peacekeepers not acting unlawfully see *ILA Final Report 2004*, 26–7.

[41] Discussed in the context of occupation in the European Convention on Human Rights in *Loizidou v Turkey* (Preliminary Objections) Series A no 310, (23 Feb 1995) ECtHR 20 (1995) EHRR 99. On the application of the International Covenants on Civil and Political and Economic, Social, and Cultural Rights in situations of military occupation see *Legal Consequences of the Construction of a Wall in the Occupied Palestinian Territory* [2004] ICJ Rep, paras 108–111.

[42] M Hirsch, *The Responsibility of International Organizations to Third Parties: Some Basic Principles*, (Brill, 1995) pp 64–5. See also K Wellens, *Remedies against International Organizations* (Cambridge University Press 2002), pp 52–3; G Gaja, 'Second Report on Responsibility of International Organizations', ILC 55th session, UN doc A/CN.4/541 (2 April 2004) paras 33–41.

[43] G Verdirame, 'UN Accountability for Human Rights Violations in Post-Conflict Situations', in ND White and D Klaasen (eds), *The UN, Human Rights and Post-Conflict Situations* (Manchester University Press, 2005) p 81 at 89–92.

from the organ to the states. Once a decision of the Council is made it is a reflection of its will, not just an amalgam of the wills of member states.[44] 'For an international entity to be regarded as existing separately from its Member States, the entity must have a decision-making organ that is able to produce a "corporate" will, as opposed to a mere "aggregate" of the wills of Member States'.[45] That the Security Council is such an organ possessing a corporate will is deduced from the fact that it can adopt mandatory decisions binding on the whole membership by a qualified majority vote.[46]

However, it might be argued that when one or more permanent members are blocking the lifting of sanctions against a state, responsibility for any human rights violation of the target population in terms of food, water, medicine, and ultimately life should be shouldered by those states.[47] Again though, in the absence of any real legal controls on the veto,[48] it can be strongly argued that the veto is part of the constitutional make-up of the Security Council, indicating that even in those cases where the veto blocks measures or the lifting of measures with negative effects on human rights it is the Security Council that bears responsibility not individual states. Of course states bear responsibility for the violations of international organizations in a residual sense that the organization is dependent on funding by member states, some of which may be used to meet claims made against it for breaches of human rights obligations.[49]

In considering the Security Council's actions under Chapter VII in human rights terms, it can be seen that its decisions can be directed at individuals such as the Lockerbie suspects,[50] or individuals suspected of belonging to certain terrorist groups. Decisions may directly affect individuals as with economic measures imposed on states or targeted at individuals. This clearly has direct relevance to economic rights. Furthermore, one must not forget that Council decisions may directly affect a group's right to self-determination, in its political and economic, as well as external and internal aspects. The Security Council should ensure that its decisions protect a peoples' right to sovereignty over its natural resources as an aspect of economic self-determination,[51] and to ensure that it only endorses elections that 'guarantee the free expression of the will of the people'.[52]

---

[44] ND White, 'The Will and Authority of the Security Council After Iraq' (2004) 17 Leiden J of Int'l L 645.

[45] RA Wessel, 'Revisiting the Legal Status of the EU', (2000) 5 *Eur Foreign Affairs Rev* 507 at 517.

[46] Arts 25 and 27 of the UN Charter.

[47] For discussion of the reverse veto in the context of the sanctions imposed on Iraq after 1990 see DD Caron, 'The Legitimacy of the Collective Authority of the Security Council' (1993) 87 AJIL 522 at 577–88.   [48] White, 'The Will and Authority', 666–71.

[49] On the divisibility of responsibility between organizations and their member states see HG Schermers and NM Blokker, *International Institutional Law* (4th edn, Nijhoff, 2003) pp 1007–1008.

[50] SC res 731, 21 Jan 1992.

[51] See eg, A Orakhelashvili, 'The Post-War Settlement in Iraq: The UN Security Council Resolution 1483 (2003) and General International Law', (2003) 8 J of Conflict and Security L 307.

[52] Art 25(b) ICCPR 1966.

Furthermore, there are human rights issues raised by the Security Council acting increasingly and controversially as a judicial body as well as a legislator,[53] in addition to its executive function of dealing with threats to and breaches of the peace. While there are of course tremendous institutional and constitutional problems with one organ being capable of acting as judge, jury, and executioner, it is contended here that when the Council is performing a judicial function, such as endorsing the listing of individuals suspected of being in the Taliban or Al-Qaeda,[54] or implicating Libya in the Lockerbie bombings of 1988,[55] it has to respect basic principles of natural justice and due process when carrying out that function. This though is more an argument of legitimacy—if the Council wants to sit as a court on occasions and judge states and individuals, then it should give them a fair trial. This puts to one side the issue of whether it has the legal competence to act as a court.[56]

It is interesting to note that in its resolutions on terrorism, the Security Council reminds states of their obligation to respect human rights law in implementing measures to combat terrorism, but does not explicitly recognize that these standards apply to it as well. In more general terms the Council has declared that 'terrorism can only be defeated in accordance with the Charter of the United Nations and international law, by a sustained comprehensive approach, involving the active participation and collaboration of all States, [and] international and regional organizations . . .'.[57] This falls short though of a full acceptance of the Council's own responsibilities as regards human rights.

Nevertheless, reminding states of their obligations under human rights law suggests that the Council is not attempting to extend the effects of article 103 of the Charter, discussed below, which gives priority to the obligations of the Charter over inconsistent treaty obligations under other treaties. From its statements above, the Council does not appear to be attempting to use this provision to usurp the human rights obligations of states. Despite this reassurance, it is necessary to consider whether the Security Council has the competence to overrule human rights treaties if it so desired.

V. The Security Council and the human rights obligations of member states

Thus far it has been argued that the Security Council is subject to human rights obligations in its activities. In effect, a rule of law argument has been made—that

---

[53] For discussion see M Happold, 'Security Council Resolution 1373 and the Constitution of the United Nations' (2003) 16 Leiden J of Intl L 593; S Talmon, 'The Security Council as World Legislature', (2005) 99 AJIL 175.   [54] SC res 1267, 15 Oct 1999.
[55] SC res 748, 31 March 1992.
[56] For views see E Lauterpacht, *Aspects of the Administration of International Justice* (Grotius, 1991) pp 37–47.   [57] SC res 1456, 20 Jan 2003 'Declaration on Combating Terrorism'.

the same obligations being promoted by the UN system in the form of human rights guarantees are applicable to the UN itself. However, the rule of law argument may be undermined if the Security Council can affect the human rights obligations of member states themselves.

Given the Security Council's extraordinary supranational powers under Chapter VII, powers that it has exercised to a significant degree since 1990, it is necessary to consider how these impact on the human rights obligations of states. The key provision is article 103 of the Charter which provides that the obligations of the UN Charter shall prevail over inconsistent treaty obligations. Article 103 was a little used provision during the Cold War but it is one that has come into the spotlight with the increasing number of Chapter VII decisions made by the Security Council in the last fifteen years.

Although a constitutional provision in one sense, it is difficult to see article 103 buttressing a constitutional approach that applies the rule of law to the Council as well as states. In fact the opposite may be closer to the mark—by its terms article 103 can be read as permitting the Council to override inconsistent human rights treaty obligations of states. For example, this may allow the Security Council to impose economic sanctions on a state under Chapter VII, which would override any inconsistent human rights obligations of the target state and member states obliged by the resolution to embargo the target state, just as its measures against Libya in 1992 overrode the obligations of Libya under the Montreal Convention of 1971, and obliged member states to deal with Libya in a restricted manner.[58]

Clearly, article 103 is directed at states not at any obligations on the Security Council itself. However, the possibility of the Security Council being able to override the human rights obligations of states needs consideration for if this argument is accepted it would give the Council considerable discretionary power over human rights.[59]

The deliberate use by the Security Council of the combined effect of articles 25 (which provides that Council decisions are binding),[60] and 103 of the UN Charter to override or supplement existing treaty obligations was certainly not fully realized in earlier commentaries on the Charter. In these, article 103 was seen as being merely 'designed to exclude the possibility of a member state being impeded in carrying out its obligations or enforcing its rights under the Charter by conflicting obligations which it may have accepted under other international

---

[58] *Questions of Interpretation and Application of the 1971 Montreal Convention Arising from the Aerial Incident at Lockerbie* [1992] ICJ Rep 114 at 126.

[59] For a discussion on this matter in relation to international humanitarian law see R Cryer, 'The Security Council and International Humanitarian Law' (British Institute of International and Comparative Law, forthcoming). It is recognized that while international humanitarian law creates obligations for both states and individuals, human rights law only creates obligations for states. See generally HJ Steiner, 'International Protection of Human Rights' in M Evans (ed), *International Law* (OUP, 2003) pp 776–7. Thus human rights law is susceptible to the full effect of art 103.

[60] Art 25 provides that: 'The Members of the United Nations agree to accept and carry out the decisions of the Security Council in accordance with the present Chart'.

agreements'.[61] Nevertheless, the intent was not to confine the effects of article 103 to the 'primary' obligations of the Charter. The drafters certainly seem to envisage the effects of article 103 applying to the 'secondary' obligations imposed by the Security Council under articles 25 and 41 in the case of sanctions regimes,[62] where member states must accept the obligations imposed by the UN Charter and the Security Council over conflicting obligations in trade agreements, for instance. Even if confined to having a specific impact on directly applicable obligations between the target state and other states whereby 'an aviation ban would apply irrespective of prior aviation agreements, and a travel ban would be operative despite a treaty on the free movement of persons',[63] and a trade embargo would be operative despite treaties on bilateral trade (and presumably multilateral obligations derived from the WTO), it can be seen that this can affect human rights obligations of the target state and its treaty partners.

Goodrich, Hambro, and Simons assert that this overriding effect applies to all binding decisions of the Security Council.[64] Earlier commentaries on the Charter agree, however, that article 103 only came into play in particular cases of conflict 'between the two categories of obligation', in contrast to the much wider provision in the League's Covenant that purported to automatically abrogate obligations inconsistent with those arising from the constituent treaty.[65]

Nevertheless, even limiting the Charter's obligations to particular cases of conflicting norms still allows the Council to override the obligations of member states derived from human rights treaties. For instance, the Council anti-terrorist legislation which requires the listing of individuals suspected of being linked to the Taliban and Al-Qaeda may well conflict with a member state's obligations under the International Covenant on Civil and Political Rights (ICCPR). In economic, social, and cultural rights (ESC rights), the imposition of economic sanctions against a target state may well conflict with the obligations of the target state under the ICESCR to uphold basic rights to food, water, medicine, and shelter for instance. Although in general terms, ESC rights are programmatic in nature, in that the level of protection achieved varies with the level of development within a

---

[61] N Bentwich and A Martin, *A Commentary on the Charter of the United Nations* (Routledge & Kegan Paul, 1950) p 179.

[62] UNCIO, vol XIII 707. Art 41 of the UN Charter provides that: 'The Security Council may decide what measures not involving the use of armed force are to be deployed to give effect to its decisions, and it may call upon the Members of the United Nations to apply such measures. These may include complete or partial interruption of economic relations and of rail, sea, air, postal, telegraphic, radio and other means of communication, and the severance of diplomatic relations'.

[63] JA Frowein and N Krisch, 'Article 41' in Simma (ed), *The Charter*, 745.

[64] LM Goodrich, E Hambro, and P Simons, *Charter of the United Nations* (3rd edn, Columbia University Press, 1969) p 616.

[65] Ibid 615; Bentwich and Martin, *A Commentary*, 180. See art 20 of the League of Nations Covenant 1919 para 1 of which provided that 'members of the League severally agree that this Covenant is accepted as abrogating all obligations and understandings *inter se* which are inconsistent with the terms thereof, and solemnly undertake that they will not hereafter enter into any engagements inconsistent with the terms thereof'.

state, the basic rights listed are in the nature of core obligations deriving from the right to life.[66] The ESCR Committee makes a similar statement:

the Committee is of the view that a minimum core obligation to ensure the satisfaction of, at the very least, minimum essential levels of each of the rights is incumbent upon every State party. Thus, for example, a State party in which any significant number of individuals is deprived of essential foodstuffs, of essential primary health care, of basic shelter and housing, or the most basic forms of education is, prima facie, failing to discharge its obligations under the Covenant. If the Covenant were to be read in such a way as not to establish such a minimum core obligation, it would largely be deprived of its raison d'etre.[67]

The Security Council is bound to respect these core rights. Although the Council has on several occasions stated that it will try to avoid 'negative humanitarian consequences as much as possible',[68] but this seems an inadequate basis upon which to argue it has accepted that it must not violate human rights.

However, by its terms, at least, article 103 only applies to treaty rights. It was clearly the intent of the drafters that it was not to apply to customary international law.[69] It has been argued, however, that 'Article 103 must be seen in connection with Article 25 and with the character of the Charter as the basic document and "constitution" of the international community' so that 'the ideas underlying Art. 103 are also valid in the case of conflict between Charter obligations' and those arising for instance in customary international law.[70] This argument cannot be fully accepted, for a constitutional approach to the Charter is not just based on the fact that the obligations it contains and those derived from it are hierarchically superior to obligations found in other international laws. Viewing the UN Charter as a constitution in a more fundamental sense would see it as comprising a set of laws and institutions that are designed to uphold and implement the core values of the system. Within the UN system, peace and security and human rights are both core values.[71] Although the human rights obligations contained in the UN Charter are weaker than those protecting the value of peace and security, it cannot be the case that the human rights elements of the Charter and all those laws derived from them, both soft and hard (custom and treaty), are swept away in the face of an inconsistent Security Council decision. To allow an executive body the discretionary power to push aside fundamental guarantees would clearly be the antithesis of a constitutional system. The core values underpinning the UN system have also

---

[66] The rights to food, water, shelter, and health are derived from arts 11 and 12 of the International Covenant on Economic, Social and Cultural Rights, while the right to life is contained in art 6 of the International Covenant on Civil and Political Rights. For their linkage see ND White, 'Towards a Strategy for Human Rights Protection in Post-Conflict Situations', in ND White and D Klaasen (eds), *The UN, Human Rights*, 465.

[67] 'The Nature of States Parties Obligations: Article 2(1) of the Covenant', *General Comment* 3, UN doc E/1991/23, para 10.

[68] UN doc S/PRST/1999/34, 30 Nov 1999. See further Simma (ed), *The Charter*, 746.

[69] R Bernhardt, 'Article 103', in Simma (ed), *The Charter*, 1293.   [70] Ibid 1299.

[71] White, *UN System*, 47–78.

passed into customary international law and it can be strongly argued that certain economic and social rights are customary, especially the core obligations specified by the ESCR Committee mentioned above.[72] This is not without controversy though as noted by Chinkin:

Although the ICESCR has been widely accepted, argument continues as to whether economic and social rights are properly so regarded. Despite post-cold war reaffirmation of the indivisibility of human rights (Vienna Declaration), there remains an unwillingness to regard such government action as mass evictions or failure to feed its population in terms of human rights abuses because this would entail scrutiny of governmental policies of distributive justice, not of human rights.[73]

Despite these misgivings it cannot be the case that Security Council sanctions somehow free the target state and its treaty partner states from respecting the core values of the Charter, and their core obligations as regards economic and social rights.

In order to respect fully the constitutional values of the UN system, a textual interpretation of article 103 is followed because it reflects a fully contextual understanding of the Charter as a constitution.[74] Article 103 should be confined to cases of conflicting treaty obligations and only where it is necessary to free states from certain treaty obligations in order for them to respect a mandatory Council decision to impose measures against a target state. The effect of Security Council resolutions is not to free the target state, other member states, or itself from compliance with basic economic and social rights. Sanctions regimes have to be designed and implemented with this in mind.

Sanctions regimes with their humanitarian exceptions and increasing use of smarter sanctions are designed to avoid the use of starvation as a weapon. The obligation to protect the basic economic and social rights of the population of the target state is still upon that state itself, but it is also an obligation on the Council to ensure that its sanctions regimes are properly designed to minimize the impact on the population.[75] Arguably too, if the target state fails to use the humanitarian exceptions correctly, for instance by distributing food and medicine only to favoured groups within the state, the Council has a duty to try and ensure that it is

---

[72] For support that the Universal Declaration of Human Rights of 1948 (which contains civil and political, and economic, social, and cultural rights) has become customary law see *Filirtiga v Pena-Irala* (1980) 19 *ILM* 966.

[73] C Chinkin, 'International Law and Human Rights' in T Evans (ed), *Human Rights Fifty Years On: A Reappraisal* (Manchester University Press, 1998) p 105 at 113.

[74] On rules of treaty interpretation see art 31 of the Vienna Convention on the Law of Treaties 1969.

[75] On the development of smart sanctions see D Cartwright and GA Lopez, *The Sanctions Decade: Assessing UN Strategies in the 1990s* (Lynne Rienner, 2000) pp 3–5; D Cartwright and GA Lopez, *Sanctions and the Search For Security: Challenges to UN Action* (Lynne Rienner, 2002) pp 63–84; and ND White and A Abass, 'Countermeasures and Sanctions' in M Evans (ed), *International Law* (2nd edn, OUP, 2005) section IVB.

corrected. This follows from the fact that the Council itself is bound by fundamental customary human rights so that its actions have to respect those rights.

VI. Remedies

Having established that the Security Council is bound to respect human rights law, including core economic and social rights, it is essential to consider whether there are any remedies available against it for breach of its obligations. The term remedy is used in the wider sense of accountability as stated in the ILA Committee's report:

The term 'remedy' is used as a form of shorthand for an acceptable outcome arrived at through a procedure instigated by an aggrieved party and is intended to include, in addition to the remedies of a formal kind, other means of redress which might be more appropriate to the circumstances of the case e.g. prospective changes of policy or practice by the [organization].[76]

Thus, non-legal remedies may be available in different forms at the levels of administrative and financial as well as political and, very occasionally, democratic accountability. The ILA Committee correctly identifies that 'accountability mechanisms may be intended to protect or restore not only legal interests, but also political, administrative and financial interests' giving rise to different mechanisms of accountability including non-legal ones such as the Ombudsman office (to deal with maladministration), Inspection Panels (to investigate complaints by groups of individuals), and Commissions of Inquiry (for serious matters of public concern).[77] Such mechanisms may be found within the UN system,[78] but they tend to be within specific institutions and their powers are very limited.

Injured individuals and groups have limited entitlements within the UN system, even before international or regional courts more generally. The European Court of First Instance and the European Court of Justice have considered the legal effects of Security Council Resolutions as implemented by the European Community, but have not reviewed them.[79] The ICJ and the European Court of

---

[76] *ILA Final Report 2004*, 39.

[77] Ibid, 39. See further 55–57. See eg, *Report of the Independent Inquiry into the Actions of the United Nations During the 1994 Genocide in Rwanda* (United Nations, 1999).

[78] See ND White, *The Law of International Organisations* (2nd edn, Manchester University Press, 2005) 224–7.

[79] Case T-306/01 *Yusuf and Al Barakaat International Foundation v Council and Commission*, CFI, (21 Sept 2005); Case C-84/95 *Bosphorus v Minister of Transport* [1996] ECR I-3953, ECJ. For discussion see RA Wessel, 'The UN, to EU and Jus Cogens' (2006) 3 Intl Organizations L Rev 1. For discussion see P Eeckhout, *External Relations of the European Union* (OUP, 2004) pp 425–44. See further the European Court of Human Rights decision in *Bosphorus Hava Yollari Turizm v Ireland* (2006) 42 EHRR 1, discussed in C Costello, 'The *Bosphorus* Ruling of the European Court of Human Rights, Fundamental Rights and Blurred Boundaries' (2006) 6 Human Rights L Rev 87.

Human Rights (ECtHR) have considered cases concerning the actions of states when acting under the authority of NATO.[80] Individuals and other non-state legal persons have *locus standi* before the ECtHR and the European Court of Justice, but not before the ICJ.

Endemic in the development of judicial review within the UN system is its sporadic and incidental nature. The human rights obligations of the Security Council may be mentioned in advisory opinions of the ICJ, or may even be the subject of an advisory opinion. In reviewing state reports or in making general comments, human rights bodies may comment on the legality under human rights law of institutional actions, thereby pointing out the effect that institutional actions have on human rights. The ESCR Committee has a developing body of critical opinion on economic sanctions and economic rights.[81] In its *General Comment 8* of 1997, it stressed that 'whatever the circumstances [economic] sanctions should always take full account of the provisions of the International Covenant on Economic, Social and Cultural Rights'. It noted that such regimes:

Often cause significant disruption in the distribution of food, pharmaceuticals and sanitation supplies, jeopardize the quality of food and the availability of clean drinking water, severely interfere with the functioning of basic health and education systems, and undermine the right to work. In addition, their unintended consequences can include the reinforcement of the power of oppressive elites, the emergence, almost invariably, of a black market and the generation of huge windfall profits for the privileged elites which manage it, enhancement of the control of the governing elites over the population at large, and restriction of opportunities to seek asylum or to manifest political opposition. While the phenomena mentioned in the preceding sentence are essentially political in nature, they also have a major additional impact on the enjoyment of economic, social and cultural rights.

The Committee criticized the notion that the humanitarian exceptions built into regimes actually protected ESC rights, and that most studies point out that they do not. The Committee considered that ESC rights could not be considered inapplicable 'solely because a decision has been taken that considerations of international peace and security warrant the imposition of sanctions', and that both the target state and the international community must protect 'at least the core content of the economic, social and cultural rights of the affected peoples of that State'. This should be taken into account in the design of the sanctions regime, and when the regime is implemented its effects should be monitored, and any adverse effects should be addressed. The Committee's Comment is clearly designed to address the problem that sanctions regimes present—that they treat

---

[80] *Legality of the Use of Force* cases [1999] ICJ Rep; *Bankovic v Belgium,* Appl no 52207/99, 2001-XII 333.

[81] See for instance UN doc E/C.12/1/add 40, 8 Dec 1999, para 10 (report on Cameroon); UN doc E/C.12/add 44, 23 May 2000, para 28 (report on Egypt). See further A Clapham, 'Sanctions and Economic, Social and Cultural Rights', in V Gowlland-Debbas (ed), *United Nations Sanctions and International Law* (Kluwer, 2001) p 131.

the population of the state as a whole as being responsible for the sins of their government.[82] The Committee concluded its Comment by stating

In adopting this general comment the sole aim of the Committee is to draw attention to the fact that the inhabitants of a given country do not forfeit their basic economic, social and cultural rights by virtue of any determination that their leaders have violated norms relating to international peace and security. The aim is not to give support or encouragement to such leaders, nor is it to undermine the legitimate interests of the international community in enforcing respect for the provisions of the Charter of the United Nations and the general principles of international law. Rather, it is to insist that lawlessness of one kind should not be met with lawlessness of another kind which pays no heed to the fundamental rights that underlie and give legitimacy to such action.[83]

The ESCR Committee clearly sees core rights as immovable in the face of security measures. In contrast, the more limited jurisprudence of the African Commission on Human Rights has been less critical of sanctions regimes and their impact on the human rights of the target state, seemingly accepting that an institutional basis for sanctions, combined with the support of the Security Council, was sufficient.[84]

Organizations may be held accountable within national legal systems as well as at the international level. In considering international organizations before national courts, Reinisch concludes that such courts 'often find ways to exercise their adjudicative power over disputes involving international organizations. The method most frequently used in order to do so is the application of a restrictive immunity concept...'.[85] The ILA Committee suggests that a 'functional immunity approach... be accompanied by laying down a stringent requirement that the actions of the' organization 'must be inherent or essential for its institutional purposes'.[86] Even if immunity is still applicable and there is no waiver of immunity by the executive head, the organization 'remains bound by its obligation to provide adequate alternative procedures for settling the dispute'.[87] This obligation

---

[82] E Zoller, *Peacetime Unilateral Remedies: An Analysis of Countermeasures* (Transnational, Dobbs Ferry, 1984) p 101.

[83] UN doc E/C.12/1997/8, CESCR *General Comment 8, (The Relationship Between Economic Sanctions and the Respect for Economic, Social and Cultural Rights)*, paras 1, 3, 8, 10, 12–14, 16.

[84] *Association Pour la Sauvegarde de la Paix au Burundi v Tanzania, Kenya, Uganda, Rwanda, Zaire, and Zambia*, ACHPR Communication no 157/96 (2003). See chapter on 'The African Commission on Human and Peoples' Rights and the Implementation of Economic, Social and Cultural Rights in Africa' by Mashood Baderin in this book.

[85] A Reinisch, *International Organizations Before National Courts* (Cambridge University Press, 2000) p 391.

[86] *ILA Final Report 2004*, 51. See further Reinisch, *International Organizations*, 348–56; 359–65; E Gaillard and I Pingel-Lenuzza, 'International Organisations and Immunity from Jurisdiction: To Restrict or to Bypass', (2002) 51 ICLQ 1.

[87] *ILA Final Report 2004*, 58. See art VIII, s 29 Convention on Privileges and Immunities of the United Nations, 1946.

and the important distinction between immunity and liability was put in clear terms by the ICJ when it stated:

the Court wishes to point out that the question of immunity from legal process is distinct from the issue of compensation for any damages incurred as a result of acts performed by the United Nations or by its agents acting in their official capacity.... The United Nations may be required to bear responsibility for the damage arising from such acts.[88]

'Immunity is used to prevent international organizations from being subject to an outside judiciary; it does not affect the rights and obligations of the organization.'[89] Absolute immunity is becoming increasingly discredited in the era of human rights. The ILA Committee points to the contradiction that arises between the obligation of states under human rights law to provide a remedy, and domestic courts denying a remedy by giving immunity to organizations. 'This human rights imperative may result in a limitation or rejection (even by domestic courts?) of jurisdictional immunity claimed' by organizations, and the 'actual exercise of adjudicatory jurisdiction'.[90] In effect, by creating organizations with wide immunities, it can be argued that states are potentially transgressing their human rights obligation to provide effective remedies for their citizens.[91]

The ILA Committee concludes on judicial remedies by stating that 'there is no inherent reason why the remedial outcomes of restitution, damages, specific performance, satisfaction and injunctive relief should not become available under the law of organizational responsibility'.[92] However, this statement is clearly *de lege ferenda* for, as Wellens concludes in his excellent study, 'there is, at present, a lack of a reasonable level of coherence in the (emerging) law of remedies against international organizations'. He further states that such a lack of coherence needs urgent attention given that it is 'pointless to envisage a comprehensive set of primary rules governing the conduct of international organizations without putting into place, both at domestic and international levels, appropriate remedial mechanisms for their enforcement'.[93]

VII. Conclusion

Institutional and international law has moved a long way in recent years to recognize that international organizations are part of the international legal order and as such have rights and duties. However, while the primary rules of international law, including fundamental economic and social rights, are applicable to the

---

[88] *Difference Relating to Immunity from Legal Process of a Special Rapporteur of the Commission on Human Rights*, ICJ Rep 1999, 88–9.
[89] HG Schermers and NM Blokker, *International Institutional Law* (4th edn, Nijhoff, 2003), 1005.   [90] *ILA Final Report 2004*, 59.
[91] See *Matthews* case (1999) 28 *EHRR* 316, at para 22.   [92] *ILA Final Report 2004*, 53.
[93] K Wellens, *Remedies against International Organizations* (Cambridge University Press, 2002) p 269–270.

activities of the Security Council, the UN system is woefully inadequate in ensuring the accountability of the Security Council in this, or in any other, regard. The latest spate of reform proposals coming out of the UN system have little to say in this regard.

The Secretary General's report 'In Larger Freedom', the title of which is taken from the preamble of the UN Charter—'to promote social progress and better standards of life in larger freedom'—creates an expectation that the report will consider the improvement of the protection of economic and social rights in the UN system including by the Security Council. However, this expectation is not met when considering the content of the report.[94] Admittedly, the report calls for reforms of the Council that would make it more representative, more democratic and accountable, while not impairing its effectiveness; and makes a very firm link between the values of security and human rights. It should have taken these encouraging suggestions together and have recommended the establishment of mechanisms of accountability to ensure that the Council's coercive and interventionist actions are subject to scrutiny to ensure they do not breach its human rights obligations.[95]

There are different mechanisms and modes of accountability to choose from, and many of these are present in different parts of the UN system—ombudsmen, inspection panels, inquiries, supervisory committees, auditors, and some judicial bodies. There is very little of this that currently touches upon the activities of the Security Council. One suggestion for introducing greater accountability for sanctions regimes would be to have each proposed regime reviewed by the UN High Commissioner for Human Rights before any enabling resolution is adopted, to build into the regime, as far as possible, human rights protection. Regular scrutiny of the effect of sanctions on the target state (and other affected states) by the High Commissioner should occur thereafter. In addition, those individuals or groups whose rights have allegedly been violated by Security Council sanctions should have recourse to an Inspection Panel along the lines of that established by the World Bank in 1993.[96] Though such mechanisms are a rarity within the UN system, the Security Council's human rights credentials, which have been eroded over the 1990s, would be greatly improved by the introduction of such a body.

---

[94] See also 'We the Peoples—the Millennium Report of the Secretary General' (2000), paras 229–233 on targeting sanctions, also para 321, 362.

[95] See 'In Larger Freedom: towards Development, Security and Human Rights for All' (2005) paras 14–16, 110, 169. In add 1 the report states that the proposed new Human Rights Council would 'interface' with other UN organs including the Security Council. Add 5 on the proposed Peace building Commission makes no mention of human rights. See further the 2005 World Summit Outcome Document, GA res 60/1, 24 Oct 2005, paras 97–105.

[96] HG Schermers and NM Blokker, *International Institutional Law* (4th ed, Brill, 2004), p 468.

6

Non-State Actors and Economic, Social, and Cultural Rights

*Manisuli Ssenyonjo**

I. Introduction

Making space in the international legal regime to take account of the role of non-state actors (NSAs) in the realization of economic, social, and cultural rights (ESC rights), and their accountability for the violations of ESC rights, remains a critical challenge facing international human rights law today. Under traditional approaches to human rights generally, and to ESC rights in particular, NSAs are considered to be beyond the direct reach of international human rights law.[1] Traditionally, human rights relations are conceptualized as 'vertical' in the sense that they involve the obligation of a governing actor (the state or agents of the state) towards individuals (or groups of individuals) within a state's jurisdiction.[2] This is based on the principle of state responsibility to guarantee human rights on the basis that the state/individual relationship involves unequal power dynamics between the parties.[3] A state's potential to abuse its position of authority to the detriment of an individual's interests was the basis for human rights to insulate the latter against state interference.

The United Nations (UN) Charter,[4] widely considered as the centre of an international 'constitutional order',[5] imposes obligations on member states to

---

* I wish to thank Professor David Harris for supervising my PhD at Nottingham (2001–02). Parts of this chapter will appear in the Human Rights Q (2006).

[1] M Ssenyonjo, 'Accountability of Non-State Actors in Uganda for War Crimes and Human Rights Violations: Between Amnesty and the International Criminal Court' (2005) 10(3) J of Conflict & Security L 405–434.

[2] See eg, W Nelson, 'Human Rights and Human Obligation', in J Pennock and J Chapman (eds), *Human Rights* (New York University Press, 1981) at pp 275–291; *The Restatement (Third) of Foreign Relations Law of the United States* (The American Law Institute, 1987), pt VII, introductory note, at 144–45 does not fully commit to any position, but states: 'how a state treats individual human beings . . . is a matter of international concern and a proper subject for regulation by international law'.

[3] See R Higgins, *Problem and Process: International Law and How We Use It* (Clarendon Press, 1994) at 39–55, 146–159.   [4] 1 UNTS xvi.

[5] N White, 'The United Nations System: Conference, Contract or Constitutional Order?' (2000) 4 Singapore J of Intl and Comparative L 281, at 291.

achieve international co-operation in promoting and encouraging respect for
human rights.[6] In this context, human rights are viewed primarily as being exer-
cisable against the state, and the state has the primary responsibility to respect,
protect, and fulfil human rights. For example, under the two principal human
rights treaties—the International Covenant on Civil and Political Rights
(ICCPR)[7] and the International Covenant on Economic, Social and Cultural
Rights (ICESCR)[8]—it is only each 'state party' to the each Covenant that undertakes human rights obligations.[9] All branches of government (executive, legislative, and judicial), and other public or governmental authorities, at whatever
level—national, regional, or local—are in a position to engage the responsibility
of the state.[10]

It is, therefore, clear that human rights treaties are principally addressed to
states[11] and NSAs cannot, at present, be parties to the existing human rights
treaties. The general obligations under article 2(1) of the ICCPR and the ICESCR
'are binding on States [Parties] and do not, as such, have direct horizontal effect as
a matter of international law'.[12] As such NSAs are currently only bound to the
extent that obligations accepted by states can be applied to them by states. The
result is that a wide range of actors other than states including international financial institutions, notably the International Monetary Fund (IMF) and the World
Bank; international organizations concerned with trade such as the World Trade
Organization (WTO); and transnational corporations (TNCs), along with many
others, are generally considered not to be bound directly by human rights law.
This means that NSAs are only indirectly accountable through states, while the
states will be directly liable for human rights violations committed by NSAs
within their respective jurisdictions. The major argument against the direct application of human rights obligations to NSAs stresses that this would carry the risk
that states might defer their responsibility to these actors, which might diminish
existing state obligations and accountability.[13]

---

[6] See preamble of the UN Charter, together with art 1(3), 55 and 56; Z Stavrinides, 'Human
Rights Obligations under the United Nations Charter' (1999) 3(2) The Intl J of Human Rights,
38–48.
   [7] 999 UNTS 171, Human Rights Committee (HRC), *General Comment 31 (Nature of the
General Legal Obligation on States parties to be Covenant)*, UN doc CCPR/C21/rev/Add 13
(2004) para 4.   [8] 993 UNTS 3.
   [9] ICCPR, art 2(1), 'Each State Party to the present Covenant undertakes to respect and to ensure
to all individuals within its territory and subject to its jurisdiction the rights recognised in the present
Covenant . . .'. ICESCR, art 2(1) 'Each State Party to the present Covenant undertakes to take steps,
individually and through international assistance and co-operation, especially economic and technical, to the maximum of its available resources, with a view to achieving progressively the full realisation of the rights recognised in the present Covenant . . .'.
   [10] HRC *General Comment 31*, para 4.
   [11] See eg, Committee on Economic, Social and Cultural Rights (ESCR Committee), *General
Comment 3*, The Nature of States Parties' Obligations (5th session, 1990), UN doc E/1991/23, annex
III at 86 (1991), para 1.   [12] HRC, *General Comment 31*, para 8.
   [13] See Kalliopi K Koufa, *Final Report of the Special Rapporteur: on Terrorism and Human Rights*,
E/CN.4/Sub.2/2004/40 (25 June 2004), para 55.

This situation threatens to make a mockery of the international system of protecting human rights generally, and ESC rights in particular, and accountability for human rights violations. This is especially so given the fact that since the end of the Cold War, there has been a trend in all regions of the world to reduce the role of the state and to rely on private actors to resolve problems of human welfare, most of which directly relate to ESC rights to work, social security, adequate food, education, health, housing, and water.[14] By virtue of the increasing powers of NSAs, they are uniquely positioned to affect, positively and/or negatively, the level of enjoyment of ESC rights. Despite this, the means by which NSAs might be held accountable for human rights violations remain unclear.[15]

This chapter attempts to examine the role of NSAs in the progressive realization of ESC rights. It addresses the following questions: Who are NSAs? Can the state be held accountable for human rights violations caused by NSAs? Can NSAs ignore ESC rights as long as states don't hold them accountable? Do international human rights treaties relevant to ESC rights impose responsibilities on NSAs? Can NSAs be accountable directly under human rights law? Finally, is there a need for the human rights regime to adapt to take account of the role of NSAs if it is to maintain its relevance?

II. Defining Non-State Actors

The term 'non-state actor' is virtually open-ended.[16] Its meaning depends on the context in which it is used. For example, the International Campaign to Ban Landmines has used the term NSAs to refer to 'armed opposition groups who act autonomously from recognised governments'.[17] In this context (of arms control), NSAs include 'rebel groups, irregular armed groups, insurgents, dissident armed forces, guerrillas, liberation movements, and de facto territorial governing bodies'.[18]

There have been several attempts to define NSAs.[19] According to Josselin and Wallace, NSAs include all organizations meeting the following three characteristics.[20] First, NSAs include organizations (emanating from civil society, or from the market economy, or from political impulses beyond state control and direction) that are largely or entirely autonomous from central government funding and

---

[14] See generally K De Feyter and F Gomez Isa (eds), *Privatisation and Human Rights in the Age of Globalization* (Intersentia, 2005).

[15] Thus, for instance, the Commission on Human Rights, in its resolution 1998/47, noted 'in particular the need to study further the role and responsibility of non-State actors in the sphere of human rights'.

[16] See P Alston, 'The "Not-a-Cat" Syndrome: Can the International Human Rights Regime Accommodate Non-State Actors?' in P Alston (ed), *Non-State Actors and Human Rights* (OUP, 2005) pp 3–36 at 5.   [17] <http://www.icbl.org/problem/solution/ban/nsa> accessed 20 April 2006.

[18] Ibid.   [19] Alston (n 16 above), pp 14–19.

[20] D Josselin and W Wallace, 'Non-State Actors in World Politics: A Framework', in D Josselin and W Wallace, *Non-State Actors in World Politics* (Palgrave, 2001) pp 1–20 at 3–4.

control. It is not clear, however, what level of governmental funding or control might disqualify an organization as a NSA. Secondly, NSAs include organizations operating or participating in networks which extend across the boundaries of two or more states. Therefore, they engage in 'transnational' relations, linking political systems, economies, and societies. Under this criterion, actors engaged solely at the domestic level in one state are not part of the definition since the focus is limited to those actors with a transnational dimension. Thirdly, NSAs include organizations acting in ways that affect political outcomes, either within one or more states or within international relations—either purposefully or semi-purposefully, either as their primary objective or as one aspect of their activities. This is very widely defined and has the potential to include a diverse range of actors.

In this chapter, the term NSA is used broadly to refer to all 'actors other than states'. This includes TNCs, professional bodies, and other non-governmental organizations (NGOs). It also extends to the UN Agencies, other international organizations, and other relevant bodies within the UN system.[21] It further includes international organizations concerned with trade such as the WTO, and international financial institutions, notably the World Bank, the IMF, and regional development banks.[22]

III. State obligations to protect against human rights violations by NSAs

A. Obligation to protect

Both the universal and regional human rights systems emphasize that states have a duty to protect those living within their jurisdictions from human rights violations. By article 2(1) of the ICESCR each 'State Party' to the Covenant undertakes the obligation:

to take steps, individually and through international assistance and co-operation, especially economic and technical, to the maximum of its available resources, with a view to achieving progressively the full realisation of the rights recognised in the present Covenant by all appropriate means, including particularly the adoption of legislative measures.

Thus, states are required by article 2(1) to adopt legislative measures[23] and/or non-legislative measures (eg the provision of judicial or other effective remedies,

---

[21] Examples include the World Health Organization (WHO), the International Labour Organization (ILO), the United Nations Development Programme (UNDP), United Nations Children's Fund (UNICEF), the United Nations Population Fund (UNPF), Food and Agriculture Organization (FAO), United Nations Environment Programme (UNEP), UN-Habitat, International Labour Organization (ILO), International Fund for Agricultural Development (IFAD). See ESCR Committee, *General Comment 14 (The right to the highest attainable standard of health* (22nd session, 2000), UN doc E/C.12/2000/4 (2000), para 63–65; *General Comment 15 (The right to water)* (29th session, 2003), UN doc E/C.12/2002/11 (2002), para 60.   [22] Ibid.
[23] See eg, ESCR Committee, *General Comment 3*, para 3; *General Comment 14*, para 56: 'States should consider adopting a framework law to operationalize their right to health national strategy.'

administrative, financial, educational/informational campaigns, and social measures) to protect ESC rights.[24] Legislative measures include not only the adoption of new legislation, but also the duty to reform, amend, and repeal legislation manifestly inconsistent with the progressive realization of ESC rights.[25] In *Purohit and Moore v The Gambia*[26] the African Commission on Human and Peoples' Rights found the Lunatics Detention Act (LDA) of The Gambia incompatible with several provisions of the African Charter on Human and Peoples' Rights (ACHPR)[27] because it failed, *inter alia*, to 'meet standards of anti-discrimination and equal protection of the law'.[28] The Commission strongly urged the government of The Gambia to repeal the LDA and replace it with a new legislative regime for mental health compatible with the ACHPR.

However, 'the ambivalence of many States in dealing with economic, social, and cultural rights' affect the state obligation to protect ESC rights.[29] The debate about ESC rights has continued,[30] and some states still do not recognize ESC rights as human rights because no state can allegedly 'fulfil' such rights. In 2003, for example, the United States of America (US) delegate to the UN Commission on Human Rights remarked that 'the communist system promised to fulfil economic, social and cultural rights but failed to deliver them'.[31] Thus the US government continues to oppose ESC rights within the UN and has claimed:

At best, economic, social and cultural rights are *goals* that can only be achieved progressively, *not guarantees*. Therefore, while access to food, health services and quality education are at the top of any list of development goals, to speak of them as rights turns the citizens of developing countries into objects of development rather than subjects in control of their own destiny.[32]

Despite this, it is clear that the goal of full realization of ESC rights, like other human rights, imposes three types or levels of obligations on states parties: the

[24] ESCR Committee, *General Comment 3* (1990), paras 5 and 7.
[25] See eg, ESCR Committee, *Concluding Observations, Cyprus*, E/C.12/1/add28 (4 Dec 1998), para 26.   [26] Communication no 241/2001 (2003).
[27] 21 ILM 58 (1982) entered into force 21 Oct 1986. arts 2, 3, 5, 7(1)(a) and (c), 13(1), 16, and 18(4).   [28] (Note 26 above) para 54.
[29] M Shaw, *International Law* (5th edn, Cambridge University Press, 2003), p 287.
[30] See eg, K Roth, 'Defending Economic, Social and Cultural Rights: Practical Issues Faced by an International Human Rights Organisation' (2004) 26 Human Rights Q 63; LS Rubinstein, 'How International Human Rights Organisations Can Advance Economic, Social and Cultural Rights: A Response to Kenneth Roth' (2004) 26 Human Rights Q 845; K Roth, 'Response to Leonard S Rubinstein' (2004) 26 Human Rights Q 873; L S Rubinstein, 'Response by Leonard S. Rubinstein' (2004) 26 Human Rights Q 879; M Robinson, 'Advancing Economic, Social, and Cultural Rights: The Way Forward' (2004) 26 Human Rights Q 866; K Tomaševski, 'Unasked Questions about Economic, Social, and Cultural Rights from the Experience of the Special Rapporteur on the Right to Education (1998–2004): A Response to Kenneth Roth, Leonard S. Rubenstein, and Mary Robinson' (2005) 27 Human Rights Q 709.
[31] Remarks by US Delegate Richard Wall, UN ESCOR, UN Commission on Human Rights, 59th Session, Agenda Item 10 (2003).
[32] Comments submitted by the United States of America, *Report of the Open-Ended Working Group on the Right to Development*, UN ESCOR, Commission on Human Rights, 57th Session, UN doc E/CN.4/2001/26 (2001), para 8 (emphasis added).

obligations to respect, protect, and fulfil.[33] This approach has been applied by the Committee on Economic, Social and Cultural Rights (ESCR Committee) in its General Comments,[34] and the African Commission on Human and Peoples' Rights in its decisions.[35]

The state obligation to protect requires states to take measures that prevent NSAs (third or private actors/parties)[36]—individuals, groups, corporations, and other entities as well as agents acting under their authority[37]—from interfering with ESC rights. For example, the protection of the freedom of action and the use of resources against other, more assertive or aggressive subjects—more powerful economic interests, such as the protection against the marketing and dumping of hazardous or dangerous products,[38] or the protection against the use of inhuman or degrading disciplinary measures such as corporal punishment or public humiliation in the (public or private) schools so as to protect the child's dignity and right to education.[39]

---

[33] See A Eide, 'Realisation of Social-Economic Rights and the Minimum Threshold Approach', (1989) 10 Human Rights L J, 35 at 37; A Eide, *The Right to Adequate Food as a Human Right*, E/CN.4/Sub.2/1987/23, para 66; A Eide, 'Economic and Social Rights', in J Symonides (ed), *Human Rights: Concepts and Standards*, (UNESCO Publishing, Aldershot, 2000) at 109–174; A Eide, 'Economic, Social and Cultural Rights as Human Rights' in A Eide, C Krause, and A Rosas (eds), *Economic, Social and Cultural Rights: A Textbook* (2nd edn, Nijhoff, 2001), pp 9–28. See also *The Maastricht Guidelines on Violations of Economic, Social, and Cultural Rights*, Maastricht, 22–26 Jan 1997, (1998) 20 Human Rights Q, pp 691–705 and UN doc E/C.12/2000/13, 2 Oct 2000), para 6; M Craven, *The International Covenant on Economic, Social, and Cultural Rights: A Perspective on its Development*, (Clarendon Press, 1995) pp 109–114; H Shue, *Basic Rights: Subsistence, Affluence, and U.S. Foreign Policy* (2nd edn, Princeton University Press, 1996) for the view that every basic right entails duties to *avoid, protect*, and *aid*; D Brand, 'Introduction to Socio-Economic Rights in the South African Constitution' in D Brand and C Heyns (eds), *Socio-Economic Rights in South Africa*, (Pretoria University Law Press, 2005), pp 1–56, at 9–12.

[34] See eg, ESCR Committee, *General Comment 18* (2005), para 25; *General Comment 17* (2005), para 55; *General Comment 16* (2005), para 17; *General Comment 15* (2002), paras 20–29; *General Comment 14* (2000), para 33; and *General Comment 13* (1999), para 46.

[35] See eg, *The Social and Economic Rights Action Center & the Center for Economic and Social Rights v Nigeria*, Communication no 155/96, para 44.

[36] See *X and Y v Netherlands*, judgment of 26 March 1985, Series A no 91, (1986) 8 EHRR 235; *Hatton v UK* Appl No 36022/97, judgment of Grand Chamber of 8 July 2003, (2003) 37 EHRR 611, para 98 (ECtHR); *Velásquez Rodriguez v Honduras* judgment of 19 July 1988, Series C No 4 (IACtHR) holding that a state has a positive duty to prevent human rights violations occurring in the territory subject to its effective control, even if such violations are carried out by third parties; *Union des Jeunes Avocats v Chad* Communication 74/92 (ACmHPR).

[37] ESCR Committee, *General Comment 15* (2002), para 23.

[38] A Eide, 'Economic and Social Rights', in J Symonides (ed), *Human Rights: Concepts and Standards*, (UNESCO Publishing, 2000) p 127.

[39] ESCR Committee, *General Comment 13*, para 41 'corporal punishment is inconsistent with . . . the dignity of the individual . . . . A State Party is required to take measures to ensure that discipline which is inconsistent with the Covenant does not occur in any public or private educational institution within its jurisdiction'. See also CRC, *Concluding Observations, Zimbabwe*, CRC/C/15/ add55, (1996) para 18: The Committee expressed 'its concern at the acceptance in the legislation of the use of corporal punishment in school, as well as within the family. It stresses the incompatibility of corporal punishment, as well as any other form of violence, injury, neglect, abuse or degrading treatment, with the provisions of the Convention'. See also CRC, *Concluding Observations, Guyana* CRC/C/15/add224 (30 Jan 2004), paras 31–32; *India*, CRC/C/5/add 228 (30 Jan 2004),

The obligation to protect, therefore, generally demands that the state has to protect against harmful activities carried out by NSAs and to prevent violations by NSAs. For example, with respect to the right to work, under article 6(1) of the ICESCR, states parties 'recognise the right to work, which includes the right of everyone to the opportunity to gain his living by work which he freely chooses or accepts, and will take appropriate steps to safeguard this right'. To this end, the ESCR Committee has noted:

Obligations to protect the right to work include, *inter alia*, the duties of States parties to adopt legislation or to take other measures ensuring equal access to work and training and to ensure that privatization measures do not undermine workers' rights. Specific measures to increase the flexibility of labour markets must not render work less stable or reduce social protection of the worker. The obligation to protect the right to work includes the responsibility of States parties to prohibit forced or compulsory labour by non-State actors.[40]

It follows that a state's 'failure to regulate the activities of individuals, groups or corporations so as to prevent them from violating the right to work of others' amounts to a violation of the right to work.[41] For example, the failure to protect workers against unlawful dismissal or against being subjected to forced or compulsory labour, slavery, or servitude by NSAs would be a clear violation of a state's positive obligation to protect. In the case of *Siliadin v France*[42] the European Court of Human Rights (ECtHR) considered the issue of whether France had fulfilled its positive obligations to protect effectively the applicant against forced labour or servitude as required by article 4 of the European Convention on Human Rights (ECHR).[43] The applicant (a Togolese national), Ms Siliadin, had worked for years for Mr and Mrs B almost fifteen hours a day and seven days a week, without respite, against her will, and without being paid. The applicant, who was an adolescent girl and a minor (fifteen and a half years old) at the relevant time, was unlawfully present in a foreign state and was afraid of being arrested by the police.

paras 44–45; *Indonesia* CRC/C/15/add 223 (30 Jan 2004), paras 43–44; *Japan*, CRC/C/15/add 231(30 Jan 2004), paras 35–36; *Papua New Guinea*, CRC/C/15/add 229 (30 Jan 2004), paras 37–38; *Campbell and Cosans v UK*, judgment of 25 Feb 1982, Series A no 48, (1982) 4 EHRR 293 (ECtHR). See also CRC, art 28(2); African Charter on the Rights and Welfare of the Child, art 11(5). See also CRC, *General Comment 8 (The right of the Child to protection from corporal punishment and other cruel or degrading forms of punishment)* (42nd session, 2006), UN doc CRC/C/GC/8 (21 Aug 2006), paras 16–29.

[40] ESCR Committee, *General Comment 18*, (adopted on 24 Nov 2005), para 25. Under art 2 of the International Labour Convention (No 29) Concerning Forced or Compulsory Labour (adopted on 28 June 1930 by the General Conference of the ILO at its 14 session, Geneva, Switzerland, entered into force 1 May 1932), the term 'forced or compulsory labour' is defined to mean 'all work or service which is exacted from any person under the menace of any penalty and for which the said person has not offered himself voluntarily'.   [41] Ibid para 35.

[42] Appl No 73316/01, judgment of 26 July 2005 (2006) 43 EHRR 16 <http://www.humanrights.ch/cms/upload/pdf/050726_EGMR_siliadinvsfrance.pdf> accessed 22 April 2006.

[43] 213 UNTS 222 art 4 '(1) No one shall be held in slavery or servitude. (2) No one shall be required to perform forced or compulsory labour'.

The applicant was entirely at Mr and Mrs B's mercy, since her papers had been confiscated and she had been promised that her immigration status would be regularized, which had never occurred. In these circumstances, the Court considered that Ms Siliadin had, at the least, been subjected to forced labour and had been held in servitude (ie obliged to provide services under coercion) within the meaning of article 4 of the ECHR at a time when she was a minor.

Accordingly, it fell to the Court to determine whether French legislation had afforded the applicant sufficient protection in the light of the positive obligations incumbent on France under article 4 of the ECHR. In that connection, it noted that the Parliamentary Assembly had regretted in its Recommendation 1523(2001) that 'none of the Council of Europe member States expressly [made] domestic slavery an offence in their criminal codes'. Slavery and servitude were not as such classified as criminal offences in the French criminal law.

Mr and Mrs B, who were prosecuted under articles 225–13 and 225–14 of the Criminal Code, were not convicted under criminal law. In that connection, the Court noted that, as the Principal Public Prosecutor had not appealed on points of law against the Court of Appeal's judgment of 19 October 2000, an appeal to the Court of Cassation was made only in respect of the civil aspect of the case and Mr and Mrs B's acquittal thus became final. In addition, according to a report drawn up in 2001 by the French National Assembly's joint committee on the various forms of modern slavery, those provisions of the Criminal Code were open to very differing interpretation from one court to the next.

In those circumstances, the Court considered that the criminal-law legislation in force at the material time had not afforded the applicant specific and effective protection against the actions of which she had been a victim. In paragraph 112 of the judgment, the Court noted that 'in accordance with contemporary norms and trends in this field, the member States' positive obligations under article 4 of the Convention must be seen as requiring the penalization and effective prosecution of any act aimed at maintaining a person in such a situation [slavery, servitude and forced or compulsory labour]'. It emphasized (in paragraphs 121 and 148) that the increasingly high standard being required in the area of the protection of human rights and fundamental liberties correspondingly and inevitably required greater firmness in assessing breaches of the fundamental values of democratic societies. Consequently, the Court concluded that France had not fulfilled its positive obligations under article 4 of the ECHR.

B. Protection against discrimination

The protection against human rights violations by NSAs is very essential in the area of discrimination since the elimination of discrimination is fundamental to the enjoyment of all ESC rights on a basis of equality. Women in particular, are often denied equal enjoyment of their human rights, by virtue of the 'lesser status ascribed to them by tradition and custom or as a result of overt and covert discrimination'.[44] It is an indisputable fact that 'many women experience distinct forms of discrimination, due to the intersection of sex with such factors as race, colour, language, religion, political and other opinion, national or social origin, property, birth, or other status, such as age, ethnicity, disability, marital, refugee or migrant status, resulting in compounded disadvantage.'[45]

In the context of non-discrimination and equality, article 2(2) of the ICESCR states a guarantee of non-discrimination on the basis of sex among other grounds.[46] Discrimination includes 'any distinction, exclusion, restriction or preference' between individuals or groups of individuals, made on the basis of any of the prohibited ground(s),[47] 'unless the distinction is based on objective criteria'.[48] Therefore, discrimination might arise when 'States treat differently persons in analogous situations without providing an objective and reasonable justification'.[49] A distinction will not be based on objective and reasonable justification if it does not pursue a 'legitimate aim' or if there is not a 'reasonable relationship of proportionality between the means employed and the aim sought to be realised'.[50] Discrimination might also arise 'when States without an objective and reasonable justification fail to treat differently persons whose situations are significantly different'.[51] Discrimination might also arise as a result of a state's failure to monitor and regulate the conduct of NSAs in relation to ESC rights. This might arise where a state fails to ensure that NSAs do not treat differently persons in analogous situations without providing an objective and reasonable justification, and where a state fails to ensure that NSAs, without an objective and reasonable justification, do not fail to treat differently persons whose situations are significantly different.

The principle of non-discrimination mentioned in article 2(2) of the Covenant is immediately applicable and is neither subject to progressive implementation nor dependent on available resources.[52] It is reinforced by article 3 of the ICESCR, which provides for the equal right of men and women to the enjoyment of the ESC rights it articulates.[53] This provision is founded on article 1(3) of the UN

---

[44] ESCR Committee, *General Comment 16*, para 5.   [45] Ibid.

[46] ICESCR, art 2(2): 'The States Parties to the present Covenant undertake to guarantee that the rights enunciated in the present Covenant will be exercised without discrimination of any kind as to race, colour, sex, language, religion, political or other opinion, national or social origin, property, birth or other status.'

[47] Revised General Reporting Guidelines, E/C.12/1991/1 (17 June 1991), para 3; ESCR Committee, *General Comment 5*, para 15; *General Comment 16*, para 11.

[48] ESCR Committee, *Concluding Observations, Japan*, E/C.12/1 add67 (30 Aug 2001), para 39: The Committee requested 'the State party to take note of its position that the principle of non-discrimination, as laid down in art 2(2) of the Covenant, is an absolute principle and can be subject to no exception, unless the distinction is based on objective criteria'. See also ESCR Committee, *Concluding Observations, Croatia*, E/C.12/1/add73 (30 Nov 2001), para 11.

[49] *Thlimmenos v Greece*, Appl 34369/97 (2001) 31 EHRR 411, para 44.

[50] *Koua Poirrez v France*, Appl No 40892/98 [2003] ECtHR 459, para 46; *Gaygusuz v Austria*, Appl 17371/90 [1996] ECtHR 36, para 42.

[51] *Thlimmenos v Greece*, Appl 34369/97 (2001) 31 EHRR 411 para 44.

[52] ESCR Committee, *General Comment 16*, para 33.

[53] ICESCR, art 3: 'The States Parties to the present Covenant undertake to ensure the equal right of men and women to the enjoyment of all economic, social and cultural rights set forth in the present Covenant.'

Charter and article 2 of the Universal Declaration of Human Rights (UDHR).[54]
In relation of NSAs, the ESCR Committee noted in its *General Comment 16*:

19. The obligation to protect requires States parties to take steps aimed directly towards
the elimination of prejudices, customary and all other practices that perpetuate the notion
of inferiority or superiority of either of the sexes, and stereotyped roles for men and
women. States parties' obligation to protect under Article 3 of the ICESCR includes *inter
alia*, the respect and adoption of constitutional and legislative provisions on the equal right
of men and women to enjoy all human rights and the prohibition of discrimination of any
kind; the adoption of legislation to eliminate discrimination *and to prevent third parties
from interfering directly or indirectly with the enjoyment of this right*; the adoption of administrative measures and programmes, as well as the establishment of public institutions,
agencies and programmes to protect women against discrimination.

20. *States parties have an obligation to monitor and regulate the conduct of non-state actors to
ensure that they do not violate the equal right of men and women to enjoy economic, social and
cultural rights. This obligation applies, for example, in cases where public services have been
partially or fully privatised.*[55]

It is thus clear that while only states are parties to international human rights
instruments protecting ESC rights and held accountable for its compliance, states
are nevertheless required to consider regulating the responsibility resting on NSAs
to respect ESC rights.[56] A state's failure, for example, to prohibit racial discrimination in the admission of students to private educational institutions would be a
clear violation of the obligation to protect the right to education.[57]

IV. Global actors/institutions

The main international institutions which form the backbone of the current
international economic system and which have had an impact on ESC rights are:
the IMF,[58] the World Bank,[59] and the WTO.[60] It is noteworthy that '[t]oday the

---

[54] GA res 217A (III), UN doc A/810 at 71 (1948).
[55] ESCR Committee, *General Comment 16* (2005) (emphasis added).
[56] See eg, ESCR Committee, *General Comment 17*, para 55.
[57] See the International Convention on the Elimination of All Forms of Racial Discrimination,
660 UNTS 195, arts 5(e)(v) and s(1)(d).
[58] For an introduction to the IMF see E Riesenhuber, *The International Monetary Fund under
Constraint: Legitimacy of its Crisis Management* (Kluwer, 2001), pp 3–73. See also F Gianviti,
'Economic, Social and Cultural Rights and the International Monetary Fund' in P Alston (ed), *Non-
State Actors and Human Rights* (OUP, 2005), pp 113–140.
[59] The 'World Bank Group' consists of the International Bank for Reconstruction and Development (IBRD) created in 1946; the International Finance Corporation (IFC) established in 1956;
the International Development Association (IDA) created in 1960; the International Centre for
Settlement of Investment Disputes (ICSID) operational in 1966; and the Multilateral Investment
Guarantee Agency (MIGA), 1988. For an overview of these institutions see I Shihata, *The World Bank
in a Changing World: Selected Essays*, Vol I (Nijhoff, 1991), pp 7–15; I Shihata, *The World Bank in a
Changing World: Selected Essays*, Vol III, (Nijhoff, 2000); D L Clark, 'The World Bank and Human
Rights: The Need for Greater Accountability', (2002) 15 Harvard Human Rights J 205–226; K
Marshall, *The World Bank: From Reconstruction to Development to Equity*, (Routledge, 2006).
[60] See C Dommen, 'Raising Human Rights Concerns in the WTO: Actors, Processes and Possible
Strategies', (2002) 24 Human Rights Q 1–50; G Loibl, 'International Economic Law' in M Evans

IMF and World Bank lend exclusively to developing and emerging economies. Furthermore, their loans are linked to [externally imposed] conditions that increasingly impinge on the domestic policies of the state'.[61] Similarly, the unfair trade rules and policies of the WTO (such as dumping of products of interest to African States, such as cotton; lack of duty-free, quota-free access to rich-states' markets for Least Developed Countries; overly complex rules of origin; and non-tariff barriers) impede developing states' capacity to raise resources from trade to invest in ESC rights.[62] With respect to such global actors, it has been observed that:

States determine the policies of some global actors, including the World Bank, the IMF and the WTO. When determining the policies of such global actors, a State must conform to its international human rights duties and must be respectful of other States' international human rights obligations. How a State discharges its duties when determining the policies of global actors must be subject to monitoring and accountability procedures as outlined in the preceding section.[63]

Therefore, influential states parties to human rights treaties as members of the IMF, the World Bank, and the WTO, are obliged to do all that they can 'to ensure that the policies and decisions of those organisations are in conformity with the obligations of states parties under the Covenant [ICESCR]'.[64] This may be achieved by, for example, voting against policies sought to be implemented by states seeking IMF/World Bank loans, such as Structural Adjustment Policies (SAPs) and Poverty Reduction Strategy Papers (PRSPs), where such policies fail to adequately integrate ESC rights and make provision for adequate Social Safety Nets (SSNs) or human rights impact assessments in implementing all the programmes. As a matter of law, a state's failure to take into account its human rights obligations when entering into agreements with NSAs would amount to a violation of the obligation to respect human rights. To this end, the ESCR Committee noted with respect to the right to work that:

The failure of States parties to take into account their legal obligations regarding the right to work when entering into bilateral or multilateral agreements with other States,

(ed), *International Law* (2003), 689–710; Report of the United Nations High Commissioner, 'The Impact of the Agreement on Trade Related Aspects of Intellectual Property Rights on Human Rights' E/CN.4/Sub2/2001/13 (27 June 2001). For overview of the WTO, see B Hoekman and M Kostecki, *The Political Economy of the World Trading System: The WTO and Beyond* (2nd edn), (OUP, 2001); Peter Van den Bossche, *The Law and Policy of the World Trade Organization: Text, Cases and Materials*, (Cambridge University Press, 2005).

[61] UNDP, *Human Development Report* (OUP, 2002), 114.

[62] Oxfam, *Africa and the Doha Round: Fighting to Keep Development Alive* (Oxfam Briefing Paper, Nov 2005) <http://www.oxfam.org.uk/what_we_do/issues/trade/downloads/bp80_africa_doha.pdf> accessed 22 April 2006.

[63] OHCHR, *Draft Guidelines: A Human Rights Approach to Poverty Reduction Strategies* (2002), para 244, at <http://www.unhchr.ch/development/povertyfinal.html> accessed 22 April 2006.

[64] See ESCR Committee, *Concluding Observations, United Kingdom of Great Britain and Northern Ireland*, E/C.12/1/add79, para 26; *Ireland*, E/C.12/1/add77, para 37; *Italy*, E/C.12/1/add43, para 20; *Germany*, E/C.12/1/add68, para 31; *Belgium*, E/C.12/1/add54, para 31; *Japan*, E/C.12/1/add67, para 37.

international organisations and other entities, such as multinational entities, constitutes a
violation of their obligation to respect the right to work.[65]

Similarly, when states are dealing with NSAs, the obligation to protect demands
that states take into account their domestic and international human rights obligations in all their activities with NSAs (including global actors like the World
Bank, the IMF, and the WTO) to ensure that the ESC rights, in particular, of the
most vulnerable, disadvantaged and marginalized groups of society, are not
undermined.[66] In a highly indebted state, this would mean that the state must pay
priority to the obligation to respect, protect, and fulfil its international human
rights obligations rather than the obligations relating to membership and agreements with the IMF and the World Bank.[67] It follows, therefore, that it is legitimate, for example, for a debtor state to 'integrate fully human rights, including
economic, social and cultural rights, in the formulation of the Poverty Reduction
Strategy Paper (PRSP)'[68] or refuse to implement loans and credit conditions that
conflict with its international human rights obligations assumed under the UN
Charter and international human rights treaties if this is necessary to ensure that
its human rights obligations are duly protected.[69] However, in practice the need
for financial resources (in the least developed states) could outweigh human rights
considerations, which limits the practical effectiveness of this approach.

In order to ensure that human rights issues are integrated into the policies of
global NSAs there is a need for a more concerted engagement with such actors.
It is essential to ensure that there is greater complementarity between the
basic tenets of international economic law and international human rights law,
while also combating some of the recent theorizing that seeks to privilege trade
law.[70] In addition, it is necessary to re-engage in a dialogue with the member
states of the WTO, the IMF, and the World Bank who, in the final analysis, will be

    [65] ESCR Committee, *General Comment 16*, para 33.
    [66] The ESCR Committee has affirmed this position in several of its Concluding Observations. See
eg, *Colombia*, E/C.12/1/add74, para 29; *Ecuador*, E/C.12/1/add100 (2004), para 53; *Egypt*,
E/C.12/1/add44 (2000), para 28; *Morocco*, E/C.12/1/add55; (2000), para 38; *Honduras*,
E/C.12/1/add57 (2001), paras 30 and 34; *Syrian Arab Republic*, E/C.12/1/add63 (2001), para 29.
    [67] This conclusion can be drawn from the recommendations of the ESCR Committee. See ESCR
Committee, *Concluding Observations, Zambia*, E/C.12/1/add106 (23 June 2005), para 36;
Concluding Observations, Senegal, E/C.12/1/add62 (24 Sept 2001), para 60.
    [68] ESCR Committee, *Concluding Observations, Senegal*, E/C.12/1/add62 (24 Sept 2001), para 50.
    [69] ESCR Committee, *Concluding Observations, Zambia*, E/C.12/1/add106 (23 June 2005),
para 36.
    [70] See eg, E Petersmann, 'Time for a United Nations "Global Compact" for Integrating Human
Rights Law into the Law of Worldwide Organization: Lessons from European Integration'
(2002)13(3) Eur J of Intl L 621. For a response to Petersmann see P Alston, 'Resisting the Merger and
Acquisition of Human Rights by Trade Law: A Reply to Petersmann' 13(4) Eur J of Intl L 815. See also
L Helfer, 'Human Rights and Intellectual Property: Conflict or Co-existence?' (2004) 22(2) *NQHR*,
167–179; C Dommen, 'The WTO, International Trade, and Human Rights' in M Windfuhr (ed),
Beyond the Nation State—Human Rights in Times of Globalization (Global Publications, 2005), ch 3.

vital to a determination of the extent to which the policies and decisions of these global actors are in conformity with the human rights obligations of states parties.[71]

V. Remedies against violations by NSAs

When violations by NSAs occur the state must not acquiesce to such violations. The state is obliged to take appropriate measures or to exercise due diligence to prevent, investigate, and punish the harm caused by NSAs[72] and, where appropriate, provide access to effective judicial or other appropriate remedies at the national level to any person or group who is a victim of a violation of any ESC rights by NSAs. All victims of human rights violations by NSAs should be entitled to adequate reparation, which may take the form of restitution, compensation, satisfaction, or guarantee of non-repetition. The ESCR Committee, for example, strongly urged Honduras to adopt and implement legislative and 'other measures' to protect workers from the occupational health hazards resulting from the use of toxic substances, such as pesticides and cyanide, in the banana-growing and gold-mining industries.[73] Similarly, the Committee recommended to the Russian Federation that 'action be taken to protect the indigenous peoples from exploitation by oil and gas companies'.[74] In Bosnia and Herzegovina, following privatization, employers arbitrarily dismissed employees or failed to pay employees' timely salaries or social security contributions.[75] The ESCR Committee recommended that 'the State party take effective measures to ensure that [private] employers respect their contractual obligations towards their employees, namely by refraining from arbitrarily dismissing them or by paying their salaries or social security contributions on time'.[76]

However, states where human rights protection is most needed are often those least able to enforce them against NSAs, such as TNCs, who possess much desired

---

[71] See eg, ESCR Committee: *Concluding Observations, United Kingdom of Great Britain and Northern Ireland*, E/C.12/1/add79 (2002), para 26; *Germany*, E/C.12/1/add68 (2001), para 31; *France*, E/C.12/1/add72 (2001), para 32; *Japan*, E/C.12/1/add67 (2001), para 37; *Belgium*, E/C.12/1/add54 (2000), para 31.

[72] See eg, R McCorquodale and R La Forgia, 'Taking off the Blindfolds: Torture by Non-State Actors' (2001)1(2) Human Rights L Rev, 189 at 217; ESCR Committee, *Concluding Observations, Ecuador*, E/C.12/1/add100 (2004), para 35. The Committee strongly urged 'the State party to implement legislative and administrative measures to avoid violations of environmental laws and rights by transnational companies'. See also *The Maastricht Guidelines on Violations of Economic, Social and Cultural Rights* (Maastricht, 22–26 Jan 1997), reproduced in (1998) 20 Human Rights Q, 691–705, para 18.

[73] ESCR Committee, *Concluding Observations, Honduraus*, E/C.12/1/add57 (21 May 2006) paras 24 and 38.

[74] ESCR Committee, *Concluding Observations, Russian Federation*, E/1998/22, paras 100 and 116.

[75] ESCR Committee, *Concluding Observations, Bosnia and Herzegovina*, E/C.12/BHI/CO/1 (24 Jan 2006), para 15.   [76] Ibid para 36.

investment capital or technology.[77] Given there current limitations of state power with respect to NSAs, what is presently required is to secure broad agreement among NSAs as to their human rights responsibility and the effective implementation of norms applicable to NSAs,[78] so that they are directly accountable to human rights standards for their actions that impact on human rights, particularly of vulnerable groups, such as women.[79] Establishing an effective framework acknowledging the human rights responsibilities of NSAs remains a challenge. One of the main problems in such arrangements is the question of who the NSAs will be responsible and accountable to in respect of ESC rights, which is now addressed below.

VI. Direct human rights responsibilities of NSAs with respect to ESC rights

While there is no doubt that the UDHR, the ICCPR, and the ICESCR envisage positive or negative obligations of states, and that the procedures for the implementation of the ICCPR and the ICESCR envisage actions only against states, it is obvious that NSAs—groups or persons—can also act in violation of the human rights of other persons enumerated in the above instruments.[80] As noted above, this is particularly true in the case of ESC rights given the general marginalization of this category of rights. As noted above, human rights law has traditionally concentrated on the actions of states. The assumption has been that it is states that have the obligation both for protecting human rights and for ensuring that human rights are not infringed, either by the state (or its agents) or by NSAs. But in the era of globalization, how credible is this concentration on state action? A plethora of NSAs now act on the international stage, but what direct human rights responsibilities, if any, do NSAs have under human rights law?

---

[77] P Redmond, 'Transnational Enterprise and Human Rights: Options for Standard Setting and Compliance' (2003) 37 (1) The Intl Lawyer, 69–102.

[78] Commission on Human Rights, Norms on the Responsibilities of Transnational Corporations and other Business Enterprises with regard to Human Rights, E/CN.4/Sub.2/2003/12/rev 2 (2003).

[79] R McCorquodale, 'Women, Development and Corporate Responsibility' in S Rees and S Wright (eds), *Human Rights, Corporate Responsibility: A Dialogue* (Pluto Press, 2000), at 174–190; J Oloka-Onyango, 'Who's Watching "Big Brother"? Globalization and the Protection of Cultural Rights in Present Day Africa' (2005) 4 Human Rights Q 1245–1273.

[80] See eg, the European Court of Human Rights acknowledgement in *Ireland v UK*, judgment at 18 Jan 1978, Series A no 25, (1979–80) 2 EHRR 25, para 149, that 'it is not called upon to take cognizance of every single aspect of the tragic situation prevailing in Northern Ireland. For example, it is not required to rule on the terrorist activities in the six counties of individuals or groups, *activities that are in clear disregard of human rights*' (emphasis added), quoted by C Warbrick, 'Terrorism and Human Rights', in J Symonides (ed), *Human Rights: New Dimensions and Challenges* (UNESCO, 1998), p 225.

A. Responsibilities of NSAs in international human rights instruments

The International Law Commission (ILC) Articles on the Responsibility of States for Internationally Wrongful Acts indicates that responsibility for human rights violations 'may accrue directly to any person or entity other than a State'.[81] The UDHR, arguably, establishes the basis of responsibility for NSAs. Article 29 of the UDHR provides that everyone has 'duties to the community'. In its preamble, it provides:

every individual and every organ of society . . . shall strive . . . to promote respect for these rights and . . . to secure their universal and effective recognition and observance.

This statement recognizes that human rights obligations apply not only to states but also to NSAs, in particular to 'every individual' and 'every organ of society'. NSAs such as corporations can be seen as 'organs of society' and, therefore, responsible under the UDHR to respect human rights.[82] More significantly, it implies that NSAs may shoulder more than the negative obligation engendered by human rights since they are obliged to 'secure' the observance of human rights. As Barbara Alexander noted:

if the drafters of the [Universal Declaration] intended to limit the scope of who should promote and recognise human rights to public, state actors, they could have used the phrase 'every State' rather than 'every organ of society'.[83]

In addition, both the ICESCR and the ICCPR expressly declare in their preambles that the individual is 'under responsibility to strive for the promotion and observance of the rights' recognized in the Covenants. With respect to the right to health, for example, the ESCR Committee has stated unambiguously:

While only States are parties to the Covenant and thus ultimately accountable for compliance with it, all members of society—individuals, including health professionals, families, local communities, intergovernmental and non-governmental organisations, civil society organisations, as well as the private business sector—have responsibilities regarding the realisation of the right to health.[84]

The implication here is two-fold. First, states should provide an environment that facilitates the discharge of such human rights responsibilities of NSAs. It follows

---

[81] ILC, *Final Articles on the Responsibility of States for Internationally Wrongful Acts*, UN doc A/56/10 (2001), art 33(2).

[82] See eg, J Paust, 'Human Rights Responsibilities of Private Corporations', (2002) 35 (3) Vanderbilt J of Transnational L, 810–815.

[83] See eg, BC Alexander, 'Lack of access to HIV/AIDS Drugs in Developing Countries: Is there a Violation of the International Human Rights to Health?' (2001) 8 (3) Human Rights Brief, 12 at 14.

[84] ESCR Committee, *General Comment 14* (2000) para 42; See also *General Comment 12* (1999) para 20.

that there may be circumstances in which a failure to progressively realize ESC rights as required by article 2(1) of the ICESCR would give rise to violations by states parties of those rights, as a result of states parties' permitting or failing to take appropriate measures or to exercise due diligence to prevent, punish, investigate, or redress the harm caused by such acts by private persons or entities. In *The Social and Economic Rights Action Center and the Center for Economic and Social Rights v Nigeria*,[85] it was alleged that the military government of Nigeria had been directly involved in oil production through the state oil company, the Nigerian National Petroleum Company (NNPC), the majority shareholder in a consortium with Shell Petroleum Development Corporation (SPDC), and that these operations had caused environmental degradation and health problems resulting from the contamination of the environment among the Ogoni People. It was argued that this breached several rights guaranteed under the ACHPR.[86] The African Commission on Human and Peoples' Rights observed, *inter alia*, in para 54:

> Undoubtedly and admittedly, the government of Nigeria, through NNPC has the right to produce oil, the income from which will be used to fulfil the economic and social rights of Nigerians. But the care that should have been taken ... and which would have protected the rights of the victims of the violations complained of was not taken. To exacerbate the situation, the security forces of the government engaged in conduct in violation of the rights of the Ogonis by attacking, burning and destroying several Ogoni villages and homes.

The Commission concluded in para 58:

> despite its obligation to protect persons against interferences in the enjoyment of their rights, the Government of Nigeria facilitated the destruction of the Ogoniland. Contrary to its Charter obligations and despite such internationally established principles, the Nigerian Government has given the green light to private actors, and the oil Companies in particular, to devastatingly affect the well-being of the Ogonis. By any measure of standards, its practice falls short of the minimum conduct expected of governments, and therefore, is in violation of Article 21 of the African Charter.[87]

Consequently, states must ensure that there are accessible, transparent, and effective monitoring and accountability mechanisms to regulate the conduct of NSAs like TNCs in order to ensure compliance with human rights responsibilities.[88] Secondly, NSAs—local, national, regional, and transnational—should take into account the human rights dimension of their policies and activities. In the context of the right to health, for example, drug companies have a 'soft law' obligation under the multilateral corporate codes of conduct to respect developing states'

---

[85] Communication no 155/96 (2001).

[86] Specifically, alleged violations of art 2, 4, 14, 16, 18(1), 21, and 24 of the ACHPR.

[87] Art 21(1) ACHPR provides: 'All peoples shall freely dispose of their wealth and natural resources. This right shall be exercised in the exclusive interest of the people. In no case shall a people be deprived of it.'

[88] See eg, R. Wai, 'Transnational Lift off and Juridical Touchdown: The Regulatory Function of Private International Law in an era of Globalisation', (2002) 40 Columbia J of Transnational L, 209.

efforts to protect the right to affordable HIV/AIDS treatment for all, including socially disadvantaged groups.[89]

It is also vital to note that both universal and regional human rights instruments prohibit both states and NSAs from engaging in any activity aimed at the destruction of human rights. For example, article 30 of the UDHR prohibits groups or persons any right to 'engage in any activity or to perform any act aimed at the destruction of any of the rights and freedoms set forth herein'. Similarly, both the ICCPR and ICESCR, in common article 5(1)—using almost identical language to that of article 30 of the UDHR stipulate that:

Nothing in the present Covenant may be interpreted as implying for any State, group or person any right to engage in any activity or perform any act aimed at the destruction of any of the rights and freedoms recognised herein or at their limitation to a greater extent than is provided for in the present Covenant.

Similar provisions are in the American Declaration of the Rights and Duties of Man[90] (articles 29–38), the ECHR (article 10(2)), the American Convention on Human Rights[91] (ACHR) (articles 13, 17, and 32), and the ACHPR (articles 27–29). Although these provisions are widely considered as mere guidelines for the behaviour of both individuals and states as opposed to imposing any direct accountability for NSAs,[92] they are not without legal implications. As at the time of writing, the jurisprudence on these provisions is scarce, but the Committee on the Elimination of Racial Discrimination has commented that a person's exercise of the right to freedom of opinion and expression carries special duties and responsibilities, specified in article 29(2) of the UDHR, 'among which the obligation not to disseminate racist ideas is of particular importance'.[93]

In sum, these provisions clearly apply not only to states but also to NSAs—groups and individuals. They forbid the abuse of human rights and forbid the misuse and exploitation of human rights instruments as a pretext for violating human rights.[94] As the ESCR Committee has observed with respect to the right to work:

Private enterprises—national and multinational—while not bound by the Covenant, have a particular role to play in job creation, hiring policies and non-discriminatory access to

[89] See generally, L Ferreira, 'Access to Affordable HIV/AIDS Drugs: The Human Rights Obligations of Multinational Pharmaceutical Corporations', (2002) 71 Fordham Law Review, 1133–1179.

[90] OAS res XXX, adopted by the Ninth International Conference of American States (1948).

[91] OAS Treaty Series 36; 1144 UNTS 123.

[92] See the study prepared for the Sub-Commission by the Special Rapporteur, Ms E-IA Daes, *Freedom of the Individual under Law: An Analysis of Article 29 of the Universal Declaration of Human Rights*, (United Nations, 1990), Human Rights Study Series no 3, Sales no E.89.XIV.5, para 2.

[93] General Recommendation XV on art 4 of the Convention, UN doc HRI\GEN\1\Rev 1 at 68 (1994), para 4.

[94] See, eg, P Sieghart, *The International Law of Human Rights*, (Clarendon Press, 1990), p 105 and T Opsahl, 'Articles 29 and 30: the other side' in A Eide, G Alfredsson, G Melander, LA Rehof, and A Rosas (eds), *The Universal Declaration of Human Rights: A Commentary* (Scandinavian University Press, 1992) p 465.

work. They should conduct their activities on the basis of legislation, administrative measures, codes of conduct and other appropriate measures promoting respect for the right to work, agreed between the government and civil society. Such measures should recognise the labour standards elaborated by ILO and aim at increasing the awareness and responsibility of enterprises in the realisation of the right to work.[95]

Therefore, while only states are parties to the existing human rights treaties and thus ultimately accountable for compliance with them, all members of society (NSAs—individuals, local communities, trade unions, civil society, and private sector organizations) have responsibilities regarding the realization of ESC rights. As a minimum, NSAs must respect states' human rights obligations. They must, therefore, refrain from acts or omissions that violate all human rights. Respecting ESC rights requires NSAs not to adopt, and to repeal laws and rescind policies, administrative measures and programmes that do not conform to states' human rights obligations including those with respect to ESC rights. One has to note that the shift in state sovereignty accompanying globalization has meant that NSAs are increasingly getting more involved in activities that impact (directly and/or indirectly) on human rights, and have gained more power to violate human rights.[96] Therefore, limiting human rights obligations to states only would defeat the object and purpose of human rights since:

Human rights are about upholding humans and protecting individuals and groups from oppressive power primarily in the context of the communities within which they live. That oppressive power can come from any source [which may be a State or a NSA]. It does not have to be political; it can be economic, social, cultural, or any other type of power.[97]

According to the UN Truth Commission on El Salvador, NSAs—in this case referring to the Farabundo Marti National Liberation Front—are subject to international human rights law. In the words of the Commission: '[w]hen insurgents assume government powers in territories under their control, they too can be required to observe certain human rights obligations that are binding for the State under international human rights law'.[98] As shown below, this view should extend to all other NSAs exercising powers akin to or even greater than that of a state especially in the field of marginalized ESC rights.[99]

However, the great majority of NSAs pay little more than lip service to ESC rights and are based in, or funded by those living in, developed states and they

---

[95] ESCR Committee, *General Comment 18*, para 52.

[96] See D Shelton, 'Protecting Human Rights in a Globalized World', (2002) 25 Boston College Intl and Comparative L Rev 273–322.

[97] See R McCorquodale, 'Overlegalizing Silences: Human Rights and Non-State Actors', (2002) 96 American Society of Intl L Proceedings 384, at 387.   [98] UN doc S/25500, annex, p 20.

[99] See J Oloka-Onyango, 'Reinforcing Marginalised Rights in the Age of Globalization: International Mechanisms, Non-State Actors and the Struggle for Peoples Rights in Africa', (2003) 18 (4) American U Intl L Rev, 851–914; M Freeman, *Human Rights: An Interdisciplinary Approach*, (Polity, 2002), 166; S Agbakwa, 'Reclaiming Humanity: Economic, Social and Cultural Rights as the Cornerstone of African Human Rights' (2000) 5 Yale Hum Rts & Dev LJ 177 at 178.

tend to be concerned primarily with civil and political rights. This means that most NSAs are able to violate ESC rights without being questioned.[100] This is partly because of the view that 'economic and social human rights are costly to secure',[101] or that ESC rights are non-binding 'principles and programmatic objectives rather than legal obligations that are justiciable'.[102] Such views reflect the marginalization of vulnerable individuals and groups, who are meant to be the primary beneficiary of this category of rights. It is vital to note that the continuing reluctance to accord ESC rights the same level of recognition and enforceability demonstrates the 'gendered' character of international human rights law.[103] This is because it is generally girls and women as a social class and as primary care givers who most acutely experience the violation and non-realization of this category of rights.[104]

It is important to recall that treaties are made to be performed.[105] NSAs, therefore, should not (as a minimum) contribute to a state's failure to comply with a treaty obligation concerning ESC rights.[106] Indeed human rights treaties are of a special character since they:

are not multilateral treaties of the traditional type concluded to accomplish the reciprocal exchange of rights for the mutual benefit of the contracting States. Their object and purpose is the protection of the basic rights of individual human beings, irrespective of their nationality, both against the State of their nationality and all other contracting States.[107]

[100]   C Jochnick, 'Confronting the Impunity of Non-State Actors: New Fields for the Promotion of Human Rights', (1999) 21(1) Human Rights Q 56–79.

[101]   See eg, P Harvey, 'Human Rights and Economic Policy Discourse: Taking Economic and Social Rights Seriously', (2002) 33 Columbia Human Rights L Rev 363 at 471.

[102]   See eg, ESCR Committee, *Concluding Observation: United Kingdom* E/C.12/1/add 79, para 11 (June 2002) and E/C/12/1/add 19, para 10 (Dec 1997). See also V Gauri, *Social Rights and Economics: Claims to Health Care and Education in Developing Countries*, Policy Research Working Paper 3006 (World Bank Development Research Group), (20 March 2003) p 16.

[103]   H Charlesworth and C Chinkin, *The Boundaries of International Law: A Feminist Analysis*, (Manchester University Press, 2000) pp 231–244. D Buss and A Manji (eds), *International Law: Modern Feminist Approaches* (Hart, 2005).

[104]   By the end of 2003, a UNESCO study disclosed that girls in fifty-four states still faced discrimination in access to education, with girls in sub-Saharan Africa, Pakistan, India, and China especially affected. See EFA, *Global Education Monitoring Report* 2003/4, ch 3. Se also J Spectar, 'The Hydra hath but One Head: The Socio-Cultural Dimensions of the Aids Epidemic & Women's Right to Health' (2001) 21 Boston College Third World L J 1–34.

[105]   P. Reuter, *Introduction to Law of Treaties* (2nd edn, Kegan Press, 1995) para 44.

[106]   See Vienna Convention on the Law of Treaties (VCLT) 1969, UKTS (1980) No 58, vol II, art 26: 'Every treaty in force is binding on the parties to it and must be performed by them in good faith.' (Although this provision of the VCLT does not apply directly to NSAs since they are not 'parties to it', the object and purpose of the VCLT would be defeated if NSAs undermine states' obligations to perform treaty obligations in good faith. Indeed, art 26 VCLT might be seen as declaratory of customary international law.) See D Harris, *International Law: Cases and Materials* (6th edn, Sweet & Maxwell, 2004), ch 10; A Aust, *Modern Treaty Law and Practice* (Cambridge University Press, 2000), ch 10.

[107]   Inter American Court of Human Rights, *The Effect of Reservations on the Entry in Force of the American Convention*, Advisory Opinion OC-2/82 of 24 Sept 1982, para 29. See also European Commission on Human Rights, *Austria v Italy*, Appl 788/60 (1961). 4 Eur Ybk of Human Rights 116, at 140.

If this object and purpose is to be meaningfully achieved, NSAs must not undermine state efforts to comply with their human rights obligations. Therefore, there is a dire need for NSAs to take more seriously their human rights responsibilities with respect to ESC rights on the international, regional, and domestic fronts.[108] In many respects, violations of ESC rights, are treated far less seriously by states and NSAs than if they occurred in relation to civil and political rights, when they would provoke 'expressions of horror and outrage'.[109] It is rare, for example, to hear of discussions of 'massive and direct denials of economic, social and cultural rights'[110] (such as systematic and large-scale violations of rights to food, housing, health, and education) in relation to the subject of torture or cruel, inhuman, or degrading treatment,[111] genocide, or crimes against humanity.[112] The denial of civil and political rights is considered as a 'violation', while the denial of ESC rights is generally viewed as an 'injustice'.[113] As the world increasingly becomes internationalized, decisions, policies, and operations of NSAs may have significant effects on lives (and human rights) of individuals and groups in local communities. Some two examples—the IMF and the World Bank—are briefly reviewed below.

B. The IMF, World Bank, and human rights

Since the formation of the IMF and the World Bank, they have showed very little interest in human rights when dealing with states claiming that these are 'political' issues within a state's domestic affairs.[114] This was first clearly manifested when both the IMF and the World Bank declined the invitation from the UN Commission on Human Rights to participate in the drafting of the ICESCR.[115]

---

[108] S Ruxton and R Karim, *Beyond Civil Rights: Developing Economic, Social, and Cultural Rights in the UK* (Oxfam, 2001) pp 1–49; C Puta-Chekwe and N Flood, 'From Division to Integration: Economic, Social, and Cultural Rights as Basic Human Rights' in I Merali and V Oosterveld (eds), *Giving Meaning to Economic, Social, and Cultural Rights* (University of Pennsylvania Press, 2001), pp 39–51; and generally T Merish, *Protecting Economic, Social and Cultural Rights in the Inter-American Human Rights System: A Manual on Presenting Claims* (Yale Law School, 2002).

[109] See Statement of ESCR Committee to the Vienna World Conference, UN doc E/1993/22, annex III, para 5.

[110] ESCR Committee, *Report on the Seventh Session*, ESCOR, 1993, supp no 2 (UN doc E/1993/22), annex III.

[111] J McBride, 'The Violation of Economic, Social and Cultural Rights as Torture or Cruel, Inhuman or Degrading Treatment' in G Van Bueren (ed), *Childhood Abused: Protecting Children against Torture, Cruel, Inhuman and Degrading Treatment and Punishment* (Ashgate, 1998) pp 107–116.

[112] S Skogly, 'Crimes Against Humanity-Revisited: Is There a Role for Economic and Social Rights', (2001) 5 (1) The Intl J of Human Rights 58.

[113] See, 'Composite Flows and the Relationship to Refugee Outflows, including Return of persons not in need of international protection, as well as facilitation of return in its global dimension', in UNHCR Standing Committee, 12th meeting (EC/48/SC/CRP.29).

[114] For an overview of the case for and against using the World Bank to enforce and/or monitor human rights, see H Moris, 'The World Bank and Human Rights: Indispensable Partnership or Mismatched Alliance?' (1997) 4 ILSA J of Intl & Comp L, 174–200.

[115] UN Economic and Social Council, Co-operation Between the Commission on Human Rights and the Specialised Agencies and Other Organs of the United Nations in the Consideration of Economic, Social and Cultural Rights, UN doc E/CN.4/534 (1951), annex, 4–5.

Likewise, in the 1960s, the UN General Assembly passed a series of resolutions successively 'inviting', 'urging', and 'requesting' the Bank to stop lending to South Africa and Portugal because of their respective apartheid and colonial policies, but the Bank insisted on its apolitical character and approved several loans in defiance of the UN resolutions.[116] Both institutions may affect the lives and rights of the people through their policies, and in case of the World Bank through the projects it funds directly.[117] For example, the IMF and World Bank's policy of privatization of hitherto public enterprises (without adequate social safety nets) has, in some respects, had a negative effect on ESC rights in several states.[118]

Despite this, the World Bank and IMF have argued that they are bound by their Articles of Agreement to be 'non-political' in their approach and give due regard to 'only economic considerations'.[119] In paying limited or no attention to human rights by the two institutions, it has been stressed that there is 'need to honour the charter of each organization and to respect the specialization of different international organs as reflected in the statutory requirements of their respective charters.'[120] It is claimed, for example, that drawing the Bank, which is 'an international financial institution, directly into politically charged areas, with their typical vagaries and double standards, can only politicise its work and jeopardise its credibility, both in the financial markets from which it borrows and in the member countries to which it lends'.[121] To this end, Shihata has argued:

The role of the Bank is to promote the economic development of its member countries. Its success in this role helps to create an environment for the enjoyment by individuals in these countries of all their human rights. . . . But it demeans the organisation to ignore its charter and act outside its legal powers.[122]

---

[116] See SA Bleicher, 'UN v IBRD: A Dilemma of Functionalism' (1970) 24 *Intl Organisation* 31.

[117] See DD Bradlow and C Grossman, 'Limited Mandate and Intertwined Problems: A New Challenge for the World Bank and IMF' (1995) 17 Human Rights Q 411 at 426; B Sadasivam, 'The Impact of Structural Adjustment on Women: A Governance and Human Rights Agenda' (1997) 19 (3) Human Rights Q 630 at 648–9.

[118] This has been noted in several Concluding Observations of the ESCR Committee. See eg, *Algeria*, E/C.12/1/add 71 (2001); *Argentina*, E/C.12/1/add 38 (1999); *Bulgaria*, E/C.12/1/add 37 (1999); *Cameroon*, E/C.12/1/add40 (1999); *Colombia*, E/C.12/1/add 74 (2001); *Egypt*, E/C.12/1/add 44 (2000); *El Salvador*, E/C.12/1/add 4 (1996); *Honduras*, E/C.12/1/add 57 (2001); *Republic of Korea*, E/C.12/1/add 59 (2001); *Nepal*, E/C.12/1/add 66 (2001); *Netherlands*, E/C.12/1/add 25 (1998); *Nicaragua*, E/C.12/1993/14 (1994); *Romania*, E/C.12/1994/4 (1994); *Senegal*, E/C.12/1/add 62 (2001); *Senegal*, E/C.12/1993/18 (1993); *Solomon Islands*, E/C.12/1/add 33 (1999); *Venezuela*, E/C.12/1/add 56 (2001). See also Commission on Human Rights, Report of the Expert Seminar on Human Rights and Extreme Poverty, 7–10 Feb 2001, E/CN.4/2001/54/add 1, para 14.

[119] See eg, IBRD Articles of Agreement, art IV, s 10, art III, s 5(b); IDA Articles of Agreement, art V, s 6, art V, s 1(g); IMF Articles of Agreement, art IV, s 3(b). For the analysis, see I Shihata, *The World Bank in a Changing World: Selected Essays and Lectures*, vol II (Nijhoff, 1995) pp 557–576; I Shihata, *The World Bank in a Changing World*, vol III (Nijhoff, 2000) pp 155–186; J Gold, 'Political Considerations are Prohibited by Articles of Agreement When the Fund Considers Requests for the Use of Resources', *IMF Survey* 146–148 (IMF 23 May 1983).

[120] I Shihata, 'Democracy and Development' (1997) 46 Intl and Comparative L Q 635 at 638.

[121] Shihata (1995) (n 119 above) p 578; Shihata (2000) (n 119 above) p 152.

[122] Shihata (1995) (n 119 above) pp 567 and 574.

Likewise, the IMF argued that human rights are a full responsibility of the individual governments and that 'rights cannot be realised in the absence of structural adjustment'.[123] The IMF has also argued that human rights protection was not explicitly included within its mandate[124] and that its founding Charter mandates that (as a monetary agency) it pays attention only to issues of an economic nature[125] and requires it to 'respect the domestic social and political policies of members'.[126]

The question that arises here is whether the World Bank and the IMF will be acting outside their charters or legal powers when they respect (or even promote) all human rights in the formulation of their policies and activities. In other words are human rights issues 'political' affairs and thus barred from any consideration by the two institutions? In fact, except for references to 'raising conditions of labour'[127] and 'maintenance of high levels of employment and income',[128] there are no direct human rights links from the Articles of Agreement of the two institutions. In addition, the two institutions are not parties to human rights treaties protecting ESC rights,[129] and accordingly not bound, *strictu sensu*, by human rights treaties and have not accepted the implementation mechanism for the existing human rights treaties.

It is essential to note that in the agreements between the UN Economic and Social Council (ECOSOC) and the IMF[130] and the World Bank,[131] entered into in accordance with articles 63 and 57 of the UN Charter establishing the latter's status as UN specialized agencies, greater autonomy, and independence is left to the two institutions from the UN[132] and neither human rights nor even articles 55 and 56 of the UN Charter are referred to. However, article 103 of the UN

---

[123] UN doc E/C4/Sub2/1991/63, para 7. It is argued that costs from SAPs are short-term and give rise to greater long-term benefits. It is also claimed that deterioration would be further in absence of SAPs.   [124] E/C.12/1994/SR.20, paras 1 and 18.

[125] J van Themaat, 'Some Notes on IMF Conditionality with a Human Face' in P De Waart, P Peters, and E Denters, *International Law and Development* (Nijhoff 1988) p 229; B Rajagopal, 'Crossing the Rubicon: Synthesizing the Soft International Law of the IMF and Human Rights', (1993) 11 Boston Intl L J 81, at 93; G Bird, 'The IMF and Developing Countries: A Review of the Evidence and Policy Options', (1996) *International Organisations*, 477–511.

[126] Articles of Agreement of IMF, 2 UNTS 39, art IV, s 3(b). The Articles were subsequently amended in 1969, 1978, and 1992 available at <http://www.imf.org/external/pubs/ft/aa/index.htm> accessed 25 April 2006.   [127] World Bank's Articles of Agreement, art I (iii).

[128] IMF's Articles of Agreement, art I (ii).

[129] Art 26 (1) ICESCR refers only to states as being capable to become parties and it would seem that international organizations cannot directly become parties to the Covenant.

[130] Agreement entered into force 15 Nov 1947, printed in *Selected Decisions of the IMF and Selected Documents* (13th issue) (IMF 1987) p 475.

[131] Agreement between the UN and the IBRD. (The Agreement formalized the relationship between the UN and the IBRD. It was approved by the United Nations General Assembly on 15 Nov 1947.) See World Bank Group Archives, <http://web.worldbank.org/external/default/main?pagePK=64319200&piPK=64323128&theSitePK=29506> accessed 25 April 2006.

[132] For eg, art 1(2) of the Agreement between UN and the IMF states, *inter alia*, that: 'The Fund is a specialized agency.... By reason of the nature of its international responsibilities... the Fund is, and is required to function as, an independent international organisation.' The IBRD/UN Agreement has a similar provision.

Charter links the two institutions' Articles to the Charter.[133] As such it has a direct influence on the way in which human rights come into play in terms of policies of the IMF and the World Bank.[134] Therefore, the IMF and the World Bank Articles of Agreement should be interpreted and applied in a manner that respects all human rights. To achieve this, the IMF and the World Bank (through their credit agreements and policies) must refrain from undermining ESC rights for all persons, especially disadvantaged and marginalized individuals and groups. This calls for the integration of human rights in the formulation of the policies of the two institutions.

In fact, human rights issues are implicitly part of the development[135] mandate of the World Bank and central to the success of the poverty alleviation programmes of the Bank and the IMF. As a result of several criticisms of the World Bank policies, the Bank has acknowledged in its Comprehensive Development Framework (CDF) that '[w]ithout the protection of human and property rights, and a comprehensive framework of laws, no equitable development is possible'.[136] It has also noted that 'creating the conditions for the attainment of human rights is a central and irreducible goal of development'.[137] Thus, the World Bank issued a set of guidelines linking its activities to human rights[138] and acknowledged that 'ensuring sustainable development requires attention not just to economic growth but also to environmental and social issues'[139] including poverty and inequality reduction and prevention of armed conflicts and terrorism.[140] In the Bank's view 'ending global poverty is much more than a moral imperative—it is the cornerstone of a sustainable world'.[141] To this end the World Bank together with the IMF have since 1995 been active in designing mechanisms to address the issue of

---

[133] Art 103 of the UN Charter provides that the obligations of the Charter prevail over other international agreements. In (1982) YILC, vol I, p 20, para 12, one member of the ILC interpreted art 103 to mean that 'the UN Charter... (is) hierarchically superior to those of any other treaty, whether earlier or later.'

[134] SI Skogly, *The Human Rights Obligations of the World and the International Monetary Fund* (Cavendish, 2001) p 27.

[135] The UN Declaration on the Right to Development, adopted by GA res 41/128 of 4 Dec 1986 states in its preamble that 'all human rights and fundamental freedoms are indivisible and interdependent and that, in order to promote development, equal attention and urgent consideration should be given to the implementation, promotion and protection of civil, political, economic, and social rights...'. See also I Brownlie, 'The Human Right to Development' in D Hunter *et al*, *International Environmental Law and Policy* (Foundation Press 1998), p 331; A Sen, *Development as Freedom* (Anchor Books, 1999); AK Sengupta, UN doc E/CN.4/2001/WG.18/2, para 9.

[136] <http://www.worldbank.org/cdf> accessed 25 April 2006.

[137] 'Development and Human Rights: The Role of the World Bank' (1998) at <http://www.worldbank.org/html/extdr/rights/hrintro.htm> accessed 25 April 2006.

[138] IBRD/World Bank, *Development and Human Rights: The Role of the World Bank* (The World Bank, 1998). For a background to status of human rights in the World Bank, see Lawyers Committee for Human Rights and Institute for Policy Research and Advocacy (ELSAM), *In the Name of Development: Human Rights and the World Bank in Indonesia* (ELSAM, 1995) pp 13–33.

[139] IBRD/World Bank, *World Development Report 2003: Sustainable Development in a Dynamic World* (The World Bank, 2003), 1.   [140] Ibid pp 2 and 157.

[141] Ibid p 184.

debt burden, culminating in what came to be known, in 1996, as the Heavily Indebted Poor Countries (HIPC) initiative[142], which was later broadened in October 1999 to increase the number of eligible states under the Enhanced HIPC Initiative. For a debtor state to qualify for this initiative, it must demonstrate, *inter alia*, that it will 'implement a full-fledged poverty reduction strategy, which has been prepared with broad participation of civil society, and an agreed set of measures aimed at enhancing economic growth'.[143] It is worth noting, first, that although the alleviation of poverty and debt relief is essential for enjoyment of ESC rights, the Bank, like the IMF, still lacks a coherent human rights policy to fully integrate human rights in the PRSPs and its debt relief is not enough to lift the HIPC out of poverty. Secondly, the Bank has claimed that it is 'concerned by human rights' but 'its mandate does not extend to political human rights'.[144]

It has to be noted, however, that internationally recognized human rights (whether civil and political or economic, social, and cultural) are of international concern that transcends 'political affairs' and autonomous jurisdiction of a state.[145] As a result, since the projects funded by the World Bank and programmes of the Bank and the IMF impact on the enjoyment of human rights, it is essential to ensure that they do not negatively impact on or violate human rights, even if they are to lead to economic development in the long run. International human rights instruments must not be subordinated to the charters of the agencies in question when, as a matter of law, the reverse should be the case.[146]

In conformity with articles 22 and 23 of the ICESCR, the IMF, and the World Bank should (through their lending policies and credit agreements) co-operate effectively with states to implement ESC rights at the national level, bearing in mind their own mandates. The minimum core obligation incumbent directly upon both the World Bank and the IMF as specialized agencies of the UN system and subjects of international law is a duty of vigilance to ensure that their policies and programs do not facilitate breaches of their member states' human rights treaty obligations.[147] This calls for a clear and consistent human rights impact

---

[142] I Shihata, *The World Bank in a Changing World: Selected Essays*, vol III (Nijhoff, 2000), pp 365–379. There are about 40 HIPC, most of which are located in Sub-Saharan Africa.

[143] IMF, 'IMF and World Bank Support Debt Relief for Uganda' Press Release No 00/34, (2 May 2000).

[144] World Bank, *The Inspection Panel Report and Recommendation on Request for inspection, Chad: Petroleum Development and Pipeline Project*, (2001), xxviii.

[145] JD Ciorciari, 'The Lawful Scope of Human Rights Criteria in World Bank Credit Decisions: An Interpretive Analysis of the IBRD and IDA Articles of Agreement', (2000) 33 Cornell Intl L J, 331; G Brodnig, *The World Bank and Human Rights: Mission Impossible?*, Carr Centre for Human Rights Policy Working Paper, T-01–05, 18.

[146] J Oloka-Onyango and D Udagama, 'Human Rights as the primary objective of international trade, investment and finance policy and practice', UN doc E/CN.4/Sub.2/1999/11, para 33; Skogly (n 134 above) 108–9.

[147] M Darrow, *Between Light and Shadow: The World Bank, the International Monetary Fund and International Human Rights Law* (Hart, 2003) p 295.

assessment[148] (to give effect to the universality of human rights) in project/programme identification, preparation, appraisal, loan negotiation, implementation, and evaluation (post-audit) for the World Bank and similar stages in negotiations and release of funds for the IMF.[149]

This would ensure, at the very minimum, that the policies and programmes of the two institutions (such as privatization of social security schemes, health care, and education) in pursuit of their respective charter obligations do not violate already existing human rights or make it worse.[150] With respect to Zambia, for example, the ESCR Committee expressed its concern in June 2005 'about the fact that privatized social security schemes in the state party have not been financially sustainable, thereby leaving its beneficiaries without adequate social protection'.[151] It recommended:

Zambia's obligations under the Covenant be taken into account in all aspects of its negotiations with international financial institutions, such as the International Monetary Fund and the World Bank, so as to ensure that the rights enshrined in the Covenant are duly protected, for all Zambians, and, in particular for the most disadvantaged and marginalized groups of society. The Committee refers the State party to its statement to the Third Ministerial Conference of the World Trade Organization adopted at its twenty-first session in 1999 (E/2000/22-E/C.12/1999/11, annex VII).[152]

Therefore, there is dire need for integration of international human rights into policies of the IMF including the poverty reduction strategies[153] to make them 'effective, sustainable, inclusive, equitable and meaningful to those living in poverty.'[154]

VII. Conclusion

This chapter has focused on only a handful of the many issues that arise in the debate over the human rights obligations of NSAs. From the foregoing, the following conclusions can be drawn. First, international human rights law is historically, and will remain (at least in the near future), essentially state-centred.

[148] K Tomasevski, 'International Development Finance Agencies', in A Eide *et al* (eds), *Economic, Social and Cultural Rights: A Textbook,* (Nijhoff, 1995) 403–413, 410.
[149] Skogly (n 134 above) 163–166.
[150] IMF Staff, 'Policies for Faster Growth and Poverty Reduction in Sub-Saharan Africa and the Role of the IMF', (Dec, 2000).
[151] ESCR Committee, *Concluding Observations, Zambia*, E/C.12/1/add106 (23 June 2005), para 22.   [152] Ibid para 36.
[153] For guidelines see OHCHR, *Draft Guidelines on a Human Rights Approach to Poverty Reduction Strategies*, 10 June 2002. Also E Carrasco, 'Critical issues facing the Bretton Woods system: Can the IMF, World Bank, and the GATT/WTO promote an enabling environment for social development?' (1996) 6 Transnational L & Cont. Problems, i–xx.
[154] ESCR Committee, *Statement on Poverty and the ICESCR*, 10 May 2001, E/C.12/2001/10, para 13.

Currently, there are limited direct human rights obligations for NSAs. As noted above, states where protection of human rights against violations by NSAs is most needed are often those least able to enforce them against NSAs, such as international financial institutions and TNCs—the main driving agents of the global economy, exercising control over global trade, investment, and technology transfers—who possess much desired investment capital or technology. Secondly, given the current limitations of state power with respect to NSAs, it is necessary that NSAs (defined broadly to include international organizations) should accept some moral human rights obligations but at present they have no clearly defined legal obligations to respect human rights apart from compliance with the legal regime of the particular state in which they are operating. Undoubtedly, however, NSAs do have a role to play in the progressive realization of ESC rights. As this chapter makes clear, the era of NSAs to respect ESC rights has arrived. The question is how can this be legally realized; should NSAs be directly liable for their violations of ESC rights under international human rights law or should they continue to be indirectly liable through states and should states have a duty under international human rights law to move against NSAs that violate ESC rights within their respective jurisdictions?

Although there is no consensus on the above issue, it is clear that in the era of globalization, it is not enough to look only to the state as the primary actor to respect, protect, and fulfil human rights. A considerable number of other actors other than states—with powers akin to, or even more than state power—(including multilateral institutions like the World Bank and IMF, and TNCs), should be equally obliged to respect human rights. In short, therefore, human rights should be everyone's responsibility. Thus, NSAs should support the emerging global framework for human rights responsibilities of NSAs as a means to achieve good governance, encourage participation, strengthen their own anticorruption controls, and provide assistance in ways that strengthen states human rights obligations.[155] Consequently, making space in the legal regime to take account of the role of NSAs in the realization of ESC rights, and their accountability for the violations of ESC rights, remains a critical challenge facing international human rights law today. In this arrangement, it should be possible to bring claims of human rights violations (including violations of ESC rights) not only against the state but also against NSAs directly. As privatization, outsourcing, and downsizing place ever more public or governmental functions into the hands of NSAs, the human rights regime must adapt to those changes if it is to maintain its relevance.[156] It is in this

---

[155] The World Bank, *Global Monitoring Report 2006: Millennium Development Goals: Strengthening Mutual Accountability, Aid, Trade, and Governance,* (The World Bank, 2006), 177 noting that 'international financial institutions (IFIs) are essential parts of the global governance framework, especially for poor countries. Their efforts include bolstering their own anticorruption controls, improving transparency, encouraging adherence to internationally recognized standards and codes, and working with their clients to encourage domestic accountability.'

[156] See, generally, K De Feyter and F Gomez Isa (eds), *Privatisation and Human Rights in the Age of Globalization,* (Intersentia, 2005); Alston (n 16 above).

context that there is increasing recognition that 'it is essential to ensure human rights obligations fall where power is exercised, whether it is in the local village or at the international meeting rooms of the WTO, the World Bank or the IMF'.[157]

It is vital for the effectiveness of international human rights law that NSAs take more account of human rights in their decision-making in order to ensure that they remain relevant for all members of the international community. Indeed, it is becoming increasingly important that all decision-making by NSAs—local, national, regional, and global—should take consistently and comprehensively human rights issues into account. As a minimum, policies and programs of NSAs must not facilitate breaches of their member states' human rights treaty and customary obligations. With respect to international financial institutions, they should pay greater attention to the protection of ESC rights in their lending policies, structural adjustment programmes, poverty alleviation programmes, and credit agreements. Whether international human rights law will develop to protect adequately against violations of human rights by NSAs, and hold, effectively, all NSAs directly accountable for violations of ESC rights, remains to be seen. The challenge that faces human rights activists is to reflect on the most appropriate manner in which to enhance the obligations of NSAs with respect to ESC rights. As a starting point, it is necessary to integrate consistently the human rights principles of non-discrimination, monitoring, democratic participation, and accountability at each step of the process of making and applying the policies and decisions of NSAs.

---

[157] M Robinson, 'From Rhetoric to Reality: Making Human Rights Work' (2003) 1 Eur Human Rights L Rev 1 at 5–6; M Robinson, 'Shaping Globalisation: The Role of Human Rights' in ASIL, *Proceedings of the 97th Annual Meeting*, 1–12.

PART III

REGIONAL AND COMPARATIVE
UNDERSTANDINGS OF
ESC RIGHTS

7

The African Commission on Human and Peoples' Rights and the Implementation of Economic, Social, and Cultural Rights in Africa

Mashood A. Baderin*

I. Introduction

In Chinua Achebe's African novel, *Arrow of God*, Ezeulu, an African chief priest, broke kola nut[1] and prayed to the gods thus:

[M]ay you live, and all your people. I too will live with all my people. *But life alone is not enough. May we have the things with which to live it well. For there is a kind of slow and weary life which is worse than death.*[2]

The last three sentences of that prayer depict what the concept of economic, social, and cultural rights (ESC rights) is all about, that is, to ensure that human beings have the things with which to live life well and prevent a slow and weary life which is worse than death. However, this can hardly be realized by prayers to the gods or by wishes alone without concerted human effort in that regard, particularly the concerted efforts of managers of the affairs of state. Owing to the connection of ESC rights to good governance and human development, and given the prevailing socio-economic malaise and poor governance in African states generally, the importance of promoting the full realization of ESC rights in Africa cannot be over-emphasized to prevent the type of slow and weary life despised by the chief priest in the *Arrow of God*. Many human rights scholars and

* I thank Professor David J Harris for his academic guidance as my personal tutor during my LLM studies and as my PhD supervisor at the School of Law, University of Nottingham and for his continued support thereafter.
    [1] Kola nut is a fruit with lobes, which, in the custom of many African tribes, is traditionally broken into small pieces by chiefs and/or elders on special occasions, shared, chewed, and prayers offered to the gods.   [2] C Achebe, *Arrow of God* (Heinemann Ltd, 1989) p 95 (emphasis added).

activists have, in the last few years, re-echoed the call that an earnest recourse to the guarantee of ESC rights by African states is the 'only means of self-defence for millions of impoverished and margnalized individuals and groups' in Africa.[3]

The African Charter on Human and Peoples' Rights (ACHPR or the Charter) was adopted in 1981, seventeen years after that prayer by the chief priest in the *Arrow of God*,[4] and was twenty years in force on 21 October 2006. The preamble of the Charter expressed the conviction of African states and members of the then Organization of African Unity (OAU) that the realization of ESC rights was necessary for both the guarantee of civil and political rights and for the promotion of development on the continent.[5] The Charter not only provided for the guarantee of specific ESC rights in Africa but also provided for the establishment of the African Commission on Human and Peoples' Rights as its implementation mechanism. Although the ACHPR is relatively younger than both the International Covenant on Economic, Social and Cultural Rights (ICESCR)[6] and the European Social Charter,[7] twenty years in force is long enough for an evaluation of the implementation of the ESC rights under the ACHPR in Africa.

This chapter will therefore assess the implementation of ESC rights under the African human rights system through a critical evaluation of the activities of the African Commission on Human and Peoples' Rights (the Commission). In the process, the chapter will also highlight possible ways of enhancing the realization of the ESC rights guaranteed under the Charter. We will begin with an analysis of the scope of the ESC rights under the Charter.

II. The scope of ESC rights under the ACHPR

An important uniqueness of the ACHPR is that, unlike the two United Nations (UN) Covenants,[8] the European Convention on Human Rights (ECHR)[9], and

---

[3] R Kunnemann, 'A Coherent Approach to Human Rights' (1995) 17 Human Rights Q 323 at 332.   [4] The *Arrow of God* (n 2 above) was first published in 1964.
[5] See preambular para 8 of the African Charter of Human and Peoples' Rights (OAU doc CAB/LEG/67/3 rev 5; reprinted in (1982) 21 International Legal Materials, 58) adopted on 27 June 1981, which provides that the African States and Members of the OAU were convinced 'that it is henceforth essential to pay particular attention to the right to development and that civil and political rights cannot be dissociated from economic, social and cultural rights in their conception as well as universality and that the satisfaction of economic, social and cultural rights is a guarantee for the enjoyment of civil and political rights'.
[6] Adopted on 16 Dec 1966; 993 UN Treaty Series, p 3.
[7] Adopted on 18 Oct 1961; Council of Europe Treaty Series, no 035.
[8] Under the UN system, economic, social, and cultural rights (ESC rights) are provided for separately in the International Covenant on Economic, Social and Cultural Rights (ICESCR), while civil and political rights (CP rights) are provided for in the International Covenant on Civil and Political Rights (ICCPR).
[9] Under the European system, the European Convention on the Protection of Human Rights and Fundamental Freedoms (1950) provides mainly for CP rights, while ESC rights are provided for under the European Social Charter later adopted in 1961.

the American Convention on Human Rights (ACHR),[10] it provides for ESC rights and civil and political rights (CP rights) in a single instrument without distinction. It follows therefore that both categories of rights are theoretically subjected to the same implementation regime under the African system. However, most scholars are of the view that, practically the ESC rights guaranteed under the Charter must, in contradistinction to the CP rights, be achieved progressively owing to the lack of resources and the poor economic situation confronting African states.[11]

Together with CP rights, the ACHPR provides specifically for the following traditional ESC rights: the right of every individual to work under equitable and satisfactory conditions,[12] the right of every individual to equal pay for equal work,[13] the right of every individual to enjoy the best attainable state of physical and mental health,[14] the right of every individual to education,[15] the right of every individual freely to take part in the cultural life of his/her community,[16] family rights and the right of every individual to family life.[17] The Charter also provides for some unique rights of economic, social, and cultural significance, namely: right of the aged and disabled to special measures of protection in keeping with their physical and moral needs;[18] peoples' right to existence and self-determination;[19] peoples' right freely to dispose of their wealth and natural resources;[20] peoples' right to economic, social, and cultural development;[21] peoples' right to national and international peace and security;[22] and peoples' right to a general satisfactory environment favourable to their development.[23] Of relevance, too, are the right of every citizen to equal access to the public service of his/her state;[24] the right of very individual to access to public property and services;[25] and the right of every individual to property.[26] It is important to note that some of these rights also overlap as CP rights[27] such as: the right of every citizen to equal access to the public service of his state; the right of very individual to access to public property and services; the right of every individual to property; peoples' right to self-determination and peoples' right to national and international peace and security. The article 2 prohibition of 'distinction of any kind' in the enjoyment of the rights guaranteed under the Charter also applies to the ESC rights and so these rights must be enjoyed by every individual without distinction of any kind.

---

[10] Under the Inter-American system, the American Convention on Human Rights (1969) provides mainly for CP rights, while ESC rights are provided for in a Protocol on Economic, Social and Cultural Rights later adopted in 1988.

[11] See eg, EA Ankumah, *The African Commission on Human and Peoples' Rights: Practice and Procedures* (Nijhoff, 1996) p 144.   [12] Art 15.

[13] Ibid.   [14] Art 16.   [15] Art 17.   [16] Ibid.   [17] Art 18.

[18] Art 18(4).   [19] Art 20.   [20] Art 21.   [21] Art 22.   [22] Art 23.

[23] Art 24.   [24] Art 13(2).   [25] Art 13(3).   [26] Art 14.

[27] See eg, CA Odinkalu, 'Analysis of Paralysis or Paralysis by Analysis?: Implementing Economic, Social and Cultural Rights Under the African Charter on Human and Peoples' Rights' (2001) 23 Human Rights Q, 327 at 336–348, where the ESC rights under the ACHPR are divided into five categories.

Although the African Charter provides for some novel collective ESC rights, as indicated above,[28] it omits some important classic individual ESC rights found in other treaties, such as the rights to rest, leisure, reasonable limitation of working hours, periodic holidays with pay, and remuneration for public holidays;[29] trade union rights;[30] the right to social security;[31] the right to adequate standard of living including adequate food, clothing, housing, and continuous improvement of living conditions;[32] and the prohibition of forced labour.[33] According to a former Secretary of the African Commission, Germain Baricako, the omission of the right to social security was 'not an oversight but rather takes into account the current economic environment in the majority of African states, whose resources could not adequately support a social security system. It is therefore left to the discretion of each state to provide its own social security system.'[34] The question of underdevelopment and lack of resources creates a paradox for ESC rights in Africa. While the realization of ESC rights will lead to both human and economic development in Africa, yet ESC rights cannot be fully realized without economic resources in the first place. This paradox must be broken through careful resource balancing by African states, which is currently hampered by mismanagement of resources and a high level of corruption in governance in most African states. The traditional practice of trying to justify the non-guarantee of certain important ESC rights by African states on grounds of general lack of resources and poor economic conditions in Africa has therefore been rightly criticized. It has been observed in that regard as follows:

Conditions in many African states today arise not out of a lack of wherewithal to satisfy the socio-economic rights of the people to a minimum of human dignity. Rather, they are partly the direct consequence of an active process of impoverishment and de-development. In some cases, international loans and grants purportedly secured to provide essential facilities have ended up lining private pockets, securing safe nests for the advantaged class or being spent to protect that class from the ire of the dispossessed, all in the name of development and security. It is unconscionable for those who participate in the squandering of development opportunities to point to the conditions they create as grounds for marginalizing enforcement of ESCR.[35]

Thus, the problem, in most cases, is that of poor governance and economic mismanagement by African leaders rather than lack of resources per se.

[28] Arts 21–24.   [29] Art 7(d), ICESCR.   [30] Art 8, ICESCR.
[31] Art 9, ICESCR.   [32] Art 11, ICESCR.
[33] Y Klerk, 'Forced Labour and the African Charter on Human and Peoples' Rights' in African Law Association (eds), *The African Charter on Human and Peoples' Rights: Development, Context, Significance* (African Law Association, 1990) 1.
[34] G Baricako, 'The African Charter and the African Commission on Human and Peoples' Rights: A Mandate to Promote and Protect Economic, Social and Cultural Rights in Africa' in ICJ Rep, *Report of a Regional Seminar on Economic, Social and Cultural Rights*, 9–12 March 1998 (International Commission of Jurists, 1999) pp 45–61 at 51.
[35] SC Agbakwa, 'Reclaiming Humanity: Economic, Social and Cultural Rights as the Cornerstone of African Human Rights' (2002) 5 Yale Human Rights and Development L J, 177 at 189–190.

It is also often argued that the traditional African communitarian and familial system can replace the need for a state social security system, whereby family members and children are considered as a form of social security for other needy members and for the elderly respectively. This is reflected in article 29 of the ACHPR, which places a duty on every individual to, *inter alia*, 'work for the cohesion and respect of the family; to respect his parents at all times, to maintain them in case of need'.[36] However, this provision is, at best, only morally viable in practice. It is unlikely that there can be any legal redress where this duty is not fulfilled by individuals. Ankumah has rightly observed that 'the provision is not directly enforceable as states not individuals, are parties to the African Charter'[37] and that states could actually use the provision to abdicate from other rights, such as social security rights. In reality, the socio-economic hardship faced by most individuals in African states makes it difficult, if not impossible, for them to fulfil the duty to maintain their parents in case of need even where they are morally inclined to do so.

The deliberate omission of a specific provision on the right to social security from the ACHPR can therefore be considered either as an act of short-sightedness or a lack of political will or both. Rather than omitting that right on grounds of lack of resources, it could have been included in the Charter but subject to the obligation of progressive realization by states. The African states would then have been encouraged to adopt well planned and well administered contributory systems for the funding of effective social security systems as is the practice in the developed states that operate such systems.[38]

Odinkalu has optimistically argued that some of the omitted rights 'are not outside the scope of interpretive possibilities' open to the Charter.[39] In my view, interpretive possibilities are, however, only exploratory and do not provide the same certainty attributable to specific provisions in the Charter. In a similar vein, Ankumah also argued that the right to rest, leisure, and limited working paid holidays are covered by the right to work 'under equitable and satisfactory conditions' as provided under article 15 of the Charter and that 'the right to assembly could be interpreted as the right to join a trade union', but acknowledged regrettably that in its Resolution on the Right to Freedom of Association adopted in 1992,[40] which explained the scope of the right to freedom of association under the Charter, the Commission failed to go as far as interpreting that right to include trade union rights as could have been expected.[41] The extent of any interpretive latitude within the provisions of the Charter depends largely on how far the Commission is prepared to exercise its interpretative mandate under article 45(3) of the Charter,

---

[36] Art 29(1) ACHPR.   [37] Ankumah (n 11 above) p 171.

[38] Note that the South African Constitution provides for justiciable ESC rights, which includes, under art 27(1)(c), the right to 'social security, including, if they are unable to support themselves and their dependants, appropriate social assistance'.   [39] Odinkalu (n 27 above) at 341.

[40] ACHPR /res 5(XI)92 (1992).   [41] Ankumah (n 11 above) 145.

which will be examined below. It is notable, however, that the Commission apparently attempted to remedy the omission of some ESC rights in the Charter by providing in the Guidelines for National Periodic Reports under the African Charter,[42] adopted in 1989, that states should provide, *inter alia*, information on rights to rest, leisure, limitation of working hours, and holiday with pay, trade union rights, and the right to social security,[43] even though these rights are not specifically provided for in the Charter.

Despite the preambular conviction of the African states regarding the importance of ESC rights and their specific guarantee under the ACHPR, the effects of these rights in action is yet to be fully realized in Africa generally and yet to be fully enjoyed in African states individually. It has mostly been a case of ESC rights *inaction* rather than ESC rights *in action* in Africa. The 2005 National Development Report published by the United Nations Development Programme (UNDP) shows that most of the states at the bottom of the table on issues relevant to ESC rights are African states and parties to the ACHPR.[44] The important need for promoting the actualization of ESC rights in Africa beyond mere aspirations and rhetoric therefore continues to be a matter of concern for both scholars and advocates of the African human rights system.[45]

III. The African Commission and the implementation of ESC rights

In addition to the political will of states to fulfil their obligations under human rights treaties, the treaty bodies established to monitor implementation under relevant human rights treaties constitute the main mechanisms for ensuring that

[42] Reprinted in R Murray and M Evans, *Documents of the African Commission on Human and Peoples' Rights* (Hart, 2001) p 249.

[43] Ibid, paras 9, 10, and 17 under General Guidelines Regarding the Form and Contents of Reports on Economic and Social Rights.

[44] UNDP, *Human Development Reports 2005, International cooperation at crossroads: Aid, trade and security in an unequal world*, pp 219–329, available online at: <http://hdr.undp.org/reports/global/2005/> accessed 12 Nov 2005. See also D Olowu, 'Human Development Challenges in Africa: A Rights-based Approach' (2004) 5 San Diego Intl L J, 179 at 184–188, particularly at 185 where the author observed that: 'A quick look at any of the *Human Development Reports* (the Reports) produced by the UNDP since 1990 shows that Africans have remained parlous in terms of the overall trends of poverty and human deprivation.'

[45] See eg, J Oloka-Onyango, 'Beyond the Rhetoric: Reinvigorating the Struggle for Economic and Social Rights in Africa (1995) 26 California Western Intl L J, no 1, pp 1–73; Odinkalu (n 27 above); Agbakwa (n 35 above); C Mbazira, 'A Path to Realising Economic, Social and Cultural Rights in Africa? A Critique of the New Partnership for Africa's Development' (2004) 4 African Human Rights L J, no 1, pp 34–52; Final Statement of Meeting on Priorities for Human Rights Research to Advance Economic, Social, and Cultural Rights in Africa, organized by the Addis Ababa University in co-operation with UNESCO from 9–11 March 2005, available at: <http://portal.unesco.org/shs/en/ev.php-URL_ID=8536&URL_DO=DO_TOPIC&URL_SECTION=201.html> accessed 12 Nov 2005; Olowu (n 44 above).

rights guaranteed under the treaties are brought into action by the states parties. Before the recent creation of the African Court on Human and Peoples' Rights in 2004,[46] the African Commission was the main treaty body established under the ACHPR to monitor its implementation. To fulfil its role, article 45 of the Charter conferred three specific mandates on the Commission, namely: the mandate to promote,[47] the mandate to interpret,[48] and the mandate to ensure the protection[49] of the rights guaranteed under the ACHPR. These mandates of the Commission to promote, interpret, and ensure the protection of the rights obviously extends to ESC rights under the Charter.

A. Promotion of ESC rights in Africa

In promoting the rights guaranteed under the Charter, the Commission has the particular mandate to, *inter alia*, collect documents, undertake studies and researches, organize seminars, symposia and conferences, disseminate information, and encourage national and local institutions concerned with human and peoples' rights.[50] It is also to give its views or make recommendations to governments, formulate and lay down principles and rules, and co-operate with other African and international institutions concerned with the promotion and protection of human and peoples' rights.[51]

Since its inauguration in 1987,[52] the Commission has undertaken many of the activities listed above in fulfilling its general mandate on the promotion of human rights.[53] However, its specific focus on the promotion of ESC rights has only recently begun. Professor Umozurike, a former Chairman of the Commission, had observed in 1988 that the Commission was 'likely to concern itself with civil and political matters; any attempt to venture into economic and social ones will result in too many cases and in too many states for the commission to cope with'.[54] That observation suggests, apparently, that the lack of initial focus on the promotion of ESC rights by the Commission was informed by the fact that most

---

[46] The Protocol on the Establishment of an African Court on Human and Peoples' Rights was adopted in 1998 and entered into force on 25 Jan 2004.   [47] Art 45(1).

[48] Art 45(3).

[49] Art 45(2). *See also* Arts 60 and 61 of the ACHPR, which empowers the Commission to draw inspiration from, and to take into consideration, other relevant international human rights instruments in fulfilling its mandate under the Charter.   [50] Art 45(1) ACHPR.

[51] Ibid.

[52] The Commission was officially inaugurated on 2 Nov 1987 in Addis Ababa, Ethopia, after its members had been elected in July of the same year by the OAU 23rd Assembly of Heads of State and Government. See OAU, *African Commission on Human and Peoples' Right Information Sheet No 1: Establishment*, p 3.

[53] A summary of the Commission's activities are provided in its Annual Activity Reports. The 10th to 16th Annual Activity Reports are available on its website at: <http://www.achpr.org/english/_info/index_activity_en.html> accessed on 12 Nov 2005.

[54] UO Umozurike, 'The Protection of Human Rights under the Banjul (African) Charter on Human and Peoples' Rights' (1988) 1 African J of Intl L, 65 at 81.

individuals in the different African states that were parties to the ACHPR were already victims of violations of the ESC rights guaranteed under the Charter and thus an attempt by the Commission to focus on ESC rights at the early stage would have inundated it with too many cases against too many states, which it could not have been able to cope with. In my view, that initial neglect has contributed to the unnecessary prolongation and continuation of the general state of ESC rights *inaction* in most African states today. In its resolution on the situation of human rights in Africa adopted in 1994, the Commission acknowledged that the deplorable human rights situation in many African states was 'characterised by the violations of economic, social and cultural, civil and political rights' and also observed that the 'persistent economic crises in Africa has exaggerated the human rights situation of vulnerable groups in African societies, in particular women and children'.[55] An early focus on the promotion of ESC rights by the Commission could have increased the awareness about those rights amongst the African populace. The importance of this is that, awareness by the populace of their guaranteed rights could serve as an empowering first step towards a quicker realization of those rights.

In March 1998, the International Commission of Jurists (ICJ) organized a regional seminar on ESC rights in Abidjan with representation from the Commission.[56] That seminar spurred the 34th Summit of Heads of State and government of the OAU held in Ougadougou in June 1998 to request, in its decisions adopted after the summit, that the OAU Secretary-General should 'convene, in co-operation with the African Commission on Human and Peoples' Rights, a high level meeting of Experts to consider ways and means of removing obstacles to the enjoyment of economic, social and cultural rights' in Africa.[57] As a follow-up, the Commission, in collaboration with the International Centre for Legal Protection of Human Rights (INTERIGHTS), the Cairo Institute of Human Rights Studies, and the Centre for Human Rights of the University of Pretoria, organized a seminar on ESC rights in South Africa in September 2004. The Pretoria Statement on Economic, Social and Cultural Rights in Africa was adopted after that seminar and was later adopted by the Commission in its Resolution on Economic, Social and Cultural Rights of December 2004.[58]

This resolution, *inter alia*, requested the Secretary of the Commission to forward the Pretoria Statement 'to the Commission of African Union, Ministries of Justice and Social Affairs and Justice; National Human Rights institutions of all states parties, International institutions working in African and Regional economic communities, Bar Associations and Law Schools in Africa and civil society

---

[55] ACHPR res 14(XVI) 94 (1994), preambular paras 2 and 6.

[56] See ICJ, *Report of a Regional Seminar on Economic, Social and Cultural Rights Abidjan, Cote d'Ivoire, 9–12 March 1998* (International Commission of Jurists, 1999).

[57] See Declaration and Decisions Adopted by the 34th Ordinary Session of the Assembly of Heads of State and Government, AHG/DEC.126, para 6, 8–10 June 1998, Ouagadougou, Burkina Faso.   [58] ACHPR /res 73 (XXXVI) 04 (2004).

organizations including non-governmental organizations with observer status'.[59] The Commission also urged its members, Special Rapporteurs, and working groups to pay particular attention to economic, social, and cultural rights,[60] which, in my view, was long overdue.

To pursue the recommendations in the Pretoria Statement, the Commission further decided to establish a separate working group composed of members of the Commission and non-governmental organizations (NGOs) with the mandate to:

(i) develop and propose to the African Commission on Human and Peoples' Rights a draft Principles and Guidelines on Economic, Social, and Cultural Rights;

(ii) elaborate a draft revised guidelines pertaining to economic, social, and cultural rights for State reporting;

(iii) undertake, under the supervision of the African Commission on Human and Peoples' Rights, studies and research on specific economic, social, and cultural rights; and

(iv) make a progress report to the African Commission on Human and Peoples' Rights at each Ordinary session.[61]

The Commission has also requested the support and assistance of the African Union for the working group. This is very important in terms of provision of the necessary resources for the effective functioning of the working group.

The Pretoria Statement is the most comprehensive statement so far adopted by the Commission in respect of ESC rights and represents a commendable attempt towards rejuvenating its mandate to promote ESC rights under the African human rights system. The events leading to the adoption of both the Pretoria Statement and the Commission's Resolution on Economic, Social, and Cultural Rights reveals the important role of NGOs and civil society in pursuing the implementation of human rights generally and of ESC rights particularly in Africa. The Charter had anticipated, and rightly made room for, such collaboration by providing in article 45(1)(c) that, in pursuing its mandate of promoting human rights, the Commission can 'co-operate with other African and international institutions concerned with the promotion and protection of human rights'. By adopting the Pretoria Statement, the Commission has now set an important parameter for the future assessment of how well it has fulfilled its mandate of promoting ESC rights under the Charter.

B. Interpretation of the scope of ESC rights under the Charter

Article 45(3) of the Charter confers on the Commission the mandate to interpret all the provisions of the Charter 'at the request of a State party, an institution of the Organization of African Unity or an African organization recognized by the

---

[59] Ibid, para 2.   [60] Ibid, para 3.   [61] Ibid, para 4.

Organisation of African Unity'. It is not on record that any state, organization, or institution has requested for the interpretation of the scope of the rights provided under the African Charter, but the Commission has on its own initiative exercised its interpretative mandate under article 45(3) by adopting some resolutions, interpreting the scope of some of the rights guaranteed under the Charter.[62] However, despite observations by many scholars on the vagueness of the ESC rights guaranteed under the Charter,[63] the Commission did not adopt an interpretative resolution specifically on any of the ESC rights under the Charter prior to the Pretoria Statement, which has now addressed this by elaborating on the scope of some of the ESC rights guaranteed under the Charter.

It is clear that the Pretoria Statement is also very significant in relation to the Commission's interpretative mandate under the Charter. By its adoption of the Pretoria Statement, the Commission has accepted the Statement's interpretations, which greatly broaden the scope and bridges the gap in the vagueness of the rights to property, work, health, education, and culture guaranteed under the Charter. However, the Statement's interpretation does not cover all the ESC rights under the Charter. It only 'highlighted' those rights it considered as the 'core contents'[64] of ESC rights under the African Charter but noted that the 'social, economic and cultural rights explicitly provided for under the African Charter, read together with other rights in the Charter, such as the right to life and respect for inherent human dignity, imply the recognition of other economic and social rights, including the right to shelter, the right to basic nutrition and the right to social security'.[65] It would therefore be a step in the right direction for the Commission to follow up the Pretoria Statement with interpretative resolutions clarifying the scope of the remaining ESC rights under the Charter, which were not covered by the Statement. Apart from adopting interpretative resolutions, the Commission is also able to discharge its interpretative mandate through the consideration of communications alleging violations of ESC rights as will be analysed in section III of this chapter below.

C. Protection of ESC rights in Africa

In ensuring the protection of the rights under the Charter, the Commission has the mandate to receive biennial reports from states parties under article 62 of the

---

[62] See eg, 9. ACHPR /res 4 (XI) 92: Resolution on the Right to Recourse and Fair Trial (1992); 10. ACHPR /res 5 (XI) 92: Resolution on the Right to Freedom of Association (1992).

[63] See eg, Agbakwa (n 35 above) at 192–193; M Mutua, 'The African Human Rights System in a Comparative Perspective' (1993) 3 Rev of African Commission on Human and Peoples' Rights 5; Oloka-Onyango (n 45 above) at 47–51; GW Mugwanya, 'Realising Universal Human Rights Norms through Regional Human Rights Mechanisms: Reinvigorating the African System' (1999) 10 Indiana Intl and Comparative L Rev, p 35; W Benedek, 'The African Charter and Commission on Human Rights and Peoples' Rights: How to Make it More Effective' (1993) 11 Netherlands Q of Human Rights, p 25.

[64] Pretoria Statement on Economic, Social and Cultural Rights in Africa 2004, para 11.

[65] Ibid, para 10.

ACHPR, through which the states are required to report 'on the legislative and other measures taken with a view to giving effect to the rights and freedoms recognised and guaranteed' under the Charter. The Commission is also conferred with the mandate of receiving and considering communications from states[66] and from non-state entities[67] claiming violations of the rights guaranteed under the Charter.

Regarding state reports, the Commission adopted Guidelines for National Periodic Reports under the African Charter[68] in 1989 with a section on ESC rights that required states parties to provide information on specific ESC rights such as the right to work, the right to social security, the right to education, the right of the family to an adequate standard of living and the highest attainable level of health. The Guidelines were, however, criticized by some states and NGOs as being too complex and confusing. Thus, in 1998, the Commission issued a simplified summary of the Guidelines, which provides generally that the states parties should provide information on how they are implementing ESC rights among others.[69]

Since 1981 the African state parties' compliance with their reporting obligations under the Charter has been relatively poor. The Commission has taken some steps, such as writing letters, adopting resolutions, appealing, offering to assist states where they have difficulties in preparing their reports and even called on specific states in a communiqué to submit their reports.[70] The Commission has, however, been criticized for not responding effectively to this problem of poor compliance or non-compliance by the African states parties to their reporting obligations under the Charter.[71] Considering the importance of state reporting to the Commission's monitoring of states' obligations under the Charter, it is imperative for the Commission to find ways of addressing this problem effectively. The Commission currently publishes the status of submissions of state periodic reports on its website, which can serve as a sort of 'naming and shaming' to compel defaulting states to comply with their obligations in that regard, but this is not regularly updated.[72] This would be more effective if the relevant information on the Commission's website were updated regularly and the status of submissions were also included in the annual report of the Commission for further publicity.

Regarding inter-state communications, there has so far been only one submitted to the Commission.[73] Despite the widespread violation of ESC rights in most African states, there has been no inter-state communication regarding the violation of ESC rights. Generally, this has been seen as not being unique to the African system.[74] Specifically it could be argued that this is because none of the African

---

[66] Art 47–54 ACHPR (1981).   [67] Art 55, ibid.   [68] Note 42 above.

[69] *See* M Evans, T Ige, and R Murray, 'The Reporting Mechanism of the African Charter on Human and Peoples' Rights' in M Evans and R Murray (eds), *The African Charter on Human and peoples' Rights: The System in Practice, 1986–2000* (Cambridge University Press, 2002) 36 at 48.

[70] *See* Ankuma (n 11 above) at 108.   [71] *See* Evans, Ige, and Murray (n 69 above) at 39–44.

[72] <http://www.achpr.org/english/_info/status_submission_en.html> accessed 25 Aug 2006. On 25 August 2006, the website indicated the status of submission 'as of May 2003'.

[73] Communication no 227/99 (1999), *Democratic Republic of Congo v Burundi, Rwanda and Uganda.*   [74] *See* Ankumah (n 11 above) at 24.

states can be said to have adequately fulfilled its Charter obligations in respect of the ESC rights and thus be in a better position of bringing a communication against another state regarding the violation of ESC rights under the Charter. Communications alleging violation of ESC rights against states parties under the Charter has therefore been by individuals and NGOs.

D. Consideration of non-state communications regarding violations of ESC rights

With the exception of the right of every individual to take part freely in the cultural life of his/her community under article 17(2) of the Charter, the Commission has had opportunity to consider allegations of violations of each of the other ESC rights guaranteed under the Charter in different non-state communications brought before it as analysed below.

1. *The right of every citizen to equal access to public service of his/her state*

Article 13(2) of the Charter guarantees the right of every citizen to equal access to the public service of his/her state. The restriction of this right to every citizen, rather than every individual, is in the light of the fact that certain public service positions may be reserved only for citizens in all states. This right is apparently a CP right if considered in relation to the right of every citizen to participate freely in the government of his state under article 13(1) of the Charter.[75] However, if access to public service is considered in relation to the right to work, it crosses into the sphere of ESC rights. Pursuant to article 2 of the Charter, where certain public service positions are reserved for the citizens of a state, all citizens of that state must have equal access to such public service positions without distinction of any kind. The denial of a citizen's access to such public service positions will be a violation of an ESC right of that citizen on grounds of discrimination.[76]

This was reflected by the Commission's decision in the case of *John K Modise v Botswana*,[77] where the complainant was allegedly denied, for political reasons, Tswana citizenship by descent even though his father was a national of Botswana and thus entitled to citizenship by descent. The defending state was prepared to grant the complainant citizenship by registration, which would have limited the complainant's access to certain public service positions which were restricted to citizens by descent under the constitution of Botswana. On the facts, the Commission held that denying the complainant of citizenship by descent, in those circumstances, would consequently lead to 'a denial of his right to equal access to the public service of his state guaranteed under article 13(2) of the Charter'.[78]

---

[75] *See* Ankumah (n 11 above) p 141, where the author lists this right as a CP right. See also art 25 of the ICCPR.   [76] Art 2, ACHPR.

[77] Communication no 97/93 (2000).   [78] Ibid, para 96.

This was a commendable decision by the Commission that rightly protected the complainant's ESC right to public service positions available only to citizens by descent, which he was entitled to by his descent and would not otherwise have had a right to as a citizen by registration, under the constitution of Botswana, which the state was prepared to grant him.

2. The right of every individual to property

Article 14 of the Charter guarantees the right to property, which 'may only be encroached upon in the interest of public need or in the general interest of the community and in accordance with the provisions of appropriate law.' While the right to property is also conceivable as a CP right,[79] the Pretoria Statement listed it specifically as an ESC right under the African Charter.[80] Baricako has observed that this right 'does not confer upon each person the right to own private property, but grants individuals the right to defend themselves against expropriation of a legally acquired asset',[81] which apparently only places a negative obligation on the state not to expropriate arbitrarily private property and not to prevent the acquisition of private property by individuals.

The Commission has found violations of the right to property under the Charter in at least seven communications as analysed below. The relevant issues in the respective communications related to seizure, closure, or confiscation of private property by government agents, as well as forced abandonment of private property due to arbitrary deportation of individuals.

In *Media Rights Agenda and Others v Nigeria*[82] and *Constitutional Rights Project and Others v Nigeria*,[83] the then military regime in Nigeria had proscribed certain newspapers, confiscated copies of the newspapers, sealed off the newspaper companies' premises, and prevented the proprietors and employees from accessing the premises. These actions were carried out under military decrees issued by the government in response to certain publications by the affected newspapers that were considered offensive by the military regime. The Commission held that both the sealing of the newspaper premises and seizure of copies of the newspapers violated the right to property and that the grounds for doing so did not fall within the exception of public need or general interest of the community under article 14. The Commission observed, *inter alia*, that:

The government did not offer any explanation for the sealing up of the premises of many publications. Those affected were not previously accused in a court of law, of any wrongdoing. *The right to property necessarily includes a right to have access to property of one's own*

---

[79] See Ankumah, (n 11 above) p 142 where the author lists this right as a CP right. See also art 21 of the American Convention on Human Rights (1969).

[80] See the preamble and para 5 of the Pretoria Statement (n 64 above).

[81] Baricako (n 34 above) p 53.

[82] Communication nos 105/93, 128/94, 130/94, 152/96 (1998).

[83] Communication nos 140/94, 141/94, 145/94 (1999).

and the right not for one's property to be removed. The Decrees which enable these premises to be sealed up and for the publications to be seized cannot be said to be 'appropriate' or in the interest of the public or the community in general.[84]

The Commission reiterated the above view in *Huri-Laws v Nigeria*,[85] in which government agents were alleged to have raided the office of a human rights NGO and seized some property of the organization, by stating that '[t]he Complainant further contends that no evidence was ever offered of public need or community interest to justify the search and seizure. The said encroachment therefore is a violation of article 14 of the Charter'.[86]

In *Union Inter Africaine and Others v Angola*,[87] the complainants were West African nationals, who were expelled from Angola in 1996 and lost their belongings in the process. In finding a violation of article 14 of the Charter, the Commission observed that:

The Commission concedes that African States in general and the Republic of Angola in particular are faced with many challenges, mainly economic. In the face of such difficulties, States often resort to radical measures aimed at protecting their nationals and their economies from non-nationals. Whatever the circumstances may be, however, such measures should not be taken at the detriment of the enjoyment of human rights. Mass expulsion of any category of persons, whether on the basis of nationality, religion, ethnic, racial or other considerations 'constitute a special violation of human rights'. *This type of deportations calls into question a whole series of rights recognised and guaranteed in the Charter; such as the right to property (article 14).*[88]

Similarly, in *Malawi African Association and Others v Mauritania*,[89] various black ethnic groups from the south of Mauritania, who had criticized the government for marginalizing black Mauritanians, were allegedly subjected to series of persecutions by government agents. This culminated in the expulsion of almost 50,000 people to Senegal and Mali in 1989 on grounds that they were Senegalese, even though many of them were bearers of Mauritanian identity cards, which were allegedly collected and torn up by government agents. Government security forces were alleged to have confiscated land and livestock belonging to the expelled black Mauritanians and those who were forced to flee due to persecutions. In relation to article 14, the Commission found that:

The confiscation and looting of the property of black Mauritanians and the expropriation or destruction of their land and houses before forcing them to go abroad constitute a violation of the right to property as guaranteed under article 14.[90]

---

[84] Note 77 above (emphasis added); re-stated in *Constitutional Rights Project, Civil Liberties Organisation and Media Rights Agenda v Nigeria* (n 54 above).
[85] Communication no 225/98 (2000).   [86] Ibid, para 53.
[87] Communication no 159/96 (1997).   [88] Ibid, para 16, 17, and 20 (emphasis added).
[89] Communication no 54/91, 61/91, 98/93, 164/97, 196/97, 210/98 (2000).
[90] Ibid, para 128.

Also in *John K Modise v Botswana*,[91] the Commission found 'an encroachment of the Complainant's right to property guaranteed under article 14 of the Charter',[92] where the complainant had, for political reasons, been denied of citizenship, deported from Botswana, and his belongings and property confiscated by the government. The Commission equally found a violation of article 14 in *The Social and Economic Rights Action Center for Economic and Social Rights v Nigeria*,[93] where the homes and shelter of the complainants had been destroyed by government agents due to oil exploration activities in the area.

It is important to note that the protection of the right to property in the above cases only required a negative obligation on the part of the respective states not to arbitrarily confiscate or destroy properties of the respective individuals and organizations. The fulfilment of this obligation mainly required an adherence to the rule of law by the respective states and did not impose any positive obligation that required huge resources, which the respective states could not afford, as is often argued in respect of ESC rights. The question of lack of resources can therefore not be an excuse, by African states, for not respecting this important ESC right under the African Charter.

However, the Pretoria Statement has further broadened the scope of the right to property under the African Charter to include the provision of equal opportunities for individuals to acquire private property, by providing that the scope of the right included '(e)quitable and non-discriminatory access to affordable loans for the acquisition of property' and '(e)quitable redistribution of land through due process of law to redress historical and gender injustices',[94] which apparently places some positive obligations on African states in that regard. The Commission has not yet had the opportunity to address this broadened interpretation of the right in any Communication.

3. The right of every individual to work

Article 15 of the Charter provides that: 'every individual shall have the right to work under equitable and satisfactory conditions, and shall receive equal pay for equal work'. The Commission addressed a violation of this right in the case of *Annete Pagnoulle (on behalf of Abdoulaye Mazou) v Cameroon*.[95] The complainant, a magistrate, was sentenced to five years' imprisonment by a military tribunal in Cameroon in 1984 for hiding his brother, who was later sentenced to death for an attempted coup d'état. The complainant continued to be placed under house arrest even after serving his sentence until 1991 when he benefited from a law of amnesty. The amnesty law provided, *inter alia*, that persons 'who have been granted amnesty and who had public employment will be reintegrated.' The complainant was

---

[91] Communication no 97/93 (2000).   [92] Ibid, para 94.
[93] Communication no 155/96 (2001).   [94] See para 5 of Pretoria Statement (n 64 above).
[95] Communication no 39/90 (1997).

however not reinstated to his position as a magistrate. The Commission held that 'by not reinstating Mr. Mazou in his former position after the Amnesty Law, the government has violated article 15 of the African Charter because it has prevented Mr. Mazou to work in his capacity of a magistrate even though others who have been condemned under similar conditions have been reinstated'.[96]

Although the Commission did not refer to article 2 of the ACHPR on non-discrimination, the reasoning in the decision that 'others who have been condemned under similar conditions have been reinstated' suggests that the non-reinstatement of the complainant was apparently discriminatory and thus prohibited by the Charter in relation to article 15. Perhaps, the Commission's non-reference specifically to the issue of non-discrimination implies that the decision could stand even in situations without elements of discrimination as in the above case.

It is important to note that the Pretoria Statement has further broadened the scope of the right to work to include a wide range of elements that are not specifically provided for in the Charter. [97]

4. The right of every individual to enjoy the best attainable state of health

Article 16 of the Charter provides that:

(1) Every individual shall have the right to enjoy the best attainable state of physical and mental health.
(2) States parties to the present Charter shall take the necessary measures to protect the health of their people and to ensure that they receive medical attention when they are sick.

The Commission has pronounced on this right in at least six communications brought before it. The communications related to shortage of medicines in hospitals, denial of detainees' access to a medical doctor or health care, and pollution of environment which leads to direct health hazards.

In *Free Legal Assistance Group and Others v Zaire*,[98] four NGOs alleged that, owing to the mismanagement of public finances, the government had failed to provide basic services to the populace and that 'there was a shortage of medicines' in the hospitals.[99] The Commission held that '[t]he failure of the Government to provide basic services such as safe drinking water and electricity and shortage of medicine as alleged in the communication... constitutes a violation of article 16'.[100] This was a very bold decision by the Commission, but which, did not have the opportunity to address obvious questions relating to availability of resources and progressive realization[101] because the case was heard *ex parte* due to the non-appearance of the defendant

---

[96] Ibid, last para of decision.   [97] See para 6 of Pretoria Statement (n 64 above).
[98] Communication no 25/89, 47/90, 56/91, 100/93 (1995).   [99] Ibid, para 4.
[100] Ibid, para 47.
[101] These issues were subsequently addressed by the Commission in 2003 in the case of *Purohit and Moore v The Gambia*, which is examined below.

state. The state did not respond to any of the Commission's notices regarding the communication.[102]

In *Media Rights Agenda and Others v Nigeria*,[103] the communication alleged that a detainee was denied access to doctors and received no medical help even though his health was deteriorating.[104] The Commission held that '[t]he responsibility of the government is heightened in cases where the individual is in its custody and therefore someone whose integrity and well-being is completely dependent on the activities of the authorities. To deny a detainee access to doctors while his health is deteriorating is a violation of article 16.'[105] The Commission restated this decision in *International Pen and Others v Nigeria*,[106] where Ken Saro-Wiwa had been detained by the state and denied access to the medicine he needed to control his blood pressure despite requests by a qualified prison doctor. The Commission added that: 'The State has a direct responsibility in this case. Despite requests for hospital treatment made by a qualified doctor, these were denied to Ken Saro-Wiwa, causing his health to suffer to the point where his life was endangered.... This is a violation of article 16.'[107] Similarly, in *Malawi African Association and Others v Mauritania*,[108] where it was alleged that some political prisoners died in detention due to malnutrition and lack of medical attention and that 'the cells were infested with lice, bedbugs and cockroaches and nothing was done to ensure the hygiene and provision of health care'.[109] The Commission held that: 'The general state of health of the prisoners deteriorated due to the lack of sufficient food; they had neither blankets nor adequate hygiene. The Mauritanian State is directly responsible for this state of affairs.... Consequently, the Commission considers that there was violation of article 16.'[110]

In the decisive case of *Social and Economic Rights Action Center for Economic and Social Rights v Nigeria*[111] the complainants alleged that the defendant state violated, *inter alia*, the right to health as recognized under article 16 by failing to fulfil the minimum duties required by this right, through: '[d]irectly participating in the contamination of air, water and soil and thereby harming the health of the Ogoni population; Failing to protect the Ogoni population from the harm caused...; Failing to provide or permit studies of potential or actual environmental and health risks caused by the oil operations' in the area.[112] The Commission held that article 16 'obligate governments to desist from directly threatening the health and environment of their citizens'.[113] In this case the guarantee of the right to enjoy the best attainable state of physical and mental health was linked with the right to a general satisfactory environment favourable to development under article 24 of the Charter, which will be further examined below.

---

[102] *Free Legal Assistance Group and Others v Zaire* above paras 6 and 40.   [103] Above.
[104] *Media Rights Agenda and Others v Nigeria* (1998) above para 9.   [105] Ibid, para 91.
[106] Communication nos 137/94, 139/94, 154/96, 161/97 (1998).   [107] Ibid, para 112.
[108] Communication nos 54/91, 61/91, 98/93, 164/97 à 196/97, and 210/98 (2000).
[109] Ibid, para 12.   [110] Ibid, para 122.   [111] Above.   [112] Above para 50
[113] Above, para 52.

In *Purohit and Moore v The Gambia*,[114] the Commission emphasized the importance of the right to health by observing that '[e]njoyment of the human right to health as it is widely known is vital to all aspects of a person's life and well-being, and is crucial to the realisation of all the other fundamental human rights and freedoms. This right includes the right to health facilities, access to goods and services to be guaranteed to all without discrimination of any kind.'[115] The Commission however, also noted that it was 'aware that millions of people in Africa are not enjoying the right to health maximally because African states are generally faced with the problem of poverty which renders them incapable to provide the necessary amenities, infrastructure and resources that facilitate the full enjoyment of this right. Therefore, having due regard to this depressing but real state of affairs, the African Commission would like to read into article 16 the obligation on the part of states party to the African Charter to take concrete and targeted steps, while taking full advantage of its available resources, to ensure that the right to health is fully realised in all its aspects without discrimination of any kind.'[116]

The right to health is an ESC right that is obviously subject to available resources as acknowledged by the Commission in this case. Nevertheless, the Commission emphasized the 'obligation on the part of states party to the African Charter to take concrete and targeted steps' within their available resources to ensure the full realization of this right. Practically, the poor economic situation in many African states has adversely affected the full enjoyment of the right to health by many people in Africa. Thus, the need for international co-operation in fully realizing the right to health in Africa cannot be overemphasized, even though the ACHPR does not specifically call for international co-operation in that regard.[117] Both the Alma-Ata Declaration adopted after the International Conference on Primary Health Care held in Alma-Ata, USSR in September 1978,[118] and *General Comment 14*[119] on the right to the highest attainable standard of health under article 12 of the ICESCR adopted by the UN Committee on Economic, Social and Cultural Rights (ESCR Committee) have emphasized the importance of international co-operation and assistance for developing states for the full realization of this right. This is especially so in the light of the Pretoria Statement which has now broadened the scope of the right to health under the African Charter to include many other elements such as '[e]ducation, prevention and treatment of HIV/AIDs, malaria, tuberculosis and other major killer diseases',[120] etc.

---

[114] Communication no 241/2001 (2003).   [115] Ibid, para 80.   [116] Ibid, para 84.

[117] However, the African States reaffirmed in the 4th preambular para of the Charter 'to coordinate and intensify their cooperation and efforts to achieve a better life for the peoples of Africa and to promote international cooperation having due regard to the Charter of the United Nations and the Universal Declaration of Human Rights'.   [118] Alta-Ama Declaration, 1978, paras 2 and 9.

[119] UN Committee on ESC rights, *General Comment 14*, paras 39 and 45.

[120] See para 7 of Pretoria Statement (n 64 above).

It is, however, important to note that African states themselves would need to demonstrate a high sense of responsibility and commitment to the realization of the right to health to justify and benefit from necessary international co-operation and assistance from developed states in that regard.

5. *The right of every individual to education*

Article 17(1) of the Charter provides for the right of every individual to education. The violation of this right was addressed by the Commission in *Free Legal Assistance Group and Others v Zaire*,[121] where the complainants alleged that, owing to mismanagement of public finances, the government had failed to provide basic services, including that 'the universities and secondary schools has been closed for two years'. The Commission held that: '[t]he closure of universities and secondary schools as described in communication 100/93 constitutes a violation of article 17'. It is arguable whether or not this will be applicable to all types of closures, such as when students go on riot or rampage and universities are closed for a long time by the authorities in some African states.

The right to education was also addressed in *Association Pour la Sauvegarde de la Paix au Burundi v Tanzania, Kenya, Uganda, Rwanda, Zaire, and Zambia*.[122] In reaction to a military coup that changed, unconstitutionally, the government of Burundi on 25 July 1996, the states of the African Great Lakes region[123] adopted a resolution at a sub-regional summit in Tanzania on 31 July 1996 imposing economic sanctions on Burundi.[124] The resolution was later supported by the UN Security Council[125] and the Summit of Heads of State and government of the OAU.[126] The Association for the Preservation of Peace in Burundi, an NGO based in Belgium, brought this communication challenging the sanctions on the grounds that the sanctions violated article 17(1) of the ACHPR 'because the embargo prevented the importation of school materials' to Burundi.

One of the respondent states, Zambia, argued that 'the said sanctions were aimed at putting pressure on the regime of Major Buyoya with a view to causing it to restore constitutional legality, reinstate Parliament, which is the symbol of democracy, and lift the ban on political parties' and thus the Great Lake States 'were right in imposing sanctions on Burundi to bring about the restoration of democracy and discourage coups d'état in Africa'.[127] Zambia further argued that 'the sanctions monitoring committee had authorised the importation into Burundi, through United Nations agencies, of essential items' and thus contended that the embargo was not a total blockade.[128] Another respondent state,

---

[121] Above.   [122] Communication no 157/96 (2003).
[123] The African Great Lakes region is designated by five lakes, Lake Albert, Lake Edward, Lake Kivu, Lake Tanganyika, and Lake Victoria, all lying in and around the Great Rift Valley. The Great Lakes States are Burundi, Democratic Republic of Congo, Kenya, Rwanda, Tanzania, and Uganda.
[124] Joint communiqué of the Second Arusha Regional Summit on Burundi, 31 July 1996.
[125] UN SC res 1072 (1996).   [126] AHG/res 257 (XXXII) 1996.
[127] Communication no 157/96 (2003), para 14 and 20.   [128] Ibid, para 18.

Tanzania, argued that 'education and educational institutions were not the targets of the embargo; however due to its multiplier effect, they were affected'. Tanzania further argued that: 'the enjoyment of economic, cultural and social rights cannot be effective in the morass that Burundi has fallen into [and that] Constitutional legality has first to be restored'. In agreeing with the respondent states, the Commission found that there was no violation of article 17 (1) on the grounds, *inter alia*, that:

The Respondent States took collective action as a sub-regional consortium to address a matter within the region that could constitute a threat to peace, stability, and security. Their action was motivated by the principles enshrined in the Charters of the OAU and the United Nations. The Charter of the OAU stipulates that 'freedom, equality, justice and dignity are essential objectives for the achievement of the legitimate aspirations of the African people.... The resolution to impose the embargo on Burundi was taken at a duly constituted summit of the states of the Great Lakes Region who had an interest in or were affected by the situation in Burundi. The resolution was subsequently presented to the appropriate organs of the OAU and the Security Council of the United Nations. No breach attaches to the procedure adopted by the states concerned. The embargo was not a mere unilateral action or a naked act of hostility but a carefully considered act of inter-vention which is sanctioned by international law. The endorsement of the embargo by reso-lution of the Security Council and the summit of Heads of State and Government of the OAU does not merit a further enquiry as to how the action was initiated.[129]

The Commission also observed that the critical question—and one which could affect the legitimacy of the action—was whether the actions taken were excessive, disproportionate, indiscriminate, and sought to achieve ends beyond the legit-imate purpose. It found that these principles were not violated in the actions taken, and thus, even though education was affected by the sanctions, this did not violate article 17(1) of the Charter.

It is notable that the approach of the African Commission regarding the effect of legitimate international sanctions on ESC rights differs from that adopted by the UN ESCR Committee. Nigel White has observed that the ESCR Committee 'clearly sees core rights as immovable in the face of security measures'.[130]

In my view, this decision of the African commission regarding the adverse effect of legitimate sanctions on the right to education, and by implication ESC rights in general, must be treated with caution. The current trend within human rights dis-course on this point sways more in favour of the view that ESC rights must be respected and protected as much as possible in the enforcement of economic sanc-tions on any state.[131]

---

[129] Ibid, paras 71 and 72.

[130] See chapter on 'Applicability of Economic and Social Rights to the UN Security Council' by Nigel White in this book.

[131] See eg, ESCR Committee, *General Comment 8 (the Relationship Between Economic Sanctions and Respect for Economic, Social, and Cultural Rights)*, UN doc E/C.12/1997/8.

The right to education under the African Charter has also now been very broadly defined in the Pretoria Statement to include a long list of relevant elements.[132]

6. *The right of every individual to family life*

Article 18 of the Charter provides that: '(1) The family shall be the natural unit and basis of society. It shall be protected by the State which shall take care of its physical and moral health. (2) The State shall have the duty to assist the family which is the custodian of morals and traditional values recognised by the community.' The Commission has addressed the right to family life in at least seven communications, which related to allegations regarding separation from family due to illegal deportation and due to detention without access to one's family.

In *Union Inter Africaine des Droits de l'Homme and Others v Angola*,[133] which alleged the illegal expulsion of some West African nationals from Angola, the Commission held that the state violated 'its obligations under article 18 paragraph 1.... By deporting the victims, thus separating some of them from their families, the Defendant state has violated and violates the letter of this text.'[134] Also in *Constitutional Rights Project and Civil Liberties Organisation v Nigeria*[135] the communication alleged that several human rights, pro-democracy activists, and opposition politicians were detained by the government and denied access to their families. The Commission held that '[i]t is ... a violation of article 18 to prevent a detainee from communicating with his family'.[136] Similarly, in *Malawi African Association and Others v Mauritania*[137] the Commission observed that holding people arbitrarily in solitary confinement and thereby depriving them their right to a family life constitutes a violation of article 18.[138]

The case of *Amnesty International v Zambia*[139] alleged unlawful exiling of the complainants by the defendant state based on political malice. The Commission held that the forcible expulsion of the complainants 'by the Zambian government has forcibly broken up the family unit which is the core of society thereby failing in its duties to protect and assist the family as stipulated in article 18(1) and 18(2) of the Charter'.[140] A similar decision was reached in *John K Modise v Botswana*,[141] which was also a complaint against unlawful deportation of the complainant by the state and where the Commission observed that the deportation deprived the complainant of his family, and his family of his support.[142]

In *Social and Economic Rights Action Center for Economic and Social Rights v Nigeria*,[143] the Commission linked the right to family life to the right to housing or shelter, even though the latter right is not specifically provided for in the African Charter. The Commission noted that '[a]lthough the right to housing or

---

[132] See para 8 of Pretoria Statement (n 64 above).   [133] Communication no 159/96 (1997).
[134] Ibid, para 17.   [135] Above.   [136] Above para 29.   [137] Above.
[138] *Malawi African Association and Others v Mauritania* (above) para 124.
[139] Communication no 212/98 (1999).   [140] Ibid, para 59.   [141] Above.
[142] *John K Modise v Botswana* (above) para 92.   [143] Above.

shelter is not explicitly provided for under the African Charter, the corollary of the combination of the provisions protecting the right to enjoy the best attainable state of mental and physical health, ... the right to property, and the protection accorded to the family forbids the wanton destruction of shelter because when housing is destroyed, property, health and family life are adversely affected.'[144]

This decision was a bold and commendable attempt by the Commission to accommodate, jurisprudentially, the issue of right to housing, which was not specifically provided for in the Charter, prior to the adoption of the Pretoria Statement which has now interpreted the scope of the right to property to include the right to housing.[145]

7. The right of the aged and disabled to special measures of protection

Article 18(4) of the Charter provides that: 'The aged and the disabled shall also have the right to special measures of protection in keeping with their physical or moral needs.' As earlier noted, this is one of the unique ESC rights provided under the ACHPR. The violation of this right was addressed in the case of *Purohit and Moore v The Gambia*,[146] which concerned the rights of mental health patients under article 18(4). In finding a violation of the right of mentally disabled patients under this provision, the Commission observed that 'as a result of their condition and by virtue of their disabilities, mental health patients should be accorded special treatment which would enable them not only to attain but also sustain their optimum level of independence and performance in keeping with article 18(4) of the African Charter and the standards applicable to the treatment of mentally ill persons as defined in the Principles for the Protection of Persons with Mental Illness and Improvement of Mental Health Care.'[147]

In my view this was a landmark decision by the Commission, which appropriately addressed the rights of a section of the community whose human rights generally and ESC rights particularly are not considered top of the list in African human rights discourse—mental health patients, which by implication would extend to the rights of other disabled persons under the Charter.[148]

8. Peoples' right to existence and self-determination

The right of self-determination is protected under both the ICCPR and ICESCR, and thus is reflected both as a CP right and an ESC right. The ACHPR identified this right as a peoples' right and combined with it the right to existence. Article 20 of the ACHPR provides that: '(1) All peoples shall have right to existence. They shall have the unquestionable and inalienable right to self-determination.

---

[144] Above para 60.   [145] See para 5 of Pretoria Statement (n 64 above).   [146] Above.
[147] *Purohit and Moore v The Gambia* (above) para 81.
[148] See MA Baderin, 'Recent Developments in the African Regional Human Rights System' (2005) 5 Human Rights L Rev, no 1, 117 at 137–140.

They shall freely determine their political status and shall pursue their economic and social development according to the policy they have freely chosen.'

In *Dawda Jawara v The Gambia*[149] the complainant, a former Head of State of the Gambia, who was overthrown in a military coup in 1994 alleged that the military coup was 'a blatant abuse of power . . . by the military junta' that violated the Gambian people's right of self-determination. He claimed that 'the policy that the people freely choose to determine their political status, since independence has been 'hijacked' by the military [and that] the military has imposed itself on the people'.

The Commission held in that regard that '[i]t is true that the military regime came to power by force, albeit, peacefully. This was not through the will of the people who have known only the ballot box since independence, as a means of choosing their political leaders. The military coup was therefore a grave violation of the right of Gambian people to freely choose their government as entrenched in article 20(1) of the Charter.'[150]

This decision is very commendable in the light of the fact that the protection of democracy is an important means of ensuring the guarantee of ESC rights through good governance.[151]

9. Peoples' right freely to dispose of their wealth and natural resources

Article 21(1) of the Charter provides that: 'All peoples shall freely dispose of their wealth and natural resources. This right shall be exercised in the exclusive interest of the people. In no case shall a people be deprived of it', and article 21(5) provides that: 'States parties to the present Charter shall undertake to eliminate all forms of foreign economic exploitation particularly that practised by international monopolies so as to enable their peoples to fully benefit from the advantages derived from their national resources.'

The nature of this right as an ESC right was brought out clearly in the case of *Social and Economic Rights Action Center for Economic and Social Rights v Nigeria*,[152] where the complainants alleged, *inter alia*, that the defendant state violated article 21 of the Charter by paving 'a way for the Oil Consortiums to exploit oil reserves in Ogoniland' without involving 'the Ogoni communities in the decisions that affected the development of Ogoniland' and that the lack of material benefit to the Ogoni people in that regard constituted a violation of article 21.[153]

In finding a violation of article 21, the Commission began by first identifying the origin of the provision contained in article 21 as follows:

The origin of this provision may be traced to colonialism, during which the human and material resources of Africa were largely exploited for the benefit of outside powers,

---

[149] Communication no 147/95 and 149/96 (2000).   [150] Ibid, para 73.

[151] See chapter on 'Democracy and the Promotion and Protection of Socio-Economic Rights' by Richard Burchill in this book.   [152] Above.

[153] Above para 55

creating tragedy for Africans themselves, depriving them of their birthright and alienating them from the land. The aftermath of colonial exploitation has left Africa's precious resources and people still vulnerable to foreign misappropriation. The drafters of the Charter obviously wanted to remind African governments of the continent's painful legacy and restore co-operative economic development to its traditional place at the heart of African Society. Governments have a duty to protect their citizens, not only through appropriate legislation and effective enforcement but also by protecting them from damaging acts that may be perpetrated by private parties.... This duty calls for positive action on part of the governments in fulfilling their obligation under human rights instruments.[154]

The Commission then held that:

[I]n the present case, despite its obligation to protect persons against interferences in the enjoyment of their rights, the Government of Nigeria facilitated the destruction of the Ogoniland. Contrary to its Charter obligations and despite such internationally established principles, the Nigerian Government has given the green light to private actors, and the oil Companies in particular, to devastatingly affect the well-being of the Ogonis. By any measure of standards, its practice falls short of the minimum conduct expected of governments, and therefore, is in violation of article 21 of the African Charter.[155]

This decision of the African Commission has been highly commended as a landmark decision for the enhancement of ESC rights as would be further analysed below.

10. Peoples' right to economic, social, and cultural development

Article 22 of the Charter provides that: (1) 'All peoples shall have the right to their economic, social and cultural development with due regard to their freedom and identity and in the equal enjoyment of the common heritage of mankind.' (2) 'States shall have the duty, individually or collectively, to ensure the exercise of the right to development.'

This is another of the unique ESC rights guaranteed under the ACHPR and one of the issues addressed by the Commission in *Association Pour la Sauvegarde de la Paix au Burundi v Tanzania, Kenya, Uganda, Rwanda, Zaire, and Zambia*.[156] The communication alleged that the sanctions imposed on Burundi violated article 22 of the ACHPR 'because the embargo prevented Burundians from having access to means of transportation by air and sea', which in essence led to a violation of their right to economic, social, and cultural development.

As stated above, the Commission found that the sanctions imposed did not violate article 22 as it was a legitimate action under both the Charters of the OAU and the UN, even though its effects impeded on aspects of the rights guaranteed under article 22 of the ACHPR. We have argued that this view by the Commission needs to be treated with caution.[157]

---

[154] Ibid, para 56–57.   [155] Ibid, para 58   [156] Above.
[157] See text to n 130 above.

11. Peoples' right to national and international peace and security

Peace and security are necessary requirements for the realization of economic, social, and cultural development in any state. While the need for the maintenance of international peace and security is an important aspect of international law, the specific provision of the right of all peoples to national and international peace and security is unique to the ACHPR.[158] The right may be considered as an enabling right for ESC rights generally under the Charter because without the existence of peace and security, hardly can a state fully pursue the guarantee of ESC rights for its populace. In pursuance of the realization of this right, states parties undertake under article 23(2) to ensure that: (a) 'any individual enjoying the right of asylum under article 12 of the present Charter shall not engage in subversive activities against his state of origin or any other State party to the present Charter' and (b) 'their territories shall not be used as bases for subversive or terrorist activities against the people of any other State party to the present Charter'.

In the case of *Association Pour la Sauvegarde de la Paix au Burundi v Tanzania, Kenya, Uganda, Rwanda, Zaire, and Zambia,*[159] examined above, the complainants also alleged a violation of article 23(2) on the grounds that 'Tanzania, Zaire and Kenya sheltered and supported terrorist militia'[160] that were attacking Burundi.[161] The respondent states denied this allegation and the Commission found no violation of this right on grounds that the sanction imposed on Burundi was in conformity with the OAU Charter and international law.[162]

12. Peoples' right to a general satisfactory environment favourable to their development

Article 24 of the Charter provides that: 'All peoples shall have the right to a general satisfactory environment favourable for their development.' The relevance of this right as an ESC right was demonstrated vividly in the case of *The Social and Economic Rights Action Center for Economic and Social Rights v Nigeria.*[163] The complainants alleged, *inter alia*, that the Nigerian government had 'not required oil companies or its own agencies to produce basic health and environmental impact studies regarding hazardous operations and materials relating to oil production, despite the obvious health and environmental crisis in Ogoniland'. The government was alleged to have 'even refused to permit scientists and environmental organisations from entering Ogoniland to undertake such studies [and] ignored the concerns of Ogoni Communities regarding oil development'.

---

[158] Art 23(1).   [159] Above.
[160] *Association Pour la Sauvegarde de la Paix au Burundi v Tanzania, Kenya, Uganda, Rwanda, Zaire, and Zambia*, above para 3.   [161] Ibid, para 37.
[162] See text to n 130 above.   [163] Above.

In finding a violation of article 24 of the ACHPR, the Commission observed as follows:

These rights recognise the importance of a clean and safe environment that is closely linked to economic and social rights in so far as the environment affects the quality of life and safety of the individual.... The right to a general satisfactory environment, as guaranteed under Article 24 of the African Charter... therefore imposes clear obligations upon a government. It requires the State to take reasonable and other measures to prevent pollution and ecological degradation, to promote conservation, and to secure an ecologically sustainable development and use of natural resources.[164]

The Commission further observed that '[u]ndoubtedly and admittedly, the government of Nigeria, through the NNPC has the right to produce oil, the income from which will be used to fulfil the economic and social rights of Nigerians. But the care that should have been taken as outlined in the preceding paragraph and which would have protected the rights of the victims of the violations complained of was not taken.'[165]

This decision regarding the right to a healthy environment by the Commission has been hailed by academics and activists in the area of both ESC rights and environmental rights.[166] The decision has been followed by a Nigerian Federal High Court in a recent case, *Jonah Gbemre v Shell Petroleum Development Company Nigeria Ltd and Others*[167] where, in granting the application for leave by the applicants to enforce their fundamental human rights under the Nigerian Constitution, the Court observed that the fundamental rights to life and dignity guaranteed by sections 33 and 34 of the Nigerian Constitution 'inevitably includes the rights to clean poison-free pollution-free healthy environment'.

Overall, the Commission has endeavoured in most of the above cases to ensure that it upholds the protection of the ESC rights guaranteed under the Charter through its decisions in the respective communications brought before it. The jurisprudence of the Commission, in this regard, boldly establishes the justiciability of ESC rights and thereby challenges the outdated notion of the non-justiciability of ESC rights. It also demonstrates that institutions of the global North do not have any supremacy in dictating the nature and obligation of human rights generally and that of ESC rights in particular.

One worrying decision, however, is the Commission's submission to a sanction regime imposed in accordance with international law, without full consideration for its adverse effect on ESC rights, especially in African states. It is submitted, in the light of the position adopted by the UN ESCR Committee in that regard,

---

[164] Above para 51 and 52.   [165] Ibid, para 54.

[166] See eg, D Shelton, 'Decision Regarding Communication 155/96 (Social Economic Rights Action Center/Center for Economic and Social Rights v Nigeria) Case No ACHPR/COMM/A044/1' (2002) 96 AJIL, no 4, pp 937–942.

[167] Federal High Court of Nigeria, Holden at Benin City, Suit no FHC/B/CS/153/05.

that the African Commission should revisit its position on this point at the earliest opportunity.[168]

IV. Conclusion

The importance of the full realization of ESC rights cannot be overemphasized owing to its necessity for achieving development, especially in African states. Agbakwa has rightly observed that '[a]ny quest for meaningful development ought to be predicated on the effective protection, enforcement, and realization of ESC [rights]'.[169]

It is clear that the ACHPR provides for a significant range of ESC rights, some of which are unique to the Charter. Yet it does omit some specific classical ESC rights, which the Commission has attempted to rectify through its case law and the adoption of the Pretoria Statement on Economic, Social and Cultural Rights in Africa of 2004. Despite any shortcomings, it would be wrong to conclude that the African Commission has failed in its mandates regarding the implementation of ESC rights in Africa. The Commission has endeavoured, albeit after an initial slow start on ESC rights, to adopt a wide and commendable approach in its interpretation of the scope of most of the ESC rights under the African Charter and also demonstrated the justiciability of ESC rights under the ACHPR. There can, however, be further improvement to ensure the full and practical realization of ESC rights under the African regional human rights system.

Under its interpretative mandate, the Commission has adopted resolutions explaining the scope of only a couple of ESC rights under the ACHPR. These have not gone far enough. It is suggested that the Commission should issue more comprehensive resolutions similar to the General Comments issued periodically by the UN ESCR Committee under the ICESCR, elaborating the scope of the remaining ESC rights guaranteed under the Charter, which are not currently covered by the Pretoria Statement. This will go a long way to elevating the status and standard of ESC rights under the African system. Under its protective mandate, the Commission has through its case law also endeavoured to establish a broad interpretation of most of the ESC rights provided under the Charter, which the African Court on Human and Peoples' Rights (ACrtHPR) will hopefully build upon when it commences operation. The role of the different NGOs and individuals who have summoned courage to bring the relevant communications before the Commission must also be appreciated.

Most importantly, the African states, who are the primary obligation bearers for the rights guaranteed under the Charter, must develop a positive political will

---

[168] See text to n 130 above.
[169] Agbakwa (n 35 above) at 179. *See also* Olowu (n 44 above).

towards the guarantee of ESC rights, through a culture of compliance with the decisions of the Commission now and with that of the Court later on.

With the creation of the ACrtHPR it is envisaged that the Commission will be able to focus much more on its mandate of promoting human rights generally under the Charter.[170] In that regard, it is suggested that equal emphasis be given by the Commission to the promotion of both ESC rights and CP rights. The Commission must be committed to achieving the laudable principles outlined in the Pretoria Statement through enhanced promotional activities that will aim at placing ESC rights in the limelight of human rights in Africa, to empower the African populace with the understanding that they not only have a right to life but a right to 'the things with which to live it well'[171] and to emphasize that African states have an important responsibility, individually and collectively, to make that happen for the African populace.

---

[170] For an analysis of the relationship between the African Court on Human and Peoples' Rights and the African Commission on Human and Peoples' Rights see MA Baderin, n 147 above, 117 at 146.   [171] Achebe (n 2 above).

8

Economic, Social, and Cultural Rights in the Inter-American System

*Verónica Gómez**

I. Introduction

The member states of the Organization of American States (OAS)[1] have granted recognition to economic, social, and cultural rights (ESC rights) for the inhabitants of the Americas in pivotal instruments adopted by the Organization, such as the 1948 OAS Charter,[2] the 1948 American Declaration on the Rights and Duties

---

* Any opinions expressed in this contribution belong to the author and should not be attributed to the IACHR or the OAS. The author thanks Commissioner Victor Abramovich and attorney Oscar Parra for their advice during the preparation of this chapter. This effort to evaluate the role of the Inter-American System in promoting and enforcing ESC rights though the eyes of someone more regularly dedicated to dealing with issues commonly labelled as civil and political rights is of course dedicated to Professor David J Harris, whose teachings and advice are remembered, cherished, and shared with others on a daily basis.

[1] The current members of the Organization of American States [hereinafter 'the Organization' or 'the OAS'] are: Antigua and Barbuda, Argentina, Bahamas, Barbados, Belize, Bolivia, Brazil, Canada, Chile, Colombia, Costa Rica, Dominica, Dominican Republic, Ecuador, El Salvador, Grenada, Guatemala, Guyana, Haiti, Honduras, Jamaica, Mexico, Nicaragua, Panama, Paraguay, Peru, St. Kitts and Nevis, St. Lucia, St. Vincent and Grenadines, Suriname, Trinidad and Tobago, United States, Uruguay, and Venezuela. The Eight Meeting of Consultation of Ministers of Foreign Affairs (1962) resolved to exclude the current government of Cuba from participation in the Organization. The Cuban State, however, is still deemed to be an OAS Member to the effect of compliance with the standards of the American Declaration on the Rights and Duties of Man.

[2] Charter of the Organization of American States, adopted by the 9th International Conference of American States, Bogotá, Colombia, 1948 OAS, Treaty Series, Nos 1-C and 61. Protocol of Amendment of the Charter of the Organization of American States adopted at Buenos Aires, Argentina, 27 Feb 1967 at the 3rd Special Inter-American conference. The Protocol entered into force 27 Feb 1970 (OASTS No 1-A). Protocol of Amendment to the Charter of the Organization of American States ('Protocol of Cartagena de Indias'), adopted at Cartagena de Indias, Colombia, on 5 Dec 1984 at the 14th Special Session of the General Assembly. The Protocol entered into force on 16 Nov 1988 (OASTS no 66). Protocol of Amendment to the Charter of the Organization of American States ('Protocol of Washington') adopted at Washington DC, United States, 5 Dec 1992 at the 16th Special Session of the General Assembly of the OAS. The Protocol entered into force on 25 Sept 1997 (1-E rev *OEA Documentos Oficiales* OEA/Ser.A/2 add 3). Protocol of Amendment to the Charter of the Organization of American States adopted at Managua, Nicaragua, 10 June 1993 at the 19th Special Session of the General Assembly of the OAS. The Protocol entered into force on 29 Jan 1996 (1-F rev *OEA Documentos Oficiales* OEA/Ser.A/2 add 4).

of Man,[3] the 1969 American Convention on Human Rights,[4] and especially in the Convention's 1988 Additional Protocol on Economic, Social, and Cultural Rights (usually referred to as the 'Protocol of San Salvador').[5] If the declaration of these commitments occasionally follows the path established by universal instruments, such as the United Nations Covenant on Economic, Social and Cultural Rights (ICESCR), their motivation is rooted in aspirations common to a majority of states in a region particularly afflicted by structural inequalities.[6] Poverty and social conflict, coupled with suppression of political participation, have been identified as causes of cycles of political instability and state sponsored violence common to many states of Central and South America in past decades.[7]

---

[3] American Declaration on the Rights and Duties of Man, adopted on 2 May 1948 at the International Conference of American States, OAS res XXX, OAS doc OEA/Ser.L/V/I.4 (1948) 'the American Declaration'.

[4] American Convention on Human Rights, adopted at the Inter-American Specialized Conference on Human Rights, San José, Costa Rica, 22 November 1969, *OASTS No. 36* ('the American Convention' or 'the Convention'). The Convention entered into force on 18 July 1978. The current states parties are: Argentina (1984), Barbados (2000), Bolivia (1979), Brazil (1992), Chile (1990), Colombia (1973), Costa Rica (1970), Dominica (1993), Dominican Republic (1978), Ecuador (1977), El Salvador (1978), Grenada (1978), Guatemala (1978), Haiti (1977), Honduras (1977), Jamaica (1978), Mexico (1982), Nicaragua (1979), Panama (1978), Paraguay (1989), Peru (1978), Suriname (1987), Uruguay (1985), and Venezuela (1977). On 26 May 1998, the Republic of Trinidad and Tobago—a state party since 1991—notified the Secretary General of the OAS of its denunciation of the American Convention. In accordance with art 78(1) of the American Convention, the denunciation came into effect one year from the date of notification. See *Basic Documents Pertaining to Human Rights in the Inter-American System* OEA/Ser.L/V/I.4 rev 10, p 56.

[5] Additional Protocol to the American Convention on Human Rights in the Area of Economic, Social, and Cultural Rights, adopted at San Salvador, El Salvador, on 17 Nov 1988 at the XVIII Regular Session of the OAS General Assembly, *OASTS no 69* ('the Protocol of San Salvador'). The Protocol entered into force on 16 Nov 1999. The current states parties are: Argentina (2003), Brazil (1996), Colombia (1997), Costa Rica (1999), Ecuador (1993), El Salvador (1995), Guatemala (2000), Mexico (1999), Panama (1993), Paraguay (1997), Peru (1995), Suriname (1999), Uruguay (1996). See *Basic Documents Pertaining to Human Rights in the Inter-American System* OEA/Ser.L/V/I.4 rev 10 (2004), p 85.

[6] See eg, G Perry, O Arias, H López, W Maloney, and L Servén, *Poverty Reduction and Growth: Virtuous and Vicious Circles* (World Bank, Latin America, and the Caribbean Studies, 2006). The report indicates that the Latin American and the Caribbean regions are the most unequal with the exception of Sub-Saharan Africa. The richest 10% of the population in these regions earns 48% of total income, while the poorest 10% earns only 1.6%. In industrialized states, by contrast, the top tenth receives 29.1%, while the bottom tenth receives 2.5%. It is argued (at p 45) that if Latin America had the level of inequality of the developed world, its income poverty levels would be closer to 5% than to the actual rate of 25%.

[7] See eg, 'Areas in which Further Steps Are Needed to Give Effect to the Human Rights Set Forth in the American Declaration of the Rights and Duties of Man and the American Convention on Human Rights' in IACHR, *Annual Report of the IACHR 1979–1980* OEA/Ser.L/V/II.50 doc 13 rev 1, 2 Oct 1980, ch VI, where the Commission indicates that it has established 'the organic relationship between the violations of the rights to physical safety on the one hand, and neglect of economic and social rights and suppression of political participation, on the other. That relationship, as has been shown, is in large measure one of cause and effect. In other words, neglect of economic and social rights, especially when political participation has been suppressed, produces the kind of social polarization that then leads to acts of terrorism by and against the government.' See also 'Status of Economic, Social, and Cultural Rights in the Hemisphere' in IACHR, *Annual Report of the IACHR 1991*, OEA/Ser.L/V/II.81 doc 6 rev 1, 14 Feb 1992, ch VI.

Special country reports and decisions on individual cases condemning egregious violations of the rights to life, physical integrity, and liberty, perpetrated during these cycles have historically been perceived as a symbol for the prevalent type of regional human rights supervision in the Inter-American System. The protection and enforcement of ESC rights, for their part, have been on many occasions linked to compliance with positive obligations on the part of member states and therefore commonly associated with progressive development.[8]

In a continent where little ground has been gained in terms of the reduction of poverty *vis-à-vis* economic growth,[9] the call for regional scrutiny of member states' efforts to comply with ESC rights is compelling. More persistent still have been the demands that the human rights organs of the OAS—the Inter-American Commission on Human Rights and the Inter-American Court of Human Rights[10]—ensure reparations are awarded and prevent irreparable harm in cases connected with ESC rights.

This outline of ESC rights in the Inter-American System reviews the substantive recognition granted to ESC rights by OAS member states followed by an account of the tools available for monitoring and assessing compliance with ESC rights. Strategies so far employed towards the judicial and quasi-judicial protection of ESC rights will be addressed in the final section of this chapter.

II. Substantive sources of ESC rights in the Inter-American System: aspirations, rights, duties, and standards

An overview of the substantive sources of ESC rights in the Inter-American System involves referencing a variety of treaties, declarations, and resolutions

[8] For the debates regarding positive obligations in the Inter-American System see T Melish and A Aliverti, 'Positive Obligations in the Inter-American Human Rights System' in 15 Interights Bulletin (2006), p 114, where it is argued that the reality of human rights abuse and prevention requires extensive positive action on the part of the State, even to ensure against breach of negative duties and that, as established by the Inter-American Court, states' negative and positive duties in the field of human rights are inseparable in practice. See also A Mowbray *The Development of Positive Obligations under the European Convention on Human Rights* (Hart, 2006).

[9] It has been argued that while China experienced annual per capita growth rates of about 8.5% between 1981 and 2000, reducing poverty by 42%, Latin America's per capita GDP declined by 0.7% during the 1980s and increased by about 1.5% per year in the 1990s, with no significant changes in poverty levels. See G Perry *et al*, above p 21.

[10] The Inter-American Commission on Human Rights ('the Inter-American Commission', 'the IACHR', or 'the Commission'), created in 1959 by a resolution of the Organization, is an autonomous organ of the OAS, with the function of promoting the observance and protection of human rights. It is composed of seven commissioners elected in their capacity as independent experts, by the General Assembly of the OAS. The Inter-American Court of Human Rights ('the Inter-American Court', 'I/A Court', or 'the Court'), created in 1979 after the entry into force of the American Convention, is an autonomous organ of the OAS with the function of adjudicating individual cases and of issuing advisory opinions regarding applicable human rights instruments. It is composed of seven judges, elected in their capacity as independent experts, by the General Assembly of the OAS.

adopted during the last six decades. The instruments expressly intended to provide a catalogue of rights and duties in the area of ESC rights—the American Declaration and the Protocol of San Salvador—are accompanied by others such as the OAS Charter and the American Convention, which infuse the protection of ESC rights with aspirations geared towards economic and social development or to provide a mechanism for follow up.

The OAS Charter enshrines aspirations towards economic and social development as a progressive goal to be achieved through international co-operation. The amendments to the Charter introduced by the Protocols of Buenos Aires, Cartagena de Indias, and Managua[11] emphasize a number of eminently macro-economic objectives, such as increased agricultural productivity and accelerated and diversified industrialization (article 34), as well as bilateral and multilateral objectives relating to foreign trade and finance (article 39), and the integration of the developing member states (articles 42, 43, 44, and 46).

In the same chapter of the Charter, concerns for prevailing structural inequalities and the lack of adequate participation of the population, manifest themselves as objectives towards the elimination of extreme poverty, the equitable distribution of wealth, the establishment of equitable land-tenure systems, the equitable distribution of income, and the introduction of acceptable working conditions, proper nutrition, and adequate housing for all inhabitants (article 34). The adoption of systems of fair wages and social security are proposed as 'mechanisms' to overcome structural inequalities. The Charter declares as a 'principle' that marginal sectors of the population and organizations of civil society must be allowed to participate in the pursuit of these objectives, without discrimination (article 45).

Member states acknowledge in the text of the Charter two rights only: the right to work and the right to an education. Specifically, the Charter singles out certain aspects of the right to work, such as collective bargaining and the workers' right to strike (article 45), and then details a number of positive obligations regarding the duty of states to ensure the enjoyment of the right to education (article 49). The priority to be given to the eradication of illiteracy; the provision of compulsory elementary education free of charge; the progressive extension of diversified middle-level education; and the general availability of higher education are acknowledged as member states' obligations in a language similar to that in the Protocol of San Salvador.

For all its limitations in terms of the lack of recognition of substantive rights, the OAS Charter is nonetheless a crucial instrument for the protection of ESC rights: it encapsulates a number of aspirations and principles relating to social security, equality, and participation that aid the interpretation of state obligations under other instruments; and, as explained below, as the treaty is universally binding on all member states in the System, it provides an anchor for the enforcement of the rights protected by the American Declaration.

[11] See n 2 above.

The 1948 Ninth International Conference of American States that adopted the original OAS Charter also produced the instrument that became the cornerstone of human rights protection in the Inter-American System for three decades: the American Declaration.[12] It has been established that the text of the American Declaration is a 'source of international obligations related to the Charter of the Organization' and that the latter 'cannot be interpreted and applied as far as human rights are concerned without relating its norms to the corresponding provisions of the Declaration'.[13]

The American Declaration gives substantive recognition to ESC rights by establishing the right to special protection, care, and aid of women during pregnancy and the nursing period (article VII); the right to the preservation of health through sanitary and social measures relating to food, clothing, housing, and medical care (article XI); the right to receive free primary education (article XII); the right to work and to a fair remuneration (article XIV); and the right to social security and protection from the consequences of unemployment, old age, or disability (article XVI). The Declaration does not condition the enjoyment of these rights on progressive development or on the availability of resources but simply enshrines them alongside other rights more commonly labelled as civil and political.

In 1969, the member states of the OAS adopted the American Convention on Human Rights which entered into force in 1978. Chapters I and II of the Convention's text enshrine general obligations for the states parties and a catalogue of civil and political rights, respectively. Chapter III, entitled 'Economic Social and Cultural Rights', provides an undertaking to 'achieve progressively... the rights implicit in the economic, social, educational, scientific and cultural standards' set forth in the OAS Charter (article 26).[14] The absence of an explicit catalogue of ESC rights in this Chapter of the American Convention—that is only one Article long—and the reference back to the Charter in this provision have been the cause of much debate on what degree the OAS Charter and/or the American Declaration and other instruments could be considered as a substantive source of obligations for the states parties.[15]

Finally, in 1988, the member states adopted an additional instrument in which they recognized the need that ESC rights 'be reaffirmed, developed, perfected and

[12] For an analysis of the ESC rights provisions in the American Declaration see M Craven 'The Protection of Economic, Social and Cultural Rights under the inter-American System of Human Rights', in D Harris and S Livingstone (eds), *The Inter-American System of Human Rights* (Clarendon Press, 1998).

[13] I/A Court HR, *Interpretation of the American Declaration of the Rights and Duties of Man within the Framework of Article 64 of the American Convention on Human Rights*, Advisory Opinion OC-10/89, Opinion of 14 July 1989, Series A no 10, paras 43 and 45.

[14] For an analysis of the preparatory works of art 26 of the American Convention see M Craven (n 12 above).

[15] Ch Courtis, 'La protección de los derechos económicos, sociales y culturales a través del artículo 26 de la Convención Americana sobre Derechos Humanos' in Ch Courtis, D Houser, and G Rodríguez Huerta (eds), *Protección internacional de los derechos humanos: nuevos desafíos* (Porrua-ITAM, México, 2005).

protected': the Protocol of San Salvador, which entered into force more than a decade later in November 1999.[16] This additional protocol to the American Convention recognizes and reinforces the right to work and the enjoyment of satisfactory working conditions, the enjoyment of trade union rights, the right to social security, the right to health, food, education, and access to the benefits of culture, and to special protection of families, women, children, the elderly and the handicapped, first acknowledged in the American Declaration.

It has been argued that the substantive recognition of rights and obligations afforded by the above instruments, both individually and collectively, fail to address many of the pressing issues afflicting large sectors of the population in the member states, such as the situation of migrant workers, the situation of the internally displaced, or the exclusion of ethnic minorities and indigenous peoples.[17] In fact, the Protocol of San Salvador declares in its Preamble the need to 'consolidate in the Americas . . . the right of its peoples to development, self-determination and the free disposal of their wealth and natural resources'. Yet the catalogue of rights adopted by the member states fails to address many of the circumstances in which these structural inequalities particularly impinge upon the well-being of vulnerable groups. The Declaration and the Protocol fail to impose clear obligations upon the contracting states in areas where discrimination and lack of adequate participation contribute to perpetuate inequality.

As a response, access to health services, food and housing, among other ESC rights, by vulnerable groups such as indigenous peoples,[18] afro-descendant communities, displaced persons and migrant workers[19] have been frequently analysed

---

16 Preamble of the Protocol of San Salvador (n 5 above).

17 See M Craven (n 12 above).

18 The Commission has indicated that 'approximately 400 aboriginal ethnic groups exist in [the American Continent], with different cultures, languages, and lifestyles. They comprise a population surpassing 30 million people, according to conservative estimates. This figure represents approximately 10% of the total population of Latin America, with an increasing demographic importance. . . . These peoples share common basic problems such as: the direct attempts at physical or cultural genocide; the legal or de facto disregard for their institutions or rights; the usurpation of their lands or the infringement of their right to collective and permanent use of their ancestral land; their legal or de facto condition as second-class citizens; the rejection or ignorance of their cultural and pedagogical practices; and consequently, the generalized destruction and erosion of their standards of living.' See *Annual Report of the IACHR 1988–1989* OEA/Ser.L/V/II.76 doc 10, 18 Sept 1989, ch VI, on the grounds for the adoption of an instrument on the rights of indigenous peoples in the Americas.

19 According to the Commission's Rapporteur on Migrant Workers: 'migration in the Americas has seen a notable increase in recent decades. As in the rest of the world, this increase has been due to a convergence of the economic and social factors that have historically spurred migration. . . . Traditional migratory flows, especially the exodus of Mexicans to the United States, have continued their pace or even picked up speed. [I]n recent years, new migratory movements have also emerged, especially in South America. Immigrant receiving states, discussion has centred on ways to restrict entry, on the social, cultural and economic consequences of immigration and on which social services immigrants may legally be denied. In states of origin, however, the debate focuses more on the basic rights of the millions of migrants who are in danger of being exploited abroad and how they can be protected. Further attention is given to which rights and social benefits should be extended to migrant workers and members of their families.' See 'Second Progress Report of the Special Rapporteur on Migrant

in the light of the obligation to ensure, *inter alia*, the rights to life, to physical integrity, to equality before the law, to freedom of conscience, to access to information, to property, and to judicial protection pursuant to the American Convention and/or the American Declaration. What many call the indirect enforcement of ESC rights through the expansive interpretation of civil and political rights has predictably been the object of understandable criticism[20] and pragmatic support.[21]

In any case, the connection and interdependence between civil and political rights and ESC rights is recognized in the Protocol's preamble,[22] as well as in other instruments,[23] and has been consistently emphasized by the organs of the Inter-American System.[24] In addition, individuals and organizations of civil society increasingly bring to the attention of the Inter-American System situations where the redress of human rights violations associated with civil rights demands the modification of social policy or other measures related to ESC rights protection.[25]

Other instruments that define standards and obligations in specific areas of the international law of human rights at the universal, regional, and even national levels, may also have an indirect, yet significant, impact in the protection of ESC rights in the Inter-American System. Article 29 of the American Convention bars any interpretation that may restrict the rights and freedoms recognized in domestic or international law.[26] Therefore, whenever state conduct is under scrutiny

Workers and their Families in the Hemisphere' in *Annual Report of the IACHR 2000*, OEA/Ser.L/V/ II.111 doc 20 rev 16 April 2001, ch VI.

[20] See for instance, M Craven 'Assessment of Progress on Adjudication of Economic, Social and Cultural Rights' in J Squires, M Langford, and B Thiele (eds), *The Road to a Remedy: Current Issues in the Litigation of Economic, Social and Cultural Rights* (UNSW Press, 2005), p 27 and afterwards.

[21] See for instance, V Abramovich and Ch Courtis *Los derechos sociales como derechos exigibles*, Trotta, 2002, p 168 and afterwards.

[22] The Protocol of San Salvador's Preamble recognizes 'the close relationship that exists between economic, social and cultural rights, and civil and political rights, in that the different categories of rights constitute an indivisible whole based on the recognition of the dignity of the human person, for which reason both require permanent protection and promotion'.

[23] The Inter-American Convention on the Prevention, Punishment, and Eradication of Violence Against Women (Convention of Belem do Para), which is the inter-American human rights instrument more widely ratified by OAS member states (thirty-two states)—indicating that violence against women 'prevents and nullifies' the free and full exercise of civil, political, economic, social, and cultural rights: the Convention was adopted in Belem do Para, Brazil, on 9 June 1994 at the XXIV Regular Session of the General Assembly of the OAS, and entered into force in March 1995.

[24] See 'The Realization of Economic Social and Cultural Rights in the Region' IACHR, *Annual Report of the IACHR 1993* OEA/Ser.L/V.85 doc 9 rev, 11 Feb, 1994, Chapter IV.

[25] For examples on dissemination of ESC rights litigation strategies before the Inter-American System see Centro por la Justicia y el Derecho Internacional (CEJIL) *La protección de los derechos económicos, sociales y culturales y el sistema interamericano*, (CEJIL, 2005); T Melish *La protección de los derechos económicos sociales y culturales en el sistema interamericano de derechos humanos: manual para la presentación de casos*, (CDES-Ecuador & Yale Law School, 2003).

[26] Article 29 of the American Convention provides that 'no provision of this Convention shall be interpreted as: a. permitting any State Party, group, or person to suppress the enjoyment or exercise of the rights and freedoms recognized in this Convention or to restrict them to a greater extent than is provided for herein; b. restricting the enjoyment or exercise of any right or freedom recognized by virtue of the laws of any State Party or by virtue of another convention to which one of the said states is a party; c. precluding other rights or guarantees that are inherent in the human personality or

pursuant to the provisions of this Convention, the Inter-American Commission
and Court bring into consideration specific standards regarding the rights of displaced persons, indigenous peoples, prisoners held under the custody of the state
or special protection for children, among others. Some of the international standards more frequently used are those established in instruments such as the UN
Guiding Principles on Internal Displacement,[27] the ILO Convention 169,[28] and
the Standard Minimum Rules for the Treatment of Prisoners.[29] Standards regarding the states' duty to afford special protection to children, contemplated in the
American Convention (article 19), are interpreted in the light of the UN
Convention of the Rights of the Child.[30]

The programmatic nature of many provisions in the American Declaration and
the Protocol of San Salvador (or their silence in areas covered by national law in
many member states) have led local standards to play a main role as substantive
sources of ESC rights in the Inter-American System. Legislation and judicial
decisions that incorporate and make operative standards contemplated in international instruments are crucial to the assessment of compliance with state obligations in many areas of ESC rights.[31]

III. Monitoring and assessment of ESC Rights:
Fact-finding and reporting

The text of the 1969 American Convention requires states parties to share with
the Inter-American Commission periodic reports on the progress achieved in the
area of ESC rights. Almost twenty years later, when concluding the 1988 Protocol
of San Salvador, the member states once more decided to resort to a system of periodic reporting by states parties as the main tool to follow-up on compliance with

derived from representative democracy as a form of government; or d. excluding or limiting the effect
that the American Declaration of the Rights and Duties of Man and other international acts of the
same nature may have.'

[27] UN Guiding Principles on Internal Displacement, adopted on 11 Feb 1998, E/CN.4/
1998/53/add 2.
[28] Convention concerning Indigenous and Tribal Peoples in Independent Countries (ILO no
169), 72 ILO Official Bull 59, entered into force on 5 Sept 1991.
[29] Standard Minimum Rules for the Treatment of Prisoners, adopted by the First United Nations
Congress on the Prevention of Crime and the Treatment of Offenders, held at Geneva in 1955, and
approved by the Economic and Social Council by Res 663 C (XXIV) of 31 July 1957 and 2076
(LXII) of 13 May 1977.
[30] UN Convention on the Rights of the Child, adopted and opened for signature, ratification and
accession by GA res 44/25 of 20 Nov 1989.
[31] See eg, the observations made by the Inter American Commission on the decisions of the
Colombian Constitutional Court regarding the obligations of state agencies towards displaced persons and their importance in terms of respect for human rights in *Annual Report of the IACHR 2005*,
OEA/Ser.L/V/II.124 doc 5, ch IV.

the substantive rights enshrined in the Protocol. Years after the adoption and entry into force of these instruments, efforts continue to define an appropriate system of periodic reporting while avoiding duplication with similar United Nations mechanisms, in which the member states of the OAS also participate. In the meantime, the Commission has made an effort to follow-up on compliance with ESC rights through the general mechanisms available in its Statute and the American Convention.

A. Reporting by the Inter-American Commission

The original 1960 Statute of the Inter-American Commission provided that this organ was to submit in its annual report to the Inter-American Conference (now the General Assembly of the OAS) or to the Meeting of Consultation of Ministers of Foreign Affairs 'a statement of progress achieved in the realization of the goals set forth in the American Declaration of the Rights and Duties of Man'.[32] The Commission dutifully complied by requesting the pertinent information from member states every year and by reproducing in its annual report summaries of the responses received. The entries included information on measures adopted for the provision of health services, labour, social security, and education. No comments or recommendations were made by the Commission in reaction to the information provided by the states.[33] The Commission reserved any observations and recommendations for the statements, reports, and studies, both carried out and made public at its own initiative, in areas considered a priority and where official data was assessed in light of other sources. In 1982, four years after the entry into force of the American Convention and three years after the adoption of its new Statute, the Commission removed the statements concerning 'progress achieved in the realization of the goals set forth in the American Declaration of the Rights and Duties of Man' from its annual report.[34]

In 1969, the contracting states of the American Convention agreed that the Inter-American Commission was to watch over the promotion of rights implicit in the standards in the economic, social, educational, scientific, and cultural fields set forth by the OAS Charter as amended by the Protocol of Buenos Aires (articles 30 to 52). To that effect, article 42 of the Convention indicates that the Inter-American Commission is to receive copies of the reports and studies submitted annually by the member states to the Executive Committees of the Inter-American Economic and Social Council and the Inter-American Council for Education,

[32] Art 9(bis) of the Statute of the Inter-American Commission on Human Rights, approved by the Council of the OAS at the meeting held on 25 May 1960, amended on 8 June 1960 and res XXII of the Second Special Inter-American Conference, in *IACHR Ten Years of Activities 1971–1981*, General Secretariat of the OAS, p 44.

[33] See eg, *Annual Report of the IACHR 1974* OEA/Ser.L/V/II.34 doc 31 rev1 30 Dec 1974, s II, pt I.

[34] See *Annual Report of the IACHR 1982–1983* OEA/Ser.L/V/II.61 doc 22 rev 1, 27 Sept 1983.

Science, and Culture, on issues relevant to the aforementioned area. Article 42 fails to indicate in which specific manner the Commission is to oversee the promotion of ESC rights standards set forth in the OAS Charter.

After the entry into force of the American Convention in 1978 and its new Statute in 1979 the Commission failed to construct a mechanism to comply with the mandate to watch over the ESC rights standards in the OAS. In its 1983–1984 Annual Report the Commission made public its frustration, indicating that 'the lack of precision of the standards cited, combined with the undeniable difficulty involved in the consideration of economic, social, and cultural rights, have brought about the inoperability, in practice, of article 42 of the American Convention'.[35] This critical view regarding substantive recognition of ESC rights in the OAS Charter (as well as the challenges faced in terms of their assessment) were accompanied by an unequivocal statement that the Convention had 'solved the problem of the institution responsible for the protection and promotion of the economic, social, and cultural rights, by entrusting this task to the Inter-American Commission' and that it had advanced 'in the subject of operational mechanisms through the system of reports'.[36] Consequently it should come as no surprise that the following annual reports contained little or no reference to information or reports shared with Inter-American Economic and Social Council or the Inter-American Council for Education, Science, and Culture.

It became clear that, rather than overseeing ESC rights under article 42 of the American Convention, the Commission was prepared to report on this area under articles 41(b) and 41(c)—which provide for the function of making recommendations to member states 'for the adoption of progressive measures in favour of human rights', as well as for the adoption of 'appropriate measures to further the observance of those rights' and 'to prepare such studies or reports as it considers advisable in the performance of its duties'. Article 18 of the Commission's Statute sets forth similar functions *vis-à-vis* all member states of the OAS, regardless of whether they have ratified the American Convention. On some occasions these studies are prepared by Special thematic Rapporteurs created by the Commission in order to gather expertise and information on certain areas often specifically geared towards ESC rights. The existing Rapporteurships are devoted to indigenous peoples, migrant workers, afro-descendants, persons deprived of their liberty, children, and women.[37]

---

[35] 'Areas in Which Further Steps are Needed to Give Effect to Human Rights Set Forth in the American Declaration of the Rights and Duties of Man and the American Convention on Human Rights' *Annual Report of the IACHR 1983–1984* OEA/Ser.L/V/II.63 doc 10, 24 Sept 1984, ch V. In a later annual report the Commission repeated its view on the inconvenience of 'mechanisms such as that regulated under art 42 of the American Convention on Human Rights which established an inadequate system of protection and therefore has not been applicable in the years in which the Convention has been in force'. *Annual Report of the IACHR 1985–1986* OEA/Ser.L/V/II.68 doc 8 rev 1, 26 Sept 1986, ch V.

[36] *Annual Report of the IACHR 1983–1984* OEA/Ser.L/V/II.63 doc 10, 24 Sept 1984, ch V.

[37] For a review on the current activities of the Rapporteurs see *Annual Report of the IACHR 2005* OEA/Ser.L/V/II.124 doc 5, 27 Feb 2006, ch II D.

Commission studies on the human rights situation in one or more member states may be made public independently through country reports, through special thematic reports or as a component of its annual report to the General Assembly of the OAS. Country reports present an analysis of the situation of human rights in a member state and offer pertinent recommendations on the basis of fact-finding during *in loco* visits to the state and from other sources, such as reports issued by intergovernmental and non-governmental organizations, hearings, and other information received by the IACHR. The Commission issued its first country report in 1962[38] and since then it has issued more than fifty of them. Thematic reports examine an issue of special interest in a member state[39] or a general concern in a specific area of human rights of interest to all member states, such as those covered by the thematic Rapporteurs.[40] The Commission has issued a dozen reports of this kind. Annual Reports include a chapter in which the Commission highlights its concern for the situation in a number of member states.[41] They also include a chapter on issues of interest such as the need to adopt new inter-American instruments or highlight certain areas of human rights that are in need of review.

During the mid-1980s the Commission presented its views, in its annual reports, on discussions leading to the adoption of the Protocol of San Salvador. Between 1990 and 1993, the Commission reported on the situation of ESC rights in the region at the request of the General Assembly of the OAS.[42] A first chapter was prepared on the basis of reports submitted by a number of member states to other intergovernmental bodies and on information made public by the Pan-American Health Organization.[43] A chapter to be included in the subsequent annual report was prepared on the basis of information obtained in response to special questionnaires sent to the member states.[44] A third and final study was made public in the annual report for 1993, where the Commission referred, *inter*

---

[38] IACHR *Report on the Situation of Human Rights in Cuba* OEA/Ser.L/V/II 4 doc 30, 1962. This first report on the situation of human rights in Cuba, like other studies on that state adopted through the years, is not the product of an observation *in loco* by the IACHR.

[39] See for instance, IACHR *Report on the Situation of Human Rights of a Sector of the Nicaraguan Population of Miskito Origin* OAS/Ser.L/V/II.62.doc 10 rev 3 and doc 26, 29 Nov 1983.

[40] See eg, *The Human Rights Situation of the Indigenous Peoples in the Americas* OEA/Ser.L/V/II.108 doc 62, 20 Oct 2000.

[41] See eg, ch IV of the Annual Report for 1989–1990 where the Commission makes observations regarding the human rights situation in Paraguay by assessing *inter alia* issues relating to land ownership, and the situation of indigenous peoples. *Annual Report of the IACHR 1989–1990* OEA/Ser.L/V/II.77 rev 1 doc 7, 17 May 1990, ch IV, section on Paraguay.

[42] See resns AG/res 1044 (XX-O/90), AG/res 1112 (XXI-91), AG/res 1169 (XXII-92), and res AG/res 1213 (XXIII-0/93) adopted by the General Assembly of the OAS at its XX, XXI, XXII, and XXIII regular sessions.

[43] See *Annual Report of the IACHR 1991* OEA/Ser.L/V/II.81 doc 6 rev 1, 14 Feb 1992, ch VI 'Areas in which Steps Need to Be Taken Towards Full Observance of the Human Rights Set Forth in the American Declaration of the Rights And Duties of Man and the American Convention on Human Rights'.

[44] See 'Status of Economic, Social and Cultural Rights in the Hemisphere' in *Annual Report of the IACHR 1992–1993*, OEA/Ser./L/V/II.83 doc 14 corr 1, March 12 1993, ch V.

alia, to the principles of indivisibility of civil and political rights and economic, social, and cultural rights; and that of achieving progressively the full realization of ESC rights through the effective use of resources available to guarantee a minimum standard of living for all.[45] No further general studies were published in the annual reports for the following twelve years.

Leaving aside the fact-finding and promotional activities carried out by the Special Rapporteurs, more fruitful reporting on ESC rights by the Commission has been made public through country reports. Starting in 1978,[46] the Commission introduced the study of ESC rights in special chapters of many of its country reports by invoking the standards in the American Declaration, the American Convention and, eventually, the San Salvador Protocol, when applicable. Through these chapters the Commission adopted and reinforced the principles regarding the immediacy required in the adoption of measures to realize ESC rights;[47] the effective enjoyment of minimal conditions required for a dignified life;[48] and the permanent obligation of progressive achievement of ESC rights without the adoption of regressive measures.[49]

The methodologies for the assessment of progressive achievement and compliance with ESC rights are based in the main on the following factors: the appreciation of compliance from the perspective of international legal obligations in light of the adoption of compatible legislation; the evaluation of planning and execution of policy; and the complaints received through individual petitions, or during *in loco* observations.[50] Statistical data regarding extreme poverty, income, unemployment,

---

[45] See 'The Realization of Economic Social and Cultural Rights in the Region' IACHR, *Annual Report of the IACHR 1993* OEA/Ser.L/V.85 doc 9 rev,11 Feb, 1994, ch IV.

[46] IACHR *Report on the Situation of Human Rights in El Salvador* OEA/Ser.L/V/II.46 doc 23 rev 1, 17 Nov 1978, ch XI.

[47] The Commission has indicated that 'the progressive nature of the duty to ensure the observance of some of these rights, as is recognized in the language of the provisions cited, does not mean that the State can delay in adopting all measures needed to make them effective. To the contrary, [it] has the obligation to immediately begin the process leading to the complete realization of the rights contained in those provisions. In no way can the progressive nature of the rights mean that [the state] can indefinitely postpone the efforts aimed at their complete attainment.' IACHR *Third Report on the Situation of Human Rights in Colombia* OEA/Ser.L/V/II.102 doc 9 rev 1, 26 Feb 1999, ch III, para 6.

[48] The Commission has indicated that 'it is essential that the economic, social, and cultural rights recognized in international and constitutional provisions have real effect in the daily lives of each of the inhabitants of [the state], thereby guaranteeing minimal conditions for leading a dignified life'. Ibid (n 47 above) para 5.

[49] The Commission stated in its 2000 Report on Peru that 'the progressive nature that most international instruments confer on state obligations related to economic, social, and cultural rights imposes on states, with immediate effect, the general obligation to constantly seek to attain the rights enshrined in the instruments, without any backsliding. Therefore, a worsening in the effective observance of economic, social, and cultural rights may constitute a violation, among other provisions, of Article 26 of the American Convention.' IACHR *Second Report on the Situation of Human Rights in Peru* OEA/Ser.L/V/II.106 doc 59 rev 2, June 2000, ch VI, para 11.

[50] In its 1999 Report on Colombia, the Commission analysed constitutional safeguards for the protection of ESC rights in detail. See IACHR *Third Report on the Situation of Human Rights in Colombia* OEA/Ser.L/V/II.102 doc 9 rev 1, 26 Feb 1999, ch III. In its 2003 Guatemala report the Commission evaluated the situation of indigenous peoples in light of ILO Convention 169 and

and human development have also been taken into account by the Commission in its assessments.[51] Indicators such as concentration of land and income have been used to determine social exclusion, and access to services relating to education and sanitation, among others, contribute to determining the degree of coverage of measures adopted by the state.[52]

B. The reporting system under the Protocol of San Salvador

In 1983, while preparing the draft Protocol of San Salvador, the Commission issued a warning on the importance of endowing the protection and promotion of ESC rights enshrined in that treaty upon an independent institution.[53] However, in 1988, when adopting the text of the Protocol, member states opted for a mechanism of reporting based on the submission of periodic reports to the then Inter-American Economic and Social Council and the Inter-American Council for Education, Science, and Culture (article 19), both being political organs of the OAS.[54]

In 1996, with the entry into force of the Managua Protocol to the OAS Charter, the Economic and Social Council and the Council for Education, Science, and Culture were replaced by the Inter-American Council for Integral Development (CIDI). CIDI is a decision-making body composed of a representative of each of the OAS member states, at the ministerial level or the equivalent. CIDI reports to the General Assembly of the OAS and its key objectives are to serve as a forum for technical policy level discussions on matters related to development, and to strengthen a partnership among OAS states to promote co-operation for development and the elimination of extreme poverty in the region.[55]

domestic legislation regarding national languages. See IACHR *Justicia e inclusión social: los desafíos de la democracia en Guatemala* OEA/Ser.L/V/II.118 doc 5 rev 2, 29 diciembre de 2003, (available in Spanish only), ch IV.

[51] IACHR *Report on the Situation of Human Rights in Mexico* OEA/Ser.L/V/II.100 doc, 24 Sept 1998, ch VII and IACHR, *Fifth Report on the Situation of Human Rights in Guatemala* OEA/Ser.L/V/II.100 doc 7 rev 1, 24 Sept 1998, ch III.

[52] In the 1999 report on Colombia the Commission assessed the degree of compliance with the duty to provide health care by comparing the percentage of the population with access to health care that had fallen from 88% to 87% between 1980 and 1993 and indicated that 'the obligation to develop these rights progressively requires at a minimum that their observance and access to them not be diminished over time'. IACHR *Third Report on the Situation of Human Rights in Colombia* OEA/Ser.L/V/II.102 doc 9 rev 1 26 Feb 1999, ch III, para 7.

[53] The Commission indicated that there was 'consensus among the experts in pointing out that one important element in the operational failure in the protection and promotion of those rights in the system of the Covenant has been leaving that matter within the sphere of a political agency such as the U.N. Economic and Social Council'. See 'Areas in Which Further Steps are Needed to Give Effect to Human Rights Set Forth in the American Declaration of the Rights and Duties of Man and the American Convention on Human Rights' Annual Report of the IACHR 1983–1984 OEA/Ser.L/V/II.63 doc 10, 24 Sept 1984, ch V.

[54] Pertinent parts of the reports may also be sent to the Inter-American Commission of Women, the Inter-American Children's Institute, or the Inter-American Indian Institute, for observations in their capacity as specialized organs of the OAS.

[55] Its sessions take the form of regular annual meetings or special meetings to deal with specific topics. An executive committee of member states acts on behalf of CIDI to ensure the execution of its

With the entry into force of the Protocol of San Salvador in 1999,[56] the General Assembly of the OAS was left with the task of formulating a set of rules for the submission of reports to CIDI on progressive measures taken to ensure the rights set forth in the Protocol. It was only in 2005 that the standards for the preparation of reports pursuant to the Protocol of San Salvador were issued: the Permanent Council[57] was instructed to establish a working group within the CIDI to examine the reports to be submitted by the states parties to the Protocol; and the Inter-American Commission was instructed to propose 'progress indicators to be used [by the working group] for each group of protected rights on which information is to be provided' by the states in their reports.[58] At the time of writing these tasks are pending and the procedure envisaged for the study of these reports remains untested.[59]

In any case, the Inter-American Commission has retained its function of issuing observations and recommendations regarding the adoption of measures to further the observance of human rights under the Protocol. The Secretary General of the OAS must send to the Inter-American Commission a copy of the reports presented to the CIDI so that the Commission may formulate the observations it deems pertinent in its annual report or a special report, at its discretion (article 19.7). Everything indicates that the information at the disposal of the political organs of the Organization may be scrutinized independently by the Inter-American Commission.

Efforts continue to define an appropriate system of periodic reporting on the progress achieved by states in providing education, health services, social security

decisions. CIDI also has created specialized committees on trade, social development, and sustainable development. See <http://www.cidi.oas.org/backg.asp> accessed May 2006.

[56] The Protocol entered into force on 16 Nov 1999 with the deposit of the 11th instrument of ratification (by Costa Rica), pursuant to art 21(3).

[57] The Permanent Council of the OAS is composed of one representative of each member state and within the limit of the Charter and of inter-American treaties and agreements it takes cognizance of any matter referred to it by the General Assembly or the Meeting of Consultation of Ministers of Foreign Affairs (arts 80 and 82 of the OAS Charter).

[58] AG/res 2074 (XXXV-0/05) adopted on 7 June 2005. The notes in the appendix to the resolution indicate that ('the idea is not to construct indices in the sense of algebraic measurements that compare all states in the region in terms of their progress. On the contrary, the progress indicator system studies processes and makes it possible to evaluate different areas of rights in terms of progress; identify, *inter alia*, trends, favourable conditions, and recurring obstacles; and, in that way, recommend concrete measures. Initially, a simple structure common to all the protected rights would be adopted, in order to establish a base to be developed in depth and detail.')

[59] The standards prepared by the General Assembly indicate that the Working Group shall present its preliminary conclusions on the national report to the state party concerned. Following receipt of those preliminary conclusions, each state party shall have sixty days to make additional comments for analysis by the Working Group. The Working Group shall adopt final conclusions on the analysed reports by consensus. Those conclusions shall be notified to the state party in a written communication and at a meeting with the accredited permanent representative to the Organization of American States. The Working Group shall submit a report with a view to its presentation to the General Assembly of the Organization. Appendix to Resolution AG/res 2074 (XXXV-0/05) adopted on 7 June 2005.

and ensure labour rights, etc. In the meantime, the Commission has made an effort to stimulate compliance with ESC rights through the procedural mechanisms provided in the American Convention, its Statute, and Rules of Procedure. The following sections illustrate the procedures for the examination of petitions and requests for protective measures, and examine some of the consequences in terms of the protection of ESC rights.

IV. The adjudication of claims on the alleged violation of ESC rights

Individuals, groups of individuals, and organizations may bring before the Inter-American System claims regarding the alleged violation of the rights protected in the American Declaration; the substantive provisions of the American Convention; articles 8(a) and 13 of the Protocol of San Salvador (rights to organize trade unions and to education);[60] article 7 of the Convention of Belém do Pará;[61] and any other applicable Inter-American human rights treaty ratified by the interested state. The procedure for the processing of claims on the alleged violation of these instruments is divided into two stages: a first stage—that can be seen as quasi-judicial—is designed to stimulate the possibility of a friendly settlement between the claimant and the state and to expedite the resolution of the controversy through an amicable

---

[60] Art 8(1)(a) of the San Salvador Protocol provides that the states parties shall ensure 'the right of workers to organize trade unions and to join the union of their choice for the purpose of protecting and promoting their interests. As an extension of that right, the States Parties shall permit trade unions to establish national federations or confederations, or to affiliate with those that already exist, as well as to form international trade union organizations and to affiliate with that of their choice. The States Parties shall also permit trade unions, federations and confederations to function freely.' Article 13 provides that '1. Everyone has the right to education. 2. The States Parties to this Protocol agree that education should be directed towards the full development of the human personality and human dignity and should strengthen respect for human rights, ideological pluralism, fundamental freedoms, justice and peace. They further agree that education ought to enable everyone to participate effectively in a democratic and pluralistic society and achieve a decent existence and should foster understanding, tolerance and friendship among all nations and all racial, ethnic or religious groups and promote activities for the maintenance of peace. 3. The States Parties to this Protocol recognize that in order to achieve the full exercise of the right to education: a. Primary education should be compulsory and accessible to all without cost; b. Secondary education in its different forms, including technical and vocational secondary education, should be made generally available and accessible to all by every appropriate means, and in particular, by the progressive introduction of free education; c. Higher education should be made equally accessible to all, on the basis of individual capacity, by every appropriate means, and in particular, by the progressive introduction of free education; d. Basic education should be encouraged or intensified as far as possible for those persons who have not received or completed the whole cycle of primary instruction; e. Programs of special education should be established for the handicapped, so as to provide special instruction and training to persons with physical disabilities or mental deficiencies. 4. In conformity with the domestic legislation of the States Parties, parents should have the right to select the type of education to be given to their children, provided that it conforms to the principles set forth above. 5. Nothing in this Protocol shall be interpreted as a restriction of the freedom of individuals and entities to establish and direct educational institutions in accordance with the domestic legislation of the States Parties.' Note 5 (above).   [61] See n 23 (above).

solution, with the good offices of the Commission. A second stage, available only in relation to claims filed against states party to the American Convention that have accepted the jurisdiction of the Court, is mostly devoted to producing evidence that might lead to the adequate reparation of the damage caused by the alleged violation, through a judgment. Claims on the alleged violation of rights under the Declaration and the American Convention relating to ESC rights issues have been brought before the Commission and the Court.

A. Quasi-judicial protection of ESC rights

The Commission receives approximately 1,400 petitions annually. The trends of the last few years[62] reveal that little more that ten per cent of them satisfy the requirements established in the Commission's Rules of Procedure regarding the presentation of colourable claims, clear information on exhaustion of remedies, and timely submission, and can therefore be processed and transmitted to the interested state.[63] Since the inauguration of the procedure for the study of petitions in the late 1960s the Commission has processed and transmitted more than 13,000 petitions.

The Commission is competent to process and decide upon claims under both the Declaration and the American Convention. Member states that are not a party to the American Convention[64] are still bound to respect the substantive guarantees set forth in the Declaration, and the Commission is competent to examine complaints filed against them under that instrument.[65] These complaints are

---

[62] See IACHR *Annual Report of the IACHR 2005*, OEA/Ser.L/V/II.124 doc 5, 27 Feb 2006, ch III 'Statistics'.

[63] The requirements for the consideration of petitions under art 28 of the Rules of Procedure provide that 'Petitions addressed to the Commission shall contain the following information: a. the name, nationality and signature of the person or persons making the denunciation; or in cases where the petitioner is a nongovernmental entity, the name and signature of its legal representative(s); b. whether the petitioner wishes that his or her identity be withheld from the State; c. the address for receiving correspondence from the Commission and, if available, a telephone number, facsimile number, and email address; d. an account of the act or situation that is denounced, specifying the place and date of the alleged violations; e. if possible, the name of the victim and of any public authority who has taken cognizance of the fact or situation alleged; f. the State the petitioner considers responsible, by act or omission, for the violation of any of the human rights recognized in the American Convention on Human Rights and other applicable instruments, even if no specific reference is made to the article(s) alleged to have been violated; g. compliance with the time period provided for in Article 32 of these Rules of Procedure; h. any steps taken to exhaust domestic remedies, or the impossibility of doing so as provided in Article 31 of these Rules of Procedure; and, i. an indication of whether the complaint has been submitted to another international settlement proceeding as provided in Article 33 of these Rules of Procedure.' *Rules of Procedure of the Inter-American Commission on Human Rights*, Approved by the Commission at its 109th special session held from 4 to 8 Dec 2000, amended at its 116th regular period of sessions, held from 7 to 25 Oct 2002 and at its 118th regular period of sessions, held from 7 to 24 Oct 2003.

[64] The OAS states which are not party to the American Convention are: Antigua and Barbuda, Bahamas, Belize, Canada, Cuba, Dominica, Guyana, Saint Lucia, Saint Vincent and the Grenadines, St. Kitts and Nevis, Trinidad and Tobago (since 1999), and the United States.

[65] See I/A Court HR *Interpretation of the American Declaration of the Rights and Duties of Man within the Framework of Article 64 of the American Convention on Human Rights, Advisory Opinion OC-10/89, July 14, 1989, Series A no 10*, paras 45–46.

processed under the authority of the Commission's Statute (article 20)[66] and the procedure established in the Rules of Procedure. The Commission's final decision on these claims is published in its annual report to the General Assembly.

As far as states that have ratified the Convention are concerned, in those cases where there is duplication between the rights protected in the Convention and those in the Declaration, the Commission only rules upon possible violations of the Convention. In those cases where the allegations refer to rights enshrined in the Declaration that are not specifically protected under the American Convention—such as the right to health and other ESC rights—the Commission has found that the Convention cannot be interpreted as excluding or limiting the effect of the American Declaration.[67] Consequently, the study of a claim might involve findings relating to the violation of both instruments.

The flexible *inter partes* procedure contemplated in its Rules allows the Commission to hear arguments and counter arguments on jurisdiction presented by both parties until it is satisfied about the admissibility or inadmissibility of the claims (articles 30 and 37). Once its decision on admissibility is made public, the Commission must place itself at the disposal of the parties in order to reach a friendly settlement of the matter under study. The Commission may also choose to do so even before a pronouncement on admissibility is made (article 41).

Amicable solutions involve mutual agreement regarding the manner in which some or all the claims are to be satisfied, thus avoiding a pronouncement on the merits of the claim and on the possible responsibility of the state by the Commission. Friendly settlement agreements may be reached in the early stages of the procedure and made public immediately, as in the case of the agreement reached with the government of Paraguay in 1999 on the acquisition of ancestral lands to be reconveyed to the Enxet-Lamenxay and Kayleyphapopyet indigenous communities.[68] In many other instances, especially those connected with the

---

[66] Art 1(2)(b) of the Statute of the Inter-American Commission on Human Rights, Approved by res 447 of the General Assembly of the OAS at its 9th Regular Session, held in La Paz, Bolivia, Oct, 1979.

[67] See IACHR Rep no 3/01 (Amílcar Menéndez, Juan Manuel Caride *et al*—case 11.670) Argentina, *Annual Report of the IACHR 2000* OEA/Ser./L/V/II.111 doc 20 rev, 16 April 2001, paras 41 and 42, where the Commission declared admissible a claim on the alleged violation of the rights protected under Articles 1(1), 2, 8(1), 21, 24, and 25(2)(c) of the Convention and those protected under Articles XI, XVI, XXXV, and XXXVII of the Declaration. See also the original decisions of the Commission regarding the right to health of indigenous communities IACHR res 12/85 (Yanomami-Case 7615-Brazil) *Annual Report of the IACHR 1985*, OEA/Ser.L/V/II.66, doc 10 rev 1; IACHR res (without number) (*Aché People*-Case 1802-Paraguay) *Annual Report of the IACHR 1977* OEA/Ser.L/V/II.43, doc 21 corr 1, 1978.

[68] Report no 90/99, Friendly Settlement, (Case 11.713-Enxet-Lamenxay and Kayleyphapopyet (Riachito) Indigenous Communities-Paraguay) *Annual Report of the IACHR 1999* OEA/Ser.L/V/II.106 doc 6 rev 13, April 1999. The Commission describes the proceedings in the following manner: 'On December 12, 1996, the Commission received the complaint, and, on January 8, 1997 transmitted the pertinent parts of the complaint to the Paraguayan State. On 8 May, 1997, the Commission made itself available to the parties in order to attempt a friendly settlement. On July 3, 1997, a friendly settlement hearing was held in Paraguay. On March 25, 1998, a friendly settlement agreement was signed in

adoption of public policies with an impact on social security, the parties tend to pursue protracted negotiations that are thereby wholly at the mercy of the benefits and risks of changes in government. In any case, friendly settlement negotiations provide a valuable opportunity for the claimant to influence public policy through dialogue and consensus, with the Commission assisting the parties by framing the issues under discussion within the standards established by the international law of human rights.

Whenever it is not possible for the parties to reach an amicable solution and the procedure to examine the parties' positions on the merits of the claim has thus been exhausted, the Commission may issue a report ruling on whether the Declaration, the American Convention or the San Salvador Protocol have been violated. A large majority of decisions on the merits adopted by the Commission during the last five years have not been made public. New criteria on the referral of cases to the jurisdiction of the Court introduced in the Rules of Procedure in force since 2001 have increased the number of complaints filed with the Court exponentially to the detriment of the publication of findings on the merits in the Commission's annual report.[69]

The Commission continues to make public its decisions on admissibility that aid in the identification of trends in the protection of ESC rights. For example, the awaited interpretation on the protection of trade union and education rights under the San Salvador Protocol;[70] the protection of the right to a dignified life and the right to health, through the expansive interpretation of the right to physical integrity and the right to life as protected in the American Convention in favour of detainees without access to medical attention or sanitation,[71] and patients infected

Washington DC and, subsequently, several meetings between the Commission, the State, and the petitioners were held in order to follow up on the commitments acquired under the friendly settlement agreement. On July 30, 1999, at an event in Asunción attended by the IACHR, Dr. Luis Angel González Macchi, President of the Republic of Paraguay, presented the representatives of the indigenous communities with documents testifying to Paraguay's compliance with the commitments contained in the friendly settlement agreement.' Compare the agreement reached in this case with the claims brought before the Inter-American Court in the *Sawhoyamaxa Community Case*, considered below.

[69] Art 51 of the American Convention has so far been interpreted in a manner that precludes the publication of the Commission's findings on the merits once this organ refers the matter to the contentious jurisdiction of the Court. Therefore, the Commission has grounded the complaints filed with the Court on the findings of fact and law and the conclusions reached in its reports on the merits but it has interpreted that it is not at liberty to publish them once the matter is under the jurisdiction of the Court. See the reasoning of the Court in I/A Court HR Advisory Opinion OC-13/93 of 16 July 1993, *Certain Attributes of the Inter-American Commission on Human Rights* (arts 41, 42, 44, 46, 47, 50, and 51 of the American Convention on Human Rights) requested by the governments of the Republic of Argentina and the Republic of Uruguay, paras 45 to 56.

[70] IACHR Rep no 23/06 (Union of Ministry of Education Workers ATRAMEC—El Salvador), adopted on 2 March 2006, where the Commission declared admissible a claim on the violation of art 8 of the Protocol of San Salvador. IACHR Report no 39/02 (adolescents in the custody of the FEBEM-P12328-Brazil) *Annual Report of the IACHR 2002* OEA/Ser.L/V/II.117 doc 1 rev 1, 2003, where the Commission declares admissible a claim on the violation of art 13 of the Protocol of San Salvador.

[71] See eg IACHR Rep no 51/05 (Mendoza Prison Inmates-P 1231/04-Argentina) *Annual Report of the IACHR 2005* OEA/Ser.L/V/II.124 doc 5, 27 Feb 2006. See also IACHR Rep no 38/02 (*Damião Ximenes Lopes*-C12237—Brazil), *Annual Report of the IACHR 2002* OEA/Ser.L/V/II.117

with HIV/AIDS;[72] the admission of new claims on the alleged violation of article 26 of the American Convention, which might lead the Commission and the Court to revisit the interpretation issued in the *Five Pensioners Case* (discussed below).[73]

B. Judicial protection of ESC rights

The contentious jurisdiction of the Inter-American Court is activated by the Inter-American Commission through the filing of a complaint against a state party to the Convention that has accepted the jurisdiction of the Court. These complaints are based on the Commission's own findings and recommendations issued in reports on the merits of claims on the violation of the American Convention and other applicable Inter-American instruments. Once the complaint has been lodged, the original claimant is brought into the procedure and is given an opportunity to present arguments, evidence and requests on the reparations sought. The state involved can file preliminary objections to the jurisdiction of the Court that might be resolved separately or jointly with the merits of the case. The Court may summon the parties to a public hearing where they can produce oral testimony from witnesses and experts. After receiving final written allegations from the state, the claimant and the Commission, the Court issues its judgment.

Between 1979 and 2006 the Court issued approximately seventy-five judgments on the merits, several of which have related to ESC rights. For example, it established that there was state responsibility for failure to comply with positive obligations to afford protection to children, persons held under custody of the state, children held under such custody, and indigenous and afro-descendant communities.[74] In many cases, these judgments ordered the states to implement measures relating to the provision of health services, education, and housing as reparations for violations to the right to life and physical integrity, or the consequences of displacement, among others.[75] The Court has not yet had the chance

doc 1 rev 1, 2003; and I/A Court HR *Ximenes Lopes v Brazil*, Preliminary Exceptions, judgment of 30 Nov 2005. Series C no 139.

[72] Rep no 32/05 (Luis Rolando Cuscul Pivaral and others infected with HIV/AIDS-Petition 642/05—Guatemala) *Annual Report of the IACHR 2005* OEA/Ser.L/V/II.124 doc 5, 27 Feb 2006.

[73] The Commission has declared admissible claims on the violation of art 26 in the case regarding the alleged responsibility of Ecuador for the impact of oil-exploration activities in the ancestral lands of the *Sarayaku indigenous community*. IACHR Rep no 64/04 *(Kichwa Peoples of the Sarayaku Community and its Members—P167/103—Ecuador) Annual Report of the IACHR 2004*, OEA/Ser.L/V/II.122 doc 5 rev 1, 2005.

[74] See eg, I/A Court HR, *Case Aloeboetoe et al v Suriname*, judgment of 4 Dec 1991, Series C no 11; I/A Court HR, *Case Villagrán Morales et al v Guatemala (Street Children case)*, judgment of 19 Nov 1999, Series C no 63; I/A Court HR, *Case of Children's Rehabilitation Centre v Paraguay*, judgment of 2 Sept 2004, Series C no 112; I/A Court HR, *Case of Yakye Axa Indigenous Community v Paraguay*, judgment of 17 June 2005, Series C no 125; I/A Court HR *Case of the Sawhoyamaxa Indigenous Community v Paraguay*, judgment of 29 March 2006, Series C no 146.

[75] See eg, I/A Court HR, *Case Aloeboetoe et al v Suriname* reparations (art 63.1 of the American Convention on Human Rights), judgment of 10 Sept 1993, Series C no 15; I/A Court HR, *Case of Villagrán-Morales et al v Guatemala (Street Children case)* reparations (art 63.1 American Convention on

to rule upon the interpretation of articles 8(a) and 13 of the Protocol of San Salvador. It has, however, had an opportunity to interpret the obligation to adopt measures with a view to the progressive realization of the ESC rights under the American Convention, in the context of an individual case regarding social security in Peru: the *Five Pensioners Case*.[76]

In this case, the Commission argued that the state had violated article 26 of the American Convention when passing legislation deemed to be an unjustified regression in terms of the social security due to five pensioners under legislation previously in force. It was alleged that the legislation imposed a cap substantially lower than the amount of the equalized pension that the petitioners were originally receiving, to the point of reducing it to one-fifth of its original value.[77] In response, Peru submitted that the pension that the claimants were receiving as a result of the judicial proceedings they filed, was considerably higher than the one to which they would have been legally entitled had their pensions been regulated by the regime applicable to public sector employees. It also argued that article 26 could not be interpreted so extensively as to suggest that payment of pensions should not be limited by law.[78]

The Court explained in its judgment that, under the individual and collective dimension of ESC rights, progressive development should be 'measured in function of the growing coverage of [these rights] in general, and of the right to social security and to a pension in particular, of the entire population, bearing in mind the imperatives of social equity, and not as a function of the circumstances of a very limited group of pensioners, who do not necessarily represent the prevailing situation'.[79] The Court therefore abstained from ruling on whether the state had progressively realized the right to social security; but it did declare the rights to property and to judicial protection had been violated by Peru under the American Convention, and found that the state had failed to adopt legislative and other measures needed to give effect to the rights protected under the treaty.

The Court's reasoning regarding the individual and collective dimension of the right to social security under article 26 has been criticized for precluding individuals from alleging direct violations of ESC rights autonomously and forcing them to prove harm compared with the majority of the population.[80] More worryingly might be the Court's self-imposed limitation of evaluating the public policy impact based on a factor such as evidence on its overall effect on a large sector of the population. It has been suggested that this implication might have a negative effect on the protection of groups prone to discrimination.[81]

Human Rights), judgment of 26 May 2001, Series C no 77; I/A Court HR, *Case of Yakye Axa Indigenous Community v Paraguay*, judgment of 17 June 2005, Series C no 125; I/A Court HR *Case of the Sawhoyamaxa Indigenous Community v Paraguay*, judgment of 29 March 2006, Series C no 146.

[76] I/A Court HR *Case 'Five Pensioners' v Peru*, judgment of 28 Feb 2003, Series C no 98.

[77] Ibid para 142.   [78] Ibid para 143.   [79] Ibid paras 147 and 148.

[80] T Melish 'A Pyrrhic Victory for Peru's Pensioners: Pensions, Property and the Perversion of Progressivity' in *1 Revista CEJIL Debates sobre Derechos Humanos (2005)* 51.

[81] C de Roux Rengifo, 'La protección judicial de los derechos económicos, sociales y culturales en el sistema interamericano' in Renato Zerbini Robeiro Leao (ed), *Os rumos do Directo Internacional dos directos humanos: ensayos em homenagem ao professor Antonio Augusto Cançado Trindade* (Fabris, 2005).

As mentioned before, the Court has approached the protection of ESC rights indirectly, through the expansive interpretation of the rights protected in the American Convention. It has also considered ESC rights at the moment of ruling on reparations in favour of vulnerable groups such as indigenous peoples, afro-descendant communities, and displaced populations or in favour of children and detainees, towards whom states have a duty of special protection.

The decision in the *Sawhoyamaxa Case*[82] provides a clear example of the Inter-American Court's approach to determining a state's duty to ensure the right of indigenous peoples to inhabit and use ancestral lands, and to provide access to food, water, education, and health services, through findings on the violation of the rights to life and property as protected in the American Convention. The case highlighted the situation of the Sawhoyamaxa indigenous community in Paraguay that lived by the side of a road, without access to basic services, on the boundaries of their ancestral lands where they were considered trespassers under Paraguayan law.[83]

The Commission brought the case before the Court alleging that, by failing to recognize and ensure the right of the Sawhoyamaxa community to the enjoyment of their ancestral land, Paraguay had failed to ensure access to their traditional means of subsistence. The Commission and the representatives of the Sawhoyamaxa community indicated that more than thirty people—the majority of them children of three years of age or younger—had died as a result of preventable diseases and lack of access to food and potable water. They argued that the deaths were attributable to the state, in support of which assertion evidence was produced to prove that state agencies had failed to provide diligent assistance to the members of the indigenous community.[84] Paraguay argued that private companies—whose rights were protected under a bilateral agreement with the Republic of Germany—held legitimate title over the lands under dispute and that these entities had refused to sell their property to the state, thereby impeding the restitution of the land claimed by the Sawhoyamaxa community. It indicated that indigenous peoples had access to health services in similar conditions to those available to the rest of the population and that the community itself was responsible for contacting health agencies by visiting their premises or requesting their services. It argued that the gravity of

---

[82] I/A Court HR *Case of the Sawhoyamaxa Indigenous Community v Paraguay*, judgment of 29 March 2006, Series C no 146.

[83] By the end of the 19th century debts acquired by the state as a consequence of the disastrous war of the Triple Alliance were discharged through the acquisition of large tracts of land in the Paraguayan Chaco by British businessmen through the London Stock Exchange. These lands—largely inhabited by indigenous peoples who were hunter-gatherers—were later partitioned and sold as individual *estancias*, which eventually incorporated the indigenous peoples as workers in exploitative conditions. By the 1990s most members of the Sawhoyamaxa ('from the place where there are no more coconuts') community—composed of approximately 400 persons belonging to the Lengua-Enxet South and Enhelt North peoples—decided to abandon the *estancias* of Loma Porá, Maroma, Diana, Naranjito, Menduca cué, Yakukay, Ledesma, Santa Elisa, and Kilometre 16 and settle by the boundaries of their ancestral land, by the side of the road that connects Pozo Colorado and Concepcion, where they lived while they pursued their claim to recover their land. Ibid para 73.

[84] Ibid paras 145 and 146.

the situation of the Sawhoyamaxa community had been duly acknowledged by a presidential decree that declared it in a state of emergency to which official agencies had responded, within their available means.[85]

The Court found that the state had failed to ensure the effective use and enjoyment of the ancestral land by the Sawhoyamaxa community and had therefore violated the right to property and the undertaking to adopt measures to protect the rights enshrined in the American Convention (art 21, 2, and 1.1). As a measure of reparation, the Court ordered the restitution of ancestral land to the Sawhoyamaxa community—by purchase or expropriation pursuant to national law and the American Convention—or the provision of an alternative piece of land in full agreement with the indigenous community, within three years as from the date of the judgment.[86] This finding on the right to property is similar to that previously issued by the Court against Paraguay in relation to the *Yakye Axa Case*, relating to another indigenous community with an identical ethnic background, situation of vulnerability, and claim to land as that of the Sawhoyamaxa.[87] The finding on the violation on the right to life (article 4) in the light of non-compliance with positive obligations in the *Sawhoyamaxa Case* expands on the standards employed by the Court in *Yakye Axa*, which had led to a split decision on the interpretation of positive obligations under article 4 of the American Convention.[88]

In the *Sawhoyamaxa* judgment, the Court stated that the enforcement of positive obligations under the American Convention—including the adoption of measures destined to ensure a dignified existence or to comply with special duties toward vulnerable subjects that require special protection—cannot be automatic. The Convention, the Court said, ought to be interpreted so as not to impose an impossible or disproportionate burden upon the authorities, in view of the difficulties involved in the adoption of public policies and of operative choices, influenced by priorities and availability of resources. The Court established that the standard for the enforcement of positive obligations requires confirmation that having been aware, or having had the responsibility to be aware, of the risk to the life or lives of an identified individual or group of individuals, the authorities failed to adopt the measures reasonably required to prevent the situation, within their competence.[89]

In application of this standard, aided by the evidence provided by the parties, the Court established a date in 1997 as from which the state had full knowledge of the

[85] Ibid, para 147.   [86] Ibid, paras 135 to 141 and 210 to 215.

[87] I/A Court HR, *Case of Yakye Axa Indigenous Community v Paraguay*, judgment of 17 June 2005, Series C no 125.

[88] Ibid *Case of Yakye Axa Indigenous Community v Paraguay*, judgment of 17 June 2005, Series C no 125, dissenting opinion of Judge Alirio Abreu Burelli and joint dissenting opinion of judges Antonio Augusto Cançado Trindade and Manuel Ventura Robles, where they consider that the majority decision excluding state responsibility for the deaths of ten members of the Yakye Axa Community fails to follow the jurisprudence of the Court regarding the positive obligations of the states parties to ensure the right to life under the American Convention, as established in *Case Villagrán Morales et al v Guatemala (Street Children case)*, judgment of 19 Nov 1999 para 199.

[89] Ibid *Case of the Sawhoyamaxa Indigenous Community v Paraguay*, para 155.

situation faced by the members of the Sawhoyamaxa community—in particular regarding the children and the elderly who were dying—as a consequence of the conditions in which they lived by the road, without sanitation and proper access to food. The Court chose not to rule upon the alleged responsibility of the state regarding deaths that occurred before this date but analysed the evidence produced regarding any loss of life that occurred afterwards, caused by preventable diseases, treatable at low cost.[90] It found that eighteen children and one adult had died of diseases such as tetanus, diarrhoea, dehydration, and other common childhood aliments, even after the state had issued a decree highlighting the state of emergency afflicting the community in 1999: in some cases their parents lacked the means to reach health centres; in others, they were told to buy medicines they could not afford—or were simply turned away. Consequently the Court unanimously declared the state responsible for failing to adopt 'positive measures within its power that could be reasonably expected in order to prevent or avoid risk to the lives of members of the Sawhoyamaxa community' and that therefore nineteen deaths caused by preventable diseases were directly attributable to the state.[91] Paraguay was found responsible for the violation of the right to life and its duty to protect children and ensure compliance with the rights enshrined in the American Convention (articles 4, 19, and 1.1). The Court ordered, *inter alia*, the payment of monetary compensation to the family members of the deceased to be distributed in accordance with the cultural practices of the community; and detailed a number of basic goods and services to be provided by the state, in agreement with the community, until the ancestral lands were duly reconveyed: fresh drinking water and food; medical attention and vaccinations; sanitation services; and bilingual schooling.[92]

The reparations granted in favour of the Yakye Axa and the Sawhoyamaxa indigenous communities are based on the provision of goods and services commonly associated with the satisfaction of the right to a dignified life. Up until the present time, the Inter-American Court has enforced the corresponding positive obligations in favour of vulnerable groups that enjoy reinforced protection of their rights under international law; unfortunately, the judicial enforcement of the provision of health, education, food, and housing for all persons under the jurisdiction of the OAS member states still remains for the Court explicitly to define.

C. Protective measures

Protective measures may be invoked as injunctions to preserve either the Commission's or the Court's jurisdiction *vis-à-vis* an imminent change of circumstance

---

[90] The Court chose to exclude the death of a child afflicted by an abnormal condition of the blood, as not attributable to the state and also found that the deaths of members of the community that had surpassed the life expectancy in Paraguay could not be entirely attributed to the state in view of the available evidence. Ibid *Case of the Sawhoyamaxa Indigenous Community v Paraguay*, paras 172 and 180.   [91] Ibid para 178. Translation by the author.
[92] Ibid paras 226 and 230.

that might affect a claim pending before them. They can also be invoked as urgent measures to prevent irreparable harm to persons where a violation of the American Convention might be imminent and there is still no claim pending before the organs of the system. They are denominated as 'precautionary' or 'provisional' measures depending on whether they have been granted by the Commission or ordered by the Court.

Precautionary measures can be granted by the Commission pursuant to its Rules of Procedure (article 25) at the request of any individual or organization.[93] The Commission is competent to consider requests regarding all member states, including those that have not ratified the American Convention.[94] Precautionary measures are issued by means of a letter addressed to the state concerned where grounds for the decision are brought to its attention, and the adoption of a number of urgent measures in co-ordination with the beneficiaries, is requested.[95] These communications also institute a mechanism of periodic reports by the parties. Follow up mechanisms with the participation of state agencies and beneficiaries have provided an opportunity to agree upon the adoption of positive measures

---

[93] Art 25 of the Rules of Procedure currently in force states that: '1. In serious and urgent cases, and whenever necessary according to the information available, the Commission may, on its own initiative or at the request of a party, request that the State concerned adopt precautionary measures to prevent irreparable harm to persons. 2. If the Commission is not in session, the President, or, in his or her absence, one of the Vice-Presidents, shall consult with the other members, through the Executive Secretariat, on the application of the provision in the previous paragraph. If it is not possible to consult within a reasonable period of time under the circumstances, the President or, where appropriate, one of the Vice-President shall take the decision on behalf of the Commission and shall so inform its members. 3. The Commission may request information from the interested parties on any matter related to the adoption and observance of the precautionary measures. 4. The granting of such measures and their adoption by the State shall not constitute a prejudgment on the merits of a case.' *Rules of Procedure of the Inter-American Commission on Human Rights*, Approved by the Commission at its 109th special session held from 4 to 8 Dec 2000, amended at its 116th regular period of sessions, held from 7 to 25 Oct 2002 and at its 118th regular period of sessions, held from 7 to 24 Oct 2003.

[94] The Commission has indicated that 'OAS member states, by creating the Commission and mandating it through the OAS Charter and the Commission's Statute to promote the observance and protection of human rights of the American peoples, have implicitly undertaken to implement measures of this nature where they are essential to preserving the Commission's mandate'. See IACHR, Report no 52/01 (Case 12.243-United States of America), *Annual Report of the IACHR 2001*, OEA/Ser./L/V/II. 114 doc 5 rev, 16 April 2002, para 117.

[95] Although precautionary measures have functioned as a mechanism for urgent protection in the Inter-American System since 1980, the Commission only started publishing summaries of the measures granted in its annual report for 1996. These summaries provide factual information on the Commission's initial decision to invoke art 25 of its Rules. At least for the moment, no other information regarding follow up on measures adopted by the states concerned and the situation of the individual beneficiaries is made public. Only two circumstances facilitate the publication of further details on the processing of these measures: the publication of a report on the admissibility or the merits of a claim where precautionary measures have been granted either as an injunction or to protect the lives of victims, witnesses, or petitioners; and the referral of the issue to the Court for the adoption of provisional measures pursuant to art 63(2) of the American Convention. Approximately 50% of the precautionary measures granted so far are not linked to individual cases and a very small number of these have been referred to the Court. Consequently, many of the considerations made by the author in this section of the chapter are *per force* the result of her own observation and direct contact with the beneficiaries of precautionary measures granted during the last decade.

tailored to the traditions and culture of indigenous peoples and the way of life of afro-descendant communities. In many cases follow up on compliance with the measures requested is also carried at public hearings and during *in loco* visits.[96]

The Commission has explained that the binding nature of precautionary measures rests on the general duty of the states to respect and guarantee human rights, to adopt legislative or other measures necessary for ensuring effective observance of human rights, and to carry out in good faith the obligations contracted under the American Convention and the OAS Charter.[97] In cases where the measures in force fail to establish an effective mechanism to prevent the commission of violations of the Convention or a state does not implement the measures requested, the Commission has to decide whether to refer the matter to the Court whenever the state in question is a party to the Convention and has accepted its jurisdiction.[98] Since the mechanism was first incorporated into the Rules of Procedure in 1980, the Commission has issued more than 500 precautionary measures.[99]

Provisional measures can be ordered by the Court pursuant to the American Convention (article 63.2) at the request of the Commission or of a claimant in relation to a matter pending before its jurisdiction. The Court may also order provisional measures at the request of the Commission in matters that have not yet been submitted to its contentious jurisdiction. For the Court to be competent to hear it, the request must refer to a state that has ratified the American Convention and accepted the jurisdiction of the Court. Provisional measures are ordered by means of a resolution containing a statement of the grounds for the request and the Court's decision, a list of the measures to be adopted by the state in agreement with the beneficiaries, and a description of the follow up mechanism, usually relying on the presentation of periodic reports by the state, the beneficiaries and the Inter-American Commission. The Court has ordered more than seventy provisional measures, so far.

Precautionary and provisional measures have been invoked, *inter alia*, to ensure access to humanitarian aid by indigenous and afro-descendant communities suffering the impact of forced displacement from their ancestral lands or communal

---

[96] See eg, IACHR Press Release 15/03 issued on 27 June 2003, available at <http://www.cidh.org/Comunicados/English/2003/15.03.htm> accessed on 7 Nov 2006, on an *in loco* visit to follow up on precautionary measures granted in favour of a displaced afro-descendant community in Colombia.

[97] IACHR *Report on the Situation of Human Rights Defenders in the Americas*, OEA/Ser.L/V/II. 124 doc 5 rev 1, 7 March 2006, para 241. For its part, the Inter-American Court has established that 'the ultimate aim of the American Convention is the effective protection of human rights, and, pursuant to the obligations contracted under it, the States should ensure the effectiveness of their mechanisms, which implies implementing and carrying out the resolutions issued by its supervisory organs, whether the Commission or the Court'. I/A Court HR, *Case of the Mendoza Prisons v Argentina*, Order of 22 Nov 2004, operative para 16.

[98] See for instance, I/A Court HR, *Case of Eloisa Barrios et al v Venezuela*, Order of 23 Nov 2004 paras 2 and 6.

[99] Summaries of the precautionary measures granted as from 1996 are made public in the annual reports of the Commission.

territories.[100] They have also been invoked to protect communities afflicted by environmental hazards and ensure access to health services. For instance, on 17 August 2004, the IACHR granted precautionary measures in favour of 5,000 families in San Mateo de Huanchor, Peru, whose health, food, farming, and live-stock were affected by deposits from an open-air mine in the vicinity of the Rimac River. The studies conducted by the Peruvian Ministry of Health had concluded that the cumulative power and chronic effect of arsenic, lead, and cadmium in the deposits generated a high risk of exposure for the communities of the zone and that children were suffering from very high levels of lead concentration in their blood. In view of the risks to the beneficiaries, the Commission granted precautionary measures and requested that Peru implement a health assistance and care program for the population, particularly for children, to identify the persons who might have been affected by the consequences of pollution and to provide the relevant medical care; and to begin transferring the deposits in accordance with the best technical conditions as determined by the relevant environmental impact study.[101]

The Commission has also granted precautionary measures to ensure that states that did not offer universal treatment to patients infected with HIV/AIDS through their respective national health services, adopt positive action to provide medical attention to patients pursuant to the standards established by the Pan American Health Organization in terms of diagnosis and access to antiretroviral medications.[102] Many of the states approached by the Commission managed to obtain external funds to cover the high cost of medications and make the treatment available.

Protective measures have also been crucial to ensure that states comply with their duty to provide medical treatment to persons under custody, whenever the condition—if untreated—could generate irreparable harm to health. The Commission and the Court have also ordered the adoption of measures to improve sanitation in penitentiaries, detention centres for adults, rehabilitation centres for children, and police stations whenever conditions of detention could cause harm to the health of the detainees.[103]

The Commission has adopted a similar approach regarding mentally disabled patients confined in hospital. For instance, on 17 December 2003 the Commission granted precautionary measures on behalf of 458 patients of a neuro-psychiatric hospital in Paraguay, where children were held together with adults; patients were

---

[100] See eg, I/A Court of HR, *Case of the Communities of Jiguamiandó and Curbaradó v Colombia*, Order of 15 March 2005.

[101] See *Annual Report of the IACHR 2004* OEA/Ser.L/V/II.122 doc 5 rev 1, 23 Feb 2005, ch III, s C.1, para 44.

[102] Between 1999 and 2002 the Commission requested Chile, El Salvador, Bolivia, Ecuador, Guatemala, Honduras, Nicaragua, Peru, Dominican Republic, and Venezuela the adoption of measures to provide diagnosis and, when appropriate, antiretroviral treatment to persons infected with HIV.

[103] I/A Court of HR, *Case of the Mendoza Prisons v Argentina*, Order of 22 Nov 2004.

held for years in solitary confinement; and poor sanitation posed a threat to their health. The Commission requested Paraguay to evaluate the beneficiaries' medical condition, improve sanitation, and apply pertinent international standards regarding confinement. In response, the then President of Paraguay visited the hospital, launched an official investigation and made changes in its administration.[104]

The protective measures available in the Inter-American System have proved to be among the more effective mechanisms in ensuring the immediate prevention of foreseeable human rights violations in situations where there is a risk of irreparable harm to persons. When individuals or communities are at risk owing to lack of access to medical treatment or to the consequences of internal armed conflict, among other circumstances, compliance with urgent measures ordered by the Commission or the Court may bring short-term relief, and avert irreparable consequences for the enjoyment of the rights to life and physical integrity and therefore, the right to health.

V. Conclusion

The Inter-American System has been frequently confronted with situations where the redress of human rights violations associated with civil and political rights demands the modification of social policy or other measures related to ESC rights advancement and protection. Large sectors of the population in the member states of the OAS—in particular, vulnerable groups such as indigenous peoples and ethnic minorities, internally displaced persons, and migrant workers, among others—enjoy little access to services and information; and yet discrimination and obstacles to participation contribute to perpetuate inequality and poverty.

Years after the adoption and entry into force of the Protocol of San Salvador, efforts continue to define an appropriate system of periodic reporting on progress achieved in providing education, health services, social security and ensure labour rights, among others. In the meantime, the Commission has made an effort to stimulate compliance with ESC rights through the procedural mechanisms provided in the American Convention, its Statute and Rules of Procedure, in the light of progressive standards adopted in international and domestic law.

The severe impact of inequality and discrimination on the enjoyment of basic rights has led the Commission and the Court to enforce state obligations to provide health services, food, and housing through the adjudication of individual cases and their reparations in a manner commonly associated with the satisfaction of the right to a dignified life. This has been achieved mainly through the expansive interpretation of civil and political rights in the light of the obligation to ensure, *inter alia*, the rights to life, to physical integrity, to equality before the law,

---

[104] See *Annual Report of the IACHR 2003* OEA/Ser.L/V/II. 118 doc 5 rev 2, 29 Dec 2003, ch III, s C.1, p 60.

to access to information, to property, and to judicial protection, pursuant to the American Convention. The Inter-American Court has played a role in strengthening precedents on the enforcement of positive obligations in favour of vulnerable groups, so that they can enjoy reinforced protection of their rights under international law.

The organs of the Inter-American System face several challenges regarding the substantive definition of ESC rights, the evaluation of policies directed to achieving progress in this area, and the direct adjudication of the rights to health, education, food, and housing for all persons under the jurisdiction of the OAS member states.

9

Violations of Economic, Social, and Cultural Rights: The Current Use and Future Potential of the Collective Complaints Mechanism of the European Social Charter

*Robin R. Churchill and Urfan Khaliq**

I. Introduction

The European Social Charter (ESC)[1] is the counterpart, in the field of economic and social rights, of the Council of Europe's much better known European Convention on Human Rights (ECHR).[2] Originally the only machinery that the Charter provided for seeking to ensure that its parties[3] complied with their obligations was a system of reporting, under which states parties report every two years on their implementation of the Charter. Such reports are first examined by the European Committee on Social Rights (ECSR), a 15-member body of independent experts in international social questions (formerly known as the Committee of

* Professor of International Law, University of Dundee and Lecturer in Law, Cardiff University, respectively. This chapter is a revised and updated version of the authors' article, 'The Collective Complaints System of the European Social Charter—An Effective Mechanism for Ensuring Compliance with Economic and Social Rights?' (2004) 15 EJIL 417. The authors would like to take this opportunity to acknowledge the enormous benefit that they have derived in their teaching and research from David Harris' many books and articles, in particular his seminal writings on the European Social Charter. Urfan Khaliq would like to express his gratitude for the assistance, support, and encouragement David Harris provided to him while he was a postgraduate student at Nottingham University.

[1] The Charter was originally adopted in 1961. A Protocol adding further rights was adopted in 1988, while a revised version of the Charter, which updates and extends the rights protected, was adopted in 1996. The texts of these three instruments can be found at CETS nos 35, 128, and 163; and I Brownlie and G Goodwin-Gill, *Basic Documents on Human Rights* (4th edn, OUP, 2002) (hereafter *Basic Documents*) pp 423, 439, and 455. References to the 'Charter' in this chapter refer to all three instruments unless otherwise indicated.　　　　[2] CETS no 005; and *Basic Documents*, at p 398.

[3] Nine members of the Council of Europe are parties to the Charter only in its 1961 version. Seven states are parties to the 1961 Charter as supplemented by the 1988 Additional Protocol, while a further twenty-two states are parties to the Revised Charter.

Independent Experts (CIE)). Thereafter reports and the ECSR's views on them are considered by the Governmental Committee (a body of national senior civil servants) and the Committee of Ministers. The latter may make recommendations to states parties that are not fully complying with the Charter.[4]

In the early 1990s, the Council of Europe embarked on a process of revitalizing the Charter. As part of this process (which also included overhauling the reporting system and drawing up the Revised Charter), the Council in 1995 adopted a Protocol to the Charter that provides an additional compliance mechanism in the form of a system of collective complaints.[5] This Protocol came into force in July 1998, the first complaint under the new system was made in October 1998, and by July 2006 a total of thirty-four complaints had been made, in twenty-nine of which proceedings had been completed.

The aims of this chapter are to review the operation of the collective complaints system to date and to assess its future potential. The chapter describes the genesis of the system and then goes on to explain, in the light of practice so far, how complaints are made and dealt with, before offering some thoughts about the utility and effectiveness of the system and its future prospects. In order to place the system in a general human rights context, the chapter begins by discussing the question of the justiciability of economic and social rights and then goes on to give an overview of mechanisms for seeking to ensure compliance by states with their obligations under other treaties concerned with such rights.

II. The question of justiciability and mechanisms to protect economic and social rights

A. The justiciability of economic and social rights

Although the international community puts increasing emphasis on the indivisibility between economic, social, and cultural rights on the one hand and civil and political rights on the other,[6] this is in contrast to many of the assumptions underlying the mechanisms for their enforcement. Economic and social rights have traditionally been considered as lacking justiciability, a quality which civil

---

[4] For further discussion of the reporting system, see DJ Harris, 'Lessons from the Reporting System of the European Social Charter' in P Alston and J Crawford (eds), *The Future of UN Human Rights Treaty Monitoring* (Cambridge University Press, 2000) p 347 and DJ Harris and J Darcy, *The European Social Charter* (2nd edn, Transnational Publishers, 2001) pp 293–354.

[5] Additional Protocol to the European Social Charter Providing for a System of Collective Complaints, CETS no 158; (1995) 34 *ILM* 1453; and *Basic Documents* p 451.

[6] Emphasis on this relationship has existed since the Universal Declaration of Human Rights (UDHR) 1948, UN doc A/811; *Basic Documents* at p 18. Also see the Vienna Declaration and Programme of Action—World Conference on Human Rights Vienna, 14–25 June 1993, UN doc A/CONF.157/23.

and political rights are deemed to possess.[7] The reason usually given is that economic and social rights are often progressive in nature and that many such rights are couched in language that is too imprecise to be judicially enforceable. Thus a traditional view has been that only bodies that are charged with the enforcement of civil and political rights treaties should be able to provide remedies, of some sort, for their violation and be given powers to that effect.[8]

Although there is a degree of merit in these arguments, they do not always hold true. As is well known, the mechanisms adopted for the enforcement of the International Covenant on Civil and Political Rights (ICCPR) and International Covenant on Economic, Social and Cultural Rights (ICESCR) were the results of political compromise and the categorization of rights was hardly an exact science.[9] To consider that all of the rights that are found in treaties that promote and protect economic and social rights are incapable of being judicially determined is an oversimplification. Some such rights (for example, the right to equal pay) are sufficiently precisely drafted to be judicially enforceable; and for some rights (such as equal pay or consultation rights in the workplace) a judicial remedy may be suitable. While not all economic and social rights are immediately justiciable, it is clear that some can become so over time, as states parties take measures to give them effect.[10] There are, of course, some methodological problems in determining whether a state is complying with its obligations,[11] but these are far from being insurmountable.

---

[7] For detailed discussion of the issue of justiciability see M Addo, 'Justiciability Re-Examined' in D Hill and R Beddard (eds), *Economic, Social and Cultural Rights* (Macmillan, 1991) p 93; M Craven, 'The Justiciability of Economic, Social and Cultural Rights' in R Burchill, D Harris, and A Owers (eds), *Economic, Social and Cultural Rights: Their Implementation in UK Law* (University of Nottingham Human Rights Law Centre, 1999) p 1; M Craven, *The International Covenant on Economic, Social and Cultural Rights: A Perspective on its Development* (OUP, 1995) p 106 and following; A Eide, 'Economic, Social and Cultural Rights as Human Rights' in A Eide, C Krause, and A Rosas (eds), *Economic, Social and Cultural Rights: A Textbook* (2nd edn, Nijhoff, 2001) p 9; M Scheinin, 'Economic and Social Rights as Legal Rights' in the above p 29; *Report of the Expert's Roundtable Concerning Issues Central to the Proposed Optional Protocol to the International Covenant on Economic, Social and Cultural Rights* (Geneva, 2002); and H Steiner and P Alston, *International Human Rights in Context: Law, Politics, Morals* (2nd edn, OUP, 2001) p 275.

[8] See the discussion in Eide (n 7 above) p 10 and T Novitz, 'Are Social Rights Necessarily Collective Rights? A Critical Analysis of the Collective Complaints Protocol to the European Social Charter' (2002) *EHRLR* 50 especially at 57–65.

[9] International Covenant on Civil and Political Rights 1966, 999 United Nations Treaty Series (UNTS) 171; *Basic Documents* p 182 and International Covenant on Economic, Social and Cultural Rights 1996, 993 UNTS 3; *Basic Documents* p 172. For a discussion of the debates at the time and on the splitting up of the rights and perceptions of the protagonists see M Craven, 'The UN Committee on Economic, Social and Cultural Rights' in Eide *et al* (eds) (n 7 above) p 455, at p 456 and following.

[10] See eg, the Limburg Principles on the Implementation of the International Covenant on Economic, Social, and Cultural Rights, UN doc E/CN.4/1987/17, annex, pt I, reproduced in (1987) 9 *HRQ* 122 and Committee on Economic, Social and Cultural Rights (hereafter ESCR Committee) *General Comment 9* UN doc E/1999/22 annex IV. It is also worth noting that the Convention on the Rights of the Child, 1577 UNTS 3; *Basic Documents* at p 241, which includes some economic and social rights, does not, unlike the ICESCR, require their 'progressive' realization, but does make allowances for the means available to a state.

[11] For a discussion of this issue see S Leckie, 'Another Step Towards Indivisibility: Identifying the Key Features of Violations of Economic, Social and Cultural Rights' (1988) 20 Human Rights Q 81;

There is now ample jurisprudence on these issues to illustrate that they can be overcome.[12] Furthermore, some national courts have adopted decisions as to the obligations imposed by provisions of national constitutions, many of which are couched in terms similar to those found in treaties protecting economic and social rights, in which they have not only defined the obligation but also the remedy.[13] It is important to note, therefore, that there is nothing inherent in economic and social rights that prevents judicial determination of their content.[14]

B. Mechanisms for the enforcement of economic and social rights

At the international level, there are various mechanisms for ensuring compliance with treaties containing economic and social rights, some of which illustrate the justiciability of such rights. In the case of treaties which primarily or only contain economic and social rights, the normal mechanism is a system of reporting. This is the case with the ICESCR. It is also largely the case with the San Salvador Protocol of 1988 to the American Convention on Human Rights,[15] although there is a right to individual petition with regard to the right to education and the right to organize.[16]

There are also treaties which contain both civil and political rights as well as economic and social rights.[17] Right-specific treaties, such as the Children's Convention,

---

Craven (n 7 above), pp 106–150; P Alston and G Quinn, 'The Nature and Scope of States Parties' Obligations Under the International Covenant on Economic, Social and Cultural Rights' (1987) 9 Human Rights Q 156 ; G Van Hoof, 'The Legal Nature of Economic, Social and Cultural Rights: A Rebuttal of Some Traditional Views' in P Alston and K Tomaševski (eds), *The Right to Food* (Nijhoff, 1984), p 97; E Vierdag, 'The Legal Nature of the Rights Granted by the International Covenant on Economic, Social and Cultural Rights' (1978) 7 *NYIL* 69, esp 83 and following; and ESCR Committee, *General Comment 3* UN doc E/1991/23 annex III.

[12] In *General Comment* 9, (n 10 above), the ESCR Committee considered the domestic application of the Covenant and clearly envisaged the use of judicially determined remedies for violations of it. See also on this issue M Craven, 'The Domestic Application of the International Covenant on Economic, Social and Cultural Rights' (1993) *NILR* 367.

[13] See in particular, the jurisprudence of the Indian Supreme Court and the South African Constitutional Court. For an excellent discussion of this issue, see S Liebenberg, 'The Protection of Economic and Social Rights in Domestic Legal Systems' in Eide *et al*, (eds) (n 7 above), at p 55 and Steiner and Alston (n 7 above) at pp 283–302. In the context of South Africa see P de Vos, 'Pious Wishes or Directly Enforceable Human Rights? Social and Economic Rights in South Africa's 1996 Constitution' (1997) 13 South African J of Human Rights 67.

[14] ESCR Committee *General Comment 3* (n 11 above) expressly recognizes this in para. 5. Also see *General Comment 9* (n 10 above), which recognizes that judicial remedies will not always be necessary but will be where administrative remedies are not adequate.

[15] Additional Protocol to the American Convention on Human Rights in the Area of Economic, Social, and Cultural Rights, 1988, OAS Treaty Series 69 (1988); *Basic Documents*, at p 693.

[16] Art 19(6). However, claims with regard to all other protected economic and social rights may be brought under the American Declaration of the Rights and Duties of Man 1948, OAS res XXX; *Basic Documents* at p 665. For discussion see M Craven, 'The Protection of Economic, Social and Cultural Rights Under the Inter-American System of Human Rights' in D Harris and S Livingstone (eds), *The Inter-American System of Human Rights* (OUP, 1998) p 289.

[17] Furthermore, some civil and political rights have been deemed to have an economic or social rights aspect to them. In practice this has primarily been limited to inhuman treatment and health

the Race Convention,[18] and the Women's Convention,[19] cover a broad spectrum of different rights. While reporting is the principal mechanism in all these treaties, the now functioning Optional Protocol to the Women's Convention provides a petition system that can be utilized by individuals, for all of the rights protected.[20] Similarly, article 14 of the Race Convention, which establishes the right to individual petition, does not distinguish for enforcement purposes between the different types of rights protected by article 5 of that treaty. In addition, the African Charter on Human and Peoples' Rights,[21] also contains a mixture of rights. The experience of the African Commission illustrates that individual complaints that seek to ensure the protection of economic and social rights are certainly possible, even if they have not yet been utilized to their full potential.[22]

The ILO system, in particular the eight core ILO Conventions,[23] protects many rights that are found in economic and social rights treaties. The main compliance mechanism is a reporting system. However, there are also other mechanisms. Of particular importance, in our context, is the procedure under article 24 of the ILO Constitution which provides for examination, in certain circumstances, of representations by employers' or workers' organizations concerning an ILO Member state's alleged failure to apply the ILO Conventions on Freedom of Association.[24] The Collective Complaints Protocol (the 'CCP')of the European Social Charter was consciously modelled on this system.

Outside the human rights context, in the strict sense, other international mechanisms exist that judicially protect and enforce economic and social rights. The

conditions in prisons under art 3 of the ECHR and art 7 and 10 of the ICCPR, although see HRC *General Comment 6 (Right to Life)* of 30 April 1982.

[18] International Convention on the Elimination of all Forms of Racial Discrimination, 660 UNTS 195; *Basic Documents* at p 160.

[19] Convention on the Elimination of all Forms of Discrimination Against Women, 1249 UNTS 13 ; *Basic Documents* at p 212.

[20] UN doc A/54/49 (vol I); *Basic Documents* at p 224.

[21] (1982) 21 *ILM* 58; *Basic Documents* at p 728.

[22] See C Odinkalu, 'Implementing Economic, Social and Cultural Rights Under the African Charter on Human and Peoples' Rights' in M Evans and R Murray (eds), *The African Charter on Human and Peoples' Rights: The System in Practice, 1986–2000* (Cambridge University Press, 2002) p 178.

[23] Convention nos 29, 87, 98, 100, 105, 111, 138, and 182. Although these Conventions are defined as core, many of the ILO's other Conventions also protect aspects of economic and social rights.

[24] The ILO Committee on Freedom of Association has now examined over 2000 complaints. For detailed discussion of this procedure and the ILO's human rights work, see V Leary, 'Lessons From the Experience of the International Labour Organisation' in P Alston (ed), *The United Nations and Human Rights—A Critical Appraisal* (OUP, 1992) p 580; A Rosas and M Scheinin, 'Implementation Mechanisms and Remedies' in Eide *et al* (eds), (n 7 above) p 425; and K Samson and K Shindler, 'The Standard-Setting and Supervisory System of the International Legal Organisation' in R Hanski and M Suski (eds), *An Introduction to the International Protection of Human Rights: A Textbook* (Abo Akademi, 1999) p 185. The ILO Committee on Freedom of Association's web page also contains details of the procedure at <http://www.ilo.org/public/english/standards/norm/applying/freedom. htm> accessed on 27 Sept 2006 and the cases brought before it at <http://www.ilo.org/ilolex/ english/caseframeE.htm> accessed on 27 Sept 2006.

European Court of Justice, for example, is competent to adjudicate on the compliance of member states with obligations imposed by Community law dealing with issues such as health and safety at work, equal pay and treatment, and conditions of employment, among others.

The preceding discussion highlights a number of issues. First, many economic and social rights and the obligations they impose upon states are capable of judicial determination. The fundamental issues are the manner in which the provision in question is drafted and the extent of the obligation it contains. Secondly, while the right to individual and/or collective petition exists in a number of international and domestic fora, there is no generally accepted approach as to who has *locus standi* to bring claims nor with regard to which particular economic and social rights.

III. The collective complaints system

A. Genesis of the collective complaints system[25]

As mentioned earlier, the collective complaints system was introduced as part of the revitalization process of the Charter, a process that began in December 1990 with the establishment by the Committee of Ministers of a Committee on the European Social Charter (generally known as the Charte-Rel Committee) to draw up proposals for reform. At its second meeting in May 1991, the Committee decided to set up a working party to draw up proposals for a collective complaints system. On the basis of proposals produced by this working party, the Charte-Rel Committee adopted draft articles for a Protocol in September 1991. These draft articles were discussed at the Ministerial Conference held in Turin in October 1991 to mark the thirtieth anniversary of the signing of the Charter, but no agreement could be reached on them.[26]

The Charte-Rel Committee resumed its examination of the draft Protocol and succeeded in finalizing the text of a draft Protocol in May 1992, which it transmitted to the Committee of Ministers. The latter, after consulting the CIE and the Parliamentary Assembly, adopted the text of the Protocol in June 1995 and opened it for signature on 9 November 1995. Under article 14 (1) the Protocol requires five ratifications for its entry into force. This condition was met in May 1998 and the

---

[25] This section draws heavily on Council of Europe, *Explanatory Report on the Collective Complaints Protocol* (1995), paras 1–8: <http://conventions.coe/int/Treaty/en/Reports/html/158.htm> accessed on 27 Sept 2006.

[26] DJ Harris, 'A Fresh Impetus for the European Social Charter', (1992) 41 ICLQ 659, 673 says that the reason for the failure to agree was not so much the opposition from certain governments as the fact that representatives of the ILO and international employers' associations and trade unions did not think that the system proposed at that time would be of much interest to employers' associations and trade unions.

Protocol accordingly entered into force on 1 July 1998. In brief outline, the Protocol allows certain types of organization to make complaints to the ECSR of non-compliance with the Charter by a state party. The ECSR first decides whether the complaint is admissible, and, if it is, it then draws up a report with its conclusions on the merits of the case. On the basis of this report the Committee of Ministers takes the final decision as to whether the complaint is upheld.

According to the Explanatory Report on the Protocol,[27] the introduction of a system of collective complaints is 'designed to increase the efficiency of supervisory machinery based solely on the submission of governmental reports. In particular, this system should increase participation by management and labour and non-governmental organizations ... The way in which the machinery as a whole functions can only be enhanced by the greater interest that these bodies may be expected to show in the Charter.' These views are reflected in the preamble to the Protocol, which speaks of the resolve of the signatories to the Protocol to 'take new measures to improve the effective enforcement of the social rights guaranteed by the Charter', an aim which 'could be achieved in particular by the establishment of a collective complaints procedure, which, *inter alia*, would strengthen the participation of management and labour and of non-governmental organizations.' Unlike the reporting system, which applies to all states parties to the Charter, acceptance to be bound by the collective complaints system is optional. The first way in which a state may manifest such acceptance is by ratifying the 1995 Protocol. So far twelve states have done so—Belgium, Croatia, Cyprus, Finland, France, Greece, Ireland, Italy, the Netherlands, Norway, Portugal, and Sweden. The second way is by a state which is a party to the Revised Charter (but which is not a party to the Protocol) making a declaration under Article D2 of the Revised Charter that it accepts to be bound by the collective complaints system. So far two states—Bulgaria and Slovenia—have made such a declaration. Thus, of the thirty-eight states parties to the Charter, only fourteen are currently bound by the system.

Discussion of the collective complaints system will begin by considering who is eligible to make a complaint and then go on to examine the procedure by which complaints are made and dealt with. The practical operation of the system so far will be reviewed in the following two sections.

B. Who may complain?

It is important to note at the outset that the system is one of collective, not individual, complaints. At the time the Protocol was being negotiated, the members of the Council of Europe were not prepared to accept a right to individual petition. Nor was there any suggestion of having an inter-state complaints procedure, probably because of the failure of such procedures in other human rights treaties

---

[27] Note 25(above), 2.

to be widely utilized. This means that complaints may only be made by some kind of organization, not by one or a number of individuals or a state. There are four types of organization that are eligible to make complaints under the system.[28] The first comprises international organizations of employers and trade unions that are observers at meetings of the Governmental Committee under the reporting system. There are three such organizations—the European Trade Union Confederation, the Union of Industrial and Employers' Confederations of Europe, and the International Organization of Employers.[29] The second type of organization entitled to make a complaint are other international non-governmental organizations (NGOs) that have consultative status with the Council of Europe and have been put on a list drawn up by the Governmental Committee for the purpose of making complaints. To be put on this list, an NGO must show that it has 'access to authoritative sources of information and is able to carry out the necessary verifications, to obtain appropriate legal opinions etc in order to draw up complaint files that meet the basic requirements of reliability'.[30] Organizations are put on the list for renewable four year periods.[31] There are currently sixty-eight NGOs on this list.[32] Harris and Darcy comment that this number is surprisingly small, given that several hundred NGOs have consultative status with the Council of Europe. They criticize the restriction of international NGOs that may make complaints to those on the list, and argue that if the intention was by this means to exclude badly prepared or propagandistic complaints, this would be better done through admissibility criteria rather than a list of approved NGOs.[33] Organizations in this second category are only entitled to submit complaints in respect of those matters in which they have been recognized as having 'particular competence'.[34]

The third type of organization entitled to make complaints comprises 'representative national organizations of employers and trade unions within the jurisdiction of the Contracting Party against which they have lodged a complaint'.[35] It is up to the ECSR when dealing with the admissibility of a complaint to determine whether a national employers' association or trade union is a 'representative' one.

---

[28] Arts 1 and 2, 1995 Protocol.

[29] It has been argued that the International Confederation of Free Trade Unions should be included in this category of complainant, even though it does not currently take part in meetings of the Governmental Committee: see K Löchner, 'The Social Partners' Opinion' in Council of Europe, *The Social Charter of the 21st Century. Colloquy Organized by the Secretariat of the Council of Europe* (Council of Europe, 1997) p 130 at 133.

[30] Committee of Ministers decision of 22 June 1995, as summarized by the Explanatory Report (n 25 above) at para 20. This paragraph also summarizes that part of the Committee of Ministers decision setting out the procedure by which the list is drawn up.

[31] See the Explanatory Report (n 25 above) at para 20.

[32] For this list, see <http://www.coe.int/t/e/human_rights/esc/4_collective_complaints/organisations_entitled/default.asp#TopOfPage> accessed on 27 Sept 2006. Harris and Darcy (n 4 above) at p 357, state that the process of dealing with applications to be put on the list has operated without controversy and that nearly all applications have been accepted.

[33] Harris and Darcy (n 4 above) p 357.   [34] Art 3, 1995 Protocol.

[35] Art 1(c), 1995 Protocol.

The ECSR has taken the view that the representativeness of a trade union is 'an autonomous concept, beyond the ambit of national considerations as well [as] the domestic collective relations context'.[36] In the first two cases (Complaint nos 6/1999 and 9/2000) brought by complainants in this third category (both complainants were French trade unions), the ECSR, after making the observation just referred to concerning the autonomous nature of the concept of representativeness, simply noted that having made an overall assessment of the documents in the file, its conclusion was that the trade union concerned was a representative one. This has generally been the ECSR's approach in nearly all the later complaints made by employers' organizations or trade unions, although in two early complaints brought by this type of complainant, the ECSR made a rather more thorough examination of the representativeness of the complainant. This was despite the fact that, as with Complaints nos 6/1999 and 9/2000, the representativeness of the organization concerned had not been challenged by the defendant state. In Complaint no 10/2000 the ECSR noted that the complainant Finnish trade union represented the great majority of employees in the sector concerned (health care) and participated in the collective bargaining process in that sector. It thus held that the complainant was a representative trade union.[37] In Complaint no 12/2002, brought by a Swedish employers' association, the ECSR noted that the association was the largest body of its kind in Sweden, representing 47,000 companies with about 1.45 million employees; that it had concluded several central level collective agreements in the private sector; and that it sought to promote general understanding of the needs of enterprise and its contribution to society. The ECSR therefore concluded that the complainant was a representative employers' organization.[38] In Complaint no 23/2003, the French government challenged the representativeness of a regional trade union in the education sector, pointing out that the union was not considered a representative one under French law. The ECSR, in rejecting this challenge, again stated that the representativeness of a trade union is 'an autonomous concept'. More importantly, however, it considered the union to be representative on the basis that it represented a considerable number of employees in the education sector in the geographic region in which it was based and was completely independent of employers.[39] On the basis of this

---

[36] Complaint no 6/1999, *Syndicat National des Professions du Tourisme v France*, Decision on Admissibility, para 6. The ECSR made a similar observation in Complaint no 9/2000, *Confédération Française de l'Encadrement—CGC v France*, Decision on Admissibility, para 6, to which the ECSR has usually referred in later complaints. The texts of the ECSR's decisions on both admissibility and the merits of collective complaints can be found on the Council of Europe's webpage. Some of the decisions on the merits are also reproduced in Intl Human Rights Rev, and these references will also be given where they exist. After their initial reference, complaints, both in the text and in the footnotes, will be cited by number only.

[37] Complaint no 10/2000, *Tehy ry and STTK ry v Finland*, Decision on Admissibility.

[38] Complaint no 12/2002, *Confederation of Swedish Enterprise v Sweden*, Decision on Admissibility, para 5.

[39] Complaint no 23/2003, *Syndicat occitan de l'éducation v France*, Decision on Admissibility, paras 3–5.

relatively limited practice, it would seem that the main tests of whether a trade union or an employers' association is a 'representative' organization will be its size (in terms of the number of its members) relative to the sector or region in which it operates and the degree to which it has participated in collective bargaining in the sector concerned.[40] Rather surprisingly, the ECSR has held that once a trade union is 'deemed to be representative for the purposes of the collective complaints procedure . . . , [it] has the right to lodge a complaint . . . on *any* point, within the bounds of article 4 of the Protocol, on which it alleges unsatisfactory application of the Charter', it would seem, even though that point concerns the position of employees on whose behalf the union concerned has no authority to act.[41]

The final category of complainant organizations comprises 'other representative national' NGOs with 'particular competence in the matters governed by the Charter.'[42] Again it will be up to the ESCR in its decisions on admissibility to determine whether such an organization is 'representative' and has the 'particular competence' referred to. While the latter qualification may not be so difficult to assess, the former is not so straightforward, certainly not as straightforward as with a trade union or employers' association. Presumably the kinds of factors the ECSR will look for when it comes to making an assessment about representativeness (which it has not yet had to do) are likely to be the number of members (although an organization could have a lot of members but nevertheless such members could still be a small proportion of the total potential membership, eg a pensioners organization); the size of an organization in terms of its income/turnover and number of staff; the degree to which it is recognized/consulted by public authorities; and the relationship of all these qualities to other national NGOs working in the same field.[43] A national NGO falling into this fourth category of complainant may only make complaints if the state in which it is located has made a declaration allowing it to do so.[44] Finland is the only state so far to have made such a declaration. According to the Explanatory Report on the Protocol, a state that has made such a declaration may not draw up a list of national NGOs permitted to make complaints, nor may it restrict such organizations to making complaints in respect of only certain provisions of the Charter.[45] Cullen has suggested that the fact that states may not draw up a list of approved organizations may discourage them from

---

[40] These factors are in fact suggested by the Explanatory Report on the 1995 Protocol as being the relevant ones: (n 25 above) para 23.

[41] Complaint no 24/2004, *Sud Travail Affaires Sociales, SUD ANPE and SUD Collectivités Territoriales v France*, Decision on Admissibility, para 11 (emphasis added). The ECSR's decision was adopted by nine votes to four. There was a vigorous dissenting opinion by Mr Belorgey.

[42] Art 2(1), 1995 Protocol.

[43] For a fuller discussion of this issue and a somewhat similar viewpoint, see R Birk, 'The Collective Complaint: A New Procedure in the European Social Charter' in C Engels and M Weiss (eds), *Labour Law and Industrial Relations at the Turn of the Century: Liber Amicorum in Honour of Prof Dr Roger Blanpain* (Kluwer, 1998) p 261 at 266–8. See also N Prouvez, 'Opinion of the Non-Governmental Organizations' in Council of Europe (n 29 above) p 140 at 144–5.

[44] Art 2(1), 1995 Protocol.   [45] Explanatory Report (n 25 above) para 28.

making the necessary declaration since the number of groups which could make complaints is open-ended, unlike the international NGOs in the second category of complainant.[46] Where a state has not made a declaration, it may be possible for a national NGO to act through an international NGO, if there is an appropriate such body on the list.[47]

Organizations of the second and fourth types may make complaints 'only in respect of those matters in which they have been recognized as having particular competence'.[48] Again, it will be up to the ECSR, when considering the admissibility of a complaint, to decide if a complainant in one of these categories has brought a complaint in relation to a matter in which it has such competence. In practice, the ECSR, when considering this question *proprio motu* in admissibility proceedings, does not carry out a very rigorous assessment. For example, in Complaints nos 7/2000 and 14/2003 the International Federation of Human Rights Leagues (IFHR) brought complaints against Greece[49] and France[50] concerning the unsatisfactory application of article 1(2) of the Charter (prohibiting forced labour) and the unsatisfactory application of articles 13 and 17 and E of the Revised Charter (the right of persons with disabilities and children to protection, and discrimination), respectively. In neither of these complaints did the French or Greek governments contest the admissibility of the applications. The ECSR, at the admissibility phase, nevertheless considered whether the IFHR had 'particular competence' in relation to the subject matter of the complaints. The IFHR's goal is to 'promote the implementation of the Universal Declaration of Human Rights and other international instruments of human rights protection ... and to contribute to the enforcement of the rights guaranteed by these instruments'.[51] This was considered by the ESCR, in both complaints, to satisfy the stipulation that the organization had 'particular competence' in relation to the subject matter of those complaints. While it is undeniable that the IFHR, as a major international human rights NGO, has some competence with regard to the specific issues raised in both complaints, it is worth noting that the ECSR did not examine the scope of the IFHR's activities nor where its 'particular competence' stemmed from.[52] In

---

[46] H Cullen, 'The Collective Complaints Mechanism of the European Social Charter' (2000) 25 ELRev HR/18 at HR/22. She probably goes too far when she suggests that a national NGO could be formed purely for the purpose of bringing a complaint, because it is necessary under art 2 both that it is 'representative' and that it has 'particular competence' in a matter governed by the Charter.

[47] D Harris, 'The Collective Complaints Procedure' in Council of Europe (n 29 above) p 103 at 115; and Harris and Darcy (n 4 above) at p 359.

[48] Art 3, 1995 Protocol. The relevant part of the equally authentic French text reads 'dans les domains pour lesquels elles [ie organizations] ont été reconnues particulièrement qualifiées'.

[49] Complaint no 7/2000, *International Federation of Human Rights Leagues v Greece*.

[50] Complaint no 14/2003, *International Federation of Human Rights Leagues v France*.

[51] See FIDH, home page <http://www.fidh.org/> accessed on 27 Sept 2006 and Complaint no 14/2003, Decision on Admissibility, para 5.

[52] For further examples of the ECSR's approach, see its decisions on admissibility in Complaint no 1/1998, *International Commission of Jurists v Portugal* (1999) 6 Intl Human Rights Rev 1142;

the few cases so far in which a challenge was made by the defendant state that a complainant did not comply with article 3, the ECSR seems to have adopted a relaxed reading of the provision. In Complaint no 8/2000, the Quaker Council for European Affairs brought a complaint that Greece was not in compliance with the Charter in respect of the way its legislation dealt with the conditions of conscientious objectors performing civilian service as an alternative to military service. The Greek government challenged the competence of the Council to make such a complaint. The ECSR rejected this challenge. It pointed out that the Council's objective, according to its Statute, was to promote the traditions of the Quakers and, to this end, its task was to bring to the attention of the European institutions the concerns of Quakers, which relate to peace, human rights, and economic justice. The Committee, therefore, concluded that the Council had made a complaint in a field in which it had 'particular competence' within the meaning of article 3.[53] Secondly, in Complaint no 17/2003, the World Organization Against Torture alleged that Greek law was not in compliance with the Charter because it did not prohibit the corporal punishment or other forms of degrading punishment or treatment of children. The Greek government challenged the competence of the Organization to make such a complaint because it was 'not particularly qualified in the field of degrading treatment of children'. The ECSR rejected this challenge, simply pointing out that the Organization was a body 'whose aim is to contribute to the struggle against torture, summary executions, disappearances, arbitrary detention, psychiatric internment for political reasons, and other cruel, inhuman and degrading treatment, regardless of the age of the persons against whom such treatments are directed' and therefore was 'particularly qualified' in relation to the subject matter of the complaint.[54] On the whole, therefore, it would seem that in practice the test is one of 'some competence' with regard to the issue raised by the complaint rather than 'particular competence' in the matters governed by the Charter.

Of the four categories of complainant, the first and the third are concerned with employment issues (broadly, economic rights), while the second and fourth categories may cover such issues but will predominantly be concerned with other aspects of the Charter (broadly, social rights). The fact that the second and fourth categories of complainant are more restricted than the first and third (in that they must be included on a list or operate in a state which has made a declaration accepting their competence to make complaints) illustrates the historic bias of the Charter

---

Complaint no 2/1999, *European Federation of Employees in Public Services v France*; Complaint no 15/2003, *European Roma Rights Centre v Greece*; Complaint no 31/2005, *European Roma Rights Centre v Bulgaria*; and Complaint no 33/2006, *International Movement ATD Fourth World v France*.

[53] Complaint no 8/2000, *Quaker Council for European Affairs v Greece*, Decision on Admissibility, para 9.

[54] Complaint no 17/2003, *World Organization Against Torture v Greece*, Decision on Admissibility, paras 2 and 6. See also Complaint no 30/2005, *Marangopoulos Foundation for Human Rights v Greece*, Decision on Admissibility, paras 3, 7, and 12, where the complainant's competence was challenged.

in favour of employers' organisations and trade unions.[55] All of the first three categories of complainant have links with the reporting system—the first category comprises the organizations that participate in meetings of the Governmental Committee; the second consists of those bodies that are to be sent copies of national reports and may be consulted by the Governmental Committee;[56] while the third category comprises organizations that are to be sent national reports on which they may comment.[57] The fact that the fourth category does not feature in the reporting system may help to explain why it is optional under the complaints system. In linking the categories of complainant to the reporting system, the collective complaints system helps to achieve one of its aims, which (as noted above) is to 'strengthen the participation of management and labour and of non-governmental organizations' in the operation of the Charter.

C. The complaints procedure

1. Initiating a complaint

The procedure begins by a qualified complainant making a complaint in writing to the secretary of the ECSR[58] alleging that a state party 'has not ensured the satisfactory application' of one or more of the provisions of the Charter by which it is bound.[59] Complaints made by the first two categories of complainant (ie international organizations) must be in one of the official languages of the Council of Europe: complaints by national employers' associations, trade unions, and NGOs may be submitted in another language.[60]

The terminology of a failure to ensure 'the satisfactory application' (or, as it is put more bluntly in article 1 of the Protocol, the 'unsatisfactory application' ('application non satisfaisante')) of the Charter is a somewhat unusual one. Birk, along with a number of other commentators, points out that the term 'satisfactory application' is not a legal one: it may be equated with 'compliance', which is the term used in the Charter in connection with the role of the ECSR in the reporting system.[61] The reason for the change in terminology is not apparent, and the Explanatory Report

---

[55] Harris (n 47 above) 126.

[56] Arts 23(2) and 27(2), European Social Charter, as amended.

[57] Art 23(1), European Social Charter, as amended. In practice not many national employers' organizations or trade unions show much interest in the reporting system: see T Novitz, 'Remedies for Violation of Social Rights within the Council of Europe: The Significant Absence of a Court' in C Kilpatrick, T Novitz, and P Skidmore (eds), *The Future of Remedies in Europe* (Hart, 2002) p 231 at p 243.

[58] Rule 22 of the ECSR's Rules (2004). This explains that the secretary of the ECSR acts on behalf of the Secretary General of the Council of Europe, who is specified as the addressee of complaints in art 5 of the 1995 Protocol.

[59] Art 4, 1995 Protocol. The French text reads: 'n'aurait pas assure d'une manière satisfaisante l'application . . .'. Note that a state party is not required to accept all the rights contained in the Charter, only a certain minimum.   [60] Rule 24 of the ECSR's Rules.

[61] Art 24 Charter, as amended.

frequently uses the term 'compliance' instead of 'satisfactory application' (eg in paras 11 and 31).[62] The terminology of unsatisfactory application may also be contrasted with that of most civil and political rights treaties, where an individual applicant must claim to be the 'victim of a violation' of one of the recognized rights.[63] It may be that the terminology of unsatisfactory application which, according to Sudre,[64] is broadly inspired by article 24 of the Constitution of the ILO, is used rather than 'violation' because some (but certainly not all) of the provisions of the Charter are sufficiently vague and general and/or programmatic that they do not lend themselves to a straightforward determination that there has been a 'violation'. Novitz, one of the themes of whose writings on the Charter is that economic and social rights are unjustifiably much more weakly protected by the Council of Europe than civil and political rights, argues that the difference in terminology between the ECHR and the Charter indicates the 'inferior status of social rights' protected under the Charter because a 'violation' is implicitly a 'much more serious matter' than 'unsatisfactory application'.[65]

The terminology generally utilized in practice by the ECSR and the Committee of Ministers when referring to a defendant state considered not to be ensuring the 'satisfactory application' of the Charter is of the state concerned having committed a 'violation' of the Charter, although in some of the early complaints the terms 'breach' or 'not in conformity' with the Charter were used. The use of such language was challenged, on one occasion, in the dissenting opinion of Alfredo Bruto da Costa in Complaint no 1/1998. Mr da Costa considered that the approach of the ECSR, which he felt focused on the situation in the defendant state (rather than on its performance), was not in conformity with the idea of 'satisfactory application'. There is a degree of merit in this argument, as the idea of 'satisfactory application' can be deemed to be concerned with the overall approach of the state party to the issue in question and not necessarily with assessing 'violations' of Charter provisions out of the context of overall policy and approach to the protected right(s) in question. Although the choice of terminology in the Charter is probably not a case of semantics, the language utilized by the ECSR in practice is noteworthy. In particular, the use of 'violation' and 'breach' lends further weight to the idea of the justiciability of economic and social rights.

A complainant, when bringing a complaint, must 'indicate in what respect' there has been unsatisfactory application of the Charter.[66] This means that a complainant must provide some evidence to support its allegation of unsatisfactory application. It seems that such evidence need not be extensive or comprehensive.

---

[62] Birk (n 43 above) at p 270.

[63] Eg art 34, ECHR; art 14, CERD; and art 1, Optional Protocol to the International Covenant on Civil and Political Rights, 1966, 999 UNTS 171; *Basic Documents*, at p 199.

[64] F Sudre, 'Le protocole additionel à la Charte Sociale Européenne prévoyant un système de réclammations collectives' (1996)100 Revue Générale de Droit International Public, 715 at 724–5.

[65] Novitz (n 8 above) at p 53.   [66] Art 4, 1995 Protocol.

In Complaint no 5/1999 Portugal argued that the complainant had not indicated in what respect it had failed to ensure satisfactory application of the provision of the Charter dealing with the rights to organize and bargain collectively as far as members of the armed forces were concerned, and therefore should be rejected as inadmissible. The ECSR rejected this challenge to admissibility. It pointed out that the complainant had referred to provisions of the Portuguese Constitution and legislation which were alleged to contravene the Charter. 'The reasons given in the complaint, although succinct, are sufficiently indicative of the extent to which the Portuguese government is alleged not to have ensured the satisfactory application of the provisions concerned.'[67] On the other hand, in Complaint no 2/1999 (which dealt with a similar issue in France) the ECSR found at the merits stage that the complainant had produced no evidence to rebut the defendant government's claim that French armed forces enjoyed certain rights of consultation and thus that the requirements of article 6 were satisfied. The complaint was therefore dismissed.[68] The ECSR will also take account of evidence supplied by those other than the complainant. Thus, for example, in Complaint no 1/1998, which concerned child labour in Portugal, the ECSR took account of information supplied by the Portuguese Government itself to conclude that in fact there had been unsatisfactory application of the Charter in that case. Where a complaint relates to legislation which is alleged to be incompatible with the Charter, that is normally sufficient by way of evidence to support an allegation of unsatisfactory application: the ECSR does not normally require the complainant to provide examples of the practical application of the legislation to support a claim of unsatisfactory application of the Charter.[69] On the other hand, where legislation on its face is compatible with the Charter, the ECSR obviously requires evidence that the application of the legislation in practice is contrary to the Charter in order for a complaint to be upheld. This was successfully shown in the case of Complaint no 1/1998 (child labour in Portugal), but not in respect of certain aspects of Complaint no 9/2000 (the right to bargain effectively in France).

A somewhat related issue is the question of the level of generality at which a complaint must be made. The Explanatory Report on the 1995 Protocol notes that it was agreed during the negotiation of the Protocol that because of their collective nature, complaints could only raise questions concerning non-compliance of a state's law or practice with one of the provisions of the Charter: individual situations could not be submitted.[70] Clearly, if a complaint alleges that legislation as such is incompatible with the Charter, this is a general (or collective) complaint

---

[67] Complaint no 5/1999, *European Federation of Employees in Public Services v Portugal*, Decision on Admissibility, para 10.

[68] Complaint no 2/1999, Decision on the Merits, (2001) 8 Intl Human Rights Rep 564 para 32. For another example of insufficient evidence, see Complaint no 16/2003, Decision on the Merits, paras 65 and 71.

[69] See eg, Complaints nos 7/2000 and 8/2000 on forced labour in Greece and Complaint no 9/2000 on the length of working hours in France.   [70] Note 25 above, para 31.

and therefore permissible. On the other hand, a complaint that there has been a breach of, say, article 4(3) (on equal pay) because Ms X has been paid less than her male colleagues performing work of equal value, would be an individual complaint and, therefore, impermissible. An example of this is provided by Complaint no 29/2005, where the complaint concerned a series of alleged infringements of the rights of the president and the secretary-general of a French trades union that had already been referred to the European Court of Human Rights. In its decision on admissibility the ECSR noted that 'the complaint does not pertain to the rules applicable in a country but rather to the manner in which those rules are being applied to a particular case . . .'. This situation did not 'fall within the remit' of the ECSR and the complaint was therefore inadmissible.[71] However, there may be a grey area in between these two extremes where complaints may be made that the practical application of legislation or an administrative practice, as shown in its application to particular individuals, is contrary to the Charter. It would seem that as long as there are a reasonably significant number of groups of individuals involved demonstrating a generality of practice, complaints of this nature will be admissible. Thus, in Complaint no 6/1999 the ECSR accepted as admissible a complaint that concerned the treatment of guides at general categories of historical and cultural sites in France and which also referred specifically to the position at the Louvre. Likewise, in Complaint no 10/2000 the ECSR accepted as admissible a complaint that concerned workers in general in the Finnish health service exposed to radiation. Although individual complaints as such may not be made, there seems no reason why an individual who believes his/her rights under the Charter have been violated should not contact an organization entitled to make complaints to request it to make a complaint about that individual's situation. That organization should then be entitled to make a complaint, provided that the situation concerned can be generalized, by showing that the alleged violation of the individual's rights is an example of a general pattern of non-compliance applying in the same way to others in the same position as the individual concerned.[72] A final point is that issues that are abstract in nature will not be dealt with by the ECSR in the collective complaints procedure. Thus, in Complaint no 2/1999 the complainant sought to argue that as a general principle the right to collective bargaining under article 6 of the Revised Charter could be exercised only through trade unions. The ECSR considered that this was an issue that in the context of a collective complaint could not be assessed in the abstract, but needed to be assessed on a concrete case-by-case basis.[73]

---

[71] Complaint no 29/2005, *SAIGI-Syndicat des Hauts Fonctionnaires v France*, Decision on Admissibility, para 8.

[72] If the complaint is successful, it should lead to the offending legislation or practice being amended, but the individual who initiated the complaint will not, of course, obtain a remedy himself/herself. In practice, this is also often the situation where human rights treaties permit individual complaints.   [73] Complaint no 2/1999, Decision on the Merits, paras 30–31.

2. Admissibility

Once it has received a complaint, the ECSR must first decide whether the complaint is admissible. Unlike many human rights treaties, the CCP does not contain an explicit or comprehensive list of conditions that must be met before a complaint will be considered admissible. A number of conditions are, nevertheless, referred to in the Protocol and applied in practice by the ECSR. The complainant must be a qualified organization; the complaint must be in writing, against a state party to the Charter, and relate to a provision or provisions of the Charter that has/have been accepted by that state; and the complaint must state in what respect that state has not ensured the satisfactory application of the provision(s) concerned.[74] The Explanatory Report to the 1995 Protocol says that the ECSR may stipulate the conditions governing admissibility in its Rules of Procedure.[75] In fact, the ECSR has not (yet) done so, except in one minor respect. Rule 23 of the ECSR's Rules provides that the complaint must be signed by a person authorized to represent the complainant organization. In practice in its decisions on admissibility the ECSR considers whether this condition has been satisfied.[76]

The Explanatory Report then goes on to say that should the ECSR decide to include conditions for admissibility in its Rules of Procedure, it must take account of the fact that the following points were agreed in the course of negotiating the Protocol. First, a complaint may be declared admissible 'even if a similar case has already been submitted to another national or international body', such as the ILO.[77] This differs from the ECHR, for example, which takes the opposite position.[78] An interesting question, not raised in the Explanatory Report, is whether a second complaint may be raised in relation to the same issue. For example, suppose a complaint is made and found to be well-founded and the defendant state fails to take corrective action, may a second complaint be made? Common sense suggests that as long as the defendant state has been given a reasonable period of time within which to take corrective action, a second complaint may be made. If it were not so, the effectiveness of the collective complaints system would be significantly impaired. On the other hand, where a complaint has been found not to be substantiated, it would seem impermissible to bring a new complaint relating to the same issue unless there were new material that might alter the view of a

---

[74] Art 4, 1995 Protocol.   [75] Explanatory Report (n 25 above) para 31.

[76] For examples of unsuccessful attempts by a defendant state to argue that r 23 had not been complied with, see Complaints no 6/2000, no 15/2003, and no 17/2003. For a partially successful attempt, see Complaint no 24/2004, where the ECSR held that the person who had signed the complaint had been authorized to do so by only one of the three trade unions making the complaint. The complaint was therefore inadmissible in respect of the other two unions.

[77] Sudre (n 64 above) at 731 questions whether this should be so, and says the point is a difficult one. It has also been questioned whether a 'similar' case also includes the same case: see M Jaeger, 'The Additional Protocol to the European Social Charter Providing for a System of Collective Complaints' (1997) 10 Leiden Jof Intl L 69 at 74.   [78] See art 35(2)(b).

state's compliance with the Charter. This seems to be the implication of the ECSR's decision on admissibility in Complaint no 16/2003. Here the ECSR noted that the complaint was not identical to Complaint no 9/2000 (in which the Committee of Ministers had found France to be in compliance with the Charter) because it involved new legislation that had been enacted since the earlier complaint. The complaint was therefore admissible.[79] The same was also the position in Complaint no 34/2006, where the complainant was able successfully to allege that the law in Portugal had changed as a result of a Supreme Court judgment given since it had made a similar complaint (Complaint no 20/2003) in which the ECSR had found Portugal to be in conformity with the Charter as regards the corporal punishment of children.[80]

A second point that the Explanatory Report says that the ECSR must take account of is the fact that the substance of a complaint has been examined as part of the normal governmental reporting procedure 'does not in itself constitute an impediment to the complaint's admissibility. It has been agreed to give the ECSR a sufficient margin of appreciation in this area.'[81] The relationship between the collective complaints system and the reporting system is explored in more detail in section V(D) below.

In two recent cases the ECSR appears to have added two further requirements for admissibility, although neither seems controversial and both are arguably inherent in the system of collective complaints. First, in Complaint no 28/2004 the ECSR rejected a complaint as inadmissible because what it was being asked to determine (whether the difference in treatment between categories of specialist medical practitioners in private practice regarding the fees that they could charge amounted to discrimination) was 'not of such a nature as to allow it to conclude that there has been a violation' of the Charter.[82] Secondly, the ECSR will only regard complaints as admissible if they engage the responsibility of the state. However, as the ECSR has held that 'the state is responsible for enforcing the rights embodied in the Charter within its jurisdiction' and has an obligation to put an end to violations of the Charter,[83] it will only be exceptionally that the responsibility of the state will not be engaged: no such instances have occurred to date.

Compared with an individual application under the ECHR, for example, the conditions for the admissibility of a collective complaint differ quite considerably: in particular, a number of conditions for the admissibility of an individual

---

[79] Complaint no 16/2003, *Confédération française de l'Encadrement CFE-CGC v France*, Decision on Admissibility, para 8. Complaint no 22/2003 raised similar issues to Complaints no 9/2000 and 16/2003, but this fact was not discussed at the admissibility stage, possibly because the defendant state, France, had not contested the admissibility of the complaint.

[80] Complaint no 34/2006, *World Organization against Torture v Portugal*, Decision on Admissibility, para 1. Whether the law has actually changed since the previous complaint will, of course, be something that the ECSR will have to decide in the merits stage.

[81] Explanatory Report (n 25 above) para 31.

[82] Complaint no 28/2004, *Syndicat National des Dermato-Vénérologues v France*, Decision on Admissibility, paras 7–8.   [83] Complaint no 30/2005, Decision on Admissibility, para 14.

application under the ECHR have no counterpart under the collective complaints procedure. First, there is no time limit for bringing a complaint. This is presumably because as the complaint relates to non-compliance of a law or practice with the Charter, the non-compliance is a continuing one.[84] However, in accordance with the principle of the non-retroactivity of treaties, a complaint may only relate to an alleged instance of non-compliance with the Charter that has occurred after the defendant state became bound by the collective complaints system, unless alleged non-compliance occurring before that date continues to occur afterwards, 'thus potentially constituting a continuing violation.'[85] A second difference is that there is no requirement to exhaust domestic remedies: the ECSR has rejected arguments by defendant states that it should read in such a requirement.[86] The reason for this is probably because according to its appendix the Charter contains obligations of an international character 'the application of which is subject to the supervision' procedures of the Charter. Thus, even those provisions of the Charter that in monist states would be regarded as self-executing cannot be invoked by individuals before national courts. Even if they could be, it is doubtful whether in many cases an individual would have the necessary *locus standi* to be able to challenge domestic legislation. A third difference with the ECHR is that a complaint may not be declared inadmissible because it is manifestly ill-founded. Arguments by defendant governments that a complaint should be rejected as inadmissible because it is manifestly ill-founded have been consistently rejected by the ECSR, which has held that this issue is a matter for the merits stage.[87] Presumably the reason why there is no threshold of *prima facie* non-compliance is because it is anticipated that complainant organizations will not bring frivolous claims, but will bring only complaints with a considerable degree of plausibility. If this is the assumption, then it has certainly been borne out in practice so far. Finally, unlike the ECHR, there is no requirement that a complaint must not be an abuse of the right of petition. An attempt by the Portuguese government to invoke such a requirement in Complaint no 11/2001 was unsuccessful. The government's argument that the complainant (the European Council of Police Trade Unions) was motivated by

[84] In fact under the ECHR the six-month rule for bringing an application does not apply to continuing violations of the Convention: see *De Becker v Belgium* (1958), 2 Ybk of the Euro Convention on Human Rights 214 at 230–234.

[85] Complaint no 30/2005, Decision on Admissibility, paras 15–16.

[86] Complaint No 26/2004, *Syndicat des Agrégés de l'Enseignement Supérieur v France*, Decision on Admissibility, paras 11–12; and Complaint no 31/2005, Decision on Admissibility, para 10.

[87] See eg, Complaint no 4/1999, *European Federation of Employees in Public Services v Italy*, Decision on Admissibility, para 12; Complaint no 8/2000, Decision on Admissibility, para 10; Complaint no 11/2001, *European Council of Police Trade Unions v Portugal*, Decision on Admissibility, paras 7 and 8; and Complaint no 18/2003, *World Organization Against Torture v Ireland*, Decision on Admissibility, para 7. Similarly, arguments by a defendant state that it has taken or is taking the necessary measures to amend the legislation/practice alleged to contravene the Charter have also been rejected as irrelevant to admissibility and considered to be a matter for the merits stage: see eg, Complaint no 1/1998, Decision on Admissibility, para 14; Complaint no 7/2000, Decision on Admissibility, para 9.

political considerations was rejected by the ECSR as being 'invalid, not being one which may be relied on to establish the inadmissibility or ill-foundedness of a complaint'.[88]

As far as procedure in admissibility proceedings is concerned, once the ECSR is seized of a complaint, a rapporteur for the complaint is appointed.[89] The ECSR 'may' request the defendant state and the complainant to submit written information and observations on the admissibility of the complaint within such time limit as it shall prescribe.[90] In practice, the defendant state will be asked to submit its observations unless a complaint appears clearly inadmissible or manifestly admissible.[91] Occasionally a complainant is asked for its views on the defendant state's observations. Otherwise, the complaint and the documentation attached to it appear to have been regarded as sufficient to give the complainant's viewpoint on the question of admissibility. The written submissions of the parties are all the material that the ECSR has in order to determine the admissibility of a complaint: unlike the merits stage (as will be seen) there is no provision for oral hearings. On the basis of the written submissions, the rapporteur then drafts a decision on admissibility, which is considered by the ECSR in private session.[92] At these meetings, as with the ECSR's meetings to examine the reports of states parties to the Charter, a representative of the ILO is invited to be present.[93] According to the published decisions on admissibility, an ILO representative has participated in the ECSR's deliberations on admissibility only in a handful of the early complaints.[94] Once the ECSR has deliberated, it takes a decision on admissibility, which must be reasoned. The decision is then notified to the parties to the complaint and to the states parties to the Charter, and made public.[95] Even if there has been no challenge to the admissibility of a complaint, which has been the position in about half of the complaints so far, the ECSR nevertheless goes through the conditions of admissibility outlined above[96] in order to satisfy itself that they have been fulfilled. Where a challenge has been made to the admissibility of a complaint, the ECSR first satisfies itself that the unchallenged conditions of admissibility have been met, before considering the challenge(s) to admissibility put forward by the defendant state.

Overall, the ECSR has taken a rather relaxed attitude to admissibility so far. Cullen has suggested that if complaints become more numerous, the ECSR may

---

[88] Complaint no 11/2001, Decision on Admissibility, para 8.

[89] Rule 27 (1) of the ECSR's Rules.   [90] Art 6, 1995 Protocol and r 29 of the ECSR's Rules.

[91] Rule 29(3) of the ECSR's Rules. For a rare example of a case being declared admissible without the defendant state being asked for its observations, see Complaint no 34/2006. The reason why the complaint appeared manifestly admissible was probably because a similar complaint had been made only three years earlier by the same organization that had been found to be admissible (Complaint no 20/2003) and the circumstances relating to admissibility had not changed.

[92] Rules 27(3) and 30(1) of the ECSR's Rules.

[93] Rule 13 of the ECSR's Rules; Explanatory Report (n 25 above) para 34.

[94] Complaints nos 1/1998, 7/2000, 8/2000, and 10/2000.

[95] Rule 30(3)(7) of the ECSR's Rules.

[96] Viz that the complaint is in writing; made by a qualified organization; signed by an authorized person; relates to a provision of the Charter accepted by the defendant state; and sets out the grounds for the allegation of unsatisfactory application of the provision concerned.

need to be more restrictive in its approach.[97] As things stand at present, however, there seems to be little likelihood of this situation occurring in the immediate future.

3. The merits stage

If the ECSR decides that a complaint is admissible, it then asks the defendant state to submit its views on the merits of the complaint in writing and for the complainant to submit a response to those submissions, both within specified time limits.[98] Other states parties to the Protocol and organizations belonging to the first category of complainant referred to above (ie international organizations of employers and trade unions) are also invited to submit their views on the complaint.[99] In practice so far only on one occasion has a state party to the Protocol submitted observations on a complaint not involving itself.[100] Of international organizations of employers and trade unions, the European Trade Union Confederation has submitted observations in many of the complaints that have so far been dealt with at the merits stage. The International Organization of Employers, on the other hand, has submitted observations on only one occasion.[101] Following the receipt of all the written material referred to, each of the parties to the complaint may submit any additional information or observations it wishes within such time limit as the ECSR may prescribe.[102] The ECSR may then, if it considers it desirable, either on its own initiative or at the request of one of the parties, organize a hearing with the representatives of the parties.[103] Of the twenty-six complaints that have so far been dealt with on the merits, a hearing has been held in seven cases.[104] Harris' argument that hearings should generally be held in order both to give the ECSR 'a better sense of the issues and arguments' and to promote the familiarity of complainant organizations with the system,[105] appears generally not to have been heeded.

On the basis of the written materials, the hearing (if held) and a draft report prepared by the Rapporteur,[106] the ECSR deliberates in private[107] on the merits of the complaint and draws up its report. In this it is required to describe the steps it has

[97] Cullen (n 46 above) HR/22.

[98] Art 7(1), 1995 Protocol; r 31 of the ECSR's Rules. Time limits are usually quite short: eg the defendant state is normally given around two months from the date of the decision on admissibility to submit its views.   [99] Art 7(1) and (2), 1995 Protocol; r 32 of the ECSR's Rules.

[100] Belgium, in Complaint no 23/2003. Cf practice before the European Court of Human Rights, where states have from time to time submitted observations in cases brought against other states because they had a particular interest in the subject matter of the case.

[101] In Complaint no 12/2002, the only complaint so far to have been brought by an employers' association.   [102] Art 7(3), 1995 Protocol.

[103] Art 7(4), 1995 Protocol and r 33 of the ECSR's Rules. As well as the parties, states, and organizations that have submitted observations shall be invited to attend.

[104] Complaint nos 2/1999, 4/1999, and 5/1999 (a joint hearing for the three cases which were concerned with the same matter), and Complaint nos 9/2000, 12/2003, 13/2002, and 15/2003.

[105] Harris (n 47 above) 106.   [106] Rule 27(3) of the ECSR's Rules.

[107] Again, as with admissibility proceedings, an ILO representative may take part, and has in fact done so in five complaints so far—Complaint nos 1/1998, 2/1999, 4/1999, 5/1999, and 6/1999.

taken to examine the complaint and to give, with reasons, its conclusions as to whether or not the defendant state has 'ensured the satisfactory application' of the provision(s) of the Charter referred to in the complaint.[108] In this latter respect the ECSR's role is essentially a quasi-judicial one, applying law to the facts to reach a considered conclusion. In so doing, the ECSR frequently refers to and follows the 'case law' as to the meaning and scope of Charter rights that it has developed in the reporting procedure and in earlier complaints. The ECSR's conclusion on the merits is not final and binding, however, as its report has to be transmitted to the Committee of Ministers for a definitive disposal of the complaint. At the same time the report is also sent to the complainant and the states parties to the Charter.[109] Subsequently, the report is also transmitted to the Parliamentary Assembly and made public, either at the same time as the resolution of the Committee of Ministers concluding proceedings for the complaint concerned or four months after the report has been sent to the Committee of Ministers, whichever is the earlier.[110]

In its report the ECSR is limited to expressing a view as to whether the defendant state has complied with the Charter or not. It seems that it is not entitled to award or suggest compensation if it finds the defendant state in non-compliance. A request in Complaint no 9/2000 for it to do so, for the sum of FF78 billion, was summarily dismissed without any discussion of the issue.[111] While it may be possible that the Committee did not entertain the request owing to the size of the claim, a power to award compensation is not in accordance with the nature and purpose of the Protocol.[112] Likewise, it seems that the ECSR has no power to award costs to a successful complainant. In Complaint nos 15/2003 and 16/2003 the ECSR, after noting that the Collective Complaints Protocol did not regulate 'the issue of compensation for expenses incurred in connection with complaints', considered that 'a consequence of the quasi-judicial nature of the proceedings under the Protocol is where there has been a finding of a violation of the Charter, the defending state should meet at least some of the costs incurred'.[113] Accordingly, it invited the Committee of Ministers to recommend that the defendant states concerned, Greece and France, pay a sum of 2,000 euros to each of the complainants. The Committee of Ministers, however, decided 'not to accede to the request for the reimbursement of costs transmitted by' the ECSR.[114] It is not clear whether the Committee was declining to recommend an award of costs in these particular

---

[108] Art 8(1), 1995 Protocol. The requirement of reasons is found in r 34 of the ECSR's Rules.
[109] Art 8(2), 1995 Protocol.   [110] Art 8(2), 1995 Protocol; r 34(2)–(4) of the ECSR's Rules.
[111] Complaint no 9/2000, para 58.

[112] Harris and Darcy, however, argue that it would be open to the Committee of Ministers, when making a recommendation to a defendant state found to be in non-compliance with the Charter, to make a recommendation suggesting that appropriate reparation be made to anyone particularly affected by such non-compliance: Harris and Darcy (n 4 above) at p 367.

[113] Complaint no 15/2003, Decision on the Merits, para 54 and Complaint no 16/2003, Decision on the Merits, para 75.   [114] ResChS (2005)7 and ResChS (2005)11.

cases, or whether it was rejecting the possibility in principle of costs being awarded: the latter appears the more likely. Furthermore, it seems clear that the ECSR does not have the power to promote a friendly settlement or order provisional measures, something that Harris has argued is regrettable.[115]

As mentioned above, it is up to the Committee of Ministers to make a definitive disposal of the complaint. Its role in so doing is described in article 9(1) of the 1995 Protocol as follows:

On the basis of the report of the Committee of Independent Experts [now the ECSR], the Committee of Ministers shall adopt a resolution by a majority of those voting. If the Committee of Independent Experts finds that the Charter has not been applied in a satisfactory manner, the Committee of Ministers shall adopt, by a majority of two-thirds of those voting, a recommendation addressed to the Contracting Party concerned. In both cases, entitlement to voting shall be limited to the Contracting Parties to the Charter.

Of this provision the Explanatory Report says:

The duties of the Committee of Ministers are similar to those it carries out as a supervisory body in the procedure instituted by the Charter [i.e. the reporting procedure]. On the basis of the report of the Committee of Independent Experts, the Committee of Ministers adopts a resolution by a majority of those voting. However, if the conclusions of the Committee of Independent Experts are negative, the Committee of Ministers must adopt a recommendation addressed to the state concerned....The Committee of Ministers cannot reverse the legal assessment made by the Committee of Independent Experts. However, its decision (resolution or recommendation) may be based on social and economic policy considerations.[116]

These somewhat opaque texts, which are equally unclear in their French versions, have given rise to differing views among commentators. It is generally agreed that if the ECSR reaches the conclusion that the defendant state has ensured the satisfactory application of the Charter, the Committee of Ministers shall do no more than adopt a resolution, by a simple majority of those voting,[117] concurring with the finding of the ECSR. This is indeed what has happened in practice.[118] Where the views of commentators diverge widely is over what the position should be where the ECSR reaches the conclusion that the defendant state has not ensured the satisfactory application of the Charter. Harris, relying on the use of the mandatory term 'shall' in article 9(1), is of the view that the Committee of Ministers may not make its own findings of compliance but must endorse the findings of the ECSR and

---

[115] Harris (n 47 above) at p 120. See also Harris and Darcy (n 4 above) at p 365.

[116] Explanatory Report (n 25 above) para 46.

[117] It is arguably anomalous that all parties to the Charter are permitted to vote, and not simply those bound by the collective complaints system.

[118] See resChS (2001)2, (2001) 8 Intl Human Rights Rep 570; (2001)3; (2001)4; (2002)5; (2005)1; (2005)2; (2004)6; (2005)13; and (2005)14, relating to Complaints nos 2/1999, 4/1999, 5/1999, 11/2001, 19/2003, 20/2003, 23/2004, 25/2004, and 26/2004, respectively. In these Resolutions the Committee of Ministers simply 'takes note' of the ECSR's report.

address a recommendation to the defendant state. He regards the reference in the Explanatory Report to account being taken by the Committee of Ministers of economic and social considerations as confusing (even though admittedly this happens in the reporting procedure) and contrary to the clear wording of article 9(1), and notes that the Explanatory Report is not an authoritative source of interpretation.[119] Trechsel has queried Harris' view on the basis that if the Committee of Ministers was bound to follow the ECSR's conclusion, what would be the point of giving the Committee of Ministers the power to consult the Governmental Committee in certain circumstances (a point dealt with below) or requiring a two-thirds majority, which implies that states have a discretion to vote against the ECSR's findings?[120] To this Harris and Darcy have responded that 'although there is a vote on the adoption of the recommendation, the vote concerns the content of the recommendation and not whether any recommendation should be addressed to the contracting party concerned at all'.[121] They also respond to the point in the Explanatory Report about account being taken of 'social and economic policy considerations' that this relates to the content of the resolution and/or recommendation, not to whether a recommendation should be adopted at all.[122] Although discussing the issue only briefly, Brillat appears to share the views of Harris.[123]

Sudre and Cullen take a very different position, however. Sudre, placing considerable reliance on the passage of the Explanatory Report quoted above, concludes that while the Committee of Ministers may not question the ECSR's findings on compliance, it may reach a decision contrary to that implied by the legal position and take account of non-legal considerations, so that in essence the Committee of Ministers, while legally bound by the opinion of the ECSR, politically is free to disregard that opinion.[124] Similarly, but more precisely, Cullen concludes that 'the Committee of Ministers may decide, on the basis of economic and social factors, not to make a recommendation to the defendant state to redress the area of non-compliance found by the ECSR in its conclusions, but it may not reject the legal basis of the conclusions'.[125] All commentators are agreed, however, that any recommendations or resolutions adopted by the Committee of Ministers are not legally binding.

Recently, the ECSR has expressed its own view of the role of the Committee of Ministers under article 9(1). In Complaint nos 16/2003 and 22/2003, the subject matter of which was similar to Complaint no 9/2000 (the length of working hours in France), the French government sought to argue that the Committee of Ministers had found that there was no violation in Complaint no 9 (even though

---

[119] Harris (n 47 above) at pp 107 and 121. See also Harris and Darcy (n 4 above) at pp 365–367.
[120] S Trechsel, 'Conclusion' in Council of Europe (n 29 above) at p 185.
[121] Harris and Darcy (n 4 above) at p 366.   [122] Ibid.
[123] R Brillat, 'A New Protocol to the European Social Charter Providing for Collective Complaints' (1996) 1 EHRLR, 52 at 61.   [124] Sudre (n 64 above) at 737.
[125] Cullen (n 46 above) at HR/27.

the ECSR had found that there was) and thus there could be no violation in the two later complaints. The ESCR roundly rejected this argument. It observed:

It is clear from the wording of the Protocol providing for a system of collective complaints that only the European Committee of Social Rights can determine whether or not a situation is in conformity with the Charter. This applies to any treaty establishing a judicial or quasi-judicial body to assess contracting parties' compliance with that treaty. The explanatory report to the Protocol explicitly states that the Committee of Ministers cannot reverse the legal assessment made by the Committee of independent experts, but may only decide whether or not to additionally make a recommendation to the state concerned.

Admittedly the Committee of Ministers, when it decides to use this power may take account of any social and economic policy considerations in its reasoning, but it may not question the legal assessment.[126]

Interestingly, the ECSR has put a gloss on the passage in the Explanatory Report quoted above. Whereas the latter states that the Committee of Ministers 'must adopt a recommendation' in cases where the ECSR has found a violation, the ECSR suggests in the passage above that the Committee of Ministers has the option whether to adopt a recommendation.

The practice of the Committee of Ministers so far is much closer to the position of Sudre and Cullen (and the ECSR) than that of Harris (and Harris and Darcy). Of the seventeen complaints where the ECSR reached the conclusion that the defendant state had not ensured the satisfactory application of the Charter (and where, therefore, in Harris' view the Committee of Ministers should have addressed a recommendation to the defendant state), in only one case (Complaint no 6/1999) did the Committee of Ministers in fact address a recommendation to the defendant state (in which it endorsed the ECSR's findings).[127] In the other cases the Committee of Ministers merely adopted a resolution concluding the proceedings. These resolutions are examined in detail in the next section of this chapter. The broader issues raised by the role of the Committee of Ministers are examined towards the end of the chapter.

As mentioned at the beginning of this chapter, the Governmental Committee plays a role in the reporting procedure. One of the most contentious issues in negotiating the 1995 Protocol was what kind of role (if any) the Governmental Committee should play in the collective complaints procedure. Initially the Charte-Rel Committee proposed that the Governmental Committee should have a role similar to the one that it has in the reporting procedure, but this was opposed by the social partners and some governments, which did not wish the Governmental Committee to have any role at all because of its composition (national civil servants) and the delay that its involvement might entail.[128]

---

[126] Complaint no 16/2003, Decision on the Merits, paras 20 and 21; and Complaint no 22/2003, Decision on the Merits, paras 23 and 24.   [127] ResChS (2000) 1.

[128] D Gomien, D Harris, and L Zwaak, *Law and Practice of the European Convention on Human Rights and the European Social Charter* (Council of Europe, 1996), at p 428.

The Charte-Rel Committee, therefore, amended its draft Protocol accordingly, and in that form (with no role for the Governmental Committee) the draft was sent to the Committee of Ministers.[129] The draft was not acceptable to a majority of the Committee of Ministers and, as a compromise, the draft was amended to give a modest role for the Governmental Committee in what is now article 9(2). This provides that where the report of the ECSR raises 'new issues', the Committee of Ministers may decide, at the request of the defendant state and by a two-thirds majority of the parties to the Charter, to consult the Governmental Committee. It is not altogether clear what is meant by 'new issues' in this context. Commentators have suggested that the term refers to a new point of interpretation or application of the Charter.[130] The 1995 Protocol is silent on the procedure to be followed where the Governmental Committee is consulted and as to the significance of any opinion that it might give. In practice, the Committee of Ministers has not yet consulted the Governmental Committee in relation to a complaint.[131]

If the Committee of Ministers endorses the findings of non-compliance by the ECSR and addresses a recommendation to the defendant state, the latter is to 'provide information on the measures it has taken to give effect' to the recommendation of the Committee of Ministers in the 'next report' that it submits under the reporting procedure.[132] If that report shows the defendant state to have complied with the recommendation of the Committee of Ministers, all well and good. If not, the Committee of Ministers could presumably address a further recommendation to the defendant state urging it to comply. Given that recommendations of the Committee of Ministers are not legally binding, it is unrealistic to expect the collective complaints system to have any stronger sanction against recalcitrant states. The Committee of Ministers has to date not adopted a further recommendation addressed to a state which has subsequently been found by the ECSR under the reporting system still not to be in compliance with the Charter. For example, in the one recommendation addressed by the Committee of Ministers to a defendant state the state concerned (France) reported at the next opportunity in the reporting cycle on the various steps that it had taken. The ECSR was only partially satisfied with these measures, and asked the French government both to take further measures and to supply it with more detailed information.[133] In 2004, possibly in

---

[129] Brillat (n 123 above) at 61. See also Harris (n 47 above) at pp 108 and 122.

[130] Harris (n 47 above) at p 122; Harris and Darcy (n 4 above) at pp 367–368; and Sudre (n 64 above) at 735. Less convincingly perhaps, Sudre suggests that the term could also concern the essential interests of the defendant state.

[131] The writers assume this to be the case, as none of the resolutions or recommendations so far made by the Committee of Ministers refer to it having consulted the Governmental Committee.

[132] Art 10, 1995 Protocol. It should be noted that the term 'next report' means literally that. Thus, if the provision of the Charter with which the defendant state has failed to comply is a non-core right, and the next report due covers only core rights, the response to the recommendation of the Committee of Ministers must nevertheless be contained in that report: see Explanatory Report (n 25 above) para 50.

[133] ECSR, *European Social Charter (Revised): Conclusions 2002 (France)*, p 26. In ECSR, *European Social Charter (Revised): Conclusions 2006 (France)*, at p 7 the Committee specifically

response to this case, the ECSR added a provision to its Rules whereby in cases where the ECSR has found a 'violation' of the Charter, the defendant state 'shall present in every subsequent report on the provisions contained in the complaint the measures taken to bring the situation into conformity'.[134] Despite the continued finding of French non-compliance with this aspect of the Charter by the ECSR, the Committee of Ministers has not adopted a further recommendation on the matter.

Having now examined at considerable length how the collective complaints system operates in general terms, it is time to consider how it has worked in practice and to see what the outcome of the first lot of complaints has been, before making a critical assessment of the system.

IV. An overview of the operation of the collective complaints system so far

By July 2006, eight years after the entry into force of the CCP, thirty-four complaints had been made. These complaints have been made against nine of the fourteen states that are bound by the system (thirteen complaints against France; six against Greece; five against Portugal; three against Italy; two each against Belgium and Bulgaria; and one each against Finland, Ireland, and Sweden). With one partial exception (Complaint no 32/2005, where the European Trade Union Confederation, one of the first category of complainants, joined two Bulgarian trade unions in making a complaint[135]), the complainants have all come from the second or third categories of those organizations entitled to make complaints.[136] Thus, Harris' prediction that the first category of complainant (international employers' organizations and trade unions) would want to make complaints[137] has not yet been borne out.

The complaints to date concern: child labour in Portugal;[138] the capacity of members of the armed forces to form trade unions and bargain collectively in France,

refers to its ECSR, *European Social Charter (Revised): Conclusions 2004 (France)*, p 211 where referring to Complaint no 6/1999 the Committee notes, 'In its previous conclusions...the Committee notes that the situation it had found not to be in conformity with art 1§2 in its decision on the merits dated 10 Oct 2000 was still not in conformity with the revised Charter. The report fails to provide any new information on the situation. Therefore the Committee concludes that the situation is still not in conformity with art 1§2 of the revised Charter.' It has similarly followed up Complaint 14/2003, at ibid, p 31 and Complaint 9/2000 in ECSR, *European Social Charter (Revised) Conclusions 2003 (France)*, p 9. The Committee of Ministers has not adopted any resolutions in relation to these findings.

[134] Rule 35 of the ECSR's Rules.

[135] Complaint no 32/2005, *Confederation of Independent Trade Unions in Bulgaria, Confederation of Labour 'Podkrepa' and European Trade Union Confederation v Bulgaria*.

[136] Sixteen from the second category and seven from the third category (six of which are national trade unions and the other an employers' association).   [137] Harris (n 47 above) at 111.

[138] Complaint no 1/1998. For comment, see Cullen (n 46 above).

Greece, Italy, and Portugal,[139] and of the police to do the same in Portugal;[140] discrimination against certain tourist guides in France;[141] certain forms of forced labour in Greece;[142] the working hours of certain categories of employees in France;[143] the working conditions of health care workers in Finland exposed to radiation;[144] the closed shop in Sweden;[145] educational provision for autistic children in France;[146] discrimination in the provision of social and medical assistance in France;[147] discrimination against the Roma in the field of housing in Greece, Italy, and Bulgaria;[148] the absence of effective prohibition against corporal punishment of children in Belgium, Greece, Ireland, Italy, and Portugal;[149] the prohibition on non-representative professional organizations from presenting candidates in professional elections in France;[150] the exclusion of certain categories of employee from French anti-discrimination legislation;[151] the alleged failure of Belgian law to guarantee the right to bargain effectively in the public sector; [152] the right to organize in the higher education and public sectors in France;[153] the payment of private medical practitioners in France;[154] the health hazards of working in lignite mines in Greece;[155] the right to strike in parts of the public sector in Bulgaria;[156] and the housing situation of the very poor in France.[157]

Of the thirty-four complaints, all but three have been declared admissible.[158] Of the thirty-one admissible complaints, the ECSR has upheld the complaint (wholly or partially) in seventeen cases,[159] rejected the complaint in nine cases,[160] and in five cases has not yet concluded its consideration of the merits.[161] In the nine cases where the ECSR rejected the complaint, the Committee of Ministers adopted a resolution taking note of the ECSR's report.[162]

---

[139] Complaint nos 2/1999, 3/1999, *European Federation of Employees in Public Services v Greece*, 4/1999 and 5/1999.   [140] Complaint no 11/2001, (10) Intl Human Rights Rev 572 (2003).

[141] Complaint no 6/1999.

[142] Complaint no 7/2000 (2001) 8 Intl Human Rights Rep 1153 and Complaint no 8/2000 (2001) 8 Intl Human Rights Rev 1158. For comments on these complaints see J Darcy, 'Forced Labour in Greece', (2002) 27 ELRev, 218.   [143] Complaints nos 9/2000, 16/2003, and 22/2003.

[144] Complaint no 10/2000, (2003) 10 Intl Human Rights Rev 554.

[145] Complaint no 12/2002.   [146] Complaint no 13/2002.

[147] Complaint no 14/2003.   [148] Complaints no 15/2003, 27/2004, and 31/2005.

[149] Complaints nos 17/2003, 18/2003, 19/2003, 20/2003, 21/2003, and 34/2006.

[150] Complaint no 23/2003.   [151] Complaint no 24/2004.

[152] Complaint no 25/2004, *Centrale générale des services public v Belgium*.

[153] Complaints no 26/2004 and 29/2005.   [154] Complaint no 24/2004.

[155] Complaint no 30/2005.   [156] Complaint no 32/2005.

[157] Complaint no 33/2006.

[158] Complaint nos 3/1999, 28/2004, and 29/2005. That such a high proportion of complaints has been found admissible is scarcely surprising, given the nature of those entitled to make the complaints and the limited admissibility criteria.

[159] Complaints nos 1/1998, 6/1999, 7/2000, 8/2000, 9/2000, 10/2000, 12/2002, 13/2002, 14/2003, 15/2003, 16/2003, 17/2003, 18/2003, 21/2003, 22/2003, 24/2004, and 27/2004.

[160] Complaints nos 2/1999, 4/1999, 5/1999, 11/2001, 19/2003, 20/2003, 23/2003, 25/2004, and 26/2004.   [161] Complaints nos 30–34.

[162] See (n 118 above).

Of the seventeen complaints where the ECSR found non-compliance with the Charter by the defendant state, in only one case did the Committee of Ministers address a recommendation to the defendant state, as article 9(1) appears to suggest it should. This was Complaint no 6/1999, which concerned a complaint of discriminatory treatment by the French government against certain kinds of tourist guides. Here the Committee of Ministers addressed a number of quite specific recommendations to the French government to take certain action to put an end to the discriminatory treatment.[163] Compared with recommendations addressed to states parties at the end of the reporting procedure, this recommendation is unusual because of its detail and specificity. In the recommendations adopted in the reporting procedure, the Committee of Ministers usually does no more than recommend that the state concerned 'takes account, in an appropriate manner, of the negative conclusion' of the ECSR.[164]

The fifteen cases where the Committee of Ministers adopted a resolution following a finding of a violation of the Charter by the ECSR rather than addressing a recommendation to the defendant state reveal a number of trends.[165] In just over a third of the cases the Committee of Ministers has adopted a resolution in which it has taken note of measures that the defendant state has already taken since the ECSR's decision on the merits, or is planning to take, to address the violation found by the ECSR.[166] In such cases it would be a rather pointless exercise for the Committee of Ministers to address a recommendation to the state concerned. It follows from the division of roles between the ECSR and the Committee of Ministers in relation to the merits stage of a complaint, that it is beyond the Committee of Ministers' competence to assess whether the measures a defendant state has taken or is planning to take satisfactorily address the violation found by the ECSR and bring the state into compliance with the Charter. This will be a matter for the ECSR to assess in the next report submitted by that state under the reporting procedure. If the ECSR should find that the violation has been adequately addressed, the complainant will then have achieved its objective without it having been necessary for the Committee of Ministers to seek to persuade the defendant state to act through the adoption of a recommendation. By and large the actions of the Committee of Ministers in these cases seem acceptable and in keeping with the spirit of the Collective Complaints Protocol, although on occasions it may be that the Committee of Ministers shows undue faith in appropriate measures being taken to curb a violation when the plans of a defendant state appear speculative and uncertain. For example, in the case of Complaint no 18/2003, where the ECSR found that Ireland had violated the Charter in providing insufficient protection from

---

[163] ResChS (2001)1.   [164] See eg, ResChS (2001)3 (addressed to Malta).

[165] There is one complaint (no 24/2004) where the ECSR found a violation but where the Committee of Ministers has yet to respond.

[166] ResChS (2004)1, (2005)6, (2005)11, (2005)12, (2005)9, and (2006)4 in respect of Complaints nos 13/2002, 14/2003, 15/2003, 17/2003, 18/2003, and 27/2004. The measures taken or to be taken by the defendant state are in some cases set out in an appendix to the resolution.

corporal punishment for children in the home and in care, the Committee of Ministers noted the intention of the Irish Department of Health and Children 'to seek legal advice in relation to amending the regulations to make more explicit the prohibition of corporal punishment of children in care, and on the need for any change required in primary legislation', as well as the Irish government's intention 'to keep the introduction of an outright ban on corporal punishment under review'.[167]

A second trend is superficially similar to the first, but much less acceptable. In three cases the Committee of Ministers in its resolution has simply had 'regard to the information communicated' by the defendant state and taken 'note of the report' of the ECSR.[168] There is no indication what the nature of the information is that the defendant state has communicated, and there is no reason to suppose that it necessarily relates to measures proposed to put an end to the violation found by the ECSR. It is this lack of transparency that gives rise to concerns about this form of the practice by the Committee of Ministers. The ECSR is proving, however, to be vigilant in subsequent reporting cycles in trying to ensure that the defendant state's response to a successful complaint has been adequate.[169]

The practice of the Committee of Ministers in the early complaints where the ECSR found a violation reveal no particular pattern, but each resolution adopted by the Committee of Ministers is in its own way unsatisfactory and worrying. In Complaint no 1/1998 the ECSR found that Portugal was not fully complying with article 7(1) of the Charter, which prohibits the employment of children below the age of fifteen. In its subsequent resolution the Committee of Ministers took note of the ECSR's report and, after pointing out that it had adopted a recommendation to Portugal on the same issue the previous year,[170] 'recalls that the government of Portugal will present, in its next report on the application of the European Social Charter, the measures taken in application of the said recommendation'.[171] This action by the Committee of Ministers has been criticised as being 'a very weak response' and as taking insufficient account of the differences between the collective complaints system and the reporting procedure.[172] More might have been achieved if the Committee of Ministers had adopted a second recommendation calling on Portugal to improve the enforcement of its child labour legislation, a recommendation on which Portugal would subsequently have had to report. Although Portugal has now taken some action to rectify the situation,[173] the ECSR, in its conclusions on Portugal's report for the period 1996–1998, still did not consider that Portugal was fully in compliance with article 7.[174]

---

[167] ResChS (2005)9.

[168] ResChS (2005)7, (2005)10, and (2005)8 in relation to Complaints nos 16/2003, 21/2003, and 22/2003.   [169] See eg, nn 174 and 178 and accompanying text.

[170] ResChS (1998) 5.   [171] ResChS (1999) 4.

[172] Harris and Darcy (n 4 above) at p 367. Cf Cullen (n 46 above) at HR/26, who describes the Committee of Ministers' actions as 'minimalist'.

[173] See Governmental Committee of the European Social Charter, 15th Report (II) (2001) at 11.

[174] ECSR, *European Social Charter: Conclusions XV-2 (Portugal) (2001)* at p 4. In ECSR, *European Social Charter (Revised) Conclusions 2006 Portugal*, p 17 and following, the Committee noted

In Complaint no 7/2000 the ECSR found Greece in non-compliance with the Charter's provisions prohibiting forced labour in respect of three particular pieces of legislation. These instances of non-compliance had been pointed out by the ECSR under the reporting system and had been the subject of a series of recommendations by the Committee of Ministers dating back to 1993. When the Committee of Ministers came to consider the first piece of legislation at issue in Complaint no 7/2000, it took note of the fact that the Greek government had advanced additional considerations not relied on during the examination of the merits of the complaint by the ECSR, namely a law of 1995, and the Committee went on to note that the Greek government 'will give a full account of these' in its next report due under the reporting system.[175] That the Greek government should be allowed to raise arguments before the Committee of Ministers which it did not raise (but presumably could have raised) before the ECSR, seems questionable. And even more surprising is the fact that those arguments related to a piece of legislation of 1995 which presumably the Greek government could have advanced when its failure to comply with the Charter was being revealed in the 1995, 1997, and 1999 reporting cycles. In relation to the second and third pieces of legislation at issue in this complaint, the Committee of Ministers 'takes note that ... the Greek government undertakes to bring the situation into conformity with the Charter in good time'.[176] Given that the reporting system had revealed failures of compliance of the relevant legislation with the Charter going back nearly ten years, it seems feeble in the extreme that the Committee should simply wait for the Greek Government to take action in its own good time. Complaint no 8/2000 also concerned alleged forced labour in Greece, this time in respect of conscientious objectors performing civilian service as an alternative to military service. The ECSR, by a majority of 6–3, found that the greater length of civilian service compared with military service, while not as such forced labour, was nevertheless a disproportionate restriction on the freedom to earn one's living in an occupation freely entered upon and thus was contrary to article 1(2) of the Charter. The fact that the ECSR was quite deeply divided as to the scope of article 1(2) may help to explain why the Committee of Ministers did not address a recommendation to Greece but instead adopted a resolution.[177] In this resolution the Committee of Ministers noted that the ECSR's report had been 'circulated to the competent authorities' and was being translated into Greek; noted recent developments in Greece, including a decrease in the length of *military* service; and finally 'takes note that the Greek Government undertakes to take the matter into consideration with a view to bring the situation into conformity with the Charter in good time'. This final part of the resolution constitutes the same feeble response as was seen in Complaint no 7/2000, a feebleness which is compounded by the

---

subsequent developments but considered that it did not have enough information to determine whether Portugal was in compliance with its obligations or not.

175　ResChS (2001) 6.　　176　Ibid.
177　ResChS (2002) 3, (10) Intl Human Rights Rep 583 (2003).

fact that the earlier part of resolution noted a decrease in the length of military service, thus if anything making the disproportionate length of civilian service worse.[178]

In Complaint no 9/2000 the ECSR (by a 5–3 majority) found two breaches of the Charter by France in respect of the length of the working hours of managers. The Committee of Ministers, however, did not endorse this finding. Instead, it noted a number of factors, which collectively appear to amount to a view as to the meaning and application of the relevant provisions of the Charter quite different from that of the majority of the ECSR (but close to the views expressed in a dissenting opinion by two members of the minority), and therefore implicitly finding no breach by France.[179] In so doing the Committee of Ministers effectively substituted its own view of the law for that of the ECSR—something which, as noted earlier, all commentators are agreed that the Committee of Ministers is not supposed to do and which, as has been seen, was firmly rejected by the ECSR in Complaints 16/2003 and 22/2003.

Another early case which raises concerns about the role of the Committee of Ministers is Complaint no 10/2000. Here the ECSR found that the exposure of health workers to ionizing radiation was dangerous and unhealthy work within the meaning of article 2(4) of the Charter and that therefore the failure of the Finnish government to ensure that such workers were entitled to additional paid holidays or reduced working hours (as article 2(4) requires) amounted to non-compliance with that article. The Committee of Ministers in its resolution[180] began by noting that the primary concern of the Finnish government was to eliminate risks created by working with ionizing radiation and that workers in the health sector in Finland were exposed to doses of radiation well below the max-imum limits required by international standards. The Committee of Ministers then went on to take note of the impending ratification by Finland of the Revised Social Charter, including the revised article 2, paragraph 4, which puts the emphasis on elimination of risks rather than on additional paid holidays or reduced working hours. The Committee of Ministers' resolution is again open to criticism. The complaint and the ECSR's report are couched purely in terms of the original Charter. It was, therefore, at best premature, at worst irrelevant, for the Committee of Ministers to consider the issue in terms of the Revised Charter (which Finland did in fact ratify six months after the resolution was adopted). The resolution can be read as suggesting that once Finland ratified the Revised Charter, it would be in compliance with it. This would mean that the Committee of Ministers had formed a view about the standard of protection required by

---

[178] Greece has subsequently introduced new legislation which provides for a significant reduction in the length of alternative service but this was still found by the ECSR not to be in conformity with art 1(2) of the Charter. ECSR, *Conclusions XVIII-1 (Greece)* p 10.

[179] ResChS (2002) 4, (10) Intl Human Rights Rep 571 (2003).   [180] ResChS (2002) 2.

article 2(4) of the Revised Charter and Finland's compliance with it. These are issues for the ECSR, not the Committee of Ministers.[181]

The last of the early cases giving rise to concern is Complaint no 12/2002, where the ECSR had found Sweden to be in breach of the provisions of the Revised Charter concerning collective bargaining. At the meeting of the Committee of Ministers to consider the ESCR's report, the Swedish representative had declared that Sweden intended to rectify the breach by renegotiating collective agreements (of which at that time there were 4,388 requiring renegotiation).[182] The Committee of Ministers in the operative part of its resolution[183] simply stated that it 'looks forward to Sweden reporting that the problem has been solved at the time of the submission of the next report' on article 5 of the Revised Charter. The Committee of Ministers seems unduly complacent here as there was no guarantee that such a large number of agreements would be renegotiated within the timeframe envisaged. In any case the ECSR had called on Sweden to use legislative, regulatory, or judicial means in order to bring about conformity with the Charter, rather than renegotiating agreements.[184]

V. Some reflections on the collective complaints system and its potential

A. The degree of use of the complaints system

Since the CCP entered into force, thirty-four complaints have been lodged, which works out at about four complaints a year on average. Whether the number of complaints that has so far been made is more or less than might have been expected is an impossible question to answer, and one that is perhaps not even worth asking. Instead, it is more fruitful to consider the factors that are likely to influence the degree of use that has been made and probably will be made of the complaints system. These factors include the following. The first is the number of states that have accepted the system. Obviously the more states that have accepted the system, the more complaints it is likely that there will be (although it should be noted that just over a third of the states that have so far accepted the system have not yet had a complaint made against them). Currently the number of states that have accepted the system is disappointingly low—only just over one third of parties to the Charter. A second factor is the degree of knowledge of the system by potential complainants. Obviously the more well-known the system is, the greater

---

[181] In ECSR, *Conclusions XVI-2 (Finland)* at p 8 the Committee referred to its own decision in Complaint no 10/2000 to conclude that the situation was not in conformity with art 2(4) of the Charter. The ECSR has not subsequently considered the provision under the reporting procedure.
[182] Appendix to ResChS (2003) 1.   [183] ResChS (2003) 1.
[184] Complaint no 12/2002, Decision on the Merits, para 28.

the likelihood of complaints. Complainants coming into the first two categories of complainant will by definition know about the system. The third category of complainant, national organizations of employers and trade unions, will know about the Charter generally from their involvement in the reporting system, but they may not be very familiar with the collective complaints system. This is likely especially to be the case in states that have been parties to the Charter for a relatively short period of time. The Council of Europe is trying to promote awareness and knowledge of the collective complaints system among potential complainants by holding occasional conferences on the system. Such knowledge appears already to be quite well-developed among French trade unions, which are responsible for around a quarter of all complaints so far. One has the impression that there may be a strategy among French trades unions to use the collective complaints system as a mechanism for trying to improve the working conditions of their members.

A third factor influencing the degree of use of the collective complaints system is the general perceived level of compliance with the Charter (as revealed, at least in part, by the reporting system). The more instances of non-compliance that are revealed, the more likely it is that complaints will be made. Fourthly, the number of complaints will to some degree be influenced by the suitability of provisions of the Charter to be subject to complaints. Not all provisions are so suitable, being too general in nature. A fifth factor is the willingness of potential complainants to bear the costs and effort of making a complaint. Sixth, the speed of the system will be a factor. The quicker that complaints are processed, the more attractive the collective complaints system is likely to be perceived. As will be seen below, the system currently deals with complaints quite quickly. Finally, the degree of use that will be made of the collective complaints system is heavily dependent on the perceived effectiveness of the system by potential complainants. Such perceptions will depend, in part, on the outcome of the complaints already made under the system. As has been seen, the picture so far is rather mixed.

B. Speed of the system

It is a common feature of human rights compliance systems that they are not particularly speedy. However, the collective complaints system has so far functioned relatively speedily. The period of time taken to reach a decision on admissibility is between four and five months on average, while the complete disposal of a complaint takes on average a little under twenty months. Of course, the fact that the complaints have been dealt with quite quickly is at least, in part, a consequence of there being relatively few complaints so far. It must be remembered that the bodies that deal with complaints, the ECSR and the Committee of Ministers, are part-time and also exercise a considerable role under the reporting system. Thus, should the number of complaints significantly increase, it is to be expected that it will take longer to deal with them.

C. The role of the Committee of Ministers

As has been seen, the Committee of Ministers has been reluctant to address rec-ommendations to states found by the ECSR not to be complying with the Charter. On some occasions this reluctance is understandable where defendant states appear to be actively putting an end to the non-compliance in question. However, there have been quite a number of complaints where the lack of an adequate response by the Committee of Ministers gives rise to disquiet. This may be symptomatic of a fundamental problem with the role of the Committee of Ministers, which is that it is in principle undesirable that a political body should be involved in what ought to be an independent, quasi-judicial process.[185] Even if one does not accept this principle, there are nevertheless a number of features about the way in which the Committee of Ministers functions that are unsatisfac-tory. The defendant state, unlike the complainant, takes part in the Committee's proceedings and may vote; the decisions of the Committee are unreasoned; and a finding of non-compliance requires a two-thirds majority, whereas the ECSR decides by a simple majority.[186] Many of the same criticisms were made about the role that the Committee of Ministers originally had under the European Convention on Human Rights, when it ruled on the merits of cases that were not referred to the European Court of Human Rights.[187] This role was removed by Protocol 11 to the Convention. It is unfortunate that the Council of Europe per-sisted with a determinative role for the Committee of Ministers when drafting the Collective Complaints Protocol, even though the latter was adopted a year after Protocol 11. As a consequence, the collective complaints system is now the only international human rights mechanism where a governmental body has a decisive say in the outcome of the proceedings.

The efficacy of the collective complaints system is to a considerable degree dependent upon the Committee of Ministers showing the necessary political will and playing a full role by making detailed recommendations to states parties if they are found by the ECSR to be in breach of the Charter and have not taken, or are not in the process of taking, measures to put an end to the breach.[188] Above all,

---

[185] The same comment can be made about the possible involvement of the Governmental Committee in the collective complaints system under art 9(2) of the Collective Complaints Protocol, given that the Committee consists of national officials. So far such criticism is purely theoretical, as up to now this Committee has not in practice been involved in a complaint.

[186] See further Sudre (n 64 above) 733–737.

[187] See further P Leuprecht, 'The Protection of Human Rights by Political Bodies—The Example of the Committee of Ministers of the Council of Europe' in M Nowak, D Steurer, and H Tretter (eds), *Progress in the Spirit of Human Rights, Festschrift für Felix Ermacora* (Kehl am Rhein, 1988); and A Tomkins, 'The Committee of Ministers: Its Roles under the European Convention on Human Rights' 1 EHRLR 49 (1995).

[188] For criticism of this approach see R Brillat, 'The Supervisory Machinery of the European Social Charter: Recent Developments and Their Impact' in G de Búrca and B de Witte (eds), *Social Rights in Europe* (OUP, 2005) p 31, at p 33.

the Committee of Ministers must refrain from implicitly questioning the legal assessment of the ECSR. If in future the Committee of Ministers continues to adopt resolutions that display the worst features of some of its past resolutions that were identified earlier (such as questioning the judgment of the ECSR or simply taking note of unspecified information provided by defendant states), there is a real danger that this will undermine the credibility of the collective complaints system and dissuade potential complainants from utilizing it.

D. The relationship between the collective complaints and reporting systems

One of the issues concerning the Protocol which in practice seems to have been largely already settled is the relationship between it and the pre-existing reporting mechanism. The existence of more than one compliance mechanism in a human rights treaty is nothing new. However, the fact that the same body engages in both constructive dialogue through the reporting procedure with state representatives and also sits in judgment upon a state's compliance with its obligations under the same treaty is not without problems. The first is a concern for the workload of the individuals involved. If the collective complaints system is used more extensively in the future, the burden that this will impose on the part-time ECSR members, in addition to their duties under the reporting system, will become more difficult to manage.

A more fundamental problem, however, may be the potential incompatibility of the two functions of the ECSR. The Independent Expert on the Draft Optional Protocol to the ICESCR has noted '[i]t is a hard assignment for one body, first to engage a state party in constructive, fruitful dialogue... on the steps it has taken... a non-confrontational, consultative exercise—and then to behave as a quasi-judicial investigative and settlement body. It should opt for one or the other.'[189] He observes that as a consequence a state may become reluctant to engage in a frank and constructive dialogue about its problems in the reporting phase, if it is likely to have to face that same committee in a quasi-judicial context.[190] The establishment of a complaints system under the Social Charter may thus have some adverse consequences for the reporting system.

The preamble to the Collective Complaints Protocol refers only to the fact that it is designed to improve the effective enforcement of the social rights guaranteed by the Charter. It does not elaborate on the relationship between the complaints and reporting mechanisms. This matter is to some extent addressed in the

---

[189] *Report of the Independent Expert on the Question of a Draft Optional Protocol to the International Covenant on Economic, Social and Cultural Rights*, UN doc E/CN.4/2002/57 at 10. The view of the Independent Expert has been challenged by the participants to the ICJ-organized roundtable on the Draft Optional Protocol to the ICESCR (n 7 above) at 10.

[190] *Report of the Independent Expert* (n 189 above) at 10.

Explanatory Report to the Protocol, which states that the reporting system is to remain the 'basic mechanism' for enforcement, with the collective complaints system designed to 'increase the efficiency' of the existing machinery[191] and be seen as a 'complement' to the pre-existing system. The exact details of how the two interrelate are for the ECSR to work out.

The relationship between the two procedures was examined by the ECSR in its very first decision on admissibility in Complaint no 1/1998, which concerned the existence of child labour in Portugal. The Portuguese government argued that the complaint should be rejected as inadmissible because the matter had already been the subject of a recommendation by the Committee of Ministers to Portugal in an earlier reporting cycle. The ECSR rejected Portugal's argument. It considered that the object of the system of collective complaints, 'which is different in nature from the procedure of examining national reports, is to allow the Committee to make a legal assessment of the situation of a state in the light of the information supplied by the complaint and the adversarial procedure to which it gives rise'.[192] The fact that the Committee had already examined the situation relating to the object of the complaint within the framework of the reporting system, and would do so again, did not in itself imply the inadmissibility of a collective complaint. Furthermore, Portugal's compliance with article 7 of the Charter (the article at issue) was examined only once every four years, and so the situation would not be assessed again for a further two years. Also the recommendation of the Committee of Ministers related to the period 1994–95, whereas the complaint referred to legislation and factual circumstances subsequent to that period. The complaints procedure therefore allowed Portugal to furnish information and evidence relating to the actions it had taken since the reporting period concerned.

Portugal also argued that for the ECSR to declare the complaint admissible and subsequently adjudicate on it, would contravene the principles of *res judicata* and *non bis in idem*.[193] If the ECSR had accepted this line of reasoning, the collective complaints system would have become largely redundant as it would, in practice, have prohibited examination of a complaint if the matter had been addressed by the ECSR, possibly even in passing, in the reporting procedure. The ECSR firmly rejected Portugal's argument, declaring that:

[n]either the fact that the Committee has already examined this situation in the framework of the reporting system, nor the fact that it will examine it again during subsequent supervision cycles do not in themselves imply the inadmissibility of a collective complaint concerning the same provision of the Charter and the same Contracting Party.[194]

---

[191] Explanatory Report (n 25 above) at paras 1–2.
[192] Complaint no 1/1998, Decision on Admissibility, para 10.   [193] Para 4.
[194] Para 10. However, the fact that the ECSR found the complaint admissible was to some extent undermined by the decision of the Committee of Ministers not to issue a recommendation to Portugal on the ground that a recommendation had already been issued under the reporting procedure. See text at n 172 above.

The ECSR went on to note that these principles, ie, *res judicata* and *non bis in idem*, 'do not apply to the relation between the two supervisory procedures'.[195]

If the Protocol is to be effective, the ECSR's approach is essential as it will allow detailed legal analysis and determination of the extent to which a state party is complying with its obligations. Criticism of the duplication of effort can be rebutted on the basis that as the same body will be involved in both compliance mechanisms, it can utilize its own work for both procedures. In declaring Portugal's application admissible, the ECSR also noted that one of the objectives of the collective complaints system was to consolidate the participation of the social partners and non-governmental organizations.[196] This in itself is quite interesting as one of the distinguishing features of the system is the increased involvement of such organizations compared with the reporting mechanism. Thus to declare an application inadmissible, owing to the fact that the issue with which it is concerned may already have been addressed in the reporting procedure, would effectively deprive such organizations of their enhanced status and role.[197] It is worthy of note that in subsequent complaints no state has objected to admissibility on the grounds raised by Portugal in Complaint no 1/1998. It is worth questioning, however, whether the ECSR will or should maintain its current approach if or when its workload increases significantly. This point can be seen in relation to Complaint no 7/2000. Unlike Complaint no 1/1998, the provision at issue in Complaint no 7/2000 was a core right and thus was examined every two years. It is, therefore, questionable whether the finding under the collective complaint system of a violation really added anything to the earlier finding of non-compliance under the reporting procedure, as the complainant did not refer to any developments subsequent to the most recent report. Darcy has questioned whether complaints that have nothing new to add to the reporting procedure, such as Complaint no 7/2000, should be declared admissible.[198]

Although the ECSR did not reject Complaint no 7/2000 as inadmissible, the fact that according to the Explanatory Report the ECSR has a 'margin of appreciation' in this matter means that it may in future, if it so wishes, follow the point of view advocated by Darcy and Sudre, especially if it becomes over-burdened by complaints. However, to do so would be to overlook the advantages of a mechanism like the collective complaints system. First, because it is based on comprehensive written

---

[195] Ibid para 13.   [196] Ibid.

[197] The Collective Complaints Protocol is, as far as is known, the first international instrument that specifically recognises the standing of NGOs other than workers' and employers' organizations to bring a complaint. The fact that the complaints procedure allows more detailed analysis of state obligations under the Charter can also be seen from the fact that the ECSR is in the reporting system now referring to complaints submitted under the CCP to outline the obligations that other states parties owe. See eg, ECSR, *Conclusions 2006, Albania* at p 7 where the ECSR refers to Complaint no 13/2000 against France to emphasize the nature of the obligation Albania owes under art E of the Charter.

[198] Darcy (n 142 above), at 218. A similar point has also been made by Sudre (n 64 above) at 731.

proceedings presented by both complainants and governments, it will allow the ECSR to analyse the legislation and the situation in practice, in a manner that is unlikely to happen under the reporting procedure. It will thus highlight in more detail the extent of the non-compliance and will allow the ECSR to provide the state party with greater guidance as to the measures that need to be taken to ensure compliance.[199] This should ensure that national provisions are brought fully into compliance with the Charter. Secondly, complaints under the collective complaints system should not only lead to a consolidation of standards but should also allow their progressive development. In numerous complaints to date the ECSR has referred to its conclusions from the reporting cycles to define the standards and the basic requirements of the Charter provisions in question. That much is to be expected. The collective complaints system importantly, however, provides an opportunity for non-governmental bodies to try to persuade the ECSR towards the progressive development of standards. Complaint no 2/1999 is an instance in question. Here the allegation was that France did not comply with articles 5 and 6 of the Charter in so far as members of the armed forces did not enjoy the right to organize and there was no right to bargain collectively.[200] One of the fundamental questions for the ECSR was not only the scope of the obligation but also the construction of the exception clause in the final sentence of article 5 as regards military personnel.[201] The Committee had elaborated over the years in the reporting procedure what this actually meant, but it is clear from the submissions made that one of the express purposes of the complaint was to push for a more restrictive interpretation of the exception[202] and for the interpretation of the Charter as a 'living instrument'.[203] However, on this matter the complainant was not successful.[204]

In terms of substance, a complaint can involve a variety of situations vis-à-vis the reporting system and offer a number of strategies to supplement it. These situations include the following:

(i) the complaint concerns a matter where in the reporting system the ECSR found non-compliance and the Committee of Ministers addressed a recommendation to the defaulting state with which the latter has not complied. Here a complaint can be used to put pressure on the recalcitrant state to comply. Complaints no 1/1998 and 7/2000 are examples of this;

(ii) the complaint concerns a matter where in the reporting system the ECSR found non-compliance, but the Committee of Ministers failed to address a recommendation to the state concerned. Here a complaint can be used to try to persuade the Committee of Ministers to issue a recommendation;

(iii) the complaint concerns a matter where in the reporting system the ECSR found the state concerned to be complying with the Charter. Here the purpose of the complaint will be to persuade the ECSR to reverse its earlier finding.

---

[199] See eg, Complaint no 6/1999.
[200] Substantively Complaints nos 3/1999, 4/1999, and 5/1999 are identical.
[201] See para 26.   [202] See para 27.   [203] See para 14.   [204] See para 29.

Complaint no 23/2003 appears to be an example of such a kind of complaint, although its attempt to persuade the ECSR to change its mind was unsuccessful;[205]

(iv) the complaint concerns a matter in respect of which the ECSR has recently articulated new or revised standards in the reporting procedure. Here the purpose of the complaint is to see whether the law and practice of a particular state comply with the newly articulated standards. Examples of this are the complaints brought by the World Organization against Torture against five states in 2003[206] alleging non-compliance with the norms of the Charter prohibiting violence against children, including corporal punishment, that the ECSR had articulated in 2001;[207] and

(v) the complaint concerns a matter that does not appear (yet) to have been addressed under the reporting system or that has arisen since the previous report. Here the complaint is essentially designed to raise an issue under the Charter *de novo*. Many of the complaints appear to be of this nature.

Although the collective complaints and reporting systems are different procedures operating in different ways, they do have a number of similarities. The same bodies (the ECSR and the Committee of Ministers) are involved in both procedures, although the ECSR acts in a more quasi-judicial way in the complaints procedure, especially at the admissibility stage, than in the reporting system.[208] Secondly, each procedure involves an examination of the law and practice of the state concerned in general terms, rather than their application to specific individuals. Finally and most importantly, the outcome in cases of non-compliance is the same in each system—the issuing of a non-binding recommendation to the state concerned, to which the latter is then required to give its response in the next cycle of the reporting procedure.

E. The desirability/feasibility of bringing more states into the collective complaints system

It is obviously disappointing that only fourteen out of thirty-eight parties to the Charter have so far become bound by the collective complaints system. Such a low level of participation reduces the utility of the system, and to some extent undermines its legitimacy and credibility. It would clearly be desirable to have more states bound by the system. This would make the system a standard part of the Charter machinery, rather than an optional minority extra as at present; would

---

[205] See especially paras 25, 29, and 30 of the Decision on the Merits.
[206] Complaints nos 17/2003, 18/2003, 19/2003, 20/2003, and 21/2003.
[207] *General Introduction to Conclusions* XV-2, vol 1 (2001).
[208] Cullen (n 46 above) HR/27–8.

increase awareness and knowledge of the Charter; and would make the Charter more effective as more instances of non-compliance were identified and hopefully rectified. Now that the collective complaints system is working regularly and frequently, states may soon become more confident in it. It might, therefore, at some stage be possible to amend the Collective Complaints Protocol to remove some of its more obvious defects, notably the current role of the Committee of Ministers.

It is not clear why more states have not ratified the Protocol (or made the necessary declaration under the Revised Charter). There are a number of possible reasons (which are not mutually exclusive). In some cases it may be bureaucratic inertia or inability/unwillingness by governments to find the necessary Parliamentary time in those states where Parliamentary approval is necessary for ratification. In other cases states may be waiting to see how the collective complaints system operates in practice before taking a decision whether to ratify.[209] In the case of Central and East European states (where only three out of seventeen such states party to the Charter have so far accepted the collective complaints system), it may well be that their relative inexperience with the Charter system (all have ratified the Charter since 1997 and some have still to go for the first time through a full cycle of reporting) has led most of them to decide to obtain more experience with the Charter generally (not least to see how far they are considered to be complying with it as revealed by the reporting system) before deciding whether to take the further step of becoming bound by the collective complaints system. Then there are a small number of older members of the Council of Europe that seem to have limited interest and enthusiasm for the Charter as evidenced by the fact that they have ratified only the Charter in its original form and not any additional or amending protocols or the Revised Charter. Such states include Germany, Iceland, Luxembourg, and the United Kingdom. States (such as Turkey) that have been shown by the reporting system to have a poor compliance record with the Charter are obviously less likely to accept the collective complaints system, although it is in such states that the system is potentially most useful.[210] Finally, it may be that there are states that are opposed to the collective complaints system for reasons of principle or that simply have a poor record of accepting optional petition systems in other human rights treaties.

[209] For an example of such a 'wait and see' approach (but in relation to the Revised Charter rather than the Collective Complaints Protocol) see the answer by Mr Macshane, the UK Minister of State for Foreign and Commonwealth Affairs, to a Parliamentary question dealing with these issues. WA 14 May 2003 Col 289 W. It has been suggested that some states may fear that the collective complaints system will be abused, will lead to the unrestrained development of social rights, and disturb the way the Charter has operated up until now. See comment by F Vandamme in Council of Europe (n 29 above) p 181 at pp 183–184.

[210] Nevertheless, four states with indifferent records of compliance (ie having been found to comply with less than half the Charter provisions they have accepted)—Belgium, Greece, Ireland, and Italy—have accepted the collective complaints system.

What can be done to persuade states to accept the collective complaints system? Four states (Austria, Czech Republic, Denmark, and Slovakia) have so far signed the Collective Complaints Protocol but have not yet ratified it. Such signature indicates that these states are seriously considering ratification, and it may, therefore, be only a matter of time before they ratify. In the case of other states, the Council of Europe, particularly through the Parliamentary Assembly and the Committee of Ministers, should encourage participation in the collective complaints system. More effective will probably be domestic political pressure from potential complainants, notably employers' organizations and trade unions. Where such bodies already play an active role in the reporting procedure, pressure to ratify will be greatest. Unfortunately, however, in too many states parties to the Charter such organizations do not get actively involved in the reporting procedure and therefore are unlikely to campaign for their state to participate in the collective complaints system.

While encouraging increased participation in the Protocol is in principle desirable, such participation may be of limited benefit in the case of states parties only to the original Charter. Many of the rights contained in the latter are outdated and lag behind the national laws of states parties and EU law (where applicable), so that the bringing of collective complaints is likely to be of limited use. The collective complaints system is likely to be of greatest utility in those states parties to the Revised Charter where the level of protection afforded by the rights of that instrument is higher and less likely to be met by the national laws of its parties. In practice, twelve of the fourteen states that are so far bound by the collective complaints system are parties to the Revised Charter, and these twelve states represent just over a half of the twenty-two parties to the Revised Charter.

As well as increasing participation in the collective complaints system generally, it would also be desirable to increase the number of acceptances of the optional fourth category of complainant, national NGOs, from its current pitiful total of one (Finland). Allowing such organizations to make complaints would generate more complaints about social rights and increase the level of domestic awareness of the Charter, and also move the Charter away from its historic bias towards employment rights. It is not clear why more parties to the system have not made the necessary declaration under article 2 of the Protocol to accept national NGOs as complainants. It may be that some states have been put off by the rather openended nature of this category of complainant.

Finally, it needs to be borne in mind that a substantial number of new accessions to the Protocol or widespread acceptance of national NGOs as complainants may not be entirely desirable or deliver some of the expected benefits without some further reform of the overall supervisory system. The increased workload of the ECSR in carrying out its functions should not be underestimated, nor should the repercussions that this could potentially have on both the quality of its work and the length of time taken to reach its conclusions.

F. The relationship between the collective complaints system and other economic and social treaty provisions

One of the consequences of the existence of the collective complaints system is that it will bring into sharper focus the issue of the difference in standards and the obligations imposed upon states by different treaties in relation to certain economic and social rights and the mechanisms available for their enforcement. The former issue has already been illustrated in a number of the complaints. While the ECSR has frequently quoted the findings of other human rights bodies to support the position that it has taken,[211] there have also been occasions when the standards that it has adopted have been different from those of other human rights bodies.[212]

As regards the availability of different mechanisms, a decision by potential complainants whether to use the collective complaints system or whether to try an alternative mechanism will always be strategic in attempting to achieve a certain objective, but will also depend on their standing to bring a complaint. As an *actio popularis*, the collective complaints system cannot and is not designed to provide individual remedies and thus is of limited utility to provide redress for individual grievances, even if an organization with standing can be convinced to lodge a complaint. Any action taken by the defendant state seeking to rectify the situation will almost certainly not be retrospective in effect and will seek only to ensure that the Charter is not breached in future, no matter the degree of detriment already suffered by individuals. The same is also true of ILO procedures. By contrast, there is the possibility of an individual remedy under, for example, the European Convention on Human Rights and EU law. The choice of remedy may depend on a comparison of Charter rights with any comparable rights under the Convention and EU law. The content of a right under one instrument may be superior to that under another. Thus complainants may have to choose between a higher standard of rights under the Charter but with limited potential for their enforcement (especially in individual cases), and a lower standard under the Convention or EU law but with the availability of individual remedies and a greater prospect of compliance by the member states.

VI. Conclusions

Although the collective complaints system has been in force for over eight years, there is still relatively little experience with its practical operation. Nevertheless,

---

[211] See eg, Complaint no 13/2002, Decision on the Merits, para 52 (European Court of Human Rights); Complaint no 15/2003, Decision on the Merits, para 40 (UN Committee on Economic, Social and Cultural Rights); and Complaint no 17/2003, Decision on the Merits, paras 24 and 31 (UN Committee on the Rights of the Child and the European Court of Human Rights).

[212] See eg, Complaint no 16/2003, Decision on the Merits, para 30 (EC law) and Complaint no 20/2003, Decision on the Merits, para 24 (UN Committee on the Rights of the Child).

there is enough to reveal a number of serious concerns. First, as an alternative to the reporting system as a method of trying to secure the compliance of states parties with the Charter, the collective complaints system is still very much a minority option. Only about one third of the states parties to the Charter have accepted the system. The reasons behind the lack of acceptances are not entirely clear. Nevertheless, it is desirable, in principle, that the collective complaints system should become generally accepted and used as a compliance mechanism: this will strengthen its legitimacy and probably result in more complaints, thereby helping to increase knowledge of the Charter. The Council of Europe and NGOs (both national and international) ought therefore to lobby governments that have not yet done so, to accept the collective complaints system. Likewise the fact that only Finland, so far, has exercised the option of permitting national NGOs other than trade union and employers' associations (the fourth category of complainant) to make complaints is another worrying factor. Again, governments need to be encouraged and pressured into accepting this category of complainant.

Once a complaint has been made, the role of the ECSR in dealing with the admissibility of the complaint and giving an opinion on the merits has worked well. The ECSR has acted speedily, has not been unnecessarily restrictive on issues of admissibility, and has generally given well-reasoned opinions on the merits. Unfortunately, however, it is not possible to be anything like as positive about the role of the Committee of Ministers. While it has generally acted speedily, its handling of those complaints where the ECSR has found non-compliance with the Charter by the defendant state has been unsatisfactory. Only in one of the complaints has it addressed a recommendation to the defendant state. In many of the other cases it has either effectively decided not to pursue the matter further or improperly adopted an interpretation of the Charter quite different from that of the ECSR. If this trend continues, it will serve only to discredit the system and discourage complaints because complainants will feel that there is little point in utilising the system if a finding of non-compliance by the ECSR will not be endorsed by the Committee of Ministers. More fundamentally, it is undesirable that the Committee of Ministers, a political body, should have any role to play in what is, or at least ought to be, a quasi-judicial process. Before 1998 the Committee of Ministers was an alternative to the European Court of Human Rights as a body for determining breaches of the European Convention on Human Rights, and both the principle of this and its exercise in practice were rightly criticised.[213] The states members of the Council of Europe decided in Protocol 11 to the ECHR to abolish this role. In view of the fact that the CCP was adopted one year after Protocol 11, it is unfortunate, to say the least, that those same states decided that it was nevertheless appropriate for the Committee of Ministers to have a determinative role in the collective complaints system.

---

[213] See the literature referred to in n 187 above.

A more fundamental issue than any of the above concerns is whether the CCP actually serves a useful purpose. While the complaints system has a number of advantages over the reporting procedure, the real test is whether complaints will actually induce any changes in behaviour on the part of defendant states. It is too early to say yet whether states will amend their behaviour if they are found in violation of the Charter under the collective complaints system. The evidence from the reporting procedure is inconclusive; some states are taking some action in response to a finding of non-compliance under the CCP, others are not.[214] In this sense, the CCP is so far proving no different from the reporting procedure where similarly there is evidence of both compliance and non compliance by states parties with the findings of the ECSR. The action (or lack of it) taken by defendant states in response to successful complaints is a matter that will deserve close attention in the future.

If it turns out that states do not take action to remedy violations of the Charter, then various approaches could be adopted. First, the Collective Complaints Protocol could be amended so that decisions of the ECSR became legally binding, with the Committee of Ministers having the same role of supervising the execution of decisions as it has under the European Convention on Human Rights. If the collective complaints system is to achieve its objectives, it is imperative that the Council of Europe learns from the experiences of the ILO mechanisms upon which it is modelled. States, such as the UK in the *GCHQ* case for example, have for many years simply ignored findings of violations by the Freedom of Association Committee primarily because its decisions are not legally binding.[215] It is unlikely that the UK would have taken the same approach if the then functioning European Commission of Human Rights had found the application concerning the same issues admissible and the European Court had subsequently found it in violation.[216] But strengthening the collective complaints system in this way is an approach that some Council of Europe states are unlikely to agree to in the foreseeable future. Even less likely are they to support proposals made by some for a right to individual petition to a new European Social Rights Court or a specialized chamber of the European Court of Human Rights.[217]

Secondly, the ECSR should try to ensure compatibility between the standards it defines for the Charter, under both the collective complaints system and the

---

[214] See eg, text accompanying nn 133, 173, and 178.

[215] Although, as Novitz has noted, the current Labour government in the UK has now given effect to the ILO finding in the GCHQ case, whereas the previous Conservative government, whose policy it was to abolish unions at GCHQ, ignored it. See T Novitz, 'International Promises and Domestic Pragmatism: To What Extent Will the Employment Relations Act 1999 Implement International Labour Standards Relating to Freedom of Association?' (2000) 63 Modern L Rev 379.

[216] *Council of Civil Science Unions v United Kingdom*, Appl 11603/85, (1987) 50 DR 228. It is worth noting that the UK was not found in breach of the European Social Charter, CIE, *European Social Charter: Conclusions XI-1 (United Kingdom)* at p 80.

[217] See eg, Parliamentary Assembly Rec 1354 (1998); Harris and Darcy (n 4 above) at pp 373–374; Novitz (n 57 above).

reporting procedure, and other relevant treaties. Ensuring such compatibility is more likely to mean that the ECSR's findings will not be ignored because similar breaches under other treaties are more likely to be enforceable, especially in the case of EU law. In taking this approach, however, there is a risk that the ECSR may need to water down its approach to the obligations imposed by certain Charter provisions, thus to some extent defeating the object of the exercise.

The omens for the collective complaints system, in its current form, are not particularly encouraging. There is a palpable danger that without some reform the practical long-term impact of the system will not be significant in increasing the utility of the rights protected by the Charter.

10

Economic and Social Interests and the European Convention on Human Rights

Colin Warbrick

I. Introduction

The argument of this chapter is that the European Convention on Human Rights (ECHR)[1] does not protect economic and social rights, explicitly (with the exception of the right to education) or impliedly. This chapter does not dispute that there may be overlaps between certain civil and political rights and economic and social rights, for instance, the trade union aspects of the political right of association with the economic right to organize for the protection of workers' interests—but they are not the same thing, certainly they are not the same in the ECHR and the European Social Charter (ESC).[2] What the Convention sometimes protects are economic and social aspects of explicit Convention rights, for instance, protection against state-inflicted destitution as an aspect of article 3, but again, this is not the protection of an economic and social right to social security (ESC, article 11) or even to social and medical assistance (ESC, article 12).

Of more practical significance is the protection of collateral aspects of economic and social interests, where these involve civil and political rights, notably procedural provisions and protection against discrimination. The development of these notions has depended first on the identification of rights in national law (not necessarily human rights), such that the interest might be perceived as being a 'civil right' in the sense of article 6(1) of the Convention and second on the interpretation of the idea of 'possessions' in article 1 of Protocol no 1[3] to embrace economic and social benefits, which allows for the attachment of non-discrimination obligations to both the enjoyment of the right and to any interference a state may seek to make with it. Both these processes are testimony to the significance of the

---

[1] CETS no 5, adopted on 4 Nov 1950.
[2] CETS no 35, adopted on 18 Oct 1961.
[3] CETS no 9, Protocol to the Convention for the Protection of Human Rights and Fundamental Freedoms adopted on 20 March 1952.

European Court's invocation of the principles of effectiveness and dynamic interpretation as key elements in the life of the Convention—but they do not result in the transformation of economic and social rights into civil and political ones or vice versa.

II. The Council of Europe regime for the protection of human rights

For the purposes of this chapter, it is necessary to present only the briefest account of the European human rights systems, to the degree necessary to explain what follows. I take the view that legal human rights are creations of positive law. There are no interests which, *a priori*, ought to be converted into positive human rights and none which must be excluded. Accordingly, I do not say that economic and social rights are not/cannot be human rights nor do I say that these human rights cannot be made the subject of individual judicial procedures. I should reject the scepticism of writers such as Dennis and Stewart on the necessary non-justiciability of economic and social human rights.[4] From the point of view of international law, it is not necessary for me to concede that all human rights are individual human rights but equally I have no difficulty with the proposition that individuals may enjoy individual rights in international law, if the states make their intentions clear (and, more controversially, I should say, make appropriate institutional arrangements so that individuals can protect their international rights in an international forum). In the European (viz Council of Europe (CoE)) context, we have the European Convention on Human Rights and its Protocols, which list a catalogue of rights and establish a machinery for their protection, a process in which individuals may participate. The preamble to the ECHR says the states were taking 'the first steps for the collective enforcement of certain of the rights stated in the Universal Declaration [of Human Rights] (UDHR)...'.[5]

While not every civil and political right in the UDHR appears in the ECHR, the most signal omission is of any of the economic and social rights the inclusion of which in the UDHR had been a matter of such controversy.[6]

Just as the members of the United Nations (UN) ultimately embarked upon the drafting of two Covenants, the one on civil and political rights, the other on economic, social, and cultural rights, with different kinds of obligations for states under each and different means for their implementation, the CoE states eventually agreed on a discrete regime of economic and social rights, though again, one

---

[4] MJ Dennis and DP Stewart, 'Justiiciability of Economic, Social and Cultural Rights: Should there be an International Complaints Mechanism to Adjudicate the Right to Food, Water, Housing and Health?' (2004) 98 AJIL 462. It is worth emphasizing that they were writing about the International Covenant on Economic, Social and Cultural Rights.   [5] 6th preambular para.

[6] The right to education was included in protocol no 1, art 2.

founded in a treaty, the European Social Charter. The Charter has its own catalogue of rights, expressed in some cases in great detail, but it does not have a protection mechanism which can be activated by the individual. The conclusions of a
recent study on the Collective Complaints Mechanism of the ESC are scarcely
encouraging. Its authors write:

The omens for the CCP [Collective Complaints Protocol] in its current form are not
positive. There is a palpable danger that without some reform the practical long-term
impact of the CCP will not be significant in increasing the utility of the rights protected by
the Charter.[7]

I shall use the ESC as my reference point for European economic and social rights,
even though it does not fit my earlier prescription for the idea of individual
human rights, in deference to the claim of the states in the Preamble that the
Charter is for 'the maintenance and further realisation of human rights and fundamental freedoms . . .'.[8]

III. Positive obligations

I do not spell out sides in the 'justiciability' debate about the nature of economic
and social rights. I am prepared to accept that disputes about some or even all such
rights might be made subject to judicial determination at the suit of an aggrieved
individual, but note that in most cases this would involve subjecting to the determination of the courts' questions of the content of and compliance with positive
obligations.[9] I have a few words about positive obligations under the ECHR. The
first and obvious one is that there are justiciable obligations of this kind (or, rather
of these kinds) in the Convention—indeed, it has become the standard method of
analysis of the Convention to disentangle the various obligations of states
imposed by the substantive provisions of the Convention, instead of trying to
determine the rights of individuals which they comprehend and, Mowbray shows,
these developments have emerged from individual cases. One result of this has
been the identification of positive obligations, not only by inference but also by
interpretation. Positive obligations are far more pervasive in the Convention than
is often understood. They are by no means resource-free symbols, allowing ready
satisfaction by the states, neither are they necessarily found only by implication.
The most important—and the ones that give the lie to the argument that there is

---

[7] On the new system of implementation of the ESC, see Robin Churchill and Urfan Khaliq, 'The
Collective Complaints System of the European Social Charter: An Effective Mechanism for Ensuring
Compliance with Economic and Social Rights?' (2004) 15 Eur J of Intl L 417 at 456.

[8] 2nd preambular para Pt1 of the ESC sets out a series of rights, but they are the rights of discrete
groups of people—workers, children, migrant workers—not the rights of 'everyone' as in the ECHR.

[9] For an extended description of positive obligations, see A Mowbray, *The Development of Positive
Obligations under the European Convention on Human Rights by the European Court of Human Rights*
(Hart, 2004).

no overlapping (it appears to be different as to content) between civil rights and economic rights—are the rights to remedies, expressly in articles 5, 6, and 13; impliedly in articles 2 and 3 and on practically every occasion when a state claims the right to interfere with a protected right.[10] The procedural rights attached to detention and the whole schemes for civil and criminal fair trials cannot be dismissed as obligations with only trivial resource implications for states but we should note that they are set out in more detail than most of the other provisions of the Convention and, what is more, have generated far and away the biggest segments of the case law of the Convention. They are programmatic rights, not in the sense that they are rights incapable of immediate realization[11] but because they cannot be reduced to simple standards, capable of elaboration by judicial decisions alone.[12]

Positive obligations are not confined to procedural obligations. Another category is preventative positive obligations under which a state is required to take steps to reduce or eliminate actual violations of the Convention by its officials. So, duties to train law enforcement staff about the safe use of lethal weapons and to plan carefully the deployment of armed force,[13] obligations of medical assessment of those in the state's custody,[14] and to police effectively environmental hazardous activities of the state can be found expressly or impliedly in the ECHR.[15] Further, protective positive obligations to secure against private action which infringes the enjoyment of Convention rights, such as the duties considered in the cases of *Osman*[16] and *Z*,[17] are examples where the state is required to act in advance of the infliction of material harm to an individual. Finally, there is a category of duties which is more difficult to locate as either negative or positive—that is the duty not to take action which runs the risk of another person, usually but not invariably an official of another state, treating a person in a way which would be incompatible with his Convention rights if coming from a state party to the Convention—the *Soering*[18] principle. However it is categorized, the *Soering* duty is important when the Court is faced with future harm and there is no reason why its test should be restricted to anticipated harm beyond the jurisdiction of the defendant state.[19] All

---

[10] For an early example, *Leander v Sweden* (1987) ECtHR A/116, 9 EHRR 433; for a more recent one see *TP and KM v UK* (2001) ECtHR no 28945/95, 34 EHRR 34/42.

[11] Quite the opposite—see *Guincho v Portugal* (1984) ECtHR A/81, 7 EHRR 223.

[12] See *Bornewood* [1999] AC 458 (House of Lords) and *HL v UK* (2004) ECtHR No 45508/99, 40 EHRR 761—*Bornewood* is *HL* in Strasbourg.

[13] *McCann* (1995) ECtHR A/324, 21 EHRR 97.

[14] *McGlinchey v UK* (2003) ECtHR Appl no 50390/99, 37 EHRR 821. The state must have procedures to determine who needs supervision and provide treatment if the supervision system shows it to be necessary.

[15] *Oneryildiz v Turkey* (2004) ECtHR no 48939/99, 39 EHRR 253; *Fadeyeva v Russia* (2005) ECtHR no 55723/0, (2005) ECtHR 376. See (Council of Europe) Steering Committee for Human Rights (CDDH), *Final Activity Report—Human Rights and the Environment*, CM(2005) 186, add 2.

[16] *Osman v UK* (1998) ECtHR no 23452/94, 29 EHRR 245.

[17] *Z et al v UK* (2001) ECtHR no 29392/95.   [18] (1989) ECtHR A/161, 11 EHRR 439.

[19] Consider the risk assessment required of a state with respect to potential environmental damage after the judgments referred to in n 15 above.

these varieties of duty may be relevant in assessing whether or not a Convention state has a duty to take or abstain from action in order to respect the economic and social interests of persons within its jurisdiction.

IV. First steps—the *Airey* case[20]

It did not need the Vienna Declaration[21] to establish that there is an inter-relationship between civil and political and economic and social rights. Indeed, the economic and social interests of individuals are often of the greatest importance to them. In the CoE system, describing these interests as 'rights' does not add much for an individual, however important the designation might be for other purposes, because the system of supervision of the obligations under the ESC does not find a place for the individual who feels that he/she is not enjoying one of his/her rights. It is understandable that such a person should turn to the ECHR with its individual-friendly system to see if protection may be found there, protection which would be capable of identifying a violation of a state's specific obligation to a particular individual. In *Airey*, the Court was asked to adjudicate upon what the state identified as a claim to civil legal aid, a right which does not appear in the ECHR and an obligation with respect to which Ireland had, in any case, made a reservation. The applicant characterized it as a right of access to a court under article 6(1), on which point she ultimately prevailed.[22]

Ireland argued that:

the Convention should not be interpreted so as to achieve social and economic developments in a contracting state: such developments [could] only be 'progressive'.[23]

This is the language of the incremental implementation of economic and social rights with which we are all familiar. The Court responded that it was

... aware that the further realisation of social and economic rights is largely dependent on the situation—notably financial—reigning in the State in question. On the other hand, the Convention must be interpreted in the light of present-day conditions ... and it is designed to safeguard the individual in a real and practical way as regards those areas with which it deals. ... While the Convention sets forth what are essentially civil and political rights, many of them have implications of a social or economic nature. The Court considers ... that the mere fact that an interpretation of the Convention may extend into the sphere of social or economic rights should not be a decisive factor against such an interpretation: there is no water-tight division separating out that sphere from the field covered by the Convention.[24]

The Court seemed to overstate its dilemma. There was no identification of which economic or social right was in issue here. Mrs A pleaded poverty but, even if there

---

[20] (1979) ECtHR A/32, 2 EHRR 305.
[21] Vienna Declaration, World Conference on Human Rights Vienna, 14–25 June 1993), UN doc A/CONF.157/24 (Pt I) at 20 (1993).   [22] Airey (1979), para 28 (n 20 above).
[23] Ibid para 26.   [24] Ibid.

were an economic right not to be poor, it is not clear that it would extend to being able to run expensive litigation—and neither the Court's judgment finding a violation nor the state's response suggested that it did. The judgment found a violation of Mrs A's right of effective access to a tribunal. The government's response was not to give her and persons like her the resources to enable them to take advantage of Ireland's existing, expensive procedure but to create a simpler, cheaper, less intimidating process which would allow people in same economic position of Mrs A access to a process which would satisfy their article 6(1) rights, either at a price they could afford or before which they could represent themselves. It cannot be said that the ultimate resolution of the case in any way satisfied an economic or social right of Mrs A; indeed, hardly even an economic or social *interest*.

I include here one other early judgment, the *Marckx* case.[25] The case concerned various elements of discrimination in Belgian law against illegitimate children and their families. Two Convention rights were in point—the right to respect for family life and the right to enjoyment of possessions. Belgium argued that some discrimination at least could be justified as being in the interest of encouraging legitimate families. Though taking a hard line against discrimination within the reach of Convention rights based on the badge of illegitimacy, the Court seemed as if it would have allowed, for example, enhanced social security support for the legitimate family, the discrimination there not touching a Convention right.[26] If this be right, it showed then an unwillingness to discern economic and social rights as being even within the ambit of the existing Convention framework. One can add the case of *Andersson and Kulman*,[27] where the Court refused to find a positive obligation in the right to respect for family life which would have required social security support for the parents of children who preferred not to work in order to develop a strong family life.

V. Trade unions

Union rights are often given as an example of rights which are both civil and political and economic and social. There are overlaps between the kinds of rights, but they are not identical. The protection of the individual right to form and be a member of a trade union, protected by article 11 of the ECHR can be contrasted with the protection of the rights of trade unions under articles 5 and 6 of the ESC.[28] In the first instance, what is at stake is the right to freedom of association and, even where the Court has gone beyond the mere formal aspects of association,[29] it is to ensure

---

[25] (1979) ECtHR A/31, 2 EHRR 330.
[26] Para 40. This suggestion, even if good at the time, could not survive *Stec*, see n 43 (below).
[27] (1986) ECommHRs 46 DR 251.
[28] D Harris and J Darcy, *The European Social Charter* (2nd edn, Transnational Publishers, 2001), pp 88–112.   [29] *Wilson* 30668/96 (2002), 35 EHRR 523.

the effective exercise of the right to associate, not the right of the trade union to function effectively. Article 11 of the ECHR is more like article 5 of the ESC (The Right to Organize). The European Court of Human Rights has held that there is no right to collective bargaining or to strike contained in article 11 of the ECHR (compare article 6 of the ESC (The Right to Bargain Collectively)).[30] These conclusions can be contrasted with the terms of the ESC and decisions of the ILO, directed to the rights of trade unions as economic and social rights, which protected a range of activities of the collectivity.[31] It should be noted that the difference is not because of the status of trade unions under the Convention. They are capable of enjoying rights independently of the rights of their members or officials. It is because of the different content of the rights guaranteed by article 11 of the ECHR and articles 5 and 6 of the ESC.

VI. Collateral protection of economic and social interests

The most important contribution of the Convention to the protection of economic and social interests (whether or not economic and social rights) has come through two separate developments, now apparently combined into a single idea. The chronological story shows the way in which the ECHR can be developed by the Court, apparently limited steps at the beginning resulting in conclusions which would have been unlikely, even unthinkable, when the interpretative process started.

A. Procedure—fair trial of civil rights

We start with the idea of 'civil right' in article 6(1) of the Convention:

In the determination of his civil rights and obligations...everyone is entitled to a fair trial...

The Court had initially decided that the idea of 'civil right' was an 'autonomous concept', that is, the characterization of an individual interest in national law, say as a public law privilege or conditional entitlement, was not decisive for Convention purposes.[32] The Court's task was to see if the legal provision in national law 'really' did create a 'civil right' in the Convention sense, that is to say, a situation in which, if the applicant established his/her case in law and on the facts, he/she would be

---

[30] *National Union of Belgian Police v Belgium* (1975) ECtHR A/191 EHRR 578; *Swedish Engine Drivers' Union v Sweden* (1976) ECtHR A/20, 1 EHRR 578.

[31] See eg ILO Declaration of Fundamental Rights (1998); Complaint against Government of United Kingdom presented by Trades Union Congress, Report no 294, Case no 1730 (1994), Committee on Freedom of Association; B Gernigon, A Odero, and H Guido, 'ILO Principles Concerning Collective Bargaining' (2000) 33 Int Labour Rev, 139.

[32] *Konig v Germany* (1978) ECtHR A/27, 2 EHRR 170.

legally entitled to some benefit or, as the case may be, not to be deprived of some advantage. The Court had already rejected the claim that all Convention rights were 'civil rights',[33] so it would have availed an applicant nothing to argue that his economic or social interest was, in fact, an economic or social human right. The matter was first considered by the Court in a pair of cases involving health insurance, *Feldbrugge*[34] and *Deumeland*.[35] Participation in the schemes under which the applicants claimed benefits was compulsory in the national laws but the benefits to them were provided under private insurance policies. The Court held that the balance of factors in each of the arrangements favoured their characterisation as 'private' rather than 'public', and so as 'civil rights', for the purposes of article 6(1) of the Convention. A significant factor in the Court's analysis was the economic nature of the benefit to the claimant, a quality no different in reality to the economic benefit gained under a contract of employment—and, though it did not seem important at the time, a claim not unlike a property right to the applicant. The consequence here for the applicants was not that they obtained under the Convention a right to any money but a right to a procedure— the fair trial before an independent and impartial tribunal required by article 6(1)—to decide whether or not, under the national arrangements, they were entitled to compensation. So, national law must create a right for people like the applicants such that if a claimant shows that he/she falls within its terms, the result would be the conferring of a benefit, in most cases, payment of a sum of money under a social insurance scheme. Thus, the Court removed from the sphere of national public law procedures at least some schemes which would fall within the ambit of economic or social human rights but it did not do this by focusing upon their quality as human rights but as 'civil rights' within the ECHR understanding of such things.

The Court continued this development, allowing the application of article 6(1) to a variety of contributory schemes in a number of national systems. The limit, of course, was that article 6(1) did not oblige a state to create any particular welfare scheme, nor to provide for any particular level of benefit in any scheme it did create. The procedural advantage could help persons already privileged under national law to secure their entitlements but it did not broaden the class of those so entitled.

B. Substance—possessions (property)

The next phase of the development of the case law began with the *Gaygusuz*[36] case. A Turkish national, relying in part on the principle established by *Feldbrugge/ Deumeland*, sought protection in Strasbourg from what he said was the

---

[33] *Golder v UK* (1975) ECtHR A/18, 1 EHRR 524.
[34] *Feldbrugge v Netherlands* (1986) ECtHR A/9, 8 EHRR 425.
[35] *Deumeland v Germany* (1986) ECtHR A/100, 8 EHRR 448.
[36] *Gaygusuz v Austria* (1996) ECtHR no 17371/90, 23 EHRR 365.

discriminatory operation of a welfare scheme in Austrian law. The scheme provided for emergency assistance to the unemployed after the termination of ordinary unemployment benefit. However, the emergency scheme benefited only Austrian nationals, so that the applicant, although in all other respects qualified, was not entitled under national law to assistance by reason of his Turkish nationality. Here, G was seeking more than a procedure. His problem under the Convention was, of course, that it protects against discrimination only with respect to the enjoyment of Convention rights but, wanting a benefit and not a procedure, G could not, on the basis of the previous case law, point to a Convention right which he had been denied. Instead, and relying on the explanation given by the Court for characterizing welfare payments as 'civil rights', viz their economic importance to claimants, G argued that the welfare entitlement was a 'possession', a property right, protected under article 1 of Protocol no 1. The Court agreed. It then found that the discrimination against non-nationals could not be justified on any grounds which satisfied article 14 of the Convention. The result was, assuming that G could show that he was entitled under Austrian law, that he became entitled to the benefit. It was apparently of importance to the Court that the Austrian scheme was a contributory one, regardless of nationality. Although the outcome does show the possibility of protecting the enjoyment of some economic and social interests under the Convention, the contingency of the judgment needs to be appreciated. Austria could simply have abolished the emergency scheme for everyone without violating any Convention obligation, so that there would have been no putative possession for the article 14 claim on which to latch. Much of this discussion about non-discrimination (though not about article 6(1) procedures) will become redundant when the Protocol no 12 comes into force.

C. Procedure and substance

These two strands—procedural protection and protection against discrimination, relying on the classification of benefits as possessions—have been brought increasingly together. The protection of interests as property has been expanded—pensions in *Wessels-Bergovert*,[37] for instance. Pensions have always caused difficulties for the Court because of the contingent nature of the benefit and, therefore, in identifying what is the 'possession' to which an applicant has a claim. Each extension of interests as possessions then carries with it the obligation to provide an article 6(1) procedure to resolve disputes about claims to benefits, without the need to go through the *Feldbrugge/Deumeland* analysis of each national arrangement to see if what is at stake is a 'civil right'—all property rights are 'civil rights'. In *Koua Poirrez*,[38] the Court has held that benefits arising from non-contributory schemes

---

[37] *Wessells-Bergevoet v Netherlands* (2002) ECtHR no 34462/97, 38 EHRR 793.
[38] *Koua Poirrez v France* (2003) ECtHR no 40892/98, 40 EHRR 34.

may be possessions for the purpose of article 1 of Protocol no 1. This confirms a development which started with *Salesi*[39] and *Schuler-Zgraggen*[40] in 1993. The shift then has been from procedure to substance and recently the Court has set out in broad terms which benefit claims constitute possessions. In *Carson*,[41] Lord Hoffmann described the Convention cases 'artificial'. He said:

[The European Court of Human Rights] has clearly felt frustrated by the need to find a Convention pigeon-hole into which to fit every objectionable form of discrimination. Social security benefits are a good example. In principle it does not seem at all unreasonable that in distributing public money in the form of social security benefits, the state should be obliged to treat all like cases alike. . . . But the virtual absence of economic rights in the Convention has made it difficult to relate this principle to the enjoyment of any specified right.[42]

In the admissibility decision in *Stec*,[43] the Court said:

It is in the interests of the coherence of the Convention as a whole that the autonomous concept of 'possessions' in Article 1 of Protocol No.1 should be interpreted in a way which is consistent with the concept of pecuniary rights under Article 6(1). It is moreover important to adopt an interpretation of Article 1 of Protocol No.1 which avoids inequalities of treatment based on distinctions which, at the present day, appear illogical or unsustainable.[44]

This is a remarkable extension of the idea of non-discrimination as an aid to interpretation of the Convention, as distinct from its meaning as a Convention right under article 14. We know that article 14 applies only to Convention rights, it does not generate rights on its own, not even a general right not to be discriminated against. Yet here, the Court relies on the idea of non-discrimination to create (or at least, to fill out) rights. Because some 'benefits' fall within article 6(1), claimants to them enjoy certain procedural benefits. Non-discrimination, the Court seems to be saying, requires that anyone with a claim to a similar (ie welfare) benefit, even if not based on a contributory scheme which gave rise to the *Feldbrugge/Deumeland* judgments, requires the same procedural protections and, what is more, that the claim will be a 'possession' understood in the same way as a claim under a contributory scheme.[45]

The reasoning to support this conclusion might go rather further than the Court intends. It says, with some justification, that the way a particular welfare scheme is funded is to some degree a matter of chance. It notes that the two provisions considered in *Stec* had once been funded on a contributory basis and now were funded out of general taxation but it then says,

. . . to exclude benefits paid for out of general taxation would be to disregard the fact that many of the claimants under this latter type of system also contribute to its financing, through payment of tax.[46]

---

[39] *Salesi v Italy* A/257 E (1993) ECtHR no 13023/87, 26 EHRR 187.
[40] *Schuler-Zgragenn v Netherlands* A 263 (1993) ECtHR no 14518/89, 16 EHRR 405.
[41] *R v Secretary of State for Work and Pensions, Ex p Carson* (2005) UKHL 37.   [42] Ibid para 11.
[43] *Stec v UK* (2005) ECtHR no 65731/01 (decision).   [44] Ibid para 49.
[45] In his separate opinion in *Stec*, Judge Borrego Borrego accused the Court of seeking to apply Protocol no 12 prematurely against a state which had not even signed it.   [46] Ibid para 50.

The notion that the payment of taxation gives sufficient interest in any project financed by the proceeds of tax creates a 'possession' for each and every taxpayer in the benefits of every public enterprise surely goes too far. Each public benefit, now a property right, would be accompanied by the obligation not to discriminate. To take an extreme example—does the funding of the police out of taxation give every taxpayer a right to police services, a right admittedly which can be qualified under article 1 of Protocol no 1, but which must not, for instance, be qualified in a discriminatory manner? It is not just that the public authorities might find their policy decisions subject to over-turning as that they might also face multiple claims to give accounts for their decisions which would raise difficulties for them. We may then yet be thrown back on something like the economic and social interest/right as an additional element to determine when a public benefit becomes a possession.

It seems likely that it will be better to think in terms of economic and social interests than fully-fledged human rights, because the Court said:

[Article 1 of Protocol No. 1] does not create right to acquire property. It places no restriction on a Contracting State's freedom to decide whether or not to have in place any form of social security scheme, or to choose the type or amount of benefits to provide under any such scheme . . . [47]

Stec was decided by the Grand Chamber.[48] The judgment followed the admissibility decision and was to decide whether differential treatment between men and women on the ages at which certain work-related benefits were terminated (by now decided to be 'possessions', even though the benefits were paid out of general taxation) was in breach of article 14. The Grand Chamber found that there was no violation. This part of the judgment is not germane to our present concerns, except perhaps to notice that the Grand Chamber affirmed that 'a wide margin [of appreciation] is usually allowed to the State under the Convention when it comes to general measures of economic or social strategy'[49] and that the Grand Chamber restated the freedom of a state to decide whether or not to have any particular scheme of social benefit,[50] quoted above from the admissibility decision.[51]

D. Other substance—medical treatment

It might be possible to limit the effect of *Stec* by reference to a different criterion— the entitlement to money (or perhaps goods and services or vouchers for them, like food or accommodation). Then, of course the question becomes how the Court will treat claims to other kinds of social benefit, such as medical treatment. The Court has not pronounced in favour of a general right to medical treatment. Certain specific facilities might be necessary as part of discrete Convention rights—abortion, gender-reassignment, treatment to preserve life, or avoid inhuman or degrading

---

[47] Ibid para 54; and see *Kopecky v Slovakia* [GC] (2003) ECtHR no 44912/98 (2004), ECHR 446.
[48] *Stec v UK* (2006) ECtHR no 65731/01 [GC].   [49] Ibid para 52.   [50] Ibid para 53.
[51] Note 43 above.

treatment—but all would be subject to broad powers of appreciation and interference. There would be protection against discriminatory allocation of access to treatment but not much scope for review against Convention standards of good faith or setting of priorities. In *Powell*, the Court said,

It cannot be excluded that the acts and omissions of the authorities in the field of health care policy may in certain circumstances engage the responsibility under the positive limb of Article 2. However, where a contracting State has made adequate provision for securing high professional standards among health professionals and the protection of the lives of the patients, it cannot accept that matters such as errors of judgment on the part of a health professional or negligent co-ordination among health professionals, in the treatment of a particular patient are sufficient of themselves to call a contracting State to account from the standpoint of its positive obligations under Article 2 of the Convention to preserve life.[52]

Any claim to a particular treatment would seem to be an *a fortiori* case. Although in a rather special context, *D*[53] suggests that circumstances in which an individual can claim the continuation of a course of treatment will be restricted to circumstances in which withdrawal would lead to treatment contrary to article 3, a high threshold. One can see a parallelism between any rights to medical treatment under the Convention and economic and social human rights but the similarities are not because they are the same in substance but because they are the same in nature—they are positive obligations, with respect to which the remedial obligations are significant. If they are in place, supplemented by article 13 if necessary, only the most egregious failures by a state might involve its responsibility.

VII. A right to subsistence?

It is thirty years ago since Francis Jacobs[54] suggested that the Convention states should add a right of subsistence to the list of rights protected by the Convention and about fifteen years since Antonio Cassese[55] suggested that, properly interpreted, the Convention already included this right. There has not been much by way of reaction to either intimation at the Convention level. There has, however been a recent decision—*Limbuela*[56]—of the House of Lords under the Human Rights Act in which this question—or something like it—has been subjected to intense scrutiny. In keeping with the thesis which I have set out, it is perhaps better to say that the House of Lords was concerned with a right not to be made

---

[52] *Powell v UK* (2000) ECtHR no 45305/99 (decision).

[53] *D v UK* (1997) ECtHR no 30240/96, D 24 EHRR 425.

[54] F Jacobs, 'To What Extent have New Restrictions on the Enjoyment of Freedoms Evolved?' (1976) *Eur Forum*.

[55] A Cassese, 'Can the Notion of Inhuman and Degrading Treatment be Applied to Socio-Economic Conditions?' (1991) 2 Eur J of Intl L 141, referring to *van Volsem* (1990) EComHR no 14641/89 (decision).

[56] *R v Home Secretary, Ex p Adam, Limbuela, Tesema* [2005] UKHL 66; also [2004] EWCA Civ 540.

destitute—those who would contest whether even a right of subsistence caught the idea of the economic right to an adequate standard of living or social assistance would be even more dismayed by the suggestion that the 'right' envisaged in this case at all represents an economic human right.

L's was one of more than 600 emergency applications made to the Administrative Court in which applicants complained that their conditions of life amounted to inhuman and degrading treatment within the meaning of article 3 of the Convention. It was one of three chosen as test cases which went to the Court of Appeal, which found for the applicants and to the House of Lords which refused the government's appeal. *L* was an asylum-seeker and the victim of a policy of humane deterrence. Parliament had provided that asylum-seekers who did not present themselves to the immigration authorities as soon as reasonably practicable after their arrival in the UK were not to receive social benefits; the Minister was under an express duty not to provide them with benefits in cash or in kind.[57] Such people were already forbidden to work. There was a saving exception to the Minister's duty of abstention. He could take action to the extent necessary to avoid the risk of a breach of a person's Convention rights under the Human Rights Act.[58] The number of people caught by the general duty was high because 'reasonably practicable' was construed strictly and those falling within it had to rely on private or charitable support—and there was not much of it, particularly the latter. As Lord Brown recognized, the policy of the Act 'intended'[59] that individuals would suffer severe privation. Only where individuals were driven to prostitution or begging would the government have been satisfied that their Convention rights were infringed;[60] mere 'rough sleeping' would not be enough.[61] The attitude of some of the judges was not quite as dismissive of these claims as one might have expected. There were remarks bordering on the facetious by Lord Scott and Baroness Hale about the delights of sleeping under the stars (though, in the end, as we shall see, even these enthusiasts for the outdoor life recanted). The condition of most persons affected would deteriorate over time, so it was a necessary ingredient of the policy that some at least of them should approach total destitution without being entitled to any relief. Facing starvation and homelessness, the only alternative would be to go home and, since it was accepted that some of these people would be refugees, this would have meant them returning to a state where the applicants had a well-founded fear of persecution. There was, it turned out, another route—emergency application to the Administrative Court. By the time that the cases reached the House of Lords, the cases of *L* and the two other applicants has been resolved but it was thought right to offer 'guidance' to the Minister for outstanding cases and for the future.

The starting point was Lord Scott's undoubtedly correct remark that it was 'not the function of article 3 [of the Convention] to prescribe a minimum standard of

---

[57] Section 55(1) Nationality, Immigration and Asylum Act 2002.   [58] Ibid s. 55(5)(a).
[59] *Limbuela* (above) para 101.   [60] Ibid para 59.   [61] Ibid para 60.

social support'.[62] In the view of Lord Bingham, treatment was 'inhuman and degrading' within the terms of article 3 if it 'denies the most basic needs of any human being'[63]—this sounds as though there is some protection of economic and social interests. The judges were agreed that the applicants were being subjected to treatment by the state, not the victims of mere inaction, on the basis that entitlement to social support had been withdrawn by the state, while at the same time the state had forbidden them to work (and the authorities knew or ought to have known about the scant nature of the private assistance available). The state was by its actions responsible for their fate—and so the apparently rather harsh case of *O'Rourke*[64] could be distinguished. O'Rourke had been made homeless by his own conduct and decisions and could not, in the face of his own obduracy, claim that his conditions of life involved the state's responsibility under article 3. The case has sometimes been said to be authority for the proposition that there is no right to subsistence in the Convention, but that clearly goes too far. What is more, Lord Bingham said that this state of affairs, if it resulted in conditions incompatible with article 3, violated an express duty in article 3, a duty which, like any other express duties was 'absolute', admitting no arguments about the proportionality of the state's interference with the enjoyment of the right to promote some public interest.[65]

Where was the line to be drawn between destitution sufficient to persuade the government to invoke the s 55(5)(a) exception and the enjoyment of full social support? Lord Bingham put it this way:

As in all Article 3 cases, the treatment to be proscribed must achieve a minimum standard of severity, and I would accept that in a context such as this, not involving the deliberate infliction of pain or suffering [a generous concession, if I may say so], the threshold is a high one. A general duty to house the homeless or provide for the destitute cannot be spelled out of Article 3. But I have no doubt that the threshold may be crossed if a late applicant with no means and no alternative means to support himself is, by the deliberate action of the state, denied shelter, food or the most basic necessities of life.[66]

Lord Bingham recognized that the court could provide only the most general guidance as to when article 3 would be violated—most turned on the facts of the individual's circumstances. Other members of the court did offer more specific instruction. Lord Hope, while conceding that the mere withdrawal of support would not, of itself amount to a violation (of course, for the applicant might receive community support or be one of the few who finds charitable assistance), and was even unwilling to say that being driven to sleeping rough in an urban

---

[62] Ibid para 66.   [63] Ibid para 7.   [64] 39022/97 (2001) (decision).
[65] The House of Lords discarded Laws LJ's introduction of the idea of a spectrum of seriousness of ill-treatment corresponding to a gradually weakening duty on the state, as art 3 was unpicked to reveal its levels of obligation. Lord Hope expressed himself 'uneasy' with this innovation (para 53) and Baroness Hale and Lord Brown agreed with him (paras 77 and 89 respectively).
[66] *Limbuela* (above) para 7.

setting were not enough,[67] eventually conceded that the degradation and humiliation attached to living on the streets would take these conditions over the threshold. Lord Scott was of like view—rooflessness and cashlessness would be enough[68] and, most damning of all, Lord Brown, that intended street homelessness would be sufficient.[69] Since this is what was intended, that should have done for the scheme of s 55 completely. Baroness Hale drew attention to the particularly dire predicament which faced women consigned to these living conditions.[70]

It did not quite, but Lord Brown's focus on the intention—perhaps better, necessary consequence—of the policy raised another issue—at what stage was the responsibility of the state engaged? Lord Hope emphasized that the Minster's power in s 55(5)(a) was *to avoid* violations of a person's Convention rights. The Minister could not wait until an applicant was actually suffering treatment which was incompatible with article 3. It is true, as Lord Scott somewhat superfluously pointed out, that the Minister could not do anything until he knew of a person's plight,[71] though when the Minister did know, his duty required him to act then. But, if, as I indicated earlier, in most cases, the condition of individuals caught in the scheme would decline over time, the duty *to avoid* violating a person's rights demanded pre-emptive action. The Lords were agreed that 'imminence' was the test but, especially given Lord Simon Brown's position, for many applicants, imminence of conditions of destitution serious enough to engage responsibility under article 3 was not merely the foreseeable but the immediate consequence of being subjected to the 'no support' regime. If the House of Lords had used the 'real risk' test from *Soering et al*, which is the European Court's test for assessing when future harm is sufficient to make a person a victim *now*, then, again given Lord Simon Brown's analysis, many, maybe most, applicants could show that they were at risk of destitution. Although the judgments make only oblique reference to this, it needs emphasizing that the people who were caught up in the policy were refugee applicants, in some cases later shown to be genuine refugees. They were engaged in a process involving interviews with officials, visits to lawyers, appearances before tribunals about a matter of the greatest consequence for them. To be expected to give even a decent account of themselves while enduring the privation contemplated by the legislation is to set an impossible burden. The Convention right found in article 3 goes some way to righting this. The government response to the Court of Appeal judgment was set out in 'Policy Bulletin No 75' of National Asylum Support Service. It might be said that the instruction accommodates to the Court of Appeal's judgment rather than embraces it.[72]

But did the House of Lords find an 'economic or social human right' in article 3? If it did, it discovered a very restricted one, a right to be saved from imminent destitution caused by the action of the state. This is hardly an economic right of any

---

[67] Ibid para 60.   [68] Ibid para 78.   [69] Ibid para 101.   [70] Ibid para 78.
[71] Ibid para 72.
[72] NASS-Policy Bulletin 75: section 55 (Late Claims) 2002 Act Guidance, 25 June 2004.

consequence for most people in most circumstances. Lord Scott, as mentioned, explicitly denied that article 3 was a source of a right to social support. Lord Bingham's judgment, with its emphasis on action by the state as a necessary ingredient of 'treatment' for the purposes of article 3, appears to leave inaction out of account, inaction, perhaps, even in the face of natural disaster or emergency economic adversity.

VIII. Conclusion

The civil and political right not to have destitution thrust upon one by the state looks a long way from an economic and social right to social support, a right which, it has been argued, is a necessary condition for the enjoyment of those civil and political rights affecting the democratic process. Sure, what was at stake in *Limbuela* were economic and social interests, they might even be seen as at the core of an economic or social right to social assistance but they were not the right itself and it would be a misapprehension to understand it so. The state does have obligations to provide for the economic and social needs of those compulsorily in its control in prisons and mental hospitals and, though the standards insisted on by the Court are not high, they are superior to the near-destitution tolerated even after *Limbuela*. And this is the worst of all, of course, that conflating the civil right explicated in *Limbuela* with the economic and social right might lead to setting the bar so low that the economic or social right loses all its useful purchase. Reference to economic and social interests might expand the substance of civil and political rights under the Convention—there is less evidence that this process will work in reverse.

11

The United Kingdom and the International Covenant on Economic, Social and Cultural Rights

Ed Bates

I. Introduction: progress in the supervision of economic, social, and cultural rights at the international level?

Over the last ten to fifteen years the protection of economic, social, and cultural rights (ESC rights) has risen up the international human rights law agenda. Major international Non-governmental Organizations (NGOs) have shown a greater willingness to focus on issues relating to ESC rights.[1] The former UN Commission on Human Rights (now the Human Rights Council) has paid significantly more attention to this subject since the 1990s,[2] as the mandates of the Thematic Rapporteurs reveal and the subject matter of annual resolutions have indicated. One of the first acts of the new Human Rights Council was to mandate[3] the Open-Ended Working Group on an Optional Protocol to the

[1] See generally K Roth, 'Defending Economic, Social and Cultural Rights: Practical Issues Faced by an International Human Rights Organization' (2004) 26 Human Rights Q 63; L Rubenstein, 'How International Human Rights Organizations Can Advance Economic, Social and Cultural Rights' (2004) 26 Human Rights Q 845 and *The Economist* (editorial), 'Special Report: Human Rights; Righting Wrongs' 18 Aug 2001 at 9 and 19–21.

[2] See M Robinson, 'Advancing Economic Social and Cultural Rights: The Way Forward' (2004) 26 Human Rights Q 866 at 866–868. Compare this, however, with apparent 'Governmental ambivalence' toward ESC rights, see H Steiner and P Alston, *International Human Rights in Context* (OUP, 2000) ('Steiner and Alston') 249–250.

[3] Human Rights Council res 2006/3. The background documents for the Optional Protocol are available at <http://www.ohchr.org/english/issues/escr/group3.htm> accessed on 15 Nov 2006. See especially C de Albuquerque (Chairperson-Rapporteur of the OP Working Group), 'Elements for an Optional Protocol to the International Covenant on Economic, Social and Cultural Rights (Advanced Edited Version)', E/CN.4/2006/WG.23/2, 21 Nov 2005 ('Albuquerque Report') and C de Albuquerque, 'Report of the Open-Ended Working Group to consider options regarding the elaboration of an Optional Protocol to the International Covenant on Economic, Social and Cultural Rights on its third session', E/CN.4/2006/47, 14 March 2006.

International Covenant on Economic, Social and Cultural Rights[4] (hereafter the treaty will be referred to as the ICESCR) to prepare a first draft Optional Protocol (OP) as a basis for future negotiations. Some states, notably the United States of America,[5] oppose an OP and the United Kingdom has indicated that it has significant reservations about the idea.[6] The Working Group has yet to address the many significant issues of principle that need to be tackled regarding the specific form that any OP might take.[7]

An OP could mark the 'coming of age' of ESC rights as justiciable rights at the international level and for this reason it has been enthusiastically supported by a coalition of NGOs.[8] However, failure to agree an OP, or the creation of a very weak instrument may have a very negative effect on the way ESC rights are viewed, in particular whether in practice they are regarded as of equal importance to civil and political rights.[9] Against this background this chapter explores how the ICESCR has been of relevance for the British government in recent years and the British government's view on the nature and status of Covenant rights, in particular their susceptibility to incorporation into domestic law. To do this it looks at the 1996 United Kingdom (UK) Report to the Committee on Economic, Social and Cultural Rights (ESCR Committee) under the Conservative administration (section II, below) and the 2001 UK Report under the 'new' Labour administration (section III). As we shall see, both these reporting rounds revealed a significant disparity of views between the ESCR Committee and the British government as regards the susceptibility of Covenant rights to incorporation into UK law. Such views and the British government's commitment to the ICESCR generally came under the spotlight further when in 2003 the UK Parliament's Joint Committee on Human Rights (JCHR) launched an 'Inquiry into the Concluding Observations of the UN Committee on Economic Social and Cultural Rights'. Section IV of this chapter looks at the progress and outcomes of that inquiry insofar as it is relevant to the British perspective on the nature of Covenant rights. This involves a look at the Report produced by the JCHR[10] and the government's response to it. Section V

---

[4] International Covenant on Economic, Social and Cultural Rights, GA res 2200A (XXI), 21 UN GAOR supp (no 16) at 49, UN doc A/6316 (1966), 993 UNTS 3.

[5] See M Dennis and D Stewart, 'Justiciability of Economic, Social and Cultural Rights: Should there be an International Complaints Mechanism to Adjudicate the Rights to Food, Water, Housing and Health?' (2004) 98 AJIL 462. The USA has not ratified the ICESCR.

[6] The writer requested details of British policy on the proposed OP from the Foreign and Commonwealth Office (FCO). However, the request was denied on the basis of exemptions under Freedom of Information legislation (letter on file with author). It is evident nonetheless that the British position has been sceptical, see FCO, *Human Rights Annual Report 2005* (Cm 6606, July 2005) at 169 and JCHR, *Government Responses to Reports from the Committee in the Last Parliament*, 8th Report (2005–06) (HL 104; HC 850) ('Government Responses to JCHR Reports') at para 34.

[7] See *Albuquerque Report* at 4–12.

[8] <http://www.escr-net.org/resources/resources_show.htm?doc_id=431533> accessed on 14 Jan 2007. The site contains a wealth of material in favour of the creation of an OP.

[9] See B Porter, 'The Right to be Heard: The Optional Protocol to the International Covenant on Economic, Social and Cultural Rights. What's at Stake' (2005) 11 *Human Rights Tribune* 3.

[10] JCHR, *The International Covenant on Economic, Social and Cultural Rights*, 21st Report (2003–04) (HL 183; HC 1188) ('JCHR ICESCR Report').

provides a critique of the government's position as regards incorporation of ESC rights into UK law.

II. The UK and ICESCR: background to the justiciability debate

The UK signed the Covenant in 1968,[11] ratified it in 1976, and has never incorporated it into domestic law.[12] In the years that have followed there were few, if any, statements made by the British government regarding ESC rights and their relevance for domestic law. Through the 1970s and 1980s various general statements were made by the government at the international level arguing that in principle ESC rights and civil and political rights were interdependent and indivisible.[13] Apparently it was not until the mid-1990s that the UK government was pressed by the ESCR Committee, which supervises the implementation of the ICESCR, to fully explain its position as regards the potential incorporation of Covenant rights into domestic law. The occasion was the ESCR Committee's examination of the UK's Third Periodic Report (of 1996) under that treaty. In its report the British government stated that 'the greater part of [the covenant's] provisions do not purport to establish norms which lend themselves to translation into legislation or justiciable issues, but are statements of principle and objectives'. The UK, it was stated, had both before and since the coming into operation of the Covenant, 'taken measures, including legislation and the adoption of policies and programmes, which advance the same principles and objectives as are set out in the Covenant'.[14] And it was added '[w]here an instrument such as the Convention [*sic* Covenant] imposes a more precise obligation not hitherto reflected in the common law, existing legislation or administrative procedures, it is the practice of the UK to bring the law or procedure into line with the obligation'.[15] No specific examples were provided of how this 'practice' had worked to date.

When the UK delegation appeared before the ESCR Committee for discussion of the 1996 Report there was an extended dialogue, lasting virtually the whole of the first session, on the nature of the obligations derived from the Covenant.[16] Various members of the ESCR Committee strongly took issue with the British

---

[11] See E Schwelb, 'The UK signs the Covenants on Human Rights' (1969) 18 Intl Comparative L Q 457.

[12] The UK constitution reflects a broadly 'dualist' approach to international law, ie it adopts a distinction between international and domestic law, requiring an international treaty to be specifically incorporated into domestic law for it to take full legal effect, see DJ Harris, *Cases and Materials on International Law* (3rd edn, Sweet & Maxwell, 2002) at 66–69.

[13] See eg, the statement made by the UK representative (Mr Steel) in the UN Commission on Human Rights in 1988, recounted in (1988) 59 British Y of Intl L at 459–460. On interdependence and indivisibility see Office of the High Commissioner for Human Rights & International Bar Association, *Human Rights in the Administration of Justice: A Manual of Human Rights for Judges; Prosecutors and Lawyers*, (United Nations, 2003) at 692–696.

[14] E/1994/104/add 11, 17 June 1996 at para 9.   [15] Ibid.   [16] E/C.12/1997 SR.36.

representative's view that the ICESCR was merely a 'programmatic document', not really having any effect in law and being only really a 'guideline'[17] at best. The British government was accused of not taking the Covenant seriously and 'muddling through'[18] with respect to the protection of ESC rights. The ESCR Committee's Concluding Observations stated that it found '*disturbing* the position of the state party that provisions of the Covenant, with certain minor exceptions, constitute principles and programme objectives rather than legal obligations, and that consequently the provisions of the Covenant cannot be given legislative effect'.[19]

A. The ESCR Committee's views on the status of Covenant rights[20]

The frustration of the members of the ESCR Committee may be seen in the context of the Committee's repeated attempts to draw attention to the concrete nature of the rights established by the ICESCR and so reject the contention that ESC rights are not justiciable at all.[21] In its *General Comment 3* (1990) on 'The nature of States parties obligations (art 2, para 1 of the Covenant)'[22] the Committee noted that freedom from discrimination of all Covenant rights[23] could be promoted, in part, through the provision of judicial or other effective remedies, and it stated that there 'are a number of. . . provisions in [the Covenant] including articles 3, 7 (*a*) (*i*), 8, 10 (3), 13 (2) (*a*), (3) and (4) and 15 (3) which would seem to be capable of immediate application by judicial and other organs in many national legal systems'.[24] It pointed out that '[a]ny suggestion that [such covenant] provisions. . . are inherently non-self-executing would seem to be difficult to sustain'.[25]

---

[17] Ibid Mr Sadi para 20.   [18] Ibid Mr Ahmed para 31.

[19] ESCR Committee, *Concluding Observations United Kingdom of Great Britain and Northern Ireland* E/C.12/1/add19, (4 Dec 1997), para 10, emphasis added. Like the ESCR Committee's General Comments, such Observations are not binding though they represent an authoritative view of compliance with standards that bind the UK in international law.

[20] A detailed analysis of the legal obligations of states to protect ICESCR rights is beyond the scope of this work, see, however, M Craven, *The International Covenant on Economic, Social and Cultural Rights: A Perspective on its Development* (OUP, 1995); M Sepúlveda, *The Nature of the Obligations under the International Covenant on Economic, Social and Cultural Rights* (Intersentia, 2003) and Office of the High Commissioner for Human Rights and International Bar Association (above) at 701–705.

[21] Cf E Vierdag, 'The Legal Nature of the Rights Granted by the ICESCR' (1978) 9 Netherlands Ybk of Intl L 69. It has been argued that the suggestion that ESC rights are non-justiciable was never accepted in the course of the elaboration of the ICESCR, see Office of the High Commissioner for Human Rights and International Bar Association, ibid at 690–692.

[22] ESCR Committee, *General Comment 3* (1990) E/1991/23, annex III. Art 2(1) ICESCR reads, 'Each State Party to the present Covenant undertakes to take steps, individually and through international assistance and co-operation, especially economic and technical, to the maximum of its available resources, with a view to achieving progressively the full realization of the rights recognized in the present Covenant by all appropriate means, including particularly the adoption of legislative measures.'   [23] Art 2(2) ICESCR.

[24] *General Comment 3* (above) para 5.   [25] Ibid.

Moreover the Committee also expressed the view that there was 'a minimum core obligation [under the ICESCR] to ensure the satisfaction of, at the very least, minimum essential levels of each of the rights' protected.[26] From *General Comment 3* it was apparent too that the British government's view, as set out in its 1996 report, had also understated the role of ESC rights in other ways. For example, article 2(1) ICESCR creates an obligation not only to 'take steps' in the field of Covenant rights, but also to monitor the extent of their realization or non-realization, plus to devise strategies and programmes for their promotion bearing in mind the criteria of 'achieving progressively the full realization' of Covenant rights and 'maximum available resources'. Again, the rather shallow view of the rights presented by the British failed to appreciate that, as the ESCR Committee had put it in *General Comment 3*, 'any deliberately retrogressive measures [in the otherwise progressive realisation of ESC rights]...would require the most careful consideration and would need to be fully justified by reference to the totality of the rights provided for in the Covenant and in the context of the full use of the maximum available resources'.[27]

Soon after its examination of the 1996 UK Report, the ESCR Committee produced *General Comment 9* on 'The domestic application of the Covenant'.[28] Here the ESCR Committee noted that the ICESCR does not require states to fully incorporate the Covenant into domestic law,[29] however it stated that this was 'desirable':

Direct incorporation avoids problems that might arise in the translation of treaty obligations into national law, and provides a basis for the direct invocation of the Covenant rights by individuals in national courts. For these reasons, the Committee strongly encourages formal adoption or incorporation of the Covenant in national law.[30]

Nonetheless, even when direct incorporation was not undertaken: 'Covenant norms must be recognised in appropriate ways within the domestic legal order, appropriate means of redress, or remedies, must be available to any aggrieved individual or group, and appropriate means of ensuring Governmental accountability must be put in place.'[31] A strong preference was expressed for judicial remedies in particular,[32] but the ESCR Committee also pointed out that administrative remedies can suffice provided they are 'accessible, affordable, timely and effective'.[33] Under the heading of 'justiciability' the ESCR Committee argued that neither the nature of Covenant rights nor the relevant Covenant provisions justified a discrepancy between ICESCR rights and civil and political rights.[34] The ESCR

---

26 Ibid para 10.   27 Ibid para 9.
28 ESCR Committee, *General Comment 9* (1998) UN doc E/1999/22, annex IV.
29 Ibid paras 5 and 8.   30 Ibid para 8.   31 Ibid para 2.   32 Ibid para 3.
33 Ibid para 9, although 'an ultimate right of judicial appeal from administrative procedures of this type would also often be appropriate'. Also 'whenever a Covenant right cannot be made fully effective without some role for the judiciary, judicial remedies are necessary', as with obligations concerning non-discrimination.   34 Ibid para 10.

Committee went on to emphasize the need to 'distinguish between justiciability (which refers to those matters which are appropriately resolved by the courts) and norms which are self-executing (capable of being applied by courts without further elaboration)'. Noting that 'the general approach of each legal system needs to be taken into account', the ESCR Committee insisted nonetheless 'there is no Covenant right which could not, in the great majority of systems, be considered to possess at least some significant justiciable dimensions'.[35]

On the topic of separation of powers (although it did not use that expression) the ESCR Committee recognized the traditional view that, generally speaking, issues relating to allocation of resources should be left to the political authorities rather than the courts. But it also noted in practice that 'courts are generally already involved in a considerable range of matters which have important resource implications'.[36] The ESCR Committee was therefore firm in its view that there could be no 'rigid classification' placing ESC rights as by definition 'beyond the reach of the courts', for this would be 'arbitrary and incompatible with the principle that the two sets of human rights are indivisible and interdependent'. Moreover, 'it would also drastically curtail the capacity of the courts to protect the rights of the most vulnerable and disadvantaged groups in society'.[37] In view of the fact that, as the ESCR Committee saw it, 'the formulations used in the Covenant are, to a considerable extent, comparable to those used in treaties dealing with civil and political rights', it opined that a state would need to have a 'compelling justification' for treating protection of civil and political rights differently from ESC rights in its legal system.[38]

More recently, against the backdrop of discussions regarding a proposed OP for the ICESCR, the justiciability of ESC rights has been strongly promoted by the current and the former UN High Commissioners for Human Rights (Louise Arbour and Mary Robinson). Both have sought to demonstrate how outdated the view has become that the two classes of rights (civil and political as against ESC) should be categorized into separate, watertight compartments.[39] It has been said that a 'new era'[40] in human rights protection was reached with the end of the Cold War and that the 'time had finally come', according to Mary Robinson, 'to take the two sets of rights equally seriously, as the drafters of the Universal Declaration of Human Rights[41] intended, and to find the most effective ways to promote and protect them'. She has also pointed to examples of European states such as Norway,[42]

---

[35] Ibid.   [36] Ibid.   [37] Ibid.
[38] Ibid para 7. The point is relevant for the UK given the passage of the Human Rights Act 1998.
[39] L Arbour, 'La Fontaine-Baldwin lecture 2005 "Freedom from want"—from charity to entitlement, 3 March 2005' and 'Statement to the Open-Ended Working Group' (n 3 above).
[40] (Note 2 above) at 866.
[41] Universal Declaration of Human Rights, GA res 217A (III), UN doc A/810 at 71 (1948). The Universal Declaration addressed not only civil and political but also and ESC rights, see arts 22–27.
[42] In 1999 Norwegian legislation incorporated the Covenant into domestic law giving it priority over conflicting legislative provisions.

which had incorporated the ICESCR, and she questioned why this example could not be followed in the UK or in Ireland.[43] As she put it, 'one part of the transition from human rights rhetoric to human rights reality in developed countries, such as Britain and Ireland, is to take the indivisibility of rights seriously'.[44]

B. UK law and ESC rights

It is certainly the case that the ICESCR, and the idea of ESC rights generally, have had a very low profile within UK law. The JCHR commented in 2004 that ICESCR international obligations and the five-yearly reviews by ESCR Committee 'have generated little domestic discussion, in contrast with the lively and informed debate in relation to civil and political rights'.[45] Volume 8(2) of Halsbury's Laws of England, devoted to 'Constitutional Law and Human Rights'[46] contains three simple references to the ICESCR and there are a mere four lines of main text under the heading 'Economic and Social Rights'.[47] However, as the UK government has continually pointed out in its reports to the ESCR Committee there exist in the UK a series of Statutes creating legal obligations on public authorities in fields corresponding to the rights protected by the ICESCR notably housing, social security, employment, anti-discrimination (for certain areas), and health care. Pursuant to such legislation public authorities may be the subject of judicial review proceedings based on their actions or omissions. Indeed it has been noted that '[t]he application of what might be considered ESC rights through judicial review of statutory duties suggests that consideration of their substance is by no means alien to the UK courts'.[48] However, with respect to ESC rights, UK law fails to 'provide constitutional level protection of universally-applicable human rights standards of the type provided by the Human Rights Act in relation to civil and political rights'.[49] The JCHR has warned '[t]his may leave vulnerable marginalised groups or individuals, who fall outside of the scope of the legislation [corresponding to ESC rights protection]'[50] and so may have no standing in court to bring a claim for judicial review as regards the application of that legislation. Furthermore, insofar as

---

[43] M Robinson, 'From Rhetoric to Reality: Making Human Rights Work' (2003) 1 Eur Human Rights L Rev 1.   [44] Ibid at 4.
[45] *JCHR ICESCR Report*, para 7. All JCHR publications referred to in the chapter are available from the JCHR's website: <http://www.parliament.uk/parliamentary_committees/joint_committee_on_human_rights.cfm> accessed on 2 Nov 2006.
[46] Halsbury's Laws of England vol 8(2) (4th edn, Butterworths, 1996).   [47] Ibid para 121.
[48] *JCHR ICESCR Report* at 19.
[49] The Human Rights Act 1998 incorporated only those Convention rights (with the exception of art 13) covered by the main European Convention text and the First Protocol to it. Additional civil and political rights protected by, eg, the International Covenant on Civil and Political Rights (GA res 2200A (XXI), 21 UN GAOR supp (no 16) at 52, UN doc A/6316 (1966), 999 UNTS 171) and Protocols 4, 7, and 12 (none of which have been ratified by the UK) of the Convention, have not been incorporated into UK law, see J Wadham and R Taylor, 'Bringing More Rights Home' (2002) 6 Eur Human Rights L Rev 713.   [50] *JCHR ICESCR Report* at 11.

primary legislation itself may provide for a breach of fundamental ESC rights there may be no way of challenging this, unless the claim can be addressed through 'Convention rights'[51] and so under the Human Rights Act.

It is arguable too that the fact that the Covenant expresses legal commitments at international law which have not been incorporated into domestic law may have an impact on how such 'rights' are generally perceived in the UK. The Covenant has seldom been even cited by the courts in the UK.[52] It is mentioned only very rarely in Parliament, although the JCHR has been making efforts to try to change this.[53] It is striking to note, for example, that the only reference to article 11(1)[54] of the ICESCR during the passage of the Homelessness Act 2002 through Parliament was by the JCHR itself.[55] The 2002 Act creates a statutory duty (which was first established by legislation in 1977) to accommodate most (but not all) homeless persons. However the debates on the floor of both Houses concerning this legislation were not informed by any discussion of the internationally recognized 'right to housing'.[56] More generally, the writer is not aware of any instance when a law or administrative practice in the UK has been explicitly amended on the strength of the legal obligations derived specifically from the ICESCR.

It is perhaps a telling illustration of the 'official' British view of the status of ESC rights that only in December 2004 did the Foreign and Commonwealth Office (FCO) relinquish its responsibility for the handling of Reporting under the ICE-SCR to the Department for Constitutional Affairs (DCA).[57] As the 1996 UK report revealed, even as a treaty binding the UK at international law it seems that the British government traditionally took the view that the Covenant was the 'softest' of human rights treaties in terms of the legal obligations created. It has been the 'UK Government's long-standing position' that ESC rights found under not only

[51] The Human Rights Act 1998, s 1.

[52] A search of the 'All [UK] Law Reports' database on 'Westlaw UK' reveals that the ICESCR has been cited (and literally no more than this) in only seven judgments (including Privy Council rulings) in the last ten years.

[53] A search of the 'Commons Hansard' and 'Lords Hansard' databases <http://www.parliament.uk> accessed 31 Jan 2006 for the last five years reveals that the ICESCR has been mentioned (and no more) in connection with domestic law on only a handful of occasions.

[54] Art 11(1) ICESCR reads, 'The States Parties to the present Covenant recognize the right of everyone to an adequate standard of living for himself and his family, including adequate food, clothing and housing, and to the continuous improvement of living conditions. The States Parties will take appropriate steps to ensure the realization of this right, recognizing to this effect the essential importance of international co-operation based on free consent.'

[55] See JCHR, *Homelessness Bill*, 1st Report (2001–02) (HL 30; HC 314).

[56] The ESCR Committee had referred to problems relating to homelessness and housing in its Concluding Observations of 2002 (published after the passage of the Homelessness Act 2002), see paras 6 (commending the UK for action taken), 19 (criticism of persistence of homelessness, particularly among certain groups of society, such as ethnic minorities), and 38, see *Concluding Observations: United Kingdom of Great Britain and Northern Ireland* E/C.12/1/add79, (5 June 2002).

[57] The DCA is the department of government responsible for upholding justice, rights, and democracy. It has taken the lead role in reporting to the appropriate UN Committee in relation to various other international instruments, notably the International Covenant on Civil and Political Rights (above) and the United Nations Convention Against Torture (GA res 39/46, annex, 39 UN GAOR supp (no 51) at 197, UN doc A/39/51 (1984)).

the ICESCR, but also, in fact, those ESC rights within the UN Convention on the Rights of the Child,[58] the Convention on the Elimination of Racial Discrimination,[59] and the Convention on the Elimination of Discrimination Against Women,[60] 'should be considered not as legally enforceable rights to be adjudicated on in the courts, but as "programmatic objectives"', aspirational goals to be taken into account by the executive arm of Government in its development of policy on economic and social issues'.[61] The pages that follow will examine how the new Labour government maintains this stance with respect to the ICESCR. They illustrate that, despite mounting criticism from both the ESCR Committee and the JCHR the UK government continues to refuse to accept the justiciability of ESC rights and countenance their direct incorporation into domestic law.

III. New Labour and ESC rights: taking indivisibility seriously?

In its Concluding Observations with respect to the 1996 report the ESCR Committee had suggested that the British government 'take appropriate steps to introduce the Covenant into legislation, so that the rights covered by the Covenant may be fully implemented'.[62] It added that it was 'encouraged that the state party has taken such action with respect to the European Convention on Human Rights [via the Human Rights Act 1998] and is of the view that it would be appropriate to give similar due regard to the obligations under the Covenant'.

The 'new' Labour administration took office amidst talk of an ethical, human rights focussed foreign policy, but it was soon evident that this prioritized the protection and promotion of core civil and political rights.[63] It seems that there was an assumption that foreign policy objectives on ESC rights were covered by the government's commendable commitment to the relief of poverty and sustainable development.[64] Ministers with foreign-policy briefs made statements on indivisibility and emphasized that the needs of economic development should not allow

[58] Convention on the Rights of the Child, GA res 44/25, annex, 44 UN GAOR supp (no 49) at 167, UN doc A/44/49 (1989).

[59] International Convention on the Elimination of All Forms of Racial Discrimination, 660 UNTS 195.

[60] Convention on the Elimination of All Forms of Discrimination against Women, GA res 34/180, 34 UN GAOR supp (no 46) at 193, UN doc A/34/46.

[61] JCHR, *The Work of the Committee in the 2001–2005 Parliament,* 19th report (2004–05) (HL 112; HC 552), para 188. As regards the government's stance on the rights protected by the UN Convention on the Rights of the Child and the JCHR's criticism of it, see JCHR, *The UN Convention on the Rights of the Child,* 10th report (2002–03) (HL 117; HC 81), paras 21–23. See also D Feldman, 'The Internationalization of Public Law' in D Oliver and J Jowell, *The Changing Constitution,* (OUP, 2004) at 127 and 134. [62] Above, para 21.

[63] See eg Robin Cook (Foreign Secretary), 'Human Rights into a New Century', 17 July 1997 and various other speeches available at <http://www.fco.gov.uk> accessed 3 Nov 2006.

[64] See chapters dedicated to protection of ESC rights in each volume of the FCO's *Annual Report on Human Rights,* available at <http://www.fco.gov.uk> accessed 3 Nov 2006.

a prioritization of ESC rights over civil and political rights.[65] Occasionally statements from the FCO were in sympathy with the view that more could and should be done to constitutionalize the protection of ESC rights within the UK legal system. The FCO Annual Human Rights Report for 1999[66] spoke in favour of enshrining ESC rights in the Kenyan Constitution for this would help to 'strengthen the negotiating position of poor and vulnerable people and increase their chances of securing these rights for themselves'.[67] It would help 'people to know what their rights are so that they are empowered to challenge policies that affect them and to demand accountability against these rights from their political representatives'. Thus, '[h]aving human rights enshrined in the national constitution will create space for organisations representing poorer and more vulnerable people to advocate on their behalf'. The very same report acknowledged that '[f]or most British people human rights are synonymous with civil and political rights. . . . One of the consequences of this has been to marginalise—in the public debate—economic and social rights, and to downplay their importance'. 'The British Government', the report continued, 'is committed to redressing this imbalance. For us, economic and social rights are as important as civil and political rights.'[68]

It has transpired, however, that under 'new' Labour there has been little enthusiasm for viewing socio-economic rights as 'rights' equivalent to 'Convention rights' under the UK legal system.[69] There was no groundswell in favour of incorporating ESC rights into domestic law when the Human Rights Act 1998 was passed. Indeed this does not appear to have been seriously contemplated at the political level, nor by NGOs[70] whilst at the time few academics criticized the Human Rights Act regime for its failure to include ESC rights coverage.[71] Nor since 1997 has the UK government extended international accountability for socio-economic rights within the context of regional human rights instruments. The Revised European Social Charter of 1996,[72] which contains extensions of the rights set out

[65] See Robin Cook (Foreign Secretary), 'Human Rights: Making the Difference', 16 Oct 1998 (London, Amnesty International Human Rights Festival Speech) and 'Human Rights—A Priority of Britain's Foreign Policy', 28 March 2001 (London, Foreign Office, 'Meeting of human rights NGOs') copies on file with author.

[66] FCO, *Human Rights Annual Report 1999* (Cm 4404 July 1999).   [67] Ibid at 16.

[68] Ibid at 14–15.

[69] For criticism see S Ruxton and R Karim, *Beyond Civil Rights: Developing Economic, Social and Cultural Rights in the UK* (Oxfam, 2001).

[70] In its report on *A Written Constitution for the United Kingdom (1993)*, the Institute of Public Policy Research proposed a non-legal declaration of social and economic rights which would cite the ICESCR and the European Social Charter and selected rights protected by them as a point of reference to guide Parliament, on this see R Blackburn, *Towards a Constitutional Bill of Rights for the United Kingdom* (Pinter, 1998), at 49–50.

[71] However, in 1997 Professors Ewing and Gearty did complain that 'social and economic rights have been more subject of erosion since 1979 than have civil and political rights', see K Ewing and C Gearty, 'Rocky Foundations for Labour's New Rights' (1997) 2 Eur Human Rights L Rev 146 at 151. See also K Ewing, 'The Unbalanced Constitution' in T Campbell, K Ewing, and A Tomkins (eds), *Sceptical Essays on Human Rights* (OUP, 2001).

[72] The Revised European Social Charter of 1996, CETS no 163.

in the European Social Charter of 1961[73] plus some additional rights, was signed by the UK in November 1997 but has never been ratified.[74] The collective complaints procedure under a 1995 Additional Protocol to the Charter has not been signed by the UK.[75] With respect to both instruments it has been stated on behalf of the government in 2006 that, 'the question of ratification [is]... under review, particularly in the light of the evolving interpretation of the revised Charter by the experts appointed to oversee compliance with it'.[76]

A. The UK's 2001 report to the ESCR Committee

The matter of the 'status' of the ESC Covenant rights was the subject of controversy again on the occasion of the examination of the UK's Fourth Periodic Report under the ICESCR, which was submitted in January 2001 and examined by the ESCR Committee in April 2002. Concluding Observations were published in June 2002.

The UK's report comprised 241 pages of detailed text covering the government's policies and action in the field of the rights set out in the ICESCR. It is striking, nonetheless, that within the text there was no reference, for example, to the ESCR Committee's General Comments and their relevance to UK practice[77] whilst there were only fleeting references back to the Committee's Concluding Observations on the UK's (previous) Third Periodic Report.[78] Overall it is hard to see from the report what tangible effect the ICESCR had had on the law of the UK. Certainly the UK report did not go to great lengths to make this evident, whilst NGOs questioned the general attitude of the British government towards

---

[73] The European Social Charter, CETS no 035. The Institute of Employment Rights has argued that '[t]he United Kingdom has one of the worst (if not the worst) levels of compliance with the Social Charter', see Memorandum from the Institute of Employment Rights, app to JCHR, *Review of International Human Rights Instruments*, 17th Report (2004–05) (HL 99; HC 264).

[74] It was stated on behalf of the FCO in 2000, that the UK government was to ratify the instrument 'in due course': FCO, *Human Rights Annual Report 2000* (Cm 4774: July 2000) at 150.

[75] Additional Protocol to the European Social Charter Providing for a System of Collective Complaints, CETS no 158 (this has been ratified by twelve European states and signed by a further six states): see RR Churchill and U Khaliq, 'Violations of Economic, Social and Cultural Rights: The Current Use and Future Potential of the Collective Complaints Mechanism of the European Social Charter', chapter 9 in this book. In December 2004, the UK ratified the Optional Protocol to the Convention on the Elimination of Discrimination against Women, GA res 54/4, annex, 54 UN GAOR supp. (no 49) at 5, UN doc A/54/49—the main treaty text protects both civil and political as well as ESC rights.   [76] *Government Responses to JCHR Reports* para 26.

[77] It is notable, for example, that in its Concluding Observations to the Third (UK) Periodic Report the ESCR Committee specifically requested information regarding the steps taken to provide protection from forced eviction in accordance with the Committee's *General Comment 7* (1997) on forced evictions (see para 313). Whilst the 2001 Report contained details on the legal regime concerning protection from eviction there was no reference to *General Comment 7* or its requirements.

[78] See para 9.09 (social security benefits and their 'take up'), para 8.07 (legal reform in employment), para 12.07 (waiting times for surgery).

the reporting process.[79] The 2001 report failed to address in detail the matter of the justiciability of Covenant rights despite the fact that the ESCR Committee's General Comment 9 had been produced since the UK's report of 1996.[80] Under the heading 'Implementation' the report simply stated:

2.01 The United Kingdom gives effect to its obligations under the Covenant on Economic, Social and Cultural Rights by means of specific laws, policies and practices which implement the various rights set out in the Covenant. The United Kingdom gives effect in like manner to the obligations it has assumed under the European Social Charter.

Within the 'List of Issues to be taken up', subsequently produced by the ESCR Committee a further explanation as to 'the 'effects' the UK intends to give to its 'obligations' under the Covenant' was requested. In its reply[81] the ESCR Committee was told by the UK government that '[t]he Convention [*sic* Covenant] is not directly applied as law within the territories to which these reports apply' and the paragraph 2.01 statement as extracted above was then quoted back to the ESCR Committee almost verbatim. Hence the Committee members were in effect invited to read the extensive report supplied to it so as to conclude for themselves an answer to their question. Efforts to elicit a more detailed response from the British government continued in May 2002 in Geneva on the occasion of the consideration of the UK's Fourth Periodic Report by the ESCR Committee. The summary records of the meetings[82] indicate that the first morning session was dominated by attempts on the part of the members of the ESCR Committee to get the British delegation to explain further the position with respect to article 2(1) and that these attempts met with limited success. Mr Fifoot, on behalf of the UK, put forward replies[83] to the effect that the UK government was 'determined to

---

[79] Democratic Audit, an NGO based at the University of Essex, stated that it was, 'concerned about the implicit disdain shown for the idea that the [ICESCR] could make a relevant contribution to public policy in the UK' 'Memorandum from Democratic Audit' (Human Rights Centre, University of Essex) at heading 4 (*'Democratic Audit JCHR Submission'*) (annex to *JCHR ICESCR Report*). Its view was that '[c]ertain members of the UK delegation reporting to [the ESCR Committee] in May 2002 showed no inclination to engage in a constructive dialogue with members of [ESCR Committee]' (above) The Committee on the Administration of Justice (CAJ), an independent cross community group working for the protection and promotion of human rights in Northern Ireland, has, with specific reference to the UK's Fourth report, commented on the growing length of the UK reports to UN treaty monitoring bodies. It was 'doubtful' whether the 'UN insists on reports of the detail and complexity now supplied'. In their experience, 'extremely detailed and overly complex reports tend to cloud rather than facilitate effective scrutiny'. It was added that, '[t]he UN has few sanctions available to it, and the reporting cycle is primarily intended to be a forum in which Member States are assisted to comply with their obligations'. The CAJ believed, 'more frankness as to the problems being encountered and the challenges facing the Member State, rather than tedious administrative detail is what is required', 'Memorandum from the Committee on the Administration of Justice', (Annex to *JCHR ICESCR Report*).
[80] Cf *General Comment* 3 (above) especially para 6.
[81] *Replies by the Government of the United Kingdom to the list of issues* (E/C.12/UK/2), E/C.12/4add5, E/C.12/4/add 7, E/C.12/4/add 8.
[82] See 28th session, summary record of the 12th Meeting (Geneva, 6 May 2002) E/C.12/2002/SR.11.   [83] Ibid para 21.

comply with its obligations under [the Covenant] ... but [that it] considered that the rights enshrined therein were not justiciable and that it was not for British judges to interpret the provisions of the Covenant'. A distinction was made between the 'very specific' provisions of the ECHR as against the Covenant, which 'was primarily concerned with more general commitments'. According to the summary records Mr Fifoot referred to the 'wide range of specific laws which could of course be invoked in court'. As regards the principle of human equality, so vital to the full realization of ESC rights,[84] the UK chose not to enshrine the principle of absolute equality in a general law rather it 'preferred to adopt specific, concrete laws on racial equality, gender equality, etc.'. Furthermore, the UK 'had no intention of implementing a national plan of action for human rights or of establishing a national human rights commission for Great Britain'[85] rather, as it had attempted to show in its report, 'the United Kingdom preferred to target its action by adopting sectoral programmes'. In return several members of the Committee championed the justiciability of Covenant rights.[86] In reply to this Mr Fifoot said that, 'although the Covenant as a whole could not be invoked before the courts, the economic, social and cultural rights enshrined therein were still justiciable and were, in fact, the subject of specific laws under domestic legislation'.[87] But the ESCR Committee was told that its General Comments were only intended 'to guide States in implementing the Covenant' and were 'in no way binding'. The UK, therefore, 'felt that it had fulfilled its obligations under the Covenant and would not accept any charge of having evaded them ... '.[88]

B. The ESCR Committee's Concluding Observations of 2002

In its Concluding Observations to the UK government's report of June 2002,[89] the ESCR Committee welcomed 'the constructive dialogue with the [UK] delegation ... , which consisted of Government officials with relevant expertise on the provisions of the Covenant'.[90] However it also 'regret[ed] ... that in the course of the dialogue, the delegation did not provide more cogent replies to some of the questions posed by members of the Committee'—a comment that may or may not have had regard to the exchanges just cited.

It should be stressed that overall the Concluding Observations were not a damning indictment of the UK's track record on the protection of substantive ESC rights. The government was praised for a number of 'positive aspects'[91] that had

---

[84] See ESCR Committee, *General Comment 16* (2005) E/C.12/2005/4 on 'The Equal Right of Men and Women to the Enjoyment of Economic, Social and Cultural Rights'.

[85] However, see n 261 below.

[86] Above (Summary Record). para 32 (Mr Sadi and Mr Pillay) and para 33 (Mr Malinverni).

[87] Ibid para 36.   [88] Ibid.

[89] ESCR Committee, *Concluding Observations: United Kingdom of Great British and Northern Ireland* E/C.12/1/add79 (above).   [90] Ibid para 3.

[91] Ibid paras 4–9.

been in evidence from the ESCR Committee's examination of the protection of ESC rights, for example, the introduction of the New Deal programmes for employment, the national minimum wage, and measures taken to reduce home-lessness, 'rough sleeping', and permanent exclusion from schools. Under the head-ings of 'Principal Subjects of Concern' and 'Suggestions and Recommendations' the Committee highlighted areas of UK practice that it regarded as in need of attention. The criticisms made were serious, but it could not be deduced from them that the protection of Covenant rights in the UK was in a dire state in prac-tice. Arguably the most significant criticism of the Committee was directed to the need to take more effective steps to combat *de facto* discrimination, in particular against ethnic minorities and people with disabilities, especially in relation to employment, housing, and education. On this the Committee strongly recom-mended that comprehensive legislation on equality and non-discrimination be enacted in British law, 'in conformity with article 2, paragraph 2, and article 3 of the Covenant'.[92] The other criticisms of the Committee as regards particular ESC rights can be viewed under two heads: those that focused on specific aspects of par-ticular rights[93] and those which were more general in nature.[94] Finally, it is interest-ing to note that a number of the Committee's Concluding Observations related not to the protection of specific rights as such, but to the need to elevate the quality of what might be termed the general domestic legal environment for protecting ESC rights. The Committee recommended that the Covenant be incorporated into domestic law (see immediately below). It also recommended that there be a strengthening in the 'institutional arrangements, within the Government adminis-tration, which are designed to ensure that [the UK's] obligations under the Covenant are taken into account, at an early stage, in the Government's formula-tion of national legislation and policy on issues such as poverty reduction, social welfare, housing, health and education'.[95] The Committee urged the relevant insti-tutions to have particular regard to its General Comments.[96] The Committee also recommended the establishment of a national human rights commission for England, Wales, and Scotland, with a mandate to promote and protect all human rights, including economic, social, and cultural rights.[97]

---

[92] Ibid para 14.
[93] Eg, relating to aspects of the national minimum wage (para 15) and full enjoyment of the right to strike (para 16); the need to continue to combat domestic violence and ensure a sufficient number of refuge places (para 17); and the need to prohibit child smacking (para 36).
[94] Eg, the need to continue to address problems in the field of: poverty and social exclusion (this, 'as a matter of high priority, with special focus on the needs of marginalized and vulnerable groups, and particular regions, such as Northern Ireland' (para 37)); homelessness (attention to be paid to those groups in society which are disproportionately affected, para 38); poor housing conditions and fuel poverty (para 39); financing of higher education (to ensure those from poorer backgrounds are not adversely affected, para 41); and integration of schools in Northern Ireland (para 42).
[95] Ibid para 25.   [96] Ibid.
[97] Ibid para 28, see also para 26 (encouraging the UK to promote Covenant obligations in its capacity as a member of leading global financial institutions); para 27 (prepare a national human

C. The ESCR Committee's criticism regarding non-incorporation

With specific reference to the relationship between the ICESCR and domestic law, the ESCR Committee 'deeply regret[ted]'[98] the failure to incorporate the Covenant and the fact that there was no intention of doing so in the near future. It 'reiterate[d] its concern about the state party's position that the provisions of the Covenant, with minor exceptions, constitute principles and programmatic objectives rather than legal obligations that are justiciable, and that consequently they cannot be given direct legislative effect'.[99] It 'strongly recommended' that the British government review its position. The Committee affirmed the principle of interdependence and indivisibility, and it underscored its view that 'all economic, social and cultural rights are justiciable', reminding the UK of *General Comment 9*.

It should be added that the critical remarks directed toward the UK as regards incorporation and justiciability are revealed to be far from unique when the Concluding Observations made with respect to other Covenant states are examined. A comprehensive analysis of such documentation is beyond the scope of this work. However, the writer has undertaken a brief survey of the ESCR Committee's Concluding Observations for western European states over the period from December 2000 to July 2005. Clearly this can only provide a broad impression and it should be borne in mind that only a selection of western European states were examined by the ESCR Committee during this period. Nonetheless, the ESCR Committee criticized (though in less strong terms than the UK) Malta,[100] Iceland,[101] Ireland,[102] and Sweden[103] for non-incorporation of the Covenant, whilst for Italy,[104] France,[105] and Belgium[106] (monist states[107]) it was evident from the Concluding Observations that there prevailed a view that some or all ESC rights were non-justiciable. With respect to states that had directly incorporated

rights plan of action, in accordance with the Vienna Declaration and Programme of Action); para 29 (protect of ESC rights in any bill of rights enacted for Northern Ireland); and para 30 (improve education and training as regards ESC rights).

[98] Ibid para 11.   [99] Ibid.
[100] ESCR Committee, *Concluding Observations, Malta* E/C.12/1/add101 (14 Dec 2004), para 10 though see para 3.
[101] ESCR Committee, *Concluding Observations, Iceland* E/C.12/1/add89 (23 May 2003), paras 10 and 19 though cf para 4.
[102] ESCR Committee, *Concluding Observations, Ireland* E/C.12/1/add77 (5 June 2002), paras 12 and 23.
[103] ESCR Committee, *Concluding Observations, Sweden* E/C.12/1/add70 (30 Nov 2001), paras 15 and 27.
[104] ESCR Committee, *Concluding Observations, Italy* E/C.12/1/add103 (14 Dec 2004), para 13.
[105] ESCR Committee, *Concluding Observations, France* E/C.12/1/add72 (30 Nov 2001), para 13.
[106] ESCR Committee, *Concluding Obervations, Belgium* E/C.12/1/add54 (1 Dec 2000), para 20 cf para 6.
[107] The legal system of a 'monist' state generally draws no clear division between national and international law, see Harris (above).

the Covenant in some way, which included Norway,[108] Greece,[109] and Finland,[110] there was criticism of the scarcity of court decisions on the Covenant and, in some instances, evidence of jurisprudence indicating that the Covenant was not justiciable on the basis that it did not create concrete rights and duties.[111] The Committee was frequently called upon to reaffirm the interdependence and indivisibility of all human rights, the justiciability of ESC rights and to draw attention to *General Comment 9* on domestic application of the Covenant.

It would be wrong to say, therefore, that the UK is virtually alone, even in western Europe, in its refusal to incorporate the Covenant. It may be noted, however, that it has been argued that certain other states treat the Concluding Observations more seriously than the UK to the extent that their subsequent reports illustrate that the Observations were a basis for policy change.[112] The half-hearted attitude apparently taken by the UK government to the ESCR Committee's Concluding Observations was exposed by the JCHR inquiry, to which we may now turn.

IV. The JCHR's inquiry and its influence

The publication of the ESCR Committee's Concluding Observations apparently went virtually unnoticed by Parliament,[113] met with little coverage in the media (some of which was hostile),[114] and with little response from specialist legal and academic commentators. Geraldine Van Bueren bucked the trend by devoting her inaugural lecture, duly published in the leading journal *Public Law*,[115] to the case for an Economic, Social, and Cultural Human Rights Act. She pointed to 'positive developments elsewhere' in the world as regards the judicial consideration of ESC rights and argued that in 'the age of human rights' it was time for the 'UK Constitution...to respond accordingly'.[116] However, in the shadow of 'September 11th' the hope that the British government would seriously consider incorporating further rights into UK law must have been faint. The Concluding Observations were not, however, destined to be forgotten about. Approximately

---

[108] ESCR Committee, *Concluding Observations, Norway* E/C.12/1/add109 (23 June 2005), para 4 cf para 23.

[109] ESCR Committee, *Concluding Observations, Greece* E/C.12/1/add97 (7 June 2004), para 30 cf para 4.

[110] ESCR Committee, *Concluding Observations, Finland* E/C.12/1/add52 (1 Dec 2000), para 12.

[111] Eg Norway (above).   [112] *Democratic Audit JCHR Submission* at 3 and 7, plus annex 1.

[113] A written question on the subject was posed by Llew Smith MP; it received a very limited reply from Prime Minister Tony Blair, *Hansard Written Answers 17 June 2002: Col 44W*. There was, for example, no debate in either House on the Concluding Observations—so far as the author is aware, there never has been any such debate in respect of any UN Human Rights treaty mechanism's Concluding Observations.   [114] See *Daily Telegraph*, Editorial, 21 May 2002 at 21.

[115] G Van Bueren, 'Including the Excluded: the Case for an Economic, Social and Cultural Human Rights Act', Public L (2002) 456 ('Van Bueren').   [116] Ibid at 466–467.

one year after their publication, the JCHR launched an inquiry into the UK's position with respect to the ICESCR. Its intention was 'to discover how the recommendations have been received in Government, and whether or how they are to be acted upon'.[117]

A. Parliament's JCHR

The JCHR[118] is a permanent joint Parliamentary committee which consists of members of both the House of Commons and the House of Lords. It possesses powers of inquiry akin to those of a departmental select committee in the Commons, but, like the latter, its reports do not bind the government. The JCHR's terms of reference, as set out by Parliament, include 'matters relating to human rights in the United Kingdom'. This allows it to scrutinize actions of the government in this field and its most regular function here is in providing reports on the human rights implications of legislation proceeding through Parliament. Since its creation the JCHR has taken the view, 'that its wide terms of reference represent a recognition that Parliament has responsibilities in respect of all the UK's obligations under international human rights law, not merely those which have so far been made part of domestic law'.[119] Thus the JCHR has consistently interpreted its remit as extending to all those internationally recognized human rights standards that have been accepted by the UK, including, of course, the ICESCR. The JCHR has therefore commented on legislation that may have implications for the international obligations covered by the ICESCR.[120] It has also reviewed the government's response to each set of Concluding Observations produced by the UN treaty bodies, as they have been issued, with the intention of 'facilitating scrutiny, by Parliament and by the wider public, of compliance with the UN human rights standards which the UK has undertaken to protect'.[121] The Committee's aim has been 'to ensure that the scrutiny of the UN bodies is integrated within a national

---

[117] JCHR, Press Notice 5 March 2003.

[118] See <http://www.parliament.uk/parliamentary_committees/joint_committee_on_human_rights.cfm> accessed 3 Nov 2006. On this committee see D Feldman, 'The Impact of Human Rights on the UK Legislative Process' (2004) 25(2) Statute L Rev 91 plus 'Parliamentary Scrutiny of Legislation and Human Rights' (2002) Sum. Public Law 323 and A (Lord) Lester, 'Parliamentary Scrutiny of Legislation under the Human Rights Act' (2002) 4 Eur Human Rights L Rev 432.

[119] Feldman (above) at 344.

[120] For example, when addressing the Homelessness Bill in late 2001 the JCHR cited para 8 of *General Comment 4* on the ICESCR (1991), *The Right to Adequate Housing (art 11(1) of the Covenant)*, making the point that public housing offered should be appropriate to the needs of the homeless person or family: JCHR, *Homelessness Bill*, 1st Report (2001–02) (HL 30; HC 314) para 9. See also *Nationality, Immigration and Asylum Bill: Further Report*, 23rd Report (2001–02) (HL Paper 176; HC 1255) at paras 10–15 (removing social security protection from asylum seekers and potential incompatibility with art 11(1) ICESCR). See also *Scrutiny: Final Progress Report*, 18th Report (2004–05) (HL Paper 111; HC 551) concerning the Anti-Social Behaviour Bill, references to the ICESCR at para 4.7 (re welfare contracts), and paras 4.8–4.10 (re removal of housing benefit).

[121] JCHR (above) (19th Report of Session 2004–05) para 173.

debate on human rights protection, and that this debate and scrutiny continues at a national level, between Government, Parliament, and the general public, in the intervals between UN consideration of periodic reports'.[122]

On 5 March 2003, a review process for the ICESCR was launched with the JCHR's call for written evidence.[123] Documentation was subsequently received from the FCO, NGOs, trade unions, and academic institutions.[124] A roundtable seminar was held, attended by a number of academics and NGOs concerned with ESC rights; a delegation of the JCHR visited South Africa for a seminar on South African protection of ESC rights and met representatives from the South African Constitutional Court, the South African Human Rights Commission, government officials responsible for human rights implementation, and lawyers, NGOs, and academics.[125] In September 2003, the JCHR took oral evidence from a delegation from the FCO, including Bill Rammell MP, Minister of State. November 2004 saw the publication of the JCHR's Report, a substantial document of sixty-three pages and eleven chapters. In it the JCHR stated that it intended to 'encourage a wider awareness and public discussion on the implications of economic, social, and cultural rights guarantees, under the Covenant and other international treaties [such as the European Social Charter], and the implications of these rights for UK law and policy'. It noted that compliance with the ICESCR was 'an aspect of the UK's international human rights obligations which has received scant scrutiny at a domestic level'.[126] As noted above, the FCO had lead responsibility for the ICESCR until December 2004, when 'ownership' of the ICESCR was transferred to the DCA.[127] Whilst, therefore, the FCO was the responsible department of government during the course of the JCHR inquiry itself, the timing was such that it was the DCA that provided the official governmental response to that JCHR inquiry (*The DCA Response*).[128] This was sent to the JCHR in January 2006, almost a year later than requested.

What follows is not an attempt to summarize the JCHR's extensive report[129] and *The DCA Response*. The main intention is to highlight those parts of the inquiry process that were relevant to the British view regarding the importance of as well as the nature and status of the ICESCR and the rights it protects for the purpose of domestic law. To do this reference will also be made to documentation authored by the FCO during the inquiry process and relevant to it.

---

[122] Ibid. By 31 Jan 2006 the Committee had completed consideration of the implementation of Concluding Observations issued in relation to the UNCRC, the ICESCR, and the CERD.

[123] For the full terms of the inquiry see JCHR Press Notice above.

[124] In all twenty-one Memoranda were submitted to the JCHR, see 'List of Written Evidence' attached to *JCHR ICESCR Report*.   [125] *JCHR ICESCR Report* para 14.

[126] Ibid para 7.

[127] JCHR (above) (19th report of 2004–05), app (letter from FCO to JCHR).

[128] 'Appendix 1—Government Response to the Committee's Twenty-first Report of Session 2003–04, on The International Covenant on Economic, Social and Cultural Rights' in *Government Responses to JCHR Reports* (above).   [129] For a summary see *JCHR ICESCR Report* at 3–4.

B. The ESCR Committee's Concluding Observations as a catalyst for the further realization of ESC rights?

A convenient point of departure is to examine how the JCHR inquiry exposed the very lackadaisical attitude that has been taken to date by the UK government toward the ESCR Committee's Concluding Observations. They are, of course, not binding and, it must be acknowledged, elements of them can be very general in nature. Nonetheless they do represent an authoritative view of an expert UN Committee on UK compliance with the ICESCR. They therefore deserve to be taken seriously.

A number of NGOs had submitted in their written evidence to the JCHR that they had found departmental responsibility for preparation of the UK's report to the ICESCR either unclear or difficult to establish.[130] It emerged from Mr Rammell's appearance before the JCHR that trade unions and local authorities were not consulted in the compilation of the UK's 2001 report; nor were key NGOs either before production or, for those that had been involved in the Geneva proceedings, were they consulted or engaged in any follow up of the Concluding Observations.[131] More fundamentally there was an almost complete absence of a meaningful governmental procedure and structure for engaging with the ESCR Committee's recommendations following each round of reporting. The JCHR inquiry revealed that the Concluding Observations document was placed on the FCO website, but it emerged that there were no formal procedures for dissemination of the observations. According to Mr Rammell relevant governmental departments were contacted, the gist of the communication being to point out 'these are the issues that perhaps you should address either by saying "yes, we have addressed them and we have responded" or "for all sorts of reasons, we do not accept the recommendations".'[132] After this communication there could be 'something like a three-year gap' before the FCO, anticipating the next report to the ESCR Committee, wrote to departments to ask what had been done by way of reaction. With there being, in effect, no regular monitoring at all of ESCR Committee's Concluding Observations[133] Mr Rammell acknowledged the need to have 'a more

---

[130] Ibid para 152.

[131] The JCHR was generally critical of the lack of involvement of NGOs in the reporting process, prior to the submission of the report, a fault that, it would seem, was due to the government, *JCHR ICESCR Report* paras 160–161.

[132] JCHR, Examination of Witnesses (Mr Bill Rammell) 15 Sept 2003, *Record of Oral Evidence Taken before the Joint Committee on Human Rights on Monday 15 September 2003*, app to *JCHR ICE-SCR Report*, Q3 ('Rammell Evidence'). From the FCO's written submission to the JCHR it emerged that appropriate departments were individually responsible for following up the relevant Concluding Observations, otherwise '[o]verall monitoring of the United Kingdom's compliance with the ICE-SCR' was down to the ESCR Committee itself, 'Memorandum from the Foreign and Commonwealth Office' (Annex to *JCHR ICESCR Report*) ('FCO Memoranda') para 8.

[133] Ibid Q18. The apparent lack of seriousness with which the government had addressed the implementation and dissemination of the Concluding Observation of the ESC Committee was also seen, though possibly to a slightly lesser extent, in respect of the other Concluding Observations

formalized structured procedure for analysing and responding to recommendations, department by department'. He agreed in principle that targets set by the
ESCR Committee should be reviewed at least on an annual basis.[134] Why previous
appearances by FCO representatives in Geneva had not stimulated such thoughts
is perhaps a reflection of the lack of seriousness with which the ESCR Committee
and the ICESCR have been viewed in the past.

Predictably the JCHR's report contained some stinging criticism of the UK's
handling of the reporting process to Geneva under the ICESCR: the 'current system too readily allow[ed] the concluding observations to be forgotten, or put
aside until the next reporting round';[135] 'a body within Government' was required
in order to drive 'progressive implementation of the Covenant rights', to work in
conjunction with the ESCR Committee 'through responding to the concluding
observations' and to provide cross-government co-ordination. A much more organized and structured approach to reporting was also required to involve civil society and devolved administration bodies both in the compilation of the report and
the follow up of Concluding Observations. The JCHR welcomed proposals to
involve the NGO community more closely in the future.[136]

As noted, responsibility for future reporting and follow up will now fall to the
DCA. It is a worrying sign, therefore, that *The DCA Response* document (in reaction to the JCHR's inquiry) did not even acknowledge the JCHR's criticism of the
way the ESCR Committee's Concluding Observations had been handled to
date,[137] let alone that they be used as a springboard to improve protection of
Covenant rights. It was, however, stated that in the future the DCA would consult
with civil society as regards the implementation of the ESCR Committee's
Concluding Observations.[138]

C. The FCO's and the DCA's view of the nature and status of ESC rights

The JCHR had thought that transferral of responsibility for the ICESCR to the
DCA from the FCO would help discourage a view of the ICESCR as being 'principally a matter of international diplomacy' with reporting to the ESCR
Committee being 'a largely procedural matter';[139] it might encourage 'an understanding of the Covenant as a set of rights and standards, the implementation of
which has practical implications for everyday life in the UK'.[140] However, there

received from certain other UN Treaty Monitoring bodies, see JCHR (above) (19th report of
2004–05) at paras 183–185.

[134] Ibid Q36.
[135] *JCHR ICESCR Report* para 157.   [136] Ibid para 162.
[137] Furthermore that Harriet Harman MP, Minister of State, DCA, appeared oblivious to the criticism made by the JCHR in its Report when she appeared before the JCHR in Jan 2006. See eg, her
comment in reply to Q11: JCHR, *Human Rights Policy: Oral Evidence and Memoranda given by Rt
Hon Harriet Harman QC MP* (16 Jan 2006) (HL 143; HC 830-I).
[138] *The DCA Response* para 88.   [139] *JCHR ICESCR Report* para 155.   [140] Ibid.

may be cause to wonder if the DCA takes a less enlightened view of ESC rights than the FCO. To make this point we should turn to the views expressed on behalf of the FCO and (subsequently) the DCA as regards the nature and status of ESC rights as protected by the Covenant.

In the course of the JCHR's inquiry various written questions were put to the government asking whether, in the light of the 2002 Concluding Observations, further consideration had been given to the case for incorporation of guarantees of ESC rights in UK law. The FCO's (limited) replies noted that the 'ICESCR does not require particular national implementation measures for its provisions'[141]—a statement that is somewhat hard to reconcile with *General Comment 9*[142]—and largely repeated extracts from the 1996 Report to the ESCR Committee to the effect that the greater part of the ICESCR was not susceptible to incorporation.[143] Yet in his submissions to the JCHR as part of the inquiry process Mr Rammell conceded that the government as such had not 'undertaken a detailed assessment of how, in what way and with what consequences we could legally incorporate' some or all of the Covenant's rights.[144] The JCHR inquiry may not have been without some influence in this connection and may have caused the government to start to take a closer look at the arguments for incorporation of ESC rights into domestic law. This is because, in February 2004, the FCO 'chaired a cross-Government meeting to explore the arguments surrounding justiciability of the ICESCR' and it was announced that the FCO would 'continue to examine views from across Government on each of the individual Articles of the Covenant'.[145] It seems that the meeting was also used to inform the UK's negotiating position at the UN Working Group on the OP for the ICESCR and it is understood that a second 'cross-Government' meeting took place in July 2005 to this end. According to correspondence received by this writer from the FCO[146] at that meeting, 'Whitehall departments...looked at: the extent to which the rights (in which their departments have an interest) are susceptible to some form of judicial administrative

---

[141] *FCO Memoranda* para 22 (see also para 23–24). [142] Above.

[143] When Mr Rammell was pressed on this matter by members of the JCHR, he explained that he had given 'some detailed consideration' to incorporation but he 'genuinely [did] not believe that [it]...would improve on the existing legal framework', *Rammell Evidence*, Q24. There was no duty to incorporate in any case, but above all, the Minister argued, 'there would be real difficulties with full legal incorporation'. His point was that 'rights of adequate food, clothing and housing' were 'issues for which there is no absolute standard'. They were 'rightly the business of Governments and their electorates through general elections, to determine what standard we should achieve'. According to Mr Rammell, ESC rights were not of any less importance than civil and political rights; however, the principle of progressive realization (set out in art 2(1) ICESCR) justified a different approach to their protection. Incorporation brought with it risks of judicial encroachment in important and sensitive policy areas. Thus, 'having looked at this long and hard' Mr Rammell was 'reinforced' in the view that there should be no incorporation of ESC rights; he thought that the example of protection of ESC rights in South Africa was of limited relevance to the UK, Q30. [144] Above Q30.

[145] Information extracted from document entitled *Economic, Social and Cultural Rights. Civil and Political Rights. A history and UK progress 2003–2004* ('*the FCO statement*') available on the FCO's website <http://www.fco.gov.uk> accessed 31 Jan 2006.

[146] Letter received from the FCO dated 22 Feb 2006, on file with the author.

remedy in the UK; and whether/to what extent, they consider it appropriate to include each of those rights within the scope of a mechanism allowing for individual complaints to a UN Committee'.[147] The writer requested further details of the content of the discussion at these 'Whitehall' meetings and their outcomes. However, the FCO has refused to furnish such information citing an exemption provided by the Freedom of Information Act.[148]

1. *The UK perspective on ESC rights protected by the ICESCR:* The FCO Statement

As a result the most comprehensive publicly available statement by the UK government on the nature of ESC rights is a short document entitled, 'Economic, Social and Cultural Rights. Civil and Political Rights. A history and UK progress 2003–2004' (hereafter referred to as '*The FCO statement*') available on the FCO's website. So far as the writer is aware the document was apparently[149] made available in July 2004. It was not submitted to the JCHR and takes a very negative view of the susceptibility of the ICESCR to incorporation.

The statement had some uncontroversial introductory comments on the historical background to the ICESCR and the topic of indivisibility. It next emphasized that some of the distinctions between civil and political rights and ESC rights should not be overdrawn, but recognized that they existed nonetheless: ESC rights 'tend to require more widespread positive action by the state', they carried 'very substantial budgetary implications', and so placed 'high demands on Governments'. It was in recognition of this that article 2(1)[150]—which included, *inter alia*, the concept of 'progressive implementation'—was introduced into the Covenant, a provision that entailed that 'states are expected to improve enjoyment of these rights on a continuous basis'. The statement went on to note that the 'progressive implementation' concept had led 'some states to argue that [ESC rights] are not rights in the truest sense, but more that they are aspirational aims'. However, the statement went on, '[w]hile it is clearly true that these rights are framed in aspirational terms, the UK Government believes that they are human rights just as important as any other human right'.[151] The UK took the view that asserting that some rights are 'more critical than others' created a 'hierarchy of human rights' and that this 'undermines the value to individuals of their rights and is contrary to the UK's firm belief that they are inextricably linked'.[152] There was a cautious acceptance in the statement that obligations under the ICESCR can be potentially subject to concrete violation in the case of retrogression, plus

[147] Ibid.
[148] Ibid. Details of the UK's position with respect to the proposed OP were also withheld.
[149] There is no date of publication within the text of the document itself. However, the 'PDF' file document information reveals that it was created (if not written) on 19 July 2004. The statement is a slightly amended version of text contained within the FCO's *Annual Report of Human Rights for 2003* (Cm 5967: Sept 2003) at 144–147.   [150] (Note 22 above).
[151] *The FCO statement.*   [152] Ibid.

recognition too that 'certain elements of the Covenant' were immediately enforceable, as with non-discrimination with respect to the enjoyment of ESC rights.[153]

With respect to the points referred to in the last paragraph, therefore, *The FCO statement* seemed to reveal some small yet significant advances on the British position, at least as they had been understood by not only the JCHR, but also the ESCR Committee. However, the remainder of the document expressed views that were set firmly against the idea that the ICESCR could be incorporated into domestic law in the UK. It was noted that the ICESCR did not require incorporation 'or that all the rights be given direct legal effect', but that 'some [unnamed] NGOs argue that all the rights should be incorporated directly into UK law in the same way as the Human Rights Act has incorporated the civil and political rights guaranteed under the European Convention on Human Rights into domestic law'. 'The UK Government', the statement went on, 'disagrees with this view'. It believed that 'the way in which economic and social rights are expressed in the Covenant does not lend itself easily to justiciable decision-making, meaning decisions with direct legal enforceability in UK courts'.[154] It was added: '[t]he difficulties involved in making judgements about economic and social rights compliance can also be an issue in non-judicial administrative decision-making'. There were 'several reasons' substantiating this position, and here the FCO set out four paragraphs in 'bullet point' form and they are quoted in full here:[155]

[1] The obligation on states is to take steps to improve the realisation of these rights progressively. It is not clear how courts could judge whether there had been an absence of general progress in a particular case where an individual claimed that they had not fully enjoyed, for example, the right to education.

[2] A Government would be constrained by budgetary resources in achieving the progressive realisation of these rights; thus a judicial decision that a Government should have made greater progress in one area such as health would amount to a judgement against a Government's policy decision to prioritise investment in another, such as education. This would take decision-making on the basic policy agenda and priorities away from an elected Government.

[3] Decisions on the best means to realise progressively these rights are essentially policy choices which do not lend themselves to justiciable procedures. Some people may judge that the realisation of these rights requires targeted interventionist policies. Others may judge that the best chances for improvement come from allowing the market, and broader economic policies, to advance the economic environment within which people can achieve these rights. To illustrate the point, it is logical that the right to adequate housing is not the right for everyone to have a house provided by the Government. For some people it may mean being provided with shelter when they cannot provide for themselves. For most people it means the Government providing an economic environment in which they can

---

[153] Generally the statement was devoid of detail here. There were no examples provided and there were no references to the ESCR Committee's General Comments.   [154] Ibid.
[155] The numbers are not provided in the original statement and are provided here for convenience.

earn sufficient income to be able to afford accommodation. The measure of an individual's
right to housing might therefore come down to a test of Governmental economic policy.

[4] Many of the rights are expressed in ambiguous terms. For example, the right to the
'highest attainable' standard of health or to an 'adequate' standard of living. These standards may well vary between individuals, raising questions about how courts could decide
what in each individual's case is the 'adequate standard' or the 'highest attainable standard.

It was such 'concerns' that 'ma[d]e it clear that not all economic, social, and cultural
rights lend themselves directly and suitably to justiciable decisions and procedures';
they also raised questions about 'the role of the courts'. So, whilst it was acknowledged that 'some States' might have chosen to incorporate ESC rights into their
domestic law, 'the UK Government [was] not convinced that this can be done in a
meaningful way within the British legal system'. 'Our view', the statement went on,
is that 'there is little point in directly incorporating the Covenant if it is unclear that
it will lead to meaningful and beneficial outcomes'.[156] However, it was accepted
that there was 'some degree of justiciability', for '[s]ome economic and social rights
can be incorporated into domestic law', an example being those 'related to trade
union organisation and membership'. Therefore, the 'UK's policy' had been to
'take legislative measures within the scope of each right where these will meet our
obligations under international human rights law and have practical and beneficial
effect. For example, rather than have a single 'right to education' we have several
policies, programmes, and legislative measures, such as the Education Act and
Disability Discrimination Act which are designed to help people enjoy the right to
education.'

2. The UK perspective on ESC rights protected by the ICESCR: The DCA Response *to the JCHR*

The DCA Response to the JCHR was less explicit and failed to go as far as *The FCO
statement* insofar as the latter had referred to ESC rights as human rights capable
of being violated even in clear cases of retrogression or discrimination. Moreover,
the greater part of what was said seemed consistent with the view—contrary to
The FCO statement—that ESC rights *were* mere aspirational policy aims for a government to strive to implement.

The DCA Response set out the view that 'social and economic rights [were] as
important as civil and political rights'.[157] The government did not accept the
argument that 'because the two sets of rights are not treated in identical ways (e.g.
incorporated directly into domestic law) it does not view them as equal in importance'.[158] However, the whole thrust of what followed seemed to undermine these

---

[156] *The DCA Response* also recognized that UK courts could make decisions about the implementation of ESC rights, but, 'given the way in which many of the rights in the Covenant are expressed, it
is not obvious that such decisions would be meaningful and beneficial for UK society' para 8.

[157] Ibid para 5.   [158] Ibid.

points. For example, the DCA refused to accept criticism made by the JCHR in its report that the government was reluctant to use the language of 'rights' when addressing the relevance of the ICESCR for domestic law and policy.[159] Yet, the very reply supplied on this point only seemed to verify the original criticism made by the JCHR, for *The DCA Response* stated that the government was, 'fully committed to a vigorous development of economic, social and cultural *policy* within the UK'.[160] The government, it was added, had 'consistently pursued a progressive agenda on social and economic *policy* and can point to sustained progress on social inclusion, reduction in unemployment, and increased funding for education and health care as evidence of its commitment to domestic realisation of the rights set out in the [ICESCR]'.[161] So there seemed to be an assumption on the government's part that protecting and realising ESC rights was mainly if not solely about 'improv[ing] the social and economic environment';[162] indeed the government was 'fully committed' to 'vigorous development of economic, social and cultural *policy*'.[163] With respect to the JCHR's point that there were potential gaps in the legislative protection of certain ESC *rights*, the government argued '[n]o legal system is perfect', but, whilst it accepted that there could be 'room for further improvement in the development of economic, social and cultural rights *policy* in the UK',[164] this was for the government and not for the courts to address. Overall the government believed that 'its progressive social policy is generally in compliance with the ICESCR'. However, 'in cases where existing provisions in the UK do not fully meet a particular requirement of the Covenant, its practice is to bring them into line with the relevant obligation to ensure its implementation in national law'.[165] But here it seemed to be out of the question that the courts should have the capacity to identify any such discrepancies in UK law for *The DCA Response* was defiant of the idea that ESC rights raised substantive issues that might be addressed by the judiciary: 'economic and social rights *are the very stuff of government policy*. They are the issues on which Governments are elected and unelected.'[166] It followed that '[d]ecision-making by the courts on economic and social rights to the extent envisaged by full incorporation of the treaty into domestic law would have profound implications for the role of Parliament in scrutinising Government's policies'. So, '[i]ncorporation of ESC rights into the UK legislation would take decision-making on the basic policy agenda and priorities away from an elected government, counter to the fundamental principles of our democracy'.[167] Furthermore, 'there would be real difficulties with full legal incorporation, as there are issues for which there is no absolute standard, e.g. adequate food, clothing and housing rights, the standards for which are rightly the business of governments to determine, and for democratically elected legislatures to oversee'.[168]

[159] *JCHR ICESCR Report* para 15.   [160] *The DCA Response* para 3, emphasis added.
[161] Ibid, emphasis added. Cf bullet point 3 from *The FCO statement* regarding the right to housing.   [162] Ibid para 9.
[163] Ibid para 3, emphasis added.   [164] Ibid para 4, emphasis added.   [165] Ibid.
[166] Ibid, para 10 emphasis added.   [167] Ibid.   [168] Ibid para 11.

It followed that there was no question of incorporation of ESC rights as set out under the ICESCR for these were characterized *en bloc* as simply non-justiciable on separation of powers grounds and given the commanding influence of article 2(1) ICESCR with its 'progressive realisation' concept. It was 'simply a fact', as *The DCA Response* put it, that there were significant differences in the ways civil and political rights are set out in the ICCPR (which itself has not been incorporated into UK law) and the ICESCR. This 'suggest[ed] strongly that the two sets of rights neither can nor should be implemented in precisely the same way'.[169] Hence the 'Government's approach to economic and social rights' would reflect 'the fact that although some economic and social rights require immediate realisation [no elaboration was provided], most are required to be realised progressively—and their realisation is not a precise art'.[170]

V. A critique of the government's position as regards incorporation of ESC rights

It is submitted that *The FCO statement* was correct to note that, although there are many areas of overlap and the two sets of rights are of equal importance, generally speaking the rights as set out and protected by the ICESCR are different in kind to civil and political rights. Many (though certainly not all) ESC rights are more complex in their realization than civil and political rights. Nonetheless, it is disappointing indeed that *The FCO statement* and *The DCA Response* provided, in the writer's view, such an unbalanced view of the justiciability and incorporation debate, making no reference to the ESCR Committee's General Comments in the process.

The general argument to the effect that incorporation would be 'undemocratic' as such cannot be reconciled with the fact that it would be Parliament itself that would pass any incorporating legislation,[171] plus, if a similar scheme to the Human Rights Act were followed, Parliamentary sovereignty would be preserved.[172] The point that ESC rights are expressed in ambiguous terms[173] and necessarily involve resource allocation issues overlooks the fact that similar criticisms can be levelled at many civil and political rights.[174] The argument expressed in *The FCO statement* that 'there is little point in directly incorporating the Covenant if it

---

169 Ibid para 6.   170 Ibid.

171 Cf Lord Bingham's comments on the democratic nature of the Human Rights Act, *A and Others v Secretary of State for the Home Department* [2004] UKHL 56, HL para 42.

172 Cf *JCHR ICESCR Report* para 65.   173 Cf *The FCO statement* bullet point 4.

174 Art 3 ECHR is perhaps the classic example of a civil and political right framed in inherently ambiguous terms. As regards the resource allocation point, see *JCHR ICESCR Report* paras 71–72 and note the observations of the South African Constitutional Court in *Ex p Chairperson of the Constitutional Assembly: Re Certification of the Constitution of the Republic of South Africa*, 1996 (4) SA 744 (CC) at para 78.

is unclear that it will lead to meaningful and beneficial outcomes' is hard to reconcile with the arguments previously presented by the FCO for incorporation of ESC
rights in Kenya.[175]

The greatest criticism to be made of the government's stance is, of course, the
unsophisticated assertion that the 'constitutionalised' protection of ESC rights
inevitably raises policy issues that are non-justiciable. The disappointing fact is that
the crude nature of such an argument was exposed by the JCHR Report itself[176]
and it has been evident too from the debate over the justiciability of ESC rights that
has informed the negotiations to create an OP for the ICESCR.[177] As we have seen,
to characterize ESC rights *en bloc* as indistinct and incapable of enforcement runs
counter to the ESCR Committee's *General Comments 3* and *9*, the latter of which
noted that such a stance was 'arbitrary and incompatible with the principle that the
two sets of human rights are indivisible and interdependent'.[178] Moreover, there is
now a rich literature on the subject of the justiciability of certain ESC rights,[179]
plus a growing body of case law from national courts and regional communication
mechanisms that point to both the appropriateness and effectiveness of considering specific ESC rights in a judicial context.[180] The latter give the lie to the argument that the separation of powers doctrine can be used as a blanket argument to
deny any role for the courts as regards the protection of such rights. As the editor of
a recent collection of materials on 'Judicial Protection of Economic, Social and
Cultural Rights', Dr Bertrand Ramcharan, former Deputy High Commissioner for
Human Rights, recently put it, 'there can be no doubt that the era of justiciability
of economic, social and cultural rights has arrived'.[181] His book brings together a
collection of caselaw from various parts of the world from which 'one conclusion
stands out . . . : the courts do have a role to play in providing judicial protection of
[ESC] rights'.[182]

Evidently a key difference between civil and political rights and ESC rights as set
out under the ICESCR is that the latter carry with them the obligation of 'progressive realisation' (article 2(1)). It is axiomatic that an effective approach to the full
realization of ESC rights overall will rely very largely on the economic and social

---

[175] Text accompanying n 66–68 (above). Cf the similar reasons cited by those in favour of incorporation of ESC rights for the UK, see *Van Bueren* and *Democratic Audit JCHR Submission*, heading 1.
[176] *JCHR ICESCR Report* paras 64–70. [177] See *Albuquerque Report*.
[178] Above para 10.
[179] See the excellent selection of materials within *Steiner and Alston* at 275–299 and especially
Y Ghai and J Cottrell (eds), *Economic, Social and Cultural Rights in Practice: The Role of Judges in
Implementing Economic, Social and Cultural Rights* (Interights/KKS Printing, 2004), including the
sources cited within the extensive bibliography at 111–115.
[180] See especially B Ramcharan (ed), *Judicial Protection of Economic, Social and Cultural Rights:
Cases and Materials* (Nijhoff, 2005) and *Albuquerque Report* 22–23. The justiciability of the ICESCR
has recently been confirmed by the International Court of Justice, which opined that various provisions of the ICESCR had been violated by Israel's construction of a wall in the Occupied Palestinian
Territory, see *Legal Consequences of the Construction of a Wall in the Occupied Palestinian Territory*
(Advisory Opinion), 9 July 2004, ICJ General List no 131, para 134.
[181] Ramcharan (above) at 3. [182] Ibid at 1.

policies of governments, so generally the protection of ESC rights should be left primarily to the executive and legislature. Policy choices on the best way progressively to realize protection of, for example, the right to housing and education, should be left to Parliament and the government.[183] Therefore few would disagree with the general thrust of the points numbered (1)–(3) from *The FCO statement* insofar as their theme is that in principle the judiciary do not have a major role (if any) to play in holding the executive to account with respect to general measures of economic or social strategy and as regards matters of *general* resource allocation.[184] However, it is submitted this situation stems from the courts' general constitutional position, in particular their lack of institutional capacity or competence in such fields, as opposed, to the broader issue of their democratic legitimacy to protect ESC rights as such.

The major flaw in the arguments presented by the authors of both *The FCO statement* and *The DCA Response* is the assumption that incorporation would entail the courts meddling in matters that should correctly be the exclusive province of the executive and the legislature, for it is very questionable that this would actually be so. In a number of cases over the last decade the UK courts have indirectly addressed what might be considered issues relating to socio-economic rights, for example in the field of access to health facilities and housing, and when resource allocation issues have been relevant.[185] Here case law demonstrates that the courts have addressed issues of resource allocation sensitively and respected the principle of the separation of powers, on the basis that another branch of government is institutionally better qualified to decide the matter.[186] As Lord Bingham has observed, '[t]he allocation of public resources is a matter for Ministers, not courts'.[187] Hence the courts have demonstrated that they take a realistic approach that recognizes their very limited role and institutional competence in matters relating to 'social or economic policy, where opinions may reasonably differ in a democratic society and where choices on behalf of the country as a whole are properly left to Government and to the legislature'.[188] There is no reason to believe that this deferential approach

---

[183] Cf *The FCO statement* point 3 (above).

[184] Cf the similar stance taken by the UK government during the drafting of the ICESCR, see Dennis and Stewart above at 486.

[185] See the annex entitled 'The Justiciability of Socio-Economic Rights in the UK', appended to *Democratic Audit JCHR Submission.* Cf the ESCR Committee, *General Comment 9,* para 10 and *JCHR ICESCR Report* para 72.

[186] See eg, *R v Cambridge Health Authority Ex p B* [1995] 1 WLR 898 (allocation of scarce resources for important but experimental surgery). On the notion of institutional competence or capacity in the context of human rights see J Jowell, 'Judicial Deference: servility, civility or institutional capacity?' (2003) Win, Public L 592. See also J (Lord) Steyn, 'Deference: A Tangled Story' (2005) Sum, Public L 346.

[187] *R v Secretary of State for the Environment, Transport and the Regions, Ex p Spath Holme Ltd* [2001] 2 WLR 15, HL at 396.

[188] *A and Others v Secretary of State for the Home Department* [2004] UKHL 56, per Lord Hope para 108. See also *Poplar Housing and Regeneration Community Association Ltd v Donoghue* [2002] QB48

would change even were the ICESCR to be incorporated to include the concept of 'progressive realisation', for this would not change the courts' institutional competence as such. It is submitted, therefore, that *The FCO statement* grossly exaggerates the idea that the courts will arrogate for themselves the role of executive and Parliament.[189] Of course, there is and can be no cast-iron guarantee against this in individual cases, but there is little to suggest that it would happen. Moreover, the example provided by courts from other jurisdictions[190] suggests that it would not occur. In any case, it may be borne in mind that, if a similar scheme of incorporation to the Human Rights Act were followed, on any issue of legislative interpretation Parliament could have the last word through the legislative process.[191]

In short, the courts in the UK can be trusted to know when to defer to the executive and legislative branches of government on grounds of relative institutional competence. So the 'government by judges' envisaged by *The FCO statement* points (2) and (3) in particular would not happen in practice credible though it sounds in theory. It is far too simplistic to present the separation of powers doctrine as the reason for non-incorporation of ESC rights. However, even if doubts remain a qualified form of incorporation is possible, as we shall now see and comment upon.

('The economic and other implications of any policy in this area are extremely complex and far-reaching. This is an area where, in our judgment, the courts must treat the decisions of Parliament as to what is in the public interest with particulare defence', per Lord Woolf at 72) and *R (Alconbury Development Ltd) v Secretary of State for the Environment, Transport and the Regions* [2001] UKHL 23 para 60, per Lord Nolan. It is submitted that the examination of socio-economic rights by the UK courts would most likely be instructed by the principle that the right in question is one, to adopt the parlance in place in recent judicial application of the Human Rights Act, that grants the executive and Parliament a significant, if not a very significant, 'discretionary area of judgment' with respect to sensitive areas about which the other branches of government have a greater institutional competence. See D Pannick and A Lester, *Human Rights Law and Practice* (2nd edn, Lexis-Nexis UK, 2004) para 3.19. See also *Minister of Health v Treatment Action Campaign (no 2)* [2002] 5 SA 721 at 735 where it was stated in the South African Constitutional Court that the separation of powers doctrine was not a reason for the court's lack of jurisdiction, but that this doctrine was relevant to 'the deference that Courts should show to decisions taken by the Executive concerning the formulation of policies', para 22.

[189] See also especially *JCHR ICESCR Report* paras 64–72. In its *General Comment 3* the ESCR Committee envisaged that retrogressive measures with regard to the protection of ESC rights could, in certain circumstances, be justified. It would seem fair to conclude, therefore, that a reasonably less progressive approach in one field (for example, with reference to point number (2) from *The FCO statement* above, being realization of the right to health) may potentially be justified by reference to a reasonable policy of increased advancement with respect to other rights. More generally a downturn in the economic climate might feasibly justify a less progressive approach in one field as against another, see Craven (above) at 132.

[190] See Ramcharan (above). See also *Albuquerque Report* 13–16, the Rapporteur noting that in her view national courts addressing ESC rights have respected 'the margin of discretion of public authorities to take decisions on resource allocation' (at 14); have applied 'objective standards as a means of adjudicating the compatibility of resource-related decisions of public authorities' (15); and emphasizing in conclusion that 'judicial and quasi-judicial consideration of economic, social and cultural rights [do] not raise any judicial conundrums that are substantially different from others already dealt with in other areas of the law' (at 16). For arguments opposing the justiciability of ESC rights see Dennis and Stewart (above).

[191] See Human Rights Act 1998, s 4 (primary legislation remains fully in force even if a court makes a 'declaration of incompatibility').

A. Qualified incorporation?

It will have been noticed that the authors of both the FCO and DCA documents proceeded on the assumption that the ICESCR be incorporated comprehensively or not at all. In its report the JCHR had gone to considerable lengths to point out that an acceptable model of incorporation of protection for ESC rights could be found for the UK, one that could guard against the risk of constitutional improprieties set out by the FCO and DCA.[192] The JCHR explicitly accepted that, in relation to rights that are to be progressively realized in particular, any model of incorporation could clearly mark out the court's institutional competence and so provide a safeguard against the prospect of handing over policy decisions to the courts. The mode of incorporation could specifically limit 'judicial scrutiny to grounds of reasonableness and non-discrimination'.[193]

On this topic much has been written about the experience of South Africa,[194] so what follows here may be very brief. As is well known, selected ESC rights have been introduced into the South African constitution on terms that require the state to 'take reasonable legislative and other measures, within its available resources, to achieve [their] progressive realisation'.[195] The rights in question are generally expressed in non-absolute, equality of access terms: such as the right of 'access to adequate housing'[196] and 'the right of access to (a) health care services, including reproductive health care; (b) sufficient food and water; and (c) social security, including, if they are unable to support themselves and their dependants, appropriate social assistance'.[197] In its application and interpretation of these provisions of the Constitution, the South African Constitutional Court has illustrated that the judiciary has been highly aware of the limits of its own institutional competence and correspondingly aware of

---

[192] *JCHR ICESCR Report* paras 51–74. Several NGOs submitting observations to the JCHR favoured some form of incorporation of ESC rights, including JUSTICE ('Memorandum from JUSTICE' (annex to *JCHR ICESCR Report*), Democratic Audit (*Democratic Audit JCHR Submission*), and the Committee on the Administration of Justice ('Memorandum from Committee on the Administration of Justice' (annex to *JCHR ICESCR Report*). However, contrary to the impression given by *The FCO statement*, no NGO providing submissions to the JCHR called for the incorporation of 'all' Covenant rights. JUSTICE, for example, argued that full judicial incorporation of every right was not necessarily appropriate, instead justiciability should be addressed on a 'case-by-case basis' for each right, (above) para 8.
[193] Ibid para 73. For discussion of different ways of incorporating ESC rights see *Van Bueren* at 468–471.
[194] See eg, D Brand and C Heyns (eds), *Socio-Economic Rights in South Africa* (Pretoria University Law Press, 2005); G Budlender, 'Justiciability of Socio-Economic Rights: Some South African Experiences', in *Ghai and J Cottrell*; A Sachs, 'The judicial enforcement of socio-economic rights: the Grootboom case' (2003), 56 Current Legal Problems 579; and M Pieterse, 'Coming to Terms with Judicial Enforcement of Socio-Economic Rights' (2004), 20(3) South African J on Human Rights 383.
[195] Constitution of the Republic of South Africa (1996), s 26(2) cf s 27(2).
[196] Section 26(1), emphasis added.
[197] Section 27(1), emphasis added. The 1996 Constitution also includes the right to environmental protection (s 24), state measures within available resources to foster equitable access to land (s 25(5)) and education (s 29).

the constitutional superiority of the other branches of government especially in the context of resource allocation issues. These points were made very clear by the JCHR in its report which noted that in the application of ESC rights the South African courts: 'have been sensitive to the counter-majoritarian potential of the economic and social rights guarantees in the Constitution, where they are applied by the courts to overturn the decisions of Government'.[198] The Constitutional Court in South Africa had 'not used . . . constitutional rights as a blunt instrument against Government policy, but [had] crafted standards of review which assess the reasonableness and non-discriminatory impact of Government action in complying with the constitutional imperatives of socio-economic rights protection'. As the JCHR observed, in fact the review standards employed were based on principles of judicial review and respect for the decision-making of the executive 'which are already applied in the UK courts, alongside review of the proportionality of interference with ECHR rights, under the HRA'.[199] The JCHR cited[200] in particular the South African Constitutional Court cases of *Soobramoney*[201] (access to health care; renal dialysis machinery) and *Treatment Action Campaign*[202] (government obstacles to provision of anti-HIV drug) and argued that the judicial approaches on display in those cases could be familiar to UK courts. Such case law has demonstrated that there are aspects to the protection of ESC rights that can come within the institutional competence of the courts. A clearly discriminatory approach to the provision of ESC rights would be an example, one that may not raise resource allocation issues at all.[203] The right to housing and to the highest attainable standard of health may seem to be framed in imprecise terms, but case law from South Africa and other jurisdictions has demonstrated that aspects of these rights are sufficiently determinate to be capable of judicial enforcement.[204] Moreover, a legislative policy may be *manifestly* incompatible with the nature of an ESC right and fail to promote at all the general welfare in a democratic society[205] (and so the policy, by reference to ESC rights is manifestly without reasonable foundation). If so, it is arguable that, if ESC rights are to be viewed as equally as important as civil and political rights, then such an extreme incursion into their protection should be justiciable.

---

[198] *JCHR ICESCR Report* para 66.   [199] Ibid. See also para 67. Cf *Van Bueren* at 460.

[200] Ibid para 61.

[201] *Soobramoney v Minister for Health, KwaZula Natal* (1998) (1) SA 765 (CC), 27 Nov 1997.

[202] *Minister of Health v Treatment Action Campaign* 2002 (5) SA721(CC) 5 July 2002.

[203] Art 2(2) ICESCR. For further analysis see *Albuquerque Report* para (jj).

[204] Eg, as regards the right to health, judicial safeguards may come in the form of, firstly, the enforcement of a guarantee against discrimination and procedural impropriety in the enjoyment of access to health care facilities, and, secondly, the avoidance of manifest unreasonableness as regards government policy in the delivery of health care services, see the case law within Ramcharan (above) ch 8 and *JCHR ICESCR Report* para 59.

[205] Cf art 4 ICESCR, 'the State may subject [ICESCR] rights only to such limitations as are determined by law only in so far as this may be compatible with the nature of these rights and solely for the purpose of promoting the general welfare in a democratic society'.

It was on the basis of arguments such as these that the members of the JCHR took the view that 'the case for incorporating guarantees of the Covenant rights in UK law, either by incorporating the terms of the Covenant itself, or by developing domestic formulations of the Covenant rights as part of a UK Bill of Rights, merits further attention'.[206] It is submitted that this statement has been borne out by subsequent developments, as noted below. However, *The DCA Response* failed to even respond to arguments for a qualified form of incorporation of ESC rights.

B. A case for qualified incorporation? Lessons from the *Limbuela* case

As we have observed, the DCA argued that ESC rights 'are the very stuff of government policy' and that these are 'the issues on which Governments are elected and unelected'.[207] Though this is a gross simplification of the substantive content of ESC rights, the point is consistent with the government's view that it is the democratically accountable branches of government that must be solely responsible for such rights protection. This boldly assumes that the mechanisms of political accountability, especially general elections, and reliance on the goodwill of Parliament are in themselves sufficient to ensure that the legislature's policy choice will never display a manifestly unreasonable disregard for the protection of core ESC rights. However, it will be argued in the paragraphs below that a recent example does exist of a specific instance when ESC rights have not been taken as seriously as they should by the executive and legislature. That is, even in the UK cases can arise which demonstrate the value of the courts as last-resort protectors of fundamental ESC rights, providing a constitutional check against primary legislation that is arguably incompatible with the ICESCR.

The *Limbuela* case[208] concerned section 55 of the Nationality, Immigration, and Asylum Act 2002,[209] providing the Secretary of State with power to withhold assistance from certain asylum seekers[210] who were destitute, subject to the 'safeguard' that support should be given when this was 'to the extent necessary for the purpose of avoiding a breach of the person's [*ECHR*] rights'.[211] This ruthless arrangement was secured by late amendments to a Bill[212] that was, in the words of the legal adviser to the JCHR at the time, 'steamrollered'[213] through Parliament in

---

[206] *JCHR ICESCR Report* para 73, see also para 70.

[207] *The DCA Response* para 10.

[208] *R (on the application of Limbuela) v Secretary of State for the Home Department* [2005] UKHL 66; [2005] 3 WLR 1014.   [209] The Nationality, Immigration and Asylum Act 2002 c. 41.

[210] Those asylum seekers whose claim was not made as soon as reasonably practical after their arrival in the UK.

[211] Section 55(5)(a). On the *Limbuela* case see C Warbrick, 'Economic and Social Interests and the European Convention on Human Rights', chapter 10 in this book.

[212] For an overview see JCHR, *Nationality, Immigration and Asylum Bill: Further Report*, 23rd Report (2001–02) (HL 176; HC 1255) paras 1–5.   [213] Feldman (above) at 109.

a 'chaotic joke of a legislative process' and which entailed that the JCHR had only a limited opportunity to comment on the human rights implications involved. It did, however, draw attention to the potential incompatibility of section 55 with, amongst other things, articles 3 and 8 of the ECHR, but also article 11(1) of the ICESCR.[214] A potential 'deliberate breach'[215] of the ICESCR, as one peer saw it, was therefore brought to the attention of the government and Parliament. However, this did not prevent the passage of the legislation as the government refused to accept that any human rights would be violated. In effect the Home Office took the view that the right to adequate housing protected by article 11(1) ICESCR amounted to no more than a guarantee that individuals should not be housed in such awful conditions that they amounted to 'inhuman and degrading treatment' (article 3, ECHR). The JCHR is to be applauded for its attempt, which proved in vain, to inform here.[216]

If one lesson of *Limbuela* might be that the democratic branches of government may not take ESC rights as seriously as they might in very specific instances, another is that the courts may provide a constitutional check on possible derelictions of duty, even if the case is 'intensely political' and has possible resource implications.[217] With no reference to the ICESCR,[218] the House of Lords unanimously concluded that the withdrawal of support by the Secretary of State to asylum seekers (who were also denied permission to work) could entail a breach of article 3 of the ECHR. Yet one lesson that must *not* be taken from *Limbuela* is that the ECHR provides an appropriate safeguard for the infringement of fundamental ESC rights, such as article 11(1) ICESCR and, also, arguably, 'the right of everyone to social security, including social insurance' (article 9 ICESCR). This is surely evident from the government's own submission to the House of Lords that mere rough-sleeping alone would not suffice for the purposes of article 3 ECHR, but that additional elements, such as individuals being driven to begging or prostitution, were required.[219] Although the Law Lords set the threshold for the applicability of article 3 at a higher level than this, there were differences of opinion regarding the point at which it would operate.[220] Obviously that provision should provide protection against only the worst forms of destitution. It is surely the case that, as the government refused to accept

---

[214] For the text of art 11(1) see n 54. In fact the potential violation of this provision was drawn to the government's attention not once but twice, (above) 23rd Report (2001–02) paras 11–15, see also JCHR, *Nationality, Immigration, and Asylum Bill,* 17th Report (2001–02) (HL 132; HC 961), para 66. [215] Lord Goodhart, HL Debates 24 Oct 2002 col 1465.
[216] JCHR (above) 23rd Report (2001–02) para 12. It transpired that there was virtually no reference to the ICESCR in the final debate in House of Commons, where the guillotine was applied and debate commenced after complaints that the amendments timeframe meant that MPs were unprepared, see Simon Hughes MP, HC Debates 5 Nov 2002 col 146.
[217] See Lord Hope's judgment in *Limbuela* (above) at para 13.
[218] The Covenant was not cited either in the High Court or the Court of Appeal judgment.
[219] See Lord Hope's judgment in *Limbuela* (above) at paras 59–60.
[220] An illustration, perhaps, of the ambiguous nature of civil and political rights, cf bullet point (4) from *The FCO statement* noted above.

during the passage of the Act, there *is* a significant gap between the level of protection afforded by article 3 of the ECHR and the minimum level of protection to be afforded by a state such as the UK with respect to article 11(1) of the ICESCR. Certainly, the exact content of what article 11(1) ICESCR requires is not a 'precise art' (to adopt the words of *The DCA Response*) and, arguably, *this* particular aspect of the enjoyment of this specific ESC right may not be appropriate for adjudication by the courts (cf *The FCO statement*, point 3). Yet, significant aspects of the right to housing *are* justiciable,[221] and, with respect to the facts of *Limbuela*, it is submitted that it could have been in the courts' institutional competence to identify when the executive may have breached a requirement to 'take reasonable legislative and other measures, within its available resources, to achieve the progressive realisation of'[222] the rights protected by article 11(1) ICESCR as noted above (as well as, arguably, article 9). With reference to this right was the legislative scheme in *Limbuela* not patently unreasonable or discriminatory, or both? In judging reasonableness it may be borne in mind that, with respect to ICESCR rights, the ESCR Committee has stated that every state party has 'a minimum core obligation to ensure the satisfaction of, at the very least, minimum essential levels of each of the rights' guaranteed by the Covenant, failing which the latter 'would be largely deprived of its *raison d'être*'.[223] For the avoidance of doubt it should also be stressed that the government did not justify the withdrawal of financial and other support for the category of asylum seekers concerned primarily by the issue of limited resources, but the policy of sending a message to bogus asylum seekers that the UK was not a 'soft touch' on asylum.[224]

The NGO JUSTICE argued that the section 55 scheme in issue in *Limbuela* revealed 'the very real failure of UK law to recognize ESC rights as independent and free-standing human rights'.[225] It was stated, '[i]f we are to take the provisions

---

[221] Jurisprudence on the right to housing as incorporated in the South African and Indian legal systems provides no substance at all to the claim that such a right allows the courts to address 'Governmental economic policy', see Ramcharan (above) ch 11. On the right to housing see the ESCR Committee, *General Comment 4* (13 Dec 1991) E/1992/23, annex III; S Leckie, 'The Right to Housing' in A Eide, C Krause, and A Rosas (eds), *Economic, Social and Cultural Rights: A Textbook* (2nd edn, Nijhoff, 2001); S Marks and A Clapham, 'Housing' in *International Human Rights Lexicon* (OUP, 2005) 209 and C Chinkin, 'The United Nations Decade for the Elimination of Poverty: What role for International Law?' (2001), 54 Current Legal Problems 553 at 574–580.

[222] Cf ss 26(2) and 27(2) of the South African Constitution.

[223] ESCR Committee, *General Comment 3* (above) para 10. According to the ESCR Committee 'a State party in which any significant number of individuals is deprived of essential foodstuffs, of essential primary health care, of basic shelter and housing, or of the most basic forms of education is, prima facie, failing to discharge its obligations under the Covenant', para 10. Since art 2(1) requires each State party 'to take the necessary steps to the maximum of its available resources', for a state to justify a failure to provide minimum core obligations based on lack of resources it must 'demonstrate that every effort has been made to use all resources that are at its disposition in an effort to satisfy, as a matter of priority, those minimum obligations', para 10, see also para 11. See also JCHR (above). 23rd Report (2001–02) para 12 and *JCHR ICESCR Report* para 121.

[224] Cf art 4 ICESCR (above).

[225] *Memorandum from JUSTICE* (above). In fact, this point was made with respect to the factually very similar case of *R v Secretary of State For The Home Department, Ex p Q and Others* [2003] EWCA

of the ICESCR seriously, then it must be clear that state-imposed destitution is itself a violation of ESC rights, rather than the more severe consequences of such destitution'.[226] *Limbuela* also seemed to validate the view expressed by the NGO Democratic Audit that, 'as is currently the case for civil and political rights, the Courts should be a bulwark for ESC rights against popular majoritarianism, where this threatens these human rights in practice'.[227] Similarly, Lord Lester,[228] a figure who was so influential in the campaign to incorporate the ECHR, and Colm O'Cinneide have argued (in fact two years before *Limbuela* was delivered) that '[t]he judiciary has an important role to play where there exists a sufficiently gross failure to uphold basic socio-economic rights'.[229] When 'the other two branches have comprehensively failed to fulfil their responsibilities', they argue, then 'the "least dangerous branch" has a duty to intervene'.[230] More generally the legislation in issue in *Limbuela* and the status of the individuals affected by it brings to mind the comments of Justice Albie Sachs[231] of the South African Constitutional Court when writing on the topic of the judicial enforcement of ESC rights in South Africa. He has criticized the argument that the executive and legislative branches of government should have *sole* responsibility for protection of ESC rights based on institutional competence or indeed democratic legitimacy. On certain issues, he points out, it is advantageous for the effective protection of human rights that judges are not accountable to the electorate in the same way as the government. Such a situation would be when it is popular for a government to target marginalized communities who may be the object of majoritarian prejudice and hostility. The latter may be precisely those requiring the protection offered by a branch of government that does not have to answer to the electorate and which by being independent can 'ensure that justice is done to all without fear, favour, or prejudice'.[232] Justice Sachs acknowledges that the courts are 'institutionally

---

Civ 364. JUSTICE argued that the refusal of the Secretary of State to provide support or permission to work engaged art 6 (right to work), art 9 (right to Social Security), art 11 (right to Adequate Standard of Living), and art 12 (right to Physical and Mental Health) ICESCR.

[226] Ibid. The NGO also pointed out that 'it is apparent from the judgment of *Q* that the jurisprudence of civil and political rights (in this case, arts 3 and 8 ECHR) is liable to become distorted to accommodate ESC rights-values where legal recognition of ESC rights is lacking'.

[227] *Democratic Audit JCHR Submission.*   [228] Lord Lester is a member of the JCHR.

[229] A (Lord) Lester and C O'Cinneide, 'The Effective Protection of Socio-Economic Rights', in *Ghai and Cottrell.* They add '[n]or should the possibility of such intervention be confined to the courts of the developing world. The deprivation and social exclusion inflicted on asylum seekers in the UK by the recently introduced voucher support scheme could constitute an example of a sufficiently gross failure to respect socio-economic rights so as to justify judicial intervention', at 21 (fn omitted).

[230] Ibid. Lester and O'Cinneide argued that '[t]he Indian and South African jurisprudence illustrate when this intervention can and should take place'. On the former, see S Muralidhar, 'Economic, Social and Cultural Rights: An Indian Response to the Justiciability Debate', in *Ghai and Cottrell.* See also *JCHR ICESCR Report* para 40–43.

[231] Sachs (above) at 587–589. See also A Sachs, 'Enforcement of Social and Economic Rights', Draft (uncorrected) Transcript of Lecture at LSE, 27 Feb 2003 (available at <http://www.lse.ac.uk/Depts/human-rights>) accessed 3 Nov 2006.   [232] Ibid at 588.

completely unsuited to take [policy] decisions on houses, hospitals, schools, and electricity' for they 'do not have the know-how and the capacity to handle those questions'. However, the courts 'do know about human dignity, [they] do know about oppression, and [they] do know about things that reduce a human being to a status below that which our society would regard as tolerable'.[233]

In summary, the arguments for a qualified form of incorporation, perhaps on the lines of the South African Constitution, become stronger when, contrary to what has been said by the FCO and DCA, there is clear evidence that the protection of specific ESC rights is not taken as seriously as it should by the executive and legislature. It is submitted that the facts underpinning *Limbuela* provide an example of this and the limited yet important constitutional safeguard that the courts could perform in identifying manifestly unreasonable violations of ESC rights. The government continues to argue that it protects ESC rights through various legislative schemes. But in practice specific ESC rights that are protected in this way today may be lost by repeal of such legislation tomorrow or the exclusion of certain unpopular categories of people from its remit and the consequential denial of opportunity for redress before the courts by way of judicial review. *Limbuela* demonstrated how meaningless specific international obligations under the ICE-SCR might become in practical terms. The prospect that the situation revealed by that case will be repeated, and that the limitations of article 3 of the Convention will be exposed, will persist if the view is taken that the Human Rights Act fills all lacunas in the UK constitution as regards positive protection of human rights. It may be observed that such a view seemed to be inherent in the legislative scheme in issue in *Limbuela*, since by its very design it provided for the potential denial of all rights other than Convention rights as defined under the Human Rights Act.[234] If the government is as serious about protecting ESC rights as it claims to be it should come up with more credible arguments than those presented in *The DCA Response* and engage with the debate on qualified incorporation in a meaningful way. Qualified incorporation—constitutionalizing the protection of certain core ESC rights as with the example of the South African constitution and confining judicial scrutiny to grounds of reasonableness and non-discrimination—would not lead to 'government by judges'. It would reflect a sensible distribution of powers between, on the one hand, the proper functions of the legislator and executive with their primary role in implementing ESC rights and, on the other, the role of the courts potentially acting in a very much secondary capacity as last resort 'protector' of the most fundamental manifestation of core ESC rights in rare cases of manifest unreasonableness and/or discrimination. That in turn would reflect the view that

---

[233] Ibid at 588–589.

[234] Courts in the UK will usually try to interpret legislation consistently with international obligations for they proceed on the assumption that Parliament does not intend to legislate in a manner incompatible with the UK's international legal obligations, *Garland v British Rail Engineering Ltd* [1983] 2 AC 751, HL at 771 per Lord Diplock. Would that assumption have applied in *Limbuela* with respect to the ICESCR given the specific wording of the legislation in issue?

the courts should have a role in protecting basic human dignity in a democratic society (even beyond article 3 of the Convention). It would tally with article 22 of the Universal Declaration of Human Rights insofar as it recognizes that no matter how unpopular the public perceives certain individuals to be they remain 'member[s] of society' such that the government should not take unreasonable or discriminatory steps to interfere with the realization of the (minimum) 'economic, social and cultural rights indispensable for [his/her] dignity and the free development of [his/her] personality'.[235]

Finally on *Limbuela*, it should be noted that in its ICESCR Report the JCHR specifically drew attention to the likelihood, in the JCHR's view, that articles 9 and 11 ICESCR would be violated by the legislation impugned in the case.[236] How did *The DCA Response* react to this? It requoted the extract from the JCHR Report on this point—but then failed to comment at all on the central point, rather it referred to general government policy on homelessness, which it defended.[237]

C. ESC rights and the development of policy

It was pointed out in *The DCA Response* that according to *General Comment 9* 'comprehensive incorporation is not essential so long as measures are taken to protect the Covenant rights'.[238] To this was added the statement, '[a] corollary of this... is that the justiciability of economic, social and cultural rights is ultimately a political rather than a legal question. That is to say, the language of the Covenant affords sufficient scope to states parties to determine for themselves how economic, social and cultural rights are to be protected in the domestic legal order.'[239] In fact, as we have seen, *General Comment 9* places a heavy emphasis on the desirability of incorporation[240] whilst the ESCR Committee itself was highly critical of the UK for its failures on this front.[241] Amongst other things *General Comment 9* refers to the need to have in place 'appropriate means of redress, or remedies,... available to any aggrieved individual or group' and states '*appropriate means of ensuring Governmental accountability must be put in place*'.[242] In this connection, and putting the issue of direct incorporation aside for now, the following question might be asked: if the government is as serious about protecting ESC rights as it claims to be via the statements and responses noted in this chapter, what precise measures does and will it take to ensure that Covenant rights are more fully and progressively recognized in UK law? In particular, exactly what means of 'ensuring Governmental accountability' are in place which ensure that full legal effect is given to the ICESCR?

When appearing before the ESCR Committee in 2001 Mr Fifoot had acknowledged that '[t]he United Kingdom did not have any mechanisms for ensuring the

---

[235] Universal Declaration of Human Rights, art 22.

[236] *JCHR ICESCR Report* para 121 (the Report was published over a year before the Law Lords' ruling in *Limbuela* was delivered).   [237] *The DCA Response* paras 35–38.

[238] Ibid para 12.   [239] Ibid.   [240] Above.   [241] Above.

[242] Above, emphasis added.

effective implementation of the Covenant'.[243] It had been stated, rather unconvincingly, that 'senior officials and decision-makers were perfectly aware of the state party's obligations under the Covenant and other international human rights instruments'.[244] During the JCHR inquiry written questions were put to the FCO asking what institutional arrangements were in place within the administration that were designed to ensure that obligations under the Covenant were taken into account.[245] The FCO's replies were very limited indeed.[246] The government simply asserted that it did comply with the ICESCR as 'existing arrangements already provide sufficient legal and administrative guarantees of rights contained in the Covenant'.[247] But there was virtually no expansion of this except the familiar assertion that Covenant commitments were undertaken via 'specific laws, policies and practices which implement the various rights set out in the Covenant', and that these were detailed in the Report provided to the JCHR.[248] Hence the JCHR was left to work its way through the FCO Report submitted to it and draw its own conclusions as to how the ICESCR was implemented from a detailed document that was far from clear in identifying *precisely* how individuals could vindicate their ESC rights at the domestic level.[249] *The DCA Response* provided no further clarification on these points. Thus, so far as the author is aware, there never has been any clear statement from the UK government regarding, for example, what precise aspects of the Covenant it regards as immediately enforceable and capable of violation through retrogression and/or discrimination, and the corresponding legal measures in place to address this. Meanwhile, *The DCA Response* states that it is government policy to bring UK law into line with ICESCR obligations, 'in cases where existing provisions in the UK do not fully meet a particular requirement of the Covenant'.[250] However, *specific* examples of when this practice has been employed in relation to specific provisions of the Covenant have never been provided. Has a detailed and comprehensive audit of UK law in relation to the Covenant, in particular as regards 'ensuring Governmental accountability' ever been undertaken?[251]

---

[243] Above para 22. See also para 37.

[244] In its Concluding Observations the ESCR Committee had criticized UK training programmes for legal and government officials for giving inadequate attention to ESC rights (above) para 13.   [245] Cf ESCR Committee, *Concluding Observations, UK,* 2002 (above) para 25.

[246] See *FCO Memoranda* (above) paras 22–24, 27, 29, 32–33.   [247] Ibid para 27.

[248] Ibid para 32. It was added, again rather unconvincingly, that '[t]he Government's civil service code states that all civil servants have "a duty to comply with the law, including international law and treaty obligations" and therefore all human rights treaties to which the UK is a party (including the Covenant) must be taken into account in the formulation of Government policy', para 33.

[249] The ESCR Committee had been placed in the same position some two or so years earlier, see text accompanying n 81.   [250] See text accompanying n 165.

[251] At the time of writing there is no mention at all of ESC rights within the relevant (ie human rights) section of the DCA's website (<http://www.dca.gov.uk/hract/hramenu.htm> accessed 31 Jan 2006) and no references to the same were contained in the DCA's Annual Report for 2004–5, DCA, *Delivering Justice Rights and Democracy* (Cm 653: June 2005).

Against this background, and considering the passage of the legislation subsequently in issue in *Limbuela*, plus the lackadaisical approach to the ESCR Committee's Concluding Observations, it is not surprising that the JCHR Report expressed doubts regarding the existence of a 'culture of respect for human rights'[252] to include ESC rights in the UK. It was suggested that ESC rights as set out in the Covenant were regarded as 'the poor cousins of the civil and political rights incorporated into UK law by the Human Rights Act'.[253] The JCHR inquiry had 'most particularly revealed':

> that insufficient attention is currently given within Government to the ways in which [ESC] rights can be used to provide a point of reference in the development of policy and legislation.[254]

As if to verify the continuing relevance of the very point being made, *The DCA Response* completely failed to comment on this direct statement. Indeed one could read that document and remain completely oblivious to the JCHR's far-reaching 'institutional' criticism. Worse still, when Harriet Harman MP appeared before the JCHR for general scrutiny with respect to the work of her Department on 16 January 2006 her comments in response to questioning suggested that she was unaware of the JCHR's censure of the government regarding ESC rights protection. Acknowledging that the DCA had recently taken over responsibility for the ICESCR she told the JCHR, '[i]f we are not doing as much as you think we should be doing on that [ie protecting ESC rights], and you think we are doing it in the wrong way, we would very much welcome hearing that from you'.[255] This statement was made less than a week after *The DCA Response* was delivered to the JCHR and over a year since the JCHR Report had been published.

1. Improving the culture of respect

In order to improve the culture of respect for human rights the JCHR had recommended that statements made under section 19 of the Human Rights Act could be extended to cover treaties such as the ICESCR, that in preparing legislative proposals government departments should 'look beyond' the ECHR and have in mind 'the wider international obligations which the UK has accepted in the human rights field', plus that this should be reflected in the explanatory notes to Bills.[256] *The DCA Response*, blinkered by its stance on the justiciability question, rejected the recommendation as being of little practical value.[257] *Limbuela* and the 2002 Act was a prime example of the relevance of this process. Were the government to clearly state that certain legislation in the field of specific ESC rights had been introduced in order to fulfil specific ICESCR (or other) obligations this could be

---

[252] *JCHR ICESCR Report* para 163.   [253] Ibid.   [254] Ibid para 164.
[255] Harriet Harman MP (n 137 above) at Q13.
[256] *JCHR ICESCR Report* para 166. See also paras 84–88.   [257] *The DCA Response* para 13.

significant for other reasons too. The courts assume that legislation enacted in this way is intended to be effective for that purpose and will interpret the legislation accordingly.[258]

To enhance a culture of respect for ESC rights the JCHR recommended that the DCA together with the new (then proposed) Commission for Equality and Human Rights 'develop ways of measuring, with some degree of objectivity, progress in realising the Covenant rights'.[259] In this connection the JCHR had been particularly critical of the government for viewing the progressive realization aspect of ESC rights as weakening the protection afforded. It was emphasized that this concept 'require[d] states to "take steps" with immediate and continued effect, towards the protection of each of the Covenant rights'. 'Such steps', the JCHR went on:

should be 'deliberate, concrete and targeted'. *Progressive realisation requires a clear programme or plan of action for the progressive implementation of each of the Covenant rights.* This plan of action should take into account the [ESCR Committee's] Concluding Observations . . . and general comments.[260]

The DCA Response failed to address this, albeit it did note that the future Commission for Equality and Human Rights[261] would have promotional and (chiefly) advisory functions which could cover ESC rights.[262] Nor did *the DCA Response* address the failure of the UK government to establish a 'Human Rights Plan of Action', to include the steps it would take in the progressive implementation of the ICESCR, another issue that had been highlighted by the JCHR.[263] There was no specific reply either in the Response to the JCHR's call, forming the very last words of the 'Conclusion' to its Report, for new energy to be directed to the place of 'Covenant rights . . . throughout the public sector' with the new Commission for Equality and Human Rights viewed as an institution with a key role to play for Covenant rights for it could 'provide a framework which unites the concerns of both "equality" and of "human rights"'.[264] As the JCHR had put it '[t]he Government, as well as the Commission, needs to promote the Covenant rights as a set of *positive guarantees* and aspirations—as a standard under which the endeavours of Parliament, the Government, public authorities and civil society can unite'.[265]

Finally, regarding specific substantive matters, the JCHR Report itself had addressed a number of policy issues in the field of socio-economic rights (including inequality and poverty;[266] workplace rights[267] and the right to strike;[268] and

---

[258] See eg, *R (Mullen) v Secretary of State for the Home Department* [2004] UKHL 18.
[259] *JCHR ICESCR Report* para 165.
[260] Ibid para 48 (footnotes omitted and emphasis added).
[261] A new Commission for Equality and Human Rights will be created in 2007 (by virtue of The Equality Act 2006). This Commission can have regard to ESC rights, see A (Lord) Lester and K Beattie, 'The New Commission for Equality and Human Rights' (2005) Sum, Public L 197 at 200.   [262] *The DCA Response* paras 15–18.
[263] *JCHR ICESCR Report* paras 80–83.   [264] Ibid para 167.
[265] Ibid emphasis added.   [266] *JCHR ICESCR Report* Ch 7.   [267] Ibid Ch 8.
[268] Ibid.

homelessness[269]), as the Committee sought to demonstrate that an increased determination to take into account obligations under the ICESCR might improve policy-making by the executive.[270] In its turn *The DCA Response* provided some detailed commentary that rejected the JCHR's criticism with respect to various of the substantive issues raised.[271] Arguably the most positive aspect of the Response was confirmation of the government's commitment to a Single Equality Act aiming to modernize and simplify equality legislation.[272] In this connection the Equality Act 2006 was passed in February 2006.[273]

VI. Conclusion

In a book published in 1997 and co-edited by Professor David Harris it was stated that the incorporation of civil and political rights into UK law and practice would 'inevitably raise questions about the status and implementation of other human rights standards, including socio-economic rights, in the UK'.[274] This prediction has certainly come true. In the JCHR's general report on its work over the 2001–2005 Parliament it was noted that the 'greatest dispute'[275] between UN treaty bodies and the UK government was as regards the 'susceptibility' of ESC rights to incorporation. Indeed this raised 'a fundamental question for the UK and its idea of human rights'.[276] That question, it was noted, had 'largely been avoided' as the Human Rights Act simply incorporated the ECHR, so the UK lacked the experience of 'the process of negotiating the terms of a Bill of Rights' as had been the case in South Africa and for the European Union in the development of the Charter of Fundamental Rights.[277] This situation, the JCHR opined, was 'perhaps to the detriment of our collective understanding of, and agreement on, human rights principles and standards'.[278] Back in 1997, there may have been optimism

---

[269] Ibid paras 117–121.

[270] The JCHR Report did address some substantive issues of domestic law, which it regarded as potentially at variance with the international legal obligations imposed by the ICESCR. For example, it urged the government to give higher priority to the development of a single Equality Act (para 111); it expressed concerns about the law on physical punishment of children (para 148) and welcomed law reform relating to domestic violence (para 146); it criticized the law on collective bargaining (paras 143–144) by reference to the Covenant; it also called for a review on the law relating to the right to strike (para 142).   [271] *The DCA Response* paras 19–86.

[272] Ibid para 28.   [273] The Equality Act 2006 (c.3).

[274] A Owers, 'Foreword' in R Burchill and D Harris (eds), *Economic, Social and Cultural rights: their Implementation in United Kingdom Law* (University of Nottingham Human Rights Law Centre, 1999) at xv.   [275] JCHR (above) (19th Report of 2004–05) para 188.

[276] Ibid para 190.

[277] Charter of Fundamental Rights of the European Union (2000/C 364/01). Although this does not create free-standing legal rights as such, it covers certain ESC rights including work place rights (arts 27–33), social security rights (art 34), and right of access to preventative health case (art 35). See D Ashiagbor, 'Economic and Social Rights in the European Charter of Fundamental Rights' (2004) 1 Eur Human Rights L Rev 62.

[278] Ibid. Lord Hoffman of the Judicial House of Lords has commented that 'human rights' might be equated with 'the rights essential to the life and dignity of the individual in a democratic society',

that the Human Rights Act would be but a first step in a longer term project for the creation of a UK Bill of Rights, possibly to include protection for ESC rights in some form.[279] However, ten years on it seems most unlikely that this will happen.[280]

Many of the reasons presented by the 'new' Labour government against incorporation of ESC rights are not dissimilar to those presented in the 1980s by the Conservative administration, then opposed to incorporation of the ECHR.[281] At their core the reasons presented by the government are that incorporation runs counter to fundamental principles of democratic accountability.[282] By contrast the JCHR view was that ESC rights protection under the South Africa Constitution had strengthened this very concept.[283] More generally, *qualified* incorporation of key ESC rights would be consistent with the constitutional trend represented by the Human Rights Act, ie Parliamentary recognition of the inappropriateness of total reliance upon the mechanisms of political accountability for the protection of human rights and the important role to be played by the courts in a modern democratic society as protectors of such rights insofar as to do so is within their institutional competence. With incorporation of the Convention the constitution has witnessed 'a shift from . . . a "sovereigntist" to a constitutional perception of the role of the judiciary, which emphasizes the courts' role as an integral component in a constitutional machinery that seeks to secure accountable government'.[284] This writer does not pretend that the case for incorporation of ESC rights into domestic law is as compelling as it was for the ECHR, but the truth is that from time to time even a democratic government can flagrantly abuse its power in the field of ESC rights, and it is submitted that the *Limbeula* case was an illustration of this. There seems to be little reason why the role of the courts to secure

---

Matthews v Ministry of Defence [2003] 1 AC 1163, para 26. He opined that the 'exact limits of such rights are debatable', that the ECHR had little 'trace of economic rights', but that it was 'well arguable that human rights include the right to a minimum standard of living, without which many of the other rights would be a mockery'. He was very clear, however, that human rights did 'not include the right to a fair distribution of resources or fair treatment in economic terms—in other words, distributive justice', adding, '[o]f course distributive justice is a good thing. But it is not a fundamental human right', ibid.

279 See Wadham (above) at 719.

280 Indeed in the post-'September 11th' environment some have viewed the outlook for the Human Rights Act itself as relatively bleak, see Lester and Pannick (above) paras 1.64–1.67.

281 In 1989 incorporation of the European Convention was opposed, *inter alia*, because its 'broad propositions . . . are often unsuited to the close textual analysis of Statutes'; owing to 'the risk of a damaging conflict between the courts' and the 'democratic' branches of government, with the courts 'being used as a means of challenging unpopular action by the government . . . which has received the support of Parliament; and because the 'injustice or unfairness of the kind [that the HRA] would be designed to correct could in the United Kingdom context be more suitably and more effectively challenged in Parliament', *Third Periodic Report of the UK under the ICCPR* (1989) para 7, as cited from Blackburn (n 70 above).   282 *The DCA Response* para 10.

283 *JCHR ICESCR Report* para 68.

284 Lord Irvine, 'Activism and Restraint: Human Rights and the Interpretative Process' (1999) 4 Eur Human Rights L Rev 350 at 371.

accountable government should not be extended to protect the most fundamental aspects of certain key ESC rights under a qualified model for their incorporation and here the South African version of constitutional protection provides a good example. Moreover, it is probable that qualified incorporation would do significantly more than this. As the JCHR argued it could help create 'a culture of justification and accountability to cover matters that are fundamental to the lives of most citizens'.[285] In this way it would have a 'most practical effect in protecting the rights of the people who are most marginalised and deprived in an unequal society'.[286]

The government insists that it takes its obligations under the ICESCR very seriously and that it regards ESC rights as of equal importance to civil and political rights. This is hard to reconcile with the crude stance it maintains insofar as it regards ESC rights as inappropriate for incorporation on the basis, it would seem, that the ICESCR can only be incorporated *en bloc* or not at all, and the unsophisticated arguments presented regarding the nature and status of ESC rights generally. The JCHR, a body of distinguished Parliamentarians, had placed before the government realistic arguments for constitutionalizing the protection of certain Covenant rights, in particular granting the courts adjudication powers based on non-discrimination and reasonableness of decision-making principles. However, *The DCA Response* simply ignored most of the fundamental points made here and it apparently failed to take very seriously some of the general proposals presented for a deeper and more consistent appreciation of ESC rights within the UK constitution. It may be no exaggeration to say that *The DCA Response* to the JCHR inquiry has merely served to underline the basic point made by the JCHR: in terms of their legal status, ESC rights have been, and for now at least seem destined to remain, 'the poor cousins of . . . civil and political rights'[287] in the UK legal system.

---

[285] *JCHR ICESCR Report* para 69.
[286] Ibid. On the need for creation of a human rights culture to include ESC rights see *Van Bueren* at 458, 463 and 465. It has been argued that the Human Rights Act has had little positive impact for those who experience social exclusion, see L Clements, 'Winners and Losers' (2005) 32(1) J of L and Society, 34.   [287] *JCHR ICESCR Report* para 163.

PART IV

APPLICATIONS OF ESC RIGHTS

12

A Human Rights-Based Approach
to Health Indicators

Paul Hunt and Gillian MacNaughton

I. Introduction[1]

For many years, the human rights community—that is, those actively working for
the promotion and protection of human rights—has considered the possible role
of indicators in relation to human rights. According to international human rights
law, economic, social, and cultural rights (ESC rights) are subject to 'progressive
realization'.[2] Those in the human rights community focusing on ESC rights have
given particular attention to indicators because they provide a methodology for
monitoring progressive realization. Without such a methodology, some states may
use the concept of progressive realization as a way of delaying—or altogether
avoiding—their responsibilities.[3]

---

[1] The contents of this chapter are closely based on the report of the United Nations Special
Rapporteur on the right of everyone to the enjoyment of the highest attainable standard of physical
and mental health ('Special Rapporteur') submitted to the United Nations in March 2006. See 'The
right of everyone to the enjoyment of the highest attainable standard of health', Report of the Special
Rapporteur to the Commission on Human Rights 2006, E/CN.4/2006/48 (3 March 2006). The
Special Rapporteur has submitted two previous reports to the General Assembly on indicators and
the right to the highest attainable standard of health. See 'The right of everyone to the enjoyment of
the highest attainable standard of health', Interim Report of the Special Rapporteur to the General
Assembly 2003, A/58/427 (10 Oct 2003); 'The right of everyone to the enjoyment of the highest
attainable standard of health', Interim Report of the Special Rapporteur to the General Assembly
2004, A/59/422 (8 Oct 2004). The Special Rapporteur has repeatedly sought—and gratefully
received—comments on his reports. He also invites comments on the human rights-based approach
to health indicators outlined in this chapter. In the light of experience and comments received, he will
continue to refine the human rights-based approach to health indicators, while promoting this
approach throughout his work, including when on state missions.

[2] See eg, International Covenant on Economic, Social and Cultural Rights (ICESCR), adopted
and opened for signature and ratification by GA res 2200A (XXI) of 16 Dec 1966 and entered into
force 3 Jan 1976, art 2(1).

[3] As Leckie puts it, 'recalcitrant States' may use progressive realization as an 'escape hatch',
S Leckie, 'Another Step Towards Indivisibility: Identifying the Key Features of Violations of
Economic, Social and Cultural Rights' (1998) 20 Human Rights Q 81 at 94.

In 1988, the United Nations Sub-Commission on the Prevention of Discrimination and Protection of Minorities (as it then was) appointed Danilo Turk to
prepare a study on the more effective realization of ESC rights.[4] In his reports,
Turk recognized the potential use of economic and social indicators for assessing
progress in the realization of these rights, and the Sub-Commission agreed that
indicators have 'a central role to play' in relation to ESC rights.[5] Turk recommended that a UN expert seminar discuss how to take this matter forward and, in
1993, the UN Centre for Human Rights (as it then was) convened such an expert
meeting. After an extensive review of the issues, the expert seminar 'recognized a
need to develop new human rights indicators based on the content of each ESC
right' and made numerous recommendations.[6] Also in 1993, the World Conference
on Human Rights urged examination of 'a system of indicators to measure progress
in the realization' of ESC rights.[7]

As the UN expert seminar of 1993 recognized, one of the essential pre-conditions
for the identification of human rights indicators is a degree of clarity about the scope
of the specific human rights in question. Crucially, since 1993, the contours and
content of the right to the highest attainable standard of health have become clearer
as a result of developments at the national, regional, and international levels.
Accordingly, it is now possible to make progress in relation to health and indicators
in a way that did not present itself to human rights practitioners in 1993.

There are other reasons why it is now possible and timely to make some progress
in relation to health and indicators. For example, in recent years, civil society organizations, such as the Philippine Human Rights Information Centre, have begun
to use human rights indicators at the grassroots level.[8] The Centre is leading a participatory project on ESC rights standards and indicators. Additionally, there is a
growing academic literature on human rights and indicators.[9] Also, in recent years,

---

[4] Turk delivered four reports: Preliminary Report of Mr Danilo Turk, Special Rapporteur on the
Realization of Economic, Social and Cultural Rights, E/CN.4/Sub.2/1989/19 (28 June 1989);
Progress Report of Mr Danilo Turk, Special Rapporteur on the Realization of Economic, Social, and
Cultural Rights, E/CN.4/Sub.2/1990/19 (6 July 1990); Second Progress Report of Mr Danilo Turk,
Special Rapporteur on the Realization of Economic, Social and Cultural Rights, E/CN.4/Sub.2/
1991/17 (18 July 1991); Third Progress Report of Mr Danilo Turk, Special Rapporteur on the
Realization of Economic, Social, and Cultural Rights, E/CN.4/Sub.2/1992/16 (3 July 1992).
[5] Second Progress Report of Mr Danilo Turk, Special Rapporteur on the Realization of Economic,
Social and Cultural Rights, E/CN.4/Sub.2/1991/17 (18 July 1991) para 8.
[6] Preparatory Committee, World Conference on Human Rights, Report of the Seminar on
Appropriate Indicators to Measure Achievements in the Progressive Realization of Economic, Social,
and Cultural Rights, World Conference on Human Rights, A/CONF.157/PC/73 (20 April 1993)
para 172.
[7] Vienna Declaration and Programme of Action, World Conference on Human Rights,
A/CONF.157/23 (12 July 1993) para 98.
[8] See 'Monitoring Economic, Social and Cultural Rights: The Philippine Experience' (PhilRights,
1997); 'Economic, Social and Cultural Rights: The Grassroots View' (PhilRights, 2000).
[9] See eg, A Chapman, 'Indicators and Standards for Monitoring Economic, Social, and Cultural
Rights' (2000) paper presented at UNDP's Second Global Forum on Human Development (2000)
available at <http://hdr.undp.org/docs/events/global_forum/2000/chapman.pdf> accessed 27 April
2006; M Green, 'What We Talk About When We Talk About Indicators: Current Approaches to

the Office of the High Commissioner for Human Rights (OHCHR), the World Health Organization (WHO), and others have devoted increasing attention to these important issues.[10]

The United Nations Development Programme (UNDP) *Human Development Report 2000: Human Rights and Human Development*, devotes a chapter to, and makes a compelling case for, the careful use of human rights indicators: 'Statistical indicators are a powerful tool in the struggle for human rights. They make it possible for people and organizations—from grass-roots activists and civil society to governments and the United Nations—to identify important actors and hold them accountable for their actions.'[11] Indicators, it continues, can be used as tools for:

- making better policies and monitoring progress;
- identifying unintended impacts of laws, policies, and practices;
- identifying which actors are having an impact on the realization of rights;
- revealing whether the obligations of these actors are being met;
- giving early warning of potential violations, prompting preventive action;
- enhancing social consensus on difficult trade-offs to be made in the face of resource constraints;
- exposing issues that have been neglected or silenced.[12]

Crucially, human rights indicators can help states, and others, recognize when national and international policy adjustments are required.

One of the authors of this chapter, the United Nations Special Rapporteur on the right of everyone to the enjoyment of the highest attainable standard of physical and mental health, has devoted three chapters to indicators and the right to health in his annual reports to the United Nations.[13] In his first report to the General Assembly (2003), he examined this issue 'with a view to developing

Human Rights Measurement' (2001) 23 (4) Human Rights Q 1062; P Hunt, 'State Obligations, Indicators, Benchmarks, and the Right to Education' (1998) New Zealand Human Rights Law and Practice 109; T Landman, 'Measuring Human Rights: Principle, Practice, and Policy', (2004) 26(4) Human Rights Q 906; K Raworth, 'Measuring Human Rights' (2001) 15 (1) Ethics and Intl Affairs 111; E Riedel, 'New Bearings to the State Reporting Procedure: Practical Ways to Operationalize Economic, Social and Cultural Rights-the Example of the Right to Health', in S von Schorlemer (ed) *Praxishandbuch UNO* (Springer 2002); H Watchirs, 'Review of Methodologies Measuring Human Rights Implementation' (2002) 30 (4) J of L, Medicine and Ethics 716; A Yamin, 'The Future in the Mirror: Incorporating Strategies for the Defense and Promotion of Economic, Social, and Cultural Rights' (2005) 27 (4) Human Rights Q 1236.

[10] See eg, Report of the Turku Expert Meeting on Human Rights Indicators, 1–13 March 2005 in Turku/Abo Finland, available at <http://www.abo.fi/instut/imr/research/seminars/indicators/Report. doc> accessed 27 April 2006; World Health Organization, Health and Human Rights, Consultation on Indicators for the Right to Health, Chateau de Penthes, Geneva (15 May 2003).

[11] United Nations Development Program (UNDP), *Human Development Report 2000: Human Rights and Human Development* at 89, available at <http://hdr.undp.org/reports/global/2000/en/> accessed 21 March 2006. [12] Ibid.

[13] See Interim Report of the Special Rapporteur to the General Assembly 2003, A/58/427(n 1 above); Interim Report of the Special Rapporteur to the General Assembly 2004, A/59/422(n 1 above); Report of the Special Rapporteur to the Commission on Human Rights 2006, E/CN.4/2006/ 48 (n 1 above). In this chapter, we use as a convenient shorthand 'the right to the highest attainable standard of health' or 'the right to health'.

gradually a practical, realistic and balanced approach'.[14] When preparing his first report, the Special Rapporteur was thinking in terms of identifying a number of right to health indicators. The following year he reported to the General Assembly on his 'work in progress', concluding that it is more promising to think in terms of a human rights-based approach to health indicators.[15] It was this idea that he developed in his third report on indicators, which was submitted to the Commission on Human Rights in early 2006, and which is reflected in this chapter.[16]

II. A human rights-based approach

In recent years, it has become clear that a human rights-based approach to particular issues—development, poverty reduction, trade—brings certain valuable perspectives that otherwise tend to be neglected. Very briefly, in general terms a human rights-based approach requires that special attention be given to disadvantaged individuals and communities; the active and informed participation of individuals and communities in policy decisions that affect them; and effective, transparent and accessible monitoring and accountability mechanisms.[17] The combined effect of these—and other features of a human rights-based approach— is to empower disadvantaged individuals and communities.[18]

Accordingly, a human rights-based approach to health indicators not only monitors key health outcomes, but also some of the processes by which they are achieved. Crucially, many commonly used health indicators have an important role to play in a human rights-based approach to health indicators, provided a few reasonable conditions are met. For example, many existing health indicators may be used provided they are disaggregated on various grounds, such as sex, race, and ethnicity. Disaggregated indicators can reveal whether or not some disadvantaged individuals and communities are suffering from *de facto* discrimination.[19] For the

---

[14] Interim Report of the Special Rapporteur to the General Assembly 2003, A/58/427 (n 1 above) para 6.

[15] Interim Report of the Special Rapporteur to the General Assembly 2004, A/59/422 (n 1 above) paras 81 and 83. This approach is informed by the principle confirmed in art 5 of the Vienna Declaration and Programme of Action: 'All human rights are universal, indivisible and interdependent and interrelated.'

[16] See Report of the Special Rapporteur to the Commission on Human Rights 2006, E/CN.4/2006/48(n 1 above).

[17] For a contemporary application of a human rights-based approach to a particular health issue—neglected diseases—see P Hunt, R Steward, J Mesquita, and L Oldring, *Neglected Diseases: A Human Rights Analysis* in preparation for the Special Topics in Social, Economic, and Behavioural Research, UNICEF/UNDP/World Bank/WHO Special Programme for Research and Training in Tropical Diseases (Geneva, 2006).

[18] See generally, Office of the High Commissioner for Human Rights, Frequently Asked Questions on a Human Rights Based Approach to Development Cooperation, United Nations, 2006, available at <http://www.ohchr.org/about/publications/docs/FAQ_en.pdf> accessed 20 July 2006.   [19] See section VI below.

most part, existing health indicators are rarely designed to monitor issues like participation and accountability, although these are essential features of a human rights approach. Thus, a human rights-based approach to health indicators requires the addition of some new indicators to monitor these essential human rights features.

A human rights-based approach to health indicators is not a radical departure from existing indicator methodologies. Rather, it uses many commonly used health indicators, adapts them so far as necessary (eg by requiring disaggregation), and adds some new indicators to monitor issues (eg participation and accountability) that otherwise tend to be neglected. In short, a human rights-based approach to health indicators reinforces, enhances, and supplements commonly used indicators. This is the approach that is set out here. Later in the chapter, by way of illustration, the human rights-based approach to health indicators is applied to the Reproductive Health Strategy endorsed by the World Health Assembly in May 2004.

III. The role of indicators

Although some members of the human rights community have hesitated to use indicators in their work,[20] in our view there is no alternative but to use indicators to measure and monitor the progressive realization of the right to the highest attainable standard of health. While a key question used to be '*Is* there a role for indicators in relation to the right to the highest attainable standard of health?' today the crucial question is '*How* can indicators be most appropriately used to measure and monitor this fundamental human right?' The human rights-based approach to health indicators set out in this chapter provides an answer to this crucial question. Additionally, the human rights-based approach to health indicators includes features, such as its emphasis on disaggregation, participation, and accountability that, if integrated into health policies and programmes, are likely to enhance their effectiveness.

One of the central messages of this chapter is that indicators have an important role to play in measuring and monitoring the progressive realization of the right to health. Nonetheless, the importance of their role should not be exaggerated. No matter how sophisticated they might be, indicators will never give a complete picture of the enjoyment of the right to health in a specific jurisdiction. For the most part, they provide useful indications regarding the enjoyment of the right to health in a particular national context. Just as it is misguided to deny that indicators have an important role to play in relation to the right to health, it is also misplaced to expect too much from them.

---

[20] For an early discussion of these issues, see (n 5 above) Second Report of Mr Danilo Turk, paras 6–48.

IV. The importance of indicators

As already observed, the international right to the highest attainable standard of health is subject to progressive realization. Inescapably, this means that what is expected of a state will vary over time. With a view to monitoring its progress, a state needs a device to measure this variable dimension of the right to health. The most appropriate device is the combined application of indicators and benchmarks. Thus, a state selects appropriate indicators that will help it monitor different dimensions of the right to health. These indicators might include, for example, maternal mortality ratios and child mortality rates. Most indicators will require disaggregation, such as on the grounds of sex, race, ethnicity, urban/rural, and socio-economic status. Then the state sets appropriate national targets—or benchmarks—in relation to each disaggregated indicator.[21]

In this way, indicators and benchmarks fulfil two important functions that underpin much of the discussion in this chapter. *First*, they can help the state to monitor its progress over time, enabling the authorities to recognize when policy adjustments are required. *Second*, they can help to hold the state to account in relation to the discharge of its responsibilities arising from the right to health, although deteriorating indicators do not necessarily mean that the state is in breach of its international right to health obligations, an important point which is discussed further below. Of course, indicators also have other important roles. For example, by highlighting issues such as disaggregation, participation, and accountability, indicators can enhance the effectiveness of policies and programmes. In this chapter, however, our focus is on the two functions signalled above.

Not only states, but also other actors are expected to integrate human rights into their policy-making. This was most recently affirmed by 170 Heads of State and government at the September 2005 World Summit:

We resolve to integrate the promotion and protection of human rights into national policies and to support the further mainstreaming of human rights throughout the United Nations system, as well as closer cooperation between the Office of the United Nations High Commissioner for Human Rights and all relevant United Nations bodies.[22]

The integration or 'mainstreaming' of human rights into national and international health policies is a major undertaking that demands a range of measures from a variety of actors. One such measure is the adoption of a human rights-based

---

[21] Progressive realization is also an implicit feature of the Millennium Development Goals. Indicators and benchmarks are needed to monitor progress towards the achievement of the Goals. See United Nations Statistics Division, Millennium Development Goal Indicators Database, available at <http://mdgs.un.org/unsd/mdg/Host.aspx?Content=Indicators/OfficialList.htm> accessed 30 Nov 2006 (listing framework of eight goals, eighteen target, and forty-eight indicators to monitor progress toward achieving the Millennium Development Goals).

[22] GA, 2005 World Summit Outcome, A/RES/60/1 (24 Oct 2005) para 126.

approach to health indicators.[23] The authors hope that specialized agencies and other UN bodies working on health issues will find this chapter useful as they strive to enhance their effectiveness and integrate human rights into their work.

In summary, in the context of the right to health, indicators can help:

(i) national public officials working on health issues;
(ii) legislative bodies as they monitor the performance of the executive;
(iii) courts, human rights institutions, and other national bodies responsible for adjudicating whether or not the state is discharging its right to health duties;
(iv) specialized agencies and other UN bodies working in partnership with states on health issues;
(v) UN human rights treaty bodies and other international bodies responsible for monitoring whether or not states are discharging their right to health duties; and
(vi) non-governmental organizations working on health issues.

V. Indicators for the national and international levels

The main focus of international human rights law is directed to the acts and omissions of states within their own jurisdictions. Naturally, therefore, discussions about human rights indicators tend to have the same orientation.[24] Indeed, the illustrative indicators mentioned in this chapter focus primarily on the national level. However, international human rights also place responsibilities on states in relation to their conduct beyond their own jurisdictions[25]—consider the references to international assistance and co-operation, and similar formulations, in the Universal Declaration of Human Rights (UDHR),[26] as well as in binding human rights treaties, such as the International Covenant on Economic, Social and Cultural Rights (ICESCR)[27] and the Convention on the Rights of the Child (CRC).[28]

Moreover, the outcomes of recent world conferences include passages that resonate with the international assistance and co-operation provisions of international human rights law. In the Millennium Declaration, for example, 147 Heads of State and government—191 states in total—recognize that 'in addition to our

[23] See eg, Interim Report of the Special Rapporteur 2004 (n 1 above) paras 53–54.

[24] See generally sources cited (n 9 above).

[25] See eg, 'The right of everyone to the enjoyment of the highest attainable standard of health', Preliminary Report of the Special Rapporteur to the Commission on Human Rights 2003, E/CN.4/2003/58 (13 Feb 2003) para 28.

[26] Universal Declaration of Human Rights (1948) art 28 ('Everyone is entitled to a social and international order in which the rights and freedoms set forth in this Declaration can be fully realized'). [27] ICESCR (n 3 above) arts 2(1), 11(2), 15(4), 23.

[28] United Nations Convention on the Rights of the Child (CRC), adopted and opened for signature, ratification, and accession by GA res 44/25 of 20 Nov 1989 and entered into force 2 Sept 1990, art 4.

separate responsibilities to our individual societies, we have a collective responsibility to uphold the principles of human dignity, equality and equity at the global level.'[29] The Millennium Declaration repeatedly affirms the twin principles of shared responsibility and global equity, principles that also animate the human rights concept of international assistance and co-operation.

In this context, two general observations can be made. First, international assistance and co-operation should not be understood as encompassing only financial and technical assistance: it also includes a responsibility to work actively towards equitable multilateral trading, investment, and financial systems that are conducive to the reduction and elimination of poverty.[30] Second, while lawyers may debate the legal nature and scope of international assistance and co-operation under international human rights law, nobody can seriously dispute that states have, to one degree or another, international human rights responsibilities that extend beyond their own borders.[31]

In these circumstances, human rights indicators are needed to monitor the discharge of a state's human rights responsibilities that extend beyond its borders. The international community has already begun to identify indicators that monitor these responsibilities. For example, a number of indicators have been identified in relation to Millennium Development Goal 8, one of them being the amount of a donor's official development assistance as a percentage of its gross national product.[32] In 2001, the General Assembly, at its special session on HIV/AIDS, adopted the Declaration of Commitment on HIV/AIDS 'Global Crisis—Global Action'[33] and, in the following year, the Programme Coordinating Board of UNAIDS approved a set of core indicators for implementation of the Declaration of Commitment.[34] Four of these core indicators relate to the global level.[35] One indicator is the amount of funds spent by international donors on HIV/AIDS in developing states and states in transition; another is the percentage of transnational companies present in developing states that have HIV/AIDS workplace policies and programmes.[36] This is not to argue that these are human rights indicators, but rather that they provide a precedent for the formulation of human rights indicators at the international level.

---

[29] GA United Nations Millennium Declaration, A/RES/55/2 (18 Sept 2000) para 2.

[30] Office of the High Commissioner for Human Rights, 'Human Rights and Poverty Reduction: A Conceptual Framework' (United Nations, 2006) at 27–30.

[31] For a recent contribution to this discussion see S Skogly, *Beyond National Borders: States' Human Rights Obligations in their International Cooperation* (Intersentia, 2006).

[32] Report of the Secretary General, 'Road map towards the implementation of the United Nations Millennium Declaration', A/56/326 (6 Sept 2001) annex, goal 8, target 13, indicator 32, at 58.

[33] See GA, Declaration of Commitment on HIV/AIDS, A/RES/S-16/2 (2 Aug 2001).

[34] See UNAIDS, Monitoring the Declaration of Commitment on HIV/AIDS: Guidelines on Construction of Core Indicators (July 2002) available at <http://data.unaids.org/publications/irc-pub06/jc1126-constrcoreindic-ungass_en.pdf> accessed 27 April 2006.   [35] See ibid at 20.

[36] Ibid.

The crucial point is that any attempt to identify human rights-based health indicators must encompass the responsibilities of states at both the national and international levels.

VI. An example of an indicator

By way of illustration, this section shows how one disaggregated indicator—the proportion of births attended by skilled health personnel—can be used in relation to the right to the highest attainable standard of health. The section does not set out a human rights-based approach to health indicators. After showing the role of this indicator (and its benchmarks) in relation to the right to health, subsequent sections introduce a human rights-based approach to health indicators.

Sexual and reproductive health are integral elements of the right to the highest attainable standard of health.[37] Therefore, states need a method of measuring whether or not they are progressively realizing sexual and reproductive health. There are many relevant indicators, including the proportion of births attended by skilled health personnel.[38] A state may select this indicator as one of those it uses to measure its progressive realization of sexual and reproductive health rights.

The national data may show that the proportion of births attended by skilled health personnel is 60 per cent. When disaggregated on the basis of urban/rural, data may reveal that the proportion is 70 per cent in urban centres, but only 50 per cent in rural areas. When further disaggregated on the basis of ethnicity, data may also show that coverage in the rural areas is uneven: the dominant ethnic group enjoys a coverage of 70 per cent but the minority ethnic group only 40 per cent. This highlights the crucial importance of disaggregation as a means of identifying *de facto* discrimination. When disaggregated, the indicator confirms that rural women members of the ethnic minority are especially disadvantaged and require particular attention.

Consistent with the progressive realization of the right to health, the state may decide to aim for a uniform national coverage of 70 per cent—in the urban and rural areas and for all ethnic groups—in five years time. Thus, the indicator is the proportion of births attended by skilled health personnel—and the benchmark or target is 70 per cent. The state will formulate and implement policies and programmes that are designed to reach the benchmark of 70 per cent in five years.

---

[37] See Commission on Human Rights, 'The right of everyone to the enjoyment of the highest attainable standard of physical and mental health', E/CN.4/RES/2003/28 (22 April 2003), preamble and para 6.

[38] This is one of the indicators selected to monitor progress toward the Millennium Development Goals. See Report of the Secretary General, 'Road map towards the implementation of the United Nations Millennium Declaration', A/56/326 (6 Sept 2001) annex, goal 5, target 6, indicator 17, at 56.

The data show that the policies and programmes will have to be specially designed to reach the minority ethnic group living in the rural areas.

Annual progress towards the benchmark or target should be monitored, in light of which annual policy adjustments might be required. At the end of the five-year period, a monitoring and accountability mechanism will ascertain whether or not the 70 per cent benchmark has been reached in urban and rural areas and for all ethnic groups. If it has, the state will set a more ambitious benchmark for the next five-year period, consistent with its obligation to realize progressively the right to health. But if the 70 per cent benchmark for all has not been reached, then the reasons should be identified and remedial action taken.

Importantly, a failure to reach a benchmark does not necessarily mean that the state is in breach of its international right to health obligations. The state might have fallen short of its benchmark for reasons beyond its control. However, if the monitoring and accountability mechanism reveals that the 70 per cent benchmark was not reached because of, for example, corruption in the health sector, then it will probably follow that the state has failed to comply with its international right to health obligations.

International assistance and co-operation is an important element of the right to health.[39] Donors have a responsibility to provide financial and other support for developing states' policies and programmes regarding, *inter alia*, sexual and reproductive health. Moreover, donors should be held to account in relation to the discharge of their responsibility. Therefore, in relation to the example set out in the preceding paragraphs, indicators are needed to measure what donors have done to help the state deliver sound sexual and reproductive health policies. Also, a monitoring and accountability mechanism is needed to address the question: has the donor community done all it reasonably can to help the state deliver sound sexual and reproductive health policies, enabling it to reach its benchmark of 70 per cent?

Of course, these issues—indicators and accountability mechanisms for the donor community—raise challenging questions. Nonetheless, indicators and accountability mechanisms that focus exclusively on the responsibilities of developing states and do not also encompass the responsibilities of the donor community are unfair, flawed, and lack credibility.

In summary, a disaggregated indicator, such as 'the proportion of births attended by skilled health personnel', when used with benchmarks, can help a state identify which policies are working and which are not. Moreover, it can also help to hold a state to account in relation to its responsibilities arising from the right to health. Of course, one indicator, even when disaggregated, cannot possibly capture all the dimensions that are important from the human rights perspective. For this, other indicators are needed—and these are discussed below. Nonetheless, this illustration shows how a disaggregated indicator, when used with a benchmark, can provide

[39] See section V above.

some useful information about the progressive realization of the right to the highest attainable standard of health.

VII. A human rights-based approach to health indicators

Health professionals and policy makers constantly use a very large number of health indicators, such as the proportion of births attended by skilled health personnel, the maternal mortality ratio, and the HIV prevalence rate.[40] Is it possible to simply appropriate these health indicators and call them 'human rights indicators' or 'right to health indicators'? Or do indicators that are to be used for monitoring human rights and the right to health require some special features? If so, what are these special attributes?

As the Special Rapporteur concluded in his report to the General Assembly (2004),[41] health indicators may be used to monitor aspects of the progressive realization of the right to the highest attainable standard of health provided:

A. *They correspond, with some precision, to a right to health norm.*[42] There has to be a reasonably exact correspondence—or link—between the indicator and a right to health norm or standard. In the case of the proportion of births attended by skilled health personnel, for example, there is a reasonably precise correspondence with several human rights norms, including the rights to health and life of mother and child, for example, under article 24(2)(a) and (d) of the Convention on the Rights of the Child.

B. *They are disaggregated by at least sex, race, ethnicity, rural/urban, and socio-economic status.*[43] Human rights have a particular pre-occupation with disadvantaged individuals and groups. This pre-occupation is reflected in numerous provisions of international human rights law, not least those enshrining the principles of non-discrimination and equality.[44] While a health indicator might or might not be disaggregated, from the human rights perspective it is imperative that all relevant

---

[40] See eg, World Health Organization, Reproductive Health Indicator Database, 'Definition of Indicators and Data Sources: 17 Reproductive Health Indicators' available at <http://www9.who.int/familyhealth/reproductiveindicators/definitionofindicators.asp> accessed 20 July 2006.

[41] Interim Report of the Special Rapporteur to the General Assembly 2004, A/59/422 (n 1 above) para 68.   [42] Ibid para 68(a).

[43] Ibid para 68(b).

[44] See eg, Universal Declaration of Human Rights (1948) art 2; International Covenant on Civil and Political Rights, adopted and opened for signature, ratification, and accession by GA res 2200A (XXI) of 16 Dec 1966 and entered into force 23 March 1976, arts 2(1) and 3; ICESCR (n 3 above) arts 2(2) and 3; CRC (n 24 above) art 2(1). In addition to such specific provisions, some treaties are entirely devoted to the realization of non-discrimination and equality. See eg, International Convention on the Elimination of All Forms of Racial Discrimination, adopted and opened for signature and ratification by GA res 2106 (XX) of 21 Dec 1965 and entered into force 4 Jan 1969; Convention on the Elimination of All Forms of Discrimination Against Women, adopted and opened for signature, ratification, and accession by GA res 34/180 of 18 Dec 1979 and entered into force 3 Sept 1981.

indicators are disaggregated. A more difficult issue is: on which grounds should the indicators be disaggregated? From the human rights perspective, the goal is to disaggregate in relation to as many of the internationally prohibited grounds of discrimination as possible.[45] However, the collection of disaggregated data remains an enormous challenge for many states. Because of limited capacity, reliable disaggregated data are often unavailable. There is another complication: vulnerability and discrimination are contextual. While a group might be especially vulnerable in one context, it might not be in another. Thus, in a particular national context, there might be a case for giving priority to the collection of some disaggregated data rather than others. Further, some health issues will demand disaggregation on particular grounds; for example, in the context of sexual and reproductive health, disaggregation on the grounds of age is crucial because of the importance of *adolescent* sexual and reproductive health. While keeping these observations in mind, we suggest that relevant indicators should usually be disaggregated, at a minimum, by sex, race, ethnicity, rural/urban, and socio-economic status. However, these grounds of disaggregation will have to be reviewed in the light of capacity, context and the health issue in question.

C. *They are supplemented by additional indicators that monitor five essential and inter-related features of the right to the highest attainable standard of health:*[46]

(1) *A national strategy and plan of action that includes the right to the highest attainable standard of health.* Because the right to health demands that a state has a strategy and plan of action that encompasses the right to health, including universal access, indicators are needed to measure this essential feature.[47]

(2) *The participation of individuals and groups, especially the most vulnerable and disadvantaged, in relation to the formulation of health policies and programmes.* Because participation is an essential feature of the right to health, indicators are needed to measure the degree to which health policies and programmes, including the quality control of services, are participatory.[48]

(3) *Access to health information, as well as confidentiality of personal health data.*[49] Because access to health information is an essential feature of the right to health, indicators are needed to measure the degree to which health information is available and accessible to

---

[45] According to the Committee on Economic, Social and Cultural Rights (ESCR Committee), the prohibited grounds include 'race, colour, sex, language, religion, political or other opinion, national or social origin, property, birth, physical or mental disability, health status (including HIV/AIDS), sexual orientation and civil, political, social or other status'. ESCR Committee, *General Comment* 14, para 18.

[46] Interim Report of the Special Rapporteur to the General Assembly 2004, A/59/422 (n 1 above), para 68(c). The following paragraphs (1)–(5) are intended only to signal the five essential features. While work has been done elsewhere to explore each feature, more is needed.

[47] ESCR Committee, *General Comment 14*, para 43(f).

[48] See eg, 'The right of everyone to the enjoyment of the highest attainable standard of physical and mental health', Report of the Special Rapporteur to the Commission on Human Rights 2004, Mission to the World Trade Organization, E/CN.4/2004/49/Add. 1 (1 March 2004) para 27; 'The right of everyone to the enjoyment of the highest attainable standard of physical and mental health', Report of the Special Rapporteur to the Commission on Human Rights 2005, E/CN.4/2005/51 (11 Feb 2005) paras 59–61.   [49] ESCR Committee, *General Comment 14*, para 12(b)(iv).

all. Health information enables people to, *inter alia*, promote their own health and claim quality services from the state and others. Clearly, other essential features of the right to health, such as meaningful participation, depend upon the accessibility of reliable information on health issues. Additionally, because of the requirements of confidentiality regarding personal health data, indicators are also needed to measure the degree to which such confidentiality is respected.

(4) *International assistance and cooperation of donors in relation to the enjoyment of the right to the highest attainable standard of health in developing countries.* The right to health places an obligation on developed states to take measures that help developing states realise the right to health.[50] Thus, indicators are needed to measure the degree to which donors are fulfilling this responsibility.

(5) *Accessible and effective monitoring and accountability mechanisms.* Because the right to health requires that all those holding right to health duties are held to account for their conduct, indicators are needed to measure the degree to which accessible and effective monitoring and accountability mechanisms are available.[51]

It is not possible for one indicator to possess all these features. Thus, rather than searching for individual right to health indicators, it is more helpful to think in terms of a human rights-based approach to health indicators. In other words, while it is impossible for one indicator to possess all the features signalled in the preceding paragraph, it is possible to identify *a range* of indicators that *together* have these features. In combination, various indicators can help a state monitor the progressive realization of the right to health. In short, a combination of appropriate indicators may together constitute a human rights-based approach to health indictors.

VIII. The problem of terminology

The literature reveals a multitude of health indicators.[52] However, there is a more fundamental difficulty. There is no commonly agreed and consistent way of categorizing and labelling different types of health indicators. For example, the following categories and labels for indicators can be found: performance, statistical, variable, process, conduct, outcome, output, result, achievement, structural, screening, qualitative, quantitative, core, and rated. The same indicator may appear in several categories. This multiplicity of overlapping labels is very confusing. Crucially, it confines meaningful discussion to a small elite of health experts. The lack of a common approach to the classification of health indicators is a challenge to those who wish to

---

[50] See eg, Interim Report of the Special Rapporteur to the General Assembly 2004, A/59/422 (n 1 above) paras 32–35.   [51] Ibid paras 36–46.

[52] Interim Report of the Special Rapporteur to the General Assembly 2003, A/58/427 (n 1 above) para 14. See eg, *Human Development Report 2000* (n 11 above) ch 5; World Health Organization, 'World Health Report 2005: Make Every Mother and Child Count,' statistical annex, available at <http://www.who.int/whr/2005/en/index.html> accessed 20 July 2006; UNAIDS (n 34 above).

introduce a simple, consistent and rational system for human rights-based health indicators.[53]

If progress is to be made, there must be a degree of terminological clarity and consistency. In 2003, the Special Rapporteur suggested that special attention be devoted to the following three categories of indicators: *structural, process, and outcome indicators*.[54] While there is no unanimity in the health literature, these categories and labels are widely understood.[55] They are also relatively straightforward. They are used by some departments of the World Health Organization, such as the Department of Essential Drugs and Medicines Policy.[56] Since 2003, OHCHR and others have also begun to use these three terms.[57] Eibe Riedel, Vice-Chair of the Committee on Economic, Social and Cultural Rights, has adopted these terms and categories.[58] In our view, these labels will serve as well as—if not better than—others. Since consistent terminology will greatly assist states, intergovernmental organizations, civil society groups, and others, we recommend that, when formulating human rights indicators in relation to health, they be categorized as structural, process, and outcome indicators.

The following paragraphs provide definitions of structural, process, and outcome indicators. It is, however, not always easy to draw a neat line between these categories. No doubt the definitions will need further tightening. Nonetheless, what follows will serve as working definitions.

A. *Structural indicators* address whether or not key structures and mechanisms that are necessary for, or conducive to, the realization of the right to health, are in place. They are often (but not always) framed as a question generating a yes/no answer. For example, they may address: the ratification of international treaties that include the right to health; the adoption of national laws and policies that expressly promote and protect the right to health; the existence of basic institutional mechanisms that facilitate the realization of the right to health, including regulatory agencies, etc.

B. *Process indicators* measure programmes, activities, and interventions. They measure, as it were, state effort. For example, the following are process indicators: the proportion of births attended by skilled health personnel; the number of facilities per 500,000 population providing basic obstetric care; the percentage of pregnant women counselled and tested for HIV; the percentage of people provided with health information on, for example, maternal and newborn care, family planning services, and sexually transmitted infections; the number of training programmes and public campaigns on sexual and reproductive health rights

---

[53] Ibid.   [54] Ibid para 15.   [55] Ibid.

[56] P Brudon, JD Rainhorn, and MR Reich, *Indicators for Monitoring National Drug Policies: A Practical Manual*, World Health Organization, Programme on Essential Drugs (WHO, 1999).

[57] See eg, R Malhotra and N Fasel, 'Quantitative Human Rights Indicators: A survey of major initiates,' Background Paper prepared for the Turku Expert Meeting on Human Rights Indicators, 10–13 March 2005 in Turku/Abo Finland (2005) at 28, available at <http://www.abo.fi/instut/imr/research/seminars/indicators/Background.doc> accessed 27 April 2006.

[58] Interim Report of the Special Rapporteur to the General Assembly 2003 (n 1 above) at para 16.

organized by a national human rights institution in the last five years. Such process indicators can help to predict health outcomes.

C. *Outcome indicators* measure the impact of programmes, activities, and interventions on health status and related issues. Outcome indicators include maternal mortality, child mortality, HIV prevalence rates, and the percentage of women who know about contraceptive methods.

While structural indictors will often be framed as a question generating a yes/no answer, process and outcome indicators will often be used in conjunction with benchmarks or targets to measure change over time. However, there is no conceptual reason why all three types of indicators cannot *either* generate a yes/no answer *or* be used with benchmarks to measure change over time.

We are especially interested in those indicators that can be used by states and others to measure the progressive realization of the right to health. Thus, we are especially interested in indicators that, when used with benchmarks, measure change over time. Nonetheless, indicators that only generate a yes/no answer may also provide useful information about a state's commitment to the implementation of the right to health. Such indicators have the added advantage that the necessary information can usually be rapidly collected by way of a cost-effective questionnaire.

Sometimes, plausible links may be established between a structural indicator (is there a strategy and plan of action to reduce maternal deaths?), a process indicator (the proportion of births attended by skilled health personnel), and an outcome indicator (maternal mortality). However, outcome indicators often reflect many complex inter-related factors. It will usually be difficult to establish firm causal links between structural, process, and outcome indicators—that is, between a policy, an intervention, and a health status outcome.

As we emphasized in part III, it is misguided to expect too much from indicators. For example, a structural indicator is: does the state constitution recognize the right to health? If the answer is 'yes', this is a useful piece of information. But if a constitutional right to health neither generates any successful litigation nor is taken into account in national policy-making, this particular constitutional provision is of very restricted value. With this in mind, we suggest that the answer to any indicator may be supplemented by a brief note or remark (a 'narrative'). For example, in the above example the answer might be: 'Yes—but the right has yet to be integrated into health policy-making.' Of course, a brief note of this sort does not dispel the manifold limitations of indicators. Nonetheless, it can help to provide a fuller picture of the right to health in the relevant state than a bare yes/no or numerical answer.

Additional specific examples of structural indicators, process indicators and outcome indicators are found in the annex.[59]

---

[59] See Interim Report of the Special Rapporteur to the General Assembly 2003, A/58/427 (n 1 above); Interim Report of the Special Rapporteur to the General Assembly 2004, A/59/422 (n 1 above); Report of the Special Rapporteur to the Commission on Human Rights 2006, E/CN.4/2006/48 (n 1 above).

IX. Conclusions and recommendations

Many *existing* health indicators, already commonly used by health ministries and others—such as the maternal mortality ratio and HIV prevalence rate—have an important potential role to play in measuring and monitoring the progressive realization of the right to the highest attainable standard of health. Health indicators may be used to monitor aspects of the progressive realization of the right to the highest attainable standard of health provided that they correspond, with some precision, to a right to health norm, and that they are disaggregated by at least sex, race, ethnicity, rural/urban, and socio-economic status. The grounds of disaggregation should be reviewed in the light of capacity, context, and the health issue in question. Additionally, health indicators must be supplemented by additional indicators that monitor five essential and inter-related features of the right to health:

(i) a national strategy and plan of action that includes the right to health;
(ii) the participation of individuals and groups, especially the most vulnerable and disadvantaged, in relation to the formulation of health policies and programmes;
(iii) access to health information, as well as confidentiality of personal health data;
(iv) international assistance and co-operation of donors in relation to the enjoyment of the right to health in developing states; and
(v) accessible and effective monitoring and accountability mechanisms.

While it is impossible for one indicator to possess all the features signalled in the preceding paragraph, it is possible to identify *a range* of indicators that *together* have these features. Thus, rather than searching for individual right to health indicators, it is more helpful to think in terms of a *human rights-based approach to health indicators*.

The human rights-based approach to health indicators is not only a tool to help states, and others, measure and monitor the progressive realization of the right to health. Additionally, the approach includes features, such as disaggregation, participation, and accountability that, if integrated into health policies and programmes, are likely to enhance their effectiveness. So far as necessary, states should adapt their existing indicators (eg by introducing appropriate disaggregation), and identify new indicators (eg on participation and accountability), so that their practice conforms to the human rights-based approach to health indicators outlined in this chapter.

With a view to assisting their partner states, specialized agencies and other UN bodies should also adapt their existing indicators, so far as necessary, and identify new indicators, in conformity with the human rights-based approach to health indicators outlined in this chapter. In their reporting guidelines, 'constructive dialogue', Concluding Observations and other documents, human rights treaty bodies are urged to adopt—and to encourage states parties to adopt—the human rights-based approach to health indicators outlined here. OHCHR should continue to play its crucial pivotal role in the development of a human rights-based approach to indicators generally, and a human rights-based approach to health indicators specifically. Non-governmental organizations should adopt the human rights-based approach to health indicators outlined in this chapter.

While this chapter sets out a methodology for a human rights-based approach to health indicators, further work is needed to make the methodology fully operational. In particular, further attention should be given to:

- developing indicators that measure the five essential features of the right to health: a national strategy and plan of action; participation; health information, as well confidentiality of personal health data; international assistance and co-operation; and monitoring and accountability;[60]
- exploring how the human rights-based approach to health indicators might best reflect the right to health analytical framework of accessibility, availability, acceptability, and quality.[61]

The existing multiplicity of terms for different categories of health indicators is extremely confusing and a major obstacle to a consistent, coherent, and rational approach to health policy. With a view to developing a common approach which is comprehensible to the non-specialist, it is strongly recommended that the human rights-based approach to health indicators adopts the following basic terms and categories: *structural indicators, process indicators, and outcome indicators*. In future, the definitions of structural, process, and outcome will need revising and refining in the light of experience. Further, there might be exceptional cases where additional categories of indicators are needed. Nonetheless, it is strongly recommended that the existing obscurantist proliferation of multiple overlapping terms is replaced, as a general rule, by structural, process, and outcome indicators. By way of illustration, the following Annex provides a table that applies a human rights-based approach to indicators, as set out in this chapter, to the Reproductive Health Strategy endorsed by the World Health Assembly in May 2004.

Finally, for well over a decade there have been interminable discussions about human rights and indicators. It is imperative that these discussions steadily move beyond the theoretical to the practical. Thanks to the work of innumerable health and human rights experts over many years, the essential features of a

---

[60] The starting point for further developing such indicators is to clarify the scope—or normative content—of each of the five essential features.

[61] This framework derives from the ESCR Committee's *General Comment 14* and has been elaborated upon and applied by the Special Rapporteur in several reports. See eg, 'The right of everyone to the enjoyment of the highest attainable standard of physical and mental health', Report of the Special Rapporteur to the Commission on Human Rights 2005, E/CN.4/2005/51 (11 Feb 2005) para 46.

human rights-based approach to health indicators are becoming increasingly clear. Of course, this approach will develop and mature further. Nonetheless, it is strongly recommended that all parties begin to adopt the human rights-based approach to health indicators outlined in this chapter, as a way of (1) measuring and monitoring the progressive realization of the right to the highest attainable standard of health and (2) enhancing the effectiveness of health policies and programmes.

Annex

A human rights-based approach to indicators in relation to the Reproductive Health Strategy endorsed by the World Health Assembly in May 2004

1. The following table applies the human rights-based approach to indicators, as set out in this chapter, to the Reproductive Health Strategy endorsed by the World Health Assembly (WHA) in May 2004.

2. WHA's Reproductive Health Strategy identifies five priority or 'core' aspects of reproductive and sexual health. Each is separately addressed in the following table. Human rights, including the right to the highest attainable standard of health, are a 'guiding principle' of the WHA's Strategy.

3. If we were to prepare a reproductive health strategy, it would have some features that are not found in the WHA's Strategy (generally, see the Special Rapporteur's report E/CN.4/2004/49, 16 Feb 2004). Nonetheless, for present purposes, we are taking the WHA's Strategy and endeavouring to provide a preliminary response to the question: 'Which indicators would be needed if a human rights-based approach to indicators were to be applied to the WHA's Reproductive Health Strategy?'

4. As already explained, a health indicator may be used to monitor aspects of the progressive realization of the right to the highest attainable standard of health on certain conditions, one being that the indicator corresponds, with some precision, to a right to health norm. All the health indicators in the following table correspond with sufficient precision to one or more right to health norms, including the following: article 24(2)(a) and (d) of the Convention on the Rights of the Child, article 12(2)(a), (c), and (d) of the International Covenant on Economic, Social and Cultural Rights, article 5(e)(iv) of the International Convention on the Elimination of All Forms of Racial Discrimination, and article 12 of the Convention on the Elimination of All Forms of Discrimination Against Women.

5. It is important that a human rights-based approach to indicators does not generate an excessive number of indicators. It is also crucial that the indicators are relatively straightforward and within the capacity of most states to collect. There is no point identifying a large number of indicators many of which lie beyond the capacity of most states. Thus, the indicators should either be commonly available, or available without considerable additional expense. Each indicator may be supplemented by a very brief explanatory note or comment.

6. The indicators in the following table are neither exhaustive nor definitive. A state might wish to add to, or subtract from, the table. Nonetheless, the following indicators may assist those states, and others, who are committed to monitoring the realization of the right to health.

7. We are extremely grateful to all those—especially the WHO Department of Reproductive Health and Research—who provided indispensable advice regarding this annex. While preparing the table, we have drawn from—and warmly recommend—*Using Human Rights for Maternal and Neonatal Health: A tool for strengthening laws, policies and standards of care*, co-published by the Department of Reproductive Health and Research, World Health Organization, and the Program on International Health and Human Rights, Francois-Xavier Bagnoud Center for Health and Human Rights, Harvard School of Public Health (2005). We will especially welcome suggestions on how to strengthen indicators regarding the five essential features of the right to health identified in section VII of this chapter.

Key to Table
*ICESCR = International Covenant on Economic, Social and Cultural Rights
*CRC = United Nations Convention on the Rights of the Child
*CEDAW = Convention on the Elimination of All Forms of Discrimination Against Women
*ICERD = International Convention on the Elimination of All Forms of Racial Discrimination
**Indicates a Millennium Development Goal indicator

	Structural Indicators	Process Indicators	Outcome Indicators
Basic Legal Context	S1. Has the state ratified the following international treaties recognizing the right to health? (a) ICESCR* *(yes/no)* (b) CRC* *(yes/no)* (c) CEDAW* *(yes/no)* (d) ICERD* *(yes/no)* S2. Does the state's constitution include the right to health? *(yes/no)* S3. Does state legislation expressly recognize the right to health, including sexual and reproductive health rights? *(yes/no)*	P1. Number of reports the state has submitted to the treaty-based bodies monitoring the following treaties: (a) ICESCR (b) CRC (c) CEDAW (d) ICERD P2. Number of national judicial decisions that considered sexual and reproductive health rights in the last five years	
Basic Financial Context	S4. Does the state have a law to ensure *universal access* to sexual and reproductive health care? *(yes/no)*	P3. Percentage of government budget allocated to health P4. Percentage of government *health budget* allocated to sexual and reproductive health P5. Percentage of government *health expenditure* directed to sexual and reproductive health P6. Per capita *expenditure* on sexual and reproductive health	
National Strategy and Plan of Action	S5. Does the state have a national sexual and reproductive health strategy/plan of action? *(yes/no)*	P7. Does the state collect data adequate to evaluate performance under the strategy/plan of action,	

	Structural Indicators	Process Indicators	Outcome Indicators

	S6. Does the strategy/plan of action provide for *universal access* to sexual and reproductive health care? *(yes/no)*
	
	 S7. Does the strategy/plan of action:
	(a) expressly recognize sexual and reproductive health rights? *(yes/no)*
	(b) clearly identify:
	  i. objectives? *(yes/no)*
	  ii. timeframes? *(yes/no)*
	  iii. duty holders and their responsibilities? *(yes/no)*
	  iv. reporting procedures? *(yes/no)*
	(c) specifically include measures to benefit vulnerable groups? *(yes/no)*
		particularly in relation to vulnerable groups? *(yes/no)*	

Participation	S8. Does the strategy/plan of action establish a procedure for the state to regularly consult with a wide range of representatives of the following groups when formulating, implementing, and monitoring sexual and reproductive health policy: (a) non-governmental organizations? *(yes/no)*	P8. Does the state regularly consult with a wide range of representatives of the following groups when formulating, implementing, and monitoring sexual and reproductive health policy: (a) non-governmental organizations? *(yes/no)* (b) health professional organizations? *(yes/no)*	

	Structural Indicators	Process Indicators	Outcome Indicators
	(b) health professional organizations? (*yes/no*) (c) local governments? (*yes/no*) (d) community leaders? (*yes/no*) (e) vulnerable groups? (*yes/no*) (f) private sector? (*yes/no*)	(c) local governments? (*yes/no*) (d) community leaders? (*yes/no*) (e) vulnerable groups? (*yes/no*) (f) private sector? (*yes/no*)	O1. Percentage of women who know about contraceptive methods (traditional or modern)— *Disaggregated by at least age, race, ethnicity, socio-economic status, and rural/urban* O2. Percentage of people ages 15–24 who know how to prevent HIV infection— *Disaggregated by at least sex, race, ethnicity, socio-economic status, and rural/urban*
Information	S9. Does state law protect the right to seek, receive, and impart information on sexual and reproductive health? (*yes/no*) S10. Does the state have a strategy/plan of action to disseminate information on sexual and reproductive health to the public? (*yes/no*) S11. Does the strategy/plan of action establish a procedure for the state to disseminate regularly information on its sexual and reproductive health policies to: (a) non-governmental organizations? (*yes/no*) (b) health professional organizations? (*yes/no*) (c) local governments? (*yes/no*) (d) media accessible in rural aras? (*yes/no*)	P9. Percentage of people exposed to information on: (a) maternal and newborn care (b) family planning services (c) abortion/post-abortion care (d) prevention and treatment of sexually transmitted infections (e) prevention and treatment of cervical cancer and other gynecological morbidities P10. Does the state regularly disseminate information on its sexual and reproductive health policies to: (a) non-governmental organizations? (*yes/no*) (b) health professional organizations? (*yes/no*) (c) local governments? (*yes/no*) (d) media accessible in rural areas? (*yes/no*)	

	Structural Indicators	Process Indicators	Outcome Indicators
	S12. Does state law protect the confidentiality of personal health information? S13. Does state law require informed consent of the individual to accept or refuse treatment?	P11. Percentage of health facilities with protocols on the confidentiality of personal health information P12. Percentage of health professionals who have received training on: (a) the confidentiality of personal health information (b) the requirement of informed consent to accept/refuse treatment	O3. Percentage of people who believe that personal information disclosed to health professionals remains confidential— *Disaggregated by at least age, sex, race, ethnicity, socio-economic status, and rural/urban*
National Human Rights Institutions	S14. Does the state have a national human rights institution with a mandate that includes sexual and reproductive health rights? *(yes/no)*	P13. Number of the following activities the institution has run on sexual and reproductive health rights in the last five years: (a) training programs (b) public campaigns P14. Number of complaints concerning sexual and reproductive health rights the institution has considered in the last five years	
International Assistance and Co-operation (These indicators are for donors)	S15. Is the state's overseas development assistance policy rights-based? *(yes/no)* S16. Does the state's overseas development policy include specific provisions to promote and protect	P15. Percentage of overseas development assistance directed to sexual andreproductive health P16. Do the state's reports to the human rights treaty-based bodies include a detailed account of the	

	Structural Indicators	Process Indicators	Outcome Indicators
	sexual and reproductive health rights? (yes/no)	international assistance and co-operation it is providing, including in relation to sexual and reproductive health? (yes/no/not applicable) P17. Does the state provide a state-specific annual report of its international assistance and co-operation, including in relation to sexual and reproductive health: (a) to the government of the recipient state? (yes/no) (b) to the public of the recipient state? (yes/no)	
Priority Aspect 1: Improving Antenatal, Delivery, Post Partum, and Newborn Care	S17. Does the state have a strategy/plan of action: (a) to reduce maternal deaths and their causes? (yes/no) (b) to ensure a universal system of referral for obstetric emergencies? (yes/no) (c) for access to care, treatment, and support for HIV-infected pregnant women? (yes/no)	P18. Number of facilities per 500,000 population providing: (a) basic obstetric care (b) comprehensive obstetric care P19. Percentage of births attended by skilled health personnel**— *Disaggregated by at least age, race, ethnicity, socio-economic status, and rural/urban* P20. Percentage of pregnant women counseled and tested for HIV	O4. Percentage of women with *access* to antenatal, delivery, post partum, and newborn care— *Disaggregated by at least age, race, ethnicity, socio-economic status, and rural/urban* O5. Maternal mortality ratio (number of maternal deaths per 100,000 live births)**— *Disaggregated by at least age, race, ethnicity, socio-economic status, rural/urban*

	Structural Indicators	Process Indicators	Outcome Indicators
		Disaggregated by at least race, ethnicity, socio-economic status, and rural/urban P21. Percentage of pregnant women screened for syphilis— *Disaggregated by at least age, race, ethnicity, socio-economic status, and rural/urban*	O6. HIV prevalence among pregnant women (15–24 years old)**— *Disaggregated by at least race, ethnicity, socio-economic status, and rural/urban* O7. Syphilis prevalence among pregnant women (15–24 years old)— *Disaggregated by at least age, race, ethnicity, socio-economic status, and rural/urban* O8. Neonatal mortality rate (number of infant deaths within one month of birth per 1,000 live births)— *Disaggregated by at least age, race, ethnicity, socio-economic status, and rural/urban*
Priority Aspect 2: Delivering High Quality Services for Family Planning	S18. Does state law: (a) require third-party authorization for women to receive family planning services? *(yes/no)* (b) specify that only married women may receive family planning services? *(yes/no)*	P22. Percentage of primary health care facilities providing comprehensive family planning services (full range of contraceptive information, counseling and supplies for at least six methods, including male and female, temporary, permanent, and emergency contraception)	O9. Percentage of people with *access* to comprehensive family planning services— *Disaggregated by at least age, sex, race, ethnicity, socio-economic status, and rural/urban* O10. Percentage of women at risk of pregnancy who are using (or whose partner is using) a contraceptive

	Structural Indicators	Process Indicators	Outcome Indicators
			method (all methods)**— *Disaggregated by at least age, race, ethicity, socio-economic status, and rural/urban*
	S19. Does the national essential medicines list include: (a) condoms? *(yes/no)* (b) hormonal contraceptives, including emergency contraceptives? *(yes/no)*		O11. Percentage of women at risk of pregnancy who desire to avoid pregnancy, but who are not using (and whose partner is not using) a contraceptive method— *Disaggregated by at least age, race, ethnicity socio-economic status, and rural/urban*
Priority Aspect 3: Eliminating Unsafe Abortion	S20. Does state law allow abortion: (a) on request? *(yes/no)* (b) for economic or social reasons? *(yes/no)* (c) for the physical and/or mental health of the woman? *(yes/no)* (d) to save the life of the woman? *(yes/no)* (e) for cases of rape or incest? *(yes/no)* (f) for fetal impairment? *(yes/no)* (g) in no circumstances? *(yes/no)* S21. Does state law criminalize abortion? *(yes/no)*	P23. Percentage of service delivery points providing abortion and/or post-abortion care P24. Percentage of practitioners trained in abortion and/or post-abortion care	O12. Percentage of women with *access* to abortion and/or post-abortion care— *Disaggregated by at least age, race, ethnicity socio-economic status, and rural/urban* O13. Abortion rate (number of abortions per 1,000 women of reproductive age)— *Disaggregated by at least age, race, ethnicity socio-economic status, and rural/urban* O14. Percentage of maternal deaths attributed to unsafe abortion— *Disaggregated by at least age, race,*

Structural Indicators	Process Indicators	Outcome Indicators
		ethnicity, socio-economic status, and rural/urban
S22. Does the state have a strategy/plan of action to: (a) prevent unsafe abortion? *(yes/no)* (b) provide post-abortion care? *(yes/no)*		O15. Percentage of people with *access to:* (a) health care for sexually transmitted infections (b) preventative care for cervical cancer and other gynecological morbidities— *Disaggregated by at least age, race, ethnicity socio-economic status, and rural/urban*
Priority Aspect 4: **Combating Sexually Transmitted Infections, Cervical Cancer, and Other Gynecological Morbidities**	P25. Number of condoms available for distribution nationwide (during the preceding 12 months) per population aged 15–49 years	O16. Percentage of people with self-reported or diagnosed symptoms of sexually transmitted infections [classified by condition]—
S23. Does the state have a strategy/plan of action: (a) to prevent sexually transmitted infections, including HIV? *(yes/no)* (b) to treat sexually transmitted infections? *(yes/no)* (c) to make anti-retroviral treatment available for people living with HIV? *(yes/no)* (d) to prevent cervical cancer? *(yes/no)*	P26. Percentage of family planning service delivery points offering counseling on dual protection from sexually transmitted infections/HIV and unwanted pregnancies P27. Percentage of women screened for cervical cancer within the past five years— *Disaggregated by at least age, race, ethnicity, socio-economic status, and rural/urban*	*Disaggregated by at least age, sex, race, ethnicity socio-economic status, and rural/urban* O17. HIV prevalence in sub-populations with high-risk behaviour— *Disaggregated by at least age, sex, race, ethnicity, socio-economic status, and rural/urban*

	Structural Indicators	Process Indicators	Outcome Indicators
			O18. Percentage of women with cervical cancer— *Disaggregated by at least age, race, ethnicity, socio-economic status, and rural/urban*
Priority Aspect 5: Promoting Sexual Health Including for Adolescents	S24. Does state law require comprehensive sexual health education during the compulsory school years? *(yes/no)*	P28. Percentage of people ages 15–19 years who have received comprehensive sexual health education in school— *Disaggregated by at least sex, race, ethnicity, socio-economic status, and rural/urban*	O19. Percentage of people ages 15–19 years who know how to prevent HIV infection
	S25. Does the state have a strategy/plan of action to promote adolescent sexual and reproductive health? *(yes/no)*	P29. Number of incidents of sexual violence, including marital rape, reported to law enforcement and/or health professionals in the past five years	O20. Age specific fertility rate (15–19 years and 20–24 years)— *Disaggregated by at least race, ethnicity, socio-economic status, and rural/urban*
	S26. Does state law prohibit sexual violence, including marital rape? *(yes/no)*		O21. Age at marriage— *Disaggregated by at least sex, race, ethnicity, socio-economic status, and rural/urban*
	S27. Does state law prohibit female genital mutilation and other harmful traditional practices? *(yes/no)*		O22. Percentage of women who have undergone female genital mutilation— *Disaggregated by at least sex, race, ethnicity, socio-economic status, and rural/urban*
	S28. Does state law prohibit marriage for both men and women prior to age 18 years? *(yes/no)*		
	S.29 Does state law require full and free consent of the parties to a marriage? *(yes/no)*		

13

The Rights to Social Security and Social Assistance: Towards an Analytical Framework[1]

Jennifer Tooze

I. Introduction

The provision of social security and social assistance to those in need is a highly charged political issue. Governments of rich states seek to demonstrate that any redistribution resulting from social security does not de-motivate individuals or undermine efficient functioning of the free market. Poor states are encouraged to privatize public services and pension schemes and to prioritize free trade.[2] It is undeniable that the provision of social security and social assistance impacts upon the economic and social wellbeing of many, in particular upon the wellbeing of the most vulnerable, in society. It is not surprising therefore to find the right to social security enshrined in the International Covenant on Economic, Social and Cultural Rights[3] (the Covenant). What is more surprising is that so little has been done to determine the content of that right in international law.

Certainly, there are difficulties in determining the nature of the rights[4] to social security and social assistance. There can be no single model that fits all. The precise benefit arising under the right will necessarily vary between states according to

[1] This chapter is based on work undertaken for my PhD thesis titled: 'Identification and Enforcement of Social Security and Social Assistance Guarantees under the International Covenant on Economic, Social and Cultural Rights' (2002). I am indebted to Professor David Harris for his supervision of that thesis and for the encouragement and support he has given me. The views expressed in this chapter are my own and do not represent the views of the Home Office or the UK government generally.

[2] See J Tooze, 'Aligning States' Economic Policies with Human Rights Obligations: The CESCR's Quest for Consistency' (2002) 2 Human Rights L Rev no 2, 229 from 240.   [3] 993 UNTS 3.

[4] Although the Covenant does not contain an express right to social assistance, its does contain a right to an adequate standard of living which arguably includes such a right. This, together with the fact that the equivalent European Social Charter 1961 (ESC), ETS 35 contains a right to social assistance, supports the development in this chapter of an analytical framework for a right to social assistance.

available resources. And it will necessarily vary within states over time according to the political motivation of governments. Additional challenges arise from the lack of any comprehensive body of domestic case law from which the nature of the right can be developed. However, these difficulties do not render a basic framework for the rights to social security and social assistance impossible. Rather, there are certain fundamental principles and characteristics of both social security and social assistance that enable an analytical framework to be developed within which their provision can be measured and monitored in international law and which can and should accommodate such variations.

This chapter argues that the rights to social security and to social assistance in international law can be translated into state obligations that can be effectively monitored and enforced. Challenges arising from the fact that the right is to be fulfilled progressively in international law are considered and a possible approach to monitoring progress is outlined. The tests of availability, adequacy, and accessibility (which have been used in the context of other economic and social rights) are used to identify the obligations of states under the Covenant[5] and the work of the United Nations (UN) Committee on Economic, Social and Cultural Rights (ESCR Committee) is analysed within that framework.[6] This focus on the work of the ESCR Committee is not intended to imply that the Committee is the most appropriate body to implement a right to social security. Indeed, the technical nature of the right suggests an expert organization such as the International Labour Organization (ILO)[7] may be better suited to the task. However, the ESCR Committee has unparalleled experience in examining the enjoyment of social security from a rights perspective and its work is therefore instructive and invaluable when considering how the right can be defined, monitored, and enforced.

Section II below introduces the Covenant and considers ways of monitoring and enforcing the progressive obligations in it. Section III introduces the concepts of social security and social assistance. Sections IV to VI identify state obligations by applying the tests of availability, adequacy, and accessibility and section VII considers issues relating to expenditure. Conclusions are then drawn in section VIII.

[5] The UN Committee on Economic, Social and Cultural Rights (ESCR Committee) applied the tests of availability and accessibility to the right to adequate housing, the tests of availability, accessibility, acceptability, and adaptability to the right to education, and the tests of availability, accessibility, acceptability, and adequacy/quality to the rights to food and to health: *General Comment 4* (1991) para 8(a) and (e); *General Comment 13* (1999), para 6; *General Comment 12* (1999), paras 7, 8, and 11 to 13; *General Comment 14* (2000), para 12.

[6] I have examined the vast majority of the work of the ESCR Committee from its 3rd session until its 26th session at the end of 2001. I regret that I have not been able to undertake a complete analysis of the ESCR Committee's work for the period 2002 until present for the purposes of this chapter. However, I have considered various elements of the ESCR Committee's work for this latter period when writing this chapter.

[7] The ILO is a specialized agency of the UN that has considerable expertise in labour matters and social security. There are various ILO Conventions relating to social security. They are overseen by an ILO Committee of Experts. The ILO has attended sessions of the ESCR Committee and submits an annual report to the Committee detailing the findings of its expert committee with regard to the implementation of relevant ILO standards being examined by the ESCR Committee.

II. The International Covenant on Economic, Social and Cultural Rights

The Covenant was adopted by the UN General Assembly in 1966 and entered into force in 1976 following the 35th ratification in line with its article 27. To date it has been ratified by 152 states[8]. The Covenant enshrines a wide range of economic, social, and cultural rights (ESCR) including the right to social security, in article 9, and the right to an adequate standard of living, in article 11.

Article 9 provides:

The States Parties to the present Covenant recognise the right of everyone to social security, including social insurance.

Article 11(1) provides:

The States Parties to the present Covenant recognise the right of everyone to an adequate standard of living for himself and his family, including adequate food, clothing and housing, and to the continuous improvement of living conditions. The States Parties will take appropriate steps to ensure the realisation of this right, recognising to this effect the essential importance of international co-operation based on free consent.

To date, implementation of the Covenant is monitored and enforced through a reporting system. Unlike the equivalent Council of Europe instrument, the European Social Charter (ESC), [9] it has no petition procedure.

In accordance with article 2(1) of the Covenant, all rights in the Covenant are to be realized by states parties progressively, to the maximum of available resources, 'by all appropriate means, including particularly the adoption of legislative measures'.[10] This general provision determines the obligations of states parties in relation to every substantive provision in the Covenant. Three key points[11] need to be made.

First, article 2(1) demonstrates that the Covenant was based on an assumption that economic growth would prevail and would permit continued expansion of the welfare state. Yet economic growth has declined in many developed and developing states challenging their ability to realize progressively the rights in the Covenant. Furthermore, the forces of economic globalization permit capital to

---

[8] Kazakhstan became the 152nd state party on 24 Jan 2006.

[9] The ESC contains a right to social security in art 12 that delineates an obligation to maintain and progressively improve social security systems as well as a right to social assistance in art 13. The Revised ESC of 1996 also contains those two rights, although standards are higher.

[10] Art 2(1) of the Covenant reads: 'Each State party to the present Covenant undertakes to take steps, individually and through international assistance and cooperation, especially economic and technical, to the maximum of its available resources, with a view to achieving progressively the full realisation of the rights recognised in the present Covenant by all appropriate means, including particularly the adoption of legislative measures.'

[11] For a more detailed analysis of art 2(1) see P Alston and G Quinn 'The Nature and Scope of States Parties' Obligations under the International Covenant on Economic, Social and Cultural Rights' (1987) 9 Human Rights Q 156.

relocate with increasing ease and compel states to compete for international investment, invariably by lowering labour costs. The nature of this general obligation must therefore be viewed in light of the current economic climate and enforcement bodies must resist simplistic criticism of regression.

Second, immediate obligations can be identified from article 2(1) and must be clarified so that states parties can understand what is expected of them under the Covenant. Whilst article 2(1) enshrines a broad obligation of result to achieve progressively the full realization of each right, states parties are obliged to undertake obligations of conduct with a view to achieving this broad result. The types of conduct that must be undertaken immediately will vary between states parties according to the resources available to them. The importance of identifying immediate obligations should not be underestimated. An obligation can only be violated in law if it requires satisfaction at that particular moment in time. This suggests that obligations are only justiciable where they are immediate. It is therefore essential that any monitoring body clarify those obligations which states parties are expected to fulfil immediately rather than progressively.

The ESCR Committee has observed that immediate obligations of result, which may entail resource implications, exist under article 2(1) of the Covenant. It applies a rebuttable assumption that the minimum essential levels of each of the rights are capable of immediate realization in all states parties. Where states fail to satisfy this core obligation, they bear the burden of proof and must 'demonstrate that every effort has been made to use all resources that are at its disposition in an effort to satisfy, as a matter of priority, those minimum obligations'.[12] However, the ESCR Committee has not identified the content of this minimum core obligation and therefore it is not clear whether this obligation of result is currently enforceable. Negative obligations to respect rights will most often (although not always) be cost free and therefore can be fulfilled by most, if not all, states parties.

Third, beyond these basic obligations, it is considerably more difficult for the ESCR Committee to identify positive obligations requiring resources that must be fulfilled immediately by any particular state party. The ESCR Committee will only have access to limited and very general indicators of resource availability, such as Gross Domestic Product (GDP) per capita, which is often not an adequate basis for identification of rights-specific obligations. In addition, states enjoy considerable discretion as to which affordable steps they take to realize progressively the rights and the ESCR Committee is unable to require particular steps to be adopted. Furthermore, there is little domestic litigation to assist the ESCR Committee in this task because courts are often reluctant to examine issues that go to the allocation of resources on the basis that such allocation is a political rather than a judicial function for which judges lack both expertise and accountability. (In contrast to civil and political rights, judges are unable to ignore the resource

---

[12] *General Comment 3* (1990), para 10.

implications of their work when enforcing the progressive obligation contained in article 2(1) of the Covenant.[13])

Even if it is not possible to identify particular steps that must be taken by states parties, it is possible to require states parties to justify the steps that they have taken. In particular, states should be called upon to demonstrate:

(i) that the steps adopted are reasonable, reasonableness being determined by reference to available resources and to the likelihood that progressive realization of the rights will result;

(ii) that they are using available resources equitably, effectively, and efficiently;

(iii) that they are developing societal resources;

(iv) that resources are targeted to subsistence requirements and essential services with a view to protecting the most vulnerable; and

(v) that they are monitoring progress made and modifying programmes where progress is insufficient.[14]

Under such an approach, the burden of proof resting on the state should increase as the levels of progress decline and in particular where the state regresses. It might also be greater in the case of developed states owing to their relative wealth. However, the imposition of an impossibly high burden on developed states would fail to acknowledge the relevance of resources to highly advanced states and would fail to consider the need for those states to maintain resources. It is submitted that in all cases the ESCR Committee should take full advantage of the flexibility inherent in article 2(1) and should be sympathetic where regressive measures are necessary to maintain the right in question.[15]

Such a policy-based approach moves beyond simple legislative measures and provides states with room to demonstrate the balance they have struck between long-term economic investment and short-term social expenditure. It effectively creates an immediate positive obligation to adopt reasonable policies. As evidenced in the work of the South African Constitutional Court,[16] such an approach allows

---

[13] Because states parties to the International Covenant on Civil and Political Rights (ICCPR) undertake to 'respect' and to 'ensure' the rights in that covenant, it appears that the Human Rights Committee in enforcing that covenant is neither forced to consider nor held accountable for the resource implications of its decisions.

[14] The author has taken a number of these from the Limburg Principles, in particular Principles 23, 24, 27, and 28: Limburg Principles on the Implementation of the International Covenant on Economic, Social and Cultural Rights (1986), (1987) 9 Human Rights Q 122. See also *The Maastricht Guidelines on Violations of Economic, Social and Cultural Rights* (1997) para 8, (1998) 20 Human Rights Q 691.

[15] The European Committee of Experts has adopted such an approach in the context of the right to social security under the ESC: *General Observation on Article 12(3), Conclusions XIII-4* at 143; *General Introduction, Conclusions XIV-1* at 39 and 46. This is discussed further in the context of expenditure in section VII below.

[16] See eg, *Government of the Republic of South Africa and Others v Grootboom and Others*, 4 Oct 2000, CCT 11/00 2001 (1) SA 46 (CC), available from <http://www.concourt.law.wits.ac.za> accessed 18 June 2006; *Soobramoney v Minister of Health, KwaZulu Natal*, Case CCT 32/97, available from <http://www.concourt.law.wits.ac.za> accessed 18 June 2006.

a degree of judicial control to be exercised over complex obligations without permitting the judiciary to step into the political arena of resource allocation. This should not be overlooked when considering the extent to which the rights to social security and social assistance are justiciable and the shape that any claims might take.

III. Social security and social assistance

A. Objectives

From 1600 to the end of the 19th century, social support within Europe took the form of the Poor Laws[17], which aimed to instil a work ethic in the poor and to ameliorate poverty. With the arrival of industrialization, poverty prevention and social compensation came to largely replace those aims. Industrialization brought with it the need for employee protection, and social security began to respond to particular social risks that gave rise to an interruption in earning power. Today, there are generally (at the international[18] as well as the European[19] level) nine branches of social security which respond to nine contingencies: medical care; sickness; invalidity; unemployment; employment injury; maternity; family; old-age; and survivors' benefit. Alongside social security, means-tested social assistance provides protection to non-workers who lack the means necessary for a decent existence.

However, it is not always easy to distinguish between social security and social assistance. Social security and social assistance cannot be distinguished by the form which they take since both may be provided in cash or in kind. Whilst social security will often be limited in duration, it may, like social assistance, be of unlimited duration. The key distinction would appear to rest on the basis of entitlement; whereas entitlement to social security emanates from the contingency, entitlement to social assistance emanates from need. It is on this basis that the European Committee on Social Rights (which oversees the implementation of the ESC) has sought to distinguish the two, although in doing so that Committee has recognized that this may in certain cases be a rather artificial distinction to draw.[20] By way of example, it may be rather artificial to find a payment to old persons to be social assistance as it is targeted at persons in need when it could equally be classified as being non-contributory social security (old-age branch).

---

[17] See generally TH Marshall 'Citizenship and Social Class' in TH Marshall *Class Citizenship and Social Development* (Doubleday, 1949).

[18] The ILO's key convention in this area is Convention 102 (1952) Social Security (Minimum Standards) Convention.

[19] The European Code of Social Security 1962 mirrors the ILO Convention 102, only it requires states parties to undertake to satisfy a larger number of branches (six) than ILO Convention 102 (three) and is accompanied by an Optional Protocol that provides for a higher level of benefits.

[20] *General Introduction, General Conclusions XIII-4* at 36–37.

A key question underpinning both social security and social assistance is the extent to which they should aim to maintain status differentials or aim to eradicate them. The variations that exist in the levels of redistribution effected through welfare states can be seen to reflect the relative weight accorded to particular principles that underlie social security and, to a lesser extent, social assistance, and to the balance that is struck between these principles:

(i)   individual equity: benefits give rise to a 'fair return' on contributions;
(ii)   horizontal equity: persons in identical positions should be treated equally;
(iii)   solidarity: risks are shared between those within the system;
(iv)   compulsory participation: in social security schemes;
(v)   economic viability: any system of social security or social assistance must be economically viable;
(vi)   state responsibility: social security and social assistance cannot be considered to be solely a private concern;
(vii)   right of insured to participate in the administration of a social security scheme; and
(viii) right of persons to an appeal.

The balance to be struck and therefore the degree of redistribution that is effected is essentially one of policy rather than of law and, beyond certain minimum standards, a rights-based approach to social security and social assistance need not, and arguably should not, affect this.

B. Provision

Social security and social assistance are provided through various schemes or instruments. These may be categorized in various ways and the following distinguishes between (i) contributory social security benefits; (ii) non-contributory social security and social assistance benefits; and (iii) other categories of benefits. A basic understanding of these schemes and instruments is essential when considering the content of the rights to social security and social assistance.

1. Contributory social security

Social insurance has, since it emerged in those states in which industrialization was taking place in the late 19th century, become the most popular tool of social security.[21] On the one hand, this is understandable. Social insurance is seen to support the labour market as its contingency base is the loss of earning power and it carries little stigmatization as entitlement derives from contributions rather than from financial need. Yet social insurance is limited in scope; those who do

---

[21] J Dixon, in J Dixon and R Scheurell (eds), *Social Security Programmes: A Cross-Cultural Comparative Perspective* (Greenwood, 1995) p 3 at pp 10–11.

not work and those whose work does not lend itself to regular contributions (in particular, work in the informal sector) find themselves excluded.

Social insurance contributions are paid by the employee and/or the employer. There is no single view as to how the contributory burden should be shared between the employee and the employer and, perhaps not surprisingly, the Covenant gives states discretion as to how social insurance should be financed. Nor is there any single view on how contributions should be calculated. Contributions and benefits will either be flat-rate or earnings-related. Where benefits are flat-rate (defined benefit) the employer bears the financial risk. Where benefits are earnings-related (defined contribution), the employee bears the risk. Currently the trend is for systems to move towards defined contribution.

A common funding basis for state social insurance is the Pay As You Go (PAYG) system. In such a system an individual's contributions provide the basis of their entitlement but do not actually fund their benefit. Rather, at any one moment in time, non-active beneficiaries receive benefits that are financed by the contributions of those who remain active in the labour market. Beyond a reserve fund, no separate savings fund is established. This relatively speedy transfer allows a PAYG system to accommodate inflation without creating undue hardship for contributors. However, a PAYG system is vulnerable to demographic fluctuations, does not generate income, and cannot be operated by the private sector (which must be fully funded).

A further contributory option is the savings fund, which can be run by the state (provident fund) or privately (by employers or private companies). Savings funds can give rise to flat-rate or earnings-related benefits. It has been argued that such saving can enhance national living standards where savings levels are sufficient to effect overall national saving[22] and that savings funds may also benefit states by building up financial markets.[23] However, low inflation and macro-financial stability are thought to be pre-conditions for the establishment of such funded schemes.[24]

2. *Non-contributory social security and social assistance*

Non-contributory benefits are almost always funded out of general taxation to which individuals 'contribute'. Non-contributory social security benefits can exist in all nine branches of social security and entitlement is determined independently of contributions. It is often paid where individuals are not, or are no longer, entitled to a contributory form of the same benefit.

Social assistance is non-contributory. It responds to need and therefore eligibility is most often means-tested (based on the claimant's income and assets). It is

[22] Gramlich in ER Kingson and JH Schultz (eds), *Social Security in the 21st Century* (OUP, 1997) p 147 at 147.
[23] See generally D Vittas, 'Pension Reform and Capital Market Development: "Feasibility" and "Impact" Preconditions', World Bank Working Paper 2414 (World Bank, 2000).
[24] Ibid at 7–8.

usually paid by the state (it is a moot point whether charity provided can be included in the calculation of social assistance) and usually takes the form of a regular payment in cash or in kind. Means-tested benefits have the benefit of targeting the most vulnerable. However, they run the risk of trapping people in a cycle of poverty because they reward savings with the withdrawal of benefit and a subsequent decline in savings. This is frustrated when they are family-based rather than individual-based. In other words, where an individual must have savings of less than x to be entitled to means-tested benefits, any savings by that person above x will give rise to a withdrawal of, or a reduction in, benefit. Where the savings limit is applied to a family rather than to an individual, it means that savings by *any* member of the family will give rise to such a reduction; therefore no member of the family can save without incurring a loss. Means-tested benefits also tend to create stigma and therefore low take-up levels are common.

3. *Other categories of benefits*

Categorical benefits are specific state-administered payments to persons belonging to socially defined categories. Examples include child and family allowances. Tax incentives also provide a vital element of the welfare package.

IV. Availability of social security and social assistance

A. Availability of social security

The availability of social security can be analysed by reference to the number of branches that are provided and the number of persons that are provided for. The ESCR Committee's Reporting Guidelines for article 9 of the Covenant reflect this in asking states parties to indicate which of the nine recognized ILO branches of social security exist, to 'describe for each branch existing... the main features of the schemes in force, indicating the comprehensiveness of the coverage provided, both in the aggregate and with respect to different groups within the society'.[25]

1. *Branches of social security*

It is implied in the Reporting Guidelines from the term 'existing' that states parties to the Covenant are not expected to provide all nine branches of social security. This would accord with the approach taken by the ILO. ILO Convention 102 requires states parties to accept at least three of the nine Parts of that Convention, each of which encapsulates a branch. The ESCR Committee, in its dialogue with states parties, has encouraged states to ratify ILO Convention 102[26] but has not

---

[25] E/C.12/1991/1, art 9, paras 3 and 6.
[26] See eg, E/C.12/1/add 57, paras 19 and 39 (Honduras).

expressly confirmed the acceptance of such a 'menu' system or the number of branches required of states parties under such a system. Whilst it is feasible that the Covenant envisages relatively low levels of coverage for all nine benefits, it would be difficult for such a position to be maintained when the ILO—the UN expert agency on social security—operates a menu system.

Four key questions arise if a menu system is to be adopted in the context of the right to social security under article 9 of the Covenant.

First, how many branches would need to be provided in order to satisfy the minimum core obligation in respect of article 9? As outlined in section II above, satisfaction of this minimum core obligation is an immediate and justiciable obligation. Clearly, the answer cannot be reached in isolation and must be determined in conjunction with the number of beneficiaries of each branch and the level of the benefits provided. Nonetheless, guidance can be taken from the work of the ILO. ILO Convention 102 requires at least three branches of social security to be provided. Although it has only been ratified by forty-one states,[27] which suggests that a minimum requirement of three branches would not be attainable by all states parties to the Covenant, the ESCR Committee has expected certain very poor developing states parties to provide for a number of social security branches.[28] Ultimately, only the ILO has access to the information necessary to determine whether a minimum core obligation of three branches will be feasible for all states parties to the Covenant, therefore consultation between the ESCR Committee and the ILO on this point is essential. Should the ILO consider such a minimum core obligation to be too onerous the ESCR Committee could reduce the number of branches required or the ILO could, where the number of states unable to satisfy that minimum requirement is sufficiently small, provide technical assistance to those states.

Second, should certain benefits be prioritized? ILO Convention 102 appears to accord particular value to five of the nine branches of social security (unemployment benefit; old age benefit; employment injury benefit; invalidity benefit; and survivors' benefit) by requiring states parties to accept at least one of them. However, prioritization was not discussed during the drafting of article 9 of the Covenant and there is nothing to suggest that the ESCR Committee prioritizes any particular branch.

Third, should traditional alternative forms of social security be taken into account when determining social security availability? The ESCR Committee has not addressed this issue consistently; in some cases it has expressed support for the preservation of community living that provides social security[29] and in other cases

---

[27] Poland became the 41st state party when it ratified on 3 Dec 2003.

[28] Eg, in the case of Saint Vincent and the Grenadines the ESCR Committee expressed concern at the lack of employment injury and maternity benefits and expressed hope that unemployment benefit would be introduced, E/C.12/1/add 21, paras 19, 21, and 25.

[29] E/C.12/1989/SR.6 para 50 (Cameroon); E/C.12/1990/SR.11 para 28 (Jamaica).

it has not responded.[30] As social security is a recognized institution internationally, as demonstrated by the work of the ILO, it would seem problematic to permit alternative forms of protection to be taken into account when determining whether the minimum core obligation has been met under article 9 of the Covenant. However, if the ESCR Committee is more concerned about the protection afforded to individuals than the institutions through which that protection is afforded, then, arguably, it should be sufficiently flexible to take into account such alternative forms of social security. The solution may be to take such alternative forms into account beyond the minimum core obligation. Because it is likely to be difficult for states parties to determine with any degree of precision the types and circumstances in which such traditional forms of support are available, the ESCR Committee may well need to rely on indicators such as poverty levels to determine both the availability and adequacy of those forms of support. (Poverty levels are discussed below as an indicator of adequacy.)

Fourth, should the provision of social assistance be taken into account when determining whether the number of branches of social security is sufficient under article 9? Again, it would seem problematic to permit social assistance to be taken into account when determining whether the minimum core obligation has been met under article 9. Beyond that minimum core, if a rights-based approach is to emphasize the level of protection afforded rather than the mechanism through which it is afforded, there is a good argument for taking the existence of social assistance into account when monitoring the availability of social security under article 9. Arguably, however, the extent to which the availability of social assistance can remedy low levels of social security should vary between developed and developing states parties, the former being required to provide a higher number of branches of social security.

2. Beneficiaries

The ESCR Committee's reporting guidelines also request states parties to indicate the 'comprehensiveness of the coverage provided' for each existing branch of social security. Although the ESCR Committee has expressed its appreciation to those states parties in which social security coverage[31] and coverage in respect of particular branches[32] is particularly comprehensive, it is difficult to determine from the dialogue how many people the ESCR Committee expects particular states parties to protect. There are a number of reasons for this. Contrary to the reporting guidelines, it is not unusual for coverage rates to be given for the entire social security system rather than for each branch and in such cases it is unclear how many benefits are available to how many people. In response, the Committee has tended

---

[30] Eg, no comment was made by the ESCR Committee to the suggestion that close family structure provided protection, E/C.12/1993/SR.9 para 39 (Vietnam).

[31] E/C.12/1993/15, para 5 (Iceland); E/C.12/1995/18, para 214 (Norway).

[32] E/C.12/1/add 27, para 4 (Israel).

to reserve its criticism for egregiously low levels of coverage[33] and has often failed to enquire where levels appear low.[34]

There therefore remains a dearth of standards under the Covenant regarding the numbers of beneficiaries to be covered by social security generally, as well as by individual branches of social security. Some insight may be gleaned from ILO Convention 102. Under that Convention, coverage is expressed as a percentage that varies between branches of social security. Generally, states can provide for one of four alternative groups: fifty per cent of all employees; classes of the economically active population that constitute at least twenty per cent of all residents; all residents who lack the means to live in health and decency; and a percentage of residents. However, not all four groups are available for each benefit. Furthermore, Convention 102 provides a separate standard (a fifth group) for those states 'whose economy and medical facilities are insufficiently developed', whereby coverage must be extended to fifty per cent of all employees in industrial workplaces employing at least twenty people.[35] These precise benchmarks could prove useful tools for the ESCR Committee were they to be applied under the Covenant. Of course, when considering the appropriateness of beneficiary levels adopted under ILO Convention 102, it is important to bear in mind the balance struck under ILO Convention 102 between the number of branches, the number of beneficiaries and the level of benefits.

B. Availability of social assistance

The availability of social assistance can be determined by reference to the number of beneficiaries. As it responds to a single contingency—need, the different types of assistance do not provide such a useful indicator.

1. Beneficiaries

There are two main differences between social assistance and social security with regard to coverage. First, because social assistance is designed to alleviate need and is targeted at the needy, the identity of the recipients of social assistance is more determinative than it is in the case of social security. Whereas, with social security, satisfaction of a benchmark is adequate, with social assistance, the fact that the recipient belongs to a particular group—the needy, is key. Second, because social assistance is designed to alleviate need rather than to protect persons from need, an increase in the number of beneficiaries of social assistance will not always reflect progress. Rather, an increase may simply reflect an increase in the number

---

[33] Eg, one member of the ESCR Committee suggested that 6% coverage (total population) was 'astoundingly low' in the case of the Dominican Republic, E/C.12/1997/SR.31, para 11.

[34] Eg, the partial exclusion in Belgium of part-time workers did not prompt any criticism from the ESCR Committee, E/C.12/1994/SR.16/add 1, para 30.

[35] See art 3, 9(d), 15(d), 21(c), 27(d), 33(b), 41(d), 48(d), 55(d), 61(d) of ILO Convention 102.

of persons who are in need and dependant on the state for support. This explains why states parties to the Revised ESC are under an obligation gradually to remove the need for assistance.[36]

The ESCR Committee has, to some extent, recognized these two differences. It has asked reporting states parties how a minimum income is provided to those in need[37] and has shown a particular interest in the most vulnerable groups.[38] It has also, on occasion, requested the numbers receiving assistance[39] and sought reasons for an increase in the number of social assistance claimants.[40] However, the ESCR Committee's work in this regard is not consistent.

Certainly, these complications throw up clear limitations in the use of beneficiary numbers as an indicator of the availability of social assistance. However, monitoring could be enhanced if the numbers covered by social assistance at present as well as five and ten years previously are sought on a regular basis, for example, in the ESCR Committee's Reporting Guidelines. The ESCR Committee could then ask states parties to explain any substantial variations with reference to any national poverty alleviation strategy.

V. Adequacy of social security and social assistance

Evidently, the adequacy and availability of social security and social assistance are closely intertwined and must be analysed together in a rights-based context. When determining the extent to which the right to either is being satisfied, availability can only ever be part of the picture. To reward states parties for increasing the number of branches of social security could be detrimental if it entailed the reduction in benefit levels to a negligible level.

The underlying aims of social security and social assistance determine the benchmark against which the adequacy of benefits will be determined. Adequate social security benefits enable the recipient to maintain reasonable income levels. Adequate social assistance benefits enable the recipient to live out of poverty. A rights-based approach to social security and social assistance would suggest that these objectives should be applied to individuals rather than to family units.

---

[36] *General Introduction, Conclusions XIII-4* at 55–57. Nonetheless, the European Committee on Social Rights is keen to establish reasons behind substantial decreases in claimants, *Conclusions XIV-1*, at 318–19 (Germany).

[37] E/C.12/1998/SR.14, para 60 (Netherlands (Aruba)); E/C.12/1998/SR. 35, para 58 (Cyprus); E/C.12/1998/SR.38, para 53 (Switzerland).

[38] E/C.12/Q/KYRG/1, para 28 (Kyrgyzstan), with regard to the disabled and elderly; E/C.12/Q/CAM/1, para 32 (Cameroon), with regard to the disabled; E/C.12/1999/SR.31, para 27 (Bulgaria), with regard to the elderly; E/C.12/Q/MEX/1, para 35 (Mexico), with regard to those attempting to leave Mexico illegally who are turned back at the border.

[39] E/C.12/1995/SR 41, para 37 (Mauritius), regarding free medical care.

[40] E/C.12/1993/SR 27, para 26 (Nicaragua); E/C.12/2001/SR.14, para 21 (Republic of Korea), regarding a three-fold increase in one year.

A. Adequacy of social security: maintaining reasonable income levels

To date, the ESCR Committee has tended to use a combination of 4 methods when determining the adequacy of social security benefits.

   (i) Adequacy has been monitored by reference to minimum standards, such as minimum subsistence and the minimum wage. Criticism has been made where benefit levels clearly fail to provide for a decent standard of living, where high levels of poverty persist and where beneficiaries are forced to seek supplementary non-state support.[41] Whilst this focus on minimum standards is not necessarily adequate, it reflects the underlying aim of article 9; to guarantee at least subsistence to social security recipients. Therefore those branches that must be provided under the minimum core obligation should satisfy this minimum standard, regardless of the provision of adequate social assistance. The necessary information is not, however, sought regularly and the ESCR Committee's Reporting Guidelines should be modified to request social security benefit levels as a percentage of the minimum and previous/average wages.

  (ii) Adequacy has been monitored by reference to the cost of living. The Committee has enquired as to whether benefits are adjusted in accordance with inflation,[42] whether benefits are indexed to prices,[43] and the relationship between benefits and the wage index.[44] It is far from clear whether article 9 contains a clear obligation to index benefits. However, since both indexation and adjustment provide clear indicators of adequacy, the Committee could enhance its monitoring by seeking and responding to relevant information with greater consistency. The Committee's Reporting Guidelines could therefore seek information on social security benefit levels as a percentage of the average wage and on the indexation and adjustment of benefit levels in line with inflation and the consumer price index. Whilst developing states may have difficulty providing such information without technical assistance, the more developed states should be able to comply.

 (iii) Adequacy has been measured by reference to duration. On various occasions, the ESCR Committee has enquired into the duration of benefits[45] and sought explanations where the duration of benefits has been reduced.[46]

---

   [41] See eg, E/C.12/1/add 40, para 21 (Cameroon) where pensions could fall below a minimum wage that was itself lower than the cost of a decent living standard; E/C.12/1/add 35, para 13 (Ireland) where levels of child benefit were considered to be inadequate to bring up a child; E/C.12/1999/SR.4, para 52 (Iceland) where disability benefit was set at 57% of the average wage on the basis that beneficiaries were forced to seek additional assistance from NGOs.

   [42] See eg, E/C.12/1995/SR.15/add 1, para 17 (Sweden).

   [43] E/C.12/1994/SR.9, para 62 (Morocco).

   [44] See eg, E/C.12/1997/SR.10, para 1 (Zimbabwe); E/C.12/1999/SR.4, para 60 (Iceland).

   [45] E/C.12/1995/SR.41, para 37 (Mauritius); E/C.12/1995/SR.8, para 35 (Portugal); E/C.12/1996/SR.3, para 48 (Spain).   [46] E/C.12/1996/SR.5, para 59 (Spain).

However, it is not clear whether benchmarks can be set in this regard. Some social security benefits will, on expiration, be replaced by either alternative social security or social assistance. There is no reason why alternative social security benefits should not be taken into account and why, beyond satisfaction of the minimum core obligation, social assistance should not be taken into account. Of relevance to the duration period is the waiting period; the period of time between day one of the contingency and day one of benefit payment.

(iv) On several occasions, the ESCR Committee has enquired into the specific levels of benefits. Inevitably, however, the ESCR Committee is not in a position to draw clear conclusions from such data.

Therefore, no clear benchmarks can be identified from the work of the ESCR Committee and the enquiries made by that Committee to date suggest a focus on poverty alleviation as much as on income maintenance.

Again, some assistance can be drawn from the ILO with regard to the adequacy of social security benefits. ILO Convention 102 requires the satisfaction of specific standards with regard to the level of social security benefits. As outlined above, the ILO Convention identifies five alternative groups of beneficiaries (Groups 1 to 5):

(i) fifty per cent of all employees;
(ii) classes of the economically active population that constitute at least twenty per cent of all residents;
(iii) all residents who lack the means to live in health and decency;
(iv) a percentage of residents; and
(v) fifty per cent of all employees in industrial workplaces employing at least twenty persons (available only to states with insufficiently developed economies).

Where the state provides a cash benefit to Group 1, 2, or 5, it can, with the exception of family benefit, choose a specified percentage (ranging from forty to fifty per cent) of either the beneficiary's previous earnings or an ordinary adult male labourer's earnings.[47] (The percentage does not vary between developed and developing states.) Where the state provides a cash benefit to Group 3, that benefit must be of such a level to 'maintain the family of the beneficiary in health and decency' and in any case as high as the corresponding benefit calculated for Group 5.[48] A special regime exists for family benefit.[49] Monitoring compliance with these requirements is relatively easy.

Can these benchmarks be applied under article 9 of the Covenant? Subject to remarks made above regarding the need to consider ILO standards as a package

---

[47] See art 65 and 66 and the Schedule to Part XI of Convention 102.
[48] Art 67(c) of Convention 102.   [49] See art 44 of Convention 102.

(number of branches, number of beneficiaries and benefit levels), there seems no reason why those benchmarks should not be applied to article 9 of the Covenant. However, beyond the minimum core obligation, it may be preferable to apply the benchmarks to the contingency rather than to a specific branch of social security. In this way, it would not matter for the purposes of the Covenant whether the benchmark is met by a combination of social security benefits or by a combination of social security and social assistance (where social security is topped up by a basic social assistance provision). This would seem entirely consistent with a rights-based approach to social security and social assistance.

B. Adequacy of social assistance: poverty alleviation

Since social assistance aims to alleviate poverty, the existence of poverty is a strong indicator of the availability and adequacy of social assistance. There are a number of ways in which poverty is measured[50] and the method adopted will impact considerably upon the poverty levels identified in any one situation. The means of measuring poverty include:

(i) relative/statistical poverty lines, which constitute a percentage of a macroeconomic indicator, such as the average wage, the national income per capita and the household equivalent income. There is no agreed level at which the relative poverty line should be set. By way of example, the United Nations Development Programme (UNDP) has adopted fifty per cent of the median disposable household income for measuring the standard of living in developed states.[51] Some argue that this measures income inequality rather than poverty;[52]

(ii) absolute budget poverty lines, which measures poverty by reference to the enjoyment of a basket of 'necessary' goods. The content of the basket is key to the effectiveness of this approach;

(iii) absolute legal/political poverty lines, which measure poverty by reference to the minimum wage. This assumes that the legal minimum income is sufficient to keep people out of poverty; and

(iv) deprivation indices, which measure poverty by reference to deprivation of a number of goods and services. Again, the identification of specific goods and services is key to the effectiveness of this approach.

---

[50] See H Deleeck, K Van den Bosch, and L De Lathouwer, *Poverty and the Adequacy of Social Security in the EC* (Avebury, 1992).

[51] HPI-2 Index, UNDP (2000), at 150–151 and 272–273.

[52] Deleeck *et al* (n 50 above) at 4. See also the position taken by the Icelandic delegation when examined by the ESCR Committee. It took issue with criticism arising from a relatively defined poverty line on the basis that the application of such a line would never allow for the eradication of poverty. In response the ESCR Committee noted 'the lack of a persuasive explanation', E/C.12/1999/SR.4, para 56 and E/C.12/1/add 32, para 16 (Icelend).

The ESCR Committee enquires whether states parties have adopted a poverty line, but does not oblige or encourage the adoption of any particular type of poverty line. It has therefore accepted relative[53] and absolute (both budget[54] and legal[55]) poverty lines and poverty lines that have been calculated by reference to deprivation[56]. It then uses the numbers falling below that line as an indication of the availability and adequacy of social assistance.[57] However, by adopting different measurements of poverty in its analysis, the ESCR Committee may unwittingly apply different standards to different states parties. The lack of any constant measurement of poverty has made comparison between states parties inappropriate and has made it virtually impossible for the ESCR Committee to respond consistently and in accordance with the resources available to states parties.

Regardless of the poverty line established by states parties, the ESCR Committee does, on occasion, use the minimum wage as a benchmark and in this way applies an absolute legal/political poverty line.[58] In doing so, it has also challenged the adequacy of the minimum wage itself, thus recognizing the limitation of this method of poverty calculation.[59] With a view to obtaining the necessary information, the ESCR Committee's Reporting Guidelines could be modified to request information regarding the level of social assistance benefits *vis-à-vis* the minimum wage.

However, the ESCR Committee rarely examines the extent to which people fall below the poverty line (known as the 'poverty gap'). Should it continue to do so, it may introduce undesirable incentives, whereby states parties are rewarded for directing resources to those living just below the poverty line rather than to those living in severe poverty. The ESCR Committee can reduce such incentives by requesting the mean or aggregate[60] poverty gap from states parties. Where states parties fail to produce this information, statistics collected by the World Bank may be of use.

---

[53] E/C.12/1997/SR.37, para 53 and E/C.12/1997/SR.38, para 34 (UK); E/C.12/1999/SR.4, paras 54 and 56 (Iceland).

[54] See eg, E/C.12/1995/SR.6, para 41 (Republic of Korea); E/C.12/1997/SR.41, para 9 and E/1990/5/add 30, para 122 (Azerbaijan, initial report).

[55] E/C.12/1990/SR.14, para 12 (Colombia), where the vulnerable are identified by reference to the minimum income together with access to basic services.

[56] E/1990/6/add 10, para 140 (Uruguay, 2nd Periodic Report).

[57] The ESCR Committee often requests information on the number of people living below the poverty line: E/C.12/1999/SR.39, para 49 (Armenia); E/C.12/Q/SUD/1, para 33 (Sudan); E/C.12/2000/SR.16, para 43 (Republic of Congo); E/C.12/Q/HKSAR/1, para 27 (UK (Hong Kong)).

[58] See eg, E/C.12/1989/SR.16, para 88 (UK); E/C.12/1996/SR.36 (Guatemala); E/C.12/1994/SR.9, para 62 (Morocco).

[59] See eg, E/C.12/1996/SR.14, para 25 (Guatemala); E/C.12/1997/SR.40, para 14 (Azerbaijan); E/C.12/1999/SR.9, para 10 (Solomon Islands);E/C.12/1/add 65, para 9 (Ukraine); E/C.12/1/add 66, paras 23 and 49 (Nepal).

[60] The aggregate would represent the total level of resources needed to raise the incomes of all households below the poverty line to an acceptable level, Deleeck *et al* (1992) (above) at p 5.

In addition to the use of poverty lines and the minimum wage, the adjustment of social assistance in line with inflation and the cost of living may be used as an indicator of the adequacy of social assistance. The ESCR Committee rarely enquires in this regard and would benefit from focusing more on the adjustment of social assistance benefits in line with inflation and the cost of living, an approach often adopted by the European Committee on Social Rights.[61] With a view to receiving the necessary information from states parties, the ESCR Committee's Reporting Guidelines could request information on the levels of social assistance benefits in relation to the average wage and on the adjustment and indexation of assistance benefits in line with inflation and the consumer price index.

Also relevant to the adequacy of social assistance are the duration of social assistance (the ESCR Committee has implied that social assistance must be available for as long as the need exists) and the comparative level of social assistance benefits[62] (the purchasing power of social assistance benefits may provide a more suitable basis for comparison[63]).

VI. Accessibility of social security and social assistance

A. General considerations

The means by which social security and social assistance are provided may raise issues of physical and economic accessibility. The ESCR Committee has enquired into and encouraged the uniform distribution of beneficiaries throughout states parties[64] and has enquired about the availability of social security in both the public and private sectors.[65] The privatization of social security provision may raise issues of accessibility. Where social security is provided by the private sector, states parties remain responsible for guaranteeing protection[66] and must exercise due diligence in controlling the behaviour of non-state actors.[67] The ESCR Committee has recognized that, in the context of privatization, the state will require additional mechanisms for supervision.[68]

The attachment of conditions to entitlement to social security and social assistance may raise issues of economic and non-discriminatory accessibility. A key concern in the context of social assistance is whether the means-test which is

---

[61] See eg, *General Introduction, Conclusions XIII-4*, at 56, where the European Committee on Social Rights confirms that the cost of living together with minimum subsistence is the *ultimate* text for determining the adequacy of social assistance.   [62] E/C.12/1999/SR.4, para 48 (Iceland).

[63] This was in fact proposed to the ESCR Committee by the UK delegation: E/C.12/1997/SR.37, para 53 (UK).   [64] E/C.12/1996/SR.38, para 22 (Finland).

[65] E/C.12/Q/NEP/1, para 22 (Nepal).   [66] E/C.12/1999/SR.38, add 1, para 35 (Armenia)

[67] *Maastricht Guidelines* (1997) (n 14 above) para 18.

[68] E/C.12/1989/SR.15, para 40 (Netherlands). E/C.12/1994/SR.31, para 49 and E/C.12/1994/14, paras 13 and 22 (Argentina).

commonly applied to its provision is set at such a level as to render assistance inaccessible to people in need (economic accessibility). Some states also attach workfare conditions (whereby the receipt of social assistance is conditioned to the pursuit and acceptance of available employment) and residence requirements to receipt of social assistance. The ESCR Committee has said very little about the appropriateness of conditions, although it will question conditions where large numbers are excluded,[69] where take-up is low,[70] and where discrimination is entailed. The ESCR Committee appears to accept means-testing so long as it is fairly applied and insists that the threshold ensures that 'all disadvantaged persons genuinely in need receive an adequate level of assistance'.[71] It has, on occasion, expressed concern with regard to workfare conditions[72] but has more often failed to respond to workfare measures mentioned in state reports, including reports of developed states.[73] It is submitted in section VII below, in the context of expenditure, that regressive measures, including workfare, should be acceptable under the Covenant where necessary for the long-term implementation of its provisions.

B. Discrimination

A key aspect of the accessibility of social security and social assistance relates to its provision on a non-discriminatory basis. Article 2(2) of the Covenant contains a 'parasitic' obligation of non-discrimination, whereby states parties:

'... guarantee that the rights enunciated in the ... Covenant will be exercised without discrimination of any kind as to race, colour, sex, language, religion, political or other opinion, national or social origin, property, birth or other status'.

In addition article 3 of the Covenant requires states parties to undertake to ensure the equal right of men and women in the enjoyment of all rights in the Covenant.

The requirement to guarantee the rights to social security and social assistance without discrimination is of particular importance owing to the immediate nature (and hence justiciability) of the obligation not to discriminate. As a result, there is considerable case law on the subject of discrimination in the provision of social security. However, the following suggests that it is not at all obvious that the requirement to eradicate certain types of discrimination is, or should be, immediate in nature in the context of social security and social assistance.

---

[69] E/C 12/1/add 59, para 23 (Republic of Korea), where 'eligibility criteria are apparently so rigid as to exclude many of the poor'.

[70] E/C.12/1996/SR.42, para 17 and E/C.12/1/add/ 10, para 24 (UK (Hong Kong)).

[71] E/C.12/1995/6, paras 12 and 19 (Suriname).

[72] E/C.12/1/add 31, paras 30, 31 and 55 (Canada).

[73] For examples of workfare measures to which the ESCR Committee has failed to respond see: E/1990/6/add 18, para 37 (Belgium, 2nd Periodic Report), where activity is limited to forty-five hours a months and is suitable in view of the qualifications and training of the individual; E/1994/104/add 20, paras 288–89 (Portugal, 3rd Periodic Report).

1. What do we mean by discrimination?

Discrimination is commonly recognized as arising where there is:

(i)   a difference in treatment;
(ii) which has the effect of nullifying the recognition, enjoyment, or exercise of the right;
(iii) which is based on one of a number of given grounds; and
(iv) which has no reasonable or objective justification.[74]

In practice, a step is often applied after step (i) (referred to here as step (ia)), whereby the claimant is required to demonstrate that he is in fact in an analogous position to the person who is being treated differently.[75] If he is not, then steps (ii) to (iv) will not be considered.

It would seem that step (ia) and (iv) effectively involve the same test. Under step (ia) the applicant must demonstrate that the parties that are exposed to the different treatment are in analogous situations. Whether or not two groups will be considered analogous will depend upon the difference in treatment complained of. Whilst the two groups may be analogous in the context of treatment A, the same two groups may not necessarily be analogous in the context of treatment B. Otherwise, any difference in situation between two groups will legitimize any difference in treatment, which cannot be correct. Consequently, where a state successfully contests the analogous situation of two groups, it demonstrates that the particular difference between the two groups is relevant to and justifies the difference in treatment. This is in effect a proportionality test.

Under step (iv) a state must demonstrate that a difference in treatment pursues a legitimate aim and that the means employed are proportionate to that aim. In practice states identify a legitimate aim with relative ease and the key turns on proportionality.

Since both tests apply a test of proportionality it is not surprising that both give rise to similar results. In the context of social security and social assistance where states are required to make numerous distinctions between persons and groups and where distinctions are often motivated by unattractive budgetary aims, it seems more likely that states will challenge discrimination claims under step (ia).

2. Nullifying the enjoyment of what?

Discrimination will arise where the difference in treatment nullifies the recognition, enjoyment, or exercise of 'the right'. In the context of social security and social assistance, the elements identified in the preceding parts of this chapter would seem to be elements of 'the right'. Therefore a difference in treatment in

---

[74] See *Belgian Linguistics Case* Series A no 6, (1968) EHRR 252.
[75] See, *Stubbings and Others v UK*, Appl 220 83/93 and 220 95/93, (2001) 23 EHRR 213, para 68; *Van der Mussele v Belgium* Series A no 70, (1983) 6 EHRR 163, para 46.

respect of the number of branches of social security provided, the number of beneficiaries, the level and duration of benefits, and eligibility conditions is capable of nullifying the recognition, enjoyment, or exercise of the rights. However, the rights do not cover an independent entitlement to the way in which social security and social assistance are provided. Therefore, a discrimination claim could not be made on the grounds that social security was provided to one group in a different way than another so long as the availability, adequacy and economic and physical accessibility were unaffected.

3. Difference in treatment?

Article 2(2) of the Covenant protects against both direct and indirect discrimination and therefore covers a difference in outcome that results from a *failure* to treat people differently.[76] Indirect discrimination will arise where a neutral rule (often with no intention to discriminate) affects a group disproportionately. Since the rule itself is not directly discriminatory, the applicant must demonstrate the discriminatory impact of the rule on the group in question. In the context of social security and social assistance, indirect discrimination arises most frequently against women and non-nationals. With regard to women, contributory conditions often fail to take into account breaks in employment for child-birth and rearing. With regard to non-nationals, residence requirements and the inability to export benefits or accrue benefits between states have a disproportionate effect on them.

4. Determining the legitimacy of a difference in treatment

Space does not permit a full analysis of all aspects of discrimination in the context of social security and social assistance. What follows therefore is an analysis of certain key aspects of such discrimination.

(i). Proportionality

As noted above, the test in respect of a difference in treatment is proportionality, whether it is applied under step (ia) (whereby the difference in treatment is justified by reference to the difference between people) or under step (iv) (whereby the difference in treatment is justified by reference to a legitimate aim). It is imperative that proportionality is applied rigorously. Two examples illustrate the application of the proportionality test.

First, a distinction between couples (married or cohabiting) and single persons with regard to contributions for residential care is reasonable and objective on the basis that different levels of income are freed up when these categories take up residential care.[77] This is because the level of benefit (contributions for residential care) is based upon the means available to beneficiaries and the taking up of

---

[76] E/C.12/1994/SR.3, para 30.
[77] *Snijders, Willemen and Van der Wouw v Netherlands* (1998), UN doc A/53/40, 140, para 8.4.

residential care impacted differently upon the means available to the two groups in question. The difference in treatment would not have been rational had the level of benefit been based on previous contributions or service.

Second, a reduction in the military pension payable to a soldier who serves as a national on the basis that, subsequent to his service, he becomes a non-national when his state gains independence would not be reasonable and proportionate.[78] In this case, the pension was in respect of military service undertaken which could not be affected by issues of nationality. The distinction may well have been proportionate in the context of social assistance.

(ii). Direct sex discrimination resulting from increasing analogy

In many developed states, women are coming to enjoy a position in the labour market that is increasingly analogous to that of men. This requires social security systems to adapt to reflect that analogy. Where they do not, legislation that was once non-discriminatory may come to directly discriminate against women. The considerable number of differences in treatment that exist between the sexes in social security, coupled with the gradual yet disparate evolution of factual differences, give rise to a large number of sex discrimination cases. By way of example, three cases considered by the Human Rights Committee (HRC)[79] concerned legislation which required women but not men to demonstrate their 'breadwinner' status for entitlement to unemployment benefit. In a fourth case,[80] the HRC considered legislation which entitled all women but only those men who did not have additional income to a survivor's pension. In three of those cases, the HRC identified discrimination. However, in a subsequent case, three members of the HRC issued an individual opinion, which stressed that social security necessarily lagged behind social developments and that consequently a requirement to eradicate discrimination should be interpreted as requiring periodic review of legislation by a state.[81]

It would be very controversial for the ESCR Committee to accept that the obligation to eradicate sex discrimination in the context of social security is in fact an obligation to review periodically social security entitlement. This is particularly the case because the immediacy of the obligation of discrimination in the Covenant is seen as the key to the justiciability of the Covenant rights and to the effectiveness of any petition system that may be introduced. Yet, such an approach to non-discrimination may well be necessary in certain areas of social security provision. Under European law, an exception to the principle of equal treatment has been recognized in the context of pensionable ages 'to enable [states] . . . progressively to adapt their pensions systems . . . without disrupting

---

[78] *Gueye et al v France* (1989), UN doc A/44/40, 189.

[79] *Broeks v Netherlands* (1987), UN doc A/42/40, 139; *Zwaan-de Vries v Netherlands* (1987), UN doc A/42/40, 160; *Vos v Netherlands* (1989), UN doc A/44/40, 232.

[80] *Pauger v Austria* (1992), UN doc A/47/40, 325.

[81] Ando, Herndl, and Ndiaye, individual opinion given in *Sprenger v Netherlands* (1992), UN doc A/47/40, 311, at 315 to 16.

the complex financial equilibrium of those systems'. [82] Here, states are required to consider periodically whether there is justification for maintaining differences. If such an exception is considered to be necessary in the context of Europe, where states are relatively wealthy, it would seem most likely that a similar approach may be required in less well developed states parties to the Covenant.

(iii). Direct discrimination against non-nationals

Direct discrimination against non-nationals often arises in the context of non-contributory social security and social assistance. Whilst the Revised ESC requires comparable social assistance to be provided to non-nationals who are working regularly or who are legally resident in a state party,[83] it permits a lower level of assistance to be provided to other non-nationals (namely those who are simply lawfully within the territory such as tourists and students).[84]

This suggests that the ESCR Committee will come under increasing pressure to recognize an exception to the principle of equal treatment, at least in respect of certain groups of non-nationals and certain types of non-contributory social security and social assistance. However, it is not clear how easily such an approach would sit under the Covenant. To date, individual members have been very critical of developed states which have sought to justify the unequal treatment of non-nationals in the context of welfare.[85]

(iv). Indirect discrimination against non-nationals

A common source of indirect discrimination against non-nationals in social security and social assistance is by way of residence requirements, whereby entitlement is conditioned on a certain period of residency. Clearly, such obligations will have a greater adverse impact on non-nationals than they will on nationals. The ESCR Committee has shown an interest in such requirements and has enquired into the availability of alternative protection whilst such residence periods are being completed.[86] Both ILO Convention 118[87] and the Revised ESC permit residence requirements in respect of certain non-contributory benefits on the basis that they are paid out of general taxation.[88]

---

[82] *Ex p Equal Opportunities Commission* (1992), ECR I-4297, para 15.

[83] Art 13(1). See *General Introduction, Conclusions XIII-4*, at 61.

[84] Art 13(4). See *General Introduction, Conclusions XIII-4*, at 62; *General Introduction, Conclusions XIV-1*, at 55.

[85] See E/C.12/2001/SR.42, para 11 and E/C.12/1/add 67, paras 12 and 39 (Japan).

[86] The ESCR Committee expressed concern where foreign workers could only participate in occupational/private social security schemes and were entitled to free medical assistance during the first two years within the state party, E/C.12/1995/SR.41, paras 48 and 52 and E/C.12/1995/18, para 228 (Mauritius).

[87] ILO Convention 118 (1962) Equality of Treatment (Social Security) Convention.

[88] Under ILO Convention 118, residence conditions can not be applied exclusively to non-nationals but can be applied equally to nationals and to non-nationals, see ILO, Interpretation of a decision concerning Convention 118, Canada (1966), Report V(2), International Labour Conference (1962), 46th session at 23. The Revised ESC permits residence requirements to be attached to all non-contributory social security benefits, app, art 12(4) Revised ESC.

Indirect discrimination against non-nationals often arises where persons have contributed to a social security scheme in one state and are unable to export their benefits on leaving that state; in such cases, non-nationals will be disproportionately adversely affected. The same occurs where persons who take up employment in another state are unable to transfer their contributions to date. Individual members of the ESCR Committee have identified this problem and have asked various questions.[89] However, ILO Conventions 118 and 157[90] do not require transportability for all non-nationals[91] and it is not clear that immediate eradication of such indirect discrimination will be a reasonable obligation to impose on all states parties to the Covenant.

VII. Expenditure

Expenditure can be seen as an indicator of the availability and the adequacy of social security and social assistance. Admittedly, it has its flaws as such an indicator. A reduction in expenditure on social security could simply reflect the transfer of service delivery from the public to the private sector rather than any reduction in provision. In the context of social assistance, a reduction in expenditure could reflect a reduction in the number of persons who are in need whereas an increase in expenditure on social assistance may simply reflect an increase in the numbers of needy individuals. Nonetheless, expenditure may provide a very broad indication of the availability and adequacy of social security and social assistance. Where the number of beneficiaries are known, it will provide an indicator of the level of benefits; where expenditure increases at a slower rate or decreases at a faster rate than the number of beneficiaries, questions should be asked of states.

Expenditure is treated separately in this chapter because it plays such a central role to the implementation of these rights and because the approach that is taken by monitoring bodies in respect of expenditure is fundamental to our understanding of these rights and to the political purposes underlying them.

The allocation of scarce resources to social services is a central function of the accountable executive, which must be given sufficient discretion to operate. The judiciary is neither an expert in finance nor accountable. Whilst the ESCR Committee is even worse placed to consider individual cases of resource allocation than a national judiciary, its approach to resource allocation provides an important guide to domestic and other bodies that find themselves faced with balancing cautious economic policies with open-ended progressive obligations.

Article 2(1) of the Covenant requires states parties to progress 'to the maximum of available resources' and therefore makes clear that obligations in respect of

---

[89] E/C.12/1995/SR.19, para 36 (Suriname); E/C.12/1994/SR.16/add 1, para 26 (Belgium).

[90] ILO Convention 157 (1982) Maintenance of Social Security Rights Convention.

[91] See art 5, Convention 118 (1962) and art 9(1) and (3), Convention 157.

expenditure will necessarily vary according to the level of development of the state party. This would tend to suggest that expenditure dedicated to any particular right should be measured as a proportion of the total resources available to a state party rather than in absolute terms. It would also suggest that a halt to the progressive realization of a right is not a violation where it is due to a lack of available resources.[92] The progressive nature of this basic obligation would also suggest that this proportion should be measured over a period of time with a view to identifying any trends.

Clearly, the means by which 'available resources' will be measured is of vital importance in light of the obligation to progress to the 'maximum of available resources'. Should the ESCR Committee base its assessment of expenditure solely on resources currently available (for example, GDP per capita levels) or should it accept expenditures designed to *maintain* those resource levels? Whilst the former will be easier to apply, the latter is surely more appropriate; interpretation of the Covenant should allow long-term as well as short-term enjoyment of Covenant provisions. But determining the level of expenditure which is necessary to maintain resource levels is a difficult economic exercise which will challenge the ESCR Committee. A large discretion will need to be given to states when making this determination.

A. Expenditure and social security

The ESCR Committee's Reporting Guidelines request states to 'indicate [the] percentages of... GNP as well as of... national and/or regional budget(s) [that] is spent on social security' and to indicate 'how... this compare[s] with the situation 10 years ago' giving reasons for such changes.[93] Not surprisingly, there are no clear standards in respect of expenditure under the Covenant. The ESCR Committee expresses concern in extreme cases and at resource constraints arising from foreign debt[94] and economic sanctions.[95]

1. Progressivity

Beyond such general comments, the ESCR Committee looks at expenditure over time. The ESCR Committee has welcomed increases in expenditure dedicated to social security and has sought information[96] and expressed concern[97] regarding

---

[92] *Maastricht Guidelines* (1997) (n 14 above) para 14(f). That is not to say that progress will not be possible where available resources do not multiply. Limburg Principle 23 recognizes the independence of progressive achievement from the increase in resources. See also Limburg Principle 24.

[93] E/C.12/1991/1, art 9, para 4.

[94] E/C.12/1/add 48/para 15 (Sudan); E/C.12/1/add 62, para 23 (Senegal).

[95] E/C.12/1/add 17, paras 8 and 18 (Iraq).

[96] E/C.12/199/SR.18/add 1, para 46 (Tunisia), regarding the reduction in state health spending as a percentage of overall health spending.

[97] E/C.12/1/add 39, para 14 (Armenia), where expenditure decreased without explanation; E/C.12/1/add 49, para 20 and E/1990/5/add 42, para 133 (Kyrgyzstan, initial report) where funds for social insurance decreased from 12.4% to 7.8% of GDP.

decreases. Where there has been a decrease the ESCR Committee is keen to learn what measures have been taken to cushion the impact.[98]

The Committee has not welcomed regressive measures in developed states parties[99] and, on occasion, has emphasized that economic growth will not necessarily lead to poverty reduction.[100] With regard to developing states, the ESCR Committee has stressed the need for social safety nets for the most vulnerable[101] and for human rights protection to accompany economic growth.[102] To date, it has not fully embraced the possible need for regression.

The work of the European Committee on Social Rights is instructive in this regard. The Revised ESC, like the Covenant, contains a progressive obligation 'to endeavour to raise progressively the system of social security to a higher level'.[103] Faced with a number of regressive measures in developed states, the European Committee on Social Rights has recognized that 'in view of the close relationship between the economy and social rights, the pursuit of economic goals is not necessarily incompatible' with the progressive obligation.[104] It has gone on to accept alterations to the social security systems 'to the extent that these are necessary in order to ensure the maintenance of the system in question . . . [and on the condition that] any restrictions do not interfere with the effective protection of all members of society . . . and do not tend to gradually reduce the social security system to a system of minimum assistance'.[105] The European Committee on Social Rights requests information on the nature, extent, and results of changes, the reasons underlying the changes, the necessity of reform, the adequacy of the reform in the particular situation, and the existence of social assistance measures for those consequently in need.[106]

A similar approach will need to be adopted under the Covenant if the ESCR Committee is to accept regressive measures in any, other than the least developed, states parties. The notion of necessity/proportionality, adopted in this context by the European Committee on Social Rights, is something with which the ESCR Committee could work. Such an approach could be enforced through judicial scrutiny of the reasonableness of states' policies; states parties would be called upon to demonstrate that any regressive measures adopted were necessary for the maintenance of the social security system, to provide adequate evidence in this regard and to demonstrate that the most basic human rights standards were not being violated.

---

[98] E/C.12/Q/AUSTRAL/1, para 16 (Australia).

[99] E/C.12/1993/SR.37, para 41 (New Zealand); E/C.12/1995/SR.34 para 24 (Norway); E/C.12/1997/SR.37, paras 14 and 25 (UK).   [100] E/C.12/1989/SR.16, para 92 (UK).

[101] E/C.12/1993/SR.28, para 29 (Nicaragua).

[102] E/C.12/1991/SR.3, para 43 and E/C.12/1991/SR.5, paras 23 and 28 (Panama); E/C.12/1997/SR.15, para 6 (Peru).   [103] Art 12(3) of the Revised ESC.

[104] The European Committee on Social Rights accepted that 'Contracting Parties may consider that consolidating public finances, in order to prevent deficits and debt interest from increasing, is one way to safeguarding the social security system', *General Introduction, Conclusions XIV-1*, at 39.

[105] *General Observation on Article 12(3), Conclusions XIII-4*, at 143; *General Introduction, Conclusions XIV-1*, at 39 and 46.   [106] *General Observation, Conclusions XIII-4*, at 143–44.

2. Comparison

A further means by which the ESCR Committee assesses expenditure levels is by way of comparison, whereby states parties are challenged when their welfare figures compare unfavourably with other states parties that the ESCR Committee deems to be comparable.[107] However, the ESCR Committee's selection of 'comparable' states is not scientific. Should the ESCR Committee wish to develop this line of analysis, it could base comparisons on the GDP per capita of states parties. GDP per capita is one indicator in the Human Development Index, adopted by the UNDP, which is available for the vast majority of states parties to the Covenant. The UNDP has argued that this indicator 'is a broad proxy for available resources, since it is from this resource base that government may raise revenues for eradicating human poverty'.[108] Greater collaboration between the ESCR Committee and the UNDP would be a welcome development and the possible application of UNDP statistics and indices by the ESCR Committee with a view to more objective comparison under the Covenant should be on the agenda of any meeting between the two.

B. Expenditure and social assistance

As noted above, expenditure as a percentage of GNP as well as of national and/or regional budgets currently provided and provided ten years ago is requested in the Reporting Guidelines for articles 9 and 12 of the Covenant.[109] However, similar information is only requested under article 11 with regard to housing and should be extended to cover social assistance.[110] Even if the ESCR Committee considers social assistance to fall under article 9 rather than under article 11, it is submitted that the Reporting Guidelines should request separate expenditure figures for social security and social assistance so that the ESCR Committee can monitor both with greater precision.

1. Progressivity

In the main, the ESCR Committee relies on trends in expenditure over time. States parties have been criticized where they have 'slashed' their social expenditure without protection of the vulnerable[111] and have been urged to spend more on social safety nets for the disadvantaged and marginalized.[112] The ESCR

---

[107] Eg, Canada was compared with Western European States, E/C.12/1989/SR.8, para 51 (Canada); Dominican Republic was compared to Costa Rica and Chile (E/C.12/1990/SR.44, para 51 (Dominican Republic); Japan was compared with France and Germany (E/C.12/2001/SR.42, para 54 (Japan).
[108] UNDP 'Human Rights and Human Development' United Nations Development Report 2000 (2000), at 98.   [109] E/C.12/1991/1, art 9, para 4, art 12, para 3.
[110] E/C.12/1991/1, art 11, para 3(d)(iv).   [111] E/C.12/1/add 31, para 11 (Canada).
[112] E/C.12/1/add 62, para 45 (Senegal).

Committee has also occasionally drawn comparisons between states parties.[113] However, because higher expenditures are not necessarily desirable, the ESCR Committee should be especially open to explanations by states parties regarding disparities and should reserve any criticism for remaining poverty levels. Where comparison is undertaken, use of GDP per capita levels, as gathered by the UNDP, would be equally appropriate for social assistance as for social security. Again, the ESCR Committee should be open to measures deemed necessary to maintain levels of available resources, including regressive measures, and require states parties to demonstrate the reasonableness of their policies.

2. *Targeting*

Because the identity of beneficiaries is key in the provision of social assistance (the most needy must enjoy protection), direction of expenditure to those most in need is key and must be considered alongside the level of expenditure itself. The ESCR Committee's Reporting Guidelines for article 11 enquire as to the per capita GNP for the poorest forty per cent of the population.[114] This clearly involves a level of redistribution. The ESCR Committee enquires into trends in income distribution[115] and the measures being taken to reduce growing disparities.[116]

VIII. Conclusions

It is clear from the above that meaning can be given to the rights to social security and social assistance under the Covenant. Whilst the above analysis is far from exhaustive, it offers an overview of the rights by providing an analytical framework within which the provision of social security and social assistance can be monitored and enforced. Specific benchmarks within that framework still need to be adopted. It has been suggested that when adopting such benchmarks, the ESCR Committee should work in close consultation with the ILO. It has also been suggested that the ESCR Committee's Reporting Guidelines could be amended to request information necessary to determine the provision of these rights.

Importantly, beyond a minimum core of each right, the framework leaves discretion to states parties to determine the level of redistribution which social security and social assistance schemes are to effect. Beyond that minimum core, key decisions regarding the allocation of scarce resources and the prioritization of competing economic and social rights are left to states. It has been argued that flexibility should be shown to states in respect of regressive measures and that they should be able to justify such measures where they can demonstrate that they are

---

[113] E/C.12/1989/SR.8, para 51 (Canada), compared with Western European states. See also E/C.12/1997/SR.16, para 44 (Peru), where Peru compared itself with other Latin American states.
[114] E/C.12/1991/1, art 11, para 1(c).   [115] E/C.12/Q/PAN/1, para 21 (Panama).
[116] E/C.12/Q/AUSTRAL/1, para 23 (Australia).

necessary for the maintenance of resources and for the long-term satisfaction of the rights themselves.

This approach is supported and facilitated by the adoption of policy-based approach to enforcement, whereby states are called upon to demonstrate the reasonableness of the policies they have adopted. Such an approach enables a certain degree of judicial control to be exercised over these rights beyond the adoption of legislative measures and moves the debate on from the more rigid approach associated with civil and political rights. This policy-approach would even appear appropriate in the context of discrimination, where, the above suggests, there may be exceptions to the immediacy of obligations.

With such an approach it is difficult to argue that these rights are outdated in today's global economy. Rather, these rights can be seen as safeguarding minimum standards whilst enabling states to adopt reasonable policies that fit within that economy.

14

Democracy and the Promotion and Protection of Socio-Economic Rights

*Richard Burchill**

I. Introduction

Discussions about human rights have become a standard part of the international legal discourse since the creation of the United Nations (UN). Democracy, on the other hand, has only recently been given attention as an aspect of international law; emerging from obscurity at the end of the Cold War and quickly developing into a leading principle for international law and relations.[1] The growth of democracy as part of the international legal discourse has been most evident with regard to international human rights law, with a tendency among commentators and policy makers to conflate human rights and democracy into a single identifiable idea and practice.[2] This conflation is based on a misunderstanding of both democracy and human rights, which limits the two things to a specific range of institutions and actions associated with the civil and political spheres of society. The result is that democracy is understood as elections and minimal institutional arrangements for government and human rights are understood primarily as those rights categorized as civil and political rights.[3]

This minimalist understanding of democracy and human rights in international law is problematic as it fails to consider the entirety of the human experience and undermines the fundamental nature of both ideas. Democracy and human rights have at their foundations a fundamental concern for the well-being

---

* I would like to take this opportunity to thank Professor David Harris for the generous support and inspiration he has provided over the course of my career.

[1] For an overview of this development see S Marks, *The Riddle of All Constitutions: International Law, Democracy and the Critique of Ideology* (OUP, 2000).

[2] For discussion see T Evans, 'If Democracy, Then Human Rights?' (2001) 22 *Third World Q*, p 623. Also N Gleditsch. 'Democracy and Peace: Good News for Human Rights Advocates.' in D Gomien (ed) *Broadening the Frontiers of Human Rights: Essays in Honour of Asbjørn Eide* (Scandinavian University, 1993) pp 287–288; T Carothers. 'Democracy and Human Rights: Policy Allies or Rivals?' (1994) 17 *Washington Q* pp 109–120.

[3] D Beetham, *Democracy and Human Rights* (Polity Press, 1999) pp 115–118.

of individuals and society. When democracy and human rights are understood in minimalist terms the emancipatory nature of the concepts is lost, as they no longer provide support for empowerment and a substantive concern for human dignity. Instead a minimalist understanding works to solidify and legitimize uneven power relations where the interests of the powerful—be it the state, majorities within states, or powerful minority groups—take primacy over the interests and needs of individuals not aligned with the interests of those in power, commonly classified as the dispossessed and marginalized. Democracy and human rights are often presented as promises of empowerment available to all, but with the minimalist conceptions the emancipatory potential is lost and the two ideas merely become tools for maintaining an uneven status quo.

Section II of this chapter discusses the problems that have arisen in the international legal discourse due to the minimalist understanding of democracy as equating to a limited range of civil and political rights. A case will be made for a definition of democracy that explicitly encompasses socio-economic rights as integral features. Section III examines the extent to which international human rights law has moved beyond minimalist conceptions of democracy and human rights through an examination of the International Covenant on Economic, Social and Cultural Rights (the Covenant). The discussion will look at two issues—the extent to which the rights contained in the Covenant are seen as being part of an understanding of democracy that moves beyond the minimalist confines and the role played by democracy in ensuring the effective implementation of the rights in the Covenant. Even though the Committee on Economic, Social and Cultural Rights has been reluctant expressly to discuss democracy, there is ample evidence that democratic principles underlie the Covenant framework. Section IV then takes on the necessity of explicitly articulating the role of democratic principles within the Covenant framework.

In this chapter it will be argued that for human rights and democracy to live up to their promised deals it is necessary to ensure an understanding of democracy that moves beyond minimalist conceptions and directly addresses the social and economic aspects of the human experience and society. To do this, socio-economic rights need to be given much greater attention in a way that places them at the centre of concerns for human dignity and development. The goal will be to articulate a version of democracy that is inclusionary and emancipatory, one that supports the ability of individuals to be part of the processes that impact upon their lives as a means of realizing their full potential.

II. Democracy and human rights in international law

A. Markets and minimalist approaches

The creation of the UN marked a major moment in the development of international law, as it started a process whereby international law could legitimately direct its attention to the way in which states exercised power over individuals in their territory. However, any initial euphoria surrounding the ability of the UN or international law to bring about dramatic changes to the lives of individuals was quickly lost in the realities of the post-war era. Following the initial impetus for creating an international human rights regime, the entire process slowed as states became hesitant about creating explicit legal obligations in this area. It quickly became clear that international law remained a system that is based upon the notion of state sovereignty and that the interests of states took primacy over any attempt to focus international law towards a concern on human values and needs. Despite the fact that there was declared support for fundamental human rights, the dignity and worth of the human person, and for 'better standards of life in larger freedom'[4] the ability of international law to actually address these issues was impeded by the well entrenched principles of the sovereign equality of states and non-intervention in the domestic affairs of states.[5]

Added to this, the emergence of the Cold War resulted in the polarization of ideological positions concerning the nature of state governments and the role of human rights. Democracy became a tool for the propaganda war between the East and West with both sides claiming to have the only true form of democracy, curtailing any broad acceptance of the idea in international law.[6] To a certain degree international human rights law was manipulated in a similar way with the opposing ideological adversaries each claiming to possess the 'right' approach to human rights protection.[7] But through inclusion in the UN Charter, the adoption of the Universal Declaration of Human Rights and subsequent efforts to develop a legal framework, human rights did become established in the international legal discourse in a way democracy did not.

However, owing to the prominence of state sovereignty in the international system it has proven difficult to establish widespread acceptance among states for the full range of international human rights obligations.[8] As Simma observes:

Perusing the list of parties to the major human rights treaties, any alert observer must wonder how many of these States have decided to join this great enterprise more for symbolic reasons than motivated by the desire to conform their domestic laws and practices to internationally agreed upon human rights standards and to subject themselves to international scrutiny.[9]

[4] UN Charter, preamble.

[5] A Cassese *Human Rights in a Changing World* (Polity Press, 1990) p 57. Also P Jessup, *The International Problem of Governing Mankind* (Claremont College, 1947) p 2.

[6] R Rich, 'Bringing Democracy into International Law' (2001) 12 *J of Democracy*, pp 22–23.

[7] Eg, at an international human rights conference in 1985 a delegate from the USA summed up the position well in declaring '[w]e talk about human [i.e., political and civil] rights and they [the Soviets] talk about unemployment and racism': quoted in R Goldstein, 'The Limitations of Using Quantitative Data in Studying Human Rights Abuses' (1986) 8 Human Rights Q p 609–610.

[8] R Falk, *Human Rights Horizons: The Pursuit of Justice in a Globalizing World* (Routledge, 2000) p 37–40.

[9] B Simma, 'Reservations to Human Rights Treaties—Some Recent Developments' in G Hafner (ed), *Liber Amicorium Professor Ignaz Seidl-Hohanveldern* (Kluwer, 1998) p 659.

In turn this has meant that treaty monitoring bodies have struggled to exert any sort of authority over states parties for ensuring compliance with the obligations set out in the treaties.[10] Leckie explains:

Given the nature of states and state interests, the treaty body reporting system is always liable to be circumvented or manipulated by states intent on skirting their legal obligations.[11]

This has resulted in treaty monitoring bodies taking a relatively light touch with states with regard to ensuring compliance as it has been necessary to recognize the primacy of state interests when dealing with states parties in the monitoring process.[12]

In doing so, the treaty monitoring bodies have focussed their attention on the technical details of the obligations contained in the treaties and no concerted attempt is made to address the underlying principles which form the context within which human rights protection takes place. Even though international human rights law does go directly to the relationship between the state and individuals, little was said about the nature of the political, economic, and social systems within states that has a direct bearing on this relationship.[13]

Developments in the late 1908s and early 1990s brought about a number of changes to this environment. International human rights law had continued its uphill battle in influencing the behaviour of states with some success and the treaty monitoring bodies became more active in ensuring obligations were complied with. The end of the Cold War broke down the ideological divide that had prevented any discussion of democracy within international law and the increase of democratic practices within states: the 'third wave' of democracy in the international system, established democracy as a predominant principle in international law and relations.[14] Writing in 1992, Thomas Franck argued that there was enough evidence in the international system to identify the emergence of a right to democratic governance. Franck felt that democracy had now taken on the dimension of a normative expectation in the international system, demonstrated by the

---

[10] See C Haynes and F Viljoen, 'The Impact of the United Nations Human Rights Treaties on the Domestic Level' (2001) 23 Human Rights Q, p 483 stating that 'UN treaty monitoring has 'had a very limited demonstrable impact' at p 488. Also H Steiner, 'Individual Claims in a World of Massive Violations: What Role for the Human Rights Committee' in P Alston and J Crawford (eds), *The Future of UN Human Rights Treaty Monitoring* (Cambridge University Press, 2000) p 20.

[11] S Leckie, The Committee on Economic, Social and Cultural Rights: Catalyst for Change in a System needing Reform' in Alston and Crawford (above) p 130.   [12] Ibid p 132.

[13] With regard to the specific role of democracy in the Covenant, see M Craven, *The International Covenant on Economic, Social and Cultural Rights: A Perspective on Its Development* (Clarendon Press, 1998) p 124.

[14] On the rise of democracy in international relations, see S Huntington, *The Third Wave: Democratization in the Late Twentieth Century* (Oklahoma University Press, 1991); F Fukuyama, *The End of History and the Last Man* (Penguin, 1992); D Rustow, 'Democracy: A Global Revolution?' (1990) 69 *Foreign Affairs*, p 75. For the impact on international law see T Franck, 'The Emerging Right to Democratic Governance' (1992) 86 AJIL, p 46; J Crawford, *Democracy in International Law* (Cambridge University Press, 1994).

widespread practice of individuals within states demanding that governmental authority be based on free and fair elections, and expectations from the international community that governments were to be validated by free and fair elections as a mark of legitimacy.[15] Franck's argument was based on developments in international human rights law concerning the widespread practice and recognition of the right of self-determination along with the recognition of specific rights such as freedoms of expression, thought, association, and assembly. Franck recognized that the type of democracy in question was a limited understanding of democracy and he conceded that it probably represented the extent to which the international system would recognize any sort of right to democratic governance.[16]

Franck's essay touched off a great deal of debate and discussion about democracy and international law. For the most part, support for the development of democracy in international law was placed within the context of international human rights law and election-related activities undertaken by the UN and other intergovernmental organizations.[17] It quickly became apparent that international law's embrace of democracy was concerned more with form than substance. The prevalence of election activity was undeniable but to claim on this basis that democracy exists was, and remains, based on a simplistic understanding of democracy that fails to embrace the full potential of the idea. Even at the more basic level associated with minimalist understandings of democracy, elections were not ensuring that civil and political rights were being respected.[18] Looking at the issue in more expansive terms, the focus on the existence of elections concealed the fact that the promise of democracy as a revolutionary and emancipatory concept was not being fulfilled.

Even though democracy was being seen as an indicator of legitimacy, adequate attention was not being given to questions about whether or not democracy contributed to the overturning of unequal power relations or only served to solidify these relations.[19] As Donnelly explains:

Pure procedural democracy can easily degenerate into non-democratic or even anti-democratic formalism. Substantive conceptions rightly insist that we not lose sight of the core values of popular authority and control over government.[20]

An understanding of democracy that confines itself to minimalist ideas and practices is incomplete. In just the same way as an understanding of human rights that is lim-

[15] T Franck (above), pp 47–48.
[16] T Franck, 'Democracy as a Human Right' in L Henkin, and J Hargrove (eds), *Human Rights: An Agenda for the Next Century* (Nijhoff, 1994) p 75.
[17] See eg, G Fox, 'The Right to Political Participation in International Law' (1992) 17 Yale J of Intl L, p 539; C Cerna, 'Universal Democracy: An International Legal Right or the Pipe Dream of the West?' (1995) 27 New York U J of Intl L and Politics, p 290; R Ezetah, 'The Right to Democracy: A Qualitative Inquiry' (1997) 22 Brooklyn J of Intl L, p 495.
[18] F Zakaria, 'The Rise of Illiberal Democracies' (1997) 76 *Foreign Affairs*, p 22.
[19] Marks (above), D Otto, 'Challenging the "New World Order": International Law, Global Democracy and the Possibilities for Women' (1993) 3 Transnational L and Contemporary Problems, p 371.
[20] J Donnelly, 'Human Rights, Democracy and Development' (1999) 21 Human Rights Q, p 618.

ited to civil and political rights fails to fully embrace the human experience, democracy understood as certain procedures and institutions fails to provide adequately the individual with the opportunity to participate in the various processes that impact upon their life and denies the chance to realize their full potential.

The tendency of international law to adopt a minimalist understanding of democracy is not surprising when placed in the wider context of general developments in the international system. The growth of democracy in the world in the 1990s was influenced by the supposed ideological victory of the West.[21] For the purposes of this chapter this means that prevailing views about human rights are confined to civil and political rights, democracy is seen as a process of choosing leaders, and competitive free market systems dominate the organization of all other aspects of the economy and society.[22] This general view, with the main emphasis on market mechanisms for ensuring efficiency in the use of capital and allocation of resources is commonly classified as neo-liberal thinking. In general this means that the state takes a reduced role in actively engaging with the way in which goods and services in society are organized and allocated as the market becomes the primary means for resource allocation. The emphasis behind neo-liberal thought is that the market provides the most efficient way of allocating resources, which in turn will provide the most effective way for the economic growth necessary for creating wealth societies. Democracy, for the purposes of neo-liberal thinking, is confined to the choosing of political leaders as all other decisions in society are dealt with through market mechanisms. The protection of human rights is limited to civil and political rights and does not extend to socio-economic rights as they necessarily involve tampering with the market.[23] The neo-liberal market-based agenda justifies itself on the benefits it creates for the whole of society, but individual circumstances are not taken into consideration, hence the marginalization of socio-economic rights.

The emphasis and focus on ensuring the greater good of society through the market does bring benefits in a variety of ways but it also means that individuals who do not fit the market model—the poor, unemployed, sick, disabled—are purposely excluded.[24] This is seen as a short-term price to pay for long-term efficiency.[25] Even though there is no pure market model in the world today, social welfare systems that have been created to offset the negative consequences of the market are devised in minimalist terms and do not necessarily address the needs of the dispossessed and disempowered. The pervasiveness of market-based thinking has been demonstrated in the European context, where social democracy has a long historical grounding in actual practice but the current European Union integration project places competitive free markets before socio-economic concerns.[26]

---

[21] The idea of an ideological victory was most clearly articulated by Fukuyama (above).
[22] See generally, Marks (above).   [23] Falk (above) p 90.
[24] Donnelly (above) pp 628–629.   [25] Ibid pp 629–630.
[26] R Burchill, 'The European Union and European Democracy: Social Democracy or Democracy with a Social Dimension?' (2004) 17 Canadian J of L and Jurisprudence, p 185; M Moed,

The Committee on Economic, Social and Cultural Rights (the Committee) has openly commented that the reliance on market mechanisms will not always provide the best means for meeting the needs of individuals and ensuring the effective exercise of human rights.[27] In discussing periodic reports from states making the transition to free market systems in the early 1990s, the Committee was clear that market mechanisms create a number of difficulties for socio-economic rights that must be overcome.[28] The Committee has continually emphasized the need to give appropriate emphasis to socio-economic rights along with principled commitments to areas such as social integration, solidarity, efforts towards equality, and social welfare provisions for all.[29] These ideas and practices run in direct contrast to the main ideas of the competitive free market,[30] making it difficult to convince states to adopt this sort of approach given the pervasiveness of neo-liberal ideas. However, to accept the dominance of markets and the minimalist approach to democracy and human rights is to accept the marginalization of sections of society and maintain structural inequalities, something that is contrary to the foundations of democracy and human rights.[31] Falk explains that the entrenchment of neo-liberal policies has resulted in ever increasing poverty and inequality in the world demonstrating the need for a 'greater willingness to take into balance social equity concerns against economistic goals.'[32] Therefore it becomes necessary to develop an appropriate understanding of both democracy and human rights and the relationship between the two, so that minimalist conceptions may be exposed as inadequate because of failing to account for the totality of the human experience, allowing for more expansive definitions that provide support for emancipation and empowerment.

B. Democracy and human rights: a complex and multifaceted relationship

In his study of democracy and human rights, David Beetham explains that there is no simple way to summarize the nature of the relationship between the two concepts owing to the 'enormous variation in the content of human rights'.[33] The dominance of neo-liberal thinking has resulted in a simplistic understanding

---

'The Social Dimension of the Enlargement of the European Union' (1998) 5 Maastricht J of Eur and Comparative L, p 107.

[27] See *General Comment 5*, paras 11–12 (on persons with disabilities).

[28] *Slovakia* UN doc E/C.21/1/add, 81 29th session, 19 Dec 2002, para 8; Viet Nam UN doc E/C.12/1993/8 9 June 1993, para 8; *Georgia*, UN doc E/C.12/1/add 83 19 Dec 2002, para 6.

[29] *General Comment 2*, para 9; *General Comment 3*, para 12; *General Comment 6*, para 17 in direct relation to older persons.

[30] A Eide and A Rosas, 'Economic, Social and Cultural Rights: A Universal Challenge', in A Eide *et al* (eds), *Economic, Social and Cultural Rights: A Textbook* (2nd edn, Nijhoff, 2001) p 5.

[31] See Donnelly (1999) (above) pp 618–619.

[32] R Falk, *Human Rights Horizons: The Pursuit of Justice in a Globalizing World* (Routledge, 2000) p 27.   [33] Beetham (1999) (above) p 114.

of both democracy and human rights and the relationship between the two.[34] International law's understanding of democracy and human rights has been significantly influenced by these views.[35] Beetham explains how civil and political rights are integral to democracy as the absence of freedoms of speech, association, and security of person would make any description of democracy contradictory. Without these freedoms there would be no opportunity for even the most basic forms of participation and no chance for popular control over the government. Socio-economic rights are seen to be in a relationship of mutual dependency with democracy as the long-term denial of such rights undermines the basic tenets of political equality in a democracy and the viability of effective democratic institutions.[36] So while it may be possible to suggest that there is no self-evident connection between socio-economic rights and democracy in the same way there is with civil and political rights, socio-economic rights remain integral to the efficacy of democracy, properly understood.

As stated it is necessary to move beyond the minimalist approaches and to give appropriate attention to the socio-economic sphere of society when dealing with democracy and human rights. However, it is commonly asserted that such a move is not possible or desired as it entails engaging with normative values or goals about which there can be no definite agreement.[37] International law's adherence to minimalist conceptions is not surprising as it avoids the complexities involved in dealing with normative values, providing the easiest way of ensuring objective measurements and also potentially reflects the extent to which there is widespread agreement among states.[38] But the attractions of simplicity should not preclude efforts in trying to develop understandings of international law that work in favour of human values and allow the law to be used in a way that protects and supports the needs of individuals. In this respect it is necessary to establish an understanding of democracy that represents 'an ongoing call to enlarge the opportunities for popular participation in political processes and end social practices that systematically marginalize some citizens while empowering others'.[39] This has close connections with ensuring the importance of socio-economic rights as 'the egalitarian principle inherent in democracy requires not only "one man, one vote", but also "one man, one equal right to live as fully humanly as he may wish"'.[40]

Limiting understanding and the application of human rights and democracy to the civil and political spheres of society fails to recognize fully and account for the totality of the human experience. The human experience cannot be classified into precisely defined categories and it has been shown that strict adherence to legal categories undermines the ability of international human rights law to contribute

---

[34] Ibid p 89, See also Falk (above) p 47; Eide and Rosas (above) p 3.

[35] T Evans, 'International Human Rights Law as Power/Knowledge' (2005) 27 Human Rights Q pp 1050 and 1059–1062; Falk (above) p 46–49.   [36] Beetham (1999) (above) p 114.

[37] Ibid ch 1; see also C Macpherson, *The Life and Times of Liberal Democracy* (OUP, 1977) ch 4.

[38] Franck (above) pp 47–48.   [39] Marks (above) p 109.

[40] C Macpherson, *Democratic Theory: Essays in Retrieval* (OUP, 1973) p 51.

effectively to the human experience.[41] Instead there is the need to take an overall view of the human existence where different individuals will be in different states of need. Some may need protection of the right to protest against the government, others may need protection when arrested or unlawfully detained, and others may need access to a job or health care. For any of these cases, an understanding of democracy beyond the minimalist view is necessary. The minimalist understandings of democracy and human rights fail to appreciate fully or grasp the need for expansive approaches that work in favour of human values ensuring empowerment.

Both socio-economic rights and civil and political rights contribute to the ability of individuals to be part of the processes that impact on their lives. International human rights law, though flawed in many respects, provides a basis for empowerment, a base line below which no behaviour is acceptable and recognition of the worth and value of human dignity.[42] This is not confined to certain human rights most commonly associated with political activity, as empowerment is more than being able to engage in certain political activities, especially when it comes to marginalized and subaltern groups. For example, the structural inequalities in society that impact on women are often most evident in the socio-economic sphere, which in turn 'contributes to their economic dependence, denial of personal autonomy, and lack of empowerment. These in turn limit still further the women's ability to participate in public life, including policy development and decision making.'[43] Ensuring socio-economic rights needs to be seen as essential to any understanding of democracy, and democracy must be seen as fundamental to furthering the promotion and protection of socio-economic rights.[44] Ensuring the effective promotion and protection of socio-economic rights provides individuals with an adequate standard of living and a life of dignity through the provision of food, clothing, work, education, and housing, etc. These aspects in turn provide the basis for freedom and independence, allowing the individual to participate and be part of society and the decision-making processes that occur.[45]

There is evidence that international law is developing an understanding of democracy beyond the minimalist conceptions. The High Commissioner for Human Rights has coined the phrase 'holistic democracy' to indicate that there is more to democracy than just certain procedures and that there is a need to take a view of democracy that is 'normatively grounded in the universal human rights standards' with the main UN human rights treaties 'providing democracy's essential ingredients'.[46] To ignore or minimize the role of socio-economic rights in any

[41] C Scott, 'Reaching Beyond (Without Abandoning) the Category of "Economic, Social and Cultural Rights"' (1999) 21 Human Rights Q, p 633.
[42] Donnelly (above) p 630. This point has been made strongly by the former UN High Commissioner for Human Rights Mary Robinson, *Realizing Human Rights* (1998) p 14.
[43] Montréal 'Principles on Women's Economic, Social and Cultural Rights' (2004) 26 Human Rights Q, p 762.   [44] See Beetham (above) pp 95–108; Falk (above) p 65.
[45] A Eide, 'Economic, Social and Cultural Rights as Human Rights' in Eide *et al* (eds) (above) pp 18–19.
[46] Report of the High Commissioner for Human Rights submitted in accordance with Commission Resolution 2001/41, UN doc E/CN.4/2003/59 27 Jan 2003, para 3.

understanding of democracy is to support exclusion, marginalization and disempowerment, and admits settling for an understanding of democracy that is at best 'attenuated'.[47] States that do not provide for even minimalist systems of democracy may be able to adhere to their treaty requirements under the Covenant as it would be possible to provide employment, health care, housing, etc, through a centrally controlled economic and social system that did not allow for basic participation rights. Conversely, states based on minimalist conceptions of democracy, identified by the existence of elections and the protection of a limited range of civil and political rights, can survive without any recognition of socio-economic rights, so long as inequality is accepted as part of the system. But the long-term viability of both systems is in question as they will each fail to account for the totality of the human experience and ultimately fall short of the spirit and letter of international human rights law.

Susan Marks has argued for the need to recognize a principle of democratic inclusion that is grounded in ensuring that individuals are able to be part of the processes that impact upon their lives.[48] Marks asserts the need to make use of this principle as a 'guide to the elaboration, application and invocation of international law' as well as a means of moving international law in a particular direction.[49] By making use of principles of democratic inclusion it is possible to engage in a dynamic process of identifying unequal power relations that serve to marginalize subaltern groups and to explore more desirable outcomes that correspond to the stated objectives of democracy and human rights. In the next section the extent to which democratic principles have informed the Committee's views on the obligations under the Covenant will be explored. Attention will also be given to the ways in which the Covenant can act as a tool for empowerment allowing individuals to be part of the processes that impact their lives with a view to ensuring all have the equal opportunity for realising their own human capabilities.[50]

III. Democracy and the ICESCR

A. General

The UN Charter contains no mention of democracy but does contain reference to human rights. The absence of democracy is due to the desire of the organization to

---

[47] Beetham (above) pp 102–103. For this reason it is rather unfortunate that the website entry for Democracy at the Office of the UN High Commissioner for Human Rights only mentions the UDHR and ICCPR in relation to the UN's commitment to democracy <http://www.ohchr.org/English/issues/democracy> accessed 8 Nov 2006.   [48] Mark (above) pp 109–110.

[49] Ibid p 111.

[50] On the role of human rights and participation with regard to human capabilities see A Sen, 'Elements of a Theory of Human Rights' (2004) 32 *Philosophy and Public Affairs* p 315, especially pp 330–338 and the references contained therein. Also M Nussbaum, 'Capabilities and Social Justice' (2002) 4 *Intl Studies Rev* p 123.

pursue universal membership, with the only proviso being that member states must be peace loving.[51] However, democracy does have a place in the UN international human rights regime. Article 21 of the Universal Declaration of Human Rights states that 'The will of the people shall be the basis of authority in government.' The UDHR also provides that limitations upon the exercise of rights contained in the Declaration must be 'solely for the purpose of securing due recognition and respect for the rights and freedoms of others and of meeting the just requirements of morality, public order and the general welfare in a democratic society'.[52] The inclusion of the explicit mention of democracy in the limitation clause supports the view that democracy provides the underlying context within which the rights in the Declaration are to be implemented and realized.[53] When it comes to questions over the application of rights it is on the basis of the principles of a democratic society that they will be decided and the inclusion of democracy in this way 'establishes precise limits on State action'.[54] In the International Covenant on Civil and Political Rights there is no general limitation clause similar to the UDHR but specific mentions of democracy occur in Article 14 (right to a fair trial), article 21 (right to peaceful assembly), and article 22 (freedom of association), whereby any impediment to these rights must be justified on the basis of being 'necessary in a democratic society'. Despite the lack of any overarching reference to democracy in the ICCPR, commentaries have suggested that a state could not meet all of its obligations under this treaty without being based on a democratic system.[55] The ICESCR contains a limitation clause similar to the UDHR and is discussed further below.

It is difficult to assert unequivocally that democratic principles are the underlying basis for the UN's system for the promotion and protection of human rights as the historical record provides mixed signals. In 1954, the Commission on Human Rights, in its consideration of the draft human rights covenants, stated that the texts 'represented a broad compromise between differing political, economic and cultural opinions...'.[56] This view was backed by comments that felt the UN's human rights treaties would not take any particular concern 'with the organization of the Constitution of a State but merely with the guarantee of human rights by the State'.[57] At the same time there appears to have been very little debate about the wording of the general limitation clause and the inclusion of

---

[51] UN Charter, art 4.   [52] Art 29(2).

[53] See M Reisman, 'Sovereignty and Human Rights in Contemporary International Law' (1990) 84 AJIL p 866; A Rosas, 'Article 21' in A Eide, *et al* (eds), *The Universal Declaration of Human Rights: A Commentary* (Nijhoff, 1992) p 299.

[54] Sub-Commission on the Promotion and Protection of Human Rights, 'Promotion and Consolidation of Democracy', Working Paper by Manuel Rodríquez Cuadros, UN doc E/CN.4/Sub.2/2001/32 5 July 2001, para 17; Rich (n 6 above) p 22.

[55] M Nowak, *United Nations Covenant on Civil and Political Rights: CCPR Commentary* (Kehl-Strasbourg-Arlington, 1993) p 441.

[56] UN doc A/2808 and Corr 1, 9 UN GAOR C.3 annexes at 10 para 30.

[57] Statements of Chile UN doc E/CN.4/SR.271 at 7 1952

democracy during the early years of drafting.[58] But, as discussed above, the Cold War context ensured that democracy was excluded from the international legal discourse.[59]

However, from the end of the Cold War, the UN has been developing a position whereby it is possible to view democracy as a guiding principle for the organization. It is not possible here to investigate fully the UN's activities in the promotion and protection of democracy but various commentators have come to the conclusion that democracy has become an important principle to be pursued by the UN in relation to its member states.[60] The 2005 World Summit stated that the UN was based on common fundamental values such as freedom, equality, tolerance, and respect for all human rights,[61] and the member states declared a commitment to ensure the effective promotion and protection of human rights, the rule of law, and democracy.[62] The Summit also declared democracy is a universal value with the common feature being the ability of people to determine their own political, economic, social, and cultural systems through the full participation of individuals in all aspects of their lives.[63] This is not evidence of any sort of legal requirement or obligation of democracy in general international law or in the UN's membership obligations but it does provide support for taking a more active stance in articulating democracy as an underlying principle of the UN's activities, especially with regard to human rights.

In the ICESCR, democracy is mentioned in article 8 where restrictions on the right to form trade unions and limitations on the activities of trade unions must be 'necessary in a democratic society'.[64] There is also the general limitation clause in article 4 where restrictions on rights may only be 'in so far as this may be compatible with the nature of these rights and solely for the purpose of promoting the general welfare in a democratic society'. The mention of 'democratic society' in this way creates a significant place for democracy in the Covenant system as it is possible to view the restriction clause as requiring democracy as an underlying principle for all member states. The reference in the clause that any action taken towards limiting rights must only have the purpose of promoting general welfare, not just in any society, but a democratic society. This would exclude any attempt to argue that action taken to limit or restrict the rights in the Covenant that are for the purposes of supporting the general welfare in a society that does not adhere to basic democratic standards. However, no such reading of article 4 has explicitly occurred to date. As Craven explains 'even if the Committee does view democracy as being

---

[58] The mention of democratic society was proposed by Lebanon and Uruguay and adopted without debate, see ECOSOC Official Records 7th session sup 9 para 55 p 13.

[59] Rich (n 6 above) pp 22–23.

[60] See N White, 'The United Nations and Democracy Assistance: Development Practice within a Constitutional Framework' in P Burnell (ed), *Democracy Assistance: International Co-operation for Democratization* (Frank Cass, 2000) p 67; C Joyner, 'The United Nations and Democracy' (1999) 5 *Global Governance*, p 333.

[61] UN General Assembly, *2005 World Summit Outcome* (15 Sept 2005) UN doc A/60/L.1, para 4.

[62] *2005 World Summit Outcome*, para 119.   [63] *2005 World Summit Outcome*, para 135.

[64] Art 8(1)(a) and (c).

a prerequisite for the fulfilment of the rights within the Covenant, it has not defined what it understands by that term, nor has it ever challenged a state upon that basis'.[65] Therefore it becomes necessary to investigate what the Committee potentially does view as the wider societal context within which the obligations in the Covenant are carried out.

In 1990 the Committee adopted *General Comment 3*, which deals with the nature of states parties obligations under the Covenant. The operative section of the Comment reads as follows:

The Committee notes that the undertaking 'to take steps...by all appropriate means including particularly the adoption of legislative measures' neither requires nor precludes any particular form of government or economic system being used as the vehicle for the steps in question, provided only that it is democratic and that all human rights are thereby respected. Thus, in terms of political and economic systems the Covenant is neutral and its principles cannot accurately be described as being predicated exclusively upon the need for, or the desirability of a socialist or a capitalist system, or a mixed, centrally planned, or laisser-faire economy, or upon any other particular approach. In this regard, the Committee reaffirms that the rights recognized in the Covenant are susceptible of realization within the context of a wide variety of economic and political systems, provided only that the inter-dependence and indivisibility of the two sets of human rights, as affirmed *inter alia* in the preamble to the Covenant, is recognized and reflected in the system in question.[66]

This Comment gives an indication about principles underlying the Covenant but sends a mixed message concerning the position of democracy within the Covenant's framework. The statement 'neither requires of precludes any particular form of government' is consistent with UN membership obligations which merely require a state be 'peace-loving'.[67] But following on, in the same line, the proviso that the system in question can 'only' be democratic gives support to the argument that democracy provides the underlying principles for the Covenant framework. However, the Comment reverts back to an indeterminate position with the statement that the Covenant is 'neutral' with regard to the political and economic systems of the states parties provided the interdependence and indivisibility of rights is respected and the particular commitments of the treaty are met.

In the Committee's discussions during the drafting of the General Comment there was recognition of the need to elaborate upon the underlying principles informing the Covenant as well as the necessity of being clear on the importance of democracy in ensuring the obligations of the Covenant.[68] It was explained that the Committee needed to define clearly and precisely the nature of the obligations in the treaty which entails looking beyond a literal and technical understanding of the Covenant's obligations.[69] The role of the Committee in looking beyond the

---

[65] Craven (above) p 124.   [66] *General Comment 3*, para 8.   [67] Art 4 UN Charter.

[68] Discussions of the Committee on the General Comment are to found at E/C.12/1990/SR.46. In particular see the comments of Mr Marcha Romero, paras 33–35.

[69] E/C.12/1990/SR.46, para 28.

technical details was supported by Committee member Marcha Romero, who felt the most interesting aspect of the Committee's work was its creative role in 'formulating principles and a basic doctrine for grounding the implementation of economic, social and cultural rights'.[70] To this end it was explained that the original draft of the Comment, which only included that states were to take steps by all appropriate measures, was 'vague since it implied the end justified the means' and states would be able to conclude that any system was acceptable provided the obligations in the Covenant were met.

Marcha Romero also explained that 'it was common knowledge that one of the most important principles [for implementation of the Covenant] was the principle of democracy' and this meant a direct statement calling for the existence of democratic systems.[71] This view was explicitly shared by other members of the Committee and was not refuted by any member.[72] Despite this democracy has not been explicitly articulated by the Committee at any length in its jurisprudence. Commentators on the Covenant have written that there appears to be a view that the Covenant does require states parties to 'possess certain general attributes' in order to meet their obligations.[73] Outside of the specific details necessary for states to adhere to the technical obligations contained in the specific provisions of the Covenant, the nature of any 'certain general attributes' remains unarticulated by the Committee, leaving it unclear as to the role played by democracy.

Despite the lack of mention of democracy by the Committee, the Covenant provides substantial support to furthering an understanding of democracy discussed above as it contributes to a definition of democracy that places concern for the dignity of the individual at the forefront and is grounded in the emancipatory ideals essential to democracy. Reference to the principles of democracy as part of the wider context within which the Covenant's obligations are implemented would serve to reinforce the importance of socio-economic rights. The preamble of the Covenant makes these points clearly in declaring that the rights in the Covenant 'derive from the inherent dignity of the human person' and that 'the ideal of free human beings enjoying freedom from fear and want can only be achieved if conditions are created whereby everyone may enjoy his economic, social and cultural rights, as well as his civil and political rights'. Through its General Comments and the state reporting procedures the Committee has explored a number of important areas that contribute to an understanding of democracy that is in line with principles of democratic inclusion. The Committee has demonstrated a strong concern for marginalized groups in society who are in a disadvantageous position with regard to socio-economic rights and has also reflected upon the need for democratic procedures and institutions as central elements to the effective promotion

---

[70] E/C.12/1990/SR.46, para 33.   [71] E/C.12/1990/SR.46, para 35.

[72] E/C.12/1990/SR.46, para 43. See E/C.12/1990/SR.48, para 41 where the Chairperson, Philip Alston presented the revised version with the explicit mention of democracy.

[73] Craven (above) p 124.

and protection of socio-economic rights. The following sections will explore the Committee's views with regard to democracy in the areas of participation, equality and non-discrimination, democratic institutions and conditions in society, and the right to education. Even though the Committee has refrained from any direct references to democracy it has demonstrated that the obligations in the Covenant are informed by the principles inherent in democracy and from this the importance of appropriate recognition for socio-economic rights in understanding democracy is also apparent.

B. Participation

The understanding of democracy that is adopted here depends upon the ability of individuals to participate in the decision-making and policy processes that impact their lives. For the most part, participation in a minimalist understanding of democracy is limited to voting as increased levels of widespread participation are often characterized as destabilizing.[74] It has been shown that effective participation is a crucial element for the realization of socio-economic rights as it provides individuals and groups with a sense of belonging and empowerment.[75] As shown below, the Committee has placed great emphasis not only on the need for participation in decision-making processes and the implementation of socio-economic projects but also with regard to the implementation and overseeing of the obligations in the Covenant. The Committee's views on participation also emphasize inclusion as particular attention is given to the ability of marginalized or subaltern groups to participate in the various processes that impact them.

As with the ICCPR, the ICESCR begins in article 1 with a statement on the right of self-determination that provides all peoples with the right to 'freely determine their political status and freely pursue their economic, social and cultural development' along with the right to 'freely dispose of their natural wealth and resources' for their own ends. The right of self-determination has had a heavily disputed history and the dominant view attempts to keep its application to a minimum, confining it to the external determination of territorial borders. But there is evidence and support of the idea of an internal dimension to self-determination that provides that the population of a state has the right to participate in determinations of the self in both political and popular terms.[76] The inclusion of self-determination in the Covenant suggests that the principles behind it, the ability of individuals to participate collectively in determining their lives, are directly applicable to the rights in the Covenant as the process of self-determination will include

---

[74] See Schumpeter (above) pp 267–269; R Bellamy and P Baehr, 'Carl Schmitt and the Contradictions of Liberal Democracy' (1993) 23 *Eur J of Political Research* pp 170–171; C Pateman, *Participation and Democratic Theory* (Cambridge University Press, 1970) p 104.

[75] H Schue, *Basic Rights: Subsistence, Affluence and U.S. Foreign Policy* (Princeton University Press, 1980) pp 71–78.

[76] See A Rosas, 'The Right of Self-Determination' in Eide *et al* (eds), (above) p 114.

economic and social aspects.[77] If there is a right to determine the self then by necessity there is the need to ensure participation rights involved in the various processes and procedures related to the Covenant's rights.[78] Cassese explains that the right to dispose freely of natural wealth and resources places a duty upon states to ensure the use of these resources is 'in a manner which coincides with the interests of the people' and that this has a direct relation to political rights such as participation.[79]

There is no general right to participation in the Covenant and, with one exception, there is no mention of participation in any of its provisions. The one exception is in article 13, with the right to education being seen as contributing to the ability of individuals to participate effectively in society, which is discussed further below. The Committee has linked participation with a number of specific rights in the Covenant, pointing out that participation is essential to the effective exercise of rights and that states are obligated to ensure individuals are able to participate in the implementation of rights. In the General Comment on the right to adequate housing the Committee makes specific reference to the existence of tenants organizations and other community groups involved in housing policy and views these opportunities for individuals to participate in public decision-making as 'indispensable' for realizing the right to adequate housing.[80] With regard to the right to food the Committee has explained that framework legislation on realizing the right should include measures that involve collaboration with civil society.[81]

A similar view has been expressed with regard to employment rights where individuals and worker's groups should be able to participate in decision-making processes related to policies and strategies concerning employment.[82] The right to benefit from scientific progress and its application in article 15 creates an obligation upon states to

ensure the right of authors of scientific, literary and artistic productions to take part in the conduct of public affairs and in any significant decision-making processes with an impact on their rights and legitimate interests, and to consult these individuals or groups or their elected representatives prior to the adoption of any significant decisions affecting their rights under article 15, paragraph 1 (c).[83]

The Committee has also stressed the need to include individuals and groups directly impacted by plans and strategies for dealing with issues involving the right to food, health, and water.[84] Looking beyond the specific rights in the Covenant,

---

[77] Ibid p 113.

[78] See eg, the 1986 Declaration on Development, article 1, GA res 41/128, annex, 41 UN GAOR supp (n 53) at 186, UN doc A/41/53 (1986). Also United Nations Development Programme, *Governance for Sustainable Development: A UNDP Policy Document* (1997), available at <http://magnet.undp.org/policy/> accessed 4 Nov 2006.

[79] A Cassese, *Self-determination of Peoples: A Legal Reappraisal* (Cambridge University Press, 1995) pp 55–56. [80] *General Comment 4*, para 9.

[81] *General Comment 12*, para 29. [82] *General Comment 18*, para 42.

[83] *General Comment 17*, para 34, 46.

[84] *General Comment 5*, para 14; *General Comment 12*, para 23, right to food; *General Comment 14*, para 11, right to health; *General Comment 15*, paras 16 and 48, right to water.

the Committee has explained that, in the implementation of structural adjust-ment policies, where international financial institutions determine the range of socio-economic decisions available, socio-economic rights are potentially under threat. Therefore, it is necessary to ensure widespread participation from those affected by these policies as any failure to do so will mean that the policies lack legitimacy.[85]

The Committee has also given attention to the ability of subaltern groups to par-ticipate in the processes surrounding implementation of the Covenant, especially when the group in question is in an adverse position with regard to specific rights. It has been explained that indigenous groups have the right to participate in the planning and implementation of policies in areas such as economic policy, the use of natural resources, health care, and the overall process of self-determination.[86] The Committee has pointed to the need for the very poor in society to be able to participate in the implementation of structural adjustment policies as they are often the most adversely affected by these measures. [87] With regard to those in poverty the Committee has also explained that while 'free and fair elections are a crucial component of the right to participate, they are not enough to ensure that those living in poverty enjoy the right to participate in key decisions affecting their lives.'[88] Mention has also been made of the ability of disabled persons and older persons to be able to participate in the processes impacting upon them, with the state required not only to abstain from any measures that may prevent participa-tion but also required to take necessary measures ensuring their full participation in society.[89] The ability of women to participate has also been addressed with the Committee not only addressing participation with regard to the rights in the Covenant but also there has been an emphasis on the importance of women being actively part of the political process.[90]

---

[85] ESCR Committee, *Summary Record*, 34th session 29 April 2005, UN doc E/C.12/2005/SR.3, statement by Mr Texier, para 22. In its Concluding Observations the Committee has identified structural adjustment policies as a factor impeding the implementation of the Covenant, especially with regard to disadvantaged and marginalized groups, see *Brazil*, UN doc E/C.12/1/add 87, 30th session, 23 May 2003, para 16; *Ecuador* UN doc E/C.12/1/add 100, 32nd session, 7 Jun 2004, para 9. Also see the Committee's positive comments concerning Algeria's efforts to overcome the neg-ative impact of structural adjustment policies, UN doc E/C.12/1995/17 28 Dec 1995, para 7.

[86] *Ecuador* UN doc E/C.12/1/add 100, 33rd session, 7 June 2004, para 12; *Russian Federation* UN doc E/C.21/1/add 94, 31st session, 12 Dec 2003, para 11; *Colombia* UN doc E/C.21/1/add 74, 27th session 30 Nov 2001, para 12 *General Comment 14*, para 27, right to health.

[87] ESCR Committee, *Summary Record*, 34th session 29 April 2005, UN doc E/C.12/2005/SR.3, statement by Mr Texier, para 22.

[88] *Poverty and the International Covenant on Economic, Social and Cultural Rights*, Statement adopted by the ESCR Committee 4 May 2000, UN doc E/C.12/2001/10, para 12.

[89] *General Comment 5*, para 9, persons with disability *General Comment 6*, para 39, older persons.

[90] *Russian Federation* UN doc E/C.21/1/add 94, 31st session, 12 Dec 2003, para 6; *Democratic People's Republic of Korea* UN doc E/C.21/1/add 95, 31st session, 12 Dec 2003, para 13; *China Hong Kong* SAR UN doc E/C.21/add 58, 28th session, 21 May 2001, para 33.

The Committee has expressed a very important view that goes to the heart of ensuring active and widespread participation. It has been stated that 'a policy or programme that is formulated without the active and informed participation of those affected is most unlikely to be effective'.[91] The Committee's emphasis on participation in the implementation of rights in the Covenant suggests a certain degree of obligation upon states for meeting the requirements of the Covenant. This obligation to ensure individuals are able to participate does not have explicit mention in the Covenant; therefore the Committee's position on participation must be seen as being derived from underlying democratic principles that inform the Covenant.

The Committee's perspective on participation extends to the procedures and processes involved in implementation of the Covenant. In its first General Comment, the Committee set out a number of objectives inherent in the reporting procedures, with objective 4 being to:

facilitate public scrutiny of government policies with respect to economic, social and cultural rights and to encourage the involvement of the various economic, social and cultural sectors of society in the formulation, implementation and review of the relevant policies.[92]

The Committee makes the point that it is not for states alone to be preparing the reports as it is necessary for civil society to be involved both in the preparation of reports[93] and the implementation of the Covenant.[94] The Committee views practices of this nature as a valuable part of promoting and protecting rights in the Covenant.[95] Again the Committee's position on this has been informed by general principles inherent in democracy and not from any specific obligations set out in the Covenant. The Committee has explained that by ensuring the participation of non-state entities in the implementation and oversight of the Covenant there is increased governmental accountability as widespread participation provides avenues for the evaluation of progress being made in implementation of the Covenant and the identification of problems and shortcomings in the implementation of the Covenant.[96] The Committee's view on non-state entities being able to participate in the implementation and oversight of the Covenant underlies the importance of individuals being able to participate in the processes that impact upon their lives. The Committee rejects the view that the state alone should be left to make decisions without any input from those who are directly affected by the decisions adopted. Craven has commented that 'the Committee's emphasis on participation lends weight to the argument that some form of democracy is a prerequisite to the

[91] *Poverty and the International Covenant on Economic, Social and Cultural Rights*, Statement adopted by the ESCR Committee, 4 May 2000, UN doc E/C.12/2001/10, para 12.

[92] *General Comment 1*, para 5.

[93] *China* UN doc E/C.12/1/add 107, 34th session, 13 May 2005, para 12; *Brazil* UN doc E/C.21/1/add 87, 30th session, 23 May 2003, para 14.

[94] *Serbia and Montenegro* UN doc E/C.12/1/add 108, 34th session, 13 May 2005, para 39; *Croatia* UN doc E/C.21/add 73, 27th session, 30 Nov 2001, para 38.

[95] *General Comment 1*, para 5; *Summary Record*, ESCR Committee, 28th session, 20 Feb 2003, statements by Mr Marchan Romero, 16.   [96] *General Comment 1*, para 6 and 8.

implementation of the rights within the Covenant'.[97] While the Committee has not explicitly linked participation, and the consequences of participation, to an articulation of democracy, its views on the subject give strength to an understanding of democracy that goes beyond the minimalist conception as it strives to ensure individuals are able to participate in the processes that impact their lives.

C. Equality and non-discrimination

In emphasizing the importance of participation for realizing the rights in the Covenant the Committee has also expressed the importance of ensuring that all are able to benefit from the protection offered by the Covenant. The Committee has taken a clear line on the problems of discrimination that result in exclusion from decision-making processes, planning, and implementation of the Covenant, focusing on the position of women, minorities, and indigenous groups. The Committee grounds the commitment to equality and non-discrimination in the broader framework of UN obligations with reference to both the UN Charter and the UDHR.[98] The Committee emphasizes that obligations in the Covenant include both *de jure* (or formal) equality and *de facto* (or substantive) equality, which concerns itself with alleviating the inherent disadvantages faced by subaltern groups.[99] The Committee stresses the need in this respect to move beyond neutral laws and procedures to look at the actual human experience and rectify structural situations of disadvantage.[100] It is recognized that all forms of discrimination need to be removed from society so that individuals are not prevented from being part of the processes in their lives based on arbitrary criteria. The emphasis on non-discrimination works to ensure that all individuals are not excluded from the opportunity for living 'an integrated, self-determined and independent life'.[101]

These general principles have been applied to the position of specific groups in society. With regard to women the Committee has expressed strong concern with embedded beliefs and traditions in society that place women at a particular disadvantage in socio-economic areas. The Committee has pointed out that

Gender-based assumptions and expectations generally place women at a disadvantage with respect to substantive enjoyment of rights, such as freedom to act and to be recognized as autonomous, fully capable adults, to participate fully in economic, social and political development, and to make decisions concerning their circumstances and conditions.[102]

---

[97] However, it is important to note that the Committee makes particular mention of the fact that the practices described above come from states 'reflecting different political and economic systems': *General Comment 1*, para 5.   [98] *General Comment 16*, para 2.
[99] *General Comment 16*, para 7.   [100] *General Comment 16*, para 10.
[101] *General Comment 5*, para 16–17.
[102] *General Comment 16*, para 14. Also see Montreal Principles on Women's Economic, Social and Cultural Rights (2004), 26 Human Rights Q, p 761.

The Committee has stated that there are a number of specific obligations upon states in this area, including the promotion of equal representation of men and women in public offices and decision-making bodies along with equal participation in development planning, decision-making, and the enjoyment of benefits deriving from these measures.[103] The Committee has repeatedly expressed grave concern with 'the inadequate representation of women in the decision-making bodies of the state party and the persistence of patriarchal attitudes',[104] and the prevalence of traditions, customs and cultural practices that lead to 'substantial discrimination against women and girls and prevent them from fully exercising their rights . . . '.[105] The Committee emphasizes 'equitable access to decision-making positions and processes as crucial to the enjoyment of economic, social and cultural rights'.[106] In this respect the Committee has expressed concern with gender inequality in specific sectors, such as employment,[107] the public service sector,[108] and in the political process generally.[109]

The Committee has shown similar concern with regard to indigenous groups and ethnic minorities, emphasizing the need to ensure non-discrimination and equal levels of participation for these groups in the planning and decision-making processes in areas such as employment, social programmes, housing, health, and education.[110] The Committee has taken a proactive stance in this regard addressing the broader issues surrounding the integration of minority groups into society,[111] suggesting that there are a number of positive obligations upon states to ensure all groups are adequately integrated. Importantly, the Committee has also made the point that market-based approaches for organizing the economy and society will not meet the needs of minority groups or those in the margins, and that governments have an obligation to take positive action to rectify disadvantages and ensure the necessary measures of equality and non-discrimination as required by the Covenant.[112]

---

[103] *General Comment 16*, para 21.

[104] *Slovakia* UN doc E/C.21/1/add 81, 29th session, 19 Dec 2002, para 10; *Solomon Islands* UN doc E/C.21/1/add 84, 29th session, 19 Dec 2002, para 6; *Zambia* UN doc E/C.12/1/add 106, 34th session, 23 June 2005, para 16.

[105] *Benin* UN doc E/C.21/1/add 78, 28th session, 5 June 2002, para 8; *Democratic People's Republic of Korea* UN doc E/C.21/1/add 95, 31st session, 12 Dec 2003, para 13; *Sudan* UN doc E/C.21/1/add 48, 23rd session, 1 Sept 2000, para 20.

[106] *Zambia* UN doc E/C.12/1/add 106, 34th session, 23 June 2005, para 16; *Spain* E/C.12/1/add 99, 32nd session, 7 June 2004, para 11.

[107] *Azerbaijan* UN doc E/C.12/1/add 104, 33rd session, 14 Dec 2004, para 16; *Lithuania* UN doc E/C.12/1/add 96, 32nd session, 7 June 2004, para 10.

[108] *Bolivia* UN doc E/C.21/1/add 60, 25th session, 21 May 2001, para 15.

[109] *Russian Federation* UN doc E/C.21/1/add 94, 31st session, 12 Dec 2003, para 6; *Democratic People's Republic of Korea* UN doc E/C.21/1/add 95, 31st session, 12 Dec 2003, para 13; *China Hong Kong* SARUN doc E/C.21/Add 58, 25th session, 21 May 2001, para 33.

[110] *Serbia and Montenegro* UN doc E/C.12/1/add 108, 34th session, 13 May 2005, para 41; *Azerbaijan* UN doc E/C.12/1/add 104, 33rd session, 14 Dec 2004, para 15; *Ecuador* UN doc E/C.12/1/add 100, 33rd session, 7 June 2004, para 11; *Israel* UN doc E/C.21/1/add 90, 30th session, 23 May 2003, paras 16, 21.

[111] *Lithuania* UN doc E/C.12/1/add 96, 32nd session, 7 June 2004, para 9; *Guatemala* UN doc E/C.21/1/add 93, 31st session, 12 Dec 2003, para 11.

[112] *General Comment 5*, paras 9–12.

The Committee's position on equality and non-discrimination is grounded in specific obligations in the Covenant. Article 2 (2) provides:

The States Parties to the present Covenant undertake to guarantee that the rights enunciated in the present Covenant will be exercised without discrimination of any kind as to race, colour, sex, language, religion, political or other opinion, national or social origin, property, birth or other status.

Article 3 adds to this through an obligation on states to 'ensure the equal right of men and women to the enjoyment of' the rights in the Covenant. The Committee has expressed the view that equality and non-discrimination not only constitute specific obligations upon states but also act as underlying principles to the implementation of the Covenant. In this way, the Committee is emphasizing the need for states to take an active concern for all sections of society and to take the action necessary to ensure that all are able to be part of society. In this respect the Committee has 'stressed that the Covenant is a vehicle for the protection of the vulnerable and disadvantaged groups in society',[113] and thus the Covenant acts as an important tool in overcoming unequal power relations in society as it refuses to accept adherence to the status quo. This position contributes to a substantive understanding of democracy that extends beyond the political sphere of society as it takes an active concern in the welfare of all as a goal in itself, but also as a means to ensuring all individuals may be active participants in the society. The position of an individual, or groups of individuals, in society is not determined by their market status and the fate of any individual is not accepted as an inevitable outcome of the system. Instead the Committee makes clear that it is necessary to address all obstacles preventing individuals from participating in the realization of their own capabilities.

D. Democratic institutions

Even though the Committee has shied away from any specific mention of democracy, even in minimalist terms, it has established the need for a number of institutional and societal practices directly related to understandings of democracy. It has also elaborated upon the general conditions in society[114] that work against the effective implementation of the Covenant. The Committee's views in this respect are highly significant as they are not based on any specific obligations in the Covenant. Instead they represent what the Committee believes to be the most conducive conditions for the effective promotion and protection of the rights in the Covenant.

The independence of the judiciary has been a significant aspect of the Committee's evaluation of state reports. This is directly connected to the Committee's

---

[113] Craven (above) p 132.

[114] Such as corruption, see *Republic of Moldova* UN doc E/C.21/1/add 91, 31st session, 12 Dec 2003, para 12 and social instability, see *Solomon Islands* UN doc E/C.21/1/add 84, 29th session, 19 Dec 2002, para 5; *Republic of the Congo* UN doc E/C.21/1/add 45, 22nd session, 23 May 2000, para 8.

view that socio-economic rights are justiciable and that appropriate remedies must be available in cases of alleged violations.[115] It is recognized that judicial enforcement is not the only means for the promotion and protection of rights in the Covenant but, at the same time, it is an important aspect as it provides an effective means for ensuring the protection of rights for the most vulnerable and disadvantaged groups in society.[116] Judicial measures are also seen as necessary to ensure adherence to the principles of non-discrimination in the application of the rights in the Covenant.[117] Therefore, the Committee has raised the issue of the independence of the judiciary and its ability to act as a neutral body in the application of the Covenant in the domestic sphere with a number of states.[118]

The Committee's emphasis on there being an independent judiciary is directly linked to the overall accountability of states with regard to the obligations agreed to in the Covenant.[119] In this regard, the Committee has commented upon the specific structures and practices of state governments. The Committee has made the point that governments and societies with 'undemocratic features... impede the full enjoyment of economic, social and cultural rights...'.[120] In this respect, there has been specific mention of free and fair elections,[121] increased respect for human rights commitments,[122] and recognition of the rights of indigenous groups and minorities.[123] In various General Comments, the Committee has explained that in the formulation and implementation of strategies for the realization of rights in the Covenant respect is to be given to the 'principles of accountability, transparency, people's participation, decentralization, legislative capacity and the independence of the judiciary'.[124] These principles are central to any understanding of democracy. The Committee has made the existence of democratic structures and practices central to the effective implementation of the Covenant even though any specific reference to these aspects is absent from the treaty.

E. Education and democracy

Article 13 of the Covenant states that 'education shall be directed to the full development of the human personality and the sense of its dignity, and shall strengthen

---

[115] *General Comment 9*, para 10.   [116] *General Comment 9*, para 10.

[117] *General Comment 3*, para 5.

[118] *Azerbaijan* UN doc E/C.12/1/addu 104, 33rd session, 14 Dec 2004, para 13; *Ecuador* UN doc E/C.12/1/add 100, 33rd session, 7 June 2004, para 10; *Democratic People's Republic of Korea* UN doc E/C.21/1/add 95, 31st session, 12 Dec 2003, para 9; *Kyrgyzstan* UN doc E/C.21/1/add 49, 23rd session, 1 Sept 2000, para 12; *Sudan* UN doc E/C.21/1/add 48, 23rd session, 1 Sept 2000, para 19.

[119] *General Comment 9* para 2.

[120] *China Hong Kong* SAR UN doc E/C.21/add 58, 25th session, 21 May 2001, para 13.

[121] *Mongolia* UN doc E/C.21/1/add 47, 23rd session, 1 Sept 2000, para 3.

[122] *Sudan* UN doc E/C.21/1/add 48, 23rd session, 1 Sept 2000, paras 5–6; *Croatia* UN doc E/C.21/add 73, 27th session, 30 Nov 2001, para 6.

[123] *Croatia* UN doc E/C.21/add 73, 27th session, 30 Nov 2001, para 20; *Bolivia* UN doc E/C.21/1/add 60, 25th session, 21 May 2001, para 7.

[124] *General Comment 12*, para 23 (right to food). Also see *General Comment 18*, para 42 (right to employment).

the respect for human rights and fundamental freedoms'. It is further expressed that 'education shall enable all persons to participate effectively in a free society, promote understanding, tolerance and friendship'. In its General Comment on article 13 the Committee explains that the right to education is:

[A]n indispensable means of realizing other human rights. As an empowerment right, education is the primary vehicle by which economically and socially marginalized adults and children can lift themselves out of poverty and obtain the means to participate fully in their communities. Education has a vital role in empowering women, safeguarding children from exploitative and hazardous labour and sexual exploitation, promoting human rights and democracy, protecting the environment, and controlling population growth.[125]

Education is directly linked to the ability of individuals to realize and exercise rights and to be part of society. The right to education demonstrates the interdependence of rights as it serves as both a political right and a socio-economic right.[126] Regardless of how it is categorized, the denial of education rights is extremely damaging as it creates substantial obstacles to the ability of individuals to participate in decision-making processes impacting their lives.[127]

There can be no justification for denying education rights or applying discriminatory policies in this area. A denial of education will have a significant impact upon the existence of democracy. If individuals are able to access education they are able to be active participants in their own development and contribute to the development of society. Education, understood in this sense as the freedom to gain and seek knowledge, provides individuals with the necessary intellectual and practical tools for engaging in decision-making processes and for expressing opinions. Education is an important pre-condition to the exercise of many other rights[128] which in turn are essential to the existence of democracy. To deny access to education is to deny the ability of individuals to realize basic human dignity, as education 'essentially empower[s] individuals to participate in and interact in the societies in which they live with dignity and with equal opportunities.'[129] In this respect, the right to education holds a special place in the promotion and protection of democracy.

IV. Articulating principles of democratic inclusion

It is clear from the above that the Committee's approach to the Covenant is influenced by underlying principles associated with democracy. The Committee has also asserted a number of elements that contribute to an understanding of

---

[125] *General Comment 13*, para 1.   [126] See Beetham (above) p 97.
[127] *Croatia* UN doc E/C.21/add 73, 27th session, 30 Nov 2001, para 35.
[128] See M Nowak, 'The Right to Education' in A Eide *et al* (above) pp 245–271.
[129] F Veriava and F Coomans, 'The Right to Education' in D Brand and C Heyns (eds), *Socio-Economic Rights in South Africa* (Petoria University Law Press, 2005) p 63.

democracy that extends well beyond minimalist conceptions. However, despite the views expressed about the Committee's role in articulating the principles that inform the Covenant, the Committee has, for the most part, remained silent on any direct mention of the term democracy. As discussed above, article 4 of the Covenant suggests that democratic society is an underlying principle of the Covenant. In its General Comment on the obligations of states, the Committee has said the Covenant is ideologically neutral and that the rights contained therein are realized in a variety of systems. But there is specific mention of the fact that various political, social, and economic systems are only acceptable provided they are democratic.

The reluctance of the Committee to refer expressly to the democratic principles underlying the Covenant is unusual in the current environment as the international legal discourse has come to accommodate references to democracy, especially in relation to human rights. It is useful that the Committee has not unquestionably embraced references to democracy in such as way as to make the term meaningless but, at the same time, the wariness of referring to democracy in a way that directly informs the obligations under the Covenant results in the promises for a better life that the Covenant brings remaining unfulfilled. On the other hand, the demands of international diplomacy mean that it is no surprise that the Committee has remained silent about the relationship between democracy and the Covenant.

In making greater use of democracy, understood as the principle of democratic inclusion, as a central feature to the implementation of the Covenant, the Committee would face two different sets of problems. States that do not adhere to the basic criteria of a minimalist conception of democracy may be able to provide adequate levels of protection for socio-economic rights and meet the technical obligations of the Covenant. However, if the situation exists whereby individuals are unable to participate actively in the formulation of policies and programmes and there is an absence of accountability of the government, this would be contrary to the principles articulated by the Committee necessary for the effective enjoyment of rights. The Committee would be in a difficult position in having to admit that the technical obligations of the Covenant were being met but that the wider context is inappropriate for the effective promotion and protection of human rights.[130] On the other hand, states with democratic systems often argue that political equality ensures the necessary principles for achieving their obligations under the Covenant and that there is no need to recognize fully many of the

---

[130] Eg in its Concluding Observations for states not known for their democratic practices, such as China, Libya, and Kuwait, the Committee emphasizes any positive measures taken to implement the provisions of the Covenant and does not identify any factors or difficulties preventing implementation, see *Libya* UN doc E/C.12/LYB/CO/2, 35th session, 25 Jan 2006; *China* UN doc E/C.12/1/add 107, 34th session, 13 May 2005; Kuwait, UN doc E/C.12/1/add 98, 32nd session, 7 June 2004.

rights of the Covenant as they only represent aspirations to be pursued.[131] In this regard, the Committee would need to articulate a version of democracy that moves beyond the dominant minimalist conceptions, adequately addresses the totality of the human experience, and rejects the acceptance of inequalities in society. This again would be a difficult position to pursue as questioning of the democratic nature of a state is an extremely sensitive area, which may result in states no longer co-operating with the Committee.[132]

To give greater prominence to the role of democracy in the protection of socio-economic rights the Committee has to work in two different directions in trying to impress upon states the need for protecting socio-economic rights as an inherent part of ensuring human dignity and the necessity of ensuring individuals are able to participate effectively in all aspects of their lives. In this regard, the Committee has the potential of alienating large numbers of states who are party to the Covenant, hence the silence on democracy as an underlying principle. Treaty monitoring bodies continue to struggle against the primacy of state interests in international human rights law, making it necessary to avoid contentious areas such as dealing with wider principles that inform the obligations contained in a treaty. Monitoring bodies are caught between the need to ensure that as many states as possible participate in the treaty regime and the necessity of influencing state behaviour in order to comply with the treaty obligations.[133] It is a delicate balance and it is understandable that the Committee has shied away from references to democracy as its more immediate concern is impressing upon all states parties that the Covenant creates binding legal obligations and should not be dismissed as only being non-binding programmatic goals to be pursued. The Committee is making significant progress in this regard as it has established the idea that there exists a basic core of legal obligations that is to be met by all states.[134]

Even though the Committee has made progress in impressing upon states the importance of the Covenant, the extent to which states have made substantive strides in ensuring the obligations under the Covenant are an integral part of the domestic system has been limited. As Craven has explained:

That the emergence and development of the Covenant have been a painfully slow process may be put down, to a large extent, to the political and ideological forces that have used human rights as a battleground.[135]

---

[131] See eg, the statements of the UK in its Third Periodic Report under the ICESCR, UN doc E/1994/104/add 11, 17 June 1996, para 9: 'As regards the International Covenant on Economic, Social and Cultural Rights, the greater part of its provisions do not purport to establish norms which lend themselves to translation into legislation or justiciable issues, but are statements of principle and objectives.'

[132] The most the Committee will comment on in relation to democratic states is a concern that the state views social, economic, and cultural rights as non-justiciable and suggests the state changes its view. see eg, *Concluding Observations New Zealand*, E/C.12/1/add 88, 23 May 2003, para 11.

[133] J Crawford, 'The UN Human Rights Treaty System: A System in Crisis' in P Alston and J Crawford (above) pp 10–11.   [134] *General Comment 3*, para 10.

[135] Craven (above) p 352.

Now that the contours of the ideological battle that have gripped international law since the creation of the UN have subsided, it is possible for democracy, appropriately understood, to be articulated as a necessary principle in the implementation of human rights. As a means of ensuring effective protection and promotion of all rights, it is essential for treaty monitoring bodies to make clear the nature of the system that is most conducive to their realization.[136] While democracy, as it is currently understood, is not necessarily ideal in resolving all problems associated with the effective promotion and protection of human rights, it does go a long way towards the realization of rights in ways other systems cannot. Even in minimalist terms, democracy allows for participation rights in the political process, along with rights concerning the security of the person, which in turn provides for significant levels of freedom and some element of popular control over government. When a substantive view of democracy is taken, the situation improves further as this system depends upon appropriate recognition of an extensive range of human rights that allow individuals to be part of the processes that impact upon their lives. Treaty monitoring bodies at the regional level have been able to be open and assertive about the importance of democracy in the protection of human rights in these systems owing to the clear commitment to democracy set out in the various treaties.[137] But even in these cases, the articulation of democracy as a major factor in the promotion and protection of human rights has taken time to move from tentative mentions to a substantive guiding principle in the implementation of human rights.[138]

The Committee does not have the same backing of membership obligations concerning democracy as do the regional bodies but, as discussed above, the UN has now appeared to embrace democracy as a fundamental principle.[139] By articulating the importance of democracy for the implementation of the Covenant the Committee will not only work to ensure the rights in the Covenant are realized by all but it will also provide further support for an understanding of democracy in international law that is more than minimalist and actually works to overcome inequality instead of supporting it.

[136] See the chapter by M O'Flaherty, 'Towards Integration of United Nations Human Rights Treaty Body Recommendations: The Rights-Based Approach Model' in this book.

[137] See eg, Inter-American Court of Human Rights, *The Word 'Laws' in Article 30 of the American Convention on Human Rights*. Advisory Opinion OC-6/86 (9 May 1986) I/A Court HR, Ser A no 6 (1986); European Court of Human Rights, *United Communist Party of Turkey and Ors v Turkey* (1998) 26 EHRR 121. But as David Harris explains even when there exists a strong sense of collegiality as demonstrated by the regional systems there still problems of compliance when states feel the views of monitoring bodies are unfavourable, see DJ Harris, 'Lessons from the Reporting System of the European Social Charter' in P Alston and J Crawford (above) p 360.

[138] See R Burchill, 'The Role of Democracy in the Protection of Human Rights-Lessons from the European and Inter-American Human Rights Systems' in D Forsythe and P McMahon (eds), *Human Rights and Diversity: Area Studies Revisited* (University of Nebraska Press, 2003) pp 137–156.

[139] The recent report by the Secretary General's High Level Panel on Threats, Challenges, and Changes recognized the work that had been done by regional organizations in norm-setting for requirements of democracy and that this is something the UN should consider adopting, *A More Secure World: Our Shared Responsibility* (2004) para 94.

V. Conclusions

Democracy has only recently become part of the international legal discourse but, in a short period of time, it has emerged as a fundamental principle guiding a significant amount of action in the international system. However, the type of democracy being promoted in international law does not necessarily embrace the emancipatory nature inherent in the idea, understood as the ability of individuals to be part of the processes that impact upon their lives. The adherence to minimalist conception of democracy has only served to maintain unequal power relations with disastrous consequences for those who are on the margins of society. International law's embrace of minimalist conceptions of democracy is not surprising given the influence of neo-liberal ideas in the international system.[140] But international human rights law provides the opportunity to overcome the negative consequences of adherence to minimalist conceptions of democracy based on neo-liberal ideas. As with democracy, it is necessary to overcome confined views that equate human rights with the limited range of civil and political rights.

The Covenant holds a special place in this regard, as it offers significant support for ensuring that all individuals in society are able to participate in the processes surrounding their lives and that governments must be accountable to the whole of society. The South African Constitutional Court has remarked that the state's commitment to a democratic society based on social justice would have a 'hollow ring' if socio-economic rights remained unrealized.[141] International law is currently in a similar position and the promises of democracy that were exalted in the 1990s will undoubtedly ring hollow unless there is greater emphasis on recognizing the importance of socio-economic rights for democracy and the necessity of democracy for the promotion and protection of socio-economic rights.

---

[140] Philip Allott has explained 'what is actually happening by way of the transformation of international society is the globalizing of the particular social form called democracy-capitalism', comments by Allott in Review Essay Symposium: Phillip Allott's *Eunomia* and *The Health of Nations* Thinking Another World: 'This Cannot be how the World was Meant to be' (2005) 16 Eur J of Intl L, p 259. See also Marks (above), J Macey and G Miller, 'The End of History and the New World Order: The Triumph of Capitalism and the Competition between Liberalism and Democracy' (1992) 25 Cornell Intl L J p 277.

[141] *Soobramoney v Minister of Health, KwaZulu Natal* 1998 (1) SA 765 (CC) paras 8–9.

15

Trade to Live or Live to Trade: The World Trade Organization, Development, and Poverty

Sarah Joseph[*]

I. Introduction

Poverty is the major cause of human misery in today's world. The United Nations Development Program, in its Human Development Report of 2004, estimated that 20 per cent of the world's population in 2000 lived on less than US$1 a day.[1] Ongoing extreme poverty deprives people of their economic, social, and cultural rights, undermines the right to development, and of itself represents a human rights violation.[2] The imperative of addressing poverty and underdevelopment is consistently stressed by the international community, such as in the Millennium Development Goals[3] and the UN World Summit in September 2005.[4]

The World Trade Organization (WTO) is an institution devoted to facilitating negotiation over, and the supervision of international rules governing the liberalization of, international trade. International trade clearly has an important commercial function, but from a human rights point of view, an evaluation of the 'success' of the WTO necessarily involves an assessment of its impact on poverty and development. That is, international trade should be a means to such ends, rather than an end in itself.[5]

[*] I take the opportunity to thank Professor David Harris for his mentorship and friendship over many years. I would also like to thank Mashood Baderin and Robert McCorquodale for inviting me to contribute to this book. I must thank Rowena Cantley-Smith, Adam McBeth, and Andrew Lang for their comments on earlier drafts. Rachel Ball, Marius Smith, and Marika McAdam provided research assistance for this chapter. This chapter is part of the outcomes of an Australian Research Council Discovery Grant on 'The WTO and Human Rights'.

[1] United Nations Development Programme (UNDP), *Human Development Report 2004: Cultural Liberty in Today's Diverse World*, available at <http://hdr.undp.org/reports/view_reports.cfm?type=1> accessed on 31 Jan 2005, 130.

[2] See A Sengupta, 'On the Theory and Practice of the Right to Development' (2002) 24 Human Rights Q 837, 884–6.

[3] The first and foremost Development Goal is to halve extreme poverty and hunger by 2015. See <http://www.un.org/millenniumgoals/index.html> accessed on 31 Jan 2006.

[4] UN doc A/res/60/1 (24 Oct 2005) paras 17–68.

[5] United Nations Development Programme (UNDP), *Human Development Report 2005: International Cooperation at a Crossroads: Aid, Trade and Security in an Unequal World*, available at

The WTO promotes market freedoms which, it is argued in orthodox trade theory, increase aggregate wealth, which should enhance the ability of all states to protect economic and social rights and alleviate poverty.[6] Indeed, Oxfam International estimated in 2002 that an increase of 5 per cent in the share of world trade by low income states 'would generate more than $350 billion—seven times as much as they receive in aid'.[7] Trade is a more empowering way of climbing out of poverty, and frees the poor of 'exposure to the whims and fads of donors who govern access to aid budgets'.[8] The potential positive human rights impact of the WTO is reinforced in the treaty itself. The preamble to the Marrakesh Agreement establishing the World Trade Organization states that the WTO members' trading relations should be 'conducted with a view to raising standards of living', 'ensuring full employment', and 'allowing for the optimal use of the world's resources in accordance with the objective of sustainable development'.[9]

Thus, at first glance, the WTO seems to be an organization that facilitates the enjoyment of economic and social rights and the alleviation of poverty.[10] Nevertheless, it has been assailed in recent times, most visibly on the street but also within its inner sanctum, regarding its alleged detrimental effect upon the enjoyment of certain human rights. These anti-WTO arguments can be categorized as being of two types. First are those arguments, largely emanating from Northern non-governmental organizations (NGOs), which criticize the WTO for its sharp focus on free trade to the effective exclusion and alleged detriment of other values, such as environmental protection, accountability, and human rights including labour rights.[11] Second are arguments, largely emanating from the governments of developing states, that the WTO has boosted the interests of rich developed states ('the North') at the expense of developing states ('the South').[12] The second set of arguments clearly raise human rights implications regarding the right to development, and the clear nexus between ongoing poverty and the denial of economic and social rights. While these two sets of arguments have sometimes intersected,[13] their respective proponents have divergent interests. Southern governments fear

---

<http://hdr.undp.org/reports/view_reports.cfm?type=1> accessed on 31 Jan 2005; 113; Dani Rodrik, *The Global Governance of Trade: As if Development Really Mattered* (UNDP, Oct 2001) 9.

[6] See text at n 90 (below).

[7] Oxfam, *Rigged Rules and Double Standards* (Oxfam, 2002), 48.   [8] Oxfam (n 7 above) 48.

[9] Marrakesh Agreement Establishing the World Trade Organization (15 April 1994); *The Legal Texts: The Results Of The Uruguay Round Of Multilateral Trade Negotiations* 4 (1999), 1867 UNTS 154, 33 ILM 1144 (1994), preamble. All WTO agreements are available via <http://www.wto.org/english/docs_e/legal_e/legal_e.htm> accessed on 8 Nov 2006.

[10] See also Preliminary Report of the Secretary-General, 'Globalization and its Impact on the Full Enjoyment of all Human Rights', UN doc A/55/342, 4.

[11] See eg, Global Trade Watch, 'The WTO: An Australian Guide', available via <http://www.tradewatchoz.org/guide/New_WTO_Guide.pdf> accessed on 24 Jan 2006.

[12] Rodrik, (n 5 above) 35; Robert Wai, 'Countering, Branding and Dealing: Using Economic and Social Rights in and Around the International Trade Regime' (2003) 14 Eur J of Intl L 35, 51–53.

[13] Eg, both NGOs and the South criticized the effect of the Agreement on Trade-Related Aspects of Intellectual Property (15 April 1994), Marrakesh Agreement Establishing the World Trade Organization, Annex 1C, 1869 UNTS 299; 33 ILM 1197 (1994) (TRIPS) on the price of pharmaceuticals and the right to health (see Wai (n 12 above) 72 and 79): see also text at nn 59–66 (below).

that the introduction of human rights issues into the WTO might be abused by the North for protectionist purposes.[14] For example, labour standards are generally lower in developing states, and WTO intrusion into that area could conceivably undercut legitimate comparative advantages.[15]

This chapter will address an amalgam of the two anti-WTO critiques, with a greater focus on the second 'Southern' argument. First, I will examine the argument that current WTO rules are biased in favour of developed states. Second, I will examine the argument that trade liberalization, which has been facilitated, but certainly not completely achieved, by the WTO, is good for the poor, particularly in the developing world. The differing interests of the North and South are also discussed, bearing in mind that losers from economic globalization and poverty exist in developing *and* industrialized states. Finally, I will endorse a reform proposal which addresses some of the major Southern concerns, whilst also taking into account some of the concerns of Northern progressive groups.

II. Current WTO rules and developing states

The WTO was established after the 'Uruguay Round' of GATT (General Agreement on Tariffs and Trade) negotiations. The current rules of the WTO are enshrined in the Marrakesh Agreement Establishing the WTO in 1994,[16] which transformed the GATT from a negotiating forum held together by a multilateral treaty into the WTO, an international organization.[17]

Many Southern governments feel that current WTO rules benefit the North at the expense of the South. This feeling has generated resentment amongst Southern governments which has contributed to the slow pace of the present Doha Development Round, where the South is trying to make up perceived 'lost ground' from the Uruguay round.[18] The premise that the WTO is biased against the South is examined in this section.

An initial observation is that the inherent advantages of the major trading players of the North over their Southern counterparts must be acknowledged.[19]

Furthermore, the proponents of these arguments cannot be neatly divided into two groups of Northern NGOs and Southern governments. Eg, Oxfam, a high profile British NGO, is a keen supporter of WTO reform along the lines argued by developing states (see generally n 7 (above)).

[14] See generally, Jagdish Bhagwati, 'Symposium: The Boundaries of the WTO—Afterward: The Question of Linkage' (2002) 96 AJIL 126. [15] See also Wai (n 12 above) 36 and 52.

[16] See n 9 (above).

[17] See Amrita Narlikar, *The World Trade Organization: A Very Short Introduction* (OUP, 2005), at 16 and 30. [18] Narlikar (n 17 above) 55.

[19] Note, however, the emergence of certain developing states as major trading players, particularly Brazil, Russia (which is not yet a WTO member), India, and China. See Gary Duncan, 'Hong Kong fudge leaves a sour taste', *The Times*, 19 Dec 2005, p 33, on the 'growing economic stature' of these four 'BRIC states'. Nevertheless, these states contain huge populations of 'the world's poorest people', so it is arguable they still fully 'deserve support in using trade to develop'; Oxfam, *What Happened in Hong Kong?*, Oxfam Briefing Paper 85, Dec 2005, available at <http://www.oxfam.org/en/files/bp85_hongkong/download> accessed on 31 Jan 2006, p 7.

For example, the major industrialized states enjoy an advantage with regard to the WTO's dispute settlement mechanism (DSM). The ultimate sanction for breach is for the WTO to authorize trade sanctions by the aggrieved member against the delinquent member. Clearly, the prospect of trade sanctions by an economic power such as the US, the European Union (EU), or Japan, will compel compliance far more readily than the prospect of trade sanctions by a small developing state.[20]

A. Special and differential treatment

The development needs of the South, particularly regarding the alleviation of poverty, are blatantly more pressing than those of the North. These special needs are recognized in the WTO and are served by provisions allowing for 'special and differential treatment' (SDT). SDT measures were authorized in the GATT after the Tokyo Round (1973–79) with the introduction of the 'Enabling Clause', which permits preferential market access for developing states and limits the expectations of reciprocity in negotiating rounds to levels 'consistent with development needs'.[21] Most SDT provisions in current WTO agreements permit longer timelines for compliance for developing nations.[22] Furthermore, developing states have relatively high tariff bindings,[23] so their WTO obligations in respect of granting market access to goods are not generally as onerous as those of developed states.

Finally, 'trade aid', that is aid designed to alleviate the burdens of trade liberalization, is recognized as essential, and was formalized after the Singapore Ministerial meeting in 1996. The Singapore Plan of Action provided for the creation of the 'Integrated Framework for Trade-Related Technical Assistance to Least Developed Countries',[24] which co-ordinates policy efforts in this regard between the WTO and other international financial and development agencies,[25] and identifies technical assistance needs in relevant states. Since 2000, the Integrated Framework has presided over a trust fund to finance trade reform in the least developed states.[26] Though it represents a welcome acknowledgement of the adjustment needs of developing states, binding obligations for developed states in terms of funding commitments are absent.[27]

---

[20] Joel R Paul, 'Do International Trade Institutions Contribute to Economic Growth and Development?' (2003) 44 Virginia J of Intl L 285, at 334–335.

[21] Bernard Hoekman, 'Operationalizing the Concept of Policy Space in the WTO: Beyond Special and Differential Treatment' (2005) 8 J of Intl Economic L 405, 405–406. The full name of the Enabling Clause is 'Differential and More Favourable Treatment, Reciprocity and Fuller Participation of Developing Countries', L/4903, GATT BISD 26S/203 (28 Nov 1979).

[22] Hoekman (n 21 above) 406; J. Hunter, 'Broken Promises: Agriculture and Development in the WTO' (2003) 4 Melbourne Intl L J 299, 315.

[23] Each WTO member commits to a schedule of 'tariff bindings' regarding named goods. A member may not impose tariffs above those bound rates.

[24] WTO Doc WT/MIN (96)/14 (7 Jan 1997).

[25] Those other agencies are the International Monetary Fund (IMF), the International Trade Centre, UNCTAD, the UNDP, and the World Bank.   [26] Hunter (n 22 above) 317.

[27] Hunter (n 22 above) 318; Narlikar (n 17 above) 108; Hoekman (n 21 above) 411; Joel P Trachtman, 'Legal Aspects of a Poverty Agenda at the WTO: Trade Law and 'Global Apartheid'' (2003) 6 J of Intl Economic L 3, 20.

SDT modalities have been criticized as inadequate responses to underdevelopment. One may note that no binding duties are placed on developed states regarding SDT.[28] The language of the GATT, the WTO, and post-Uruguay Ministerial Declarations in this regard is always aspirational and does not imply enforceability.[29]

Furthermore, non-reciprocity has meant that many goods of special interest to developing states were kept off the negotiating table, as developed states lacked the incentive to pursue reform in such areas. As a result, the highest Northern tariffs generally apply to such goods, particularly textiles and agricultural goods.[30] In other words, non-reciprocity probably exacerbated the tendency of, and motivation for, developed states to neglect the trade interests of the South.[31] Therefore, a significantly greater degree of commitment to trade liberalization was evident from developing states in the Uruguay Round. The resultant WTO bargain is however widely thought to favour developed states over developing states, as discussed in the next sections.

It is also worth noting that significant pressure on developing states regarding trade liberalization has been generated outside the WTO. For example, many developing states have been forced by bodies such as the International Monetary Fund (IMF) and the World Bank, as part of loan conditions, to impose much lower tariffs than those to which they are bound under the WTO.[32] The existence of such 'arm-twisting', even though the WTO is not responsible for it, undermines the WTO's SDT provisions, and is probably not taken into sufficient account in WTO negotiations.

B. The Uruguay round 'Grand Bargain'

In the Uruguay Round of GATT/WTO negotiations, developing states reluctantly agreed to the extension of the GATT into areas such as services,[33] investment,[34] and

---

[28] Whilst states are not required to implement the Enabling Clause, conditions may apply if they do, such as non-discriminatory implementation: see *EC—Tariff Preferences*, Report of the Appellate Body, WT/DS246/AB/R, 7 April 2004, and discussion in J Harrison, 'Incentives for Development: the EC's Generalized System of Preferences, India's WTO Challenge and Reform' (2005) 42 Common Market L Rev 1663.   [29] Hunter (n 22 above) 303–4.

[30] Hoekman (n 21 above) 408–409 and 422; Christine Breining-Kaufman, 'The Right to Food and Trade in Agriculture' in Thomas Cottier, Joost Pauwelyn and Elizabeth Bürgi (eds), *Human Rights and International Trade* (OUP, 2005) 358, 366.   [31] See also Trachtman (n 27 above) 11.

[32] Paul (n 20 above) 319; Oxfam (n 7 above) 126–128.

[33] General Agreement on Trade in Services (15 April 1994), Marrakesh Agreement Establishing the World Trade Organization, annex 1B, *The Legal Texts: The Results Of The Uruguay Round Of Multilateral Trade Negotiations* 284 (1999), 1869 UNTS 183, 33 ILM 1167 (1994) (GATS). It is generally felt that the GATS is geared towards dismantling trade barriers in areas where developed states have a comparative advantage, such as financial and telecommunications services (where considerable progress has been made in post-Uruguay Ministerial agreements), rather than services in which the South is advantaged. See eg, UNDP (n 5 above) 136–138; Trachtman (n 27 above) 14; Oxfam (n 7 above) 226.

[34] Agreement on Trade-Related Investment Measures (15 April 1994) Marrakesh Agreement Establishing the World Trade Organization, annex 1A, *The Legal Texts: The Results Of The Uruguay*

intellectual property (discussed below).[35] They also agreed to the imposition of rules regarding non-tariff barriers which largely reflected the standards of developed states: it is generally agreed that developing states have incurred disproportionate implementation costs regarding those new standards.[36] For example, Dani Rodrik states that it:

has been estimated that it costs a typical developing country $150 million to implement requirements under just three of the WTO agreements; [those regarding] customs evaluation, sanitary and phytosanitary measures, and intellectual property.... [T]his is a sum equal to a year's development budget for many of the least developed countries.[37]

The developed states' side of the bargain was to agree to some liberalization regarding agriculture and textiles, which had essentially been omitted from prior GATT negotiations, under the Agreement on Agriculture (AoA)[38] and the Agreement on Textiles and Clothing (ATC).[39] Of course, agricultural goods and textiles are products where many developing states have a comparative advantage.[40]

1. The Northern side of the bargain—the agriculture example

Unfortunately, the AoA and the ATC 'left vast scope for continued protectionism'.[41] In 2005, the United Nations Development Programme (UNDP) stated:

On average, low-income developing countries exporting to high-income countries face tariffs three to four times higher than the barriers applied in trade between high-income countries.... Developing countries count for less than one-third of developing country imports but for two-thirds of tariff revenues collected.[42]

This section will concentrate on the failings of the Uruguay agriculture deal. Agricultural produce in the US and especially the EU remain heavily subsidized; developing states find it very difficult to penetrate those lucrative markets.[43] Indeed, excess subsidized agricultural exports have made their way to developing

---

Round Of Multilateral Trade Negotiations 143 (1999), 1868 UNTS 186 (TRIMs Agreement). Some regulation of investment restrictions has been introduced under TRIMs though it is quite weak.

[35] See text at nn 50–86 (below).   [36] Narlikar (n 17 above) 71; Hoekman (n 21 above) 410.
[37] Rodrik (n 5 above) 26.
[38] Agreement on Agriculture (15 April, 1994) Marrakesh Agreement Establishing the World Trade Organization, annex 1a, *The Legal Texts: The Results Of The Uruguay Round Of Multilateral Trade Negotiations* 33 (1999), 1867 UNTS 410.
[39] Agreement on Textiles and Clothing, Marrakesh Agreement Establishing the World Trade Organization, annex 1a, *The Legal Texts: The Results Of The Uruguay Round Of Multilateral Trade Negotiations* annex 1a. This Agreement was a transitional arrangement which terminated on 1 Jan 2005, so trade in textiles and clothing is now subject to normal GATT rules. Much of the liberalization demanded under the ATC was delayed by developed states until the last phase of its ten-year life, so benefits thereunder for developed states accrued later than had been expected: Narlikar (n 17 above) 70–71.   [40] Paul (n 20 above) 314.
[41] Narlikar (n 17 above) 26. See generally, Hunter (n 22 above) and Christine Breining-Kaufman (n 30 above).   [42] UNDP (n 5 above) 127.
[43] Paul (n 20 above) 325–6; Breining-Kaufman (n 30 above) 368.

states, undercutting local farmers and driving them out of business.[44] Furthermore, while the AoA mandated the binding of all agricultural tariff lines, developed states committed to prohibitively high tariffs. The costs to developing states of continued agricultural protection in the North has been estimated at US $100 billion, 'more than double the total sum of development assistance',[45] a sum that would significantly increase the capacities of developing states to improve economic and social conditions and combat poverty.

Furthermore, the AoA does not combat 'tariff escalation'. Processed agricultural commodities are subjected to higher 'escalating' tariffs than raw or primary goods. Tariff escalation discourages states from developing secondary agricultural industries, and from 'diversifying into value-added production'.[46] The UNDP in 2005 reported that Japanese tariffs on processed foods were seven times higher, and Canadian tariffs twelves times higher, than on primary products.[47] Tariff escalation encourages developing states to concentrate on basic agrarian production, while further refinement of products, particularly crucial in adding value, takes place elsewhere. Tariff escalation therefore retards opportunities for people in developing states to climb out of poverty. The undesirability of such an economic strategy is exacerbated by the volatility of commodities markets, discussed below.[48]

Negotiations, and more often stalemates, regarding the need for further liberalization of agriculture have thus far dominated the Doha round.[49]

2. *The Southern side of the bargain—the TRIPS example*

The Agreement on Trade-Related Aspects of Intellectual Property (TRIPS)[50] has generated considerable concern over its effects on developing states and human rights,[51] particularly regarding its requirement for all WTO members to provide twenty-year patent protection for patentable goods. Developed states had to comply by 1 January 1996, while developing states had until 2000 and the least developed states had to comply by 2006.[52]

Patents grant inventors monopoly rights over the sale of their creations for a certain period of time. This facility encourages people to market their creations, thus making them publicly available, and also encourages research and development, which might be stymied if copycats could immediately compete with inventors: the costs of invention are high compared to the costs of copying. A rationale for the

---

[44] Breining-Kaufman (n 30 above) 368; Oxfam (n 7 above) 93 and 116.

[45] Oxfam (n 7 above) 96. Department of Foreign Affairs and Trade (DFAT), *Globalization: Keeping the Gains* (Commonwealth of Australia, Canberra, 2003), at 44 quotes the figure of $40 billion, but states that this is probably a conservative estimate.

[46] Hunter (n 22 above) 312. See also Oxfam (n 7 above) 102–103.

[47] UNDP (n 5 above) 127.   [48] See text at nn 135–144.   [49] UNDP (n 5 above) 129.

[50] See (above) n 13.

[51] See eg, Sub-Commission on the Promotion and Protection of Human Rights, 'Intellectual Property Rights and Human Rights', res 2000/7 (17 Aug 2000).

[52] The deadline for least developed states has been extended with regard to pharmaceutical products to 2016; see text at n 60 (below).

global extension of IP rights under TRIPS is to encourage greater foreign investment and local innovation in the South.[53] Further, the right to enjoy the fruits of
one's creations is recognized by article 15(1)(c) of the International Covenant on
Economic Social and Cultural Rights 1966 (ICESCR).[54]

Of course, the prices of patented goods are inflated by the lack of competition.
Therefore, patent rights must be balanced against the rights of the general community to enjoy the benefits of new technological developments. The latter rights
are also recognized in the ICESCR at article 15(1)(b). Further, 'there is substantial
evidence that the existing rules for patents and copyrights are overly protective,
providing a larger reward than is necessary and stifling competitive forces'[55] and
further innovation. Finally, it seems that the North–South technological gap has
widened since the advent of TRIPS, indicating that the Agreement has not catalyzed the anticipated greater level of innovation in developing states.[56]

TRIPS presently mandates the regressive transfer of wealth from the South to
the North, as most patent rewards are gained by people, particularly companies,
from the North.[57] People in the South, where patent rights were not generally
respected prior to TRIPS, must now pay more for patented goods. The biggest
losers are the poor in developing states, who cannot afford the price increases.[58]
This situation is particularly problematic when the goods are essential for the
enjoyment of economic, social, and cultural rights.

The most vocal criticisms of TRIPS have concerned its effect on the prices
of pharmaceuticals, undermining the right to health, particularly in light of the
HIV-AIDS epidemic in the developing world.[59] The clamour regarding pharmaceuticals prompted a WTO Ministerial Declaration in Doha in 2001 on 'The TRIPS

[53] See Shanker A Singham, 'Competition Policy and the Stimulation of Innovation: TRIPS and
the interface between Competition and Patent Protection in the Pharmaceutical Industry' (2000) 26
Brooklyn J of Intl L 363 at 375–385.
[54] International Covenant on Economic, Social and Cultural Rights, opened for signature 16 Dec
1966, UN doc A/6316, art 2(1). See generally, Sam Ricketson, 'Intellectual Property and Human
Rights' in Stephen Bottomley and David Kinley (eds), *Commercial Law and Human Rights* (Ashgate,
2002), 187–213.
[55] Paul (n 20 above) 329. See also eg, Tom G Palmer, 'Are Patents and Copyrights Morally
Justified? The Philosophy of Property Rights and Ideal Objects' (1990) 13 Harvard J of L and Public
Policy 911, 914; Peter Drahos, 'The Rights to Food and Health and Intellectual Property in the Era
of 'Biogopolies', in Bottomley and Kinley (n 54 above) 215 at 227.
[56] H Sun, 'The Road to Doha and Beyond: Some Reflections on the TRIPS Agreement and
Public Health' (2004) 15 Eur J of Intl L 123, at 141; see also Oxfam (n 7 above) 212.
[57] The UNDP reported that '[f]irms in developed countries currently account for 96% of royal-
ties from patents' (n 5 above) 135. See also FM Abbott, 'Towards a New Era of Objective Assessment
in the Field of TRIPS and Variable Geometry for the Preservation of Multilateralism' (2005) 8 J of
Intl Economic L 77 at 80.
[58] See eg, World Health Organization Commission on Macroeconomics and Health,
Macroeconomics and Health: Investing in Health for Economic Development, 2001 <http://www3.who.
int/whosis/cmh/ cmh_report/report.cfm?path=whosis,cmh,cmh_report&language=english> accessed
on 1 Feb 2006, p 87.
[59] See generally, Sarah Joseph, 'Pharmaceutical Corporation and Access to Drugs' (2003) 25
Human Rights Q 425.

agreement and public health'.[60] Paragraph 7 of this Declaration extended the deadline for TRIPS compliance by the least developed states to 2016 regarding pharmaceuticals. It also affirmed the right of members to implement safeguard measures to 'protect public health and, in particular, to promote access to medicines for all'. Article 31 of TRIPS allows exceptions, notably 'compulsory licenses', where a government may authorize the production of generic versions of a patented product without the consent of the patent-holder so long as the latter receives fair remuneration. That condition may be waived in 'national emergencies'.[61] The Declaration in paragraph 5(c) affirmed that public health crises relating to HIV/AIDS, tuberculosis, and malaria were relevant 'national emergencies'. The Declaration also noted in paragraph 6, but did not fix, a problem for states that lack the capacity to produce generic drugs. Article 31(f) of TRIPS generally prohibits the export of compulsorily licensed goods, thus limiting the ability of such states to import such products. In 2003, the WTO General Council issued a decision[62] to allow the export of compulsorily licensed copies of patented essential medicines for the purposes of combating epidemics to states that lack the infrastructure to manufacture such drugs themselves.[63] In December 2005, this Decision was transformed into a formal amendment to TRIPS.[64] Despite this breakthrough, at the time of writing no state had made use of this scheme to import generic drugs.[65] These developments have nevertheless gone some way to alleviating the impact of TRIPS on access to drugs. However, the potential narrow scope of the Doha Declaration and the TRIPS amendment, in that they may not apply outside the context of epidemics, must be noted. Lower profile health problems like diabetes, pneumonia, and cancer are not explicitly addressed,[66] yet the poor in the South cannot afford patented medicines for those maladies either.

[60] Declaration on the TRIPS Agreement and Public Health, WT/MIN/01/DEC/W/2 (14 Nov 2001).

[61] These safeguards must be acknowledged as a possible cure for many criticisms of TRIPS; their scope is unclear as they have not been interpreted by the Dispute Settlement Bodies of the WTO. Note also that art 8 of TRIPS permits members to adopt measures to 'protect public health', so long as those measures are consistent with TRIPS. It is possible that TRIPS has been abused in political rhetoric to bolster threats of sanctions. Note that the US had threatened sanctions against a number of states, such as South Africa, Brazil, and Thailand, to discourage compulsory licensing plans (Joseph, (n 59 above) 445 (see also 430)).

[62] The General Council is open to all members, and is delegated functions by the Ministerial Conference (the highest WTO body with representation of all members) and by WTO Agreements. Its power to make decisions is contained in art IX of the Marrakesh Agreement Establishing the WTO.

[63] WTO General Council, 'Implementation of paragraph 6 of the Doha Declaration on the TRIPS Ageement and public health', WTO doc WT/L/540 (30 Aug 2003).

[64] *Doha Work Programme Ministerial Declaration*, WT/MIN(05)/DEC, adopted on 18 Dec 2005, para 40. See *Amendment of the TRIPS Agreement: Decision of 6 December 2005*, WTO doc WT/L/641 (Decision of the General Council).

[65] Adam McBeth, 'When Nobody Comes to the Party: Why have no States used the WTO Scheme for Compulsory Licensing of Essential Medicines?' (2006) New Zealand Ybk of Intl L 69.

[66] UNDP (n 5 above) 136.

Concern has also been raised over article 27(3)(b) of TRIPS, which requires states to provide for either patent or *sui generis* IP rights in 'plant varieties'. This provision mandates the private commercialization of food sources and therefore may threaten enjoyment of the right to food.[67] Further, TRIPS is inherently biased towards Northern notions of invention and innovation. 'Indigenous' or 'traditional' knowledge is generally not patentable,[68] yet minor industrial modifications of indigenous discoveries are patentable. In such situations, sometimes called 'biopiracy', the patent-holder (normally a Northern company) reaps the commercial benefits without any requirement under TRIPS to somehow compensate the relevant indigenous communities, who are largely responsible for the idea and concept of the relevant product. Indeed, the 'people who originally developed [the seed varieties] must buy them back at exorbitant rates'.[69] Hence, TRIPS prescribes a discriminatory regime regarding protection of IP rights, while biopiracy, which is not discouraged by TRIPS, undermines the enjoyment of cultural rights by communities, particularly indigenous communities.[70] Alleged examples of biopiracy include the attempt by US company, Rice-Tec to patent strains of basmati rice,[71] and US company, Thermo Trilogy's attempt to patent a medicinal product derived from the Indian neem tree.[72] Another problem concerns the quest for originality, which encourages genetic modification of plant breeds. Modification can improve seeds by, for example, improving a crop's resistance to certain diseases. However, modified foods can pose dangers to unmodified crops through cross-fertilization. For example, the cross-breeding of sterile 'terminator seeds' could destroy the lifecycle of natural seeds, forcing farmers to buy seeds each season.[73] A final problem regarding TRIPS and plant varieties is that IP rights encourage their beneficiaries to concentrate on

[67] Breining-Kaufman (n 30 above) 355.

[68] Eg, indigenous knowledge lacks an identifiable author, as it has often been passed down communally from generation to generation. Its long-term evolutionary nature may also lack the requisite 'originality'. See Breining-Kaufman (n 30 above) 356.

[69] Marjorie Cohn, 'The World Trade Organization: Elevating Property Interests above Human Rights' (2001) 29 Georgia J of Intl and Comparative L 427, at 435. See also generally, Dr John Mugabe, 'Intellectual Property Protection and Traditional Knowledge', at a WIPO Discussion on Intellectual Property and Human Rights (Geneva, 9 Nov 1998) available via <http://www.wipo.int> accessed 8 Nov 2006 25 Nov 2005.

[70] Caroline Dommen, 'Raising Human Rights Concerns in the World Trade Organization: Actors, Processes and Possible Strategies' (2002) 24 Human Rights Q 1, 9.

[71] See eg, European Fair Trade Association, 'Press Release: Basmati Patent', 3 Oct 2001, available at <http://www.eftafairtrade.org/Document.asp?DocID=190&tod=63424> accessed on 8 Nov 2006; Luke Harding, 'India outraged as US company wins patents on rice', *The Guardian*, 23 Aug 2001.

[72] See Organic Consumers Association, 'EU Patent Office revokes USA 'Biopiracy' Patent on Fungicide derived from Neem Tree Seeds', Press Release of 8 March 2005, at <http://www.organicconsumers.org/patent/neemtree030905.cfm> accessed on 8 Nov 2006.

[73] Dommen (n 70 above) 40. In March 2006, a de facto UN moratorium on the use of terminator technology was reaffirmed, despite being challenged by Canada, New Zealand, Australia, and some corporations. See 'UN upholds moratorium on Terminator Seed Technology' (31 March 2006), *Ban Terminator*, at <http://www.banterminator org> accessed on 13 April 2006.

lucrative IP-protected crops, generating monocultures and diminishing biodiversity.[74] The problems with monocultures are addressed below.[75]

TRIPS permits the adoption of *sui generis* IP systems as alternatives to patent protection for plant varieties. Furthermore, article 8 of TRIPS permits members to take measures to protect 'nutrition' so long as they are consistent with TRIPS. Therefore, IP systems may perhaps be developed which are fully consistent with the protection of the right to food and other relevant human rights.[76] However, it is presently uncertain whether TRIPS allows such flexibility, as *sui generis* regimes must under article 27(3)(b) be 'effective'. Article 27(3) does not seem to recognize relevant stakeholders beyond breeders, such as farmers, so an effective *sui generis* regime under TRIPS may require greater protection for breeders than is desirable under international human rights law.[77]

Developing states have come under pressure to follow the most commonly used *sui generis* system, that developed by the International Union for the Protection of New Varieties of Plants (UPOV), which mandates patent-like monopoly rights.[78] UPOV grants monopoly rights to breeders. Farmers are permitted to reuse seeds but they cannot sell produce from those harvested seeds.[79] It is to be hoped that in the future members will make use of the more balanced regimes recommended in the UN Convention on Biological Diversity 1992 (CBD)[80] and the International Treaty on Plant Genetic Resources 2004 (ITPGR),[81] which both provide greater recognition for the rights of farmers, and that such regimes are recognized as TRIPS compliant.[82] Indeed, the CBD also acknowledges the need for recognition and compensation for the commercialization of indigenous knowledge in articles 8(j) and 10(c). At the time of writing, consultations were continuing within the WTO on 'the relationship between the TRIPS Agreement and the (CBD)'.[83]

[74] Dommen (n 70 above) 39; Shelley Edwardson, 'Reconciling TRIPS and the Right to Food', in Cottier *et al* (eds) (n 30 above) 387; Oxfam (n 7 above) 224.

[75] Text at nn 131–133 (below). [76] Edwardson (n 74 above) 383.

[77] Laurence R Helfer, in Intellectual Property Rights in Plant Varieties: An Overview with Options for National Governments, (FAO Legal Papers Online 31 July 2002), at 32 quotes D Leskien and M Flinter, Intellectual Property Rights and Plant Genetic Resources: Options for a Sui Generis System, Issues in Genetic Resources no 6, (International Plant Genetic Resources Institute, 1997), as stating that an effective sui generis regimes requires 'either an exclusive right [for breeders] to control particular acts with respect to the protected varieties or at a minimum the right to remuneration when third parties engage in certain acts'.

[78] Dommen (n 7 above) 39; Edwardson (n 74 above) 383; Oxfam (n 7 above), 221. See International Convention for the Protection of New Varieties of Plants, (of 2 Dec 1961, as revised at Geneva on 10 Nov 1972, on 23 Oct 1978, and on 19 March 1991) (UPOV Convention).

[79] UPOV Convention (n 78 above) art 15.

[80] *UN Convention on Biological Diversity*, opened for signature 5 June 1992, reprinted in 31 ILM 1004 (entered into force 29 Dec 1993).

[81] *International Treaty on Plant Genetic Resources for Food and Agriculture* (entered into force 29 June 2004). Available at <ftp://ftp.fao.org/ag/cgrfa/it/ITPGRe.pdf> accessed on 31 Jan 2006.

[82] Edwardson (n 74 above) 388–390; Breining-Kaufman (n 30 above) 357.

[83] Hong Kong Declaration, adopted 18 Dec 2005, WT/MIN(05)/W/3/rev 2, para 39 (hereafter Hong Kong Declaration). See generally, Laurence R Helfer, 'Regime Shifting: The TRIPS Agreement and the New Dynamics of International Intellectual Property Lawmaking' (2004) 29 Yale J of Intl L 1.

Even prominent free trade advocates are wary of TRIPS. Contrary to the thrust of the other WTO agreements, TRIPS restricts trade as it mandates monopoly rights. Jagdish Bhagwati has stated that the TRIPS agreement 'does not belong' and 'retards the process of trade liberalisation'.[84]

A moratorium on TRIPS enforcement with respect to patents of essential items should be imposed, during which the WTO should thoroughly review its impact on the poor.[85] Unfortunately, that is not the current trend of trade negotiations. Numerous 'TRIPS plus' agreements, that is agreements which provide even greater IP protection than that imposed by TRIPS, have been concluded on a regional (eg the North American Free Trade Agreement (NAFTA)) and bilateral basis throughout the world. 'TRIPS has now become a bottom line rather than a top line'.[86]

3. The Doha development round

A new round of WTO negotiations was launched in Doha in 2001, known as the Doha Development Round. The round's name firmly points to a focus on Southern issues. Outcomes since Doha have been disappointing. The latest meeting in December 2005 in Hong Kong yielded only modest progress.

It is beyond the scope of this chapter to examine the Hong Kong Ministerial Declaration. It will suffice to note that numerous details remain to be ironed out at the time of writing. If agreement cannot be reached promptly, the conclusion of the Doha round will be significantly postponed. US President Bush's 'Fast Track Authority' (FTA) to negotiate WTO deals expires in June 2007, and is unlikely to be renewed quickly, so there is an effective deadline of early 2007 for a Doha deal to be clinched.[87]

4. Conclusion on current WTO rules

Current trade rules, such as those allowing for the maintenance of trade barriers regarding agriculture and the mandating of IP trade barriers, are biased against developing states. This circumstance undermines the WTO's stated goal of improving living standards across the world, and its potential for promoting development and alleviating poverty, as the populations in greatest need are disadvantaged.

III. Free trade, poverty, and growth

This section will examine whether the global dismantling of trade barriers, the overriding goal of the WTO, is in fact a good thing for developing states and

---

[84] Jagdish Bhagwati, 'Symposium: The Boundaries of the WTO—Afterward: The Question of Linkage' (2002) 96 AJIL 126, 128.   [85] UNDP (n 5 above) 148.

[86] Oxfam (n 7 above) 221; see also UNDP (n 5 above) 136.

[87] Under FTA, the Congress must wholly accept or reject any deal put to it. Upon expiry of FTA, Congress will be able to demand amendments; any amendment would necessitate renegotiation within the WTO. Without FTA, US ratification of a WTO agreement is 'considered legislatively impossible': Oxfam (n 19 above) 19.

the poor generally. The apparent raison d'etre of increased free trade is that it will lead to greater economic growth which will enhance net welfare, including the lot of the poor.

At the outset, one must acknowledge the literature that seriously contests the benefits of economic growth per se. For example, some ecological economists have argued that growth beyond a certain threshold level is actually uneconomic and generally counterproductive.[88] Discussion of such theories is beyond the scope of this chapter, which will proceed on the basis that growth is, at least generally, beneficial.[89] However, these alternative arguments demonstrate that even this standard departure point for free trade arguments is contentious.

The following discussion focuses on the following question: does trade liberalization actually promote economic growth?

The theories of European economists Adam Smith and especially David Ricardo provide the theoretical underpinnings for the commonly held idea that free trade increases net welfare. In 1776, Smith proposed the theory of 'absolute advantage'—that State A should produce goods for which it has an advantage over State B, and should export those goods to B, while importing from B goods for which B has an advantage over State A. Ricardo advanced Smith's theory in 1817 by promulgating the theory of 'comparative advantage', which applied to all states, regardless of whether they had an 'absolute advantage' in the production of any goods. State A, according to Ricardo, should concentrate on producing and exporting those goods which it is best suited to produce, thus avoiding opportunity costs, while importing other goods in which State B has a comparative advantage. In this 'pure theory of trade', numerous advantages accrue to all states. The production processes brought about by specialization become more efficient and sustainable in each state, while consumers in all states enjoy access to lower priced goods. Increased efficiency and competition should increase incentives to innovate to boost competitiveness.[90]

Of course, numerous economic theories have built on or departed from these two hundred year old theories. Many modern neoliberal economists recognize qualifications and nuances to this pure trade theory.[91] However, most free trade advocates still see comparative advantage as 'offering the best description of how international trade creates wealth'.[92] The WTO's own website proclaims

[88] See eg, M Max-Neef, 'Economic Growth and Quality of Life: A Threshold Hypothesis' (1995) 15 *Ecological Economics* 115; PA Lawn, 'A Theoretical Foundation to support the Index of Sustainable Economic Welfare [ISEW], Genuine Progress Indicator [GPI], and other Related Indexes' (2003) 44 *Ecological Economics* 105. Ecological economists use differing indices to the GDP to support their argument that 'when macroeconomic systems expand beyond a certain size, the additional benefits of growth are exceeded by the attendant costs [such as resource depletion]' (Lawn, p 105).
[89] As noted below, certain types of growth can have adverse consequences, such as growth in the tobacco industry, or growth which generates extreme inequality.
[90] See Paul (n 20 above) 290–292.   [91] Paul (n 20 above) 290.
[92] G Richard Shell, 'Trade Legalism and International Relations Theory: An Analysis of the World Trade Organization' (1995) 44 Duke L J 829, 858; Michael H Davis and Dana Neacsu, 'Legitimacy, Globally: The Incoherence of Free Trade Practice, Global Economics, and the Governing Principles of Political Economy (2001) 69 U of Missouri Kansas City L Rev 733.

that comparative advantage 'is arguably the single most powerful insight into economics'.[93]

Ricardo's theory is based on a perfect market. Yet numerous distortions pervade global markets. The most obvious trade distortions arise from barriers to free trade, which still exist despite the efforts of the GATT and the WTO. As noted, certain trade barriers are actually mandated under TRIPS. Markets are also distorted by anti-competitive practices, which currently remain outside the mandate of the WTO.[94] Furthermore, much international trade today is in fact conducted within multinational corporations (MNCs).[95] An MNC will often import components from its offshore subsidiaries, even if lower priced components are available elsewhere.[96] Finally, Ricardo's theory is not easily applied to trade in services, where it may be difficult for a foreign service to substitute for a home service.[97] Therefore, the relevance of Ricardo's theory in the present day, with so many trade distorting factors and an increasing amount of trade in services, may be questioned.[98] Joel R Paul estimates that 25 per cent at the most of the world's exports are traded in a perfect market, but the real figure is 'probably significantly less'.[99]

The mantra that the dismantling of trade barriers inevitably leads to economic growth has been questioned. Certain influential studies have purported to compare groups of 'globalising' states with 'non-globalisers', reporting that the former group has recorded greater rates of economic growth.[100] However, those studies do not reveal anything about the *trade policies* of the respective states.[101] States that engage in significant international trade may nevertheless maintain highly trade restrictive policies. China (which only joined the WTO in 2001), India, the Republic of Korea, and Taiwan have all experienced outstanding rates of growth, but those growth spurts began long before those states undertook liberalizing reforms.[102] Vietnam, which is on the brink of acceding to the WTO at the time of writing, is another apparent economic success story, where growth and poverty reduction have occurred under a protectionist regime.[103] On the other hand, Haiti has one of the world's most open economies, and yet has had a stagnant economy.[104] One may also note the many impoverished states in sub-Saharan Africa that have very high export percentages of their GDPs, such as Sierra Leone, and Guinea-Bissau.[105] The studies really only demonstrate that states have reduced trade barriers as they have become richer,[106]

[93] 'Understanding the WTO: The Case for Open Trade', at <http://www.wto.org/english/thewto_e/whatis_e/tif_e/fact3_e.htm> accessed on 8 Nov 2006.
[94] DFAT (n 45 above) 49.   [95] Oxfam (n 7 above) 43.   [96] Paul (n 20 above) 295.
[97] Eg, language barriers limit the ability of an overseas labour force to substitute for another.   [98] Oxfam (n 7 above) 57–60.
[99] Paul (n 20 above) 298.
[100] See eg, D Dollar and A Kraay, 'Trade, Growth and Poverty', World Bank Research Working Paper 2615 (World Bank, June 2001), and D Dollar and A Kraay, 'Growth is Good for the Poor', World Bank Policy Research Working Paper 2587 (World Bank, April 2001).
[101] Oxfam (n 7 above) 130–131.
[102] Rodrik (n 5 above) 18 and 24; Paul (n 20 above) 312–3.   [103] Rodrik (n 5 above) 21.
[104] Rodrik (n 5 above) 21; Oxfam (n 7 above) 127.
[105] Chantal Thomas, 'Poverty Reduction, Trade, and Rights' (2003) 18 American U Intl L Rev 1399, 1406.   [106] Rodrik (n 5 above) 22.

though some states such as Haiti may have reduced trade barriers prematurely. The studies do not demonstrate that trade liberalization per se is a guarantor or a prerequisite of growth,[107] though it often boosts pre-existing growth.[108]

Indeed, after conducting a comprehensive empirical study on a number of national economies, the development economist Halit Yannikaya concluded that:

restrictions on trade can benefit a country depending on whether it is a developed or developing country, whether it is a big or a small country, and whether a country has comparative advantage in those sectors that are receiving protection.[109]

Therefore, it seems that the relationship between trade liberalization and growth is very complex, and essentially depends on 'certain characteristics of countries'.[110]

A. Globalization and inequality

Even if economic liberalization promotes economic growth, that circumstance may not translate into benefits for the poor. Growth per se does not necessarily mean that the increases in wealth are being fairly distributed. Most economic studies indicate that the advent of increased global economic integration, which is undoubtedly facilitated by the WTO, has accompanied and perhaps generated greater inequality within states.[111] The gap between states has also increased.[112]

While the rich appear to have become richer, have the poor become poorer? Economists differ on whether there has been an absolute increase or decrease in poverty. Patterns in this respect differ across the world, with globalization accompanying a decrease in poverty in East Asia, an increase in Africa and the former Eastern bloc, and static poverty lines in Latin America.[113] What therefore seems likely is that economic globalization has not notably improved the global position of the poor, whilst it has accompanied and perhaps contributed to an increase in inequality between rich and poor.

Perhaps it is arguable that increasing inequality is not objectionable if the plight of the poor nevertheless improves: it is arguably acceptable for economic globalization to improve the welfare of the poor at a lesser rate than that enjoyed by the

---

[107] UNDP (n 5 above) 119; Dan Ben-David, Håkan Nordström and Alan Winters, 'Trade, Income Disparity, and Poverty', *WTO Special Studies 5* (WTO, 1999), 59.

[108] UNDP (n 5 above) 119.

[109] H Yanikkaya, 'Trade Openness and Economic Growth: A Cross-Country Empirical Investigation' (2003) 72 J of Development Economics 57 at 84; emphasis added.

[110] Yanikkaya (n 109 above) 84. See also R Howse, 'Mainstreaming the Right to Development into International Economic Law and Policy at the World Trade Organization', paper prepared for the OHCHR Secretariat, UN doc E/CN.4/Sub.2/2004/17, 9 June 2004, para 3.

[111] Paul (n 20 above) 310; Thomas (n 105 above) 1402–3; Oxfam (n 7 above) 67–68; Working Group on the Right to Development, 'Review of progress and obstacles in the promotion, implementation, operationalization, and enjoyment of the right to development', UN doc E/CN.4/2004/WG.18/2, 17 Feb 2004, paras 12–18.   [112] Paul (n 20 above) 314.

[113] Oxfam (n 7 above) 66. See also UNDP (n 7 above) 130.

rich.[114] However, a situation of extreme inequality, termed 'global apartheid' by South African President Thabo Mbeki in 2002,[115] is inherently undesirable. Increased inequality leads to greater disempowerment and social exclusion for those at 'the bottom', as the political power exercised by those at 'the top' is more out of reach.[116] Amartya Sen has stated that '[r]elative deprivation in the space of incomes can yield absolute deprivation in the space of capabilities'.[117] Sen's 'capabilities' refer to a person's ability to function in society. While there is clearly a difference between the absolute and relative poor in terms of some capabilities, such as freedom from starvation, there may be little difference between the absolute and relative poor regarding other capabilities, such as the 'capability to live without shame' or to have self respect.[118] Finally, inequality can generate social instability and conflict: '[a]n island of affluence surrounded by an ocean of poverty feels no security in a rising tide'.[119] The WTO may be legitimately criticized for its predominant focus on trade liberalization, whilst it neglects the imperative of prompting redistribution of the fruits of economic globalization to those in greatest need.[120]

B. Trade liberalization: detrimental outcomes for the south

There are notorious examples where trade is simply disastrous for development and broader human rights outcomes. For example, the diamond trade stoked conflict in Sierra Leone,[121] while resource extraction for the export market provoked and exacerbated conflict in the Democratic Republic of the Congo (DRC).[122] Another example of 'bad' trade is the growth in tobacco markets in the developing world, and their continuation despite decline in the developed world. Tobacco consumption of course causes illnesses and deaths.[123] Rather than focus on these 'worst case scenarios' involving conflict, extreme human rights abuses, and dangerous products, the following analysis focuses on the potential detrimental consequences of more 'normal' trade scenarios.

Agricultural liberalization is generally the main demand of developing states in the Doha Round. Yet such liberalization could harm some of the poor in developing

[114] Thomas (n 105 above) 1403.
[115] Mbeki is quoted by Trachtman (n 27 above) 3. See also Oxfam (n 7 above) pp 23.
[116] See eg, C Jencks, 'Does Inequality Matter?', *Daedalus* (Winter 2002), 49 at 63–64, on inequality and political power in the US.   [117] A Sen, *Inequality Re-Examined* (OUP, 1995), p 115.
[118] See also A Sen, 'Poor, Relatively Speaking' (1983) 35 *Oxford Economic Papers* 153 at 159–163.
[119] Paul (n 20 above) 320.
[120] Trachtman (n 27 above) 4 and 21. See also Rodrik (n 5 above) 9–11; Narlikar (n 17 above) 56.
[121] See UN Security Council, *Eighteenth Report of the Secretary General of the United Nations Mission in Sierra Leone*, UN docs S/2003/663.
[122] See UN Security Council, *Reports of the Panel of Experts on the Illegal Exploitation of Natural Resources and other Forms of Wealth of the Democratic Republic of the Congo*, UN docs S/2001/357, S/2002/1146, S/2003/1027.
[123] See generally, AL Taylor, 'Trade, Human Rights, and the WTO Framework Convention on Tobacco Control: Just what the Doctor Ordered?', in Cottier *et al* (eds), above (n 30 above) at 322–333.

states. First, it is important to note that not all developing states have a comparative advantage in agriculture. Some states are dependent on imports for food,[124] and have relied on subsidized Northern exports, sometimes labelled 'food aid'. While there is little doubt that such 'food aid' has been abused to the detriment of the competitiveness of Southern farmers (and competing Northern farmers),[125] the possible dismantling of food aid is of considerable concern to net food-importing developing states.[126] The negative effects of the AoA, and of broader agricultural liberalization, are acknowledged in the 1993 *Ministerial Declaration on Measure Concerning Possible Negative Effects of the Reform Program of Least Developed and Net Food-Importing Developing Countries*.[127] While that document offers many recommendations, it introduces no binding obligations.[128]

Agricultural trade is dominated by large-scale farms owned by multinational agribusiness companies.[129] Many small farmers are unable to compete with these conglomerates, and are consequently deprived of their traditional livelihoods and their ability to provide for their own food requirements. These companies are more likely to be 'concerned with profitable trade than with local-level food security'.[130] Further, concentration of ownership and an emphasis on specialization, along with the commercial benefits of any relevant IP protection, encourages 'vast monocultures being planted with genetically identical seed'.[131] This leads to a loss of biological diversity, and magnifies the likely losses if a crop, or its market, should fail.[132] Large export operations can also place 'enormous stress' on ecological resources, including water and soil.[133] Export orientation in agriculture has prompted switches from subsistence products to non-food cash crops, such as coffee, cocoa, and tobacco. The diversion of resources from food can transform a state into a net food importing state,[134] with all of the vulnerabilities associated with that status if the state's population is poor. This situation

[124] See also 'WTO List of Net Food Importing Developing Countries', G/AG/5/rev 6 (10 April 2003).   [125] Oxfam (n 7 above) 117–119.

[126] Hunter (n 22 above) 307, n 56; Breining-Kaufman (n 30 above) 343.

[127] GATT doc LT/UR/D-1/2 (1993).

[128] Hunter (n 22 above) 312–4; Dommen (n 70 above) 33; Breining-Kaufman (n 30 above) 368. See also Hong Kong Declaration (n 83 above) para 6, and Oxfam (n 19 above) 12.

[129] Food and Agriculture Organization (FAO), *Agriculture, Trade and Food Security: Issues and Options in the WTO Negotiations from the Perspective of Developing Countries*, vol II, Country Case Studies (FAO, 1999), section IV; Carmen C Gonzalez, 'Symposium: Whither goes Cuba? Prospects for Economic and Social Development: Trade Liberalization, Food Security, and the Environment— The Neoliberal Threat to Sustainable Rural Development' (2004) Transnational L and Contemporary Problems 419, at 490–492; Dommen (n 70 above) 34–35.   [130] Dommen (n 70 above) 34.

[131] Dommen (n 70 above) 40; see also Gonzales (n 129 above) 469.

[132] Dommen (n 70 above) 40; Gonzales (n 129 above) 434.

[133] Sophia Murphy, 'WTO Agreement on Agriculture: Suitable Model for a Global Food System?' *Foreign Policy in Focus*, v 7, fn 8, June 2002, 4; Oxfam (n 7 above) 92–93.

[134] See Ben-David *et al* (n 107 above) at 57 on the example of Zambia, where the switch to cash crops 'apparently eliminated the knowledge and seed supplies required for subsistence varieties, preventing farmers from reverting to traditional methods when the cash crop market disappeared'. See also Dommen (n 70 above) 34–35.

is especially unsatisfactory considering the current volatility of agricultural commodities markets.

Agricultural commodities markets often deliver very poor returns to producers,[135] due to a number of factors. First, consumers (unless they are starving) will not generally eat more food because more is available.[136] It is difficult to tailor supply to demand owing to the vagaries of climatic conditions, and the fact that it is not easy to simply 'move land in and out of production'[137] to suit market conditions. Further, consumer prices do not reflect the fluctuating primary product prices, as the producer's costs represent only a tiny proportion of the final product's cost.[138] Most of the price reflects post-harvest processing, such as roasting of coffee beans or grinding of cocoa, which largely occurs in richer states: '[o]f the average cup of coffee sold in a coffee bar, it is likely that the farmer would receive less than one per cent of the retail price'.[139] This problem is exacerbated by tariff escalation,[140] which discourages developing states from processing their raw commodities. Finally, many commodities markets are dominated by only a few MNCs;[141] this cartelization allows buyers to exercise downward pressure on the prices paid to producers.[142] Problems regarding commodities markets are 'conspicuously absent' from binding ameliorating WTO initiatives.[143] At Hong Kong, the WTO acknowledged the problems caused by unstable commodities markets, but no solid commitments in this regard were made.[144]

Thus, while agricultural liberalization is generally felt to be a likely boon for the South, caution in moving forward must be exercised. Mauritius submitted a warning on this issue to the WTO in 2000, explicitly arguing that further AoA negotiations must be conducted with an eye on the ICESCR, 'which emphasises the importance of adequate food supply alongside the continuous improvement of living conditions'.[145]

Developing states also have a comparative advantage regarding labour costs, which has led to the relocation of many manufacturing jobs from developed to developing states. These jobs have predominantly, though not exclusively, been in low skilled areas.[146] Many of these jobs have gone to women, though the reasons behind this workforce feminization are not necessarily positive; women are viewed by export industries as 'more productive workers, better at repetitive work, and less likely to unionise or demand higher wages'.[147] Jobs growth in manufacturing has also generated mass migration to urban areas. Affected cities often lack adequate

---

[135] See generally UNDP (n 5 above) 139–142; Paul (n 20 above) 315; Gonzales (n 129 above) 434.   [136] Oxfam (n 7 above) 159; Murphy (n 133 above) 3.

[137] Murphy (n 133 above) 3.   [138] Oxfam (n 7 above) 159.

[139] Oxfam (n 7 above) 162.   [140] See nn 46–48 (above).

[141] Oxfam (n 7 above) 161–162; Dommen (n 70 above) p 34; Murphy (n 133 above) 4.

[142] See UNDP (n 5 above) 142–143; Murphy (n 133 above) 8; DFAT (n 45 above) 50.

[143] UNDP (n 5 above) 139.   [144] Hong Kong Declaration (n 83 above) para 55.

[145] Fourth Special Session of the [WTO] Committee on Agriculture, Non-Trade Concerns, Statement by Mauritius, G/AG/NG/W/75 (30 Nov 2000).

[146] See Oxfam (n 7 above) 78.

[147] Paul (n 20 above) 316; see also p 317 and Oxfam (n 7 above) 81–84.

infrastructure to cope with this influx of people many of whom, whilst employed, remain poor. Low skilled work in export enclaves can have little connection to the rest of a state's economy, and can add little value beyond labour to the final products,[148] which leads to low quality export growth. Furthermore, concerns may legitimately be raised regarding labour rights abuses on many of these assembly lines in developing states. Maintenance of the comparative advantage is dependent on maintenance of low wages, which can easily motivate a state to undermine labour rights.[149] At one level, the increase in jobs caused by export markets might create demand for labour, thus driving up wages.[150] Yet developing states face significant competition in this arena from other developing states: the demand for labour in a single state can easily be undermined by the cheaper availability of labour in another state. Foreign capital is highly mobile, and can easily relocate to cheaper states,[151] leading to significant sudden 'economic dislocations', as low skilled labourers may find it very difficult to migrate to other sectors.[152] In this respect, the unleashing of China and its huge population of low cost labourers on the international stage is of concern.[153]

Therefore, a developing state will be a very vulnerable player in the global economy if its comparative advantages lie solely in agricultural commodities and low-skill manufacturing, which is the situation of many if not most developing states.[154] Their prospects for sustained economic growth, which provides resources for poverty alleviation and development, are not high. Somehow, such states should attempt to develop more dynamic comparative advantages, in order to better access the benefits of economic globalization.[155]

C. Trade liberalization and the south: the way forward

Ongoing static protectionism is not a long-term prescription for economic success.[156] Some protectionist policies can have severe impacts on a state's

---

[148] Oxfam (n 7 above) 77, quotes a study (D Bhattacharya and M Rahman, 'Seeking Fair Market Access for Bangladesh Apparels in the USA: A Strategic View', *Centre for Policy Dialogue* (Dhaka, 2000)) showing that local value-addition in low skilled manufacturing adds on average only 25–30% of the value of exports. See also UNDP (n 5 above) 118.

[149] See UNDP (n 5 above) 124; Oxfam (n 7 above) 86–87: see also DFAT (n 45 above) 21 (noting that 'strong unions' and workplace rights can undermine labour market growth).

[150] DFAT (n 45 above) 11; Oxfam (n 7 above) 51 and 55.

[151] Oxfam (n 7 above) 40 and 82–83.

[152] Paul (n 20 above) 315; Wai (n 12 above) 50. Note that volatile investment can have a highly detrimental effect on developing states—perhaps worse than low yet stable investment; see North South Institute, *Canadian Development Report 2004: Investing in Poor Countries—who Benefits?* (Renouf Publishing, 2004), at 32–33.

[153] See B Lynn, 'Trading with a Low-Wage Tiger' (2003) 14 *The American Prospect* 10, detailing how Mexico lost 5% of its manufacturing jobs when certain foreign investors moved their operations to China in 2001 (available via <http://www.prospect.org/print/V14/2/lynn-ba.html> accessed on 8 Nov 2005. See also Oxfam (n 7 above) 79 and 139.

[154] UNDP (n 5 above) 118–119; Oxfam (n 7 above), 62, 71–73, 75, and 77.

[155] UNDP (n 5 above) 134; Oxfam (n 7 above) 74.

[156] Rodrik (n 5 above) 24; Oxfam (n 7 above) 24 and 61–62.

population.[157] Participation in world markets has certainly assisted many economies in the North and the South to grow, and to gain cheaper access to imported technologies.[158]

However, as noted above, the linkage between liberalization of trade and greater growth cannot be taken for granted:[159] growth is not necessarily stimulated by rapid liberalization. Rather, it seems that gradual liberalization, which may begin after the implementation of other appropriate domestic reforms, is a better method for improving a state's economy. A 'gradual sequenced approach' allows a state to prepare for and absorb the inevitable adjustments of globalization.[160] All industrialized states went through significant protectionist periods over many decades prior to their current liberalized conditions.[161] It is therefore legitimate for developing states, in their own self interest, to resist pressure towards rapid liberalization. 'To the extent that the [WTO] limits the ability of governments to respond to [domestic and other] market distortions, the [WTO] may reduce economic growth'.[162]

Rodrik suggests that '[t]he exchange of reduced policy autonomy in the South for improved market access in the North is a bad bargain where development is concerned'.[163] For example, the industrial success of Korean steel and automobiles, and Taiwanese electronics, were built on an initial period of restrictive and directed industrialization policies, designed to nurture those industries before exposing them to international competition.[164] Many of the strategies used to build these industries, which have catalyzed high quality growth in these East Asian economies in contrast to the low quality growth highlighted above regarding agriculture and low skilled labour, are now restricted or banned under WTO rules.[165]

There is no doubt that local and international factors outside the remit of the WTO will impact on a state's ability to maximize the benefits and minimize the detriments from global economic integration.[166] A state's levels of political stability, corruption, infrastructure and welfare support, indebtedness, and social services such as education and health are all highly determinative of a state's ability to benefit from WTO rules.[167] Reform in these areas will provide a greater fillip to a state's development prospects than rapid liberalization.[168] For example, higher health standards will lead to a more productive workforce, while higher education standards generates a higher skilled workforce.[169]

---

[157] At 62, Oxfam (n 7 above) notes that the 25% tariffs imposed by some African states on mosquito nets 'cost lives' by increasing the incidence of malaria.   [158] DFAT (n 45 above) 5.
    [159] See text at nn 94–110 (above); see also UNDP (n 5 above) 119.
    [160] Rodrik (n 5 above) 24; Oxfam (n 7 above) 139, 145, 241, and 246; Ben-David *et al* (n 107 above) p 61–62.   [161] Oxfam (n 7 above) 26.
    [162] Paul (n 20 above) 323.   [163] Rodrik (n 5 above) 27.
    [164] Thomas (n 105 above) 1406; Oxfam (n 7 above) 147.
    [165] Rodrik (n 5 above) 19; Oxfam (n 7 above) 233; UNDP (n 5 above) (on relevant restrictions in TRIMS).   [166] Rodrik (n 5 above) 25.
    [167] Thomas (n 105 above) 1408.   [168] Trachtman (n 27 above) 18.
    [169] Oxfam (n 7 above) 89–90.

The expenditure of resources by some developing WTO members on international trade reforms might 'divert human resources, administrative capabilities and political capital' away from domestic institutional reforms which should appropriately precede a drive towards WTO compliance.[170] There is a need for greater policy space and flexibility to allow developing states to devise and implement reforms prior to liberalization.[171] Such reforms should include the provision of safeguards to shield the vulnerable, particularly the poor, from the detrimental effects of globalization. Logically, such safeguards should precede or accompany the detrimental effects: a safety net does not work if someone has already fallen through it.

At the same time, the general benefits of market access for the South to the North are clear; it can provide capital for poverty alleviation and other development projects which might pave the way for future liberalization opportunities and commitments. An optimal outcome for the South from future WTO negotiations is therefore true asymmetry, arguably reflecting the intended spirit of the Enabling Clause of 1979. Implementation of the current SDT provisions are however premised on the South continuing to 'move forward' on liberalization, when a pause or deceleration in that regard may be more beneficial for some states.[172]

D. Balancing globalization winners and losers across the world

The theory of comparative advantage holds that the removal of trade barriers is beneficial for all states. From a human rights point of view, it is the effect of WTO rules on individuals and groups rather than states that is important. The process of liberalization clearly creates 'winners' and 'losers' at a sub-state level, such as those respectively employed in efficient and inefficient industries. The winners have generally been MNCs, which conduct most of the world's international trade,[173] and persons with high skill levels, who are likely to be more educated than lower skilled workers. Generally, these winners are in the wealthier sectors of society.[174] The losers, who have generally been at the lower end of the socio-economic spectrum, are certainly not confined to populations in the developing world.[175] Plenty of people in industrialized states have lost their jobs because of offshore competition.[176]

[170] See D Rodrik, 'Trading in Illusions' (March/April, 2001) *Foreign Policy* at 55. See also Rodrik (n 5 above) 27.
[171] Trachtmann (n 27 above) 5; Hoekman (n 21 above) 410 and 415; Rodrik (n 5 above) 21; see also Working Group on the Right to Development (n 111 above).
[172] See Breining-Kaufman (n 30 above) 373–376, on the need for 'affirmative action' or 'positive discrimination' within the WTO. See Thomas Pogge, 'Priorities of Global Justice' (2001) 32 *Metaphilosophy* 6, 13.
[173] See UNCTAD, *World Investment Report 2002, Transnational Corporations and Export Competitiveness*, UNCTAD/WIR/2002 (UN, 2002), p 153, stating that two thirds of world trade in the late 1990s was conducted by MNCs, including trade within MNCs.
[174] UNDP (n 5 above) 123; Paul (n 20 above) 303; Oxfam (n 7 above) 80 and 138.
[175] Trachtman (n 27 above) 5 and 13; Oxfam (n 7 above) 90–91.
[176] See Paul (n 20 above) 300–301 on statistics regarding the effect of WTO and NAFTA policies on US employment.

Certainly, one might expect many of the losers to simply change careers and move into the efficient production sectors. However, such options are not always available. As Paul notes:

You cannot turn an automotive factory into a dairy farm; a 50 year old factory worker probably will not make a good computer engineer; and a factory town in Maine cannot grow oranges.[177]

These 'sunk costs' lead to significant social costs, such as taxpayer costs to provide welfare payments to the unemployed, and the decline of and consequent social instability within communities built up around inefficient industries.[178]

Northern governments are of course politically accountable for the potential detrimental effects of trade liberalization on some within their own population. For example, the main political justification for continued agricultural protection in the North is to save the Northern farming sector, particularly in Europe, from oblivion. Northern farmers, like their Southern counterparts, also wish to protect their livelihoods and communities.[179] They would question why their rights to work or rights to enjoy their own culture should be sacrificed to help out people in the South.[180]

From a pure numbers point of view, agricultural liberalization, or at least the opening up of Northern markets, would benefit more poor people, as the South suffers from a greater level and depth of impoverishment than the North.[181] Further, the globalization losers in the North are more likely than those in the South to receive compensation from the winners (via taxation) through, for example, the provision of social security payments and public health care.

Currently, it seems more politically palatable for EU governments to subsidize their farmers and hurt the poor in developing states, rather than adopt policies that might lead to the destruction of rural communities.[182] On the other hand, taxpayers are currently subsidizing the farming sector, so it probably makes sense to transform those subsidies into welfare payments, while simultaneously allowing agricultural competition which benefits not only Southern farmers but also Northern consumers.[183] Furthermore, agriculture in the North, as in the South, is dominated by agribusiness, rather than individual 'small' farmers so 'the removal of agricultural protection does not raise . . . ethical problems'.[184] In 2005, the UNDP reported that three quarters of EU agricultural subsidies under its Common Agricultural Policy (CAP) went to 10 per cent of subsidy recipients.[185]

Do developed states have a duty to help the poor in developing nations? There are numerous references to interstate assistance as an obligation in international

---

[177] Paul (n 20 above) 300; see also Oxfam (n 7 above) 91.   [178] Paul (n 20 above) 300.
[179] Breining-Kaufman (n 30 above) 370.   [180] See also Hunter (n 22 above) 320–1.
[181] Hunter (n 22 above) 321.   [182] Paul (n 20 above) 303.
[183] Hunter (n 22 above) 321; Trachtmann (n 27 above) 13. Consumers unlike producers are a disparate group who lack political mobilization: Narlikar (n 17 above) 5.
[184] J Bhagwati, 'The Poor's Best Hope', *The Economist*, 20 June 2002, at 24.
[185] UNDP (n 5 above) 130.

human rights law.[186] Article 56 of the UN Charter[187] oblige states to take '*joint and separate action*' [emphasis added] to achieve the purposes set out in article 55. Article 55 requires the promotion of:

(i) higher standards of living; full employment, and conditions to enable social progress and development;

(ii) solutions of international, economic, social, health, and related problems, and international cultural and educational cooperation; and

(iii) universal respect for, and observance of, human rights and fundamental freedoms for all without distinction as to race, sex, language, or religion.

Article 2(1) ICESCR requires states progressively to implement economic, social, and cultural rights 'individually *and through international assistance and cooperation*'.[188] Articles 3(3) and 4 of the Declaration on the Right to Development 1986[189] also recognize a duty of interstate co-operation regarding development. In particular, article 4(2) states, *inter alia*:

As a complement to the efforts of developing countries, effective international co-operation is essential in providing these countries with appropriate means and facilities to foster their comprehensive development.

The Committee on Economic, Social and Cultural Rights, the body which monitors implementation of the ICESCR, has referred a number of times to relevant interstate obligations. For example, regarding the right to food, it has stated that:

States should recognize the essential role of international cooperation and comply with their commitment to take joint and separate action to achieve the full realization of the right to food. In implementing this commitment, States parties should take steps to respect the enjoyment of the right to food in other countries, to protect that right, to facilitate access to food and to provide the necessary aid when required. States parties should, in international agreements when relevant, ensure that the right to adequate food is given due attention and consider the development of further international legal instruments to that end.[190]

The Committee has expressed similar views regarding the right to health,[191] the right to water,[192] and the right to work.[193]

Thomas Pogge has cogently argued that there is a moral duty amongst richer states to take steps to assist the poor in developing nations:

There are at least three morally significant connections between us and the global poor. First, their social starting positions and ours have emerged from a single historical process

---

[186] Breining-Kaufman (n 30 above) 362–366.

[187] Charter of the United Nations, opened for signature 26 June 1945, 59 stat 1031, TS 993, 3 Bevans 1153, art 2(7) (entered into force 24 Oct 1945).

[188] This duty is reinforced in art 11 ICESCR regarding the right to an adequate standard of living (emphasis added).

[189] Declaration on the Right to Development, GA res 41/128 (4 Dec 1986) 97th plen mtg, UN doc A/RES/41/128.   [190] *General Comment 12*, E/C.12/1999/5, para 36.

[191] *General Comment 14*, E/C.12/2000/4, para 38–40.

[192] *General Comment 15*, E/C.12/2002/11, para 30–36.

[193] *General Comment 18*, UN doc E/C.12/GC/18, para 30.

that was pervaded by massive grievous wrongs...including genocide, colonialism and slavery, [which] play a role in explaining both their poverty and our affluence. Second, they and we depend on a single natural resource base, from the benefits of which they are largely, and without compensation, excluded. The affluent countries and the elites of the developing world divide these resources on mutually agreeable terms without leaving 'enough and as good' for the remaining majority of humankind. Third, they and we coexist within a single global economic order that has a strong tendency to perpetuate and even to aggravate global economic equality.[194]

Beyond human rights law, utilitarianism and morality, there are also undoubted benefits for the North in helping the South. First, alleviation of poverty and associated discontent can help defuse potential backlashes against the North, which has arguably been traumatically manifested by the increased incidence of terrorism.[195] Trachtmann notes that the increased intransigence of poor states within the Doha negotiations manifests a more peaceful backlash.[196] Magnanimity by the North during the Doha Round will probably facilitate more significant concessions from the South in future WTO negotiations.[197] Finally, the alleviation of poverty has a positive economic impact,[198] by helping to transform the poor into viable consumers, opening up marketing possibilities for both Southern and Northern markets in the long run.[199]

The rights of globalization 'losers' in the North should however not be bargained away for nothing. There are, in particular, legitimate concerns about advantages flowing to Southern industries due to severely inadequate regulations, such as poor or non-existent environmental and labour (including occupational health and safety) standards.[200] At some point, those standards can be so low as to be genuinely trade distorting.[201] Perhaps a bargain can be devised to provide relief for the losers in the South *and* the North.

D. A new bargain?

Agricultural and textiles reform are the main WTO demands of the developing states. In addition, significant reform of TRIPS is desirable. Despite arguments regarding the lopsidedness of the Uruguay deal, it is unlikely that the South will receive a round 'for free'.[202] Robert Wai has proposed that the introduction of labour standards as an exception within the WTO be the Southern concession in

---

[194] See Pogge (n 172 above) 4–15. See also Hunter (n 22 above) 301.

[195] Trachtman (n 27 above) 9.   [196] Trachtman (n 27 above) 9–10.

[197] Larry Elliott, 'WTO summit: No easy way out as an encore looms', *Guardian*, 19 Dec 2005, p 21.

[198] Rodrik (n 5 above) 12.

[199] See generally, CK Pralahad and Stuart L Hart, 'The Fortune at the Bottom of the Pyramid', in *Strategy + Competition Magazine*, Issue 26, First Quarter 2002.   [200] Wai (n 12 above) 49–50.

[201] Wai (n 12 above) at 60, notes how unreasonably low labour standards could perhaps be characterized as 'social' dumping or subsidization, thus permitting protectionist responses. 'Dumping' arises when a good is sold on an export market 'below cost': WTO members are permitted to retaliate against dumping practices.   [202] Elliott (n 197 above).

a new deal.[203] Certainly, lower labour costs are perfectly legitimate when accompanied by lower costs of living and lower labour productivity.[204] However, unconscionable labour practices, such as allowance of forced labour, often accompanied by systemic oppression or prohibition of labour organizations which are necessary to give workers bargaining power with employers, are genuinely trade distorting practices.[205] An agreement which promotes adherence to core international labour standards therefore has a legitimate nexus to the notion of free trade.[206]

Such a compromise would not be easy. The Singapore Ministerial Declaration of 1996 effectively eschewed the possibility of serious WTO involvement in labour rights by confirming the International Labour Organization (ILO) as 'the competent body to set and deal with these standards'.[207] Developing states in particular were opposed to inclusion of labour rights in any new round,[208] fearing that such standards would be abused for protectionist purposes.

It is arguable that the allowance of trade sanctions based on labour standards will in fact hurt the poor more than inadequate labour standards.[209] In response, it is worth noting three points. First, labour rights are designed to benefit all workers, including those in the South who suffer from exploitative work practices to facilitate export growth, and those in the North who have legitimate concerns about 'regulatory competition and fair trade'.[210] Second, such standards will also protect against unfair labour competition *between* developing states. Finally, it is proposed that this amendment be the sole quid pro quo for the opening up of Northern markets for Southern agriculture and textiles, as well as some relief from TRIPS, which will provide capital to help finance better labour rights infrastructure.

In any case, a labour rights clause could be constructed so as to minimize the chances of protectionist trade sanctions, and yet increase existing incentives for labour rights improvement. Trade sanctions could be disallowed prior to any dispute ruling.[211] Indeed, sanctions could be delayed until a target state had been given a chance to subject itself to the expert scrutiny of the ILO and to comply with any eventual ILO recommendations.[212] Of course, it would be desirable for

---

[203] Wai (n 12 above) 80–81. Wai actually argues for a more comprehensive social clause addressing issues such as health and the environment. However, art XX(b) and (g) of the GATT already permit exceptions regarding these issues (the original GATT treaty has been included as one of the WTO Agreements). [204] Rodrik (n 5 above) 30.

[205] Wai (n 12 above) 60; Rodrik (n 5 above) 30.   [206] See Wai (n 12 above) 48–50.

[207] See WT/MIN(96)/DEC/W (13 Dec 1996) para 4.

[208] Narlikar (n 17 above) 101–102.

[209] Wai (n 12 above) 55 and 62–63; Oxfam (n 7 above) 200.   [210] Wai (n 12 above) 80.

[211] States often unilaterally impose sanctions and then attempt to justify them by reference to WTO exceptions (such as art XX of the GATT (see n 203 above)) in any eventual dispute, if the targeted State makes a complaint.

[212] The ILO explicitly opposes trade sanctions on the basis of labour standards for protectionist purposes. See *ILO Declaration on Fundamental Principles and Rights at Work* (86th session, June 1998) paragraph 5. See, on the trade and labour debate, P Alston, ' "Core Labour Standards" and the Transformation of the International Labour Rights Regime' (2004) 15 Eur J of Intl L 457 at 471–474.

WTO dispute settlement bodies to be influenced in this respect by the work of the ILO as well as the Committee on Economic Social and Cultural Rights.[213]

The proposed labour rights clause could be the sole 'Southern' side of a new bargain. Current demands by the North for further concessions on liberalization of goods, services, and investment protection could be delayed. The major winners from such concessions would likely be the winners from the Uruguay round, who can afford to wait for further reform and further winnings. There is surely a greater imperative to address the needs of those left behind from previous reforms, rather than, for example, the desires of MNCs for greater profit growth. At the least, concessions now would improve the chances of major breakthroughs in future WTO bargains. Of course, the South would have a considerable stake in future bargains, which could for example address issues regarding corporate monopolies and commodities market failures. 'Failure to address concerns such as fair trade or regulatory competition [regarding labour rights], developing states' development or human rights, contributes to a lack of national support for trade liberalisation'.[214]

Reforms outside the WTO should also occur, such as increases in aid and more poverty-friendly policies from the IMF, World Bank, and regional development agencies. The Southern states can also help each other. Developing states 'impose . . . higher trade barriers on each other's imports than those imposed on industrial countries'.[215] Greater South/South cooperation should occur, to stimulate efficiency and promote each other's industries, while Northern liberalization delivers funds to assist in such liberalization.[216]

IV. Conclusion

Oxfam has noted that debates regarding trade and poverty have been dominated by 'ritualistic exchanges' between globaphobes, who are against the WTO and economic globalization, and globaphiles, who believe that increased trade is good for all.[217] The globaphile view is generally accorded more respectability by the WTO and governments (most of whom are WTO members or aspiring members) than the globaphobe view, which is often dismissed as irrational.[218] Indeed, 'globaphobes' may be criticized for their simplistic characterization of economic globalization as the cause of many of the world's problems, such as poverty and inequality, whilst failing to acknowledge the detrimental role played by poor local

---

[213] See generally, J Harrison, 'The Impact of the World Trade Organisation on the Protection and Promotion of Human Rights' (PhD Thesis, European University Institute, Sept 2005) copy on file with the author, chapter 11.   [214] Wai (n 12 above) 82.
   [215] UNDP (n 5 above) 127.   [216] See also Thomas (n 105 above) 1409–1411.
   [217] Oxfam (n 7 above) 23.
   [218] See, eg, Howse (n 110 above) at paras 15 and 29 (the latter criticizing the WTO's Trade Policy Review Mechanism for its presumption, in assessing Senegal, that trade restrictions are counterproductive, a 'neo-liberal article of faith').

government policies.[219] Yet the arguments of 'globaphiles' effectively mirror those of the globaphobes: globaphiles have a similarly intractable attachment to the idea that free trade is simply 'a good thing' for everybody, including the poor.[220] To the extent that the poor unduly suffer during the process of trade liberalization, globaphiles tend to attribute those harms to poor local governance.[221] Whilst poor local governance is undoubtedly a major contributor to ongoing poverty, it seems likely that rapid trade liberalization will exacerbate such situations by for example exposing vulnerable sectors prematurely to competition and providing greater opportunities for corruption from an influx of rich foreign investors. In the governance/globalization equation, it is not only governance that can be 'bad': it can be tantamount to asking the classic 'chicken and egg' question in attempting to allocate blame for poor outcomes to either external factors (eg globalization) or internal factors (eg bad governance). Just as globalization is not the cause of all woes, it is no universal panacea. Globaphiles should move on from a slavish adherence to the 'liberalization is good per se' argument. Faith in that argument has led the WTO to become an organization dedicated to free trade as an end in itself, rather than as a means towards ends, such as economic development and poverty alleviation.[222]

While the benefits of increased liberalization for the wealthier sectors of societies seem clear, there is considerable doubt over whether the poor in either the developed or the developing worlds are benefiting at all. Given the injustice and the dangers caused by growing inequalities, as well as doubts and enmity over the inequity of the Uruguay deal, a new WTO deal must address the need for the poor to 'win'. It seems possible to structure a deal that addresses many of those concerns involving concessions regarding agriculture, textiles, and TRIPS from the North, and labour concessions from the South. Whilst the poor in the South may continue to 'lose', or at least 'not win', from a new proposed deal because of continued poor local governance, the North should largely 'buy a round' for the South and give the relevant governments a chance to implement appropriate domestic policies in advance of a future round. The assymetric round could be 'payback' for Uruguay or perhaps even a 'down payment' for future concessions.

One cannot pretend that the proposed 'pro-poor' reforms are easy or even likely. There is a danger that lack of progress in the current Doha round, or an

---

[219] See, for a highly negative view of the WTO, Steven Shrybman, 'The World Trade Organization: A Dangerous Recipe for Unsustainable and Unaccountable Alphabet Soup Rule', at <http://www.web.net/~opirgkin/qcacg/letter1.html> accessed on 24 Jan 2006.

[220] See eg, A Oxley, 'Make Trade Free: How the Doha Round can reduce Poverty', 18 Nov 2005 (available via <http://www.worldgrowth.org/reports/report.aspx?id=2>) accessed on 8 Nov 2006. Oxley concedes that some African countries have joined the WTO prematurely, but does not concede that trade liberalization has had detrimental effects in Africa (see pp 9–10).

[221] See eg, DFAT (n 45 above) 20 and 33; David Dollar, 'Globalization, Poverty, and Inequality since 1980', World Bank Policy Research Working Paper 3333, June 2004, available via <http://papers.ssrn.com/sol3/papers.cfm?abstract_id=625296> accessed on 24 Jan 2006, at p 24; Ben-David *et al* (n 107 above) 48.   [222] Rodrik (n 5 above) pp 9–11; UNDP (n 5 above) 119.

insistence on an asymmetric deal that fails to cater for the rich, may convince the strongest states, notably the US and the EU, that regional or bilateral deals are the best way of achieving their optimal trade outcomes.[223] A move away from multi-lateralism is bad news for the South, given that the power imbalances in bilateral relationships are more open to abuse than in multilateral forums.[224] At the same time however, the South, as well as the poor in the North, should not be held hostage to dominant interests in the most powerful states, and cave into deals that may generate more harm than good. It is time for all states to take seriously the imperative of reducing global poverty and promoting human development across the world. The WTO is a crucial forum in which such initiatives must occur.

[223] See UNDP (n 5 above) 137.   [224] See Oxfam (n 7 above) 27.

16

The Right to Development as Applied in National Law

Jane Ansah

I. Introduction

The concept of the right to development is relatively recent in international human rights law. Nonetheless it is increasingly gaining acceptance, especially among the African states, some of whom have included it in their constitutions, either in the principles of national policy[1] or as a justiciable human right within the Bill of Rights.[2] In other developing states it has gained acceptance through judicial activism.[3] However, some states, particularly developed states, still question its status and application as a human right.[4]

The United Nations General Assembly adopted the Declaration on the Right to Development (UNDRD) in 1986.[5] In this Declaration, the right to development (RD) is defined as:

an inalienable right by virtue of which every human person and all peoples are entitled to participate in, contribute to, and enjoy economic, social, cultural and political development, in which all human rights and fundamental freedoms can be fully realised.[6]

The advocates of the RD have hailed it as a milestone in the human rights discourse[7] and that it deserved a place in the human rights system of the United Nations,[8] whilst others have labelled it as a distracting, if not dangerous, ideological initiative.[9]

---

[1] Eg, the constitutions of Ghana and Uganda.

[2] Eg, the constitutions of Benin, Central African Republic, Democratic Republic of Congo, Ethiopia, Malawi, and Senegal.

[3] See eg, *Madhu Kishwar v State of Bihar* (1996) 5 SCC 125.

[4] See eg, E/CN.4/1987/10. annex II.   [5] UN GR 41/133 (4 Dec 1986).

[6] Art 1, para 1.

[7] A/C.3/41/SR.61, the Chairman, Mr Hamer (Netherlands), commented after the adoption of the UNDRD.

[8] A/C.3/41/SR.61, Mrs Coll's (Ireland) comment after the adoption of the UNDRD.

[9] J Donelley, 'In Search of the Unicorn: The Jurisprudence and Politics of the Right to Development' (1985) 15 California Western Intl L J 487. See also A/C.3/41/SR.61 Miss Byrne's (United States of America) comment after the adoption of the UNDRD.

At the international level, the RD was conceived by its proponents, the developing states, to be one means of redress for the economic imbalance between the developing and developed states, and as a means to enforce the integration of development issues within the human rights discourse both at the international and national levels.[10] This has, as will be shown, brought about political and academic controversy over its scope and content.

At the national level, the RD is a very important human right, especially in former European colonies where there is underdevelopment, abject poverty, poor observance of human rights, dependency on development aid, and a lack of good governance.[11] This chapter argues that it is only through the implementation and realization of the RD that there is going to be full and effective respect of all human rights without any trade-offs that will adversely affect the state's respect and realization of the minimum core obligations towards those in its jurisdiction. Further, as the state becomes transparent, accountable and allows the people to participate in the development of their state, all human rights will be respected.

The particular national position that will be explored in this chapter is that of Malawi, as its constitution uniquely contains a guarantee of the right to development as a justiciable human right. This chapter examines this right and the public law duty on the state in order to consider the extent to which the RD is applicable and realizable, considering that its realization depends on resources and that Malawi is a developing state that is heavily dependent on donor funding. It will be argued that the RD is not solely a demand or a right for assistance or aid to be given to the vulnerable but that it provides the criteria by which the economic, social, cultural, and political performance of the state can be determined. Further, it will be argued that the main objective of the RD is the provision of equality of opportunity to access basic resources through the provision of an enabling environment and empowerment of the right holders and, in particular, the marginalized and disadvantaged persons and groups. This should facilitate their control over their resources and also foster full participation in determining their own destinies, and of their communities or societies. This should translate into access to the decision-making process, and more transparent and accountable decision-making, in the formulation and implementation of policies and programmes, as well as ensuring that the government upholds its obligation to use donor funds judiciously, equitably and in accordance with the intended purpose.[12]

[10] See I Shivji, *The Concept of Human Rights in Africa*: CODESRIA Book Series, 1989 'the contemporary demands of the Third World States for better terms on the international market, greater aid and assistance and generally in, what has to be known as, the demand for the new international economic order' (p 81).
[11] See O Micaletti, *Report of Activities 13–2-1994 to 20–5-1994 (Confidential)* (Centre for Human Rights, UN Electrol Assistance Secretariat, Lilongwe, Malawi, 1994) p 16. Also See Bampton's report (1994) *Background Considerations: Constitutional Autochthony and Legal Continuity* (unpublished, on author's file).
[12] See C Chihana, *Address by Chakufwa Chihana President of Alliance For Democracy (AFORD) to the National Constitutional Conference* (Kwacha Conference Centre, Blantyre, Malawi, 24 Feb 1994) (unpublished, on author's file) and also Bampton's interview of Feb 2001.

It is observed that power inequalities reveal themselves into unequal access to the control over resources, production, property, income, information, knowledge, and decision-making within the society, as

If those who were hungry had the economic resources to turn their need into demand for food in economic terms, then producers would supply food for the hungry.[13]

This chapter will show that the main obstacle for the realization of the RD within states is the lack of equitable policies and programmes for distribution and redistribution of resources, which, if remedied, should result into the elimination of power inequalities.

II. The right to development at the international level

A. Evolution of the right to development

Notions of the RD can be traced back to the 1940s. It is argued that the International Labour Organization (ILO) affirmed these notions at Philadelphia, when it adopted the Declaration of Philadelphia which stated that:

all human beings, irrespective of race, creed or sex, have the right to pursue both their material well-being and their spiritual development in conditions of freedom and dignity, of economic security and equal opportunity.[14]

In this assertion, the link between rights, dignity, and personal well-being was established. The Declaration was incorporated into the Constitution of the ILO in 1946.[15]

The seeds of the RD are also found in the discussions that led to the adoption of the Universal Declaration of Human Rights (UDHR), although it did not find its way into the Declaration in its present form. During its drafting, it was proposed that UDHR should include the following statement: 'the object of society is to afford each of its member equal opportunity for the full development of his spirit, mind and body.'[16] Articles 22[17] and 28[18] of the UDHR also establish the link between human rights and development, especially the importance of the

---

[13] A Eide, A Oshaug, and WB Eide (eds), 'Food Security and the Right to Food in International Law and Development' (1991) 1 Transnational L & Contemporary Problems 418.

[14] 1944 Declaration of Philadelphia: Principle II (a). This declaration was incorporated into the 1946 ILO Constitution's annex, ILO Constitution, <http://www.ilo.org/public/english/about/iloconst.htm#annex> accessed 6 Nov 2006.

[15] Constitution of the ILO annex; ILO Philadelphia Declaration Concerning the Aims and Purposes of the International Labour Organization.   [16] E/CN.4/AC/W.1, 2.

[17] Art 22: 'Everyone, as a member of society, has the right to social security and is entitled to realisation, through national effort and international co-operation and in accordance with the organisation and resources of each State, of the economic, social and cultural rights indispensable for his dignity and the free development of his personality.'

[18] Art 28: 'Everyone is entitled to a social and international order in which the rights and freedoms set forth in the Declaration can be fully realised.'

connection between an appropriate international economic and social order and the realization of human rights.[19]

The RD was also anticipated when developing states made demands for economic self-determination, which surfaced at the UN in 1952 through a General Assembly Resolution, which recognized the right of states freely to utilize and exploit their own natural resources.[20] In the 1970s, the RD is seen in the quest by the developing states for participation in decision-making and fair trade practices, envisaging affirmative action and also demands for development assistance from the developed states through the establishment of the New International Economic Order (NIEO). This was to be:

based on equity, sovereign equality, interdependence, common interest and co-operation among all States, irrespective of their economic and social systems which shall correct inequalities and redress existing injustices.[21]

The 1974 Declaration was an effort by the developing states to attain true political and economic self-determination. It was followed by two other General Assembly Resolutions, the Programme of Action on the Establishment of a NIEO[22] and the Charter of Economic Rights and Duties of States (CERDS),[23] which set standards and formulated duties for states with regard to international economic relations. The NIEO failed, owing to political differences and world recession, and thereafter, 'it became evident that the political future market was in the area of human rights and that it was, therefore, prudent to pursue the policy goals under that particular banner.'[24] Once development was linked with human rights, it led to the RD, which was envisaged as the 'driving force and the ultimate goal of the NIEO.'[25]

B. Concepts of the right to development

The notion of the RD can rightly be said to have originated from Africa.[26] The African jurist, Keba M'baye,[27] articulated the RD in its present form. In 1972 he delivered a lecture at the International Institute of Human Rights in Strasbourg entitled 'The right to development as a human right'. M'baye came to the conclusion that all fundamental rights and freedoms are linked to the right to existence, to an increasingly higher standard of living and, therefore, to the

[19] E/CN.4/Sub.2/1983/24/rev1, 29.
[20] UNGA, A/RES/626 (VIII) (21 Dec 1952), Permanent Sovereignty over Natural Resources.
[21] Preamble of the Declaration on the Establishment of the New International Economic Order, UNGA, A/RES/3201(S-VI) (1 May 1974).
[22] UNGA, A/RES/3202 (S-VI) (1 May 1974).
[23] UNGA, A/RES/3281 (XXIX) (12 Dec 1974).
[24] J Brownlie, *The Human Right to Development, Study prepared for the Commonwealth Secretariat*, Human Rights Unit (Occasional Paper, Commonwealth Secretariate, London, 1989) p 3.
[25] E/CN.4/Sub.2/1983/24/rev1, ch IX, 27.
[26] See M Bulajic, *Principles of International Development Law* (2nd edn, Nijhoff, 1993), p 157.
[27] First President of Supreme Court of Senegal, President of International Commission of Jurists and former President of the United Nations' Commission on Human Rights.

RD.[28] He dealt with the RD in four sections: the definition of development; right-holders; duty-holders; and the basis for the justification of the RD.

M'baye asserted that the RD is a human right because people cannot exist without development.[29] He examined the definition of development and concluded that true development should meet Malcolm Adiseshia's definition in which development is defined as a form of humanism, a moral and spiritual fact as well as a material and practical one. Development is further defined as the expression of the integrity of man responding to both his material needs, (which are: food, health, clothing, and shelter) and, at the same time, his moral requirements of peace, compassion, and charity.[30]

Further, M'baye asserted that the supposed incompatibility that exists between development and human rights emanates from development being looked at from an angle of economic development only. M'baye, therefore, advocated an integrated approach to development that includes human rights observance so that the means of development does not submerge the purpose of development, which is the well-being of the human being. He argues that the calculation of Gross Domestic Product gives a false picture because the poor are invisible in the society. However, M'baye did not disregard economic growth but emphasized that the individual should be at the centre of development. In the endeavour to achieve economic growth, consideration should be given to human rights, thereby linking human rights with development.

M'baye argued that the RD is a right for the individual as well as for peoples. However, he advocated the superiority of group rights in relation to individual rights. He asserted that individual rights must be temporarily limited in order to benefit the general public. He argued that one looks at the individual as the indicators of development are examined. These indicators are the birth rate, consumption, savings, life expectancy, and others. In the end, it is the individual who benefits, for he/she enjoys the fruits of development. Although M'baye appears elsewhere to argue that the RD is a group right, he does not consistently maintain that position. Instead, he concludes by asserting that development concerns 'all men', 'every man', and 'all of man'. He leaves open the question of whether the RD is a group right, individual right, or both.

M'baye blamed the developed states as the authors and perpetrators of the world's development problems. He argued that they have to take responsibility for their past and present actions. They are to make amends through helping the underdeveloped states which are in the state of underdevelopment owing to the oppression and atrocities inflicted upon them through slave trade, forced labour, and colonialism,[31] whose effects are still felt today.[32] To M'baye, the question of

---

[28] K M'baye, 'Le Droit au Developpement Comme un droit de L'homme,' 5 *Revue des droit de L'homme* (1972) pp 528–530.   [29] Ibid.

[30] Ibid p 513.

[31] R Rich 'The Right to Development as an Emerging Human Right' (1983) 23 Virginia J of Intl L 289. See also E/CN.4/1334.

[32] See A Rosas, 'So-Called Rights of Third Generation,' A Eide C Krause, and A Rosas (eds), *Economic, Social and Cultural Rights: A Textbook* (Nijhoff, 1995), p 248, where he asserts that 'Western

duty-holders is straightforward. These are the developed states, former colonial powers and the states that were involved in the slave trade. However, he does not elaborate further what criteria is to be used to determine which developed state is responsible to which developing state.

M'baye set out several justifications for the new RD. His first justification is economic. He argued that international trade is based on unfair practices. It is dominated by the developed states which have a massive share of the gains owing to the division of labour, which is a by-product of colonialism. The developing states are the sources of raw materials and the purchasers of finished products, which cost many times more than the cost of raw materials. M'baye claims that the prosperity of the European states is built on the misery of the developing states.[33] M'baye then concludes that the exploited people have the RD.

The second justification, as contended by M'baye, is that the developed states look for allies from the developing states because of ideological differences among themselves. These ideologies cause unrest and the developing states pay with human lives as the developed states give them finances and weapons.[34]

Finally, he argues that the RD is not a new right and not merely an articulation of already accepted human rights. He asserts that it is implied in several international instruments, including the United Nations (UN) Charter, the UDHR, the two International Covenants and, also, the Charter of Economic Rights and Duties of States.

M'baye's articulation of the RD has been heavily criticized by some commentators[35] while supportive commentators have interpreted, elaborated, and expanded it further.[36] However, it is observed that the justifications that M'baye expounds indicate that the RD is more than simply the assertion of already existing human rights. It is therefore submitted that the RD's claim is economic power-sharing and the redistribution of wealth and it calls for a legal obligation to be imposed on the developed states and the international community to assist the developing states, thereby making a new claim for a legal right to assistance.

From the time of M'baye's arguments, the RD was introduced into the international arena. However, it was popularized by Karel Vasak who wrote of what he called the 'third generation' of rights, called 'rights of solidarity [which include] . . . the right to development'.[37] He theorized that these rights have

---

states have expressed reservations, . . . that they would be faced with claims on the part of developing countries for entitlements to resources.'

[33] K M'baye, 'Le Droit au Developpement' in Dupuy Rene-Jean (ed) *The Right to Development at the International Level, Workshop, The Hague 16–18 October 1979* (Silthoff & Noordhoff, 1980), p 79.   [34] Ibid.

[35] Eg, J Donnelly, 'In Search of the Unicorn: The Jurisprudence and Politics of the Right to Development.' (1985), 15 Califonia Western Intl L J, 474.

[36] See eg, M Bedjaoui, 'The Right to Development' M. Bedjaoui (ed) *International Law of Development Achievements & Prospects* (UNESCO, 1991) p 1177, K Vasak, 'A Thiry Year Struggle - the Sustained Efforts to Give Force of Law to the Universal Declaration of Human Rights' (1977), *UNESCO Courier*, 29.   [37] Vasak (n 36 above).

emerged from global interdependence. He asserted that today's problems need international co-operation through the spirit of solidarity based on the special bond of mankind, which compels man to assist the under-developed or the vulnerable. Their solution is dependent on the 'combined efforts of individuals, states and other bodies, as well as public and private institutions'.[38]

Although Vasak's concept of the third generation of rights popularized the RD, it is not quite complementary to M'baye's theory. Vasak wrote of emerging rights including the RD, implying that these rights were new. In contrast, M'baye claimed that the RD was not a new right; it was already within the international instruments[39] and, therefore, it was not advisable to have a separate UN instrument for it. Albeit, both jurists had one purpose in mind: to have the right recognized and accepted in international human rights law.

C. The United Nations and the right to development

Both M'baye and Vasak, who was then the Director of UNESCO's Division of Human Rights and Peace, played an important role in the adoption by the United Nations Commission on Human Rights (UNCHR) of a resolution on the RD in 1977.[40] The resolution[41] was adopted without a vote, and it called upon the UN Secretary-General to undertake a study of: 'the international dimensions of the right to development as a human right in relation with other human rights based on international co-operation'.[42] This was 'the first recognition of the right to development as a human right and a starting signal for a series of UN activities'.[43]

After some working groups and seminars,[44] together with working papers,[45] a draft declaration on the RD was debated in the UNCHR. After a protracted debate, on 4 December 1986 the UN General Assembly adopted the UNDRD (as resolution 41/128). It also adopted resolution 41/133, based on a proposal by Pakistan,[46] which declares that:

The achievement of the right to development requires a concerted international and national effort to eliminate economic deprivation, hunger and disease in all parts of the

[38] Ibid.

[39] K M'baye, 'Le Droit au Developpement Comme un droit de L'homme,' 5 *Revue des droit de L'homme* (1972), p 532. See also E/CN.4/1334, 29.

[40] P Alston, 'Prevention Versus Cure as a Human Rights Strategy' Development, Human Rights and the Rule of Law.' *Report of a Conference held in Hague on 27 April–1 May* (Pergamon Press, 1981) p 101.   [41] UNCHR res 4 (XXXIII), 21 Feb 1977.

[42] Ibid, para 4.

[43] K de Vey Mestadagh, 'Keeping Human Life: Altering Structures of Power, Economic Benefits and Institutions' in *Development, Human Rights and the Rule of Law. Report of a Conference held in Hague on 27 April–1 May* (Pergamon Press 1981) p 30.

[44] See ST/HR/SER.A/8. See also HR/GENEVA/1980/BP, cited in M Bulajic, *Principles of International Development Law* (2nd edn, Nijhoff, 1993) p 363.

[45] These included a draft declaration by Cuba and by a non-aligned group (E/CN.4/AC.34/WP.5), as well as papers by experts from the Netherlands and the USSR (E/CN.4/AC.34/WP.18 and WP.19).   [46] A/C.3/41/L.5.

world without discrimination in accordance with the Declaration and the Programme of Action on the Establishment of the New International Economic Order, the International Development Strategy for the Third United Nations Development Decade and the Charter of Economic Duties of States:

To this end, international co-operation should aim at the maintenance of stable and sustained economic growth with simultaneous action to increase concessional assistance to developing countries, built world food, security, resolve the debit burden, eliminate trade barriers, promote monetary stability and enhance scientific and technological; co-operation.

In the preamble to the UNDRD it is stated that the General Assembly:

[R]ecognises that development is a comprehensive economic, social, cultural and political process, which aims at the constant improvement of the well-being of the entire population and of all individuals on the basis of their active, free and meaningful participation in development and the fair distribution of the benefits resulting there from.[47]

This preambular paragraph conveys an all inclusive meaning, which is not confined to economic development where growth is measured in terms of gross national product. Instead the concept of development is given a broader concept, which includes social, political, and cultural progress that is founded on respect for the dignity and value of the human person and participation in decision-making. In other words,

Development is not just providing people with adequate food, clothing, and shelter; many prisons do as much. Development is also people deciding what food, clothing and shelter are adequate, and how they are to be provided.[48]

The principle of respect for human rights is central to the concept of the RD, which is itself deemed an inalienable human right.[49] It was envisaged that the required multi-faceted development would occur in an environment where 'all human rights and fundamental freedoms can be fully realised',[50] resulting in the assurance of the respect and enjoyment of the whole spectrum of human rights.[51] Even where resources are inadequate, disrespect for human rights is unacceptable.[52] Both the rights in the ICCPR and ICESCR are to be realized simultaneously as was envisaged in paragraph 3 of the preamble of these Covenants.

After the adoption of the Declaration, the RD has been kept on the agenda of both the General Assembly and the Commission on Human Rights, and it has featured at World Conferences, leading one writer to comment that the RD

---

[47] Para 2 of the preamble.

[48] J Dioko, untitled lecture (International Council of Amnesty International, Cambridge, 21 Sept 1978) 11, cited in P Alston, 'Prevention Versus Cure as a Human Rights Strategy' in *Development, Human Rights and the Rule of Law. Report of a Conference held in Hague on 27 April– 1 May* (Pergamon Press, 1981), p 54.   [49] See Art 1(1) UNDRD.

[50] Ibid.   [51] E/CN.4.1334, 6.

[52] See Vienna Declaration and Programme of Action (1993), (n 51 above) para 10 reads: '... lack of development may not be invoked to justify the abridgement of internationally recognised human rights.' Also the RD does not allow trade-offs: see para 9(2) UNDRD.

'emerged with almost indecent haste from total obscurity to considerable prominence in the space of less than a decade'.[53]

III. The right to development at national level

A. Inclusion of the right to development in the Malawi constitution

As referred to earlier, the RD has been included in some post-independence
African constitutions.[54] It is included in the Malawi Constitution in its justiciable
Bill of Rights. Section 30 of that Constitution provides:

(1) All persons and peoples have a right to development and thereto the enjoyment of eco-
    nomic, social, cultural and political development and women, children and the disabled
    in particular shall be given special consideration in the application of this right.
(2) The state shall take all measures for the realization of the right to development. Such
    measures shall include, amongst other things, equality of opportunity for all in their
    access to basic resources, education, health services, food, shelter, employment and
    infrastructure.
(3) The state shall take measures to introduce reforms aimed at eradicating social injus-
    tices and inequalities.
(4) The state has a responsibility to respect the right to development and to justify its poli-
    cies in accordance with this responsibility.

The advocates for the inclusion of the RD in the Constitution were the disgrun-
tled Malawian elite, who were not in government,[55] and the displeased international donors, who were concerned with the prevailing culture of corruption, lack
of accountability and transparency on the part of government and the large, and
ever-increasing gap between the rich and the poor.[56] There was also considerable
pressure after a bishops' pastoral letter that was circulated and read in all Roman
Catholic churches throughout Malawi in March 1992, which called for respect of
human dignity, human rights and democracy, equitable distribution of wealth
and social justice. This letter noted the 'growing gap between the rich and the
poor with regard to expectations, living standards and development' and called for
a more just and equal distribution of the state's wealth.[57]

It was felt that including the RD in the Constitution would serve three purposes: to make economic, social, and cultural rights justiciable; to make the state

---

[53] P Alston, 'The Shortcoming of a 'Garfield Cat' Approach to the Right to Development' (1985),
15 California Western Intl L J, 510.   [54] See nn 1 and 2 (above).
[55] A well-known trade unionist, Chihana, addressed a seminar in Lusaka in 1992, where Malawi
political exiles met to discuss prospects of democracy in Malawi (above).
[56] See C Chihana 'Malawi Prospectus For Democracy: Keynote Address delivered at Lusaka,
Zambia' (20 March 1992) (unpublished on author's file). See also J Chiona, Archbishop *et al, The
Truth Will Set You Free: A Statement by the Bishops of Malawi, Malawi Beyond Banda*, Occassional
Papers no 47 (Centre for African Studies, Edinburgh University, 1992).
[57] See J Chiona, ibid, p 1.

accountable for its use of monies loaned to it for development purposes; and as an anti-corruption measure.[58] It also sought to clarify that development was not limited to economic development. In the report on the drafting of the Constitution it was stated that:

> The issue of development is regarded in Malawi as a key right, perhaps more important than the political rights are regarded in developed countries. It was also a way in which social and economic rights, which could not possibly be justiciable in the present economic circumstance, could maintain an equally valuable profile in the relationship between the government and the citizen. Fundamentally it is less based on standards but on the equality of access and prioritisation of development goals. Moreover it places the state under a justiciable duty to justify its policies in terms of social and economic development of the nation. This is a matter of considerable significance, since other than through political pressure very few other nations place this responsibility so highly. [59]

B. The scope and content of the right to development in section 30

1. 'Development'

It is surprising that, in view of Malawi's different source and motivation for the need for the RD and the circumstances surrounding the drafting of the Constitution, section 30 is largely a replica of article 8 of the UNDRD, except for minor modifications. It is not surprising therefore that section 30 has inherited most of the conceptual problems of the RD under international law and it is difficult to relate the content of section 30 to the impetus for its inclusion. It is unfortunate that, since the adoption of the Malawi Constitution in 1994, there has been no scholarly analysis or any commentary on the Constitution generally and the RD in particular.[60] The Malawi courts have also not considered the content of section 30 to any significant extent.[61] The RD has been pleaded in a few cases and in some, though not all,[62] of them the courts have found a breach of the RD.[63] However, the general scope and content of the RD in section 30 still remains unclear.

The drafting history of the RD in the Malawi Constitution shows that the very first hand-written draft of section 30 qualified 'development' with the word 'personal'.[64] This is indicative of the fact that the RD was envisaged to be human-based, as is provided in the UNDRD's article 2, where the human person is to be

---

[58] K Bampton (1994), 'Background Considerations: Constitutional Autochthony and Legal Continuity' (unpublished, on author's file) 34.   [59] Ibid.

[60] Other than the PhD (as yet unpublished) of the author.

[61] A Nyirenda, T Hansen, and D Kaunda *Comparative Analysis of the Human Rights Chapter Under the Malawi Constitution in an International Perspective* p 279 USAID.

[62] *Mkandawire and Others v The Attorney General* (1997) 2 Malawi L Rep 1. This is discussed below.

[63] See *Fredrick Banda v Dimon (Malawi) Ltd*, High Court Principal Registry, unreported, 3 Sept 1998, no 1394 of 1996, and *Bongwe and Others v Min of Education* High Court, unreported, 7 Aug 1998, no 80 of 1997.

[64] Hand-written draft by Bampton, dated 14 Jan 1994 (on the author's file).

at the centre of development. Therefore, the word 'development' in section 30 entails the individual's increased skill and capacity, greater freedom, creativity, self-discipline, responsibility, and material well-being; it also includes the individual's economic development, which is a pre-requisite condition to the whole process of development.[65] The drafting history of section 30 also reveals that the word 'development' is intended to have a general, broad meaning including the simultaneous realization of all human rights. The bishops' pastoral letter,[66] which triggered the state-wide call for multi-party democracy and respect for human rights in Malawi, supports the human-centred meaning. As seen above, this letter condemned the violation of both civil and political rights as well as economic and social rights, and called for dignity of mankind, equality, the right to education, the right to health services for all, freedom of expression, fair trial, universal and fair elections, and emphasized participation of all in public life and decision-making.[67] Indeed, the final version of section 30 shows the link between human rights and development, as 'development' is much more than having enough food to eat and water to drink. Any 'progressive' interpretation of the term must include civil and political rights (CP rights) such as the right to association and to participation.'[68]

Participation by individual members of society is pivotal to the human rights-based concept of development that is in section 30. Indeed, the preamble to the UNDRD defines 'development' as:

a comprehensive economic, social, cultural and political process, which aims at the constant improvement of the well-being of the entire population and of all individuals on the basis of their active, free and meaningful participation in development and the fair distribution of benefits.[69]

The definition clearly indicates the importance of participation, which must be active, free, and meaningful in order to achieve the individual's development. Hence,

development is not just providing people with adequate food, clothing and shelter; many prisons do as much. Development is also people deciding what food, clothing and shelter are adequate, and how they are to be provided.[70]

Thus, it is submitted that the meaning of the word 'development' in section 30 transcends purely economic factors and entails participation in the processes,

---

[65] N Udombana, 'The Third World and the Right to Development: Agenda for the Next Millennium' (2000), 22 Human Rights Q 755.   [66] J Chiona (above) pp 2–6.

[67] Ibid.

[68] See P Alston, 'Prevention Versus Cure as a Human Rights Strategy' in *Development, Human Rights and the Rule of Law. Report of a Conference held in Hague on 27 April–1 May* (Pergamon Press 1981) p 52. Also Udombana, argues that development is a broad-based process, which is both individual and societal or state-based: N Udombana, 'The Third World and the Right to Development: Agenda for the Next Millennium' (2000) 22 Human Rights Q 756.

[69] See the preamble to UNDRD (above).

[70] See P Alston, 'Prevention Versus Cure as a Human Rights Strategy' Development, Human Rights and the Rule of Law' (above) p 54, quoting from Jose Dioko's lecture at an Amnesty International meeting. This link to participation is also relevant to the right of self-determination.

which should result into dignified and respected positive change in a human being's life or a group of people's lives. There are four elements of the RD listed in section 30(1), being economic, social, cultural, and political development.

2. *Economic development*

In relation to economic development, Abi-Saab confirmed the link between economic development and human rights in the RD when he said that economic development is:

a necessary precondition for the satisfaction of the social and economic rights of the individuals ... without a tolerable degree of development, the society will not be materially in a position to grant and guarantee these rights. [71]

Indeed, the creation of an economic base is vital for the implementation of human rights including the RD.[72] In addition, the Malawi Constitution makes a specific provision for the right to freely engage in economic activity.[73]

However, although economic development might be a precondition for the realization of human rights, it cannot be achieved at the expense of human rights. Therefore, the economic development that is envisaged in section 30 is not the economic development from a solely monetarist economist's point of view. An example is food production that is related to monetary market demand rather than to the needs of human beings; where individuals experience an increase in financial resources, they are enabled to access food, which results in good health, thereby enabling them to attend school and participate in elections and other activities that pertain to a fulfilling and dignified human life.[74] In similar vein, Colliard emphasized that economic development should result in a better standard of living in a general sense and should facilitate the enjoyment of life for everybody, with the economic side of the equation never outweighing the human cost, which is objective to guarantee all human rights in order to ensure the happiness of the entire population, including that of the vulnerable.[75]

Economic development does not automatically result in guarantees of human rights. Indeed, Malawi has experienced some development, yet:

The Malawian experience has been growth without expansion of job opportunities, growth without increased access to productive resources, growth without concern for the

[71] G Abi-Saab, 'The Legal Formulation of a Right to Development' R-J Dupuy (ed), *The Right to Development at the International Level, Workshop, The Hague in 16–18 October 1979* (Silthoff & Noordhoff, 1980) p 163.

[72] In this respect note that the UNDRD resulted from the UNCHR's efforts to eliminate obstacles to the implementation of economic, social and cultural rights, particularly in the developing states. See CHR/res/4 (XXIII), E/CN.4/1257 (1977).

[73] Section 29 of the Malawi Constitution reads: 'Every person shall have the right to freely engage in economic activity, to work and to pursue a livelihood anywhere in Malawi.'

[74] See A Eide *et al*, 'Food Security and the Right to Food in International Law and Development' (1991) 1 Transnational L and Contemporary Problems 418.

[75] C Colliard, XXXIII 'L'Adoption Part L'assemblée Générale de la déclaration sur le droit au développent' (4 Dec 1986) (1987) *Annuaire Francais de Droit International* 614.

environment...growth without positive impact on the livelihoods of the majority of the people and growth without equitable distribution of incomes and services.[76]

A useful comparison of the difference between economic growth and human rights is seen in a comparison between two states:

South Africa, with a per capita income of $3,310 and Viet Nam, with a per capita income of $350. Infant mortality is 60 per 1,000 live births in South Africa, 31 in Viet Nam. The adult literacy rate is 84.6% in South Africa, but 92.9% in Viet Nam.[77]

Vietnam with a lower income per capita according to UNDP human development index has lower infant mortality and higher adult literacy than South Africa, which has a higher income per capita.[78] Although growth is measured in GDP, it has to be translated into better living standards for all, as well as a fair distribution of benefits.[79] This confirms that the decisive element for the realization of human rights is not economic development per se, but the policies that the state formulates and implements. Equitable distribution of the proceeds of economic development is very important because the poor are the least vociferous and powerful by virtue of their economic lack. The poor are the most isolated, and economic power would enable them to participate in policy formulation, planning, and implementation, thereby achieving the RD.[80] So while economic development is very important, what happens to the proceeds of that economic development is more important.

3. Social development

Social development is an important element of the RD in section 30. Whilst the section does not define social development, the United Nations Declaration on Social Progress and Development has defined social progress in article 2:

Social progress and development shall be founded on respect for the dignity and value of the human person and shall ensure the promotion of human rights and social justice, which requires:

The immediate and final elimination of all forms of inequality, exploitation of peoples and individuals...[81]

This entails the raising of the material and societal standards of living for human beings, which should result in social justice and redistribution of wealth. Social development as provided in section 30 entails distribution and redistribution of resources and services, and also accessibility of resources and services. This calls for

[76] See UNDAF, *Towards Vision 2020: United Nations Development Assistance for Poverty Eradication in Malawi* (UNDP, Lilongwe, Malawi, 1998), p 4.

[77] UNDP Report (2000), *Human Rights and Human Development*, United Nations Development Report 2000 at 81.

[78] Hence the Committee on ESRCR *General Comment 3* emphasizing that the ICESCR does not require the existence of any particular economic system GC 3, para 8.

[79] See A Lindroos, *The Right to Development* (University of Helsinki, 1999), p 40. See also J Chiona, n 56.   [80] A Sen, *Development as Freedom* (OUP, 1999), p 38.

[81] See Declaration on Social Progress and Development, Part II, GA A/res/2542 (XXIV) 11 Dec 1969, art 2.

positive action by the state on behalf of those who are not able to sell or access services by reason of disability, age, poverty, or any other hindrance beyond their
control.[82]

Social development requires equitable social inclusion as opposed to social
exclusion. It is not only limited to a person's access to pure material requirements,
including food, clean water, and adequate housing but also includes his/her access
to community-based services, like education and health services, as well as the
opportunities to benefit from labour and community market. The immaterial
aspects of life, such as personal security, access to information, and ability to influence or participate in political decisions, are also included.[83] However, the individual has the primary responsibility to provide for himself/herself. Hence,
UNDRD's article 2 provides that on the one hand, the human being should be
the active participant and beneficiary of the RD individually and collectively. The
state, on the other hand, is obligated to remove all hindrances that may obstruct
an individual's access, thus the Committee on Economic, Social and Cultural
Rights (ESCR Committee) recommended 'the adoption of appropriate economic, environmental and social policies, at both the national and international
levels, oriented to the eradication of poverty and the fulfilment of all human rights
for all.'[84]

Thus, social policies and all other policies should focus on raising the standard
of living of the human being to enable him/her to live a life of dignity and self
worth, which is attained through the elimination of poverty. Poverty, as seen in
the above quotation, is a result of lack of social development, which entails the
non-availability of resources.[85] It is also a result of human rights violations,
including the denial of economic, social, and cultural rights, such as rights to
food, health services, shelter/housing, employment, and education.[86] Social
development as provided in section 30, requires social inclusion and power
through the simultaneous realization of all human rights, taking into consideration the indivisibility and interdependence of human rights,[87] including the elimination of poverty.[88]

Further, the RD requires that emphasis is placed on ensuring that the
resources such as the health services, food and land necessary for human living
with dignity, and improvement of social life, are available and accessible to all

---

[82] See s 30(1).

[83] See N Udombana, 'The Third World and the Right to Development: Agenda for the Next
Millenium' (2000) 22 Human Rights Q 3.

[84] CESCR GC 12, para 4. See also E/C.12/1999/5.

[85] See E/C.12/2001/10, Poverty and the ICESCR.

[86] See J Häusermann, *A Human Rights Approach to Development* (Rights and Humanity DFID,
1998) p 24. See also S Skogly 'Is There a Right Not to be Poor?' (2002) 2 Human Rights L Rev 59.

[87] See G van Bueren, 'Alleviating Poverty Through the Constitutional Court' (1999) 15 South
African J Human Rights 54.

[88] See K Munthali (15 March 2002). Because of food shortage in Malawi, people have been killed
for stealing maize.

people. For example, in times of food crisis, feeding of the elderly, the infirm, orphans, children, and pregnant women should be embarked upon.[89] Consistent with this, the Malawi government and its partners in development have embarked on a poverty alleviation programme, which is based on the realization of the RD. The objective of United Nations Development Assistance Framework (UNDAF) in Malawi is to help eradicate poverty by 'creating the capacity to achieve the right to development for all Malawians'.[90] The Malawi Human Rights Commission (MHRC) has welcomed this action as such programmes have:

a role to play in empowering Malawians to fulfil their right to development by building their capacities through a right-based approach to economic and social empowerment. Active participation of the citizens and more especially the poor is key to the fight against poverty. The poor should not be seen to be on the receiving end but should be active participants in transforming their status.[91]

Thus both the material and immaterial aspects of life are important for the achievement of social progress. Of importance also is the ability of all human beings to participate in decision-making in order to influence decisions about social development.

4. Cultural development

Cultural development is also one of the important elements of the RD under section 30. Cultural rights and development are provided for in article 15 of the ICESCR, article 27 of the ICCPR and articles 17 and 22 of the ACHPR (as well as article 27 of the UDHR).[92] Culture is also rooted in other human rights guarantees, such as freedoms of thought, conscience and religion, expression, association, the rights of women, the right to self-determination, equality, the right to education, and the right to health care.[93]

Section 26 of the Malawi Constitution guarantees the right to culture and language, as 'every person shall have the right to use the language and to participate in the cultural life of his or her choice'. This gives an individual within the society the liberty to choose a particular culture, which may be different from that which the majority of the community may practice and, therefore, implies the

---

[89] W Smith, 'Malnutrition Deepens', (2002) <http.allAfrica.com>, where the Vice President of Malawi, Malewezi, was quoted saying that 'Feeding programmes need to be introduced at health centres and primary schools to reach vulnerable groups such as children, under five-olds, pupils and pregnant and breast-feeding mothers'.
[90] UNDAF, (1998), *Towards Vision 2020: United Nations Development Assistance for Poverty Eradication in Malawi* (UNDP, Lilongwe, Malawi, 1998) p iii.
[91] Malawi Human Rights Commission (e-mail communication from the Chairman, of HRC to the author (9 Nov 2001)) (on author's file).
[92] See the discussion of cultural rights by D McGoldrick, 'Culture, Cultures, and Cultural Rights', chapter 17 in this book.
[93] See R Adalsteinsson and P Thorhallson, 'Article 27' G Alfredsson and A Eide (eds), *The Universal Declaration of Human Rights: A Common Standard Achievements* (Nijhoff 1999), p 575.

right to be different. Also envisaged are notions of tolerance, inclusiveness, and change, as section 24(2)[94] of the Malawi Constitution obligates the state to 'eliminate customs and practices that discriminate against women' in order to conform to universal human rights standards.[95] Thus cultural development in section 30(1), read with sections 24 and 26, envisages opportunities that should be available to individuals and groups to explore and be creative without any hindrance due to customs, traditional practices, or discrimination.

5. Political development

Political development, as included in section 30(1), requires power and equitable participation in governance, through people's 'participation in, contribution to, and enjoyment of, . . . political development'.[96] This implies political participation in the decision-making process where the political ground is levelled and people are placed in an enabling environment for collective bargaining to achieve social justice.[97] Decentralization of political power is one way to achieve this,[98] as it can be a means of 'empowering and educating people to participate in development and governance'[99] and 'popular participation in government is an essential aspect of decentralisation; that is the process of transferring power from the centre to sub-national levels.'[100] Political development also entails the establishment of the elements necessary for political participation, such as freedom of the press, association, speech, and trade unions, and requires the elimination of obstacles

[94] Section 24 of the Malawi Constitution reads: '(1) Women have the right to full and equal protection by the law, and have the right not to be discriminated against on the basis of their gender or marital status which includes the right—(a) to be accorded the same rights as men in civil law, including equal capacity—(i) to enter into contracts; (ii) to acquire and maintain rights in property, independently or in association with others, regardless of their marital status; (iii) to acquire and retain custody, guardianship and care of children and to have an equal right in the making of decisions that affect their upbringing; and (iv) to acquire and retain citizenship and nationality; (b) on dissolution of marriage—(i) to a fair disposition of property that is held jointly with a husband; and (ii) to fair maintenance, taking into consideration all the circumstances and, in particular, the means of the former husband and the needs of any children. (2) Any law discriminates against women on the basis of gender or marital status shall be invalid and legislation shall be passed to eliminate customs and practices that discriminate against women, particularly practices such as—(a) sexual abuse, harassment and violence, (b) discrimination in work, business and public affairs; and (c) deprivation of property, including property obtained by inheritance.'

[95] See also Declaration on the Rights of People belonging to National Ethnic, Religious, and Linguistic Minorities, UNGA A/RES/47/135, (18 Dec 1992) which has a similar provision. Art 8 of the Declaration provides that the exercise of minority rights shall not be prejudicial to the enjoyment of already established universally recognized human rights and freedoms.

[96] Art 1 UNDRD.

[97] See C Ng'ong'ola, *Employment & Industrial Law in Malawi: A Prospectus for Reform* (Labour Law Unit, Cape Town South Africa, FES, 1996), p viii. Dr Traub-Merz Rudolf's foreward note.

[98] UNDP Report, *The UN Roundtable Forum on Democratisation in Malawi 21–23 July 1993*, *UNDP* [Ref.MLW/93/004] (1993) p 50.

[99] R Nyirongo, *The Nation Newspaper* of 12 March 2002.

[100] W Tordoff, 'Decentralisation, Local Government and Development' *UNDP Report on Round Table Discussion* (Ref MLW/93/004) (held at Capital Hotel, Lilongwe, 1993) app 2, 1.

that hinder participation, such as tribalism,[101] corruption,[102] and extravagance.[103] It is submitted that the political development in section 30(1), entails the equal, actual, and representative participation in decision-making.[104] However, for political reasons, participation, an important element of political development, is not explicitly provided for in section 30 as was originally envisaged.[105] Nevertheless, participation is implicit within section 30 through the tools that are provided for the realization of the right to development and the principles of non-discrimination and equality that are embedded in the section and also in section 20[106] of the constitution.

The importance of the commitment to political development in section 30 is reinforced by the fundamental principles of the Malawi Constitution as contained in section 12(iii). This section requires those in authority to exercise their power, based on the trust of the people, through an 'open, accountable and transparent Government and informed democratic choice'. This social trust obligates the leaders to take into consideration the wishes and needs of the people as they formulate and implement policies in the state, resulting in all people living a life of dignity and self-respect.

C. Rights and duties in section 30

1. Rights and rights-holders

The rights in section 30 include the following:

(i) The right to enjoy all the facets of development: economic, social, cultural, and political;
(ii) The implied right to affirmative action;

---

[101] See M Hamsungule, *Human Needs Assessment Survey in Malawi.* DCHR/HRRC (Lilongwe, Malawi, 1999), p 14 and also C Chihana, Address by Chakufwa Chihana, President of Alliance For Democracy (AFORD) at the National Constitutional Conference, Kwacha Conference Centre, Blantyre (24 Feb 1994), p 4.

[102] The formation of the Anti-Corruption Bureau to combat corruption and the enactment of the Corrupt Practices Act. See the query by the British High Commission and the withdrawal of aid by the Denmark, at <http://allAfrica.com> 'British Warns Malawi On Corruption' (12 Oct 2000) and (2 Nov 2000) accessed Nov 2001. Malawi is the third largest recipient of British Aid.

[103] Proponents of the inclusion of the RD in the Constitution included the donor community who were interested in arresting extravagance, such as the Malawi government's purchase of expensive Mercedes cars in the year 2000. See British Envoy Warns Malawi on Corruption, <http://allAfrica. com> (12 Oct 2000) accessed Nov 2001.

[104] See s 6 on the universal and equal suffrage.

[105] The draft s 30 had a sub-section 5 on popular participation that was edited by the politicians at the last minute (Bampton, interview with the author held on 13 Feb 2001, in Nottingham).

[106] Section 20 of the Malawi Constitution reads: '(1) Discrimination of persons in any form is prohibited and all persons are, under any law, guaranteed equal and effective protection against discrimination on grounds of race, color, sex, language, religion, political or other opinion, nationality, ethnic or social origin, disability, property, birth, or other status. (2) Legislation may be passed addressing inequalities in society and prohibiting discriminatory practices and the propagation of such practices and may render such practices criminally punishable by courts.'

   (iii) The right to equality of opportunity to access basic resources;

   (iv) The right to equality and non-discrimination;

    (v) The right to the introduction of reforms aimed at eradicating social injustices and inequalities;

   (vi) The right to participate in all facets of development, implied in sections 30(1) and 30(2);

  (vii) The right to development policies that aim at the eradication of poverty, implied in the obligation to ensure equal access to basic resources provided in section 30(2);

 (viii) The right to know the basis of prioritization of policies, provided in section 30(4); and

   (ix) The right to a transparent and accountable government, provided in section 30(4).

Section 30(1) states that 'all persons and peoples have a right to development'. Although the term 'persons' is not defined, it is clear from this part of the Malawi Constitution dealing with human rights that it pertains to the human person. On only one occasion has the High Court in Malawi encountered the need to define the word 'person' in human rights discourse and this was in regard to the RD. This was in the case of *Mkandawire and Others v The Attorney General* (popularly known as the AFORD case).[107] In that case two political parties, the United Democratic Front (UDF) (the then ruling party) and Alliance For Democracy (AFORD) (one of the two main opposition parties in Malawi) entered into a coalition agreement after the elections in 1994. Thereupon, the President appointed some AFORD MPs to ministerial positions. On 2 June 1996, AFORD terminated the agreement and advised its MPs who, as a result of the coalition had been appointed to ministerial positions, to withdraw from the cabinet. Some AFORD ministers declined to resign. Thereupon AFORD leaders appealed to the President to dismiss the AFORD ministers who did not voluntarily resign. The President refused. AFORD requested the Speaker of the National Assembly to declare the seats of those members vacant because they had crossed the floor but the Speaker did not oblige. The AFORD members walked out of Parliament. AFORD and its members unsuccessfully sued the government for, *inter alia*, violation of their fundamental rights, including the RD. The High Court, referring to section 30, held that the RD was not applicable to political parties, as it only concerns the RD of natural persons.[108]

Section 30(1), read together with section 15(2), clearly shows that rightholders of the RD are natural persons and groups of individuals.[109] To this extent the court was clearly correct. What is the status of a political party? The Malawi High Court did not discuss the legal personality of a political party. However, the

---

[107] *Mkandawire and Others v The Attorney General* (1997) 2 Malawi Law Reports 1.
[108] Ibid 13.
[109] A Nyirenda, T Hansen, and D Kaunda, *Comparative Analysis of the Human Rights Chapter Under the Malawi Constitution in an International Perspective* (1999) p 279 USAID.

European Commission on Human Rights dealt with the question of the personality of a political party under United Kingdom law, in the Liberal Party case,[110] where the applicants complained that they were affected adversely by the British electoral system of election by a simple majority. It was held that 'a political party as a gathering of people with a common interest can be considered as a non governmental organisation or a group of individuals'.[111] It also decided, in a different case, that 'when a church lodges an application under the Convention, it does so in reality, on behalf of its members. It should therefore be accepted that a church body is capable of possessing and exercising the rights contained in Article 9 in its own capacity as a representative of its own members.'[112]

Similarly, a political party in Malawi is a gathering of individuals with a common purpose; it is not a registered company and does not otherwise have a separate legal personality. It is submitted that according to section 15,[113] because it is a group of persons, a political party is entitled to make a claim for a violation of its human rights. Therefore, the High Court was incorrect and AFORD should have been considered as a non-governmental organization (NGO) or as a group of persons that could have been a victim of a violation of the RD. Thus it is submitted that the word 'persons' in section 30 includes individuals, political parties, NGOs, and associations.

Another category of right-holders included in section 30(1) is 'peoples'. The term 'peoples' is used in public international law in connection with the right of self-determination.[114] It cannot mean all the people in a state in international law,[115] and, even more clearly, it cannot mean this under national law protection of human rights, as it would be absurd for a state to have a claim against itself.

As discussed above, the rights enshrined in the Constitution are binding on all the organs of the government and also on natural and legal persons. This denotes both the vertical and direct horizontal application of human rights. In the case of *Blantyre Netting Company v CV Chidzulo and Others*,[116] a case that involved fair labour practices between private parties, where there was a claim by employees

---

[110] *The Liberal Party, Mrs R and Mr P v the UK* Appl 8765/69, 21 DR 211.

[111] Ibid 222. This was followed in *Fryske Nasjonale Partij and Others v the Netherlands*, Appl 11100/84, 45 DR 240.   [112] *X and Church of Scientology v Sweden*, Appl 7805/77; 16 DR 211.

[113] Section 15 of the Malawi Constitution reads: '(1) The human rights and freedoms enshrined in this Chapter shall be respected and upheld by the executive, legislature and judiciary and all organs of the Government and its agencies and, where applicable to them, by all natural and legal persons in Malawi and shall be enforceable in the manner prescribed in this Chapter. (2) Any person or groups of persons with sufficient interest in the protection and enforcement of rights under this Chapter shall be entitled to the assistance of the courts, the Ombudsman, the Human Rights Commission and other organs of Government to ensure the promotion, protection and redress of grievance in respect of those rights.'

[114] See R Higgins, *Problems and Process: International Law and How We Use It* (Clarendon Press, 1994) pp 111–128.

[115] R McCorquodale, 'A Human Rights Approach to the Right of Self-Determination' (1994), 43 ICLQ 857.

[116] *See Blantyre Netting Company v CV Chidzulo and Others*, Supreme Court of Appeal, unreported, 3 Sept 1996, no 17 of 1995.

against their employer, the Malawi court, just like the Canadian court in the case of *Manning v Hill*,[117] recognized the horizontal application of human rights. It looked at the values underlying the Constitution and used a generous interpretation of constitutional terms in order to implement the spirit of the Constitution, which, it said, is the promotion of human rights. The court held that contractual obligations entered into by private parties constitute a 'law' that has to be consistent with the Constitution, including section 31.[118] The court, just like the Irish Court in the case of *Meskell v Coras Iompair Eireann*,[119] recognized the direct effect of human rights norms on private individuals. In the Irish case, the defendant's private employers, at the recommendation of trade unions, who were concerned with the level of union membership, terminated the contracts of their employees and re-employed them on condition that they agreed to be members of the trade union. The plaintiff was not re-employed because he did not agree to the new condition although he had been a paid up member of the trade union during his employment. The plaintiff successfully sued the defendants for his dismissal claiming that it was a violation of his rights under the constitution. It is pertinent to point out that the Malawi court, in the *Blantyre Netting Company* case, used the inconsistency clause to give indirect effect to the right to fair and safe labour practices and fair remuneration provided under section 31 of the Constitution. It is surprising that the court used the inconsistency section when section 15 of the Constitution provides explicitly for horizontal application. It is submitted that, by virtue of section 15, there is direct horizontal application of human rights in Malawi.

Section 15(2) indicates the notion of *locus standi* in the enforcement of human rights in the use of the words 'sufficient interest'. Order 53 of the Rules of the Supreme Court of the United Kingdom (RSC), which is still applicable to Malawi, regulates *locus standi*. For a court to give leave for an application for judicial review to be heard, the tests of 'standing' and 'sufficient interest' must be fulfilled before leave is granted by the court. However, leave is not necessary in all instances considering that section 43 of the Malawi Constitution[120] makes provision for the right to administrative justice. To understand what is meant by the word 'interests', section 43 has to be read together with section 15(2), which uses the words 'sufficient interest'. It is submitted that the word 'interests' in section 43 means 'sufficient interest'.

The Malawi Supreme Court of Appeal considered the question of *locus standi* in the case of *Civil Liberties Committee (CILIC) v The State, The Registrar General*

---

[117] *Manning v Hill* (1995) 126 DLR (4th) 129, 156.

[118] Section 31(1) reads, 'Every person shall have the right to fair and safe labour practices and to fair remuneration'.   [119] *Meskell v Coras Iompair Eireann* [1973] IR 121, 132.

[120] Section 43. 'Every person shall have the right to—(a) lawful and procedurally fair administrative action, which is justifiable in relation to reasons given where his or her rights, freedoms, legitimate expectations or interests are affected or threatened: and (b) be furnished with reasons in writing for administrative action where his or her rights, freedoms, legitimate expectations or interests if those interests are known.'

and The Minister of Justice.[121] This case involved the ban of a newspaper (National Agenda). CILIC sued the defendants, claiming that the defendants had violated its freedom of opinion and freedom of expression under sections 34[122] and 35[123] as read with section 15(2) of the Constitution. The court considered whether CILIC had *locus standi* in this matter under section 15(2). It was held that the intention of the drafters was not to allow public interest litigation because the Constitution required that an applicant must have sufficient interest in the matter. The requirement of sufficient interest, according to the court, entails that an applicant who is not personally affected sufficiently or is not related to such affected person does not have standing. This narrow and restricted interpretation attributed to the words 'sufficient interest' by the court is unwarranted in human rights considerations, which call for a wide and far reaching interpretation. Further, the wording of sections 15(2) and 46(2)[124] do not support this interpretation. It is submitted that the words in these sections envisage the involvement of persons other than the right-holder, who, by virtue of being a victim of a violated right, has a right to be heard. This was so held in the case of *Okeke v The Minister of Home Affairs and the Controller of Immigration* [125] Mrs Thandiwe Okeke, a wife of Mr Peter John Okeke, a Nigerian citizen, who, upon arrival at the airport in Malawi, was arrested, detained, and later deported back to Nigeria for breaking immigration laws. She commenced an action against immigration officials alleging that her rights under the Malawi Constitution had been violated and sought review by the court of the immigration official's decision. The court held that the decision to detain and deport her husband had a direct impact on her life. There was sufficient connection between the applicant and the matter to which the application related. The decision made by the Controller of Immigration was held to be incorrect and was quashed. In another case, *Du Chisiza Jnr v Minister of Education and Culture,*[126] the defendants ordered a ban on video, drama, and all entertainment by outsiders in government-run educational institutions. The plaintiff, who had a drama group that used to perform at various places, including schools and other government-run educational institutions, as a business, was

---

[121] *Civil Liberties Committee (CILIC) v The State, The Registrar General and The Minister of Justice* Supreme Court of Appeal, unreported, 8 April 2004, no 55 of 1998.

[122] Section 34 of the Malawi Constitution reads: 'Every person has the right to freedom of conscience, religion, belief and thought, and to academic freedom.'

[123] Section 35 of the Malawi Constitution reads: 'Every person shall have the right to freedom of expression.'

[124] Section 46(2) of the Malawi Constitution reads: 'Any person who claims that a fundamental right or freedom guaranteed by this constitution has been infringed or threatened shall be entitled-(a) to make application to a competent court to enforce or protect such right or freedom; and (b) to make application to the Ombudsman or the Human Rights Commission in order to secure such assistance or advice as he or she may reasonably require.'

[125] *Okeke v The Minister of Home Affairs and the Controller of Immigration,* High Court, unreported, 8 July 2001, no 73 of 1997.

[126] *Du Chisiza Jnr v Minister of Education and Culture,* High Court, unreported, 22 March 1993, no 10 of 1993, 4.

affected by the Minister's ban. He applied to the court for judicial review. Although the ban did not specifically refer to the applicant, or affect the applicant's right directly, the judge said:

it would seem that it is not necessary for the applicant to show a right which has been infringed by the Minister. He is only required to show that he has sufficient interest in the matter to which the application relates.[127]

The court held that the Minister's banning order affected the interests of the applicant and concluded that the ban was invalid, null, and void. This case shows the breadth of protection afforded to human rights in the Malawi Constitution when they are interpreted appropriately.

2. *Duties and duty-holders*

The main duties under section 30 are:

(i) to ensure the enjoyment of economic, social, cultural, and political development in section 30(1);

(ii) to ensure 'equality of opportunity for all'[128] to access basic resources. By implication, the state is under a duty to eradicate poverty;

(iii) to 'take all necessary measures for the realization of the right to development';[129]

(iv) to introduce reforms aimed at the eradication of injustices and inequalities;

(v) to justify its policies;[130]

(vi) an implied obligation to be accountable and transparent in its dealings. This entails the application of democratic principles;

(vii) to give special consideration to vulnerable groups in the application of the RD;[131] and

(viii) an implied obligation to ensure equality and non-discrimination;[132]

The RD requires the creation and implementation of policies. Hence, under section 30, the main duty-holder is the state, which has the primary responsibility for the implementation and realization of the RD.[133] Section 30, read with section 15(1), obliges the state to respect and uphold the RD. However, as shown above, section 15 makes provision for the horizontal application of human rights. According to section 15, duty-holders include natural and legal persons.

Section 30 imposes both negative and positive obligations upon the state. Section 30(4) obliges the state to respect the RD. This entails a negative obligation to refrain from interfering with the individual's or a group's enjoyment of economic, social, cultural, and political development. For example, in the South African case of *The Government of the Republic of South Africa and Others v Grootboom and Others*,[134] the

---

[127] Ibid.   [128] Section 30(2).   [129] Ibid.   [130] Section 30(3).
[131] Section 30(1).   [132] Ibid.   [133] Art 3(1) of the UNDRD.
[134] *The Government of the Republic of South Africa and Others v Grootboom and Others* 2001 (1) SA, 46 (CC).

applicants in this case were evicted illegal squatters whose make-shift shelters were destroyed. The South African Constitutional Court examined the duty of the state in respect of the right to housing and found the action of the state in breach of its constitutional obligations. It also held that the state should immediately provide shelter to those applicants who were in a desperate situation.[135]

One case before the Malawi courts has considered the extent of the state's duties under section 30. In *Thomas Brown v The Republic*,[136] the Malawi High Court had to consider a case where the police arrested twenty-four people, including the appellant, who was found walking aimlessly within the city, following an outbreak of house robberies in Blantyre. Tambala J quashed the conviction of the applicant (who had pleaded guilty of being a rogue and a vagabond) and said that 'section 30(2) suggest[s] that the State has a duty to provide employment to its citizens'. This decision must be incorrect as the obligation under section 30(2) is to take measures to protect the RD, including to ensure 'equality of opportunities to access', such as the formulation and implementation of policies that target the empowerment and enablement of the vulnerable and the inclusion of all in decision-making. There is no obligation actually to provide resources.[137]

3. Special consideration

At the Constitutional Symposium to debate the draft Malawi Constitution, it was argued that there must be:

a system which can actively support the less privileged, the women, children and the disabled so that they too can fully participate in all endeavours of society. Without sufficient constitutional safeguards this dream may never be realised.[138]

Accordingly, section 30(1) provides that 'women, children and the disabled shall be given special consideration in the application of this right'. This is also supported by section 20, which prohibits discrimination and provides for equal protection (see above), and section 12 (v), which provides that 'all persons have equal status before the law'.

The term 'special consideration' in section 30(1) obliges the state to take affirmative action in favour of vulnerable groups. This is consistent with international law.[139]

₁₃₅ Ibid.

₁₃₆ *Thomas Brown v The Republic* High Court, unreported, 19 April 1996, no 24 of 1996.

₁₃₇ The realization of the RD does not primarily mean giving out resources except in cases of social security or social assistance: see art 9 ICESCR.

₁₃₈ C Chihana, Address by Chakufwa Chihana, President of Alliance For Democracy (AFORD) at the National Constitutional Conference, Kwacha Conference Centre, Blantyre (24th Feb 1994), p 7–8.

₁₃₉ See eg art 4 CEDAW, ESCR Committee, *General Comment 5*. Note that CERD art 2(2) which goes further by imposing an obligation to take necessary affirmative action measures: 'States Parties shall, when the circumstances so warrant, take, special and concrete measures to ensure the adequate development and protection of certain racial groups or individuals belonging to them, for the purpose of guaranteeing them the full and equal enjoyment of human rights and fundamental freedoms. These measures shall in no case entail as a consequence the maintenance of unequal or separate rights for different racial groups after the objectives for which they were taken have been achieved.'

The obligation of the state under section 30 is, in the formulation and implementation of policies and programmes, to ensure that vulnerable persons and groups within the community or state are targeted and, where necessary, 'special consideration' is given to ensure their participation. For example, the government should come up with programmes and policies to ensure that vulnerable persons and groups enjoy equality of opportunity to access resources without any impediments based on their vulnerable status. Implied also in the phrase 'give special consideration' is the positive obligation to ensure equality. Unlike non-discrimination, which entails a negative obligation, equality imposes a positive obligation,[140] as equal treatment of unequals results in inequalities.[141] In section 30, the state has an obligation to take special measures[142] to allow vulnerable groups to access resources on equal footing with the non-vulnerable.[143] These resources include education, food, infrastructure, and health services. That would be achieved through special programmes with a particular bias to 'eradicate massive poverty, including policies to increase purchasing power, improve access to goods and services'.[144]

Indeed, preferential treatment is sometimes recognized and applied in Malawi, especially at an administrative level. For example, in order to ensure that girls and children from very poor families access education, the state provides food to girls and children from poor families only[145] and political parties and the government are encouraged to reserve 30 per cent of leadership positions for women.[146]

D. Scarcity of resources

Section 30(2) of the Malawi Constitution uses the phrase 'all necessary measures' without any limitation concerning the availability of resources, such as found in the ICESR and in the South African and Indian Constitutions. The judiciary in Malawi has considered the question of resources in the case of *Mungomo v The Electoral Commission*.[147] In this case, the court justified the postponement of the 1999 Presidential and Parliamentary Elections because of irregularities in the voter registration that were occasioned by lack of funds.

---

[140] See S Joseph, J Schultz, and M Castan, *The International Covenant on Civil and Political Rights: Cases, Materials and Commentary* (OUP, 2000) p 519.

[141] See A Yusuf, 'A Differential Treatment as a Dimension of the Right to Development' in Dupuy Rene-Jean (ed), *The Right to Development at the International Level, Workshop, The Hague, 16–18 October 1979* (Silthoff & Noordhoff, 1980), p 237.

[142] GC no 4 of the HRC advocates affirmative action to ensure positive enjoyment of human rights.

[143] See NCC (1994a), comments of several delegates at the Constitutional Conference, Mrs E Kalyati, 57, Mrs M Nyandovi-Kerr, 67, S Latif, 62, E Chiwaula, 74.

[144] E/CN.4/2002/WG.18/4, 10.

[145] MESC, Education Sector Policy and Investment Framework (PIF) (2000) Ministry of Education, Sports and Culture (MESC) Lilongwe, Malawi, para 3.3.

[146] See MGYCS, National Gender Policy 2000–2005 (2000), Ministry of Gender, Youth and Community Services at 21.

[147] *Mungomo v The Electoral Commission* High Court, unreported, Case no 23/99.

Other jurisdictions have addressed the question of scarce resources. In the Indian Supreme Court case of *State of Andra Pradesh v Lavu Narendranath*,[148] a case involving the selection test for a college, the court conceded that financial commitments and other relevant matters were justifications for the admission into college of only a few students. The South African Constitutional Court has taken into consideration scarce resources as a limiting element in the application of social and economic rights. In the case of *Soobramoney*,[149] where a diabetic man who suffered from kidney failure and needed to be on a dialysis machine made a claim that he was entitled to emergency treatment at government expense under section 27(3) of the South African Constitution, which provides that 'no one may be refused emergency treatment', the South African Constitutional Court concluded that the phrase 'available resources' has both a wide and narrow application. In reaching this decision, Chaskalson J held that renal dialysis did not fall within emergency treatment as envisaged in article 27(3), rather the case fell within the right of access to health care services, in practice section 27(1), which was subject to 'available resources' (article 27(2)). The wide application of the term resources means the national resources, including donor aid money, and the narrow application of resources refers to the executive's budgeted resources for a particular section/department. Whilst the court took the view that budget allocation should be primarily left to the executive, the court however, could examine the use of resources.[150] On the facts of the case, the appeal was not allowed on the ground that the allocation of medical resources in that case was reasonable. In a case in the United Kingdom, where an expensive treatment for an infant was withdrawn, the judge stated that:

I would stress the absolute undesirability of the court making an order which may have the effect of compelling a doctor or health authority to make available resources (both human and material) to a particular child without knowing whether or not there are other patients.[151]

Implied in the cases in these three jurisdictions is the courts' partial deference to the executive when faced with difficult questions involving balancing of scarce resources with human rights. Although the three jurisdictions appear to take one direction in the application of economic and social rights, the situations are different in view of the nature of the claims and the extent to which the state meets its minimum core obligations. These have been explained as:

a State party in which any significant number of individuals is deprived of essential foodstuffs, of essential primary health care, of basic shelter and housing, or of the most basic forms of education is, prima facie, failing to discharge its obligations under the Covenant.[152]

---

[148] *State of Andra Pradesh v Lavu Narendranath* (1) SCC, (1971), 607 (India).

[149] *Soobramoney v the Minister of Health, KwaZulu Natal* 1998 (1) SA 765 (CC).

[150] In view of CESCR's GC 3, the court has jurisdiction to look beyond the available budget.

[151] In *Re J (A Minor) (Child in Care: Medical Treatment,* [1993] Fan 15, per Balcombe LJ (UK Court of Appeal).   [152] ESCR Committee GC 3, para 10.

In the case of the United Kingdom, it is a relatively developed state with a system that has achieved more than the minimum core obligations. In fact, it has a well developed National Health Service. Its decisions concerning scarce resources are in connection with complicated and expensive treatment. This type of treatment can be called 'luxury treatment' (my own terminology). In contrast, the situations concerning economic and social rights in the Indian, Malawian, and South African cases are different, in that they involve the satisfaction of the minimum core of the state's obligations. It is argued that courts act differently here, although much also turns upon the wording of the relevant statute. This is demonstrated by the *Grootboom*[153] case where housing rights were examined. After the court scrutinized the legislative measures, other measures, and policies that the government had adopted within its available resources, it held that programmes that catered only for medium and long-term relief but failed to provide for those in desperate and urgent immediate need, were unreasonable. Similarly, the Indian Supreme Court of Appeal has acknowledged the minimum core obligation in the case of *Francis Coralie Mullin v The Administrator, Union Territory of Delhi and Others.*[154] The applicant was in preventive detention. He applied to court for release and also for a right to consult a lawyer of his choice. Although this case concerned civil and political rights, the Supreme Court said, *obiter*, that 'a life of dignity should include at least the bare necessities of life such as adequate nutrition, clothing and shelter over the head.'

It is suggested that, in view of Malawi's economic position, the practice of other similar states and the general position in international law, it requires that courts take into account the scarcity of resources when considering the RD, despite the lack of a limitation provision in section 30.

E. Justiciability

The RD, in the context of section 30(1), is a justiciable right like the other human rights in the Malawi Constitution. In the *AFORD case* (considered above), the court confirmed that the RD was a justiciable human right, albeit not applying the right to the applicants. In *Thomas Brown v Republic*, also discussed above, the court considered (incorrectly) that the state may have an obligation to provide employment to people. Two other cases on the RD involved unfair dismissal from contractual employment. These are the cases of *Bongwe and 11 Others v Minister of Education*[155] and *Fredrick Banda v Dimon (MW) Ltd*.[156] In both cases the plaintiffs were dismissed

---

[153] 2001 (1) SA 46.

[154] *Francis Coralie Mullin v The Administratior, Union Territory of Delhi and Others AIR* (1981), SC 746 (India).

[155] *Bongwe and 11 Others v Minister of Education* High Court, unreported, 7 Aug 1998, no 80 of 1997.

[156] *Fredrick Banda v Dimon (MW) Ltd* High court, unreported, 3 Sept 1998, no 13 of 1994.

from their jobs by their employers. A breach of the RD was pleaded. Without any discussion of the scope and content of the RD, the court held in each case that there was a violation of the RD contrary to section 30. The learned judge in the *Bongwe* case said that:

the State shall take all the necessary measures for the realization of the right to development and such measures shall include, among other things, employment and infrastructure.[157]

It is submitted that a case of unfair dismissal from contractual employment does not per se amount to a violation of the RD of the employee. According to section 30, the state is obligated to create a conducive and enabling environment for all to enjoy equality of opportunity to access employment. However, in certain cases, depending on the circumstances of the case, differential treatment involving the provision of empowering devices for the enjoyment of the RD, which may include employment, may be required. In this case the plight of the individual relying upon the RD should be established in order to decide whether he qualified for special consideration to entitle him to the provision of employment or not, for example whether he was disabled. However, it should be noted that the primary objective of the RD is not the giving of resources to persons and groups of people, as this would create dependency. The objective of the RD is to empower persons and groups of people to be self-reliant and to be able to lead independent lives.

The entitlement in the RD is to the policies that are required to achieve and/or facilitate access to resources. The policies should ensure a pattern of growth, be it economic, social, cultural, or political development, to benefit all and in particular the disadvantaged and vulnerable. Therefore, the resources that are invested should target the building of capabilities in human beings. A claim for a breach of the RD would succeed where a policy has been formulated and certain individuals and groups are discriminated against or, by reason of their vulnerability, are unable to access the available resources, such as where there is free education but people from a certain group are denied access. In the case of *George Nasawa Through Zulu (Next Friend) v Attorney General*,[158] the applicant had made a fraudulent representation that he came from the district where the school to which he was admitted was located. Although the practice of restricting admission to the school to people from the locality amounted to discrimination against people from outside the locality, the practice was based on objective criteria. It was in pursuance of affirmative action in favour of people from certain district that required assistance in education.

In each of these cases, the Malawi courts had no difficulty in accepting that the RD was a justiciable human right.

---

[157] See *Bongwe and 11 Others v Minister of Education* High Court, unreported, 7 Aug 1998, no. 80 of 1997.
[158] *George Nasawa Through Zulu (Next Friend) v Attorney General* High Court, unreported, 23 Feb 1994, no 153 of 1993.

IV. Conclusions

The RD moved through the UN system at an incredible speed,[159] culminating in the adoption of the UNDRD. In contrast, the inclusion of the RD in the Malawi Constitution was a well thought-out strategy, for the purpose of achieving social justice and to make the government responsible, transparent, and accountable to all the people of Malawi. Further, it is envisaged that the RD would compel the government to act judiciously in dealing with and distributing government monies, including loans, donor monies, and assistance in any other form.

Most important is the focus of the RD on empowerment, participation, distribution, and redistribution of the proceeds of development and resources to all without any discrimination. The RD also imposes a duty on the government to justify its actions even where it has acted reasonably. This is a vital element in view of scarce resources that call for prioritization. Thus, metaphorically, the main purpose of the RD generally is the provision of wings to all and in particular to the 'have nots' for them to fly.

So far, the constitutional guarantee of the RD, despite being a justiciable human right, has not played a significant role in Malawi. However, this is not peculiar to the RD, as few of the rights in the Malawi Constitution have been considered closely by the courts primarily owing to lack of information and assistance about the RD and other rights. For example, section 20 (protecting equality) was pleaded in the case of *General Simwaka v The Attorney General*.[160] In that case General Simwaka commenced an action against the government for wrongful termination of his employment with the Malawi Army, including a claim that the government be ordered to take steps to ensure that his rights, in particular the right not to be discriminated against, should be respected and protected. The court, without examining the scope and content of section 20, said that:

> it would seem that the Public Service Act has no application to those persons employed in the Malawi Army. However, it would not be proper to discriminate against Army Officers and any such discrimination would violate section 20 of the constitution.

Violation of a number of rights was also alleged in the case of *The Malawi Law Society, Episcopal Conference of Malawi, Malawi Council of Churches v The State and The President of Malawi, The Minister of Home Affairs, The Inspector General of Police, Army Commander*.[161] The facts of the case are that there were rumours that the National Assembly was going to present a bill seeking to amend section 83(3) of the Malawi Constitution, which limits the terms that the President and Vice Presidents

---

[159] See J Donnelly, 'In Search of the Unicorn: The Jurisprudence and Politics of the Right to Development' (1985) 15 California Western Intl L Jo 475.

[160] *General Simwaka v The Attorney General* Supreme Court of Appeal, unreported, 12 Jan 2004, no 6 of 2001.

[161] *The Malawi Law Society, Episcopal Conference of Malawi, Malawi Council of Churches v The State* High Court, unreported, 22 Oct 2002, no 78 of 2002.

may serve to a maximum of two consecutive terms. The proposed amendment was to allow the President and the Vice Presidents to serve unlimited terms in their respective offices. While conducting a rally, the President issued an oral directive that there should be no demonstrations for or against the envisaged amendments and further directed the other respondents to deal with anyone violating his directive on the ban. The applicants sought an order of *certiorari* quashing the directive of the President and a declaration that the President's ban on demonstrations was unconstitutional in that it fettered the constitutional rights to freedom of association provided in section 32, freedom of conscience provided in section 33, freedom of opinion provided in section 34, freedom of expression provided in section 35, and freedom of assembly provided in section 38. The court held that if the directive were enforced, it would completely take away the rights enshrined in the Constitution in those sections and section 40.[162] Therefore, the applicants were entitled to the relief sought.

It is noted that, whilst lawyers are aware of the availability of human rights, including the RD, in the Malawi constitution, most of them do not have in-depth knowledge of their content and scope, as revealed in their court pleadings. Thus, so far, the RD has been pleaded in cases involving unfair dismissal, while situations that much more clearly warrant the use of the RD pass unnoticed.

It is also commendable that the Malawi Poverty Alleviation Programme has emphasized the realization of the RD and has focused on the RD's main target: 'economic empowerment'. Its policy framework, as indicated above, has defined the programme in the language of the main impetus of the RD as 'a process through which the poor are empowered to improve their plight and contribute to national development'.[163] Economic power will enable the poor in Malawi to take charge of their affairs and make decisions that are in accordance with their priorities.

The main problem that the RD is facing in Malawi is lack of political will. The lack of understanding and use of the RD has meant that the government has not yet been compelled to take action or to discontinue a policy that is in violation of the RD. Hence, the responsibility to realize its potential falls to non-governmental organizations, lawyers, and the courts. The work of the judiciary in Malawi with regard to human rights and, in particular, to the RD, is made easier by the Constitution's wide interpretation provisions in section 11 that call for the court's imaginative ability to deal with section 30. Section 11, broadly speaking, shows the *sui generis* nature of the Constitution. It calls for a special and unique interpretation:

(1) appropriate principles of interpretation of this Constitution shall be developed and employed by the courts to reflect the unique character and supreme status of this Constitution;
(2) in interpreting the provisions of this Constitution a court of law shall-
  (a) promote the values which underlie an open and democratic society;

162 Ibid 4.
163 Policy Framework for Poverty Alleviation Programme, Office of President & Cabinet, EPD, (1996), 1. See also UNDAF, *Towards Vision 2020: United Nations Development Assistance for Poverty Eradication in Malawi* (1998) UNDP, Lilongwe, Malawi, p 9.

(b) take full account of the provisions of Chapter III and Chapter VI; and
(c) where applicable, have regard to current norms of public international law and comparable foreign case law;

(3) where a court of law declares an act of the executive or a law to be invalid, that court may apply such interpretation of that act or law as is consistent with this Constitution; and

(4) any law that ousts or purports to oust the jurisdiction of the courts to entertain matters pertaining to this Constitution shall be invalid.

The particular uniqueness of the Malawi Constitution was emphasized in the case of *Thandiwe Okeke v The Minister of Home Affairs and The Controller of Immigration*, discussed above. In allowing the husband's entry into Malawi, Mwaungulu J said that:

it is the court's duty to interpret this Constitution understanding it ascribes to itself a potency and uniqueness not to be overshadowed by general considerations.... It is characteristic that our Constitution, anticipating the problems it intended to forestall and our aspirations for promoting democracy and fundamental human rights, provides notions unheard of or unthought of in modern constitutional and political theory, conceptualisation and thought. This goes to its uniqueness.[164]

Evidently, the interpretation of the Malawi Constitution should take into consideration the fact that the intention behind the adoption of the Constitution was to disassociate the state with its past. As a general approach to its task, the High Court, in case of *The Trustees of Malawi Against Physical Disabilities v The State and The Office of The Ombudsman*,[165] in interpreting section 123(2) with regard to the functions and powers of the Ombudsman, spelt out the principles which should be applied when the Constitution is being interpreted. The court should:

(i) take into consideration the Constitution's wording;
(ii) examine the circumstances that brought about the Constitutional change; and
(iii) construe the Constitution in a wider context, taking into consideration the state's aspirations, the democratic dispensation and the human rights regime.[166]

The trust invested in the judiciary in the Malawi Constitution for the realization of social and economic rights, and the achievement of equity, transparency, and accountability through their interpretation and application of the guarantee of the RD, is very important. It is recommended that, for the RD to achieve its envisaged purpose, there is need for judicial activism in Malawi in the same manner as the South African Constitutional Court.

---

[164] *Thandiwe Okeke v The Minister of Home Affairs and The Controller of Immigration* High Court, unreported, 8 July 2001, no 73/97, 5.

[165] Case no 22/2001, 7. In this case, the Ombudsman had investigated a matter involving unlawful dismissal of an employee. In his determination, he gave remedies. Thereupon the applicant sought judicial review of the Ombudsman's determination.

[166] *Thandiwe Okeke v The Minister of Home Affairs and The Controller of Immigration*, no 164, 5.

17

Culture, Cultures, and Cultural Rights

*Dominic McGoldrick**

I. Introduction

Cultural rights are the failed Cinderella of the international human rights lexicon—pretty to picture but they don't quite make it to the ball.[1] This has been the case notwithstanding that there are ever-widening debates on managing cultural differences and cultural diversity.[2] International human rights lawyers discuss culture and cultural wrongs a lot, but discuss cultural rights a lot less.[3] It took until 2002 for the United Nations Human Rights Commission to adopt a resolution specifically on cultural rights.[4] Even in 2005 a request from the Secretary-General for information on 'human rights and cultural diversity' received no responses.[5]

This chapter considers the challenges of dealing with culture and cultures, as well as the ideas and substance of cultural rights, especially article 15 of the International Covenant on Economic, Social and Cultural Rights 1966 (ICESCR), the core binding provision on cultural rights in the international human rights system. It will examine the two new recent international texts relevant to cultural rights: *General Comment 17* of the International Committee on Economic, Social and Cultural Rights (the Committee on ESC Rights), adopted in 2005; and the United Nations Economic, Social and Cultural Organization (UNESCO) Convention on the Protection and Promotion of the Diversity of Cultural Expressions,

* I had the privilege of being supervised by David Harris for my PhD from 1981–87. I am grateful to my colleague Fiona Beveridge and the editors of this volume for their comments. Responsibility for the views expressed is mine alone.

    [1] See YM Donders, *Towards a Right to Cultural Identity?* (Intersentia, 2002) 65–68.
    [2] W Kymlicka, *The Rights of Minority Cultures* (OUP, 1995); *Cultural Liberty in Today's Diverse World*, United Nations Human Development Programme's Report 2004 (United Nations, 2004).
    [3] See H Niec (ed), *Cultural Rights and Wrongs* (UNESCO, Institute of Art and Law, 1998).
    [4] See res 2002/26. See also GA res 58/167, 'Human Rights and Cultural Diversity' (4 March 2004), UN doc A/res/58/167.
    [5] See Note by the Secretary-General, UN doc A/60/40 (8 Sept 2005). In the report of the UK Parliament's Joint Committee on Human Rights, *The International Covenant on Economic, Social and Cultural Rights* 21st Report HL Paper 183, HC 1188 (2003–04) there is no specific discussion of cultural rights.

also adopted in 2005. Finally, it offers some concluding reflections and suggests that there may be signs of a renaissance for culture and cultural rights.[6]

II. Culture and cultures

Various notions of culture have become a central part of human rights discourse.[7] Philosophical discussion of the ideology of 'human rights' often takes place in the context of a discussion of group or societal cultures.[8] Individual human rights are often counterposed against the collective aspects of cultural rights. The idea of 'cultural relativism' has presented a strong challenge to a universal conception of human rights.[9] This was highlighted by the debate on 'Asian Values'[10] and the compromise formula of the Vienna Declaration on Human Rights, namely that account had to be taken of, 'the significance of national and religious particularities and various historical, cultural and religious backgrounds'.[11]

It can also be argued that the doctrine of the margin of appreciation under the European Convention on Human Rights serves to respect cultural relativity and sensitivity.[12] So too can interpretation of human rights law in a cross-cultural perspective.[13] More recently, debates have focused on the concept of multi-'culturalism',[14] which has led to strong calls to respect for 'cultural diversity'.[15] Cultural Diversity is

---

[6] See E Stamatopoulou, 'Why Cultural Rights Now?' (Carnegie Council, Sept 2004) <http://www.cceia.org> accessed on 7 Nov 2006.

[7] See R Stavenhagen, 'Cultural Rights and Universal Human Rights' in A Eide, C Krause, and A Rosas (eds), *Economic and Social Rights: A Textbook* (Nijhoff, 1995) 85–109.

[8] See eg, W Kymlicka, *Liberalism, Community and Culture* (Clarendon Press, 1989); JJ Shestack, 'The Philosophical Foundations of Human Rights' (1998) 20 Human Rights Q 201–234.

[9] See AD Renteln, *International Human Rights: Universalism Versus Relativism* (Sage, 1990); J Donnelly, 'Cultural Relativism And Universal Human Rights' (1984) 6 Human Rights Q 400–419; Z Androus, 'Female Genital Cutting: A Sociological Analysis' (2005) 9(4) The Intl J of Human Rights 535–38; General Assembly Resolution 56/128, 'Traditional or Customary Practices Affecting the Health of Women and Girls' (30 Jan 2002) UN doc A/res/56/128.

[10] See LS Bell, AJ Nathan, and I Peleg (eds), *Negotiating Culture and Human Rights* (Columbia University Press, 2001). By contrast it is notable that there has been little if any evidence of a cultural relativity debate with respect to international humanitarian law.

[11] Para 5 of the Vienna Declaration and Programme of Action of the World Conference on Human Rights 1993 (1993) 32 International Legal Materials 1661.

[12] See JA Sweeney, 'Margins of Appreciation: Cultural Relativity and the ECHR' (2005) 54 ICLQ 459–474. The doctrine is central to the jurisprudence of the European Court of Human Rights but the Human Rights Committee disclaims its use.

[13] See AA An-Naim (ed), *Human Rights in Cross Cultural Perspectives—A Quest for Consensus* (Philadelphia University Press, 1992); M Baderin, *International Human Rights And Islamic Law* (OUP, 2003); and 'Human Rights and Islamic Law: The Myth of Discord' (2005) Eur Human Rights L Rev 165–185.

[14] See W Kymlicka, Multicultural Citizenship (OUP, 1995); D McGoldrick, 'Multiculturalism and its Discontents' (2005) 5 Human Rights L Rev 27–56. There have recently been significant differences of opinion in the Committee on the Elimination of Racial Discrimination as to how to approach multiculturalism.

[15] See A Rosas and J Helgesen (eds), *The Strength Of Diversity: Human Rights And Pluralist Democracy* (Kluwer, 1992); S Caney and P Jones (eds), *Human Rights and Global Diversity* (Cass,

presented as a 'public good' in its own right that can challenge such human rights fundamentals as equality or liberty.[16] Indeed, much of the feminist challenge to reinterpret human rights centres on 'patriarchal cultures and structures',[17] and there has been an awareness that, by virtue of the right to self-determination, all peoples have their right to freely determine, *inter alia*, their 'cultural development'.[18] Further, part of the basis for the claims of indigenous peoples stems from the idea that their 'cultures' must at least 'survive' and preferably should be preserved and fostered.[19] Elements of this include both their natural heritage and their cultural heritage.[20] A feature of this revival of interest in 'culture' is that it is taboo to suggest that any one(s) culture is better/worse than anyone else's. In an international human rights context this is disingenuous, given that many international instruments (for example, on women, race, and children) are clearly aimed at certain 'cultural' practices that they aim to eliminate. The tendency to discuss culture particularly in relation to minorities is premised on an implicit critique of majority culture, namely that it tends to dominate, and often effectively eliminate, minority cultures.

The various and evolving notions of culture represent a continuing challenge for universal human rights discourse at the macro or conceptual level. We now turn to consider how they have been reflected and translated at the micro level of 'cultural rights'.

III. Cultural rights

The concept of 'cultural rights' as individual human rights remains ambivalent for a number of reasons.[21] First, interpretation of culture varies widely. At one end of the spectrum is an intellectual idea of culture and the processes of its creators—the arts, literature, classical music. At the other end is an anthropological sense of culture—as a way of life.[22] In the language used by UNESCO, culture is a set of distinctive spiritual, material, intellectual, and emotional features of society or a

2000); Achieving social cohesion in a multicultural Europe—Concept, situation and development (Trends in social cohesion No 18) (Council of Europe, 2006).

[16] See S Benhabib, *The Claims of Culture: Equality and Diversity in the Global Era* (Princeton University Press, 2002).

[17] See S Mullally, *Culture, Gender and Human Rights* (Hart, 2006). See also F Raday, 'Culture, Religion, and Gender' (2003) 1(4) Intl J of Constitutional L pp 663–715.

[18] See art 1 of the both the ICCPR and the ICESCR.

[19] See P Thornberry, *Indigenous Peoples and Human Rights* (Manchester University Press, 2002)

[20] See R O'Keeffe, 'The World's Cultural Heritage: Obligations to States Parties or to the International Community as a Whole' (2004) 53 ICLQ 189.

[21] See A Eide, 'Cultural Rights as Individual Human Rights', in Eide *et al* (eds), (n 7 above) 289–301; SP Marks, 'Defining Cultural Rights' in M Bergsmo (ed), *Human Rights and Criminal Justice for the Downtrodden* (Nijhoff, 2003) 293; Y Dinstein, 'Cultural Rights' (1979) 9 Israel Y of Human Rights 58.

[22] See J Cowan, MB Dembour, and R Wilson (eds), *Culture and Rights: Anthropological Perspectives* (Cambridge University Press, 2001).

social group and encompasses art, literature, lifestyles, ways of living together, value systems, traditions, and beliefs. More generally, there is the difficulty of determining 'what pertains to religion, what pertains to culture, and what is the political use of both'.[23] A good example of this relates to recent controversies concerning the regulation of the wearing of Islamic headscarves. Some of the disagreements on this issue relate to whether its wearing is mandated by religion, culture, or both, and what the wearing of it symbolizes for the individual wearer, the individual observer and for the community.[24] One possible explanation for the difficulty in making such determinations is that not all cultures or people, 'draw the same sharp distinctions between law, religion and other aspects of social and cultural life as the majority of people do in the West'.[25]

Second, modern understandings of culture present it as complex, contingent, and constantly evolving.[26] The idea of attaching rights to it runs the risk of essentializing or reifying culture.[27] The very idea that a state or an individual has a single culture is also strongly challenged. A state of multiple-cultures and individuals enveloped in an extensive system of sub-cultures are much more realistic understandings of the contemporary world.

Third, there are problems associating the concept of cultures within states and across states with that of individual or group rights.[28] As Lyndel Prott has argued, '[A]ny attempt to talk about cultural issues in terms of rights may be slippery and difficult. Culture is not a static concept: cultures change all the time.'[29] Moreover, in some states, 'distinctions are not drawn between the state and the community'.[30] Another aspect of the difficulty is that culture has a strong group or communitarian aspect whereas most human rights have an individualist perspective. Indeed, some argue that the use of culture is usually misleading and it would be better and more accurate to identify specific rights, for example, to expression, association, religion,

[23] MA Helie-Lucas, 'The Preferential Symbol For Islamic Identity: Women In Muslim Personal Laws' in V Moghadem (ed), *Identity Politics and Women: Cultural Reassertions and Feminism in International Perspective* (Westview, 1994) 391–407 at 404; WJ Talbot, *Which Rights Should Be Universal?* (OUP, 2005) 39–47.

[24] See D McGoldrick, *Human Rights and Religion: The Islamic Headscarf Debate in Europe* (Hart, 2006); C Mahabir, 'Adjudicating Pluralism: the *Hijab*, Law and Social Change in Post-Colonial Trinidad' (2004) 13(4) Social and Legal Studies 435–452.

[25] SM Poulter, *English Law and Ethnic Minority Customs* (Butterworths, 1986) para 1.03.

[26] See F Barth, 'The Analysis of Culture in Complex Societies' (1989) 3–4 *ETHNOS* 120. It is also often emphasized that cultures are created, understood or defined in creation to opposition to things eg Western, colonial, alien, or outside forces.

[27] See Cowan *et al* (n 22 above). See also D Scott, 'Culture in Political Theory' (2003) 31 *Political Theory* 92–115; T Summerfield, 'Australian Rules: The Rise Of Rights And The Demise Of The Right' (2005) 18(2) Intl J for the Semiotics of L 141–158.

[28] See B Robbins and E Stamatopolou, 'Reflections on Culture and Cultural Rights' (2004) 103 (2–3) *South Atlantic Quarterly* 419–434.

[29] L Prott, 'Cultural Rights as People's Rights' in Crawford (ed), *The Rights of Peoples* (OUP, 1988) 93 at 95. See also L Prott, 'Understanding One Another on Cultural Rights' in *Cultural Rights and Wrongs* (UNESCO, 1998) 161–175.

[30] M Kjoerum, 'Universal Human Rights: Between the Local and the Global' in K Hastrup (ed) *Human Rights on Common Ground: The Quest for Universality* (Kluwer, 2001) 75–89 at 79.

specific minority rights, etc.[31] An interesting illustration of the jurisprudential uneasiness with cultural 'rights' is evident in the title of the United Nations Human Development Programme's Human Development Report 2004: *Cultural Liberty in Today's Diverse World*.[32] Jurisprudentially, a liberty is a much weaker concept than a right.[33] Cultural rights also suffer from the more general critique on whether the rights in the ICESCR are really rights at all.[34] An aspect of this critique is their programmatic and progressive nature.[35] The Committee on ESC rights has sought to counter this by developing the idea of core obligations for each of the rights in the ICESCR, including article 15, that are open to immediate implementation.[36] As well as lawyers having problems with the idea of cultural 'rights', it is also notable that specialists in culture almost never refer to international human rights law to support their arguments or discussions.

Fourth, when the texts of international instruments are examined, the notion of cultural rights that they present is a limited one, both quantitatively and qualitatively.[37] Whilst the Universal Declaration of Human Rights (UDHR) and the ICESCR are considered below, a number of other international instruments refer to particular aspects of culture. Many discussions of cultural rights quickly turn to the cultural rights of minorities[38] or indigenous peoples.[39] The underlying assumption

---

[31] 'Instead of invoking culture, if one talks about say, local arts, one could simply say local arts; if one means language, ideology, patriarchy, children's rights, food habits, ritual practices or local political structures, one could use those or equivalent terms instead of covering them up in the deceptively cozy blanket of culture': T Eriksson, 'Between Universalism, and Relativism: A Critique of the UNESCO Concepts of Culture?' in J Cowan, MB Dembour and R Wilson (eds), *Culture and Rights: Anthropological Perspectives* (Cambridge University Press, 2001) 127.

[32] *Human Development Report 2004* (UNDP, 2004).

[33] See WN Hohfeld and WW Cook (eds), *Fundamental Legal Conceptions As Applied In Judicial Reasoning; And Other Legal Essays* (New Haven, 1923); C Gearty, 'Democracy And Civil Liberties: A Reappraisal' <http://www.lse.ac.uk> accessed 7 Nov 2006.

[34] JK Mapulanga-Hulston, 'Examining the Justiciability of Economic, Social and Cultural Rights' (2002) 6(4) The Intl J of Human Rights 29–48. The US's long-standing objections to viewing them as rights are well known. See the Introduction to this book.

[35] Art 2 ICESCR. See the discussion in Joint Committee on Human Rights, *The International Covenant on Economic, Social and Cultural Rights* (n 5 above) 20–28. Under the European Convention on Human Rights the right to education, which is often categorized as a cultural right, does not have a programmatic character. See eg *Mersel Eren v Turkey*, Appl 60856/00, ECtHR (Second Section), 7 Feb 2006, [2006] Education Law Reports 155.

[36] See eg the 3 Committee's *General Comments* (ESCR) (on the nature of States parties' obligations, art 2.1 of the Covenant) and *9* (the domestic application of the Covenant), *13* (on the right to education, paras 43–44) and *14* (on the right to health, paras 30–32), in HRI/GEN/1/rev 5, 26 April 2001; *Statement in 2001 General Comments 17*, see below; SA Hansen, 'The Right To Take Part in Cultural Life: Towards Defining Minimum Core Obligations Related To Article 15(1)(A) of the ICESCR' in A Chapman and S Russell (eds), *Core Obligations: Building A Framework for Economic, Social and Cultural Rights* (Intersentia, 2002) 279–303.

[37] See J Symonides, 'Cultural Rights: A Neglected Category of Human Rights' (1998) 158 *International Social Sciences J* 559–572.   [38] See Donders (n 1 above) ch VII.

[39] See Donders (n 1 above) chs VIII and XI. See also the references to culture in articles 4, 13, 23, 30, and 31 of the Convention concerning Indigenous and Tribal Peoples in Independent Countries <http://www.ilo.org/ilolex/english/convdisp1.htm> accessed on 7 Nov 2006; and there are references to culture in articles 8, 11, 14, 15, and 31 of the latest draft of the Universal Declaration on the Rights of Indigenous Peoples, Report of Human Rights Council, UN doc A/61/448 (6 Dec 2006).

is probably that majorities can take care of, and protect, their own dominant culture. Article 27 ICCPR states that, 'In those States in which ethnic, religious or linguistic minorities exist, persons belonging to such minorities shall not be denied the right, in community with the other members of their group, to enjoy their own culture, to profess and practise their own religion, or to use their own language'.[40] The Human Rights Committee (HRC) has given a wide interpretation to the rights of the minorities specified under article 27 ICCPR to 'enjoy their own culture'.[41] For the HRC, culture extends to 'a particular way of life associated with the use of land resources, especially in the case of indigenous peoples. That right may include such traditional activities as fishing or hunting and the right to live in reserves protected by law.'[42] Although the HRC has adopted a wide interpretation of culture, it has tended not to find violations of article 27 on the facts of the communications before it.[43] There are also references to culture or cultural life in a number of other international human rights instruments, including article 13(c) of the Convention on the Elimination of Discrimination against Women 1979 (CEDAW),[44] articles 29–31 of the Convention on the Rights of the Child 1989,[45] and article 45(3) of the International Convention on the Protection of the Rights of All Migrant Workers and Members of Their Families (1990).[46]

Finally, there is relatively little academic literature on 'cultural rights' as such, although it is now increasing.[47] Many leading texts on international human rights, and even on the ICESCR, have no index entry for cultural rights,[48] and national Bills of Rights rarely contain 'cultural rights'.[49]

---

[40] See also arts 1 and 4 of the 1992 'Declaration on the Rights of Persons Belonging To National or Ethnic, Religious or Linguistic Minorities' GA res 47/135 (18 Dec 1992). Language is a central element of culture.

[41] See S Joseph, J Schultz, and M Castan (eds); *The ICCPR—Cases, Materials and Commentary* (2nd edn, OUP, 2004) 752–793; D McGoldrick, 'Canadian Indians, Cultural Rights and the Human Rights Committee' (1991) 40 *Intl and Comparative L Q* 658–668. See also M O'Flaherty, 'Towards Integration of United Nations Human Rights Treaty Body Recommendations: The Rights-Based Approach Model', chapter 2 in this book.

[42] See *General Comment 23* on the Rights of Minorities, para 7 (April 1994).

[43] See eg *Ilmari Lansmann v Finland*, UN doc A/50/40, p 66; *Mahiuka v New Zealand* UN doc A/56/40, vol II, p 11. Cf the decision of the Inter-American Court of Human Rights in *Mayagna (Sumo) Awas Tingni Community v Nicaragua*, Series C no 79 [2001] IACHR 9 (31 Aug 2001) finding violations of the Right to Judicial Protection (art 25) and the Right to Property (art 21) in the context of a foreign companies prospecting of land without the agreement of the indigenous community.

[44] 1249 UNTS 13.   [45] 1577 UNTS 3.

[46] See also art 17(2) and 29 African Convention on Human and Peoples' Rights (1982) (no communications have ever been brought to the African Commission on this right), see M Baderin, 'The African Commission on Human and Peoples' Rights and the Implementation of Economic, Social, and Cultural Rights in Africa', chapter 7 in book; art 13 Inter-American Convention on Human Rights.

[47] See I Szabo, *Cultural Rights* (Sijthoff, 1974) (for a socialist perspective); Donders (n 1 above) A Chapman and S Russell (eds), *Core Obligations: Building A Framework for Economic, Social and Cultural Rights* (Intersentia, 2002).

[48] See eg M Craven, *The ICESCR—A Perspective on its Development* (OUP, 1998). Indeed, cultural rights only just makes it into the last chapter of this book!

[49] Exceptions are South Africa (art 10 of the 1996 Constitution) and Belarus (art 51 of the 1994 Constitution). On South Africa and ESC Rights see Joint Committee on Human Rights, *The International Covenant on Economic, Social and Cultural Rights* (n 5 above) 16–18.

IV. Article 15 ICESCR

Only one provision in each of the UDHR and the ICESCR provide for cultural rights. As Eide observed, 'they appear almost as a remnant category'.[50] Article 27(1) UDHR states that 'Everyone has the right to freely participate in the cultural life of the community, to enjoy the arts and to share in scientific achievement and benefits'. Under article 15(1) ICESCR states parties similarly recognize the right of everyone to take part in cultural life and to enjoy the benefits of scientific progress and its applications.[51] A right to participate 'in' something is important and is also covered by aspects of freedom of expression and association.[52] However, a participatory right is obviously different in nature from a right 'to' something. The article 15 right is literally to participate 'in *the* cultural life of *the* community', which unrealistically suggests a singular cultural life of a singular community. However, the participatory element has been interpreted as including a right to express one's own cultural life.[53] For example, the Reporting Guidelines of the Committee on ESC Rights refer to 'the right of everyone to take part in the cultural life which he or she considers pertinent, and to manifest his or her own culture'.[54] The contemporary understanding is that there can be more than one community in a state, all of which have cultural lives.

Article 27(2) UDHR provides that 'Everyone has the right to the protection of the moral and material interests resulting from any scientific, literary or artistic production of which he is the author'. This is restated in article 15(1)(c) ICESCR as the right to 'benefit from the protection of the moral and material interests . . . '. This has the appearance of an individual property right.[55] The idea that individual (and possibly community) intellectual property rights have to be protected to protect the human right to culture is a difficult notion for states, groups, and peoples that have historically seen property rights as collective and communal.[56] Industrialized states hold virtually all patents worldwide. Most patents granted in developing states belong to residents of industrialized states.[57] Intellectual property rights have been

---

[50] Eide (n 21 above) 289.

[51] See R O'Keefe, 'The "Right to Take Part in Cultural Life" under Article 15 ICESCR' 47 ICLQ (1998) 904–923.

[52] The right to democracy is also often presented as a participatory right. See S Wheatley, 'Deliberative Democracy and Minorities' (2003) 14 Eur J of Intl L 507. See also R Bedoya, 'Deliberative Cultural Policy Practices' (Dec 2005) <http://www.culturalcommons.org> accessed on 7 Nov 2006.   [53] See Hansen (n 35 above); O'Keefe (n 51 above).

[54] See text to n 66 below.

[55] A. Chapman, 'Core Minimum Obligations Related To ICESCR Article 15(1)(C)' in A Chapman and S Russell (eds), *Core Obligations: Building A Framework for Economic, Social and Cultural Rights* (Intersentia, 2002) 305–331.

[56] See Chapman, ibid; RL Ostergard, 'Intellectual Property: A Universal Human Rights?' (1999) 21 Human Rights Q 157. The UN Sub-Commission on the Promotion and Protection of Human Rights adopted a Resolution on Intellectual Property and Human Rights for the first time in 2000, see E/CN.4/Sub.2/2000/7 (17 Aug 2000).   [57] See Chapman (n 51 above) 321.

viewed as supporting western protectionism and capitalist exploitation,[58] which
have had a 'chilling effect on cultural creativity and the sharing of public goods' and
a generally detrimental effect on traditional and indigenous cultures.[59] Moreover, as
Rosemary Coombe has observed, the ICESCR has 'remained largely outside of the
purview of most intellectual property activists'.[60] She notes that one reason for this is
that the US has not ratified the ICESCR. However, it is increasingly recognized that
such protection of aspects of traditional knowledge may be the most effective way to
protect cultural rights.[61] The World Intellectual Property Organization (WIPO) has
recognized the need to reach out to new beneficiaries of the intellectual property system if it is to achieve global legitimacy.[62] As well as national and EU laws, there are a
range of international instruments that serve to protect such intellectual property
rights.[63]

Article 15 ICESCR contains three further provisions:

2. The steps to be taken by the States Parties to the present Covenant to achieve the full
   realization of this right shall include those necessary for the conservation, the development and the diffusion of science and culture.
3. The States Parties to the present Covenant undertake to respect the freedom indispensable for scientific research and creative activity.
4. The States Parties to the present Covenant recognize the benefits to be derived from the
   encouragement and development of international contacts and co-operation in the scientific and cultural fields.

These provisions are more in the nature of general undertakings rather than individual rights. As noted above, some analyses of article 15 proceed on the basis that there
are two approaches to cultural rights: there are rights to participate 'in' a culture and
there is also a right to 'a' culture.[64] A right to participate in a culture can only exist if
there is a culture. Hence the obligations of states in article 15(2) ICESCR to take
steps to conserve, develop, and diffuse culture. The general undertaking by states in
article 2 ICESCR to realize the rights in the Covenant includes a reference to states
taking steps, 'individually and through international assistance and cooperation'.

---

[58] See A Ngenda, 'The Nature Of The International Intellectual Property System: Universal
Norms And Values Or Western Chauvinism?' (2005) 14(1) Information & Communications
Technology Law 59–79; J Cornides, 'Human Rights and Intellectual Property: Conflict or
Convergence?' (2004) 7(2) J World Intellectual Property 135–167.

[59] R Coombe, 'Cultural Rights and Intellectual Property Debates' *Human Rights Dialogue*,
(Spring, 2005) <http://www.cceia.org> accessed 7 Nov 2006.   [60] Ibid.

[61] See J van Fleet, 'Protecting Knowledge' <http://www.carnegiecouncil.org>. For another example
of an international law approach to protect cultures by protecting their intellectual property rights in
the context of biodiversity see the UN Convention on Biological Diversity (1992), s 31 International
Legal Materials (1992) 818.

[62] See 'Traditional Knowledge, Genetic Resources and Folklore' <http://www.wipo.int/tk/en/?>
accessed 7 Nov 2006.

[63] Eg Universal Copyright Convention (1952, revised 1971); Prohibition on the Prevention of
Illicit import, Export or Transfer of Ownership of Cultural Property (1970).

[64] See Hansen (n 36 above).

With respect to cultural rights, 'International Cooperation in the preservation of cultural heritage is the pre-eminent concern of UNESCO.'[65]

The Committee on ESC Rights has issued detailed 'Reporting Guidelines'[66] to assist states on article 15 reports as follows:

1. Please describe the legislative and other measures adopted by or in your State to realize the right of everyone to take part in the cultural life which he or she considers pertinent, and to manifest his or her own culture. In particular, provide information on the following:

    (a) Availability of funds for the promotion of cultural development and popular participation in cultural life, including public support for private initiative.

    (b) The institutional infrastructure established for the implementation of policies to promote popular participation in culture, such as cultural centres, museums, libraries, theatres, cinemas, and in traditional arts and crafts.

    (c) Promotion of cultural identity as a factor of mutual appreciation among individuals, groups, nations and regions.

    (d) Promotion of awareness and enjoyment of the cultural heritage of national ethnic groups and minorities and of indigenous peoples.

    (e) Role of mass media and communications media in promoting participation in cultural life.

    (f) Preservation and presentation of mankind's cultural heritage.

    (g) Legislation protecting the freedom of artistic creation and performance, including the freedom to disseminate the results of such activities, as well as an indication of any restrictions or limits imposed on the freedom.

    (h) Professional education in the field of culture and art.

    (i) Any other measures taken for the conservation, development and diffusion of culture.

Please report on positive effects as well as on difficulties and failures, particularly concerning indigenous and other disadvantaged and particularly vulnerable groups.

The Guidelines continue with reference to detailed elements of article 15(2)–(4) in the scientific[67] and cultural fields.[68] They give greater specificity to the content on article 15 ICESCR and lay particular stress on popular participation and the promotion of cultural identity and cultural heritage.

---

[65] Eide (n 21 above) 238. However, see the recently adopted Council of Europe Framework Convention on the Value of Cultural Heritage for Society, CETS no 199, 27 Oct 2005, and its Explanatory Report at <http://conventions.coe.int/Treaty/EN/Reports/Html/199.htm> accessed on 7 Nov 2006. Art 6 of the that Convention expressly provides that it does not create any enforceable rights.

[66] 'Revised general guidelines regarding the form and contents of reports to be submitted by states parties under articles 16 and 17 of the International Covenant on Economic, Social and Cultural Rights' UN doc E/C.12/1991/1 (17 June 1991).

[67] On the science related aspects of art 15 see RP Claude, 'Scientists' Rights and the Human Rights to the Benefit of Science' in A Chapman and S Russell (eds), *Core Obligations: Building A Framework for Economic, Social and Cultural Rights* (Intersentia, 2002) 247–278.

[68] Ibid, paras 2–9.

V. General Comment 17

In the practice of the Committee on ESC Rights cultural rights had quietly disappeared,[69] at least until more recent years.[70] In 2001, after a day of general discussion, there was an extensive general statement on 'Human Rights and Intellectual Property'.[71] Many of the elements of the statement were developed in *General Comment 17* of the Committee on ESC Rights on 'The right of everyone to benefit from the protection of the moral and material interests resulting from any scientific, literary or artistic production of which he is the author', adopted until 21 November 2005.[72] This was the first General Comment adopted on article 15 and then only on article 15(1)(c).[73]

General Comment 17 draws on drafting history of article 15 ICESCR[74] and on the Committee's experience under the state reporting system. It begins by explaining the human rights rationale of article 15(1)(c) and how it is distinguished from intellectual property rights:

1. The right of everyone to benefit from the protection of the moral and material interests resulting from any scientific, literary or artistic production of which he or she is the author is a human right, which derives from the inherent dignity and worth of all persons. This fact distinguishes article 15, paragraph 1 (c) and other human rights from most legal entitlements recognized in intellectual property systems. Human rights are fundamental, inalienable and universal entitlements belonging to individuals and, under certain circumstances, groups of individuals and communities. Human rights are fundamental as they are inherent to the human person as such, whereas intellectual property rights are first and foremost means by which States seek to provide incentives for inventiveness and creativity, encourage the dissemination of creative and innovative productions, as well as the development of cultural identities, and preserve the integrity of scientific, literary and artistic productions for the benefit of society as a whole.

2. In contrast to human rights, intellectual property rights are generally of a temporary nature, and can be revoked, licensed or assigned to someone else. While under most intellectual property systems, intellectual property rights, often with the exception of moral rights, may be allocated, limited in time and scope, traded, amended and even forfeited, human rights are timeless expressions of fundamental entitlements of the human person. Whereas the human right to benefit from the protection of the moral and material interests resulting from one's scientific, literary and artistic productions safeguards the personal link between authors and their creations and between peoples, communities, or other groups and their collective cultural heritage, as well as their basic material interests which are necessary to enable authors to enjoy an adequate standard of living, intellectual property

---

[69] See O'Keefe (n 51 above). When they have been considered it has generally been in the context of the treatment of minority or indigenous groups: see Hansen (n 36 above) 302–303.

[70] See Hansen (n 36 above); O'Keefe (n 51 above).

[71] UN doc E/C.12/2001/15, 14 Dec 2001. The discussion was held in co-operation with WIPO.

[72] Ibid.   [73] Further General Comments on article 15 are in preparation.

[74] See also M Green, 'Drafting History of the art 15 (1) (c) of the International Covenant on Economic, Social and Cultural Rights', UN doc E/C.12/2000/15 (9 Oct 2000).

regimes primarily protect business and corporate interests and investments. Moreover, the scope of protection of the moral and material interests of the author provided for by article 15, paragraph 1 (c), does not necessarily coincide with what is referred to as intellectual property rights under national legislation or international agreements.[75]

3. It is therefore important not to equate intellectual property rights with the human right recognized in article 15, paragraph 1 (c)...[76]

The subsequent parts of *General Comment 17* focus on the normative content of article 15 paragraph 1 (c), states parties' obligations, violations, implementation at the national level, and the obligations of actors other than states parties. Sections of the General Comment address conditions for states parties' compliance, non-discrimination and equal treatment, limitations, general legal obligations on states parties (applying the Committee's established methodology that human rights imposes three types or levels of obligations on states parties: the obligations to *respect, protect,* and *fulfil*), specific legal obligations (including reference to the effective protection of the interests of indigenous peoples relating to their productions, and measures to preserve the distinctive character of minority cultures). It also addresses related obligations, international obligations, core obligations, violations (stating that if resource constraints render it impossible for a state to comply fully with its Covenant obligations, it has the burden of justifying that every effort has been made to use all available resources at its disposal in order to satisfy, as a matter of priority, the core obligations), national legislation, indicators and benchmarks, remedies and accountability, and finally, the obligations of actors other than state actors. The Committee provides an interpretation of the following key terms of the article: 'author' (noting that legal entities can be holders of intellectual property rights but not human rights); 'Any scientific, literary or artistic production'; 'Benefit from the protection' (stressing the need for protection to be effective); 'Moral interests' (noting the intrinsically personal character of every creation of the human mind and the ensuing durable link between creators and their creations); 'Material interests' (noting the close linkage of this provision with the right to own property); and 'Resulting'.[77]

General Comment 17 has taken a long time to arrive but it offers extremely helpful guidance for states. It reflects the lessons drawn from the Committee on ESC Rights dialogue with states parties under the reporting procedure. It will

[75] Relevant international instruments include, *inter alia*, the Paris Convention for the Protection of Industrial Property, 1883, as last revised in 1967; the Berne Convention for the Protection of Literary and Artistic Works, 1886, as last revised in 1971; the International Convention for the Protection of Performers, the Producers of Phonograms and Broadcasting Organizations ('Rome Convention'), 1961; the WIPO Copyright Treaty, 1996; the WIPO Performances and Phonograms Treaty, 1996 (which, *inter alia*, provides international protection for performers of 'expressions of folklore'); the Convention on Biological Diversity, 1992; the Universal Copyright Convention of UNESCO, 1952, as last revised in 1971; and the Agreement on the Trade-related Aspects of Intellectual Property Rights (the TRIPS Agreement) of the WTO.

[76] *General Comment 17,* paras 1–3.   [77] *General Comment 17,* paras 7–17.

assist the normative evolution of cultural rights by giving much greater specificity to its content and implications. It could therefore do much to counter the argument that cultural rights lack normative weight.

VI. The UNESCO Convention on the Protection and Promotion of the Diversity of Cultural Expressions

The most recent addition to the list of international instruments on culture has come from the United Nations Educational, Scientific and Cultural Organization (UNESCO), which makes much of its claim that it is the only UN agency with a mandate in culture.[78] This may be literally true but, as we have seen above, there are a number of international human rights bodies and treaty organs whose governing instruments include aspects of culture. The UNESCO Constitution refers to its working 'with a view to preserving... the fruitful diversity of the cultures' and to 'promote the free flow of ideas by word and image'.[79] The 'Convention on the Protection and Promotion of the Diversity of Cultural Expressions' was adopted by the General Conference of the United Nations Educational, Scientific and Cultural Organization, meeting in Paris from 3 to 21 October 2005 at its 33rd session.[80]

A. Drafting

A regular theme in UNESCO discussions is the 'cultural consequences of globalization' which include 'cultural vulnerability'.[81] One of UNESCO's responses to globalization has been to resort to standard setting. In 2001, it adopted the UNESCO Universal Declaration on Cultural Diversity[82] and its Action Plan.[83] The Declaration was not legally binding and the Director-General of UNESCO has referred to it as 'an ethical commitment'.[84] The member states then decided to draw up a binding standard-setting instrument with protection of the diversity of cultural contents and artistic expressions. This was one of the options set out in a

---

[78] See Donders (n 1 above) ch V. Cf art 151 EC on 'Culture', discussed by T Ahmed and T Hervey, 'The European Union and Cultural Diversity: a Missed Opportunity?' (2003/4) 3 *European Yearbook of Minority Issues* 43–62 who argue that art 151 can be interpreted to refer to cultures of groups within member states.   [79] See art 1(3) and (2) UNESCO Constitution.

[80] It entered into force on 18 March 2007, three months after its ratification by 30 States. On accession, including by regional economic integration organization (such as the European Union), see art 27.   [81] See UNESCO doc C/84, prov, para 52.

[82] Adopted unanimously by the 185 member states <http://www.unesco.org> accessed on 7 Nov 2006.   [83] See Donders (n 1 above) 134–137.

[84] See 'Preliminary Report By The Director-General Setting Out The Situation To Be Regulated And The Possible Scope Of The Regulating Action Proposed, Accompanied By The Preliminary Draft Of A Convention On The Protection Of The Diversity Of Cultural Contents And Artistic Expressions', UNESCO doc 33 C/23, para 2 (4 Aug 2005).

2003 report by the Director-General in a 'Preliminary study on the technical and legal aspects relating to the desirability of a standard-setting instrument on cultural diversity'.[85] The other three proposed options were (a) a new comprehensive instrument on cultural rights; (b) an instrument on the status of the artist; (c) a new Protocol to the Florence Agreement (on the Importation of Educational, Scientific and Cultural Materials of 1950 and its additional Nairobi Protocol of 1976). It is the rejection of the first option—a new comprehensive instrument on cultural rights—that is of significance in the context of this chapter. States preferred to leave the generality of cultural rights where they are—bits here and there. They went for the particular—Convention on 'Diversity of Cultural Expressions'. The aim was to adopt the Convention by consensus but in the event US objections prevented this.[86] It was eventually approved by 148 votes for, two against, four abstentions.[87]

In October 2003, the General Conference, invited the Director-General to submit to it at its 33rd session (2005) a preliminary report, accompanied by a preliminary draft convention. The drafting was done astonishingly quickly given the complexity involved. Indeed, the speed of drafting was one of the US's objections. Between December 2003 and May 2004, 15 independent multidisciplinary experts drafted, made recommendations and gave legal opinions for drafting the outline. They produced a preliminary report and a preliminary draft convention on the 'protection of the diversity of cultural contents and artistic expressions'.[88] The Director-General undertook consultations with the World Trade Organization (WTO), the United Nations Conference on Trade and Development (UNCTAD), and the World Intellectual Property Organization (WIPO). It is interesting to note that intergovernmental human rights organizations were not consulted. Three meetings of government experts were convened. An indication of the widespread interest and input was that over 500 experts from over 130 member states, two permanent observers to UNESCO and representatives from nine intergovernmental organizations and over 20 non-governmental organizations attended each session. The Director-General submitted a preliminary report to the 33rd session (2005).[89]

The draft Convention was discussed in Commission IV of UNESCO in October 2005.[90] At the end of the debate the Commission recommended in a vote by show of hands that the General Conference adopt the preliminary draft of the Convention. Five member states placed on record their explanations of their

[85] UNESCO doc 166 EX/28, March 2003.

[86] Alan Riding, 'U.S. Stands Alone on UNESCO Cultural Issue' <http://www.mediatrademonitor. org/node/view/249> accessed on 7 Nov 2006. J Pauwelyn 'The UNESCO Convention on Cultural Diversity, and the WTO: Diversity in International Law-Making?' *ASIL Insight*, <http://www. asil.org/insights/2005/11/insights051115.html> accessed on 7 Nov 2006.

[87] The other objecting state was Israel. The abstentions were by Australia, Honduras, Liberia, and Nigera.

[88] See <http://www.unesco.org/culture/diversite/convention> accessed on 7 Nov 2006.

[89] See Draft Report of Commission IV, UNESCO doc 33 C/84 Prov (33 C/COM.IV/2) 20 Oct 2005.   [90] Ibid, p 19.

vote.[91] These were Japan, the US, New Zealand, the Republic of Korea, and Mexico. The resolution adopted by the General Conference on the adoption of the Convention stated that 'this Convention pertains to the field of culture'[92] and expressed confidence that it 'shall be implemented in a manner consistent with the principles and objectives of the constitution of UNESCO'.[93]

The new Convention is a good example of how challenging it is to take any one area of human right and to make it fit harmoniously with (i) existing human rights law/indigenous peoples rights and (ii) the rest of the increasingly complex and specialized areas of international law eg trade law, environment law, and development law. The resolution adopted by the General Conference on the adoption of the Convention referred to its 'forming a coherent part within the system of international instruments'.[94]

B. The preamble

Some indication of the difficulty and sensitivities involved is revealed by the mere length and complexity of the preamble. The preambles to the International Covenants of 1966 are relatively short. The preamble to the migrant workers Convention of 1990 is much longer—some sixteen preambular paragraphs—but mainly focused on other human rights instruments and identifying the mischief being addressed. The preamble to the 2005 Convention had 21 preambular paragraphs. It links cultural diversity to such meta-concepts as sustainable development, peace and security, human rights, development, minorities, indigenous peoples, traditional cultural, social cohesion, women in society, freedom of thought, expression and information, intellectual property rights, globalization. It is helpful to reproduce part of the preamble to indicate how cultural diversity is perceived:

1. *Affirming* that cultural diversity is a defining characteristic of humanity,

2. *Conscious* that cultural diversity forms a common heritage of humanity and should be cherished and preserved for the benefit of all,

3. *Being aware* that cultural diversity creates a rich and varied world, which increases the range of choices and nurtures human capacities and values, and therefore is a mainspring for sustainable development for communities, peoples and nations,

4. *Recalling* that cultural diversity, flourishing within a framework of democracy, tolerance, social justice and mutual respect between peoples and cultures, is indispensable for peace and security at the local, national and international levels,

5. *Celebrating* the importance of cultural diversity for the full realization of human rights and fundamental freedoms proclaimed in the Universal Declaration of Human Rights and other universally recognized instruments,

---

[91] See doc 33 C/84 Prov, above, annex.

[92] Res 42 (2005) on 'Implementation of the Convention on the Protection and Promotion of the Diversity of Cultural Expressions' (Records of the General Conference, 33rd session, Paris) 3–21 Oct 2005, Vol 1, Resolutions, (Paris, UNESCO, 2005), res 42, p 96.   [93] Ibid.

[94] Ibid. See generally M Koshennlemi, 'Fragmentation of International Law: Difficulties Arising From The Diversification And Expansion Of International Law', Report of the Study Group of the International Law Commission, UN doc A/CN.4/L.682 (13 April 2006).

6. *Emphasizing* the need to incorporate culture as a strategic element in national and international development policies, as well as in international development cooperation,...

7. *Taking into account* that culture takes diverse forms across time and space and that this diversity is embodied in the uniqueness and plurality of the identities and cultural expressions of the peoples and societies making up humanity,

8. *Recognizing* the importance of traditional knowledge as a source of intangible and material wealth, and in particular the knowledge systems of indigenous peoples, and its positive contribution to sustainable development, as well as the need for its adequate protection and promotion,...

15. *Taking into account* the importance of the vitality of cultures, including for persons belonging to minorities and indigenous peoples, manifested in their freedom to create, disseminate and distribute their traditional cultural expressions and to have access thereto, so as to benefit them for their own development,...

17. *Recognizing* the importance of intellectual property rights in sustaining those involved in cultural creativity,

18. *Being convinced* that cultural activities, goods and services have both an economic and a cultural nature, because they convey identities, values and meanings, and must therefore not be treated as solely having commercial value,

19. *Noting* that while the processes of globalization, which have been facilitated by the rapid development of information and communication technologies, afford unprecedented conditions for enhanced interaction between cultures, also represent a challenge for cultural diversity, namely in view of risks of imbalances between rich and poor countries,...

The preamble was considered satisfactory because it captured the spirit of the Convention. However, the United States (US) made a formal objection to paragraph 18 concerning cultural activities, goods, and services.

C. The terms of the convention

The title of the Convention suggested by the independent experts was the 'Convention on the Protection of the Diversity of Cultural Contents and Artistic Expressions'. For these experts, the term 'cultural expressions' was to encompass both 'cultural contents' and 'artistic expressions'.[95] The experts emphasized that the term *protection*, 'should under no circumstances be taken to mean that States Parties should turn in on themselves or close themselves off from others. Rather, the diversity of cultural expressions should always be guaranteed by freedom of expression, and the public should be afforded the broadest possible access to them'.[96] In fact all the experts agreed that 'protection' must be understood in a positive sense, that is to say, not only in terms of preserving cultural expressions but also as creating the conditions in which they might develop and flourish.[97]

---

[95] UNESCO doc 33 C/23, para 7.   [96] Ibid.   [97] Ibid para 8.

A specific definition of 'protection' for the purposes of the Convention was included in article 4(7):

'Protection' means the adoption of measures aimed at the preservation, safeguarding and enhancement of the diversity of cultural expressions.

The plenary changed the title to Convention on the Protection and Promotion of the Diversity of Cultural Expressions because it was considered to reflect better the scope of application of the Convention.

D. Objectives and principles

Article 1 of the Convention sets out nine objectives. They include raising awareness of the value of the diversity of cultural expressions at local, national, and international levels; and recognition to the distinctive nature of cultural activities, goods, and services as vehicles of identity, values, and meaning. The US made a formal objection to article 1(g), which contained the objective of recognition of the dual nature of cultural goods and services.

Article 2 sets out eight 'Guiding Principles'.[98] It is notable that the first principle is respect for human rights and fundamental freedoms. It states that:

Cultural diversity can be protected and promoted only if human rights and fundamental freedoms, such as freedom of expression, information and communication, as well as the ability of individuals to choose cultural expressions, are guaranteed. No one may invoke the provisions of this Convention in order to infringe human rights and fundamental freedoms as enshrined in the Universal Declaration of Human Rights or guaranteed by international law or to limit the scope thereof.[99]

The specific reference to cultural diversity being protected on the basis of the human rights to freedom of expression, information, and communication is particularly important. In the 1970s and 1980s some of UNESCO's initiatives raised concern that they were aimed at restricting these freedoms in an effort to create a more balanced and equitable flow of information.[100] Western states, in particular, viewed the initiatives as an attempt to justify increased state controls and state censorship on the press and other information media. The concerns were partly responsible for the withdrawal of the US (in 1984, returning in 2003)[101] and the UK (in 1985, returning in 1997) from UNESCO.

The subsequent principles are the sovereign right to adopt measures and policies to protect and promote the diversity of cultural expressions within their

---

[98] The Drafting Committee had to consider sixty-three formulations of principles.
[99] Art 2(1).
[100] See K Venkata Raman, 'Towards a New World Information Order: Problems of Access and Cultural Development', in R St J MacDonald and DM Johnstone (eds), *The Structure and Process of International Law* (Nijhoff, 1984) 1027–1084.
[101] See (1985) 34 International Legal Materials 489.

territory, equal dignity of and respect for all cultures (including the cultures of persons belonging to minorities and indigenous peoples), international solidarity and co-operation (the US made a formal objection to the expression 'cultural industries'), complementarity (ie that the cultural aspects of development were of equal importance as its economic aspects),[102] sustainable development, equitable access (to a rich and diversified range of cultural expressions from all over the world and access of cultures to the means of expressions and dissemination), and openness and balance.

E. Scope and definitions

Under article 3 the 'Convention shall apply to the policies and measures adopted by the Parties related to the protection and promotion of the diversity of cultural expressions'. There was some controversy on this provision. Article 4 provides a series of definitions for the purposes of this Convention.[103] Such definitions are not uncommon in UNESCO instruments. The independent experts agreed that, the terms 'culture' and 'cultural diversity' should not be tackled in their full range of accepted meanings or manifestations, but only in relation to the term cultural expressions, which are transmitted by means of 'cultural goods and services' as well as in other ways. Although some experts made the point that the notion of 'cultural goods and services evoked the vocabulary used in agreements on international trade, it was felt that the proposed definition boiled down to a more cultural conception of this notion, thus allowing for a distancing from the strictly trade-related understanding, while recognizing the dual nature of these goods and services'.[104]

The defined terms are: 'Cultural Diversity', 'Cultural Content', 'Cultural Expressions', 'Cultural Activities', 'Goods and Services', 'Cultural Industries', 'Cultural Policies and Measures', 'Protection', and 'Interculturality'. The US made a formal objection to five of the definitions (cultural expressions, cultural activities, goods and services, cultural industries, cultural policies, and protection). Saudi Arabia expressed reservations on article 4. Argentina reserved its position with regard to the definition of cultural activities, goods, and services (article 4(4)). Nonetheless, it is very helpful to have an agreed understanding of these commonly used expressions. The defined terms were often referred to as 'cross-cutting themes'. 'Cultural diversity' refers to the manifold ways in which the cultures of groups and societies find expression. These expressions are passed on within and among groups and societies. Cultural diversity is made manifest not only through the varied ways in which the cultural heritage of humanity is expressed, augmented, and transmitted by the variety of cultural expressions but also through diverse modes of artistic

---

[102] See Note by the UN Secretary-General on the 'Effects of economic reform policies and foreign debt on the full enjoyment of human rights, particularly economic, social and cultural rights', UN doc A/60/384 (27 Sept 2005).

[103] Concensus on definitions was assisted by a joint proposal from the African Group and the European Union.   [104] UNESCO doc 33 C/23, para 10.

creation, production, dissemination, distribution, and enjoyment, whatever the means and technologies used.[105]

'Cultural content' refers to the symbolic meaning, artistic dimension, and cultural values that originate from or express cultural identities.[106] 'Cultural expressions' are those expressions that result from the creativity of individuals, groups, and societies, and that have cultural content.[107] 'Cultural activities, goods and services' refers to those activities, goods and services, which at the time they are considered as a specific attribute, use or purpose, embody, or convey cultural expressions, irrespective of the commercial value they may have. Cultural activities may be an end in themselves, or they may contribute to the production of cultural goods and services.[108] 'Cultural industries' refers to industries producing and distributing cultural goods or services as defined in article 4(4).[109] 'Cultural policies and measures' refers to those policies and measures related to culture, whether at the local, national, regional, or international level that are either focused on culture as such or are designed to have a direct effect on cultural expressions of individuals, groups or societies, including on the creation, production, dissemination, distribution of and access to cultural activities, goods, and services.[110] Finally, 'Interculturality' refers to the existence and equitable interaction of diverse cultures and the possibility of generating shared cultural expressions through dialogue and mutual respect.[111]

F. Rights and obligations

Part IV of the Convention is of central importance. It deals with the rights and obligations of the parties. It is notable that it is concerned with the rights of states rather than the rights of individuals. The independent experts recognized, 'the importance of maintaining a balance between the sovereign right of States to adopt measures to protect and promote diversity of cultural expressions within their territory and their obligations to protect and promote it at the international level also'.[112] Article 5(1) states the 'general rule regarding rights and obligations'. It reaffirms the

sovereign right to formulate and implement their cultural policies and to adopt measures to protect and promote the diversity of cultural expressions and to strengthen international cooperation to achieve the purposes of this Convention. Policies and measures to protect and promote the diversity of cultural expressions within its territory, are to be consistent with the Convention.[113]

Particularly important in this context is article 20, which is considered below.

The sovereignty focus is emphasized by article 6, which deals with the 'Rights of Parties at the national level'. This sets out a series of measures aimed at protecting and promoting the diversity of cultural expressions within its territory which,

[105] Art 4(1).   [106] Art 4(2).   [107] Art 4(3).   [108] Art 4(4).   [109] Art 4(5).
[110] Art 4(6).   [111] Art 4(8).   [112] UNESCO doc 33 C/23, para 11.
[113] Art 5(1) and (2).

'taking into account its own particular circumstances and needs', a state party may adopt. Under article 6(2) the measures include:

(a) regulatory measures aimed at protecting and promoting diversity of cultural expressions;

(b) measures that, in an appropriate manner, provide opportunities for domestic cultural activities, goods and services among all those available within the national territory for their creation, production, dissemination, distribution and enjoyment of such domestic cultural activities, goods and services, including provisions relating to the language used for such activities, goods and services;

(c) measures aimed at providing domestic independent cultural industries and activities in the informal sector effective access to the means of production, dissemination and distribution of cultural activities, goods and services;

(d) measures aimed at providing public financial assistance;

(e) measures aimed at encouraging non-profit organizations, as well as public and private institutions and artists and other cultural professionals . . . ;

(f) measures aimed at establishing and supporting public institutions . . . ;

(g) measures aimed at nurturing and supporting artists and others involved in the creation of cultural expressions; and

(h) measures aimed at enhancing diversity of the media including through public service broadcasting.

This series of measures clearly envisages significant state aid and assistance programmes. Many of them *could* have protectionist objectives and so raise issues of potential conflicts with European and international trade regulations.[114] In 2002 three states: the UK, the US, and China, produced 40 per cent of the world's cultural products. Latin America and Africa accounted for less than 4 per cent.[115] The US made a formal objection to article 6(2)(b) and (c) and Japan reserved its position on article 6(1).

Article 7 deals with measures to promote cultural expressions. Article 8 addresses measures to protect cultural expressions. It makes provision for the possibility of states taking such measures in 'special situations where cultural expressions on its territory are at risk of extinction, under serious threat, or otherwise in need of urgent safeguarding'. Measures taken have to be reported to an Intergovernmental Committee. Article 9 deals with information sharing and transparency.[116] It provides, *inter alia*, for four yearly reports to UNESCO on 'measures taken to protect and promote the diversity of cultural expressions within their territory and at the international level'. Subsequent articles deal with education and public awareness (article 10) the participation of civil society (article 11), international cooperation (article 12), the integration of culture into sustainable development (article 13),

---

[114] See J Pauwelyn 'The UNESCO Convention on Cultural Diversity, and the WTO: Diversity in International Law-Making?' ASIL Insight, <http://www.asil.org/insights/2005/11/insights051115.html> accessed on 7 Nov 2006.

[115] Report of UNESCO's Institute for Statistics, cited in 'Developing Countries Lose Out in Cultural Trade' (UNESCO Press Release, 15 Dec 2005) <http://portal.unesco.org/culture> accessed on 7 Nov 2006.   [116] Israel expressed reservations on art 9.

cooperation for development (article 14) and collaborative arrangements (article 15). Article 16 makes provision for preferential treatment for developing states. The question of preferential treatment gave rise to intense debate, mainly on account of the potential impact of that article on states' national immigration policies. Australia, New Zealand, and Canada made a declaration stating that in the light of the debate, it was understood that the text of the article allowed sufficient flexibility in the application of domestic legislation, including immigration law.[117] The New Zealand Declaration stated that:

On the basis of the discussions at the Third Intergovernmental Meeting of Experts in June, 2005, it is New Zealand's understanding that the obligation in Article 16 on developed countries to facilitate cultural exchanges with developing countries by granting preferential treatment to artists and other cultural professionals and practitioners through the appropriate institutional and legal frameworks is not intended to affect the content or implementation of domestic legislation, policies or individual decisions on the entry of persons into New Zealand territory and other immigration matters.

Article 17 deals with international co-operation in situations of serious threat to cultural expressions. Article 18 makes provision for the establishment of an International Fund for Cultural Diversity. Funds will mainly be contributed by voluntary donations and funds appropriated for this purpose by the General Conference of UNESCO. The Intergovernmental Committee on the basis of guidelines determined by the Conference of Parties, shall decide the use of resources of the Fund.[118] No political, economic, or other conditions that are incompatible with the objectives of the Convention may be attached to contributions made to the Fund.[119]

Article 19 is concerned with the exchange, analysis, and dissemination of information.[120] The independent experts had proposed the establishment of a Cultural Diversity Observatory with the task of 'collecting, analysing and disseminating information on this field, and maintaining a data bank designed to foster dynamic partnerships among all potential partners'.[121] The governmental experts did not favour this. They approved the work that such a mechanism was intended to do, but recommended the use of existing UNESCO structures, in co-operation with the Institute for Statistics, in order to avoid additional expense.[122]

G. Relationship with other international agreements

Throughout the drafting process there was concern about other international agreements that might interact with the Convention. There was acceptance of the need to ensure coherence. In the Convention the issue is addressed in article 20.

---

[117] UNESCO doc 33 C/23, para 62.   [118] Art 18(4).   [119] Art 18(5).
[120] Japan and Israel expressed reservations to art 19. See also pp 446–467, 472–473 below.
[121] UNESCO doc 33 C/23, para 12.   [122] Ibid para 25.

This has the rather ungainly title of 'Relationship to other treaties: mutual supportiveness, complementarity and nonsubordination'. Article 20 provides that:

1. Parties recognize that they shall perform in good faith their obligations under this Convention and all other treaties to which they are parties. Accordingly, without subordinating this Convention to any other treaty,

    (a) they shall foster mutual supportiveness between this Convention and the other treaties to which they are parties; and

    (b) when interpreting and applying the other treaties to which they are parties or when entering into other international obligations, Parties shall take into account the relevant provisions of this Convention.

2. Nothing in this Convention shall be interpreted as modifying rights and obligations of the Parties under any other treaties to which they are parties.

Article 20 was the subject of protracted and difficult debate. Many states considered the provision to be of fundamental importance. The final text was endorsed by a large number of delegations. Its two operative paragraphs appear to point in different directions. The US made a formal objection to article 20. Australia also requested that its objection be entered in the record. New Zealand voted for the adoption of the Convention on the basis of its understandings regarding article 20:

New Zealand considers that the clear legal effect of Article 20 is to ensure that the provisions of the Convention do not modify in any way the rights and obligations of the Parties under other treaties to which they are also parties. Accordingly, any inconsistencies between this Convention and those other treaties must be resolved in favour of the other treaties.[123]

Argentina, Israel, Japan, Chile, and Turkey also expressed reservations on the article, though Argentina and Chile subsequently withdrew their reservations.[124]

H. Follow-up

The independent experts considered that the success of the future convention would greatly depend on its follow-up mechanisms. There was a desire to avoid any mechanism that entailed unduly burdensome procedures, administrative tasks, or high costs. They proposed an independent advisory group but this was not accepted by the governmental experts.[125] A mechanism for the settlement of disputes was also considered important to the Convention's effectiveness. One difficulty was whether it was possible that disputes could be settled from a 'strictly cultural point of view'.[126] In the event, a Conference of Parties was established as the plenary and supreme body of the Convention.[127] It meets in ordinary session every two years in conjunction with the General Conference of UNESCO, to the

---

[123] Ibid.   [124] UNESCO doc 33 C/23, para 63.   [125] Doc 33 C/23, paras 26, 43.
[126] Doc 33 C/23, para 12.   [127] Art 22.

extent possible. The functions of the Conference of Parties are set out in article 22. They include the receipt and examination of reports of the parties to the Convention transmitted by an Intergovernmental Committee. article 23 provides for the establishment of an Intergovernmental Committee, initially composed of representatives of 18 states parties and elected for a term of four years. The Intergovernmental Committee meets annually. It functions under the authority and guidance of, and is accountable to, the Conference of Parties. The functions of the Intergovernmental Committee are set out in article 23. They include commenting on the reports of the states parties. In general, the follow-up system of governmental experts and a conference of states parties replicates the pattern in environmental treaties rather than the systems used in human rights treaties.

Article 25 deals with the mechanism for the settlement of disputes. It provides for recourse to conciliation at the request of only one party, accompanied by an opt-out clause, enabling a state to declare its intention not to be bound by the provision. This non-binding mechanism for the settlement of disputes allows, within a strictly cultural perspective, possible divergences of views on the interpretation or application of certain rules or principles relatives to the Convention to be dealt with. This mechanism encourages, first and foremost, negotiation, then recourse to good offices or mediation. Only if no settlement is achieved, a party may have recourse to conciliation. The Convention does not include any mechanism for sanctions.

I. The US position

The US opposed the adoption of the draft Convention. The US had left UNESCO for nineteen years and only rejoined it in 2003. It contributes 22 per cent of UNESCO's budget and will thus contribute indirectly to the International Fund for Cultural Diversity, even though it is not a party to the Convention. It was extremely disappointed with the decision to adopt the preliminary draft. It explained that it had, 'very serious concerns about the potential of the Draft Convention to be misinterpreted in ways that might impede the free flow of ideas by word and image as well as affect other areas, including trade'.[128] The US was concerned that the Convention could be used to protect culture from the effects of international trade agreements via control and censorship. For example, it could be used to 'restrict American audiovisual products, particularly Hollywood movies and television programmes'.[129] Indeed, the Convention was sponsored by France and Canada, both of which have long standing policies of using public subsidies and quotas to protect national cultural industries (radio, television, movies, etc) so as to prevent their being overwhelmed by American popular culture.

---

[128] Doc 33 C/23, para 12.
[129] Alan Riding, 'U.S. Stands Alone on UNESCO Cultural Issue' <http://www.mediatrademonitor. org/node/view/249> accessed on 7 Nov 2006.

The US clearly had major problems with the Convention and was concerned at its potential implications for human rights and for trade agreements. It considered that references to its concerns being principally the protection of Hollywood's output was to trivialize these concerns. Yet, by making a significant issue of its objections, it suggests that it considered the Convention to be an instrument of potential importance. For example, it was concerned that France will use the terms of the Convention to justify trade protection for French language books, French films, and French agricultural products, such as *foie gras*.[130] In its explanation of its vote the Permanent Delegate of the US to UNESCO was concerned that the Convention would be used to control, not facilitate, the flow of goods, services, and ideas:

[T]here have been disturbing statements by some government leaders of their intent to use this convention to block the import of agricultural and other products from the developing world and others.

The United States has achieved the vibrant cultural diversity that so enriches our society by our commitment to freedom and our openness to others, and by maintaining the utmost respect for the free flow of ideas, words, goods and services. We believe it is critical that this organization and global leaders make clear that this Convention will not become yet another tool for major world markets to shut out goods and services from developing and other markets. The goal of the United States is to ensure the free flow of diversity in all of its forms—cultural, informational, and trade. In addition, this Convention as now drafted could be used by states to justify policies that could be used or abused to control the cultural lives of their citizens—policies that a state might use to control what its citizens can see; what they can read; what they can listen to; and what they can do. We believe—in keeping with existing conventions—that the world must affirm the right of all people to make these decisions for themselves.... this text could be misused to legitimize actions by governments to deny human rights and fundamental freedoms...

We deeply regret that the flawed process that produced this Convention was driven by unnecessary haste. The document's ill-defined terminology and internal inconsistencies do not demonstrate the respect that this important subject matter deserves or the rigor that should characterize a legally binding document.... We have received repeated assurances from other delegations that the Convention is not intended to permit any restrictions or limitations on human rights and trade openness, but neither the time nor the opportunity was provided to clarify fully the intent of the text.

We have been clear that the Convention cannot properly and must not be read to prevail over or modify rights and obligations under other international agreements, including WTO Agreements. Potential ambiguities in the Convention must not be allowed to endanger what the global community has achieved, over many years, in the areas of free trade, the free flow of information, and freedom of choice in cultural expression and enjoyment....

---

[130] During the negotiations of the failed OECD Multilateral Agreement on Investments, France proposed a controversial protective clause for 'cultural industries'. The proposed exception clause read as follows: 'Nothing in this agreement shall be construed to prevent any Contracting Party to take any measure to regulate investment of foreign companies and the conditions of activity of these companies, in the framework of policies designed to preserve and promote cultural and linguistic diversity'. See N Albala, 'The Dangers of the Multilateral Agreement on Investment Shackling the State' Le Monde Diplomatique March 1998, <http://mondediplo.com/1998/03/08maialba> accessed on 7 Nov 2006.

For these reasons, the United States has requested clarity of language as to this Convention's relationship with other international instruments. The rights and obligations found in such instruments provide the legal foundation for increases in trade that have brought greater prosperity to billions of people around the world. Will the Convention place these other rights and obligations at risk? We regret that this Conference has not taken the time to fully clarify this intent in the text itself. This instrument remains too flawed, too open to misinterpretation, and too prone to abuse for us to support. . . . For these reasons, the United States voted 'no' on the adoption of this Convention.[131]

Underlying the US versus rest of the world tension around the UNESCO Convention on Cultural Diversity is a deeper ideological debate about the relationship between globalization and what we generically refer to as 'culture'. Many of the states supporting the Convention see its value as a modest check or marker on the tide of globalization in the form of economic liberalization and the de-territorialization of markets. The Convention can provide support for territorial measures that limit or correct market forces in defence of culture. In this context, the tendency of the market to commodify everything, including culture, is seen as the root of the problem. The discovery that culture is, after all, a 'human right', can be understood as resistance to this commodification tendency. The US ideology is different because it envisions 'culture' as more individualistic and property-rights oriented (the market merely allows people to live out their individual choices and it is the exercise of these choices that constitute 'culture' in the first place) rather than 'culture' being more communal, conservative, traditional, and linked to inheritance, and not necessarily being linked to an economic exchange of any sort. The UNESCO Convention can probably be understood as an attempt to mediate between these two versions of 'culture' and to prevent the hegemony of the former over the latter.

The US is thus in the same position of relative isolation that it has been with other major international instruments, such as the ICESCR,[132] the UN Convention on the Rights of the Child,[133] and the Statute of the International Criminal Court.[134] Time will tell whether the US concerns are justified. If in the course of time they prove unfounded, the US may be convinced to ratify, as it eventually did with the Genocide Convention (1948) in 1988, and the International Covenant on Civil and Political Rights (1966) in 1992.

J. The position of other states

As noted, Israel also voted against the Convention. Japan supported the adoption of the Convention on the premise that it pertained to the field of culture, and that

---

[131] <http://www.amb-usa.fr/USUNESCO/texts/GenConf33_Amb_Intervention_CD_Vote.pdf> accessed on 20 Oct 2005.   [132] 155 states parties as of 8 Dec 2006.
[133] Only the US and Somalia are not parties.
[134] See D McGoldrick, 'Political and Legal Responses to the ICC' in D McGoldrick, P Rowe, and E Donnelly (eds), *The Permanent International Criminal Court* (Hart, 2004) 389–449 at 400–437.

the measures to be taken in accordance with its provisions should not compromise the rights and obligations under international instruments in other fields. Japan shared the concerns expressed by the US but that they were overstated. It hoped that the US would remain firmly engaged with UNESCO in its many areas of responsibility, where the continued solidarity and co-operation among all member states will be essential.[135] The Republic of Korea voted in favour of the adoption of the Convention. It expressed its regret that it was adopted by voting, rather than by consensus. It regretted some of the ambiguous wordings of the Convention. It emphasized that the provisions of this Convention should not affect the rights and obligations stated in other international treaties. In particular,

Article 20 stipulating the relationship between this Convention and other treaties shall not be interpreted as being able to influence, modify and compromise rights and obligations that are stated under other treaties.... measures to be taken by the provisions of this Convention must be implemented in a way that is harmonious and consistent with rights and obligations under international instruments in other fields as well as the cultural field[136]

Mexico welcomed the adoption of the Convention. With regard to article 20, its interpretation was that the Convention would be implemented in harmony with other treaties, 'It will not be subordinate to them, nor will they be subordinate to this Convention. We also consider that Mexico's position in future international negotiations has not been predetermined.'[137]

K. The significance of the UNESCO convention

The Convention does not purport to grant or recognize individual or group human rights. The language, format and structure approximate more to those of an environmental treaty than a human rights one. In particular, the implementation systems contrast strongly with the human rights treaty organs composed of independent experts and the meetings of states parties having a merely procedural role.[138] However, there is a sense in which it can be classed as a human rights treaty.[139] It is strongly premised on the value of cultural diversity as an international public good. It defends human creativity. In those senses it is supportive of individual cultural rights. The Convention has a dual focus. First, the rights of states parties to protect and promote the diversity of cultural expressions and, second, international co-operation.

As for the significance of the Convention to the work of UNESCO, during the debate on UNESCO's medium-term strategy 2004–08 a number of states suggested that the follow up to the Convention could provide 'strategic guidance'

---

[135] See Records of the General Conference, 33rd session, Paris, 3–21 Oct 2005 vol 1, resns (UNESCO, 2005), Explanations of Vote, p 219.　　　　　[136] Ibid p 220.

[137] Ibid.

[138] Cf The Committee under the ICESCR was initially composed of governmental experts.

[139] See generally F Coomans, 'UNESCO and Human Rights' in R Hanski and M Suksi (eds), *An Introduction to the International Protection of Human Rights* (2nd edn, Abo Academy, 1999) 219–230.

for the strategy as a 'new framework for cultural policies'.[140] At the conclusion of the drafting of the Convention, several states stressed the positive contribution of the text to the development of international law, noting that its adoption would be a significant step in the history of contemporary international relations in which culture is required to play a growing role.[141] The US disassociated itself from that conclusion in its final declaration.

VII. Conclusions

There may be signs of a renaissance for culture, cultural rights, and a right to cultural identity or autonomy.[142] Cultural rights may offer a framework for resolving disputes and managing cultural differences that is not so threatening to states as the rights to self-determination and minority rights.[143] Cultural rights may still be the Cinderella of the international human rights movement but they may offer a more positive framework for addressing the increasingly difficult tensions that arise from states' multicultural and pluralist policies. *General Comment 17* (2005) of the Committee on ESCR will assist the normative evolution of cultural rights by giving much greater specificity to its content and implications. The further General Comments that are in preparation on other aspects of article 15 will enhance this.

So too might the 2005 UNESCO Convention on the Protection and Promotion of the Diversity of Cultural Expressions, which was overwhelmingly supported by 148 states. In particular, it was strongly supported by France, Canada, the European Union, Brazil, and South Africa. As noted, it expressly states that it is, in principle, intended to be consistent with existing international human rights.[144] This is reaffirmed by the provision in article 20(2) that, 'Nothing in this Convention shall be interpreted as modifying rights and obligations of the Parties under any other treaties to which they are parties'. An earlier draft that would have given priority to the cultural Convention was not adopted.[145] WTO agreements do not have a general cultural exception.[146] However, the Convention stresses the value of the

---

[140] UNESCO doc C/84, prov, para 50.   [141] UNESCO doc C/23, para 72.

[142] See also R Coomaraswamy, 'Indentity Within: Cultural Relativism, Minority Rights and the Empowerment of Women' (2002–03) 34 George Washington International L Rev 483–513.

[143] See B Robbins and E Stamatopoulou, 'Reflections on Culture and Cultural Rights' (2004) 103 (2–3) South Atlantic Q 419–34, arguing that 'If the Kosovars had been allowed both to teach the Albanian language in school and had been given the resources to do so, we might not have had to debate whether NATO's "humanitarian intervention" was just another example of Western imperialism', at 34.

[144] See text to n 99 above. The major international human rights treaties have been widely ratified and so can generally be understood to evidence 'existing international human rights'.

[145] See T Broude, 'Comment: Cultural Diversity and the WTO: A Diverse Relationship' ASIL Insight (21 Nov 2005) <http://www.asil.org/insights.htm> accessed on 7 Nov 2006.

[146] See ME Footer and CB Grabner, 'Trade Liberalization and Cultural Policy' (2000) 3 J of International Economic L 115 who argue against a broad cultural exception but in favour of the application of specific rules governing trade and culture. See also E. Cohen, 'Globalization and Cultural Diversity'

diversity of cultural expressions and this may be taken account in interpreting human rights treaties, particularly their limitations clauses,[147] and in the interpretation of WTO agreements.[148] The European Commission's Press Release on the Convention states that:

This text forms the basis of a new pillar of world governance in cultural matters.... The UNESCO Convention sets out common rules, principles and points of reference for cultural diversity at global level. It is the first time the international community has been able to reach such a consensus on these questions. The text makes a considerable contribution to recognising the role and legitimacy of public policies in protecting and promoting cultural diversity.... There is nothing in the Convention that prejudges the positions that the parties will take in trade bodies. For their part, the Community and Member States have a clear position in the WTO on cultural and audiovisual services, which is to preserve their role in maintaining and developing policies in these areas. Within the framework of the Doha Development Round, the Commission indicated that it would not ask for or offer trade commitments in audiovisual and cultural services.[149]

The 'property' element of culture and the commodification issues make the prospect of legal claims much more imminent.[150] Any dispute would be dealt with largely by the WTO Dispute Settlement Body (DSB) under GATT article XX, GATS, or TRIPs. It is open to question whether GATT article XX really lends itself to the defence of, for example, the sorts of actions envisaged by article 6 of the UNESCO Convention. If it did, the next issue would be what sort of test would the DSB apply? Presumably it would be proportionality coupled with the need to conform to the chapeau to article XX.[151]

If, as seems likely, the Convention is widely ratified, it will make an interesting addition to the corpus of binding international law relevant to culture, cultures, and cultural diversity.[152]

in Cultural Diversity, Conflict and Pluralism, UNESCO, World Culture Report 2000, ch 4 (UNESCO, 2000).

[147] See Art 20(1) of the Convention, cited in section VI above.

[148] In the US Shrimp case the WTO panel made reference to environmental treaties that had not been ratified by all of the parties concerned as a reflection of the 'contemporary concerns of the community of nations', US—Import Prohibition of Certain Shrimp and Shrimp Products, WTO Appeal Panel, 12 Oct 1998, para 129; A Qureshi, 'Extraterritorial Shrimps, NGOs and the WTO Appellate Body' (1999) 48(1) ICLQ 199–206.

[149] European Commission, MEMO/05/387 (Brussels, 20 Oct 2005) <http://europa.eu.int> accessed on 8 Nov 2006. The Commission envisaged early ratification of the Convention by the European Community. The EC ratified on 18 Dec 2006.

[150] The WTO has already had to deal with disputes that can be categorized as cultural. See DZ Cass, The Constitutionalization of the World Trade Organization (OUP, 2005) 129–131 concerning Canadian restrictions on the import of periodicals, particularly from the US.

[151] For an excellent analysis see T Voon, 'UNESCO and the WTO: A Clash of Cultures?' (2006) 55 ICLQ 635–652. Cf the discussion of GATT article XX in relation to women's rights in F Beveridge, 'Feminist Perspectives in International Economic Law' in D Buss and A Manji, International Law: Modern Feminist Approaches' (Hart, 2005) 173–201 at 182–189.

[152] As does the Council of Europe Framework Convention on the Value of Cultural Heritage for Society, CETS no 199, 27 Oct 2005, and its Explanatory Report at <http://conventions.coe.int/Treaty/EN/Reports/Html/199.htm> accessed on 8 Nov 2006. Art 6 expressly provides that the convention does not create any enforceable rights.

Index